Handbook of
Child Psychopathology

Handbook of Child Psychopathology

Edited by

Thomas H. Ollendick
Virginia Polytechnic Institute and State University
Blacksburg, Virginia

and

Michel Hersen
Western Psychiatric Institute and Clinic
University of Pittsburgh School of Medicine
Pittsburgh, Pennsylvania

Plenum Press • New York and London

Library of Congress Cataloging in Publication Data

Main entry under title:

Handbook of child psychopathology.

Bibliography: p.
Includes index.
1. Child psychopathology—Handbooks, manuals, etc. I. Ollendick, Thomas H. II. Hersen, Michel. [DNLM: 1. Child behavior disorders. 2. Mental disorders—In infancy and childhood. WS 350.6 H236]
RJ499.H33 1982 618.92′89 82-18906
ISBN 0-306-40938-0

A Division of Plenum Publishing Corporation
233 Spring Street, New York, N.Y. 10013

Printed in the United States of America

Contributors

Thomas M. Achenbach, *Department of Psychiatry, University of Vermont, Burlington, Vermont*

Judy L. Arthur, *Moore/Arthur Associates, 191 Crest Dr., Eugene, Oregon*

Magda Campbell, *Children's Psychopharmacology Unit, New York University Medical Center, New York, New York*

Susan B. Campbell, *Department of Psychology, University of Pittsburgh, Pittsburgh, Pennsylvania*

Ira L. Cohen, *Children's Psychopharmacology Unit, New York University Medical Center, New York, New York*

Diane E. D. Deitz, *Department of Learning and Development, Northern Illinois University, DeKalb, Illinois*

David Dinklage, *Department of Psychology, University of Minnesota, Minneapolis, Minnesota*

Larry A. Doke, *Center for Adolescent Rehabilitation and Education, New Mexico State Hospital, Las Vegas, New Mexico*

Daniel M. Doleys, *Behavioral Medicine Services, Brookwood Medical Center, Birmingham, Alabama*

Craig S. Edelbrock, *Department of Psychiatry, University of Pittsburgh, Pittsburgh, Pennsylvania*

Joseph R. Flippo, *Department of Behavioral Sciences, New Mexico Highlands University, Las Vegas, New Mexico*

Michel Hersen, *Department of Psychiatry, Western Psychiatric Institute and Clinic, University of Pittsburgh Medical School, Pittsburgh, Pennsylvania*

Steven A. Hobbs, *Center for Behavioral Medicine, Oklahoma College of Osteopathic Medicine and Surgery, Tulsa, Oklahoma*

Wallace A. Kennedy, *Department of Psychology, Florida State University, Tallahassee, Florida*

Benjamin B. Lahey, *Clinical Training Program, Department of Psychology, University of Georgia, Athens, Georgia*

Gloria R. Leon, *Department of Psychology, University of Minnesota, Minneapolis, Minnesota*

Johnny L. Matson, *Department of Learning and Development, Northern Illinois University, DeKalb, Illinois*

Jack I. Mills, *Department of Psychology, Claremont Graduate School, Claremont, California*

Dennis R. Moore *Moore/Arthur Associates, 191 Crest Dr., Eugene, Oregon*

Duane G. Ollendick, *Department of Psychology, Zumbro Valley Mental Health Center, Rochester, Minnesota*

Thomas H. Ollendick, *Department of Psychology, Virginia Polytechnic Institute and State University, Blacksburg, Virginia*

Richard Perry, *Children's Psychopharmacology Unit, New York University Medical Center, New York, New York*

Theodore A. Petti, *Department of Psychiatry, Western Psychiatric Institute and Clinic, University of Pittsburgh Medical School, Pittsburgh, Pennsylvania*

Alan C. Repp, *Department of Learning and Development, Northern Illinois University, DeKalb, Illinois*

Anne W. Riley, *Department of Psychology, Virginia Polytechnic Institute and State University, Blacksburg, Virginia*

Laura Schreibman, *Department of Psychology, Claremont McKenna College, Claremont, California*

Karen R. Sobotka, *Department of Psychology, Louisiana State University, Baton Rouge, Louisiana*

Michael Stefanek, *Department of Psychology, Virginia Polytechnic Institute and State University, Blacksburg, Virginia*

B. Marion Swanson, *Department of Psychology, Northeastern Oklahoma State University, Tahlequah, Oklahoma*

June M. Tuma, *Department of Psychology, Louisiana State University, Baton Rouge, Louisiana*

C. Eugene Walker, *Department of Psychiatry and Behavioral Sciences, University of Oklahoma Health Sciences Center, Oklahoma City, Oklahoma*

Carol K. Whalen, *Program in Social Ecology, University of California, Irvine, California*

Diane J. Willis, *Child Study Center, Department of Pediatrics, University of Oklahoma Health Sciences Center, Oklahoma City, Oklahoma*

Richard A. Winett, *Department of Psychology, Virginia Polytechnic Institute and State University, Blacksburg, Virginia*

Preface

Although the field of child psychopathology is of relatively recent origin, it is a healthy, burgeoning one. Within the past 10 to 20 years, numerous articles and books have been published, and the field can now be described as emerging with an identity of its own. No longer can child psychopathology be viewed simply as a downward extension of adult psychopathology. Rather, children must be viewed as children, not as miniature adults. Such a situation requires that issues of child psychology and developmental psychology be intimately considered when delineating the problems of children.

Such a focus has guided our efforts in soliciting contributors and topics for this volume. All contributors are active researchers and clinicians in the area of child psychopathology, and all are acutely aware of the special considerations of child and developmental psychology as they relate to child behavior problems. Further, all contributors are empirically minded; consequently, the various chapters are data-based and represent the most up-to-date knowledge available. However, since research-based knowledge is more abundant in some topic areas than in others, the chapters vary in length and scope.

The book is organized in three parts: General Issues, Specific Psychopathologies, and Prevention and Treatment. In the first part, historical, developmental, etiological, and taxonomic issues are considered in detail. The purpose of this section is to provide a framework for the conceptualization of the specific psychopathologies that follow. In the second part, a variety of psychopathologies are examined. Each of the chapters in this part is organized around a set of specific issues, including definitional, taxonomic, etiologic, and treatment considerations. Although not exhaustive, this part adequately samples a wide diversity of behavior problems in children. In the final section, psychoanalytic, behavioral, and psychopharmacologic treatments are reviewed, and new and exciting preventative strategies are examined. All in all, the volume is intended to be a source book, detailing the current status and directions for future research in the area of child psychopathology.

In a project such as this, many persons are to be acknowledged. Among the foremost are the contributors, whose enthusiasm and dedication to the project have been truly remarkable. Quite obviously, without them, up-to-date treatment of each topic could hardly have been possible. We would also like to acknowledge Mr. Leonard Pace and the various professionals at Plenum Publishing Corporation, whose support and assistance have been invaluable. In addition, we would like to lend a special "thanks" to the many children who, perhaps unknowingly, served as the impetus for this project. As students of child psychopathology, we are continually reminded of what they teach us, and of how much we have yet to learn. Finally, our own children, Laurie, Katie, and Jonathan, and spouses, Mary and Vicki, have been instrumental in helping us "see" the intricacies of childhood and the need for a book such as the present one. To them, we dedicate this effort.

THOMAS H. OLLENDICK
MICHEL HERSEN

Contents

I

General Issues

1

A Historical Overview of Child Psychopathology

THOMAS H. OLLENDICK AND MICHEL HERSEN

Introduction

The field of child psychopathology is of relatively recent origin. Prior to the twentieth century, psychopathology was concerned almost exclusively with adult behavioral disorders. Child behavior disorders, though occasionally acknowledged, received little concerted attention. In all likelihood, this state of affairs resulted from the then prevailing viewpoint of children being simply little adults or *homunculi* ("little men"). Children were not thought to possess "personalities" of their own; rather, they were viewed as minature adults, evincing problems similar to adults, and benefiting from reasoned advice much like their adult counterparts (Aries, 1962). A "child psychology," let alone a "child psychopathology," was nonexistent.

In contrast, the twentieth century has been characterized by extensive studies of the child. Predating the first White House Conference on Children in 1909 and advancing beyond the International Year of the Child in 1979, numerous efforts have been made to understand, assess, and treat the behavior disorders of children *as children,* not as minature adults. An explosion of knowledge has occurred, filling many child psychology texts with voluminous data. There is no doubt that advances have been made. However, it would be safe to conclude that not all aspects of child psychopathology have been tackled.

In this introductory chapter, we shall briefly examine the historical underpinnings of

THOMAS H. OLLENDICK • Department of Psychology, Virginia Polytechnic Institute and State University, Blacksburg, Virginia 24061. MICHEL HERSEN • Department of Psychiatry, Western Psychiatric Institute and Clinic, University of Pittsburgh Medical School, Pittsburgh, Pennsylvania 15261.

the field of child psychopathology. In doing so, a context for an assessment of the current status of child psychopathology will be provided. The remainder of the text will address issues related to the etiology, assessment, classification, and treatment of child behavior disorders.

The Emergence of Childhood

According to Aries (1962), the beginnings of child psychology can be traced to the seventeenth century. Prior to that time, there is little evidence that childhood was viewed any differently from adutlhood. Children were dressed as adults and were expected to behave as such. Further, there were no special play acitivites, games, or literature for children (Knopf, 1979). Even drawings and paintings of children resembled those of adults, including facial features, dress, and mannerisms.

Whereas a variety of accounts have been presented to explain these early viewpoints of children, the most plausible explanations appear to be related to the presence of child labor practices and high infant mortality rates. There simply was little time or opportunity for a child to behave childishly. As noted by Bremmer (1970) in his documentary on youth in America, "epidemics malnutrition, and ordinary diseases of childhood and those contracted from mothers, especially tuberculosis, carried off hundreds in the earliest stages of life" (p. 5). It has been estimated that as many as two-thirds of all children died before they reached 4 years of age. Those who survived became valuable "economic commodities." Their economic value was ensured by an apprenticeship system that required them to work at the age of 6, frequently under poor work conditions and for protracted periods of time. Working up to 14 hours a day in unhealthy and unsafe settings (Brown, 1939), it is little wonder that few children lived on to adolescence. Those who survived until the age of 12 quickly entered into marriage contracts, which were arranged for them by their elders to ensure their continued economic worth. The economic situation required that these young parents "be fruitful, multiply, and replenish the earth." Large families were required to exist in a society characterized by early infant deaths and inappropriate and unsafe work settings for its children.

Such practices certainly continued and prevailed into early colonial times in America. During colonial expansion, it was not uncommon for the early settlers to request the transportation of poor children to the Americas. For example, transportation of "idle" children from England to labor-starved Virginia was a common practice. One British legislative order, dated 1620 and authorizing the transportation of such children against their wishes, reads:

> so forasmuch as information is likewise made that among that number [hundreds] there were divers unwilling to be carried thither and that it is conceived that both the City [London] wanteth authority to deliver and the Virginia Company to receive and carry out these persons against their wills . . . if any of them shall be found obstinate to resist or otherwise to disobey such directions as shall be given in this behalf, we do likewise hereby authorize such as shall have the charge of this service to *imprison, punish, and dispose any of those children.* (italics added, quoted in Bremmer, 1970, p. 8)

Such treatment of children was evident in numerous other practices in the 1600s. Young girls were delivered to the colonies to reduce discontent among the primarily male colonists. Known as "tobacco brides," these young girls often were sent against their wishes and before the age of 12. In the 1640s a Massachusetts law specified that a rebellious or stubborn son could be put to death:

> If a man has a stubborn or rebellious son . . . which will not obey the voice of his father or the voice of his mother, and that when they have chastened him will not harken unto them, then shall his father and mother lay hold on him and bring him to the magistrates assembled in Court, and testify to them by sufficient evidence that this their son is stubborn and rebellious and will not obey their voice and chastisement, but lives in sundry notorious crimes. Such a son shall be put to death. (reproduced in Bremmer, 1970, p. 38)

It is obvious that the status of children and adolescents then was a precarious one, replete with expectations, subtle messages, and not-so-subtle dictates that respect, obedience, and work were mandatory. The child was to dress, behave, and work like an adult, and yet did not have the privileges of adulthood. Clearly, children and adolescents were viewed similarly to slaves and other valuable chattel. Those who survived filled a most important and vital economic role.

Aries (1962) notes that changes in the prevailing view of children became evident in the late 1600s and early 1700s, especially in upper socioeconomic families. In these families, perhaps because of better health practices, more leisure time, and the decreased necessity to work, the role of the child emerged. Parents began to "play" with their children, to express affection towards them, and to enjoy them as children. Children's games and play activities developed, and a child literature emerged. As parents and adults in general became more interested in children, concerns about their development and education increased. No longer viewed as economic pawns, children were seen as little "persons" in need of guidance and moral support. Undoubtedly, the churches played some role in these developments, as did the influence of a number of philosophers. Rousseau, writing in the mid 1700s, underscored the idea of childhood:

> We expect to find the man in the child without thinking of what the child is before he is a man. . . . Childhood has ways of seeing, thinking, feeling peculiar to itself; nothing is more absurd than to wish to substitute ours in their places. (quoted in Brown, 1939, p. 11)

Based on the philosophies of Locke, Pestalozzi, and Rousseau, the child began to be viewed as a *tabula rasa* ("blank slate") that could be affected by a variety of experiences. The duty of parents and society to help "form" the child and to shape his/her destiny emerged. This philosophy resulted in diverse developments: moral education, compulsory schooling, and improved health practices. This philosophy also served as the impetus and forerunner of early theoretical systems, including psychoanalytic and behavioral ones, developed to account for normal and pathological behavior in children.

Thus, after many centuries of virtual neglect, the importance and distinctness of childhood was acknowledged. Of course, it took many years before Rousseau's notion of the child was accepted. Some might argue that this notion still has not found total acceptance, even in highly civilized societies. Support for this lingering doubt may be found in the relatively high incidence of child abuse in the United States. Child abuse or neglect still ranks as one of the five leading causes of death for young children (along with accidents, cancer, congenital abnormalities, and pneumonia). Except for the dated language, the following account of a battered child in Plymouth, 1655, is not unlike what has been observed in the 1980s:

> having a boy whom proved sick and naughty . . . we do find that the body was blackish and blue, and the skin broken in diverse places from the middle to the hair of his head . . . and there was the knuckles of one hand and one of his fingers frozen, and also both his heels frozen . . . upon

> reviewing the body we found three gaules like holes in the hams . . . the dead corpse did bleed at the nose. (quoted in Bremmer, 1970, p. 123)

While this example may appear extreme, child abuse remained so pervasive in the late 1800s that the Society for the Prevention of Cruelty to Children was founded in the United States and England. In 1912, the Federal Children's Bureau was established to ensure the welfare of children. In 1938, the Wages and Hours Bill was passed to prohibit the employment of children under 16 years of age in hazardous occupations. Clearly, while childhood has been recognized and viewed as a distinct phase of development since the early 1700s, there has been no assurance that children have been accorded judicious treatment. To this end, the "International Bill of Rights for Children" was recently proclaimed in 1979, the International Year of the Child.

Emergence of Childhood Psychopathology

As noted by Achenbach (1974), the history of childhood psychopathology cannot be portrayed as an uninterrupted march of progress towards better treatment through greater knowledge. Rather, progress appears to have been cyclical and highly dependent upon societal attitudes about children and prevailing theories about psychopathology. Understanding and treatment of childhood psychopathology mirrored these attitudes and opinions across successive periods of time.

Because a psychology of childhood was largely nonexistent prior to the 1700s, early conceptions of child behavior disorders were identical to those hypothesized for adult disorders. As is generally well known, the early Greeks and Romans held that behavior disorders were the result of biologic or organic "imbalances." Hippocrates spoke of "humoral substances" that, when they became imbalanced, resulted in "mental" disorders. Given the organic disease perspective, children (as well as adults) were viewed as defective, and were treated as objects of scorn or persecution. In ancient Rome, children who were severely impaired (e.g., mentally retarded and/or probably psychotic) were disposed of in the Tiber by their parents to relieve themselves and society of the burden of support (Rosen, Clark, & Kivitz, 1976). Less impaired children, such as enuretics, were treated with a variety of concoctions thought to relieve the "humoral imbalance" and to restore the child to an appropriate biologic state. In a fascinating historical account of enuresis, Glicklich (1951) described the medical treatment that prevailed in 1550 B.C. at the time of the Papyrus Ebbers:

> A remedy for incontinence of urine:
>
> | | |
> |---|---|
> | Juniper berries | 1 |
> | Cyprus | 1 |
> | Beer | 1 hennu measure |

Interestingly, even in 1550 B.C., enuresis was considered sufficiently abnormal to be mentioned in one of the few medical texts of the day! Other early treatments of enuresis included: burning the crop of a cock and giving it to the child to drink in tepid water; shaving a hare's scrotum and placing it in wine for the child to drink; and giving the child the toasted seed of the wild rue to drink every third day! Many of these "treatments" prevailed until the dawn of Christianity, and some persisted well beyond it.

With the emergence of Christianity, a more compassionate attitude appeared, which served as the early precursor to "moral" treatment. In this period, it was believed that kindness and forbearance were essential in dealing with "disturbed" persons. Biblical scholars refer to the admonition of St. Paul to "comfort the feeble-minded" (Rosen, Clark, & Kivitz, 1976). This attitude, however, appears to have been short-lived and was superseded by the demonology of the "Dark Ages" and the early medieval period (Zilboorg & Henry, 1941). It was posited that evil spirits inhabit people (as well as objects and animals), and that these spirits were responsible for abnormal behavior. As a result, children and adults exhibiting behavior problems were regarded with fear and suspicion, as if "possessed" by a devil. For example, both Luther and Calvin denounced the retarded as "filled with Satan." Treatment ranged from rejection, humiliation, and imprisonment, to burning at the stake under the careful supervision of church and state authorities. Although specific treatment methods varied, a decided preference for punitive methods was evident.

As noted in our discussion of the emergence of childhood, conceptions of childhood as distinct from adulthood began to surface in the 1600s and early 1700s. Even with these developments, however, behavior problems of children continued to be viewed much like those of adults. At this time, prevailing societal attitudes fostered a resurgence of the organic disease model, first introduced by Hippocrates. In contrast, however, such resurgence of the organic model was also characterized by humane attitudes and concern much like those observed at the dawn of Christianity. As noted by Zilboorg and Henry (1941), this combined viewpoint was related to significant advances that were occurring in the fields of physiology, neurology, and general medicine, and to developing moral attitudes towards the disturbed. These moral attitudes were seen most clearly in Pinel's unchaining of the inmates when he became head of the Bicetre Hospital in Paris in 1792. Pinel stressed the natural causes (i.e., organic) of "insanity" rather than demoniacal possession; in his opinion, patients required moral treatment based on kindness and forebearance rather than punishment. According to Bockoven (1963),

> The moral therapist acted toward his patients as though they were mentally well. He believed that kindness and forbearance were essential in dealing with them. He also believed in firmness and persistence in impressing on patients the idea that a change to more acceptable behavior was expected. (p. 76)

Implicit in early moral treatment philosophies was the notion that "psychological" factors could beneficially affect the insane. This notion was not completely incompatible with the early organic theories, since organic changes were often attributed to psychological causes such as disappointment and bereavement (Achenbach, 1974). Thus, while the role of psychological factors was emerging, the prevailing viewpoint was a medical and organic one with a humane attitude superimposed upon it.

During this same epoch, a second philosophical force was emerging, which was to usher in a view of psychopathology as determined by natural environmental causes in addition to organic causes (Rie, 1971). This view essentially affirmed the humanitarian attitude but also posited that behavior problems were caused by environmental forces. Most notably, sensory stimulation, or a lack thereof, was viewed as a primary determinant of behavior. This philosophy, articulated most forcefully by Rousseau, laid the educational foundation for the early work of Itard and Seguin in the 1800s. In 1801, a young adolescent boy ("the wild boy of Aveyron") was found naked and wandering in the forest, and referred to Itard for treatment. Itard described the boy in the following manner:

> What do we see? A disgustingly dirty child affected with spasmodic movements and often convulsions who swayed back and forth ceaselessly like certain animals in the menagerie, who bit and scratched those who opposed him, who showed no sort of affection for those who attended him; and who was in short, indifferent to everything and attentive to nothing. (quoted in Harrison & McDermott, 1972, p. 727)

Here was Rousseau's "natural savage" awaiting intervention. Itard's intervention, based largely on the repetition of sensory stimulation, was designed to socialize and educate the child. Although Itard worked incessantly for 5 full years with this child, "Victor" acquired very few skills and Itard concluded that he was largely unsuccessful in his efforts. He concluded that the boy's "idiocy" (mental retardation) prevented success.

Despite Itard's failure, the principles underlying this approach were well entrenched and were introduced into the United States in 1848 by Seguin. Thus, a view of psychopathology as being determined by organic and/or environmental influences was generally accepted in the mid 1800s. Of equal importance, a humanistic attitude was also present, which was to guide the treatment of individuals displaying psychopathology. This emerging attitude was evident in 1843 when Dorothea Dix implored the Legislature of Massachusetts for more humane treatment conditions. As is amply illustrated in her observations, such humane conditions were not common at that time:

> I proceed, gentlemen, briefly to call your attention to the *present* state of insane persons confined within this Commonwealth, in *cages, closets, cellars, stalls, pens! Chained, naked, beaten with rods* and *lashed* into obedience. (quoted in Rosen, Clark, & Kivitz, 1976, p. 6)

Thus while attitudes were changing, the actual advances in treatment suggested by Itard, Seguin, and others lagged behind and were not fully incorporated until the middle to late 1800s.

As recently as 1843, Dorothea Dix observed children and adolescents being confined and placed in cages and cellars as insane persons. Although a few isolated references to disorders in children existed (Harms, 1967), there were no specific facilities designed especially for the treatment of children. Further, there appeared to be little awareness or concern with developmental disorders unique to children. Only disorders that severely impaired children (e.g., "insanity") were recognized and "treated."

In the late 1800s and early 1900s, a number of currents merged that appear to have formed the "stream" of child psychopathology. Many of these developments occurred concurrently, suggesting a zeitgeist that was conducive to change and an interaction that promoted progress (Achenbach, 1974; Knopf, 1979; Ross, 1959). Among these developments were the discovery and care of the mentally retarded, the development of intelligence tests, the formulation of psychoanalysis and behaviorism, the child study movement, and the emergence of child guidance clinics. Whereas all of these factors may seem somewhat disparate to the reader, they all appear to have focused attention on the growing child and on the developmental aspects of psychopathology. For example, psychoanalytic theory emphasized the critical role of early childhood experiences for the development of both normal and abnormal personalities, while behaviorism posited that environmental forces exerted a dominant role in influencing and shaping the growing child's behaviors. Clearly, both of these theories—though frequently viewed as antagonistic—focused attention on children and on the development of a *child* psychopathology. Although it is beyond the scope of this introductory chapter to review in detail the various currents responsible for these developments, we shall highlight aspects of the child guidance movement that illustrate this trend.

Child Guidance Movement

The child guidance movement in the United States followed the early pioneering work of G. Stanley Hall, who devised the "baby biography" as an early scientific method for studying the child. Hall's methodology, although now suspect as a research tool, consisted of sending questionnaires to parents, teachers, and children themselves. His goal was to collect normative data on children in such diverse areas as motor abilities, fears, dreams, and emotions. Although he did not obtain specific information about childhood psychopathology in his studies, Hall was one of the first individuals who addressed the scientific study of children *per se* (Watson, 1959). As such, he generated scientific enthusiasm about the study of children and provided necessary developmental norms by which abnormal behaviors in children could be judged.

Concurrent with Hall's work, Witmer established the first psychological clinic for children at the University of Pennsylvania in 1896. Witmer's primary interest involved the psychoeducational problems of children, and his methods appeared to be an extension of early sensory strategies formulated by Itard and Seguin. In addition, a reading of Witmer seems remarkably current in its emphasis upon environmental deprivation and the correlates of learning problems like aphasia and dyslexia. At that time, psychoanalysis had not yet been incorporated into American thought; the prevailing treatment philosophy remained a psychoeducational one based on early diagnosis and remediation through repetitive sensory stiumlation exercises. Two years following the opening of Witmer's clinic, juvenile courts were established in Illinois and Colorado, marking the beginning of an awareness about adolescent problems and extending avenues of treatment to "behavioral" problems. In the early 1900s, psychoanalysis was introduced into America, and shortly thereafter the first child guidance clinic (as we now know them) was founded by Healy in 1909 in Chicago. In 1912, Wallin opened a similar clinic at the University of Pittsburgh. The early psychoeducational focus fostered by Witmer, however, soon gave way to concerns with internalized neurotic problems of children, probably due to the influence of psychoanalysis (Ross, 1959). This shift in emphasis was bolstered by a 1915 study of the National Committee for Mental Hygiene, which reported widespread emotional problems in children and deplored the lack of adequate facilities to treat such children.

Growth of child guidance clinics was at first slow. Most of these clinics emphasized a team approach to the diagnosis and treatment of children's behavior problems. The clinic team included a social worker and psychologist who worked under the direction of a psychiatrist. This "holy trinity," as it became known (Redl, 1962), specified distinct roles and functions for each of the three disciplines. The child was tested by the psychologist, parents were interviewed by the social worker, and treatment was conducted by the psychiatrist. Many of the psychiatrists were psychoanalytically oriented, assuring continued focus on internalized neurotic problems. Psychotherapy offered to the child was aimed at assisting him/her in modifying basic underlying personality structures determined by early parent–child relationships. In order to reduce parental resistance to change in their children, mothers and fathers also were interviewed and provided with "guidance." Clearly, the goal of the early child guidance centers was to foster self-awareness and understanding in children, not to "adjust" children to prevailing familial and environmental circumstances.

During the first quarter of the twentieth century, behaviorism also emerged as a viable treatment model (Watson, 1913, 1919, 1924). In his early writings, Watson (1913) argued that the primary focus of treatment should be on helping the child adjust to the environment, not on helping the child derive understanding or self-awareness. While Watson approved of psychoanalysis insofar as it promoted discussion of personal problems, he argued that it was "based largely upon religion, introspective psychology and Voodooism" (1924, p. 18). Further, he predicted that behaviorism would replace psychoanalysis in the developing child guidance clinics. As history indicates, his prediction was inaccurate, at least in the short run. Psychoanalysis remained the primary force in such clinics well into the 1960s, and it continues to enjoy widespread use (Koocher & Pedulla, 1977). For reasons not completely understood, behaviorism remained relatively dormant until the 1960s, at which time it resurfaced. Presently, application of learning theory to the behavior disorders of children also enjoys widespread use (Gelfand & Hartmann, 1975; Marholin, 1978; Ollendick & Cerny, 1981; Ross, 1981; Sulzer-Azaroff & Mayer, 1977).

Child guidance clinics and the more recently established child study centers continue to be major forces in the development of child psychopathology as a special field of study. Although professional roles and functions currently overlap and are blurred in these settings, such clinics and centers continue to operate along the lines delineated in the early child guidance model. Irrespective of treatment orientation, these settings continue to be the primary loci of training in clinical child psychology (Koocher & Pedulla, 1977). Today, most of these clinics have been incorporated into broader-based institutions referred to as "mental health centers."

Summary

As we have noted, study of child psychopathology is of relatively recent origin. Prior to modern times, children were fortunate to survive to adolescence; most who did survive were valued almost exclusively for their economic worth. In such times, child psychology and child psychopathology were nonexistent. At the beginning of the twentieth century, however, the study of children *per se* emerged, and a variety of forces came together to form the beginnings of child psychopathology as a field of inquiry. Clearly, the area of child psychopathology might well be regarded as a twentieth-century phenomenon.

Currently many issues remain, and consequently the field itself is a vibrant one. Issues associated with the nature of child psychopathology, the classification and categorization of such psychopathology, the models for conceptualizing psychopathology, etiologic agents resulting in psychopathology, and viable systems for efficacious intervention *all* warrant further exploration. Moreover, the critical role of development remains to be systematically investigated as it pertains to each of these basic issues. Surely, there are other equally important issues awaiting resolution.

In the remainder of this text, several of these issues are explored in greater depth. In chapters 2 through 4, issues related to normal development, etiology, and classification are examined. In Part II, the current status of a variety of child psychopathologies is detailed. This section is not meant to be exhaustive; rather, it is intended to sample diverse behavior problems in children. In Part III, psychoanalytic, behavioral, and psychopharmacologic treatments are reviewed, and new and exciting preventative strategies are examined.

At this point, one might well ask: "What is the current status of child psychopathology?" While this volume addresses the question in considerable detail, we must caution the reader that no easy or ready answers prevail. The study of child psychopathology is complex; our current understanding must be considered rudimentary but, nonetheless, highly promising. As students of child psychopathology, we are continually impressed with the mysteries of child development, and the complexities of understanding and treating diverse forms of child psychopathology. As has been noted elsewhere, "complex problems require complex solutions" (Hersen, 1981). In the field of child psychopathology, the complex issues now are being examined with considerable care. Over time, it is our expectation that empirically verified solutions (some simple, some complex) to these problems will be forthcoming.

References

Achenbach, T. M., *Developmental psychopathology,* New York: Ronald Press, 1974.

Aries, P. *Centuries of childhood.* New York: Vintage Books, 1962.

Bockoven, J. S. *Moral treatment in American psychiatry.* New York: Springer, 1963.

Bremmer, R. H. (Ed.), *Children and youth in America: A documentary history, 1600–1865.* (Vol. 1). Cambridge, Mass.: Harvard University Press, 1970.

Brown, F. J. *The sociology of childhood.* Englewood Cliffs, N.J. Prentice-Hall, 1939.

Gelfand, D., & Hartmann, D. P. *Child behavior analysis and therapy.* New York: Pergamon Press, 1975.

Glicklich, L. B., An historical account of enuresis. *Pediatrics,* 1951, *8,* 859–876.

Harms, E. *Origins of modern psychiatry.* Springfield, Ill.: Charles C Thomas, 1967.

Harrison, S. I., & McDermott, J. F. (Eds.). *Childhood psychopathology: An anthology of basic readings.* New York: International Universities Press, 1972.

Hersen, M. Complex problems require complex solutions. *Behavior Therapy,* 1981, *12,* 15–29.

Knopf, I. J. *Childhood psychopathology: A developmental approach.* Englewood Cliffs, N.J.: Prentice-Hall, 1979.

Koocher, G. P., & Pedulla, B. M. Current practices in child psychotherapy. *Professional Psychology,* 1977, *8,* 275–287.

Marholin, D. (Ed.). *Child behavior therapy.* New York: Gardner Press, 1978.

Ollendick, T. H., & Cerny, J. A. *Clinical behavior therapy with children.* New York: Plenum Press, 1981.

Redl, F. Crisis in the children's field. *American Journal of Orthopsychiatry,* 1962, *22,* 759–780.

Rie, H. E. (Ed.). *Perspectives in child psychopathology.* Chicago: Aldine-Atherton, 1971.

Rosen, M., Clark, G. R., & Kivitz, M. S. (Eds.). *The history of mental retardation: Collected papers* (Vol. 1). Baltimore: University Park Press, 1976.

Ross, A. O. *The practice of clinical child psychology.* New York: Grune & Stratton, 1959.

Ross, A. O. *Child behavior therapy: Principles, procedures, and empirical basis.* New York: Wiley, 1981.

Sulzer-Azaroff, B., & Mayer, G. R. *Applying behavior analysis procedures with children and youth.* New York: Holt, Rinehart, & Winston, 1977.

Watson, J. B. Psychology as the behaviorist views it. *Psychological Record,* 1913, *20,* 158–177.

Watson, J. B. *Psychology from the standpoint of a behaviorist.* Philadelphia: Lippincott, 1919.

Watson, J. B. *Behaviorism.* New York: People's Publishing, 1924.

Watson, R. I. *Psychology of the child: Personal, social and disturbed child development.* New York: Wiley, 1959.

Zilboorg, G., & Henry, G. W. *History of medical psychology.* New York: Norton, 1941.

2

Developmental Perspectives in Child Psychopathology

SUSAN B. CAMPBELL

Looking at Behavior in Developmental Context

Although it is obvious to any student of child development that behavior, whether "normal" or "abnormal," must be examined within a developmental context, it is only recently that child psychiatry and clinical child psychology have paid more than lip service to this notion. Both theory and nomenclature were originally adapted from work with adults, and the important changes in behavior and cognitive capacity that occur as a function of physical maturation and psychological development were largely overlooked. Instead, attempts were made to extend adult models downward, and theories of adult psychopathology were unsuccessfully adapted to childhood problems.

While conceptualizations of adult problems may provide some insight into childhood disorders, and vice versa, both research and practice in the child field are complicated by a host of factors that influence problem definition, course, and outcome, as well as treatment decisions. Among these are the child's chronological age, level of cognitive and social development, family background, and a variety of other social and cultural factors. Indeed, it is virtually meaningless to consider child behavior in isolation from social influences and developmental stage.

At the most basic level, problem definition depends on the age of the child. Behaviors considered symptomatic of disturbance at one age may be considered typical at another. Thus, bedwetting, inability to read, stranger anxiety, or separation distress are not considered problems among 1- and 2-year-olds, but are worthy of concern in 12-year-olds. Refusal to go to sleep before midnight might be a cause of concern to parents of infants,

SUSAN B. CAMPBELL • Department of Psychology, University of Pittsburgh, Pittsburgh, Pennsylvania 15260.

but not of adolescents. Other potentially problematic behaviors appear to change with age. For example, defiant behavior is often a concern of parents, and it is more common among toddlers and adolescents than among 8-year-olds. However, its manifestations obviously vary as a function of age.

The cognitive-developmental level of the child similarly influences how a particular behavior is perceived, interpreted, and labeled by adults. For example, aggressive behavior is a common referral complaint among school-age and adolescent males seen in child mental health facilities. However, interpretations of aggressive behavior vary with the age of the child (Wenger, Berg-Cross, & Berg-Cross, 1980), and aggressive behavior in 2- and 3-year-old males rarely leads to referral. Parents may describe their youngster as "rough" and note that he does not "mean" to hurt the other child. Inherent in this is a distinction between the child's behavior and intentions as well as some notion of perspective-taking. The toddler has not yet reached the stage of cognitive development that permits him to take the viewpoints of others into account. Thus, he does not connect his behavior (i.e., hitting) with its effect on another person (i.e., inflicting pain). Further, aggressive encounters between 2- and 3-year-old peers are frequently struggles over a toy (Smith & Green, 1975), reflecting the egocentrism of this stage of cognitive and social development. Both think of "me" and do not consider the fact that their partner wants the toy just as much as they do. Thus, egocentrism and lack of perspective-taking typical of toddlerhood lead adults to construe particular negative behaviors as less problematic in young children than these same behaviors would be perceived in older children.

Similarly, the prognostic implications of behaviors at different ages vary considerably, although much empirical work remains to be done in this area. Parents of toddlers frequently complain of tantrum behavior and aggression towards peers, but they are more likely than parents of older children to perceive these behaviors as transient developmental phenomena. While data on the long-term consequences of these behaviors in young children are lacking, clinicians do not interpret such behavior as likely to predict later antisocial or interpersonal problems. On the other hand, disobedience towards adults and aggression towards peers in school-age youngsters are associated with antisocial behavior in adolescence and young adulthood (Gersten, Langner, Eisenberg, Simcha-Fagan, & McCarthy, 1976; Robins, 1966). Thus, clinicians would be more likely to be concerned about the potentially negative prognosis of such behaviors in a school-age as opposed to preschool-age child.

Age of onset and chronicity of symptoms are also relevant to the conceptualization of problem behavior in children and to probable prognosis. Thus, overactive and defiant behavior in a 10-year-old boy that is described as having been present since infancy or toddlerhood is more likely to be seen as a serious problem with a relatively poor prognosis than the same behavior occurring in a 10-year-old boy in response to parental divorce. Although early onset and chronicity would contribute to a diagnosis of a bona fide syndrome, late onset of an acute disorder in response to a specific stressor would most likely be viewed as a reactive disorder that is time-limited and has a good prognosis. Thus, the same overt behaviors in children of the same age and sex may elicit different diagnostic formulations and treatment recommendations, depending partly upon developmental factors of age of onset and chronicity.

Treatment recommendations are likewise influenced by the child's age and cognitive–developmental level. Play therapy is most often used with children in the preschool and primary grades who are less likely to be clearly aware of their problems or to have the verbal sophistication to discuss them directly in a therapeutic situation. Some clinicians find play an ideal vehicle for communicating with and gaining insight into the problems of young children (Axline, 1969). On the other hand, older children with average intelligence and good verbal skills are more likely to be seen in verbal psychotherapy.

Whereas behavioral approaches are used with children of all ages, often with parent or teacher as the behavior change agent (Berkowitz & Graziano, 1972), self-monitoring and self-reinforcement approaches (Turkewitz, O'Leary, & Ironsmith, 1975) or the use of peers as behavior modifiers (Colletti & Harris, 1977; Surratt, Ulrich, & Hawkins, 1969) are more common with older children. Type of reinforcement obviously varies with age, and tokens or other forms of delayed reinforcement are less often used with young children who may be less able to delay gratification.

Cognitive-developmental factors likewise play a role in treatment outcome. For example, cognitive behavioral approaches that attempt to teach the child more efficient problem-solving strategies appear to work better with school-age youngsters (Douglas, Parry, Marton, & Garson, 1976). They have attained a certain level of cognitive development and can think about the short-term consequences of their behavior better than younger children (Cohen, Sullivan, Minde, Novak, & Helwig, 1981), who are less likely to engage in consequential thinking.

Similarly, cognitive-developmental level is seen as influencing diagnostic labels. It has been suggested that the "here and now" orientation of children up to age 8 or 9 and a tendency not to reason about the future preclude true affective disorder. Since a feeling of hopelessness and pessimism about the future is often conceptualized as central to a diagnosis of depression (Beck, 1972), a certain degree of cognitive development is a necessary prerequisite to a sense of future time. Thus, among some clinicians a diagnosis of depression must await the transition from concrete operational to formal operational thinking in Piagetian terms (Rie, 1966).

Taken together, then, these examples illustrate the important role that cognitive and affective development play in determining who is perceived as a problem, how the problem is conceptualized and labeled, what treatment recommendations are made, and what the likely outcome of the problem is.

Problem Behavior and Adult Expectations: Whose Problem Is It?

Although most adults who reach mental health facilities initiate contact themselves and have at least some notion that they have a problem, children almost uniformly are professionally evaluated because a parent, teacher, or physician has expressed concern; they may or may not be aware of the problem themselves. Indeed, they may not have a problem at all. The first task of the clinician working with children and families is to determine whether or not a problem actually exists. Intolerance, ignorance, and misconceptions on the part of adults often lead to referral. All too often, when there is a problem, the problem may reside more in the family system or in the way parents are managing their child's behavior, though this is often a difficult concept to convey to parents. Further, parents' perceptions of child behavior are often influenced by their own emotional state. For example, Shepherd, Oppenheim, and Mitchell (1971), in a large epidemiological study of childhood psychopathology, compared a group of clinic attenders with matched controls who were rated as having problems of equivalent severity but who had never sought treatment. The main factors that differentiated clinic attenders from nonattenders were maternal perceptions of the problem as serious versus transient, maternal feelings of competence, family disruption, and maternal depression. Sandberg, Wieselberg, and Shaffer (1980) noted an association between ratings of behavior problems and maternal psychiatric distress. Similarly, Richman (1977), in a study of behavior problems in 3-year-olds, found that high ratings of behavior problems were associated with maternal depression, marital dysfunction, and high stress, suggesting that maternal tolerance plays a large role in defining behavior problems in children. Further, the association between marital problems and childhood behavior disorders (Johnson & Lobitz, 1974; Porter & O'Leary, 1980; Rutter, 1971; Whitehead, 1979) suggests the importance of the family climate in the perception and definition of childhood problems. In a study of referral patterns among general practitioners in London, Gath (1968) reported that in at least two-thirds of the cases referred to a child psychiatry clinic, parental attitudes had been the key factor leading to referral. Taken together, then, these findings suggest that parental conceptualizations of the problem and their own psychological state influence their tolerance for and ability to handle child behavior, and thus have considerable impact on referral patterns.

In our own ongoing project involving parent-defined "hyperactivity" and associated behavior problems in toddlers, we have been consistently impressed with variations we see in parental tolerance. Whereas a few parents seem to be able to rationalize as "just being a boy" a range of destructive, aggressive, and inappropriate behaviors, others seem unable to accept even the mildest temper outburst or expression of defiance in 2- and 3-year-olds, and they anxiously call the project to seek help "before things get out of hand." Many of the parents in our project are defining "normal" and age-appropriate attempts to be independent as "problem" behavior, and they are setting up a negative and escalating cycle of coercive control (Bell, 1968; Patterson, 1976). Clearly, parental tolerance and its influence on parenting style and child management skills play an important role in the definition of childhood problems as well as in their development and maintenance.

This issue is further complicated by the fact that not everyone in the child's environment will perceive a behavior as a problem or perceive a problem the same way. Thus, the parent and teacher ratings of behavior problems often show only minimal agreement (Campbell, Schleifer, & Weiss, 1978; Rutter, Tizard, & Whitmore, 1970; Sandberg *et al.*, 1980; Schleifer, Weiss, Cohen, Elman, Cvejic, & Kruger, 1975; Shepherd *et al.*, 1971), while disagreement between parents and physicians has also been reported (Jenkins, Bax, & Hart, 1980). Finally, even within families, parents do not always agree on the existence or severity of problem behavior (Ferguson, Partyka, & Lester, 1974; Speer, 1971). This is not totally surprising because children behave in different ways in different situations (Mischel, 1977) and with different individuals (Lytton, 1979; Lytton & Zwirner, 1975). Taken together, adult variations in tolerance and expectations, their differential effects on child behavior, and the situational specificity of behavior all contribute to difficulties in assessing when and whether a problem exists.

Epidemiological Studies of Childhood Behavior Problems: Prevalence Rates as a Function of Age and Sex

Although definitions of "normal" or "abnormal" behavior are impossible to arrive at, and it is clear that age, sex, cultural, and other factors determine what is and is not considered appropriate, some attempts have been made to provide normative data on the frequencies of specific behaviors in representative samples of children of a particular age. Thus, a number of large-scale survey studies of representative groups of children have been carried out to determine rates of specific problem behaviors in the general population. The bulk of these studies have been conducted in Great Britain (Richman, Stevenson, & Graham, 1975; Rutter *et al.,* 1970; Shepherd *et al.,* 1971) and the United States (Lapouse & Monk, 1958; MacFarlane, Allen, & Honzik, 1954; Werry & Quay, 1971).

Studies of very young children have been rare. However, one recent study (Jenkins *et al.,* 1980) examined parental concerns about 97% (N = 418) of the 6-week-old to 4½-year-old children in a geographic catchment area of North London. Problems in infancy were relatively rare and the focus, not surprisingly, was on sleeping problems, on feeding difficulties and colic, and on crying. Between ages 1 and 2, problems began to increase somewhat, but feeding and sleeping problems continued to predominate. Bowel and bladder problems emerged at age 2 and problems peaked at age 3 when the major complaint became difficulties with management and discipline. Although parents expressed concerns about specific behaviors, few saw their children as demonstrating significant or severe problems, an observation with which the examining general practitioner usually agreed. These cross-sectional findings generally confirm results of the Berkeley Growth Study (MacFarlane *et al.,* 1954), which followed a representative sample of children from 21 months to 14 years.

The majority of large-scale studies of children's behavior have been concerned with children of preschool and school age. Despite differences in methodology, age of child, sample characteristics, locale, and sources of data, major findings have been remarkably consistent. When frequencies of specific behaviors considered to be of psychiatric significance are studied in large populations of children, it is evident that symptomatic behaviors are very common among nonreferred children of preschool age (Kohn, 1977; MacFarlane *et al.,* 1954; Rolf, Hakola, Klemchuk, & Hasazi, 1976) and school age (Rutter *et al.,* 1970; Werry & Quay, 1971). Further, boys are perceived as having more problems than girls, especially behavior associated with conduct disorders and hyperactivity (Rutter *et al.,* 1970; Werry & Quay, 1971), although sex differences in behaviors are found less consistently with younger children (Hughes, Pinkerton, & Plewis, 1979; Kohn, 1977; MacFarlane *et al.,* 1954; Richman *et al.,* 1975; Rolf *et al.,* 1976). Age changes in specific behaviors are also apparent, with a general tendency for problems such as fears and worries, nightmares, enuresis, and tantrums to decrease with increasing age in preschool (Coleman, Wolkind, & Ashley, 1977: MacFarlane *et al.,* 1954) and school-age samples (Lapouse & Monk, 1958; Werry & Quay, 1971).

Prevalence estimates for certain behaviors are extremely high and underline the importance of considering the frequency, intensity, and chronicity of clusters of symptoms within a developmental and social context when defining psychiatric disorder (Rutter *et al.,* 1970). Isolated behaviors in and of themselves do not determine whether or not a disorder exists. Furthermore, rare behaviors do not indicate disturbance any more than frequent behaviors indicate normality. However, it is important to note that many behaviors considered of psychiatric significance are extremely common in nonclinical samples.

For example, the defining features of hyperactivity (now known as attention deficit disorder with hyperactivity in DSM-III) are restlessness, distractibility, and short attention span (Campbell, 1976; Whalen & Henker, 1976). According to Werry and Quay's (1971) data, teachers described 49.7% of kindergarten through second-grade boys in a midwestern college town as restless; 43.5% were described as having a short attention span, and 48.2% were rated distractible. Similarly, a large proportion of mothers in Buffalo, New York, rated their 6- to 12-year-old children as overactive (49%) and restless (30%) (Lapouse & Monk, 1958). Although hyperactivity is rarely diagnosed in Great Britain (Rutter *et al.,* 1970), and prevalence rates of associated behaviors are somewhat lower, Shepherd *et al.,* (1971) found that 20% of boys between 5 and 14 years sampled in the Buckinghamshire survey were described as restless. Rutter *et al.* (1970) found that parents rated 34.8% of the general population of 10- to 11-year-old boys on the Isle of Wight as restless, and 25.2% as having poor concentration. Comparable figures for teacher ratings were 15.7% and 35.3%, respectively. Across all four studies, fewer girls were rated as showing these behaviors, and younger children showed them more often than older children.

What are the implications of these data? First, if the epidemiological cutoff of 10% were utilized (Shepherd *et al.*, 1971), and it were agreed that rarity meant abnormality, we would be forced to conclude that, assuming that these ratings by teachers and parents are valid reflections of the behavior in question, these behaviors are essentially normal. That is, restlessness and attentional problems are so common in young boys as to be virtually meaningless in terms of diagnostic significance. Indeed, even calling these behaviors problematic might be misleading. An alternative interpretation might be that there is an epidemic of hyperactivity that has spread from North America to Great Britain. Furthermore, data on cross-sectional age differences might suggest that overactive behavior and attentional problems are outgrown as children mature. However, all these conclusions would be wrong.

Data on isolated behaviors cannot really answer questions about the presence of an actual psychological disorder or its course. These issues require information on patterns of symptoms that covary, and on their change over time within subjects showing the disorder. In fact, hyperactivity is one of the most common diagnoses given to school-age boys seen in child mental health facilities in North America (Miller, Palkes, & Stewart, 1973; Trites, Dugas, Lynch, & Ferguson, 1979). Furthermore, some recent studies suggest that these problems are also common in younger samples (ages 3 to 5—Behar, 1977; Coleman *et al.*, 1977; Kohn, 1977) and that they may have prognostic significance for later school functioning (Coleman *et al.*, 1977; Halverson & Waldrop, 1976; Kohn, 1977). Follow-up studies of hyperactive school-age youngsters indicate that problems in social and academic functioning persist, although the specific behavioral manifestations of the disorder change somewhat with age (Milich & Loney, 1979; Weiss, Hechtman, & Perlman, 1978; Weiss, Minde, Werry, Douglas, & Nemeth, 1971). Thus, the clinical findings parallel the epidemiological findings in that the problems are common, are more often found in boys, and show some changes with age. However, were we to conclude from the epidemiological studies that the problems were merely transient developmental disturbances or behaviors that were so common as to be clinically meaningless, we would be wrong. The frequency of occurrence of a specific behavior in the population as a whole, as well as its variation in the population as a function of age and sex, may highlight the need to be cautious in diagnosing disorder. However, it tells us little about the prevalence, course, or likely developmental outcome of a syndrome that includes the specific behavior in question.

Thus, it is important to distinguish between isolated behaviors, which may be characteristic of both "normal" and disturbed children, and clusters of symptoms, which tend to covary, which tend to interfere with adaptive functioning, and which are considered indicative of psychiatric disorder (Rutter *et al.*, 1970). Several epidemiological studies have examined prevalence rates of disorder over and above examining the frequencies of specific symptomatic behaviors. Gersten *et al.* (1967) noted that 12% of their subjects residing in midtown Manhattan had significant behavior problems, while Bower (1969) reported problems in 10% of Los Angeles school children. Rutter *et al.* (1970) screened all children who were betweeen 10 and 11 on the Isle of Wight (England) in 1965 (N = 3316), and on the basis of empirically derived cutoff scores on parent and teacher behavior rating scales, selected 13% for intensive psychiatric assessment. On the basis of this assessment, 5.4% of the total population was diagnosed as having a psychiatric disorder. Problems were more common in boys. However, sex differences were also apparent in the type of problem.

Not surprisingly, conduct disorders were more frequent among boys and neurotic problems were more common in girls. Finally, interpersonal problems and concentration difficulties were the most common symptoms found across all diagnostic groups. Here again, the findings of prevalence of disorder parallel the findings examining frequencies of specific behaviors.

Richman *et al.* (1975) reported a prevalence rate of 7% "moderate to severe" problems and 15% "mild" problems among a representative sample of 3-year-olds in London, roughly similar to the rates reported by Rutter *et al.* Richman and her colleagues did not find sex differences in rates of disorder, but family problems were associated with childhood disturbance. These findings were confirmed by Hughes *et al.* (1979) in London and by Minde and Minde (1977) in a smaller nonrepresentative sample of 3- to 4-year-olds in Toronto. Furthermore, behavior problems in toddlers appear to be associated with a high incidence of delayed language development (Baker, Cantwell, & Mattison, 1980; Richman, 1977).

Finally, there is general consensus from a large number of studies that problems in toddlers, preschoolers, and school-age youngsters fall into two primary categories of disorder: (1) internalizing or inner-directed clusters of behavior such as neurotic, withdrawn, depressed, and somatic problems; and (2) externalizing or outer-directed clusters of behavior such as conduct problems, hyperactivity, and aggressive and antisocial disorders (Achenbach, 1978; Behar, 1977; Kohn, 1977; Quay, 1979; Rutter *et al.,* 1970). Like specific symptoms, age changes and sex differences are found when clusters of behavior are examined.

In summary, symptomatic behaviors are common across the age range from early to later childhood, whereas estimates of actual disorder seem relatively low. Furthermore, family functioning and parental tolerance, as well as the age of the child, clearly influence whether or not a child will actually be referred for an evaluation and whether or not a problem will be diagnosed. Further, these factors will partly determine whether a problem is perceived by the clinician as potentially serious or as a transient developmental problem typical of a particular stage of development. It is to these transient problems that we now turn our attention.

Common Developmental Problems

Whereas problem definition and prognostic implications of specific behaviors vary with age, it is also clear that certain problem behaviors are characteristic of a particular developmental stage and are apparently transient. Common developmental problems may reflect the exaggeration of age-appropriate behaviors or difficult transitions from one stage of development to the next. While the turbulence of adolescence is the most frequently cited example of a common developmental problem, problems are common at all ages; they may be particularly intense at one age (e.g., toddlerhood) and more subtle at another (e.g., early school-age or "latency"). However common, developmental problems are often a source of serious concern to parents (Mesibov, Schroeder, & Wesson, 1977). Further, the assumption is often made by both parents and professionals that improper handling of a difficult developmental phase may lead to later problems, and conversely, if early problems are handled sensitively and appropriately, development of difficulties at a later stage may be prevented (Thomas, Chess, & Birch, 1968).

Among young children, common developmental difficulties rarely reach the mental health practitioner; rather, the family physician or pediatrician is frequently consulted about the behavioral and developmental concerns of parents of infants and toddlers. Often such difficulties reflect misunderstandings on the part of parents about the normal course of development and the particular tasks of a developmental stage; further, these common developmental problems are often exacerbated by parental mismanagement. Thus, it is important to bear in mind that these childhood problems can best be conceptualized within a model that examines the reciprocal influences of parents on children and children on parents (Bell & Harper, 1977; Sameroff & Chandler, 1975). Several typical problems characteristic of different stages from infancy through school-age will be discussed with particular emphasis on their developmental aspects, both typical and potentially problematic.

Infancy

The "Difficult" Infant

While infants are rarely referred to mental health professionals except in severe cases of gross disorder or developmental delay, parental concerns often do reach the pediatrician (Carey, 1972). Furthermore, there has been much clinical, theoretical, and research attention focused on infant temperament and its possible role as a precursor of childhood difficulties (Bell & Harper, 1977; Sameroff & Chandler, 1975; Thomas *et al.,* 1968). It is generally acknowledged that there are wide individual differences in infant behavior from the neonatal period onward. Furthermore, these differences are reflected in behaviors such as the frequency and duration of crying, infant cuddliness and consolability, activity level, alertness, and self-quieting (Brazelton, 1973; Korner, 1971; Vaughn, Taraldson, Crichton, & Egeland, 1980). These behaviors can have profound effects on parent behavior and the quality of the developing parent–infant relationship (Korner, 1971; Osofsky, 1976). It seems obvious that an active, alert, and easily consoled infant will elicit different behaviors from caretakers and have different requirements for caretaking than an active but irritable infant who cries frequently and is not easily calmed.

The possibility that early infant temperamental characteristics could influence the quality of early parenting as well as later infant development and family relationships was initially articulated by Thomas *et al.* (1968) in a classic prospective study of early infant temperament and the development of behavior disorders in young children. These authors noted the importance of "goodness of fit" between an infant's behavioral style and parental tolerance, sensitivity, and methods of childrearing. These notions of mutual regulation of parent–child interaction and individual differences in the specifics of interaction patterns have been spelled out within a more sophisticated theoretical framework in Sameroff and Chandler's (1975) transactional model of development and have been operationalized by several investigators of infant development (Brazelton, Koslowski, & Main, 1974; Stern, 1974).

Thomas and his associates suggested that infants who were irritable, slow to adapt to changes in routine, intense in reaction, and irregular in biological functioning were more difficult to care for and more likely to develop later behavior problems. However, intensive clinical follow-up of a large sample of families in New York City indicated that difficult infants who were handled sensitively, whose parents effectively modulated their intensity and permitted them time to "warm up" to new stimuli, were more likely to weather this often difficult developmental period with no ill effects. On the other hand, parents who were rough, intolerant, or who forced their difficult infants to adapt to changes in routine quickly, were often more likely to suffer the consequences later on, as their difficult infants grew into negative and defiant toddlers with early peer problems. On the other hand, easy infants, that is, infants who were positive in mood, reasonably regular in patterns of sleeping and eating, and adaptable to change, also adapted to a wider range of parental management styles and were less likely to develop later problems, although they were not immune from them. This early study has become a classic in the field and has generated a number of more sophisticated research studies into the relationship between early infant temperament and later behavior.

More recent research that has utilized systematic behavioral observation, blind observers, and independent data sources indicates that difficult infant behavior, such as prolonged crying and inconsolability, is associated with lowered maternal responsiveness (Bates, Freeland, & Lounsbury, 1979; Campbell, 1979; Crockenberg, 1980; Moss, 1967); it has been suggested that an escalating negative cycle of parent–child encounters may lead to later behavior problems in some proportion of difficult infants (Campbell, 1976; Crockenberg, 1980; Ross & Ross, 1976; Sameroff, 1978). However, continued follow-up of difficult infants will be necessary to determine the validity of this hypothesis.

Although it is clear from the longitudinal work of Thomas *et al.* (1968) that not all difficult infants become behavior-problem toddlers, retrospective data from several studies support the contention that children who are described as active and aggressive in toddlerhood, preschool-age (Campbell, 1976), and school-age (Stewart, Pitts, Craig, & Dieruf, 1966) are more likely to be described by parents as irritable and difficult-to-soothe infants, who had irregular and unpredictable patterns of eating and sleeping. Although the problems of collecting such retrospective data are obvious, the findings are at least suggestive of a relationship between difficult infant temperament and later behavior problems.

For example, in an ongoing study of behavior-problem toddlers and matched controls currently being carried out in our lab at the University of Pittsburgh, we have analyzed pilot data on 37 2- to 3-year-old youngsters. Comparisons between children who were rated by parents as showing behavior problems ($N = 23$) and nonproblem controls ($N = 14$), indicate that parent-perceived problem toddlers were also reportedly more difficult infants. Mothers report a more difficult neonatal ($\chi^2 = 6.26, p < .01$) and infancy period ($\chi^2 = 8.92, p < .01$) characterized by irregular sleep patterns ($\chi^2 = 3.98, p < .05$) and feeding difficulties ($\chi^2 = 5.27, p < .02$). Problem toddlers were also described as more active infants ($\chi^2 = 4.30, p < .05$), who cried excessively ($\chi^2 = 3.98, p < .05$), and were more difficult to console when upset than controls ($\chi^2 = 3.90, p < .05$).

Although much work remains to be done in this area to assess systematically the relationships among infant temperamental characteristics, early parent–child relations, and later behavior problems, it does seem safe to conclude that some are easier to care for than others and, further, that difficulties during this period may indeed be a precursor of later problems, although it also appears that parental behavior can influence whether or not difficult infant behavior will develop into later behavior problems or will merely reflect a difficult phase of development that is eventually outgrown. Research that evaluates specific aspects of both infant and parent behavior and changes in these behaviors over time is just beginning to address these questions.

Problems in Attachment

It has long been assumed by clinicians and theorists of child psychopathology that the early mother–infant relationship is a primary determinant of later development and subsequent mental health (Bowlby, 1958; A. Freud, 1965; Mahler, 1968; Winnicott, 1957).

While early theorists hypothesized a unidirectional and causal relationship between early maternal behavior and an infant's psychological development, recent theoretical advances underscore the complex and mutually regulated interaction that develops between mother and infant. The major reconceptualization in this area falls under the rubric of attachment theory (Ainsworth, 1969; Bowlby, 1969). Research on the nature of mother–infant interaction is beginning to confirm many of the notions put forth by attachment theorists.

Over the course of the first year of life, infants develop a specific and enduring relationship with primary caretakers (usually parents), which has been termed *attachment* (Ainsworth, 1969; Bowlby, 1969). Attachment is a reciprocal relationship that develops gradually through stages during the first year and is mediated by the quality, timing, and pacing of adult–child encounters (Ainsworth, Blehar, Waters, & Wall, 1978). Initially, the infant directs social responses (crying, smiling, sucking, clinging) indiscriminantly to any responsive adult. However, as cognitive capacities develop, the infant begins to respond differentially to familiar and unfamiliar figures, usually by the end of the third month. By the sixth or seventh month, the infant actively seeks to maintain contact with attachment figures, is active in initiating contact, protests at separation, and is beginning to show a wariness of strangers. As the attachment relationship consolidates, the primary attachment figure serves as a secure base from which the infant explores the environment and is the main source of comfort in times of distress, fear, or illness. Whereas establishment of attachment is a universal feature of infant social–emotional development (except in cases of early infantile autism, where failure to form an attachment is a significant feature of the disorder), variations in maternal and infant behavior can influence the quality of the attachment relationship that develops.

Individual differences in patterns of attachment have been explored in depth by Ainsworth and her colleagues (Ainsworth & Bell, 1969; Ainsworth & Wittig, 1969; Ainsworth *et al.*, 1978; Bell & Ainsworth, 1972; Stayton, Hogan, & Ainsworth, 1971) as well as others (Sroufe & Waters, 1977; Vaughn, Egeland, Sroufe, & Waters, 1979). Findings from a large series of studies indicate that early maternal behavior influences later infant–mother attachment. Mothers who are sensitive to their infant's cues and are responsive across a range of situations that include feeding, responsiveness to crying, early face-to-face play, and the provision of opportunities to explore, foster the development of a secure attachment relationship. Mothers who respond to their infant abruptly, who are unresponsive, or who pace their behavior to their own needs and schedules, foster development of an anxious or ambivalent attachment characterized by excessive anger, clinging, and/or avoidant behavior on the part of the infant. The mother is not utilized as a source of support or comfort in stressful situations. Quality of attachment at the first year appears to build upon earlier mother–infant interaction patterns and has also been found to relate to later problem-solving ability and competence with peers (Matas, Arend, & Sroufe, 1978; Waters, Wippman, & Sroufe, 1979). Securely attached infants appear to develop in more optimal directions, both cognitively and socially. However, studies that examine the relationship between quality of early attachment and later psychopathology have yet to be carried out, despite the central role of early maternal behavior in dynamic formulations of pathological development.

Recent research using a prospective design suggests that maternal behavior interacts with infant characteristics and life circumstances to influence the pattern of attachment. Neonatal difficulties, as measured by the Brazelton Neonatal Behavioral Assessment Scale, were associated with anxious attachments at 1-year among a sample of families at risk because of poverty and other stressful life events (Vaughn *et al.*, 1979; Waters, Vaughn, &

Egeland, 1980). It has also been suggested that child abuse and neglect, both extreme examples of disordered attachment, should be associated with anxious and avoidant infant behavior (Ainsworth *et al.,* 1978), and there is some recent evidence to support this hypothesis (Egeland & Sroufe, 1981; George & Main, 1979).

These findings are provocative and underline the importance of continued research on these questions. In particular, we require research that examines the impact of a variety of psychological and social variables on the development of attachment; research on the relationship between early attachment and later psychological adjustment and maladjustment is also sorely needed. Despite lack of empirical evidence, many clinicians working with infants and families tend to assume that early problems in attachment will inevitably lead to later problems. While it has been suggested that disordered attachment is a risk factor increasing probability of later problems, findings from high-risk research suggest that some children growing up in less than advantageous circumstances develop normally and are reasonably invulnerable to influences that would be deleterious to others (Anthony, 1974).

Toddlerhood and Preschool Age

Defiance or Independence?

The achievement of independence is among the major developmental tasks of toddlerhood. Children must make the shift from a dependent infant to a mobile, verbal child who explores the world and begins to interact outside the nuclear family. This is a stage of rapid cognitive development as the youngster begins to develop a sense of himself or herself as an individual, to learn that his or her behavior has effects on others, to spend time experimenting on the inanimate world, and to test his or her own limits. Although parents expect children to develop independence at this stage in areas such as feeding, toileting, and even dressing, independence in other areas can lead to problems. Often the child's move towards independence and environmental mastery leads to a period of intense struggle with parents over limits and control (Brazelton, 1974).

Children at this age are rarely brought to mental health clinics, but pediatricians must deal with questions about behavior and management on a daily basis. This is an extremely difficult time for parents who are often afraid to set limits or are unable to accept the defiance that is typical of this stage. Amazingly little research has been done on behavior problems in this age group, although the few survey studies previously cited (Jenkins *et al.,* 1980; MacFarlane *et al.,* 1954; Richman, 1977) indicate that noncompliance or management problems are the prominent parental concern. Jenkins *et al.* reported that while only 5% of parents of infants expressed excessive concern about behavior, 23% of parents of 3-year-olds were unsure about how to discipline their toddler. MacFarlane *et al.* (1954) found that negativism peaked at age 3 for boys and was associated with hyperactivity and tantrum behavior. This is confirmed by our own data on behavior problem toddlers, in which disciplinary problems and concerns about when and how to set limits are the major concerns expressed by parents of 2½- to 3½-year-olds.

Several research studies on compliance in this age group are enlightening. It is well known from the behavioral literature (Forehand & Scarboro, 1975) that parental commands are associated with increased noncompliance in children. In an elegant study of parent–child interaction in toddlers, Lytton and Zwirner (1975) carried out extensive home observations of a large sample of 2- and 3-year-old boys. Sequential analysis of data indicated that these youngsters were more likely to comply after a parental suggestion than after a command or prohibition. Further, less conflict-laden situations were associated with more compliant behavior. Finally, physical control and negative interaction were associated with more noncompliance, which in turn led to a negative and controlling response from the parent, and the cycle escalated. More recently, Lytton (1979) reported that when phsyical control was paired with a command or prohibition, compliance was even less likely to occur. This escalating and negative cycle of conflict has been described by Patterson (1976) with somewhat older children.

Minton, Kagan, and Levine (1971) observed 90 first-born children at home when each child was 27 months of age. They reported that children were, on the whole, obedient, and they suggested that the notion of the "terrible two's" was a myth, at least for this sample. They did, however, note social class differences in parenting style and sex differences in child behavior. Mothers from lower educational levels tended to use more prohibitions and more physical punishment; boys tended to be more disobedient than girls, especially in response to maternal prohibitions. College-educated mothers, on the other hand, tended to use more reasoning and to explain prohibitions. These findings are consistent with a number of earlier studies, which found social class differences in child rearing and differential effects of authoritarian versus democratic child-rearing practices on child behavior (Baumrind & Black, 1967; Sears, Maccoby, & Levin, 1957).

While it is obvious that parental actions can maintain noncompliant behavior at a high rate, it is also likely that some degree of "defiant" or "independent" behavior is both age-appropriate and necessary for the child's normal development as an individual. The toddler must learn to separate from the parents, to be aware of and to express his or her own needs, and to learn about his or her capacities. Often, behavior considered to be "independent" in tolerant and knowledgable parents is considered "defiant" or "noncompliant" by less tolerant parents. As with many problems of childhood, the problem may be in the eye of the beholder.

In our own work with toddlers and their families, we have been impressed with the variations in parental tolerance, their impressions of the child's intent, and the management strategies they employ. Parents who complain that their toddler "never listens" or that no form of discipline ever "works" tend to be those with inconsistent management approaches who often shout and threaten, but tend not to follow through to enforce limits effectively. Or, they use a good deal of physical punishment, which exacerbates the cycle of conflict. Their children are irritable and the battles between them are constant. They are often amazed at the cooperation a quiet, yet direct and firm approach achieves. Such parents often perceive any attempt at independence as a test of their authority as a parent—something they attempt to squelch almost automatically. At the other extreme, we see parents who are at their wit's end, unable to set appropriate limits on their toddler's defiance, parents who are being tyrannized by their 2-year-olds. We are currently evaluating the effectiveness of parent training groups and have stressed the importance of a combined developmental and behavioral approach. Training parents in the use of operant procedures alone, without additional information about what behavior is or is not developmentally appropriate, seems to have difficulties of its own, despite its effectiveness in changing specific behaviors.

In conclusion, the striving for independence typical of toddlerhood is often perceived by parents as defiance. Further, it appears that attempts by parents at overcontrol can lead to an escalation of noncompliant behavior. However, at this stage of our knowledge, little can be said about the long-term implications of such behavior. While clinical lore predicts that in most instances excessive defiance in toddlerhood is a stage-specific developmental phenomenon, it also appears that especially insensitive handling of this stage may increase the likelihood that problems will persist (Kohn, 1977; Thomas *et al.*, 1968).

Aggressive Behavior

Aggressive behavior towards peers is a common complaint of parents of preschoolers. When descriptions of the behavior of young children are analyzed, an aggressive factor invariably emerges (Behar, 1977; Bell, Waldrop, & Weller, 1972; Kohn & Rosman, 1972). Coleman *et al.* (1977) noted that 53% of their sample were described as having difficulty with peers at age 3. Rolf *et al.* (1976) found that 30% of 4- and 5-year-olds in their sample were seen as moderately to highly aggressive with peers. Observations on nonclinical samples in preschools confirm that aggressive encounters are reasonably common occurrences (Blurton-Jones, 1972; Serbin, O'Leary, Kent, & Tonick, 1973; Smith & Green, 1975).

Studies of peer interaction among preschoolers indicate that aggressive behavior is not only common, but that it tends to be successful. Both Patterson, Littman, and Bricker (1967) and Smith and Green (1975) reported that the majority of aggressive acts resulted in the aggressor getting his or her way. Studies also indicate that aggressive interchanges are more common between boys than between girls or mixed sex dyads (Pedersen & Bell, 1970; Serbin *et al.*, 1973; Smith & Green, 1975) and that the majority are property conflicts over the use of a toy (Blurton-Jones, 1972; Dawe, 1934; Houseman, 1973; Smith & Green, 1975).

Smith and Green (1975) noted that 73% of the aggressive incidents they observed in 15 different preschool classrooms were property conflicts. Houseman (1973) similarly reported that 67% of the conflicts she witnessed during 63 hours of observation in preschools were related to the possession or use of materials or space. Conflicts averaged 13.6 per hour per child and lasted a mean of 12.4 seconds. Further, frequency of conflict varied with activity setting. For example, fights were more likely to develop when children were playing with blocks than when they were engaged in an art activity. Furthermore, there is evidence that this form of instrumental or object-oriented aggression declines with age (Dawe, 1934; Hartup, 1974).

Feshbach and Feshbach (1972) suggest that aggressive behavior is a response readily available in the repertoire of young children and a direct way of reaching a goal such as obtaining a toy. With development, children learn alternate, more adaptive means such as sharing and negotiating. However, Feshbach and Feshbach point out that it is often difficult to distinguish between an instrumental aggressive act, which is determined solely by self-interest (obtaining a toy), and hostile or person-oriented aggression, where the intent is to hurt the other child. Intent may be a factor that differentiates "normal" behavior from more problematic aggressive behavior.

Studies indicate that children who are consistently aggressive in preschool are less popular with peers; conversely, prosocial behavior is associated with greater peer popularity (Charlesworth & Hartup, 1967; Hartup, Glazer, & Charlesworth, 1967). In addition, observational studies suggest that aggressive behavior elicits negative behavior from peers while positive interaction elicits more compliance and prosocial behavior (Leiter, 1977; Moore, 1967).

Several studies also indicate relationships among high-intensity behaviors. That is, preschool children who tend to be active and boisterous also tend to be more aggressive, to initiate peer interaction, and to attempt to dominate peers (Battle & Lacey, 1972; Billman

& McDevitt, 1980; Buss, Block, & Block, 1980; Halverson & Waldrop, 1973). Thus youngsters who engage in active behavior and are more involved with peers are also more likely to become aggressive than the more quiet, passive children. Moreover, there is evidence that these patterns persist into the early school years (Battle & Lacey, 1972; Buss *et al.,* 1980; Halverson & Waldrop, 1976; Kohn, 1977).

Thus, there is evidence that aggressive exchanges between young children are common, particularly between boys, and that aggressive behavior influences peer acceptance even in preschool. Short-term longitudinal studies suggest that early aggressive behavior may develop into less adaptive, competent forms of social behavior. However, the meaning or long-term implications of aggressive behavior in young children, especially young children who have not been identified as behavior problems, remains unknown. It seems unlikely that lack of sharing and struggles over toys in preschool will have long-term negative implications for later social development and peer relations. However, it is likely that peer problems in preschool, when paired with other behavior problems that are mismanaged by parents or that occur in the context of a disturbed family situation, will persist and have a poor prognosis (Minde & Minde, 1977; Richman, 1977; Rutter, 1971).

Studies that directly examine aggressive behavior in groups of clinically identified preschoolers have been rare. Schleifer *et al.* (1975) observed parent-identified hyperactive preschoolers in a research nursery and found that they were more aggressive with peers than nonhyperactive controls. Moreover, follow-up of these same youngsters into elementary school indicated that the problems persisted (Campbell, Endman, & Bernfeld, 1977).

We are currently engaged in a comprehensive follow-up study of behavior-problem toddlers and preschoolers. Preliminary data on 37 youngsters indicate that aggression towards peers is a prominent concern among mothers who report behavior problems with their child. Specific complaints about peer problems were voiced by 57% of mothers in the clinical group, but by only 14% of control mothers. Furthermore, the clinical group was rated as significantly more aggressive by both parents and teachers. Observations of peer interaction in preschool confirmed that children in the clinical group were significantly more likely to engage in aggressive encounters with peers than were control children. While most of these interchanges were struggles over a toy, consistent with the observations of Smith and Green (1975), several children were observed to approach other children and lash out physically by pushing, kicking, or biting. At times these outbursts appeared to be unprovoked; at other times they appeared to be overreactions to approaches from other children. While these data are only preliminary observations on a small number of children, they may suggest, in keeping with Hartup (1974), that a more fine-grained analysis is in order. Although conflicts and resolutions over sharing toys may be an important facet of normal social development that facilitates the development of more positive peer relations, such as sharing and perspective-taking, the angry, aggressive, and apparently unprovoked attacks we witnessed from several of our subjects may indeed be early precursors of more severe social problems. The answers to these questions require intensive study in samples of young problem children who can be followed longitudinally.

Social Withdrawal

Studies of social withdrawal are relatively rare, although factors that include shy, withdrawn, and solitary behaviors usually emerge from factor-analytic studies of behavioral descriptions of young children (Behar, 1977; Bell, Waldrop, & Weller, 1972; Kohn & Rosman, 1972). However, unlike aggressive behavior, excessively shy and withdrawn behavior appears to be relatively rare. For example, in the Rolf *et al.* (1976) study, teachers rated fewer than 10% of 2- to 5-year olds as moderately to highly bashful, avoidant of peer contact, or fearful of people. It may be that behaviors that are less attention-getting and annoying are rated as less severe problems, or noted less often because they are less salient.

However, Kohn and Parnes (1974) provide some data that suggest that teacher ratings of social withdrawal are valid reflections of the amount of peer interaction. Preschoolers who were rated high on the apathetic–withdrawn dimension of Kohn's Social Competence Scale were also observed to interact less with peers, to be more solitary, and to cope less effectively with aggression from peers.

In a detailed analysis of the peer interactions of normal and disturbed preschoolers, Leach (1972) found that 3-year-olds who had difficulty separating from their mothers were less competent with peers. They initiated less interaction with peers, were less responsive to peer initiations, and tended to withdraw or give in to aggressive interactions, for example, when a peer grabbed a toy. Over time, these children continued to interact less and to be less integrated into the peer group. Whereas newcomers into nursery school often show some initial social withdrawal and other adjustment problems (Hughes *et al.*, 1979), they become integrated into the group relatively rapidly and over time are indistinguishable from peers (Feldaum, Christenson, & O'Neal, 1980; McGrew, 1972). However, this was not the case with the youngsters in Leach's sample.

The bulk of the research on socially withdrawn preschoolers has focused on efforts to increase the frequency of peer interaction through the use of modeling (Evers & Schwarz, 1973; O'Connor, 1972; Gottman, 1977a) and peer therapists (Strain, Shores, & Timm, 1977). These attempts have met with moderate success. Intervention studies have emphasized the amount of interaction as the selection criterion for social withdrawal, on the assumption that quantity of peer contact reflects social competence. However, Gottman (1977a, b) has questioned this assumption. He reported (1977a) that children selected because of a limited amount of peer interaction were not necessarily less popular with peers as assessed by sociometric measures of peer acceptance or peer rejection.

Gottman argues that peer popularity may be the more important dimension to examine, rather than quantitative measures of peer interaction, if children "at risk" are to be identified. While there is little evidence clearly linking low frequencies of interaction in preschool with later social maladjustment, evidence indicates that children who are unpopular with peers in elementary school are likely to have problems in adulthood (Cowen, Pederson, Babigian, Izzo, & Trost, 1973). Gottman argues that children low on peer interaction are not the same children who are low on peer acceptance, and that it is the latter group that requires further study.

Observational and sociometric data obtained on a large sample of preschool-age children in Headstart programs suggested several patterns of social behavior (Gottman, 1977b). Those low on peer acceptance tended to cluster into two subgroups. One group engaged in negative interaction with the teacher. The second group was frequently "tuned out" when alone and was higher on observations of shy, anxious, and fearful behavior. Gottman argues that this group comprises true social isolates, since their incompetent social behavior is also associated with limited popularity with peers. Recent work by Peery (1979) indicates that isolated children who are ignored by peers differ from overtly rejected children in social perception. Further research on the empirical description of preschool children who are quiet and withdrawn and are either ignored or rejected by peers is obviously a priority if the socially incompetent preschool child is to be better understood.

Several studies suggest that, just as high-intensity behaviors in preschoolers tend to covary, low-intensity behaviors also tend to go together and to show some temporal stability. Buss *et al.* (1980) found that teacher ratings of 3-year-olds as shy and reserved, withdrawn, and solitary were negatively correlated with objective and independent measures of activity level at age 3, and that these relationships persisted at ages 4 and 7. Similarly, Halverson and Waldrop (1973) found that children who withdrew from peer interaction in preschool were less active during free play than children who were social participators; teacher ratings of apathy–withdrawal were also negatively related to actometer readings of activity level during free play. Kohn (1977) reported that children rated as apathetic–withdrawn in day care were less engaged with peers and continued to be perceived as socially withdrawn by their classroom teachers in third grade. They were also functioning less well academically than their more socially competent peers.

Taken together, these studies suggest that children who are perceived by their preschool teachers as socially withdrawn may continue to have problems, although these youngsters may be less likely to come to the attention of mental health professionals than their more active and aggressive counterparts. Whereas Gottman suggests that these are not necessarily the same youngsters to be selected by peers as socially incompetent, more work remains to be done on this issue. Probably the combined use of teacher and peer ratings and direct observations are the most appropriate. Furthermore, children who are shy and withdrawn may be neither chosen by peers nor overtly rejected by them; rather, they may be ignored (Peery, 1979).

It appears that extremes of behavior among preschoolers, either behavior of very high intensity or very low intensity, may not bode well for long-term social development. However, studies on the nature of low-intensity behaviors, their relationship to peer popularity, and their long-term implications for social development remain to be carried out.

School Age

School Problems

Problems related to school functioning are among the most common reasons for referral to child mental health facilities. School problems tend to be relatively pervasive and to encompass learning and achievement problems, attentional and conduct problems, and impaired relationships with teachers and peers. They can run the gamut from delayed reading achievement and distractibility, which are reasonably common complaints of both parents and teachers (Rutter *et al.,* 1970; Shepherd *et al.* 1971) to truancy, which is relatively rare, at least in the preadolescent samples studied in Britain (Rutter *et al.,* 1970; Shepherd *et al.,* 1971) and the American Midwest (Werry & Quay, 1971).

There is wide agreement in the literature that achievement and behavior problems in school tend to covary, that they are associated with family disturbance, and that they are more common in boys (Love & Kaswan, 1974: Robins, 1966; Rutter, 1971; Rutter *et al.,* 1970; Sandberg *et al.,* 1980; Shepherd *et al.,* 1971). For example, in the study by Shepherd *et al.,* teachers rated approximately one-third of the boys and one-quarter of the girls in a sample of over 6,000 youngsters as "below average" in school attainment. Poor achievers were also more likely to be rated as showing disruptive, uncooperative, and restless behavior in the classroom. However, when stricter, more specific, and more objective criteria of poor achievement are employed, rates go down. Rutter *et al.* (1970) classified a child as showing specific reading retardation only if he or she was 28 months behind in reading and of average intelligence. The prevalence rate given these criteria was only 3.7% of 10- to 11-

year-olds on the Isle of Wight. Reading disorders were associated with other cognitive deficits, including poor spelling and arithmetic achievement and language dysfunction. Furthermore, poor readers came from larger families and were more likely to have conduct disorders in school.

Several large screening studies of school maladjustment in the United States indicate that, when combined assessments are made utilizing teacher ratings and school achievement indices, roughly 30% of primary school children are classified as "at risk" (Cowen, Trost, Izzo, Lorion, Dorr, & Isaacson, 1975; Glidewell & Swallow, 1969). For example Cowen and his colleagues have been engaged in a massive screening, intervention, and follow-up study of children identified by teacher ratings as "at risk" in the primary grades. Children identified as potentially maladjusted have been found to differ from classroom controls on measures of school achievement and peer popularity. Furthermore, within the high-risk group, family variables are related to patterns of disturbance. Children coming from families low in pressure to succeed in school were rated as less socially competent and more likely to have learning problems than other referred children (Gesten, Scher, & Cowen, 1978). These findings were generally supported in a study of nonreferred children (Boike, Gesten, Cowen, Felner, & Francis, 1978). Family crises were also associated with referral patterns. Children whose parents had recently separated or divorced were more likely to be referred to the mental health project for conduct disturbances than referred children not in family crisis (Felner, Stolberg, & Cowen, 1975).

Similarly, Bower (1969) screened over 5,000 children in the fourth through sixth grades in California. Roughly 10% of the population was rated by teachers as showing some degree of maladjustment in school, while roughly 5% was referred for help. Referred children differed from classmates on a number of measures that closely parallel findings of other studies (Cowen *et al.,* 1975; Love & Kaswan, 1974). Referred children were behind their classmates in reading and arithmetic, scored lower on a measure of intelligence, had poorer self-esteem, and were more likely to be perceived negatively by peers.

Taken together, then, a number of studies indicate that problems in school are a source of concern to parents and teachers and that relatively large numbers of children do not function optimally in the school environment. Furthermore, children identified by school personnel as showing poor adjustment perform poorer than peers on measures of achievement, are less competent socially, and are more likely to have behavior problems in school. Finally, these deficits are associated with varying types and degrees of family disturbance.

Peer Problems

While it is obvious from the preceding section that school, family, and peer problems tend to go together, recent interest has begun to focus on the important role peer interaction plays in both normal (Asher, Oden, & Gottman, 1976; Gottman, Gonso, & Rasmussen, 1975; Hartup, 1970) and deviant development (Campbell & Paulauskas, 1979; Hartup, 1976). It is widely accepted among child development theorists that many aspects of socialization are facilitated by give and take within the peer group (Hartup, 1976; Lee, 1975). Furthermore, there is a converging body of evidence linking success with peers to psychological adjustment and academic achievement across a wide age span. Children who are both socially and academically competent tend to be more popular with peers (Asher *et al.,* 1976; Bower, 1969), while unpopular children or children who are not socially competent are more likely to experience adjustment difficulties and to achieve less academically (Cowen *et al.,* 1973; Kohn, 1977; Robins, 1966).

A number of studies also indicate that children with externalizing symptoms such as hyperactivity, aggressivity, and disruptive behavior in school are perceived more negatively by peers (Bower, 1969; Bryan, 1974; Klein & Young, 1979; Rolf, 1976). For example, Klein and Young reported that hyperactive boys were perceived more negatively by their classmates and were observed to engage in more negative interactions than active but normal classroom controls. Victor and Halverson (1975) found that boys who were rated as distractible by teachers were rated as "mean and noisy" by peers.

Parents and teachers also are likely to rate referred children as having more problems with peers than controls (Campbell & Paulauskas, 1979; Klein & Young, 1979; Love & Kaswan, 1974). For instance, Love and Kaswan found that children referred to a school-based mental health program were more likely to receive a high rating from teachers on a series of items reflecting "negative social impact," while they were perceived as lower in "social assets" than controls. Independent observations by "blind" observers indicated that referred children disrupted peer play on the playground more often than controls. Other studies of referral patterns to school-based mental health programs indicate that referred youngsters are perceived by teachers as having problems getting along with other children, either because they are too aggressive and domineering or too timid and unassertive (Bower, 1969; Cowen *et al.,* 1975; Gesten *et al.,* 1978).

While it is relatively clear that poor peer relations are a concomitant of problem behavior in referred groups, it is also true that behaviors that may be construed as symptomatic of peer difficulties are relatively common in the general population. For example, teachers in the Werry and Quay (1971) study rated roughly 30% of the boys in the sample as aggressive and uncooperative in group situations. Ratings of shyness were also common; 33% of boys and 41% of girls were perceived as shy. Approximately 13% of children in the Isle of Wight study (Rutter *et al.,* 1970) were rated by teachers as "not liked" by peers; 15% were rated as solitary. Furthermore, children who were rated high on number of problems were also more likely to be perceived as "not liked" by both parents and teachers.

Some recent attempts have been made to define differences between popular and unpopular children in behavioral terms. While it is obvious that problem children are less accepted by peers, the nature of their social skill deficit remains undefined. Gottman, Gonso, and Rasmussen (1975) studied the social behaviors of popular and unpopular third and fourth graders. Popular children were selected as "best friends" by classmates more often than unpopular children, suggesting that the unpopular subjects in this sample were a mixture of both rejected and ignored children. Popular children demonstrated more social skill on a role-play task assessing knowledge of how to make friends. They also gave and received more positive reinforcement when interacting with peers in the classroom and spent less time off-task. Finally, they performed more efficiently on a referential communication task, suggesting better ability to take the perspective of the listener into account. Based on the results of this study, Oden and Asher (1977) utilized a coaching procedure to instruct unpopular children in social skills. Children were instructed on participation in play, turn-taking and sharing, and communicating and giving support. Results indicated that training increased popularity and that gains were maintained at a one-year follow-up.

Several recent studies have begun to examine the social behavior of clinically defined groups. As was already noted, children with externalizing symptoms are more negative and disruptive when observed with peers (Abikoff, Gittelman, & Klein, 1980; Klein & Young, 1979; Love & Kaswan, 1974). Learning-disabled and hyperactive youngsters have also been found to communicate less efficiently than peers in some studies (Bryan, 1977; Whalen, Henker, Collins, McAuliffe, & Vaux, 1979), but not in others (Paulauskas & Campbell, 1979). Attempts to assess peer relations of referred children, however, have been hampered by variable and nonspecific definitions of social competence as well as by a focus on behaviors that may or may not be indicative of problems in the peer group.

In summary, it appears that social competence with peers is also reflected in peer popularity, and that more skilled children may be better adjusted. Continued research on the specific behaviors that contribute to more competent and less competent peer relations is an important goal. Such data will have particular relevance for selecting and intervening with children "at risk" in view of findings that suggest higher rates of long-term negative outcome in some children with poor peer relations in elementary school (Cowen *et al.*, 1973; Robins, 1966).

Longitudinal Perspectives: The Natural Course of Childhood Problems

A thorough understanding of the developmental features of childhood behavior problems hinges on knowledge of the developmental course of the more common symptoms and disorders. Although studies on the developmental course of behavior problems can only give clues to etiology, they provide important information on who is "at risk" for continued disorder, who is likely to improve without treatment, and who is likely to develop disorder at a later date. In addition, correlates of positive and negative outcome help define populations who are vulnerable to the onset or persistence of disorder. While cross-sectional studies suggest that changes occur in symptoms as a function of age (Lapouse & Monk, 1958; Werry & Quay, 1971), only follow-up studies that examine the same children over time can provide accurate information on changes in problem behaviors and the relative prognostic importance of particular clusters of symptoms. Gersten *et al.* (1976) found that several behaviors that appeared to decrease with age, when examined cross-sectionally, failed to show similar changes when data were analyzed longitudinally to examine stability and change over time in the same subjects; this highlights problems when making longitudinal inferences from cross-sectional findings.

From both a research and clinical perspective, then, it is essential that we learn more about the meaning and prognostic significance of potentially problematic behaviors. For example, which difficult infants are truly at risk to develop later problems, and which problems specifically? What aspects, if any, of preschool aggression or social withdrawal are early precursors of later problems? Only prospective studies will provide clear answers to such questions. Related issues of primary prevention and early intervention are beyond the scope of this chapter.

Early longitudinal studies of nonclinical populations (MacFarlane *et al.*, 1954) suggested that the majority of symptoms experienced by young children were transient developmental phenomena. Such findings led Robins (1979) to conclude, in a recent review, that patterns of symptoms appearing before age 6 were of little predictive significance. However, review of several recent short-term follow-up studies of young children suggests that this conclusion may be premature.

In an early study, Westman, Rice, and Bermann (1967) reported that ratings of poor adjustment in preschool were associated with use of mental health services during elementary and high school. Family problems and poor peer relationships were predictive of later problems, while "immaturity" was not. Two more recent follow-up studies of nonclinical samples of preschoolers suggest that patterns of angry–defiant behavior and apathetic–withdrawn behavior persist into the early elementary school grades and that aggressive and hyperactive behaviors are also associated with poorer cognitive functioning in the primary grades (Halverson & Waldrop, 1976; Kohn, 1977).

Several additional studies also suggest that problems experienced by preschoolers may persist, although the specific manifestations of problem behavior may change with age. Richman (1977) reported on a 1-year follow-up of 96 problem and 96 control children first seen at age 3; 60% of the problem group was still rated as a problem on the basis of maternal reports and clinicians' judgments, while changes were noted in specific symptoms. However, childhood problems were associated with marital distress and maternal depression initially, and continued family distress was related to the persistence of the child's symptoms. In the absence of data from sources other than the mother, it is difficult to interpret these findings. Maternal reports of women under stress may reflect general dissatisfaction with life circumstances and/or lowered tolerance for the typical behavior of preschoolers rather than actual child pathology.

In a similar study, Minde and Minde (1977) followed up a small sample of Toronto preschoolers. While mothers reported that problems persisted into kindergarten, there was little agreement between parents and teachers. Likewise, Coleman *et al.* (1977) found stability in the number of symptoms reported by mothers who rated their youngsters at ages 3, 4, and 5, but found little relationship between ratings of mothers and teachers. Furthermore, consistent with Richman's (1977) results, maternal ratings of childhood behavior problems were highly correlated with self-reported depression and minor physical complaints. Consistent with the earlier work of MacFarlane *et al.* (1954), these authors also noted that symptoms such as enuresis and fears declined with increasing age, while others such as discipline problems and poor peer relationships did not.

Hughes *et al.* (1979) recently followed a sample of preschoolers for 18 months after school entry; 13% were assessed by teachers as showing serious adjustment problems initially. While many of these problems were transient reactions that appeared to abate as the child adapted to school, as many as 50% of those children having initial difficulties continued to show specific problems. Similarly, Chazan and Jackson (1974) reported that 43% of 5-year-olds who were identified as having problems continued to experience problems when followed at age 7.

In a series of studies (Campbell *et al.,* 1977; Campbell *et al.,* 1978; Campbell, Schleifer, Weiss, & Perlman, 1977; Schleifer *et al.,* 1975), we followed a sample of hyperactive preschoolers into elementary school. While both parent and teacher ratings continued to differentiate hyperactive children from controls, parent ratings strongly indicated that problems persisted. However, those children in the hyperactive group who were seen as most problematic by parents were not necessarily the ones about whom teachers had the most complaints. Observational measures indicated that hyperactive children who were more aggressive and inattentive in preschool spent more time off-task in elementary school. Self-report measures indicated that hyperactive children had lower self-esteem than controls at follow-up. Thus, these findings suggest that early hyperactive and aggressive behavior did not just disappear with development, although clear predictors of outcome were difficult to pinpoint.

Taken together, these studies suggest that early problems may indeed be related to later disorders among school-age samples, although the long-term significance of early symptomatology is unknown. While some proportion of preschoolers with difficulties appear to show persistent problems, others do not. More sophisticated studies that examine predictors and correlates of outcome and attempt to define which subgroups of problem toddlers and preschoolers are "at risk" for continued school and social problems appear especially crucial. Not surprisingly, studies done to date suggest the importance of family dysfunction and maternal mental health problems as likely precursors and/or correlates of child maladjustment and suggest directions for early intervention efforts.

While the relationship between behavior problems in children under 6 and later disorder is still unclear, convergent results are beginning to emerge from follow-up studies of school-age youngsters into adolescence (Gersten *et al.*, 1976; Milich & Loney, 1979; Rutter *et al.*, 1970; Weiss *et al.*, 1971) and early adulthood (Gersten *et al.*, 1976; Robins, 1966; Weiss *et al.*, 1978). Studies indicate that externalizing disorders (hyperactivity, conduct disorder, aggressive and antisocial disorders) and associated poor school achievement are likely to persist and to be precursors of adult disorder. Robins (1966) reported higher rates of antisocial behavior, trouble with the law, alcoholism, and marital instability in a group of former child guidance clinic cases with externalizing symptoms who were followed into adulthood and compared with controls from the same neighborhood. Gersten *et al.* (1976) reported that aggressive behavior, delinquency, and conflict with parents showed marked stability from elementary school age to late adolescence. In a series of follow-up studies of hyperactive children into adolescence (Weiss *et al.*, 1971) and early adulthood (Weiss *et al.*, 1978), Weiss found that hyperactive subjects had poorer records of school achievement and lower self-esteem than controls at both time periods. Furthermore, as young adults, hyperactives were noted to be more restless, had more police contacts involving thefts, and more frequent and severe automobile accidents than nonhyperactive controls. Furthermore, within these externalizing clinical groups, early aggression, poor school achievement, family pathology, and paternal antisocial behavior were predictive of poor outcome in adolescence and early adulthood (Milich & Loney, 1979; Robins, 1966; Rutter, 1971; Weiss *et al.*, 1978).

On the other hand, internalizing disorders including neurotic, withdrawn, anxious, and psychosomatic complaints appear less persistent. Rates of adult disturbances did not differentiate Robin's (1966) neurotic child guidance cases from controls. Similarly, Gersten *et al.* (1976) found less stability among internalizing behaviors such as social isolation and anxiety than among more aggressive behaviors. Other studies of clinical groups report findings consistent with these, indicating that neurotic symptoms in childhood are less likely than externalizing symptoms to be associated with serious adult disorders (e.g., Hafner, Quast, & Shea, 1975; Warren, 1965).

Thus, there is evidence linking antisocial problems in childhood to later disorder, but the prognostic significance of these behaviors in younger children remains to be determined. Furthermore, it appears that anxiety and neurotic problems that have their onset in middle childhood do not necessarily predict serious adult disorder. While it has generally been assumed that early peer problems and social withdrawal, particularly in children under 6, are merely transient developmental disturbances, studies that examine clinical groups of young children longitudinally have not yet been carried out, and several recent studies of behavior problems in preschoolers suggest that problems persist in a significant proportion of youngsters. Continued research into early precursors of behavior disturbances and their family and environmental correlates, as well as on predictors of good and poor outcome, is a priority if we are to progress beyond the level of description and classification of childhood problems to an understanding of their developmental course. Furthermore, successful amelioration of potential problems requires design and initiation of appropriately targeted prevention and early intervention programs, which must select "at risk" populations likely to develop significant and persistent disorders. Data on precursors, correlates, and outcome of disorder in children are an essential first step in this endeavor.

Summary

This chapter examined childhood behavior problems from a developmental perspective. Several ways in which developmental factors may influence problem definitions, diagnostic formulations, treatment recommendations, and predictions about outcome were explored. Further, it was noted that patterns of childhood referral and parental help-seeking regarding childhood problems are largely a function of the expectations adults have about child behavior rather than a result of clearly deviant behavior. Furthermore, the psychological state of parents influences their tolerance and plays a role in determining which children are referred and treated.

Epidemiological studies of specific problem behaviors and prevalence rates of actual disorder as a function of age and sex were reviewed next. While it is clear that symptomatic behaviors are common in the general population, estimates of actual disorder, based on clusters of symptoms which interfere with functioning, are relatively low. Furthermore, rates of both symptoms and disorders appear to vary with the age and sex of the sample.

Several common developmental problems were examined in the next section, with emphasis on their appearance at a particular stage of development. They were conceptualized as exaggerations of age-appropriate behaviors, as reflections of difficult transitions from one developmental stage to the next, or as age-related but maladaptive reactions to environmental, particularly family, stress. Examples include attachment problems in infancy, defiance and aggression among toddlers and preschoolers, and school difficulties among older children. Research on these behaviors was critically examined, integrating studies on both "normal" and clinical populations when possible. An attempt was also made to draw inferences about the potential long-term developmental impact of such behaviors. In general, it appears that common developmental problems may be a warning signal; the skill with which they are handled at a particular stage of development will partly determine whether such problems are indeed transient or are precursors of more severe and persistent difficulties.

Finally, follow-up studies were examined. They generally suggest that problems among preschoolers are not as transient as was once assumed, especially when associated with family dysfunction or parental psychopathology. Behavior disorders in school-age samples, when they include primarily externalizing symptoms, appear to have a poorer prognosis than disorders characterized primarily by internalizing symptoms. However, research on most of these issues has barely scratched the surface; firm conclusions are unwarranted at this stage of our knowledge, and continued research will be necessary before clear guidelines for prevention or intervention can be established.

References

Abikoff, H., Gittelman, R., & Klein, D. F. Classroom observation code for hyperactive children: A replication of validity. *Journal of Consulting and Clinical Psychology,* 1980, *48,* 555–565.

Achenbach, T. M. The Child Behavior Profile: I. Boys Aged 6–11. *Journal of Consulting and Clinical Psychology,* 1978, *46,* 478–488.

Ainsworth, M. D. S. Object relations, dependency, and attachment: A theoretical review of the infant–mother relationship. *Child Development,* 1969, *40,* 969–1025.

Ainsworth, M. D. S., & Bell, S. M. Some contemporary patterns of mother/infant interaction in the feeding situation. In A. Ambrose (Ed.) *Stimulation in early infancy* London: Academic Press, 1969.

Ainsworth, M. D. S., & Wittig, B. A. Attachment and exploratory behavior of one-year-olds in a strange situation. In B. M. Foss (Ed.), *Determinants of infant behaviour.* (Vol. 4). London: Methuen, 1969.

Ainsworth, M. D. S., Blehar, M., Waters, E., & Wall, S. *Patterns of attachment.* Hillsdale, N.J.: Lawrence Erlbaum, 1978.

Anthony, E. J. A risk-vulnerability intervention model for children of psychotic parents. In E. J. Anthony & C. Koupernik (Eds.), *The child in his family: Children at psychiatric risk.* New York: Wiley, 1974.

Asher, S. R., Oden, S. L., & Gottman, J. M. Children's friendships in school settings. In L. G. Katz (Ed.), *Current topics in early childhood education.* Hillsdale, N.J.; Lawrence Erlbaum, 1976.

Axline, V. M. *Play therapy* (Rev. ed.) New York: Ballantine Books, 1969.

Baker, L., Cantwell, D. P., & Mattison, R. E. Behavior problems in children with pure speech disorders and in children with combined speech and language disorders. *Journal of Abnormal Child Psychology,* 1980, *8,* 245–256.

Bates, J. E., Freeland, C. A. B., & Lounsbury, M. L. Measurement of infant difficultness. *Child Development,* 1979, *50,* 794–803.

Battle, E. S., & Lacey, B. A context for hyperactivity in children over time. *Child Development,* 1972, *43,* 757–773.

Baumrind, D., & Black, A. E. Socialization practices associated with dimensions of competence in preschool boys and girls. *Child Development,* 1967, *38,* 291–327.

Beck, A. T. *Depression: Causes and treatment.* Philadelphia: University of Pennsylvania Press, 1972.

Behar, L. The Preschool Behavior Questionnaire. *Journal of Abnormal Child Psychology,* 1977, *5,* 265–276.

Bell, R. Q. A reinterpretation of the direction of effects in studies of socialization. *Psychological Review,* 1968, *75,* 81–95.

Bell, R. Q., & Harper, L. V. *Child effects on adults.* Hillsdale, N.J.: Lawrence Erlbaum, 1977.

Bell, R. Q., Waldrop, M. F., & Weller, G. M. A rating system for the assessment of hyperactive and withdrawn children in preschool samples. *American Journal of Orthopsychiatry,* 1972, *42,* 23–34.

Bell, S. M., & Ainsworth, M. D. S. Infant crying and maternal responsiveness. *Child Development,* 1972, *43,* 1171–1190.

Berkowitz, B. P., & Graziano, A. M. Training parents as behavior therapists: A review. *Behavior Research and Therapy,* 1972, *10,* 297–317.

Billman, J., & McDevitt, S. C. Convergence of parent and observer ratings of temperament with observations of peer interaction in nursery school. *Child Development,* 1980, *51,* 395–400.

Blurton-Jones, N. Categories of child-child interaction. In N. Blutron-Jones (Ed.), *Ethological studies in child behavior.* London: Cambridge University Press, 1972.

Boike, M. F., Gesten, E. L., Cowen, E. L., Felner, R. D., & Francis, R. Relationships between family background problems and school problems and competencies of young normal children. *Psychology in the Schools,* 1978, *15,* 283–290.

Bower, E. M. *Early identification of emotionally handicapped children in school* (2nd ed.). Springfield, Ill: Charles C Thomas, 1969.

Bowlby, J. The nature of the infant's tie to his mother. *International Journal of Psychoanalysis,* 1958, *39,* 350–373.

Bowlby, J. *Attachment.* New York: Basic Books, 1969.

Brazelton, T. B. *The Neonatal Behavioral Assessment Scale.* Clinics in Developmental Medicine, No. 50. Philadelphia: J. B. Lippincott, 1973.

Brazelton, T. B. *Toddlers and parents.* New York: Delta, 1974.

Brazelton, T. B., Koslowski, B., & Main, M. The origins of reciprocity: The early mother–infant interaction. In M. Lewis & L. Rosenblum (Eds.), *The effect of the infant on its caregiver.* New York: Wiley, 1974.

Bryan, T. H. Peer popularity of learning disabled children. *Journal of Learning Disabilities,* 1974, *7,* 261–268.

Bryan, T. H. Learning disabled children's comprehension of nonverbal communication. *Journal of Learning Disabilities,* 1977, *10,* 36–41.

Buss, D. M., Block, J. H., & Block, J. Preschool activity level: Personality correlates and developmental implications. *Child Development,* 1980, *51,* 401–408.

Campbell, S. B. Hyperactivity: Course and treatment. In A. Davids (Ed.), *Child personality and psychopathology* (Vol. 3). New York: Wiley, 1976.

Campbell, S. B. Patterns of mother–infant interaction and maternal ratings of temperament. *Child Psychiatry and Human Development,* 1979, *10,* 67–76.

Campbell, S. B., & Paulauskas, S. L. Peer relations in hyperactive children. *Journal of Child Psychology and Psychiatry,* 1979, *20,* 233–246.

Campbell, S. B., Endman, M., & Bernfeld, G. A three-year follow-up of hyperactive preschoolers into elementary school. *Journal of Child Psychology and Psychiatry,* 1977, *18,* 239–250.

Campbell, S. B., Schleifer, M., & Weiss, G. Continuities in maternal reports and child behaviors over time in hyperactive and comparison groups. *Journal of Abnormal Child Psychology,* 1978, *6,* 33–45.

Campbell, S. B., Schleifer, M., Weiss, G., & Perlman, T. A two-year follow-up of hyperactive preschoolers. *American Journal of Orthopsychiatry,* 1977, *47,* 149–162.

Carey, W. B. Measurement of infant temperament in pediatric practice. In J. C. Westman (Ed.), *Individual differences in children.* New York: Wiley, 1972.

Charlesworth, R., & Hartup, W. W. Positive social reinforcement in the nursery school peer group. *Child Development,* 1967, *38,* 993–1002.

Chazan, M., & Jackson, S. Behaviour problems in the infant school: Changes over two years. *Journal of Child Psychology and Psychiatry,* 1974, *15,* 33–46.

Cohen, N. J., Sullivan, J., Minde, K., Novak, C., & Helwig, C. Evaluation of the relative effectiveness of methylphenidate and cognitive behavior modification in the treatment of kindergarten-aged hyperactive children. *Journal of Abnormal Child Psychology,* 1981, *9,* 43–54.

Coleman, J., Wolkind, S., & Ashley, L. Symptoms of behaviour disturbance and adjustment to school. *Journal of Child Psychology and Psychiatry,* 1977, *18,* 201–210.

Colletti, G., & Harris, S. L. Behavior modification in the home: Siblings as behavior modifiers, parents as observers. *Journal of Abnormal Child Psychology,* 1977, *5,* 21–30.

Cowen, E. L., Pederson, A., Babigian, H., Izzo, L. D., & Trost, M. A. Long-term follow-up of early detected vulnerable children. *Journal of Consulting and Clinical Psychology,* 1973, *41,* 438–446.

Cowen, E. L., Trost, M. A., Izzo, L. D., Lorion, R. P., Dorr, D., & Isaacson, R. V. *New ways in school mental health. Early detection and prevention of school maladaptation.* New York: Human Sciences Press, 1975.

Crockenberg, S. *Antecedents of mother–infant interaction and infant irritablilty in the first three months of life.* Paper presented at the International Conference on Infant Studies, New Haven, March 1980.

Dawe, H. C. An analysis of two hundred quarrels of preschool children. *Child Development,* 1934, *5,* 139–157.

Douglas, V. I., Parry, P., Marton, P. M., & Garson, C. Assessment of a cognitive training program for hyperactive children. *Journal of Abnormal Child Psychology,* 1976, *4,* 389–410.

Egeland, B., & Sroufe, L. A. Attachment and early maltreatment. *Child Development,* 1981, *52,* 44–49.

Evers, W. L., & Schwarz, J. C. Modifying social withdrawal in preschoolers: The effects of filmed modeling and teacher praise. *Journal of Abnormal Child Psychology,* 1973, *1,* 248–256.

Feldbaum, C. L., Christenson, T. E., & O'Neal, E. C. An observational study of the assimilation of the newcomer to the preschool. *Child Development,* 1980, *51,* 497–507.

Felner, R. D., Stolberg, A., & Cowen, E. L. Crisis events and school mental health referral patterns of young children. *Journal of Consulting and Clinical Psychology,* 1975, *43,* 305–310.

Ferguson, L. R., Partyka, L. B., & Lester, B. M. Patterns of parent perception differentiating clinic from nonclinic children. *Journal of Abnormal Child Psychology,* 1974, *2,* 169–182.

Feshbach, N., & Feshbach, S. Children's aggression. In W. W. Hartup (Ed.), *The young child: Reviews of research* (Vol. 2). Washington, D.C.: National Association for the Education of Young Children, 1972.

Forehand, R., & Scarboro, M. E. An analysis of children's oppositional behavior. *Journal of Abnormal Child Psychology,* 1975, *3,* 27–32.

Freud, A. *Normality and pathology in childhood.* New York: International Universities Press, 1965.

Gath, D. Child guidance and the general practitioner. A study of factors influencing referrals made by general practitioners to a child psychiatric department. *Journal of Child Psychology and Psychiatry,* 1968, *9,* 213–227.

George, C. & Main, M. Social interactions of young abused children: Approach, avoidance, and aggression. *Child Development,* 1979, *50,* 306–318.

Gersten, J. C., Langner, T. S., Eisenberg, J. G., Simcha-Fagan, O., & McCarthy, E. D. Stability and change in types of behavioral disturbance of children and adolescents. *Journal of Abnormal Child Psychology,* 1976, *4,* 111–128.

Gesten, E. L., Scher, K., & Cowen, E. L. Judged school problems and competencies of referred children with varying family background characteristics. *Journal of Abnormal Child Psychology,* 1978, *6,* 247–256.

Glidewell, J. C., & Swallow, C. S. *The prevalence of maladjustment in elementary schools: A report prepared for the Joint Commission on the Mental Health of Children.* Chicago: University of Chicago Press, 1969.

Gottman, J. M. The effects of a modeling film on social isolation in preschool children: A methodological investigation. *Journal of Abnormal Child Psychology,* 1977, *5,* 69–78. (a)

Gottman, J. M. Toward a definition of social isolation in children. *Child Development,* 1977, *48,* 513–517. (b)

Gottman, J. M., Gonso, J., & Rasmussen, B. Social interaction, social competence, and friendship in children. *Child Development,* 1975, *46,* 709–718.

Hafner, A. J., Quast, W., & Shea, M. J. The adult adjustment of one thousand psychiatric and pediatric patients: Initial findings from a twenty-five-year follow-up. In R. D. Wirt, G. Winokur, & M. Roff (Eds.), *Life History research in psychopathology.* (Vol. 4). Minneapolis: University of Minnesota Press, 1975.

Halverson, C. F., & Waldrop, M. F. The relations of mechanically recorded activity level to varieties of preschool play behavior. *Child Development,* 1973, *44,* 678–681.

Halverson, C. F., & Waldrop, M. F. Relations between preschool activity and aspects of intellectual and social behavior at age 7½. *Developmental Psychology,* 1976, *12,* 107–112.

Hartup, W. W. Peer interaction and social organization. In P. H. Mussen (Ed.), *Carmichael's manual of child psychology* (Vol. 2). New York: Wiley, 1970.

Hartup, W. W. Aggression in childhood: Developmental perspectives. *American Psychologist,* 1974, *29,* 336–341.

Hartup, W. W. Peer interaction and the behavioral development of the individual child. In E. Schopler & R. J. Reichler (Eds.), *Psychopathology and child development: Research and treatment.* New York: Plenum Press, 1976.

Hartup, W. W., Glazer, J. A., & Charlesworth, R. Peer reinforcement and sociometric status. *Child Development,* 1967, *38,* 1017–1024.

Houseman, J. A. *Interpersonal conflicts among nursery school children in free play settings.* Paper presented at the American Psychological Association, Montreal, Canada, August 1973.

Hughes, M., Pinkerton, G., & Plewis, I. Children's difficulties in starting infant school. *Journal of Child Psychology and Psychiatry,* 1979, *20,* 187–196.

Jenkins, S., Bax, M., & Hart, H. Behaviour problems in pre-school children. *Journal of Child Psychology and Psychiatry,* 1980, *21,* 5–18.

Johnson, S. M., & Lobitz, G. K. The personal and marital status of parents as related to observed child deviance and parenting behaviors. *Journal of Abnormal Child Psychology,* 1974, *3,* 193–208.

Klein, A. R., & Young, R. D. Hyperactive boys in their classroom: Assessment of teacher and peer perceptions, interactions, and classroom behaviors. *Journal of Abnormal Child Psychology,* 1979, *7,* 425–442.

Kohn, M. *Social competence, symptoms, and underachievement in childhood: A longitudinal perspective.* Washington, D.C.: V. H. Winston & Sons, 1977.

Kohn, M., & Parnes, B. Social interaction in the classroom—A comparison of apathetic–withdrawn and angry–defiant children. *Journal of Genetic Psychology,* 1974, *125,* 165–175.

Kohn, M., & Rosman, B. L. A Social Competence Scale and Symptom Checklist for the preschool child: Factor dimensions, their cross-instrument generality, and longitudinal persistence. *Developmental Psychology,* 1972, *6,* 430–444.

Korner, A. F. Individual differences at birth: Implications for early experience and later development. *American Journal of Orthopsychiatry,* 1971, *41,* 608–619.

Lapouse, R., & Monk, M. A. An epidemiologic study of behavior characteristics in children. *American Journal of Public Health,* 1958, *48,* 1134–1140.

Leach, G. M. A comparison of the social behaviour of some normal and problem children. In N. Blurton-Jones (Ed.), *Ethological studies in child behaviour.* London: Cambridge University Press, 1972.

Lee, L. C. Toward a cognitive theory of interpersonal development: Importance of peers. In M. Lewis & L. A. Rosenblum (Eds.), *Friendship and peer relations.* New York: Wiley, 1975.

Leiter, M. P. A study of reciprocity in preschool play groups. *Child Development,* 1977, *48,* 1288–1295.

Love, L. R., & Kaswan, J. W. *Troubled children: Their families, schools, and treatments.* New York: Wiley, 1974.

Lytton, H. Disciplinary encounters between young boys and their mothers and fathers. Is there a contingency system? *Developmental Psychology,* 1979, *15,* 256–268.

Lytton, H., & Zwirner, H. Compliance and its controlling stimuli observed in a natural setting. *Developmental psychology,* 1975, 769–779.

MacFarlane, J. W., Allen, L., & Honzik, M. P. *A developmental study of the behavior problems of normal children between twenty-one months and fourteen years.* Berkeley: University of California Press, 1954.

Mahler, M. *On human symbiosis and the vicissitudes of individuation.* New York: International Universities Press, 1968.

Matas, L., Arend, R. A., & Sroufe, L. A. Continuity of adaptation in the second year: The relationship between quality of attachment and later competence. *Child Development,* 1978, *49,* 547–556.

McGrew, W. C. Aspects of social development in nursery school children with emphasis on introduction to the group. In N. Blurton-Jones (Ed.), *Ethological studies in child behaviour.* London: Cambridge University Press, 1972.

Mesibov, G. B., Schroeder, C. S., & Wesson, L. Parental concerns about their children. *Journal of Pediatric Psychology,* 1977, *2,* 13–17.

Milich, R., & Loney, J. The role of hyperactive and aggressive symptomatology in predicting adolescent outcome among hyperactive children. *Journal of Pediatric Psychology,* 1979, *4,* 93–112.

Miller, R. G., Palkes, H. S., & Stewart, M. A. Hyperactive children in suburban elementary schools. *Child Psychiatry and Human Development,* 1973, *4,* 121–127.

Minde, K. K., & Minde, D. Behavioral screening of preschool children: A new approach to mental health. In P. J. Graham (Ed.), *Epidemiological approaches to child psychiatry.* London: Academic Press, 1977.

Minton, C., Kagan, J., & Levine, J. A. Maternal control and obedience in the two-year-old. *Child Development.* 1971, *42,* 1873–1894.

Mischel, W. The interaction of person and situation. In D. Magnusson & N. S. Endler (Eds.), *Personality at the crossroads: Current issues in interactional psychology.* Hillsdale, N.J.: Lawrence Erlbaum, 1977.

Moore, S. G. Correlates of peer acceptance in nursery school. In W. W. Hartup & N. L. Smothergill (Eds.), *The young child: Reviews of research.* Washington, D.C.: National Association for the Education of Young Children, 1967.

Moss, H. A. Sex, age, and state as determinants of mother–infant interaction. *Merrill-Palmer Quarterly,* 1967, *13,* 19–36.

O'Connor, R. D. Relative efficacy of modeling, shaping, and the combined procedures for modification of social withdrawal. *Journal of Abnormal Psychology,* 1972, *79,* 327–334.

Oden, S., & Asher, S. R. Coaching children in social skills for friendship making. *Child Development,* 1977, *48,* 495–506.

Osofsky, J. Neonatal characteristics and mother–infant interaction in two observational situations. *Child Development,* 1976, *47,* 1138–1147.

Patterson, G. R. The aggressive child: Victim and architect of a coercive system. In E. J. Mash, L. A. Hamerlynck, & L. C. Handy (Eds.), *Behavior modification and families.* New York: Brunner/Mazel, 1976.

Patterson, G. R., Littman, R. A., & Bricker, W. Assertive behavior in children: A step toward a theory of aggression. *Monographs of the Society for Research in Child Development,* 1967, *32,* (113, Whole No. 5).

Paulauskas, S. L., & Campbell, S. B. Social perspective-taking and teacher ratings of peer interaction in hyperactive boys. *Journal of Abnormal Child Psychology,* 1979, *20,* 233–246.

Pedersen, F. A., & Bell, R. Q. Sex differences in preschool children without histories of complications of pregnancy and delivery. *Developmental Psychology,* 1970, *3,* 10–15.

Peery, J. C. Popular, amiable, isolated, rejected: A reconceptualization of sociometric status in preschool children. *Child Development,* 1979, *50,* 1239–1242.

Porter, B., & O'Leary, K. D. Marital discord and childhood behavior problems. *Journal of Abnormal Child Psychology,* 1980, *8,* 287–296.

Quay, H. C. Classification. In H. C. Quay & J. S. Werry (Eds.), *Psychopathological disorders of childhood* (2nd Ed.). New York: Wiley, 1979.

Richman, N. Short-term outcome of behavior problems in three year old children. In P. J. Graham (Ed.), *Epidemiological approaches in child psychiatry.* London: Academic Press, 1977.

Richman, N., Stevenson, J. E., & Graham, P. J. Prevalence of behaviour problems in 3-year-old children: An epidemiological study in a London borough. *Journal of Child Psychology and Psychiatry,* 1975, *16,* 277–287.

Rie, H. E. Depression in childhood: Survey of some pertinent contributions. *Journal of the American Academy of Child Psychiatry,* 1965, *5,* 653–685.

Robins, L. N. *Deviant children grown up.* Baltimore: Williams & Wilkins, 1966.

Robins, L. N. Follow-up studies. In H. C. Quay & J. S. Werry (Eds.), *Psychopathological disorders of childhood* (2nd ed.). New York: Wiley, 1979.

Rolf, J. E. Peer status and the directionality of symptomatic behavior: Prime social competence predictors of outcome for vulnerable children. *American Journal of Orthopsychiatry,* 1976, *46,* 74–88.

Rolf, J., Hakola, J., Klemchuk, H., & Hasazi, J. *The incidence, prevalence, and severity of behavior disorders among preschool aged children.* Paper presented at the Eastern Psychological Association, New York, April 1976.

Ross, D. M., & Ross, S. A. *Hyperactivity: Theory, research, and action.* New York: Wiley, 1976.

Rutter, M. Parent-child separation: Psychological effects on the children. *Journal of Child Psychology and Psychiatry,* 1971, *12,* 223–260.

Rutter, M., Tizard, J., & Whitmore, K. *Education, health and behavior.* London: Longman, 1970.

Sameroff, A. J. Infant risk factors in developmental deviancy. In E. J. Anthony, C. Koupernik, & C. Chiland (Eds.), *The child in his family: Vulnerable children.* New York: Wiley, 1978.

Sameroff, A. J., & Chandler, M. J. Reproductive risk and the continuum of caretaking casualty. In F. D. Horowitz (Ed.), *Review of child development research* (Vol. 4). Chicago: University of Chicago Press, 1975.

Sandberg, S. T., Wieselberg, M., & Shaffer, D. Hyperkinetic and conduct problem children: Some epidemiological considerations. *Journal of Child Psychology and Psychiatry,* 1980, *21,* 293–312.

Schleifer, M., Weiss, G., Cohen, N. J., Elman, M., Cvejic, H., & Kruger, E. Hyperactivity in preschoolers and the effect of methylphenidate. *American Journal of Orthopsychiatry,* 1975, *45,* 38–50.

Sears, R. R., Maccoby, E. E., & Levin, H. *Patterns of childrearing.* Evanston, Ill.: Row, Peterson, 1957.

Serbin, L. A., O'Leary, K. D., Kent, R. N., & Tonick, I. J. A comparison of teacher response to the preacademic and problem behavior of boys and girls. *Child Development,* 1973, *44,* 796–804.

Shepherd, M., Oppenheim, B., & Mitchell, S. *Childhood behaviour and mental health.* New York: Grune & Stratton, 1971.

Smith, P. K. & Green, M. Aggressive behavior in English nurseries and play groups: Sex differences and response of adults. *Child Development,* 1975, *46,* 211–214.

Speer, D. C. Behavior Problem Checklist (Peterson-Quay): Baseline data from parents of child guidance and non-clinic children. *Journal of Consulting and Clinical Psychology,* 1971, *36,* 221–228.

Sroufe, L. A., & Waters, E. Attachment as an organizational construct. *Child Development,* 1977, *48,* 1184–1199.

Stayton, D., Hogan, R., & Ainsworth, M. D. S. Infant obedience and maternal behavior: The origins of socialization reconsidered. *Child Development,* 1971, *42,* 1057–1069.

Stern, D. Mother and infant at play: The dyadic interaction involving facial, vocal, and gaze behaviors. In M. Lewis & L. Rosenblum (Eds.), *The effect of the infant on its caregiver.* New York: Wiley, 1974.

Stewart, M. A., Pitts, F. N., Craig, A. G., & Dieruf, W. The hyperactive child syndrome. *American Journal of Orthopsychiatry,* 1966, *36,* 861–867.

Strain, P. S., Shores, R. E., & Timm, M. A. Effects of peer social initiations on the behavior of withdrawn preschool children. *Journal of Applied Behavior Analysis,* 1977, *10,* 289–298.

Surratt, P. R., Ulrich, R., & Hawkins, R. P. An elementary student as a behavioral engineer. *Journal of Applied Behavior Analysis,* 1969 *2,* 85–92.

Thomas, A., Chess, S., & Birch, H. G. *Temperament and behavior disorders in children.* New York: New York University Press, 1968.

Trites, R. L., Dugas, E., Lynch, G., & Ferguson, H. B. Prevalence of hyperactivity. *Journal of Pediatric Psychology,* 1979, *4,* 179–188.

Turkewitz, H., O'Leary, K. D., & Ironsmith, M. Generalization and maintenance of appropriate behavior through self-control. *Journal of Consulting and Clinical Psychology,* 1975, *43,* 577–583.

Vaughn, B. E., Egeland, B., Sroufe, L. A., & Waters, E. Individual differences in infant–mother attachment at 12 and 18 months: Stability and change in families under stress. *Child Development,* 1979, *50,* 971–975.

Vaughn, B. E., Taraldson, B., Crichton, L., & Egeland, B. Relationships between neonatal behavioral organization and infant behavior during the first year of life. *Infant Behavior and Development,* 1980, *3,* 47–66.

Victor, J. B., & Halverson, C. F. Distractibility and hypersensitivity: Two behavior factors in elementary school children. *Journal of Abnormal Child Psychology,* 1975, *3,* 83–94.

Warren, W. A study of adolescent psychiatric in-patients and the outcome six or more years later—II. The follow-up study. *Journal of Child Psychology and Psychiatry,* 1965, *6,* 141–160.

Waters, E., Vaughn, B. E., & Egeland, B. R. Individual differences in infant–mother attachment relationships at age one: Antecedents in neonatal behavior in an urban, economically disadvantaged sample. *Child Development,* 1980, *51,* 208–216.

Waters, E., Wippman, J., & Sroufe, L. A. Attachment, positive affect, and competence in the peer group: Two studies in construct validation. *Child Development,* 1979, *50,* 821–829.

Weiss, G., Hechtman, L., & Perlman, T. Hyperactives as young adults: School, employer, and self-rating scales obtained during ten-year follow-up evaluation. *American Journal of Orthopsychiatry,* 1978, *48,* 438–445.

Weiss, G., Minde, K., Werry, J. S., Douglas, V., & Nemeth, E. Studies on the hyperactive child—VII. Five year follow-up. *Archives of General Psychiatry,* 1971, *24,* 409–414.

Wenger, S., Berg-Cross, L., & Berg-Cross, G. Parents' judgments of children's aggressive behavior. *Merrill-Palmer Quarterly,* 1980, *26,* 161–170.

Werry, J. S., & Quay, H. C. The prevalence of behavior symptoms of younger elementary school children. *American Journal of Orthopsychiatry,* 1971, *41,* 136–143.

Westman, J. C., Rice, D. L., & Bermann, E. Nursery school behavior and later school adjustment. *American Journal of Orthopsychiatry,* 1967, *37,* 725–731.

Whalen, C. K., & Henker, B. Psychostimulants and children: A review and analysis. *Psychological Bulletin,* 1976, *83,* 1113–1130.

Whalen, C. K., Henker, B., Collins, B., McAuliffe, S., & Vaux, A. Peer interaction in a structured communication task: Comparisons of normal and hyperactive boys and of methylphenidate (Ritalin) and placebo effects. *Child Development,* 1979, *50,* 388–401.

Whitehead, L. Sex differences in children's responses to family stress: A re-evaluation. *Journal of Child Psychology and Psychiatry,* 1979, *20,* 247–254.

Winnicott, D. W. *Mother and child: A primer of first relationships.* New York: Basic Books, 1957.

3

Etiological Factors

DIANE J. WILLIS, B. MARION SWANSON, AND C. EUGENE WALKER

Introduction

A critical question with which mental health professionals are confronted when studying child psychopathology is that of etiology. When a child is not developing normally, parents seek professional help; too often, however, professionals attribute causation of psychopathology to extremes such as the family constellation or minimal brain (neurological) dysfunction. Rarely does the practicing psychologist or other mental health professional actively seek to understand the genetic makeup (hereditary history) of the child or the child's constitution and temperament, and how these variables interrelate with his/her environment to produce maladaptive behavior.

Then, too, professionals are prone to ignore sociocultural influences upon the child, except for immediate family constellations. In this chapter, we shall present an overview of important sociocultural influences and their effects upon the child, recognizing that this is critical in assessing the child's problems. Some behaviors may be normal when viewed in the context of the child's environment, and the treatment course may be that of educating the teacher or referee. Finally, to some degree we are what we learn; the last section of this chapter will address the fact that some children behave as they do because of previous learning experiences.

DIANE J. WILLIS • Child Study Center, Department of Pediatrics, University of Oklahoma Health Sciences Center, Oklahoma City, Oklahoma 73117. B. MARION SWANSON • Department of Psychology, Northeastern Oklahoma State University, Tahlequah, Oklahoma 74464. C. EUGENE WALKER • Department of Psychiatry and Behavioral Sciences, University of Oklahoma Health Sciences Center, Oklahoma City, Oklahoma 73117.

In the past ten years, genetic research has advanced at an extraordinarily rapid pace. Medical diagnoses are more sophisticated, and the incidence of genetic disorders has more than doubled because of advances in medical technology, which allows us to diagnose more accurately. For example, 2.5% of all newborn infants are found to have some genetic defect. Between 12% and 20% of all hospital admissions to pediatric centers are children and youth admitted with some gene-related disorder. This is proof positive that we must become familiar with genetic disorders and the subsequent cognitive and behavioral effects of such disorders on the developing child. It is fortunate, perhaps, that genetic selection is likely occurring prenatally, since chromosomal anomalies are approximately 50 times more frequent in spontaneous abortions than in newborn infants.

A child's behavior is always the product of nature and nurture. The forces of nature include heredity and its characteristics, such as skin color, body structure, and so forth, as well as nongenetic characteristics, such as organic impairment that might result from encephalitis or anoxia at birth.

Nurture includes environmental factors such as the child's sociocultural, familial, and learning environment. McDavid and Garwood (1978) point out that it is difficult to study genetically determined behavior in distinction from environmentally determined behavior (and vice versa) because the two are so intertwined.

Genetics is the study of hereditary characteristics of an organism or person that are transmitted biologically from its parents (Kendler, 1963). We all begin life as a single egg cell from the mother that is fertilized by the union with a sperm cell from the father. The fertilized cell contains a nucleus within which reside the chromosomes: it is within chromosomes that the unitary agents of inheritance, the genes, reside. Within each cell of our bodies, there are 22 matched pairs of chromosomes and a single pair of sex chromosomes. In male offspring the sex chromosome pair consists of an *X* and a small *Y* chromosome (*XY*). In female offspring the sex chromosome pair consists of two *X* chromosomes (*XX*).

Sex-linked characteristics are transmitted through the sex chromosomes. Chromosomes, as well as the thousands of genes in each chromosome, are chemical substances. The hereditary material, DNA, is carried by the chromosomes. Without entering into a lengthy discussion, a *gene* can be defined as "a segment of DNA, the molecules of which contain genetic codes that determine what will be passed from one generation to the next" (McDavid & Garwood, 1978, p. 37). There are exceptions to the sex chromosome pattern in males. For example, there are instances when a male has 47 chromosomes and an *XXY* sex-chromosome constitution (McKusick, 1969). In other instances, some males have 47 chromosomes and an *XYY* sex chromosome. While much more research is needed to document the effects of an extra *Y* on males, preliminary studies have found that these males are tall and unusually aggressive. Many are found in penal institutions, and many, but not all, are mentally retarded to some degree (McKusick, 1969). There are, of course, exceptions to this in that some *XYY* males develop adequately, both socially and mentally (Stoll, Flori, Calvert, Beshara, & Buck, 1979). The example cited illustrates the need to adequately assess the causes of psychopathology in children and youth, medically as well as psychologically. It is reasonable to assume that environmental influences, particularly the child's family, affects expression of behavior in the *XYY* male.

Once a genetic (inherited) disorder is diagnosed, Vaughn, McKay, and Behrman (1979) suggest that management of the child is best approached by acknowledging and recognizing the inherited condition by delineating the pattern of inheritance and by identifying and clarifying clinical aspects of the disorder. The latter point is helpful in counseling parents and children because certain disorders can contribute to lowered cognitive functioning, to self-destructive behavior, or to hyperactive behavior. Couples may also desire genetic counseling when they are about to marry, when one or the other has a family history involving possible heritable disease, or when the prospective spouses are related to each other and want to know the genetic risks involved (Srivastava, 1979).

Dominant and Recessive Genes

When genes from the mother and father pair up, the gene pairs are called alleles. If we have identical alleles (e.g., *BB* genes for brown eyes), then we are said to be homozygous for that gene. But if we carry one *B* gene and one *b* (blue eyes) gene, we are said to be heterozygous for that gene pair because they are dissimilar. If a man homozygous for brown eyes (i.e., has two *BB* genes) marries a woman heterozygous for brown eyes (i.e., she has one *B* gene and one *b* gene), then their offspring would all have brown eyes. That means that brown is a *dominant* gene, and when paired with *b* (blue eyes), the child would still have brown eyes. To have a child born with blue eyes, both parents would need to be heterozygous (carry *Bb* genes) and the offspring would have a one in four chance of receiving *bb* genes, or having blue eyes. In other words, manifestation of a *recessive* condition depends upon a set of matching genes, one from each parent, passing to one or more of the offspring. The child who receives two matching genes is homozygous and carries the recessive condition (Slater & Cowie, 1971). Interfamily marriage may be more common in those children born with a recessive genetic condition (i.e., there is a high incidence of first-cousin marriage among those born with recessive traits) (Slater & Cowie, 1971). The ratio of children born with a recessive condition is about one in four when both parents are heterozygous. Phenylketonuria is an example of a recessive gene condition. There are also instances of a recessively inherited growth-hormone deficiency whereby the parents are of normal height but have a high consanguinity rate and therefore give birth to children who fail to grow.

Dominant genetic conditions have a higher incidence of occurring in offspring, and researchers will generally find that one or both parents also manifest the condition. The condition may manifest itself in a variety of ways (e.g., children found to have neurofibromatosis may have parents and other family members who show minimal clinical signs, such as café au lait spots), and it may appear fully at a later date in life, In this instance, parents may already have children and have passed on the condition before it manifests itself in one of them. Huntington's chorea is an example of this latter state.

The number of genetic, metabolic, chromosomal, and mutant gene abnormalities found in children has risen during the past 10 to 15 years due to better diagnostic procedures and to the field of cytogenetics. Mental health professionals evaluate or treat children or families with Downs syndrome, muscular dystrophy, hemophilia, tuberous sclerosis, neurofibromatosis, PKU, and a wide variety of disorders that cause mental retardation or some type of sensory impairment.

Prenatal Diagnosis of Genetic Disorders

In the last 10 years, tremendous advances have been made in diagnosing the chromosomal and hereditary biochemical disorders of metabolism. Unfortunately, the general public is slow to make use of these diagnostic techniques. In 1974, only 4.1% of pregnant women took advantage of prenatal genetic studies (Milunsky, 1976). Women over 35 years of age or couples deemed "at risk" for having produced a handicapped child could take greater advantage of prenatal genetic studies. It is not our intent here to delve into the ethical questions that might arise should parents learn that their unborn child is likely to have severe genetic problems. Rather, we will give a brief overview of these prenatal diagnostic tests.

Ultrasound is one technique used to detect possible problems with the fetus, and it is the safest technique for both fetus and mother. Fetal anomalies before the 24th week of pregnancy can be determined, and the mother may terminate her pregnancy. Both internal and external structures of the fetus can be visualized by the ultrasound method, and a diagnosis for fetal structural abnormalities can be made (Campbell, 1979). Ultrasound is also useful in diagnosing multiple pregnancy, detecting abnormalities in the fetal growth rate, and helping to determine the exact age of the fetus (Campbell, 1979). Defects such as anencephaly, hydrocephaly, microcephaly, and renal tract anomalies have been detected by ultrasound.

Perhaps the most exciting advance made in fetal diagnosis comes from fetoscopy and fetal blood sampling. The fetoscope is an instrument that provides the physician a means of directly visualizing the fetus and placental blood vessels (see Figure 1). The physician can also use this instrument to draw blood samples from the placental blood vessels which allows for diagnosis of diseases like sickle cell anemia, *B*-thalassemia, and Xerderma pigmenta (a rare and frequently fatal disease in which the skin and eyes are extremely sensitive to light) in the fetus (Mahoney & Hobbins, 1979).

Another technique used in prenatal diagnosis is amniocentesis. A transabdominal amniocentesis is usually performed and can be performed in the doctor's office. The pregnant mother lies supine with her legs extended on the examining table. Under local anes-

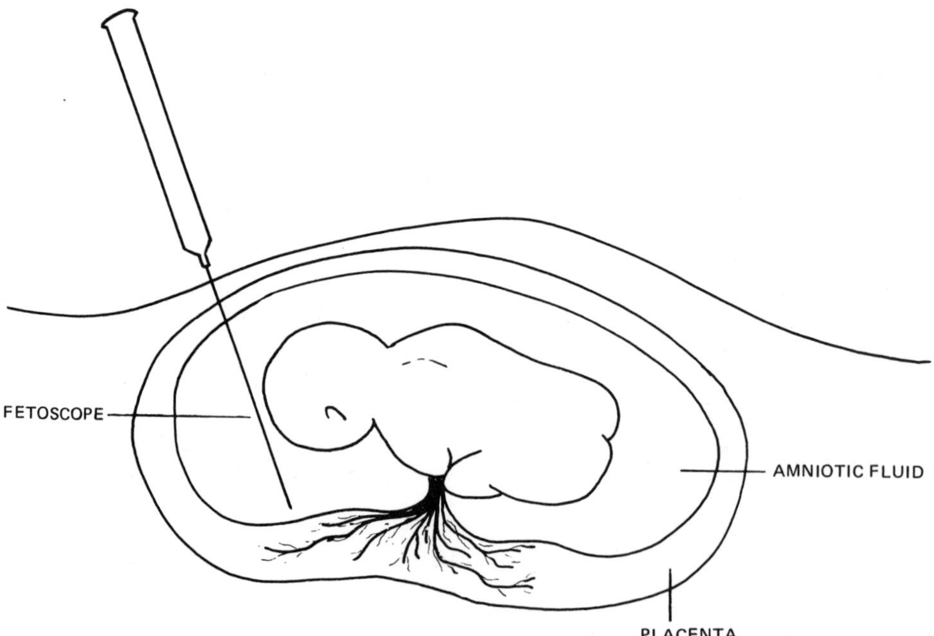

Figure 1. Diagram of the fetoscope.

thesia, a long spinal needle is inserted through the abdominal wall at a right angle toward the uterine cavity. Amniotic fluid is then aspirated from the cavity (Milunsky, 1979).

Ultrasound may be utilized prior to amniocentesis and is often used to locate the placenta. This technique is likely to cut down on the fetomaternal bleeding, allow fewer needle sticks, require fewer repeated amniocenteses, offer greater likelihood of obtaining a diagnosis, and involve fewer pregancy, labor, and delivery risks (Kerenyi & Walker, 1977). There are, however, risks involved in performing amniocentesis (e.g., spontaneous abortion and possible respiration problems at birth). Nevertheless, the amniotic fluids removed from the pregnant mother yield valuable information for prenatal diagnosis of many inborn errors of metabolism and other developmental anomalies associated with early death (e.g., Tay-Sachs disease), serious diseases, and profound mental retardation. As a result of amniocentesis, the parents may elect to abort the fetus rather than give birth to a child with serious developmental anomalies. There are, however, methods of altering the course of certain genetic diseases that occur with inborn errors of metabolism. Infants with phenylketonuria and galactosemia can be placed on special diets that alter the course of the disorder and prevent mental retardation and other developmental problems.

It will take time to improve these fetal diagnostic techniques and, as already mentioned, the general public is slow to accept and utilize such diagnostic tools. As mental health professionals, however, we need to be aware of the diagnostic procedures because they may be indicated for pregnant mothers who already have one or two handicapped children or who have been on drugs known to drastically alter the structure of the fetus.

Heredity and Schizophrenia. Studies in the past have supported the notion that schizophrenia can be inherited and that the likelihood of offspring born to a schizophrenic parent becoming schizophrenic is greater than that of offspring born to healthy parents (Kallman, 1938, 1946). Whereas Kallman (1946) found a high concordance rate for schizophrenia among identical twins, Gottesman and Shields (1966) established more elaborate procedures to study hospital admissions and found slightly lower concordance rates for schizophrenia among identical twins. Perhaps the strongest support for genetic factors contributing to the development of schizophrenia come from studies of Rosenthal, Wender, Kety, Welner, and Schulsinger (1971) and Heston (1966). These investigators studied twins given up for adoption at an early age. In the study of Rosenthal *et al.* (1971), of 69 index cases and 67 matched controls, 1 subject was hospitalized for schizophrenia, 2 were diagnosed as schizophrenic, 10 of 17 were diagnosed as borderline schizophrenics, and 9 of 14 were viewed as schizoid or borderline paranoid. The 10 of 17 and 9 of 14 subjects were index cases.

It is safe to say that children born to schizophrenic parents are also likely to be subjected to greater environmental stress. Additionally, most of the schizophrenic mothers would have been on some type of medication, and whether or not the prenatal care and birth history of offspring are as good as those for offspring of emotionally healthy mothers is something we need to study more carefully. Children born to schizophrenic parents may be susceptible, vulnerable, and perhaps less competent due to factors other than schizophrenia. For the moment, though, evidence appears to support the notion of at least a genetic predisposition to schizophrenia when one or both parents are schizophrenic.

Congenital Defects. Congenital means that a condition is present at birth, but it does not mean that the condition is hereditary. According to McKusick (1969), many congenital disorders *are* hereditary, but many are the result of environmental or extrinsic causes such as malformation that occur to the fetus when the mother contracts rubella, commonly known as German measles. McKusick also notes that most congenital malformations such as cleft lip/palate, cardiac malformations, and clubfoot are likely to be the result of a combination of genetic and environmental factors. Finally, McKusick notes that not all genetic disorders are congenital, (i.e., present, manifested, or visible at birth). Huntington's chorea is an example of an inherited condition that does not manifest itself until later in life.

Temperament

Temperament is defined as

> the individual's constitutional tendency to react to his/her environment in a certain way. Some people are more placid than others, some more vigorous, some more high strung; and it is likely that such differences are innate and recognizable from the moment of birth. (Hinsie & Campbell, 1960, p. 726)

In other words, *temperament is the behavioral style or emotional reactivity manifested by the child as the child interacts with his or her environment.*

As stated, the role of temperament in the development of the child is an important variable to consider when studying individual children. Each child is unique. A simple example of individual temperament is as follows. If we enter a newborn nursery and ring a loud bell, we probably would obtain different responses from each infant. One infant might cry out and demonstrate a startle reflex, another might sleep through the loud bell, while another might open his or her eyes and gaze at us. Each infant is demonstrating a difference in temperament. Thomas and Chess (1977) identify nine basic variables or temperament characteristics that children may demonstrate; and development of either healthy or psychopathological behavior depends upon a "goodness of fit" between these temperamental characteristics and the child's environment. Parent counseling in child management might well vary depending upon temperament of the child. The nine temperamental characteristics include: (1) activity level; (2) rhythmicity; (3) approach or withdrawal to new situations; (4) adaptability; (5) threshold or responsiveness; (6) intensity of reaction; (7) quality of mood; (8) distractibility; and (9) attention span and persistence (Thomas & Chess, 1977).

Of these nine categories, three temperamental types of children were identified, each with his or her own unique style of relating in life. They are: (1) the *easy child,* who is mild and predominantly positive in mood, approachable, adaptable, and rhythmic; (2) the *difficult child,* who is predominantly negative and intense in mood, not too adaptable, and arhythmic; and (3) the *slow-to-warm-up child,* who is low in activity, approach, and adaptability, variable in rhythm, but somewhat negative (Carey, 1981; Thomas & Chess, 1977). Additional variables consisting of fastidiousness and predictability, have been suggested by Graham, Rutter, and George (1973) and by Hegvik, McDevitt, and Carey (1980).

Mental health professionals interviewing parents of problem children may have difficulty measuring or assessing temperament. Basically, the professional will exact a good clinical and developmental history. Open-ended questions such as "Describe your infant during his first months of life" are good. In our own practice, we have parents reply to this question: "He never slept, he cried all the time, and nothing I did seemed to console him" or "She was such a good baby, she never caused me any problems." Details based on such statements can be elicited from parents, and a number of descriptive behavioral traits can be deduced by asking questions appropriate to the nine temperamental characteristics described by Thomas, Chess, and Birch (1968) and Thomas and Chess (1977). Following are some brief descriptions of questions for parents, based on temperamental characteristics.

Activity Level. In clinical practice, the activity level of the child can be assessed by asking parents how much their child moved about as a baby, whether the child was restful or fitful during sleep, (i.e., how much in disarray the crib sheets or blankets might have been), and whether the child could be left lying on something momentarily without fear that he/she would move around and fall.

Rhythmicity. Questions pertaining to ease of regulating are involved in determining the rhythm cycle of the child. Did the child feed, have bowel movements, go to sleep at predictable times, or was he/she highly variable?

Adaptability. What was the behavior of the child like when something new occurred (e.g., when unexpected company arrived, when changes in the child's bedroom, or moving to a new home occurred). Did the child warm up quickly to new people or new foods, or did it take awhile? If it took awhile, then how long?

Approach–Withdrawal. How did the baby or child react to introduction of new people or surroundings. Was there little reaction, were there mild to moderate behavioral upsets, or did the child like it?

Threshold Level. Was the child sensitive to loud noises, foods, textures of clothing, heat or cold? How responsive or aware was the child to environmental sounds such as the telephone or a siren? Describe any intense likes and dislikes the child might have had.

Intensity of Reaction. Did the child react to pleasure or displeasure in a loud or quiet way (e.g., if she did not want a particular food, how would she behave?)? Did the child whimper, cry or protest loudly, smile, coo, or laugh loudly to situations, people, foods?

Quality of Mood. Was the child mostly happy and contented or just the opposite? How did parents know when the child was content or liked something and when the child disliked something?

Distractibility. If there were environmental stimuli such as noise or people entering the room, did the child stop his or her activity or continue it? Could the child be easily distracted when sucking, feeding, or crying?

Persistence and Attention Span. How long did the child normally stay with activities? If the child dropped a toy, did he/she persist in trying to retrieve it or give up easily?

Other techniques have been devised to try to measure temperament more systematically than is possible with parent interviews or behavioral observations. Carey (1970) devised the Infant Temperament Questionnaire and later revised and improved the internal consistency of the test (Carey & McDevitt, 1978). Other parent questionnaires quickly followed. The Toddler Temperament Scale (1–3 years of age) was devised by Fullard, McDevitt, and Carey (1978), the Behavioral Style Questionnaire was devised for children 3–7 years of age (McDevitt & Carey, 1978), and the Middle Childhood Temperament Questionnaire was developed for 8- to 12-year-old children (Hegvik *et al.,* 1980). Bates, Freeland, and Lounsbury (1979), Persson-Blennow and McNeil (1979), and Buss and Plomin (1975) have developed other questionnaires assessing temperament in infants. Further, Thomas and Chess (1977) devised questionnaires that both parents and teachers can fill out for the 3–7 year age-group.

In summary, temperament is the emotional or behavioral style of a person, and although it is fairly consistent, life experiences can alter one's temperament to a degree. Mental health professionals assessing child psychopathology might want to consider temperamental characteristics of the child and how these "fit" with the family. The study of temperament continues to be an area ripe for research.

Constitution

Briefly let us review constitutional factors as they relate to psychopathology. A child's constitution is based on a number of factors. The term *constitution* can be defined as:

> the sum total of the morphological, physiological and psychological characters of an individual with additional variables of race, sex and age, all in great part determined by heredity but influenced in varying degrees by environmental factors. (Tucker & Lessa, 1940. p. 265)

Hereditary makeup (physical traits), spontaneous and artificial mutations, traumatic incidents before and at birth, and very early life experiences all contribute to the constitution of the developing child (Kisker, 1964). Broadly defined, a child's constitution is his or her total biological makeup.

Two very early theories relating physical makeup of the individual to mental illness that generated a great deal of research are those of Kretschmer (1925) and Sheldon (1940). Kretschmer described three body types and the pathology likely to be found in the individuals possessing those body types. These include: (1) the pyknic, characterized by a thick set, barrel-shaped trunk, and a round and compact body—the psychological type of a pyknic falls into one of three types of cyclothyms, ranging from the healthy, good natured "chatterbox" to the manic depressive (Hinsie & Campbell, 1960); (2) the athletic, muscular type who is strong and vigorous; and (3) the asthenic or the leptosomic, characterized by weak body type and a body that may appear tall and thin. The psychological aspects for the athletic and asthenic body types tend to be schizoids or schizothymes (Hinsie & Campbell, 1960).

Sheldon's (1940) somatotypes consist of: (1) endomorphs, who are round or fat; (2) mesomorphs, who are athletic or muscular; and (3) ectomorphs, depicting linearity.

While body types and the characteristic behavioral and psychological correlates attributed to each type are interesting to note, when working with children and determining the etiology of a child's behavior, the temperamental characteristics presented by the child are likely to lend more information. However, the study of temperament has been slow to develop in actual clinical practice, and rarely does one attribute behavior to body build.

Sociocultural Conditions

In addition to genetic, constitutional, and temperamental factors related to psychopathology, mental health professionals must consider social and cultural influences to which the child is exposed. Discussion in Part II of this volume will address specific etiology related to various behavioral disorders. However, an overview of certain conditions in the child's interpersonal relationships and cultural milieu is warranted. The interactions among biological, psychosocial, and cultural factors is paramount to understanding behavioral difficulties with only one class of factors rarely being represented as the sole causative entity.

As the newborn completes the birth process, he or she immediately becomes dependent upon members of society for basic life-sustaining measures. Subsequently, the developing child encounters a myriad of social and cultural experiences, all of which can either facilitate healthy emotional growth or, conversely, contribute to maladaptive behavior.

The child's immediate family is recognized as the first socializing agent. The child's development is facilitated by an optimal level and range of nurturant and stimulating contacts between parent and child. Wholesome progress takes place more rapidly and smoothly when both parents are present, and cooperation exists in providing the child with appropriate parental affection, proper discipline, development of a value system not in conflict with societal norms, and suitable modeling by the parents for the child's acquisition of a healthy feminine or masculine identification (Coville, Costello, & Rouke, 1969). Thus, the presence and nature of *altered* family constellations merits consideration.

Family Structure or Constellation

The presence of the nuclear family, wherein both parents regularly assume parenting responsibilities, has been affected by the rapidly increasing divorce rate in our present society. Everly estimates that approximately "11 million out of 66 million," or "about one of every six children," are living in a single-parent home, usually because of parental separation or divorce (1977, p. 7).

Divorce and Family Dynamics

Within the divorce process, the mother receives legal custody of the child or children involved in over 95% of the cases. Because most mothers emerge as the head of the household following such proceedings, and due to the fact that 9 of 10 single parents are mothers (Jauch, 1977), our discussion will address parent–child relations from this perspective. The need is acknowledged, however, for further research concerning the father as a "single parent."

The effects of a parent's absence, usually the father's, received early attention in the literature as contributing to the presence of juvenile delinquency. Haskell and Yablonsky (1978) present evidence from various studies demonstrating that a high incidence of delinquents come from broken homes. The incidence of broken homes is 1.5 to 2 times more frequent among the delinquent population as contrasted to the nondelinquent. Haskell and Yablonsky caution, however, that there is a greater chance of "a warm, stable parent . . . raising a nondelinquent" than there is of "two parents who are in conflict" (1978, p. 100).

Many mothers now singled by divorce have proven to be capable of coping with the accompanying stress and do succeed in adequately raising healthy and happy children (Jauch, 1977). In some cases, children are seen as benefiting from divorce because they no longer are subjected to the hostile and uncomfortable environment that previously existed in the home. Certainly, in many instances divorce may provide a psychologically healthier environment for the remaining family members.

However, child rearing is simply more difficult for the single parent. Many mothers are forced to seek outside employment to meet financial costs in raising a family. Census figures report that approximately 31% of female householder families were below the poverty level in 1978. The responsibility of outside employment combined with child-rearing responsibilities—even within the nuclear family—requires greater energy, effort, and coping skills on the part of the working mother.

Besides economic and coping stresses on the mother, there is the problem of adequately supervising the children. Working mothers do not usually have the luxury of setting job hours that coincide with the child's school hours, thus many children are unsupervised. Even preschoolers are often left to fend for themselves, and the consequences can be harmful. The number of children experiencing such situations is difficult to determine. However, the number of children who are left alone and termed "latch key kids" (as they leave or return to an empty house) is sufficiently high to warrant societal concern regarding this practice.

Whether the single parent is engaged in employment or remains at home, Gardner (1977) cites a variety of reactions that children may display as a result of divorce. Some may *deny* the finality of divorce and continue to ask when the absent parent will return. Others may react similarly but with repressed or suppressed feelings, with the child acting as though no changes in the family household are evident. A second type of reaction includes the occurrence of *depressive symptoms;* these, of course, may be manifested in various ways. Third, some children of divorce may react with *regressive behavior,* returning to more infantile actions in order to maintain the single parent's attention and compensate for loss of the other parent. Gardner also points to other possible reactions, including the child's *feeling angry* concerning the absence of one parent from the home and/or *feeling guilty* because the child may perceive the divorce as resulting from his or her own previous actions or presence. Last, Gardner notes that "reconciliation obsessions" are common reactions and may continue for an extended period of time. Each of these grief reactions may have detrimental effects on the child if not resolved in a manner consistent with the principles of healthy emotional adjustment. The mental health professional working with children will want to obtain a complete and in-depth history of the family situation, including the child's reaction to divorce, visitation rights (how frequently and how consistent), who cares for the child while mother works, the economic situation, and other stresses affecting the child and parent.

Teenage Pregnancy and One-Parent Families

Weiss (1980) cites that over 1 million teenagers become pregnant every year, with two-thirds of such pregnancies occurring accidently. Teenagers currently represent over 50% of the number of all unwed mothers, either choosing or being forced into single parenting. Weiss (1980) further states that many such teenagers are inadequately prepared physically, socially, and/or economically to become parents. The pregnant teenager suffers, or is likely to suffer the consequences of terminating or delaying her education, of being excluded from part of the normal teenage social scene, and of risking greater emotional friction with family members and/or the father. These social or emotional complications serve to foster hostile feelings on the part of the teenage mother. Such feelings in turn may be projected onto the child as the "reason" for present difficulties and thus may foreshadow possible maternal rejection and neglect. When marriage occurs as a result of the pregnancy, statistics indicate that 3 of 5 marriages end in divorce within 6 years (Weiss, 1980, p. 32). Thus, the impact of early pregnancy and divorce can have adverse consequences on child rearing and can contribute enormously to a child's psychopathology.

Other Factors Affecting Family Dynamics

Loss of a parent through death can profoundly disrupt family functioning as each member is faced with working through the stages of grief (Kubler-Ross, 1969). Frequently, the family's resulting instability is compounded by financial problems in the case of paternal death or, of an equally frightening nature, the future care of the children in the case of maternal death. Certainly, the surviving parent is faced with a tremendous task, as he or she is burdened not only by personal bereavement but by being the sole supportive network of child family members.

White and Gathman (1974) note:

> that school-age children and adolescents sometimes manifest their grief in the form of diffuse, angry, rebellious behavior. Smaller children respond with withdrawal, phobias and fears of being deserted, as well as with active curiosity about death. (p. 4)

White and Gathman further acknowledge that the small child, unless the occurrence of death is dealt with in a frank and appropriate way, may be subject to the trauma of his or her own unrealistic fantasies and imagination. The possible presence of severe depression being experienced by one or more family members as a result of grief must continue as a source of concern until the time when it is clear that the mourning process is of normal nature and proportion.

When a family loses a single child by death, the stability of the family is threatened. The effects of such a loss can have a negative influence on future parenting of subsequent children in that parents may tend to be overprotective or submissive toward their children. The precipitating stress situation must be dealt with by providing appropriate supportive and professional assistance, not only to the parents but to siblings as well.

Child Abuse and Neglect

Within the family environment, the child should ideally encounter the "mothering" process as an initial, positive socializing experience. Moss (1972), in studying a nonclinical sample of first-born children and their mothers in the natural home setting, observed maternal behaviors in response to stimuli elicited by the infant (e.g., crying, fussing, being actively or passively awake). Mothering responses that structured learning opportunity and shaped response patterns of the infant included (1) affectional contacts, such as holding the child closely and caressing the child; (2) attending to infant needs, as in caretaking activities; and (3) other activities serving as stimulating or arousal actions, such as holding the child in sitting or standing positions for muscular growth or stimulating the child through tactile, visual, or verbal behaviors, including looking or smiling at, talking to, or imitating infant or child behaviors such as vocalizations (Moss, 1972).

In contrast, however, to children receiving these and other positive maternal (parental) experiences, there are countless numbers of children who suffer from lack of nurturant familial interactions. Infant or child failure to thrive, because of emotional neglect by parental or surrogate figures, was reported early in the literature (Spitz, 1972). Such neglect continues to be a source of concern for it adversely affects later cognitive, social, and emotional functioning.

Estimates vary concerning actual incidence or number of children suffering from the battered child syndrome (Kempe, Silverman, Steele, Droegemueller, & Silver, 1962). Accurate reporting is clouded by the reluctance of society to label parents as abusers without tangible proof that the child is in danger of actual physical injury. However, Green (1978) cites figures reported by the National Center on Child Abuse and Neglect, which include all forms of child abuse and neglect (mental or physical injury, negligent treatment or maltreatment, sexual abuse). The Center reports 1.6 million abuse cases recorded annually; approximately 2,000 to 4,000 children die every year as the result of child abuse.

Although the extent of psychological trauma and subsequent emotional complications experienced by the abused child still need further research, various types of pathology are reflected in victims of child abuse. In a discussion of environmental components contributing to an abusive home, Green (1978), Helfer and Kempe (1968), and Green, Gaines, and Sandgrund (1974) conclude that no single factor is responsible for child abusive actions. However, environmental stress in its many varying forms (e.g., economic difficulties, divorce, separation, unplanned pregnancies, childrearing conflicts or pressures) has significant potential for tension building, which may erupt and be discharged onto the child.

That abusive parents were often abused children themselves is frequently referred to as a sociocultural factor perpetuating the incidence of child abuse (Steele, 1976). The cultural "inheritance" of proneness to abuse is cited in the literature because certain kinds of violent attitudes are learned and passed along within families (Werber & Cochran, 1978). Another environmental influence frequently cited as contributing to abuse is the lack of accurate and knowledgeable parental information concerning developmental expectations of the child (Green, 1978; Steele, 1976). Frustrated by the inability of the child to live up to faulty parental demands regarding certain types of performances, retaliation in the form of abusive action for purposes of "teaching" the child may ensue.

Ethnic Derivation and Socioeconomic Status

Other sociocultural factors studied in relation to psychopathology include ethnic identification—particularly minority group status—and socioeconomic status. As a variable *per se,* no direct correlation between ethnicity and psychopathology has been evidenced. However, when accompanied by corrolary conditions such as lowered socioeconomic status (SES), whether within the minority or Caucasion population, a higher proportion of emotional/behavioral disorders has been cited. Swanson and Willis (1979) report that approximately 24.5 million Americans qualify as "poverty level" families according to federal guidelines for such inclusion. Jauch (1977) writes:

> Many researchers believe that the reputation of so-called "broken homes" for producing more than their share of child abuse, child neglect, delinquency and other child "pathologies" is more likely to have been caused by the stress of *poverty* in these families rather than to the absence of one parent. (p. 31)

If we consider the interplay among varied facets of the individual's sociocultural environment, how do ethnic and socioeconomic status relate to presence of pathology? Among populations classified as poverty-level, the following figures are estimated concerning ethnic derivation:

> About 9 percent of the white population is included, along with 31 percent of the black population, 21 percent of the Spanish-speaking population and 38 percent of all Indians. (Swanson & Willis, 1979, p. 136)

Despite governmental attempts to eradicate poverty, the children of millions of families suffer from malnutrition. In addition to the genetic-constitutional effects of maternal nutrition on offspring, the physical and mental development of the child is at a critical phase during the first few years of life. Lack of brain growth or development due to severe dietary deficiencies resulting in mental retardation has been confirmed through various research findings.

Other factors hindering a feeling of well-being include inadequate housing conditions and facilities among the poverty striken. Overcrowding, with its resultant lack of privacy, may increase stress and tensions within families so that there is a continual feeling of frustration, fatigue, and dissatisfaction. In such poverty-ridden conditions, children do not always feel safe and secure because vandalism and destructive actions occur more frequently within depressed housing areas. Hence, children do not always grow up feeling free from danger and, indeed, may develop retaliative behaviors.

School Peer Pressures

As the child matures, he or she experiences greater dependency upon peers and teachers as socializing agents within the educational setting. Learning capabilities, academic or sports-related achievement, and physical attractiveness to others all serve as areas of concern in the search for the ego satisfaction and self-esteem necessary for positive emotional growth. The greater difficulty that many lower-socioeconomic-class students have in meeting scholastic demands of the traditional middle-class oriented school has been a concern of educators for a number of years.

In addition to the school's assuming a greater role in society's responsibility for raising children, public media—particularly television—serves as a socializing agent. Much debate exists concerning the effects that television has on the child's development. There is greater agreement that symbolic models, as viewed within television programming or advertising, emphasize that physical attractiveness is paramount to acceptance by others. As youngsters are bombarded by television and film media to maintain or emulate certain aspects of physical appearance (e.g., clothing, body build, sexual attractiveness), the task of meeting such "standards" becomes increasingly difficult for many children. The rising number of attempted or completed suicides (with younger-age children increasingly included) attests to increased pressures being inadequately mastered by children and youth. Although multiple factors are, of course, reflected in the etiology of suicidal acts, feelings of alienation (e.g., intrafamily conflict, lack of peer acceptance) and inability to cope with perceived expectations are at the core of such acts. Often, the school is ill equipped to recognize early signs of depression, for example, as it may be masked in antisocial or rebellious behaviors. Or the seriousness of withdrawn or timid behavior, perhaps precipitated by the loss of a parent through death or prolonged hospitalization, may go unnoticed because such behavior does not constitute an overt problem within the learning climate of the classroom or school setting.

Learning Basis of Psychopathology

In attempting to understand childhood psychopathology, the principles of learning have much to offer. One of the most impressive characteristics of human beings is that they are primarily creatures of learning. *Homo sapiens* is capable of a large repertoire of highly complex behaviors, involving manipulation of the environment, manipulation of abstract symbols, and manipulation of each other through socialization. While other animals have relatively simple behaviors that are frequently heavily influenced by inherited characteristics, humans appear to be minimally influenced by such characteristics and must learn virtually every behavior that characterizes them as adults. Thus, while many creatures can survive immediately or shortly after birth on their own, human beings perish without constant and intensive care for many years. In the adult, there are only a few responses, such as coughing, sneezing, the startle response, and similar behaviors, that occur without prior learning. Virtually all behaviors of the adult are the product of learning (Eysenck, 1960; Mahoney & Arnkoff, 1978; Skinner, 1953). Genetic inheritance plays a definite role in human functioning, as pointed out earlier in this chapter, but inherited predispositions and characteristics of human beings are plastic and subject to major variation based on learning experiences of the individual throughout his/her life span. The intent here is neither to oversimplify nor to deny the contributions of other factors, rather to emphasize the major role that learning plays in human behavior.

Awareness of the primacy of learning with respect to human behavior is valuable in thinking clearly with respect to childhood psychopathology. If we are aware of the fact that a given child behaves the way he or she does because of previous learning and conditioning experiences, this provides us with an invaluable means of understanding and treating that behavior (Franks, 1961; Ross, 1978).

A basic assumption of behavioral theorists is that no new principles are required to explain abnormal behavior beyond those required to explain normal behavior (Eysenck, 1960; Kanfer & Phillips, 1970). Behavior, whether it is effective and productive, or ineffective and nonproductive, is learned, and it is learned according to the same principles in either case. Because in psychological laboratories there have been several decades of research conducted on the principles of learning, we have at least a modicom of information that permits us to understand behavior and to design strategies that will result in changing that behavior in predictable ways.

Virtually any of the principles of learning that have been investigated in psychological laboratories may be employed to understand childhood psychopathology (cf. Ross, 1978). It is not possible in the space of this chapter to discuss all of the various principles that might be involved. However, some of the principles of learning that commonly result in abnormal behavior can be discussed.

In general, emotional reactions are thought to follow a classical conditioning paradigm in terms of the learning model that explains their development. That is, emotional reactions, both positive and negative, are conditioned responses based on previous experience. Thus, stimuli that were present and became associated with pleasant sensations in the past have the ability to evoke such sensations in the present. The field of marketing and advertising uses this fact very skillfully to induce people to purchase products. The color, size, and shape of the package, the name and adjectives used to describe the product, and the pictures of descriptions of the type of person who uses the product (or who will be attracted to a person who does) are all calculated to evoke pleasant responses.

However, negative emotional reactions may also be conditioned. When such reactions are sufficiently extreme or frequent that they affect an important aspect of one's life to a degree that they interfere with a person's functioning, they become a source of psychopathology. The most widely studied reaction of this sort is that of fear or phobia. However, many other unpleasant emotions doubtless condition our responses. The work with phobias extends at least back to the experiment of Watson and Raynor (1920) in which they conditioned a fear response in a child (Albert) by clanging a hammer against a piece of steel behind the child's head each time a white rat was presented. In this classic experiment, Albert's initial reaction to the animal was one of curiosity and pleasure. However, following pairing of this animal with the frightening sound, the child began to be frightened by the animal, cried, and attempted to withdraw from it. This experiment was carried out in a hospital. Unfortunately, the child was removed from the hospital before any kind of extinction or deconditioning could be carried out. However, Jones (1924), in a later demonstration, found a child with a fear that had developed naturally, but which was very similar to that experimentally conditioned in Albert. This child, Peter, was treated by engaging him in pleasant activities and gradually moving a rabbit closer to him by successive approximations. Repeated exposures under such circumstances resulted in removal of the fear.

The work with fear and phobia as conditioned reactions continued in the years following Watson, eventually culminating in research by Wolpe (1958) and others demonstrating that systematic desensitization provides a very effective treatment for such responses. While many of the phobias that have been extensively studied involve rather simple and discrete stimuli, such as fear of small animals, it is possible to view them as a partial or complete explanation for a wider range of psychopathologies. For example, sexual dysfunction and deviation are often thought to have a significant dimension of phobia with respect to sexual interaction with appropriate heterosexual partners. The result is dysfunction or deviation (turning to a less threatening outlet). Likewise, many personality disorders can be conceptualized as life-styles designed to avoid phobic stimuli that are perceived by the individual in the environment. For example, the schizoid individual may withdraw from social situations and inhibit emotional expression in order to avoid the pain and distress of the frequent phobic responses that would otherwise occur. Psychosomatic disorders may be conceptualized as stress reactions based on conditioned fear. Substance abuse is sometimes viewed as an attempt to anesthetize oneself against the effects of fear and stress induced by perceived threats in one's environment. Many of the neurotic disorders obviously contain a strong element of conditioned fear. It is also possible to conceptualize many psychotic reactions as states of prolonged panic behavior in that studies of psychotic patients have indicated a very high level of physiological arousal. Also, normal individuals, when pushed to a state of panic, behave in ways very similar to individuals who are regarded as psychotic. The main distinction appears to be the lack of ability by those regarded as psychotic to regain their equilibrium and reduce the panic state. Figure 2 illustrates how even relatively complex and abstract problems, such as marital difficulties, may be based on conditioned emotional reactions such as fear. If a male has been punished or mistreated by females while he was developing, he will have numerous negative conditioned emotional reactions that will prevent him from trusting, becoming intimate with, and being comfortable in the presence of females. As an adult, these conditioned reactions will create marital difficulties. While the same process could occur with females, perhaps a more common pattern is for the father to be aloof, unsupportive, and uninvolved during the female's developmental years. As a result, the adult female exposed to such conditioning may have difficulty relating to males, trusting them, or having very positive reactions to them.

While basic emotional reactions are often conceptualized as following a classical conditioning paradigm, skills training is more frequently conceptualized as following an operant conditioning model. It should be pointed out that these conceptualizations are primarily for heuristic purposes and do not necessarily imply any absolute truth with respect to the use of such a model. In fact, as is well known, there is still debate and discussion about the fact that either operant or classical conditioning can be seen as incorporating the other and being the most basic.

However, in terms of generating hypotheses and explaining behavior, operant condi-

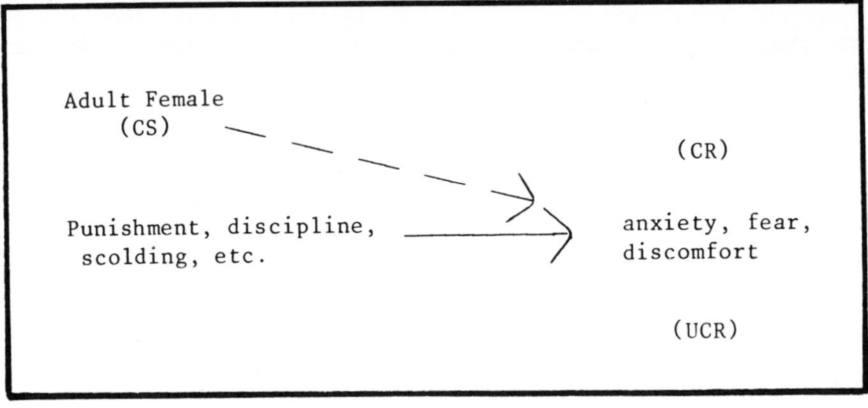

Figure 2. Conditioning history predisposing a male to marital difficulties.

tioning provides a ready model for understanding a variety of skills. Thus, every skill, whether it be eating with a fork, tying one's shoes, riding a bicycle, or relating effectively to other human beings, may be seen as learned on the basis of operant conditioning. Basically, in this paradigm, behavior is assumed to be a function of its consequences. Responses or behaviors that lead to reward tend to be repeated under similar circumstances in the future. Responses or behaviors that lead to punishment tend not to be repeated in the future. Thus, the conditioning history of the organism explains the current functioning, and skillful management of contingencies between the response and the consequence can be used for therapeutic benefit. Since responses may be viewed as having a favorable or unfavorable consequence or outcome, we can conceptualize these outcomes under the general rubric of reinforcement and punishment. Those responses that lead to a favorable outcome are likely to be repeated in the future. They are thus strengthened or reinforced. Those responses that lead to an unfavorable outcome are unlikely to occur again in the future. They are said to have been weakened or punished. Reinforcement always increases the probability of a response occurring in the future. Punishment always suppresses or decreases the tendency for that response to occur again in the future. It is important to make this distinction clear because many people confuse "negative reinforcement" with "punishment." *Positive reinforcement* involves *presentation of a pleasant stimulus* following a response. *Negative reinforcement* involves *removal of an unpleasant stimulus* following a response. Note, however, that a response that leads to a favorable outcome, whether it be presentation of a pleasant stimulus or removal of an unpleasant one, is reinforced and will be likely to occur again in the future. Thus, if we do something and are given a reward for doing so, we will attempt to repeat that behavior in the future. Likewise, however, if we have, say, a pain, and employ a certain medication that results in *alleviation* of the pain, we are likely to use that medication again in the future. In both cases the behavior has been "reinforced" or increased in terms of probability of occurring in the future. The former is referred to as positive reinforcement, the latter as negative reinforcement, but they are both reinforcement.

Punishment may also occur in two varieties. We may think of direct punishment and indirect punishment. *Direct punishment* refers to the circumstance in which *an unpleasant stimulus is applied* following a behavior. *Indirect punishment* occurs when *a pleasant stim-*

ulus is removed following a behavior. Thus, if we reach for the cookie jar and are smacked on the hand, this is direct punishment. However, if we are told that we will not be permitted to watch television for the evening because of some misbehavior, this would be indirect punishment (removal of a pleasant stimulus). Presentation of an unpleasant stimulus or removal of a pleasant stimulus both have a punishing effect.

Figure 3 demonstrates the various combinations of stimuli that result in reinforcement and punishment. However, the story does not end here because a variety of emotional reactions are observed to be concomitant with the experience of reinforcement or punishment. Thus, when an individual is reinforced, he or she generally has a number of positive emotional reactions. Such a person feels good about himself or herself, about the world, tends to be happy, is willing to work and perform harder in the future, and in general experiences a state of well-being that is often referred to as a "good self-concept." On the other hand, an individual who is experiencing repeated and/or excessive punishment for his or her behavior tends to experience a number of negative emotions such as frustration, anger, and depression, and tends to withdraw from the situation as well as to become hostile and aggressive. This may be thought of as having developed a "poor self-concept." Since many theories of psychopathology stress the social aspects of the development and definition of psychopathology, the operant conditioning paradigm appears to explain the manner in which social skills are learned, thus it has considerable relevance to our understanding in this area. That is, we might assume the major etiological factors in the development of various forms of psychopathology inherent in the difficulty the individual has in relating effectively to others. Further, "mental illness" is a concept that has strong social underpinings in its very definition (we tend to be regarded as "mentally ill" when our behavior is sufficiently annoying to others around us that they are unwilling to tolerate it). We can see, then, that a model or paradigm that enables us to conceptualize how such behaviors might have developed, what is currently sustaining them, and what strategies might change those behaviors, would have considerable relevance to our understanding of psychopathology.

While, by far, most of the research to date in the area of learning has dealt with one

Status of Stimulus

Nature of Stimulus	Presented (+)	Removed (-)
Positive (+)	1 ++ Positive stimulus presented following behavior = reinforcement	3 +- Positive stimulus removed following behavior = punishment
Negative (-)	2 -+ Negative stimulus presented following behavior = punishment	4 -- Negative stimulus removed following behavior = reinforcement

Figure 3. Consequences following responses resulting in reinforcement (squares 1 and 4) or punishment (squares 2 and 3).

variation or another of the classical and operant paradigms (as noted in the beginning of this section), human beings have the ability to deal with abstract symbols to a much greater degree than any other creature. Thus, within the organism, many important events occur that influence behavior. There is a great deal more controversy about how these processes work, research in these areas has been more limited, and much less can be said with precision about these processes. However, the importance of this area cannot be denied. Thus, the "stream of consciousness," the thoughts of the individual, can and does affect behavior. The cognitive maps, cognitions, understandings, or whatever else that an individual carries around mentally, influence perception of stimuli and help to determine which responses will be made. The ability of the person to solve problems and cope successfully with life as a human being appears to involve these higher mental processes to a great extent. The ability of the individual to perceive contingencies between behavior and consequences, particularly when time delay is involved, falls under this general rubric. The ability to form concepts and perform higher-order learning tasks appears to be a part of this phenomenon as well. In terms of psychopathology, the area of learning appears to be most useful in explaining the more bizarre behaviors characteristic of psychotics and other severely disturbed individuals, who are frequently referred to as having "thought disorders." Much psychopathology that would strain classical and operant conditioning concepts for explanation fits readily within the mediation paradigm. However, it should be emphasized again that we are dealing in heuristics at this point because it is possible to conceptualize behavior without resorting to mediational conceptualizations. But use of such terms has frequently proved more efficient in the sense of suggesting strategies for intervention. Much more needs to be known about this area. Currently, it represents an exciting frontier for psychological theorizing, research, and therapy.

It is worth noting that application of principles of learning to the field of interpersonal relationships is often referred to as social learning theory. Since we have already commented on the social aspects of psychopathology, suffice it to say that the literature of this area provides a wealth of seminal information for understanding psychopathology as well as for designing treatment interventions. We shall now turn to some more specific examples of how the development of psychopathology may be understood by employing principles of learning.

Consider the inappropriate application of reinforcers and punishers. Behavior that is reinforced tends to be repeated. Behavior that is punished tends not to be repeated. If a child is reinforced for inappropriate behavior and punished for appropriate behavior, this will result in a very deviant and maladaptive pattern (Bijou & Baer, 1961; Gelfand, 1969). Likewise, if the child fails to receive reinforcement for appropriate behavior or is not corrected or punished for inappropriate behavior, deviant patterns may develop. Clinicians who see children are constantly confronted with the fact that a given child's behavior is quite understandable when the patterns of reinforcement and punishment that have been employed by the family are known (DeNike & Tiber, 1968).

For example, if a child is systematically reinforced for being dependent and punished for attempts at assertive behavior, that child may well develop problems involving shyness, withdrawal, and fearfulness at being separated from parents. In a similar vein, Eron (1978) has described the process of learned helplessness, which may lead to a variety of forms of psychopathology. Likewise, if a child is not corrected when dishonest or is encouraged (through adult models and signs of approval) to engage in manipulative behavior, patterns begin to develop that can lead to serious behavioral and interpersonal problems.

Closely related to this phenomena is the excessive use of aversive control or punishment. In the process of socializing a child, it is necessary to exert considerable control over that child's behavior. This control can be exerted in positive ways through various types of reinforcement, or it can be exerted aversively through use of punishment and unpleasant consequences for behavior. Excessive use of punishment or aversive control is known to result in a variety of emotional behaviors such as anger, frustration, hostility, aggressiveness, depression, and withdrawal (Schwartz, 1978; Walters & Grusec, 1977). Any of these may become the complaint that leads a child patient to be initially referred to a clinician. Child abuse represents the extreme in terms of use of aversive control; the effects of such treatment are well known (Kempe & Kempe, 1978).

Some pathology appears to result from superstitious behavior (Bandura, 1968; Ferster, Culbertson, & Boren, 1975). Skinner (1938) defines superstitious behavior as cases in which responses that were in progress at the time of delivery or reinforcement are *accidentally* reinforced, even though these responses have no functional relationship to obtaining the reinforcement. Thus, pigeons have been taught to bow and scrape or turn in circles because these behaviors were, by chance, being engaged in at the time reinforcement was delivered (Skinner, 1948). Some human psychopathology appears to be a result of this kind of accidental conditioning.

The examples mentioned so far rely primarily on operant conditioning principles as a paradigm. However, the classical conditioning paradigm is also frequently employed in explaining psychopathology. As noted earlier in this chapter, traumatic conditioning appears to play a major role in the development of many anxieties and phobias, and fears. By this process, stimuli that are present at times when the organism experiences distress or discomfort, tend to become conditioned stimuli for these reactions and are capable of evoking similar reactions each time they occur. In addition, since generalization is known to occur with such types of conditioning, an individual who has been traumatically conditioned to a given stimulus will respond with fear and anxiety to a wide range of similar stimuli throughout his or her lifetime, unless some specific intervention is employed to extinguish this conditioning (Wolpe, 1958).

Related to this problem is the chronic presence of excessive stress. If a person is placed in a situation in which excessive and prolonged stress exists, the result may be a major deterioration in the functioning of that individual (Ferster *et al.,* 1975). Severe neuroses and psychoses may well develop out of such circumstances.

Perception of the stimulus is often a crucial factor in determining behavior. In order to respond effectively to the complex situations that are required of human beings each day, particularly those involving interpersonal relationships, it is necessary to perceive accurately the stimuli present in the situation (McGuigan & Lumsden, 1973). If one fails to do this, his or her behavior is regarded as inappropriate and offensive by others. In such cases, the individual has failed to master various discrimination learning tasks or, as a result of faulty learning, has a cognitive structure that does not contain adequate labels for the experiences encountered (Bandura, 1969; Kanfer & Phillips, 1970; McDavid, 1962). This results in significant personal distress and social maladjustment. Treatment involves attention to discrimination training for the individual and facilitation of his or her learning to accurately label experiences, feelings, and emotions in such a way that they may be dealt with realistically.

In addition to failures in discrimination, many individuals suffer from an impoverished behavioral repertoire. That is, they simply have failed to develop adequate coping and problem-solving skills throughout their life to deal with the complexities of social living (Patterson, 1966). As a result, they constantly fail in situations where they would like to succeed, have difficulty interacting with others, and suffer a variety of unpleasant emotions because they are not able to attain their goals. Often this impoverished repertoire appears to result from a lack of adequate models in the person's environment, or from the presence of inappropriate models (Bandura, 1968; Bandura & Walters, 1963). For example, when one sees a teenager who resorts to excessive use of somatic complaints and feigned illnesses to avoid attending school, it is not uncommon to find that one of the parents uses this same strategy in dealing with life stresses and that the child is simply modeling unhealthy behavior that is already present in the family.

Much of the research on the principles of learning has been carried out with simple organisms such as rats or pigeons. However, as was mentioned earlier in this section, humans have the ability to manipulate abstract concepts (such as language) very effectively. Thus, while it is still a somewhat inadequately explored area, there is general agreement that cognitive dysfunction also may result in psychopathology (Mahoney & Arnkoff, 1978; Payne, 1961). That is, thoughts that occur in the individual may produce effective or ineffective behavior, depending on their nature (Ellis, 1962). One simple example of this phenomenon may suffice. In talking with depressed patients, it frequently becomes apparent that their "stream of consciousness" and cognitions are all of a very pessimistic and unpleasant nature. They constantly ruminate about all the unhappy facts of their life and the feeling that "nothing will ever work out." Thinking along these lines only increases those feelings and tends to become a self-fulfilling prophecy. Thus, an individual who begins to ruminate in this manner becomes more depressed, and as this person becomes more depressed, he or she ruminates more, thus creating a vicious circle. The depressed patient is cognitively placing himself/herself in a situation in which punishment is delivered with great frequency through his/her thoughts (Beck, 1979a). A very effective treatment strategy is to change those thought patterns from overly pessimistic and punishing to a more realistic and optimistic outlook. This frequently results in alleviation of the depression (Beck, 1979b.).

In a similar vein, Kanfer and Marsten (1963a,b) have discussed the concept of internal self-reinforcement. This concept appears to have much relevance for understanding psychopathology. For example, the person whose thoughts are constantly negative may be conceptualized as delivering frequent punishment to himself or herself with predictable consequences for feelings and behavior. Kanfer and Marston (1963a,b) trained patients to reinforce themselves internally for appropriate behaviors (e.g., "That was a good thing to do. Good for me! I'm glad I did that!"). This process resulted in changes in mood and behavior. It is interesting that this approach also provides us with a model to explain self-confidence. An individual who monitors his or her own behavior (reinforcing appropriate behavior and mildly punishing inappropriate behavior) is considered by others to be a person with "self-confidence," as opposed to the individual who constantly seeks external reassurance from others regarding the appropriateness of his or her behavior.

Before concluding this section, a brief word about taxonomy systems employing a learning paradigm might be in order. One very general way of approaching cases using a learning theory model is to conceptualize the patient's problems in terms of behavioral excesses and deficits. Excesses refer to behaviors that occur too frequently; deficits refer to behaviors that do not occur frequently enough. A treatment program is then designed to increase and decrease the behaviors as desired. Walker, Hedberg, Clement, and Wright (1981) have added to this list the concept of behavioral anomalies. By anomaly, Walker *et al.* introduces the concept that some behaviors are simply inappropriate and unwanted regardless of frequency. Thus, while a behavioral excess might be excessive drinking (needing reduction), a behavioral deficit might be inability to be properly assertive in a variety of situations (needing an increase). It is a behavioral anomaly to believe that all people belonging to the Mason's lodge are plotting against one or to believe that anything less than a grade of "A" in a class represents failure. Such thought disorders cannot be readily conceptualized as excesses or deficits. Rather, they are anomalies and require elimination.

Summary

The etiological factors contributing to child psychopathology are diverse, ranging from genetic factors to temperament coupled with socioeconomic, family, and learning experiences in the environment. Some etiological factors are unalterable, such as certain inherited characteristics or disorders, but many are alterable. In assessing child psychopathology, we must thoroughly examine the child's early development and behavioral-style history. Also, parental history, including child rearing expectations, possible stresses upon the family, and the family's method of handling specific behaviors exhibited by the child, requires attention.

The child's temperament often contributes to the way he/she is handled. Difficult children or those who are presented with multiple complications before, during, and after birth may not experience adequate caretaking in early infancy if reared in a socioeconomically disadvantaged home. The behavioral style or temperament of the child has an effect on his/her surrounding environment, and vice versa. Hence, to thoroughly understand such psychopathology, we must consider the interaction effect of the child and the environment.

References

Bandura, A. A social learning interpretation of psychological dysfunctions. In P. London & D. Rosenham (Eds.), *Foundations of abnormal psychology.* New York: Holt, Rinehart & Winston, 1968.

Bandura, A. *Principles of behavior modification.* New York: Holt, Rinehart, & Winston, 1969.

Bandura, A., & Walters, R. H. *Social learning and personality development.* New York: Holt, Rinehart & Winston, 1963.

Bates, J. E., Freeland, C. A. B., & Lounsbury, M. L. Measurement of infant difficultness. *Child Development,* 1979, *50,* 794–803.

Beck, A. T. *Cognitive therapy and emotional disorders.* New York: New American Library, 1979. (a)

Beck, A. T. *Cognitive therapy of depression.* New York: Guilford Press, 1979. (b)

Bijou, S. W., & Baer, D. M. *Child development I: Universal state of infancy.* New York: Appleton-Century-Crofts, 1961.

Buss, A. H., & Polmin, R. *A temperament theory of personality development.* New York: Wiley, 1975.

Campbell, S. Diagnosis of fetal abnormalities by ultrasound. In A. Milunsky (Ed.), *Genetic disorders and the fetus.* New York: Plenum Press, 1979.

Carey, W. B. A simplified method of measuring infant temperament. *Journal of Pediatrics,* 1970, *77,* 188–194.

Carey, W. B. The importance of temperament–environment interaction for child health and development. In M. Lewis & L. A. Rosenblum (Eds.), *The uncommon child.* New York: Plenum Press, 1981.

Carey, W. B., & McDevitt, S. C. Revision of the Infant Temperament Questionnaire. *Pediatrics,* 1978, *61,* 735–739.

Coville, W. J., Costello, T. W., & Rouke, F. L. *Abnormal psychology and mental illness: Types, causes, and treatment.* New York: Barnes & Noble, 1969.

DeNike, L. D., & Tiber, N. Neurotic behavior, In P. London & D. Rosenham (Eds.), *Foundations of abnormal psychology.* New York: Holt, Rinehart & Winston, 1968.

Ellis, A. *Reason and emotion in psychotherapy.* New York: Lyle Stuart, 1962.

Eron, L. D. (Ed.). *Journal of Abnormal Psychology* (Vol. 87). Washington, D.C.: American Psychological Association, 1978.

Everly, K. New direction in divorce research. *Journal of Clinical Child Psychology,* 1977, *6,* 7–10.

Eysenck, H. J. (Ed.). *Behavior therapy and the neuroses.* New York: Pergamon Press, 1960.

Ferster, C. B., Culbertson, S., & Boren, M. C. P. *Behavior principles.* Englewood Cliffs, N.J.: Prentice-Hall, 1975.

Franks, C. M. Conditioning and abnormal behavior. In H. J. Eysenck (Ed.), *Handbook of abnormal psychology.* New York: Basic Books, 1961.

Fullard, W., McDevitt, S. C., & Carey, W. B. *Toddler temperament scale, 1978.* Unpublished test form, available from William Fullard, Ph.D., Department of Educational Psychology, Temple University, Philadelphia, PA 19922. (Please send $5.00 to cover costs.)

Gardner, R. A. Children of divorce. Some legal and psychological considerations. *Journal of Clinical Child Psychology,* 1977, *6,* 3–6.

Gelfand, D. M. (Ed.). *Social learning in childhood.* Belmont, Calif.: Brooks/Cole, 1969.

Gottesman, I. I., & Shields, J. Schizophrenia in twins: 16 years' consecutive admissions to a psychiatric clinic. *British Journal of Psychiatry,* 1966, *112,* 809–813.

Graham, P., Rutter, M., & George, S. Temperamental characteristics as predictors of behavior disorders of children. *American Journal of Orthopsychiatry,* 1973, *43,* 328–339.

Green, A. H. Child abuse. In B. B. Wolman, J. Egan, & A. O. Ross (Eds.), *Handbook of treatment of mental disorders in childhood and adolescence.* Englewood Cliffs, N.J.: Prentice-Hall, 1978.

Green, A. H., Gaines, R., & Sandgrund, A. Child abuse: Pathological syndrome of family interaction. *American Journal of Psychiatry,* 1974, *131,* 882–886.

Haskell, M. & Yablonsky, L. *Juvenile delinquency* (2nd ed.). Chicago: Rand McNally, 1978.

Hegvik, R., McDevitt, S. C., & Carey, W. B. *Middle childhood temperament questionnaire, 1980.* Unpublished test form, available from Ms. Robin L. Hegvik, 307 North Wayne Avenue, Wayne, PA 19087. (Please send $5.00 to cover costs.)

Helfer, R. E., & Kempe, C. H. (Eds.). *The battered child.* Chicago: University of Chicago Press, 1968.

Heston, L. L. Psychiatric disorders in foster home reared children of schizophrenic mothers. *British Journal of Psychiatry,* 1966, *112,* 819–825.

Hinsie, L. E., & Campbell, R. J. *Psychiatric dictionary.* New York: Oxford University Press, 1960.

Jauch, C. The one-part family. *Journal of Clinical Child Psychology,* 1977, *6,* 30–32.

Jones, M. C. A laboratory study of fear: The case of Peter. *Pediatric Seminar,* 1924, *31,* 308–315.

Kallman, J. F. *The genetics of schizophrenia.* New York: J. J. Augustin, 1938.

Kallman, J. F. The genetic theory of schizophrenia: An analysis of 691 schizophrenic twin index families. *American Journal of Psychiatry,* 1946, *103,* 309–322.

Kanfer, F. H., & Marston, A. R. Conditioning of self-reinforcement responses: An analogue to self-confidence training. *Psychological Reports,* 1963, *13,* 63–70. (a)

Kanfer, F. H., & Martson, A. R. Determinants of self-reinforcement in human learning. *Journal of Experimental Psychology,* 1963, *66,* 245–254. (b)

Kanfer, F. H. & Phillips, J. S. *Learning foundations of behavior therapy.* New York: Wiley & Sons, 1970.

Kempe, R. S., & Kempe, C. H. *Child abuse.* Cambridge: Harvard University Press, 1978.

Kempe, C. H., Silverman, F., Steele, B. F., Droegemueller, W., & Silver, H. The batterd child syndrome. *Journal of the American Medical Association,* 1962, *181,* 17–24.

Kendler, H. H. *Basic psychology.* New York: Appleton-Century-Crofts, 1963.

Kerenyi, T. D., & Walker, B. The preventability of "bloody taps" in second trimester amniocentesis by ultrasound scanning. *Obstetrics and Gynecology,* 1977, *50,* 61.

Kisker, G. W. *The disorganized personality.* New York: McGraw-Hill, 1964.

Kretschmer, E. *Physique and character.* London: Degan Paul, Trench, Trubner, 1925.

Kubler-Ross, E. *On death and dying.* New York: MacMillan, 1969.

Mahoney, M., & Arnkoff, D. Cognitive and self-control therapies. In S. L. Garfield & A. Bergin (Eds.), *Handbook of psychotherapy and behavior change: An empirical analysis.* New York: Wiley, 1978.

Mahoney, M. J., & Hobbins, J. C. Fetoscopy and fetal blood sampling. In A. Melunsky (Ed.), *Genetic disorders and the fetus.* New York: Plenum Press, 1979.

McDavid, J. W. Effects of ambiguity of environmental cues upon learning to imitate. *Journal of Abnormal and Social Psychology,* 1962, *65,* 381–386.

McDavid, J. W., & Garwood, S. G. *Understanding children.* Lexington, Mass.: D. C. Heath, 1978.

McDevitt, S. C., & Carey, W. B. The measurement of temperament in 3–7 years old children. *Journal of Child Psychology and Psychiatry,* 1978, *19,* 245–253.

McGuigan, F. J., & Lumsden, D. B. (Eds.). *Contemporary approaches to conditioning and learning.* New York: Wiley, 1973.

McKusick, V. A. *Human genetics.* Englewood Cliffs, N.J.: Prentice-Hall, 1969.

Milunsky, A. Current concepts in genetics: Prenatal diagnosis of genetic disorders. *New England Journal of Medicine,* 1976, *295,* 377.

Milunsky, A. Amniocentesis. In A. Milunsky (Ed.), *Genetic disorders and the fetus.* New York: Plenum Press, 1979.

Moss, H. A. Sex, age, and state as determinants of mother–infant interaction. In U. Brunfenbrenner (Ed.), *Influences on human development.* Hinsdale, Ill.: Dryden Press, 1972.

Patterson, C. H. Reinforcement theory. In J. Dollard & N. Miller (Eds.), *Theories of counseling and psychotherapy.* New York: Harper & Row, 1966.

Payne, R. W. Cognitive abnormalities. In H. J. Eysenck (Ed.), *Handbook of abnormal psychology.* New York: Basic Books, 1961.

Persson-Blennow, I., & McNeil, T. F. A questionnaire for measurement of temperament in six-month-old infants: Development and standardization. *Journal of Child Psychology and Psychiatry,* 1979, *20,* 1–13.

Rosenthal, D., Wender, P. H., Kety, S. S., Welner, J., & Schulsinger, F. The adopted-away offspring of schizophrenics. *American Journal of Psychiatry,* 1971, *128,* 87–91.

Ross, A. Behavior therapy with children. In S. L. Garfield & A. Bergin (Eds.), *Handbook of psychotherapy and behavior change: An empirical analysis.* New York: Wiley, 1978.

Schwartz, B. *Psychology of learning and behavior.* New York: W. W. Norton, 1978.

Sheldon, W. H. *The varieties of human physique.* New York: Harper & Row, 1940.

Skinner, B. F. *The behavior of organisms: An experimental analysis.* New York: Appleton-Century, 1938.

Skinner, B. F. "Superstition" in the pigeon. *Journal of Experimental Psychology,* 1948, *38,* 168–172.

Skinner, B. F. *Science and human behavior.* New York: MacMillan, 1953.

Slater, E., & Cowie, V. *The genetics of mental disorders.* New York: Oxford University Press, 1971.

Spitz, R. A. Hospitalization. An inquiry into the genesis of psychiatric conditions in early childhood. In U. Burnfenbrenner (Ed.), *Influences on human development.* Hinsdale, Ill.: Dryden Press, 1972.

Srivastava, P. K. *Basic genetics for health professionals.* Littleton, Mass.: PSG Publishing, 1979.

Steele, B. F. *Working with abusive parents from a psychiatric point of view* (DHEW Publication No. (OHD) 76-30070). Washington, D.C.: Department of Health, Education and Welfare, National Center for Child Abuse and Neglect, 1976.

Stoll, C., Flori, E., Calvert, A., Beshara, D., & Buck, P. Abnormal children of a 47, *XYY* father. *Journal of Medical Genetics,* 1979, *16,* 66–68.

Swanson, B. M., & Willis, D. J. *Understanding exceptional children and youth.* Skokie, Ill.: Rand-McNally, 1979.

Thomas, A., & Chess, S. *Tempêrament and development.* New York: Brunner/Mazel, 1977.

Thomas, A., Chess, S., & Birch, H. G. *Temperament and behavior disorders in children.* New York: New York University Press, 1968.

Tucker, W. B., & Lessa, W. A. *Man: A constitutional investigation.* Quarterly Revue of Biology, 1940, *15,* 265.

Vaughn, V. C., McKay, R. J., & Behrman, R. E. *Textbook of pediatrics* (11th ed.). Philadelphia: W. B. Saunders, 1979.

Walker, C. E., Hedberg, A., Clement, P., & Wright, L. *Clinical procedures for behavior therapy.* Englewood Cliffs, N.J.: Prentice-Hall, 1981.

Walters, G. C., & Grusec, J. E. *Punishment.* San Francisco: W. H. Freeman, 1977.

Watson J. R. & Raynor, R. Conditional emotional reactions. *Journal of Experimental Psychology,* 1920, *3,* 1–14.

Weiss, N. *Teenage pregnancy and prevention: Teachers guide.* New York: Human Relations Media, 1980.

Werber, P. & Cochran, P. *Violence in the family: Teachers guide.* New York: Human Relations Media, 1978.

White, R. B. & Gathman, L. T. The syndrome of ordinary grief. *Ross timesaver: Feelings and Their Medical Significance.* 1974, *18,* 1–4.

Wolpe, J. *Psychotherapy by reciprocal inhibition.* Stanford, Calif.: Stanford University Press, 1958.

4

Taxonomic Issues in Child Psychopathology

THOMAS M. ACHENBACH AND CRAIG S. EDELBROCK

Although taxonomic issues may seem remote from everyday work with disturbed children, they lurk about in many guises. We will first consider these guises and then discuss ways to give taxonomy a more open and constructive role in helping disturbed children.

The Many Faces of Taxonomy

Implicit Taxonomic Assumptions

Beginning with their professional training, mental health workers assimilate taxonomic assumptions that shape their views of psychopathology and what should be done about it. Not only concepts of specific disorders but also broad distinctions such as "organic versus psychological" and "exogenous versus endogenous" may influence all subsequent impressions. The settings in which they train and work also shape professionals' assumptions via the types of dispositional decisions required. Workers who have few treatment options to choose from, for example, may be much less conscious of taxonomic questions than those who have abundant options.

Theories of psychopathology likewise imply taxonomic distinctions among disorders, although these distinctions are seldom translated into operational definitions. Psychodynamic theory, for example, implies taxonomic distinctions pertaining to the distribution of drive energies, the structural development of personality, and defense mechanisms (A.

THOMAS M. ACHENBACH • Department of Psychiatry, University of Vermont, Burlington, Vermont 05405. CRAIG S. EDELBROCK • Department of Psychiatry, University of Pittsburgh, Pittsburgh, Pennsylvania 15261.

Freud, 1965). Behavioral theories, on the other hand, distinguish among disorders assumed to reflect operant versus respondent conditioning (cf. Achenbach, 1982, Chapter 10).

Treatment and Administrative Decisions

Treatment and administrative decisions involve taxonomic assumptions about who should receive what services, if any. These decisions are further affected by taxonomic distinctions made by insurance companies and government agencies that pay for mental health services. The impact of third-party payers has grown enormously with expansion of mental health benefits, Medicare, and proliferation of nontraditional practitioners expecting payment for mental health services. This has led to taxonomic struggles among practitioners seeking to ensure that their services would be independently reimbursable by third-party payers. These struggles became especially bitter when an early draft of the American Psychiatric Association's new *Diagnostic and Statistic Manual* (DSM–III, 1980) held that all mental disorders are medical disorders. Although later drafts moderated this claim, the chief authors of DSM–III acknowledged that third-party considerations affected their final taxonomy in other ways (Spitzer, Williams, & Skodol, 1980).

Reimbursability by third-party payers is doubtless a factor in many diagnoses assigned in clinical practice, but determination of eligibility for mental health benefits is particularly problematic for children's behavior disorders. Because children's behavior disorders may require educational and environmental interventions more often than basic one-to-one therapy, traditional models for services and reimbursement are more tenuous than for most adult disorders.

Professional Communication

Taxonomic issues also arise in communications among professionals. Terms like "schizoid," "sociopathic," "neurotic," and "borderline," for example, are bandied about to describe individual clients. Diagnosticians, case conferences, and clinical seminars often labor over questions of whether a client is "really" schizophrenic, hysterical, depressed, hyperactive, or what have you. Such diagnoses have major connotations for prognosis and assumed etiology. Yet even under research conditions designed to maximize reliability, most disorders elicit mediocre agreement among diagnosticians. Efforts to improve the reliability of DSM–III criteria for adult disorders have not borne fruit for children's disorders: Clinicians making DSM–III diagnoses from standardized case histories of children have been found to agree less often than when making DSM–II diagnoses of the same material (e.g., Mattison, Cantwell, Russell, & Will, 1979; Mezzich & Mezzich, 1979). Furthermore, reliabilities reported in DSM–III itself show a *decline* in interjudge agreement from early to later drafts of criteria for children's disorders (American Psychiatric Association, 1980, p. 471).

If clinicians cannot agree in diagnosing children from a common data base under research conditions, how can they agree under more typical clinical conditions? Considering our ignorance of specific etiologies and treatment effects, why should diagnostic disagreements matter anyway? With the possible exception of stimulant drugs for hyperactivity, few diagnostic decisions about children's disorders have implications of demonstrated validity for treatment or prognosis. Yet considerable time and effort are devoted to diagnosis.

Taxonomy in Relation to Formal Diagnoses and Diagnostic Formulations

Confusion often arises from ambiguities in the term *diagnosis*. The meaning of diagnosis can range from being almost synonymous with taxonomy or classification to much broader meanings. At the narrow extreme, a leader of efforts to operationalize psychiatric diagnosis calls diagnosis "the medical term for classification" (Guze, 1978, p. 53). At the broader extreme, diagnosis can mean (a) an "investigation or analysis of the cause or nature of a condition, situation, or problem," and (b) "a statement or conclusion concerning the nature or cause of some phenomenon" (Woolf, 1977, p. 313).

The distinction between diagnosis in the narrow sense of classification and the broad sense of an investigation and conclusion has also been stated in terms of a contrast between (a) *formal diagnosis* or *differential diagnosis,* on the one hand, and (b) a *diagnostic formulation* or *diagnostic work-up,* on the other (Roth, 1978). It might be argued that clinicians actually have little need for formal diagnoses—that is, the diagnostic categories listed in taxonomies such as the DSM. Instead, clinicians are more interested in diagnostic formulations—the comprehensive investigations and conclusions needed to guide case management. Yet diagnostic formulations require an overarching taxonomic structure with which to link a particular client to accumulated knowledge about similar clients. A taxonomic structure is also needed to aid in discriminating between a particular client and those having different needs. Taxonomic structures thus serve to highlight both similarities and differences between individual clients and classes of clients with whom experience has been gained.

Even where the goal is an idiographic formulation of the individual, judgments must be made using categories and dimensions evolved through experience with many cases. No matter how idiographically oriented they are, clinicians cannot—and should not—make judgments free of diagnostic concepts formed through their prior experience. Such concepts, however, typically reflect the clinician's personal training experiences, impressions, and quasitheoretical constructs like "schizophrenia." Although these may provide a sense of personal conviction about diagnostic judgments, they are seldom tested for validity. To make the diagnostic process more effective, we therefore need to find those characteristics that actually reveal important links and differences among cases, can be reliably assessed, and have valid implications for case management.

Research, Epidemiology, and Public Policy

More remote from everyday work with disturbed children, but nevertheless relevant to helping such children, are taxonomic issues that arise in research, epidemiology, and public policy. Without a well differentiated and reliable taxonomy, it is difficult to form groups with which to conduct research on differential etiology, course, prognosis, and response to treatment. Likewise, epidemiological studies require operationally defined taxonomies to determine how many children have what disorders and how they are distributed.

Public policy pertaining to disturbed children is made in a vacuum unless it rests on knowledge of the specific disorders they manifest. The more we know about each disorder, and about the numbers of children manifesting it, the better we can plan prevention and services.

Medical Origins

Most contemporary notions of psychopathology have been shaped by nineteenth-century taxonomic approaches. The bacteriological paradigm that proved so successful in the study of organic diseases provided an organic disease model for study of mental disorders as well. Wilhelm Griesinger's (1845/1867) influential textbook translated the disease model into the psychiatric realm with the dogma that *mental diseases are brain diseases.* It was hoped that the classification of mental diseases could proceed from *descriptions* of symptom syndromes to discovery of a specific *physical cause* for each syndrome.

There is no doubt that the organic disease model helped bring mental disorders into the purview of scientific research. The study of general paralysis (later called paresis), in particular, fueled hopes that taxonomic advances would lead to the discovery of specific organic etiologies. Progressively better descriptions from 1798 through the 1840s culminated in the definition of this disorder as a *combination* of mental symptoms, such as memory deficits and irrationality, with physical symptoms of motor impairment, typically ending in death.

Once a uniform descriptive definition of paresis was accepted, autopsy research from the 1840s through the 1870s revealed inflammation in brains of most paretics. The possible causes were gradually narrowed down to syphilis. The hypothesized role of syphilis was experimentally corroborated in 1897 when Kraft-Ebing showed that inoculation with the syphilis spirochete produced no secondary symptoms of syphilis in paretics. Why not? Because the paretics were already infected. Later research further confirmed that syphilis was the specific cause of paresis.

Inspired by the conviction that accurate description would lead to the discovery of a specific organic etiology for each disorder, Emil Kraepelin (1883) brought together in one taxonomic system the hodgepodge of phenomena that were coming to constitute the subject matter of psychiatry. Through revisions and expansions over the next 40 years, Kraepelin's descriptive taxonomy provided the structure around which concepts of psychopathology were organized. It also served as a model for subsequent taxonomies.

Although Freud undermined descriptive diagnosis by defining disorders in terms of inferred psychological mechanisms, he initially retained important assumptions about organic predispositions as well. Even when organic aspects faded out of later psychoanalytic theory (Freud, 1926/1959), vocabulary of the disease model was largely retained. In fact, psychoanalysts have probably helped entrench an illness-oriented view of psychopathology at least as much as proponents of the organic disease model. Application of the disease model to disorders unlikely to have specific organic causes was also strengthened by eventual inclusion of a category of psychogenic disorders in Kraepelin's (1883/1915) taxonomy, as well as personality disorders that Kraepelin viewed as a borderland between illness and mere eccentricity. Such extensions of the organic disease model have been a continuing source of confusion in subsequent taxonomic efforts.

The DSM Approach

The three editions of the DSM (American Psychiatric Association, 1952, 1968, 1980) are legacies of Kraepelinian taxonomy. They retain most of the same major disorders, proclaim descriptive diagnosis as the favored approach to disorders of unknown etiology, and cast even personality disorders into a diseaselike format. Despite these overall similarities, the three editions of the DSM also reflect major changes in prevailing psychiatric attitudes.

The 1952 edition (DSM–I), for example, clearly reflects Adolf Meyer's (cf. Lief, 1948) doctrine that psychiatric disorders are best thought of as *reactions types of the psychobiologic unit.* According to Meyer, a reaction type represents a particular way in which an individual—mind and body—adjusts to life stresses.

The 1968 edition (DSM–II) is an amalgam of diverse approaches embracing disease entity concepts of psychoses such as schizophrenia; psychoanalytic concepts of neuroses; an implied typology of personalities for the personality disorders; definitions in terms of single symptoms for special symptom reactions; transient situational reactions ("adjustment reactions"), defined as "acute reaction[s] to overwhelming environmental stress" (p. 48); and behavior disorders of childhood and adolescence, defined as being "more stable, internalized, and resistant to treatment than transient situational disturbances, but less so than psychoses, neuroses, and personality disorders" (pp. 49–50). (Despite the intermediate stability imputed to these behavior disorders, and despite the deletion of Meyer's term "reaction" elsewhere in DSM–II, these behavior disorders are unaccountably called "reactions"—e.g., hyperkinetic reaction of childhood, withdrawing reaction of childhood, etc.)

Although sharing the Kraepelinian heritage of earlier editions, the 1980 edition (DSM–III) features several innovations. One is that it provides explicit criteria for diagnosing disorders. Most of these criteria stem from efforts to develop operational definitions of psychiatric disorders, the so-called Research Diagnostic Criteria (or RDC; Spitzer, Endicott, & Robins, 1978). A second innovation is the division of psychiatric taxonomy into two axes: Axis I includes clinical syndromes, plus other conditions that are the focus of attention or treatment (e.g., malingering) and additional codes (e.g., unspecified mental disorder). Axis II includes personality disorders and specific developmental disorders. These axes imply different levels of conceptualization for disorders that coexisted on a single axis in DSM–I and DSM–II. A third innovation is the addition of three other axes to supplement the psychiatric diagnoses. One of these, Axis III, is merely an explicit listing of any known medical disorder. The other two involve global ratings of severity of psychosocial stressors (Axis IV) and the individual's highest level of attained functioning in the preceding year (Axis V).

Taxonomies Designed for Childhood Disorders

Beginning with Kraepelin—whose original system made no mention of children—the official psychiatric taxonomies have been designed primarily for adults. Until 1968, the DSM offered only two categories of childhood disorders: Adjustment Reaction and Childhood Schizophrenia. DSM–III has added numerous new categories of child and adolescent disorders, but these were hammered out in negotiations of the DSM task force rather than being based on empirical data or research diagnostic criteria, as major adult categories were. It is therefore unknown whether the DSM–III child and adolescent disorders reflect valid distinctions among disturbed youngsters, and, if so, whether DSM–III criteria can reliably discriminate among disorders. As mentioned earlier, comparisons of DSM–II and DSM–III child diagnoses, as well as comparisons of early and late drafts of DSM–III, indicate declining rather than improving reliability (American Psychiatric Association, 1980; Mattison *et al.,* 1979; Mezzich & Mezzich, 1979). The efforts to broaden DSM–III by adding an axis for rating psychosocial stressors and one for rating the highest level of attained functioning also seem keyed much more to characteristics of adult psychiatric contacts than to children.

Anna Freud's Diagnostic Profile. Recognition that disorders of childhood may require taxonomic approaches different from adult disorders has spurred several other approaches. One is Anna Freud's (1965) effort to derive a diagnostic profile from psychoanalytic theory. The profile comprises diagnostic assessments in terms of inferences about drive development, ego and superego development, regression and fixation points, conflicts, frustration tolerance, and sublimation potential. As diagnostic categorizations, Freud suggests possibilities such as the following: variations of normality; transitory symptoms classed as byproducts of developmental strain; infantile neuroses; character disorders; infantilisms; borderline, delinquent, or psychotic disturbances; retarded, defective, and nontypical personalities; and disruptions of mental growth. Although Freud's proposal was intended to be a draft version, its subsequent development appears to have been confined largely to illustrative applications to single cases, without systematic reliability or validity studies (e.g., Greenspan, Hatleberg, & Cullander, 1979).

The GAP Classification. A second approach has been to formulate an omnibus system resembling the Kraepelinian and DSM taxonomies but oriented specifically toward childhood disorders. This approach was adopted by the Group for the Advancement of Psychiatry (GAP, 1966). They employed the following 10 major categories: healthy responses; reactive disorders; developmental deviations; psychoneurotic disorders; personality disorders; psychotic disorders; psychophysiological disorders; brain syndromes; mental retardation; and other disorders.

In introducing its taxonomy, GAP stressed that "a traditional medical somatic model is inadequate" and that "descriptive–clinical, genetic, and dynamic dimensions must be included . . . in a manner appropriate to the developmental nature of childhood" (p. 176). The GAP classification indeed focuses on developmental aspects of psychopathology much more than Kraepelinian taxonomies have. However, its definitions of disorders are mixtures of narrative descriptions and theoretical inferences that provide no operational criteria for determining whether a child has a particular disorder. Some of the GAP categories, such as psychoneurotic disorders, are defined in terms of especially abstract constructs and inferences. It is therefore not surprising that the reliability of GAP diagnoses has been mediocre, especially for those categories involving fine-grained theoretical distinctions among disorders (Beitchman, Dielman, Landis, Benson, & Kemp, 1978; Freeman, 1971).

Multivariate Approaches. Faced with the lack of well substantiated syndromes of children's disorders, researchers have increasingly sought to identify childhood syndromes through statistical analyses of covariation among signs and symptoms. Early workers began by computing correlations among pairs of items and then attempting to discern syndromes through a combination of clinical judgment and statistical criteria (Ackerson, 1942; Hewitt & Jenkins, 1946; Jenkins & Glickman, 1946). Later efforts have taken advantage of high-speed computers to factor analyze and cluster analyze correlations among items, mainly behavior ratings. Despite differences in rating instruments, raters, subject samples, and analytic methods, these efforts have shown considerable convergence in the identification of certain syndromes. In a review of multivariate studies, we found that 4 broad-band syndromes and 14 more finely differentiated, narrow-band syndromes had been found in at least 2 studies each (Achenbach & Edelbrock, 1978). Descriptive labels for these syndromes are listed in Table 1, along with the number of studies in which each syndrome was found in ratings made from clinical records and in ratings by mental health workers, teachers, and parents.

Table 1. Number of Studies in which Syndromes Have Been Identified through Multivariate Analyses[a]

Syndrome	Source of ratings				Total
	Case histories	Mental health workers	Teachers	Parents	
Broad-band					
Overcontrolled	2	1	5	6	14
Undercontrolled	3	3	5	7	18
Pathological detachment	3	—	1	—	4
Learning problems	—	—	1	1	2
Narrow-band					
Academic disability	—	1	—	3	4
Aggressive	3	4	1	8	16
Anxious	1	2	1	2	6
Delinquent	3	1	—	7	11
Depressed	2	1	—	5	8
Hyperactive	3	2	1	7	13
Immature	—	1	—	3	4
Obsessive-compulsive	1	—	—	2	3
Schizoid	3	4	—	5	12
Sexual problems	1	2	—	3	6
Sleep problems	—	—	—	3	3
Social withdrawal	1	1	1	5	8
Somatic complaints	1	—	—	7	8
Uncommunicative	—	1	—	2	3

[a]From Achenbach & Edelbrock, 1978, plus syndromes subsequently identified in factor analyses of the Child Behavior Checklist for boys and girls aged 4–5 (see Table 2).

Comparison of the Multivariate and DSM Approaches

In terms of their impact on research, training, and practice, the DSM and multivariate approaches are clearly dominant. It is therefore worth examining relations between them.

There are differences of opinion about how many syndromes derived from multivariate analyses are robust enough to deserve confidence, and about whether a few broad-band syndromes or more numerous narrow-band syndromes better represent childhood psychopathology (cf. Quay, 1979). Nevertheless, the multivariate studies—despite their differing flaws and biases—have yielded a substantial number of distinctive syndromes among children and adolescents. Some of these syndromes resemble the child and adolescent syndromes of DSM-III, whereas others have no clearcut counterparts in DSM-III (cf. Achenbach, 1980). Conversely, DSM-III includes some syndromes that have not been clearly substantiated in multivariate studies.

The convergence of multivariate and DSM approaches on at least some syndromes is encouraging, but their lack of correspondence on other syndromes is not an indictment of either approach. Each approach may simply have different strengths and weaknesses for discovering or defining certain clinical phenomena. There are several reasons why early infantile autism, for example, was not likely to be discovered via typical multivariate research. First, autism is so rare even in clinical populations that the proportion of cases in most samples would be too small to significantly affect covariation among items. Second, its symptoms are so unusual that they would not be included in omnibus rating instruments. Third, some of its defining features occur so early that they would not be routinely reported by the time most children are assessed by mental health workers, unless the syndrome was already a target for assessment.

However, traditional taxonomic approaches also fail to make efficient use of sensitive clinical observations like those that led Leo Kanner (1943) to formulate the autistic syndrome. Over the 37 years it took for the official taxonomy to adopt Kanner's syndrome, the lack of standardized defining criteria sowed confusion among workers who evolved their own idiosyncratic notions of autism (cf. Achenbach, 1982, Chapter 12). Furthermore, although the syndrome probably would not have been discovered through multivariate methods, these methods have helped to objectify procedures for discriminating it from other severe disorders once a pool of potential defining criteria was formed (e.g., Prior, Perry, & Gajzago, 1975). Thus, multivariate approaches may complement more traditional taxonomic approaches to certain disorders.

For other disorders, the proper application of multivariate methods may be superior to traditional procedures for discovering and defining syndromes. This is especially true where the number of relevant variables is large, and where they are distinguished by particular combinations of features that are not strikingly pathognomonic by themselves. Most school-aged children referred for outpatient services do not manifest strikingly bizarre or pathognomonic behaviors, for example. Instead, most of their behavior can be observed in most children at least some of the time. A key taxonomic problem, then, is to detect those aspects of intensity, frequency, or patterning of behavior that indicate a need for special help, and to use this information in deciding what type of help is needed.

Certain behaviors—such as bedwetting, temper tantrums, overactivity, inattentiveness, and fears—are troublesome, yet typical of most children at certain ages. When should they be dismissed as not cause for concern, and when should they be used as diagnostic data? And how much of what kinds of behaviors, in what pattern and at what age, constitutes a particular disorder?

Even in the stage of refinement reached by DSM–III, the traditional taxonomic approach has been to start:

> with a clinical concept for which there is some degree of face validity. Face validity is the extent to which the description of a particular category seems on the face of it to describe accurately the characteristic features of persons with a particular disorder. It is the result of clinicians agreeing on the identification of a particular syndrome or pattern of clinical features as a mental disorder. Initial criteria are generally developed by asking the clinicians to describe what they consider to be the most characteristic features of the disorder. (Spitzer & Cantwell, 1980, p. 359)

In finalizing their criteria for the "clinical concepts" of adult disorders, the DSM task force could draw on extensive trial-and-error efforts to operationalize concepts that already had a long history of use. Although these efforts have by no means yielded full agreement among various versions of research diagnostic criteria for even such venerable clinical concepts as schizophrenia (cf. Achenbach, 1981), they provide a far stronger foundation for adult categories than child categories of DSM–III. Unlike adult categories, there were *no* research diagnostic criteria on which to base child categories, for which the "face validity" alluded to by Spitzer and Cantwell pertains only to the clinical concepts of those who formulated the DSM taxonomy. It remains to be seen whether their clinical concepts or their necessarily arbitrary decisions about how to operationalize them have any other type of validity.

Until the DSM–III categories of childhood disorders can be applied reliably and be shown to discriminate validly among significant numbers of clinically referred children, we will not know whether they represent actual differences among childhood disorders. If they are found to represent such differences accurately, then they can be tested for validity with respect to other important variables, such as differential etiology, prognosis, and responsiveness to treatment.

Utilizing the Multivariate Findings

The DSM offers categories that are not based on empirical findings but are designed to be used; the multivariate studies, by contrast, offer empirical findings, but these findings have seldom been designed for practical use. How can we make practical use of the ability of the multivariate approach to derive syndromes from data too complex to be reduced through clinical judgment alone?

Many multivariate studies have ended with the presentation of groups of items found to covary when scored from a particular rating instrument completed by particular raters for a particular sample (cf. Achenbach & Edelbrock, 1978). In some cases, the rating instrument has then been used in other studies, and conventions have been adopted for scoring individual children on groups of covarying items.

As an example, Borkovec (1970) had correctional staff fill out Quay and Peterson's (1968, 1975) Behavior Problem Checklist on incarcerated male delinquents (age unspecified). Those who scored above the group mean on items of a "psychopathic" factor but below the mean on items of a "neurotic" factor were categorized as psychopaths. Those who showed the reverse pattern were classified as neurotics. The groups thus formed were then found to differ in galvanic skin responses to experimental auditory stimuli.

Although such findings indicate that the Checklist scores may have interesting correlates, they do not add much to the utility of the syndromes for other workers; scores obtained from ratings of delinquents by correctional workers in one institution may bear little relation to scores that might be obtained for other samples, raters, and settings. Furthermore, the psychopaths and neurotics were defined categorically by their standing relative to the mean scores of their particular sample. This procedure tells other workers little about how to categorize individual cases as psychopaths or neurotics. Linear variations on taxonomic variables are also obscured by categorical aggregation of individuals. The applicability of the findings to girls and to other ages is not known either.

Practical Applications

In order to translate the multivariate findings into procedures for assessing individual children, it is necessary to establish uniform criteria for scoring the empirically-derived syndromes, for relating specific scores to appropriate normative populations, and for making taxonomic assignments. This requires long-term programmatic research, with considerable trial and error to optimize reliability, validity, comprehensiveness, and utility for purposes as diverse as clinical assessment, research, training, epidemiology, and program planning. Although trying to fulfill all these aims simultaneously requires compromises among their differing requirements, a common data language might overcome some of the existing obstacles to communication between alien realms. Interfacing basic and applied objectives seems especially essential in order to make research more relevant to mental health services and to improve services through research.

The Child Behavior Checklist

We will use our own work to illustrate the kind of efforts we advocate, but others have also sought to translate multivariate findings into practical procedures for assessing children (e.g., Miller, 1977).

The assessment of child psychopathology is subject to a principle of uncertainty like the Heisenberg principle in physics—there is no way to make a perfectly veridical assessment, because the assessment procedures inevitably interact with target phenomena in ways that we cannot ascertain with complete precision. It is also subject to a Rashomon principle—truth is always a function of who is telling it. Recognizing the impossibility of obtaining totally unbiased assessments of children's behavior disorders, we have used ratings by parents, teachers, clinicians, trained observers, and youngsters themselves. This enables us to compare the predictive power of various informants. However, we chose parents' reports as the keystone of our assessment system for several reasons:

1. Referral for mental health services is usually instigated by adults rather than the child who is the identified patient.
2. Parents are the adults who are most universally involved in assessment of children.
3. Parents typically know more about more aspects of their child's history than any other adult.
4. Even though parents, like other adults, see a biased sample of their children's behavior and are biased in what they perceive, their perceptions are a central part of what needs to be assessed. These perceptions typically play an important role in what can be done to help their child and in evaluating the outcome.

Our basic assessment instrument is called the Child Behavior Checklist. It comprises 20 social competence and 118 behavior problem items designed to be filled out by parents or parent surrogates of children aged 4 through 16 (see Achenbach, 1978, 1979; Achenbach & Edelbrock, 1979, 1981, for details). We chose this age range because few children under 4 are referred for mental health services, and because parents' ratings are less susceptible to satisfactory norming for behavioral competencies and problems below the age of 4 and over the age of 16: Below 4, vicissitudes of biological maturation and specific home environments play an inordinate role, and there are fewer ecologically standard situations such as school and neighborhood environments to provide a basis for comparison among children; above the age of 16, there is once again less uniformity in situations and cultural expectations that youngsters face, as some leave school, those who remain follow increasingly diverse paths, and parents often become less knowledgeable about their own offspring.

The Child Behavior Checklist is the product of a long series of pilot editions and revisions. It takes about 17 minutes to complete and is typically filled out at the beginning of a clinical contact. It can also be readministered periodically to assess change as a function of time or intervention. Intraclass correlations in the .90s have been obtained for test–retest and interparent reliabilities of item scores, and nearly all items discriminate significantly between demographically matched normal and clinically referred children (Achenbach & Edelbrock, 1981).

Factor Analysis of the Checklist. In order to derive empirically based multivariate syndromes, we have factor analyzed the behavior problem items scored from Checklists filled out as part of intake procedures of some 30 outpatient mental health settings. These include child guidance clinics, university psychiatry departments, private practices, health maintenance organizations, and community mental health centers.

Because the prevalence and patterning of behaviors vary with age and sex, we have performed separate analyses for each sex at ages 4 to 5, 6 to 11, and 12 to 16. The sample sizes were 450 in each of the four older groups, 250 for boys aged 4 to 5, and 170 for girls aged 4 to 5. The smaller samples in the youngest age-groups reflect the low frequency of their referral for mental health services. Despite the cooperation of 30 mental health settings, it took 7 years to accumulate 170 Checklists for 4- and 5-year-old girls. This was fewer than we sought for our analyses, but, with a rate of only about 25 cases per year, it seemed pointless to wait much longer. We will do reanalyses if we ever get substantially more data on 4- to 5-year-old girls.

The details of the factor analyses have been reported elsewhere (Achenbach, 1978; Achenbach & Edelbrock, 1979), but Table 2 summarizes descriptive labels for behavior problem syndromes that we retained. Our separate analyses for each sex and age-group revealed some syndromes that were peculiar to one sex or age and that were probably obscured in studies that combined the sex and age-groups. For example, the syndrome designated as *Cruel* in Table 2 was found in our samples of 6- to 11- and 12- to 16-year-old girls, but not in most studies that combined the sexes. The distinctive covariation

Table 2. Syndromes Found through Factor Analysis of the Child Behavior Checklist

Group	Internalizing syndromes[a]	Mixed syndromes	Externalizing syndromes[a]
Boys aged 4–5	1. Social withdrawal 2. Somatic complaints 3. Immature 4. Depressed	1. Sex problems	1. Delinquent 2. Aggressive 3. Schizoid
Boys aged 6–11	1. Schizoid 2. Depressed 3. Uncommunicative 4. Obsessive-compulsive 5. Somatic complaints	1. Social withdrawal	1. Delinquent 2. Aggressive 3. Hyperactive
Boys aged 12–16	1. Somatic complaints 2. Schizoid 3. Uncommunicative 4. Immature 5. Obsessive-compulsive	1. Hostile withdrawal	1. Hyperactive 2. Aggressive 3. Delinquent
Girls aged 4–5	1. Depressed 2. Somatic complaints 3. Schizoid 4. Social withdrawal	1. Sex problems	1. Obese 2. Aggressive 3. Hyperactive
Girls aged 6–11	1. Depressed 2. Social withdrawal 3. Somatic complaints 4. Schizoid-obsessive		1. Cruel 2. Aggressive 3. Delinquent 4. Sex problems 5. Hyperactive
Girls aged 12–16	1. Anxious-obsessive 2. Somatic complaints 3. Schizoid 4. Depressed withdrawal	1. Immature hyperactive	1. Cruel 2. Aggressive 3. Delinquent

[a]Syndromes are listed in descending order of their loadings on the second-order Internalizing and Externalizing factors.

between items such as "Cruel to animals," "Cruelty, bullying, meanness to others," and "Physically attacks people" that appears among disturbed girls was probably missed in samples comprising both sexes, because these items do not covary so systematically among boys as girls. Similarly, the clearcut *Depressed* factors found for 6- to 11-year-olds of both sexes did not emerge when we tried combining 6- to 11-year-olds and 12- to 16-year-olds for analysis: The depressive items that grouped together on a single factor among 6- to 11-year-olds were spread across several factors for 12- to 16-year-olds, and combining the age-groups obscured the distinctive covariation that was confined to the younger samples.

Besides those syndromes that were limited to particular sex or age-groups, several syndromes were found in some form in all six groups. These include the *Aggressive, Somatic complaints,* and *Schizoid* syndromes. The replication of these syndromes across six age/sex samples indicates considerable generality; yet these syndromes vary somewhat between sexes and from one age-group to another. This suggests that—even where there may be similarities between sex and age-groups—precise assessment requires taking account of age and sex differences in the patterning and prevalence of specific behaviors.

Second-Order Factor Analysis. Once we had identified robust factors for each age/sex group, we retained items loading .30 or higher as the basis for behavior problems scales. A child's raw score on a scale is the sum of his or her scores on the individual behavior problem items of the scale. Because previous research had revealed hierarchical relations between a few broad-band syndromes and more numerous narrow-band syndromes of the sort shown in Table 2, we performed second-order factor analyses of the behavior problem scales derived from our first-order factors.

The second-order analyses yielded two major groupings of scales in each age/sex sample. One grouping resembled a broad-band syndrome designated in other studies as overcontrolled, personality disorder, inhibition, and internalizing (cf. Achenbach & Edelbrock, 1978). The second grouping resembled a broad-band syndrome designated elsewhere as undercontrolled, conduct disorder, aggression, and externalizing. Table 2 lists our narrow-band behavior problem scales in descending order of their loadings on these groupings, which we have designated as *Internalizing* and *Externalizing,* respectively. For five of the six age/sex groups, there is also a scale that had moderate loadings on both the Internalizing and Externalizing second-order factor. We have therefore designated these scales as *Mixed* in Table 2.

The Child Behavior Profile. To provide a normative basis for assessing a child's behavior problem score on each scale, the raw scores are transformed into *T* scores derived from Checklists filled out by 1300 parents of normal children (Achenbach & Edelbrock, 1981). A child's scores are displayed in a profile format showing how the child compares with normal children of the same age and sex on each narrow-band scale. Standard scores are also computed for the child's total score on all items of the Internalizing scales, Externalizing scales, and entire behavior problem portion of the Checklist. These scores provide more global comparisons between the behavior problems reported for a particular child and his or her normal peers. The social competence items of the Checklist are scored on three *a priori* scales entitled *Activities, Social,* and *School.* These are normed on the same nonclinical sample as the behavior problem scales.

We have also determined the prevalence of every behavior problem and competence item as reported by parents of 1,300 clinically referred and 1,300 demographically matched normal children aged 4 through 16. This enables users to evaluate children in relation to peers in terms of individual items, narrow- and broad-band scales, and total scores for behavior problems and social competence. By reassessing children at intervals, changes as a function of time or treatment can also be identified. But how do we move from these multitiered, quantifiable descriptions of reported behaviors to *taxonomic* distinctions among children? This is the topic of the rest of our chapter.

From Multivariate Description to Taxonomy

The previously summarized behavior problem syndromes reflect covariance among specific behaviors, but they do not necessarily reveal the overall patterns that characterize individual children. Such syndromes do afford a basis for constructing taxonomies of children's behavior disorders, however. A variety of quantitative methods, such as cluster analysis, have been developed for constructing taxonomies from multivariate profiles describing individuals. We will use the term *taxometric* in reference to quantitative procedures for constructing taxa and classifying individuals according to the resulting taxonomy (cf. Achenbach, 1981; Meehl, 1978). Clustering algorithms, for example, can be applied to profile data in order to identify groups of individuals manifesting similar profile characteristics. Such groups can serve as taxonomic constructs or "types" constituting a taxonomy. Quantitative criteria or decision rules can then be formulated for classifying individuals according to their similarity to the various types.

Taxometric methods are powerful heuristic tools for empirically deriving taxonomies and for classifying individuals. However, such taxonomies do not necessarily yield "true" types, in the sense of a one-to-one correspondence between taxa and underlying genotypes. Instead, they are provisional frameworks that can serve many purposes in the study of child psychopathology. For example, they can aid in reduction and ordering of complex multivariate data, generation and testing of hypotheses, and prediction of group differences. The predictive power of such taxonomies can be evaluated in terms of their relations to such criteria as neurological functioning, cognitive level, prognosis, course, and treatment response.

Numerous methods are available for constructing empirically based taxonomies, and each method raises diverse options, problems, and issues. The choices required often entail trade-offs with respect to the nature of the taxonomies they produce. There are no definitive rules for employing taxometric methods, and even general rules of thumb are meager. Despite these problems, such methods offer the advantage of using explicit quantitative criteria to construct taxonomies, which, in turn, permit more precise discriminations among individuals. Moreover, decisions and compromises made when using taxometric methods can be systematically compared with respect to the heuristic value and predictive power of the taxonomies they produce.

The following sections present an overview of taxometric methods. The procedures and results of a program of taxometric research will then be described to illustrate several methodological alternatives, problems, and issues encountered in using such methods.

Cluster Analysis

Before selecting a clustering method, we must first ask a most basic question: Does the structure of the data warrant any clustering efforts whatsoever? That is, are there any homogeneities or densities within the data that indicate inherent clusters of individuals?

This is an important consideration because many clustering methods produce groupings even when applied to random data. Instead of the "garbage in, garbage out" maxim often applied to statistical analysis, a catch phrase for cluster analysis is "garbage in, clusters out." In other words, in addition to revealing existing structure, clustering methods can impose artificial structure on the data, even when no natural structure exists. Cluster analysts have only recently become concerned with the question of cluster validity and the appropriateness of cluster analysis for a given data set.

Dubes and Jain (1979) have offered a useful review of the methods for testing data for inherent cluster structure. These methods are aimed at determining the *clustering tendency* of the data—that is, the degree to which there are homogeneous yet distinct groupings embodied in the data. (For specific methods, see Dubes & Jain, 1979; Ling, 1973, 1975; Ling & Killough, 1976; Strauss, 1975). Because these methods do not always agree regarding the existence of clusters, it is advisable to use more than one method to evaluate the data before applying a clustering method. Moreover, none of the proposed measures provides a definitive test of clustering tendency. The results of such methods should therefore be used only as guidelines for decisions about subsequent analyses.

The essential point is that multivariate data sets do not *automatically* qualify for cluster analysis. It is possible, for example, that no homogeneous clusters exist in the data. The failure to detect clustering tendency may indicate that the variables under consideration are inappropriate for taxonomic purposes, or that the instruments or procedures for assessing variables are inadequate. The unreliability of measures used in behavioral sciences, for instance, may obscure distinct subgroups in the data. An additional, and often ignored, possibility is that the data may contain only one cluster. Uniform admission criteria for a study, for example, may produce samples that are homogeneous with respect to variables being measured. If so, there is no point in trying to subdivide such a sample according to scores on these variables.

Choosing a Clustering Method

If there is sufficient evidence of clustering tendency, we must then choose an appropriate method of cluster analysis. This is a difficult but critical decision because dozens of clustering methods have been developed, and they may yield different taxonomies when applied to the same data. The choice of clustering method will help to determine the nature of the resulting taxonomy, including the size, homogeneity, and number of groups, and the profile characteristics that distinguish one group from another. Comprehensive and detailed reviews of clustering methods and the types of taxonomies they produce are available elsewhere (Anderberg, 1973; Everitt, 1974; Sneath & Sokal, 1973).

There are many ways of categorizing clustering methods (Anderberg, 1973; Bailey, 1974; Everitt, 1974), although some methods defy categorization. In general, it is useful to distinguish between *hierarchical* and *nonhierarchical* methods. The hierarchical methods do not produce a discrete number of clusters, but a heirarchical arrangement of individuals and groups. At low levels in the hierarchy, several small, homogeneous groups exist, whereas at higher levels in the hierarchy these clusters are combined into larger, more heterogeneous groupings. Thus, hierarchical techniques permit the identification of homogeneous groups of individuals and the relations among these groups. Hierarchical methods include *agglomerative* procedures, which build clusters by the stepwise amalgamation or joining of individuals into larger groups, and *divisive* techniques, which begin with all profiles in one cluster and split the sample into successively smaller and smaller clusters.

Among hierarchical methods, agglomerative procedures have been more widely used and studied than divisive procedures. The most commonly used agglomerative methods are the so-called linkage algorithms, including single, complete, average, and centroid linkage, as well as Ward's (1963) minimum variance technique. The agglomerative methods all produce a hierarchical ordering of groups, although they employ different statistical criteria in forming these groups. Blashfield (1976) has reviewed heirarchical agglomerative methods and their applications in behavioral sciences.

In contrast to the hierarchical methods, the nonhierarchical procedures produce a specific number of clusters. Many of the nonhierarchical methods require the choice of an initial grouping as a starting point. Individual profiles are then rearranged to "improve" the grouping according to some statistical criterion. Various procedures have been developed for selecting the initial "seed" clusters, for determining the relocation of profiles, and for evaluating the quality of the subsequent partitions (see Anderberg, 1973, for a review of such procedures). Initial "seed" clusters, for example, may be selected according to procedures that seek an initially random partition (e.g., MacQueen, 1967; McRae, 1971) or a partition that is representative of the range of profile characteristics (e.g., Ball & Hall, 1967).

Despite refinements, such nonhierarchical procedures have several drawbacks in taxonomic research. Certain *K*-means methods, for example, require the user to specify an initial grouping that often has no objective justification or theoretical merit. Not only is it difficult to determine the appropriate number of clusters in advance, but differences in the membership of the "seed" clusters may bias the final clustering solution. New methods are being developed that may overcome some of these problems, however (cf. Milligan, 1980).

Q-Factor Analysis

In addition to the heirarchical and nonhierarchical clustering procedures, *inverse* or *Q-type factor analysis* has been used to generate typologies of individuals (Butler & Adams, 1966; Collins, Burger, & Taylor, 1976; Monro, 1955; Stephenson, 1936). Ordinary *R*-factor analysis is typically used to identify groups of items that covary. However, simple modifications of the factoring procedure permit identification of groupings of individuals having similar profile patterns. Specifically, in *Q*-factor analysis, profiles describing individuals are intercorrelated to produce a matrix of correlations among *individuals* rather than among *items*. When these correlations are factor analyzed, the result is a set of dimensions defined by individuals having similar profile patterns, rather than groups of items that correlate highly. The factor loadings indicate the degree to which the individuals are similar to the "type" represented by the factor. Despite the historical precedence of this method, factor analysis has been widely criticized as a taxonomic tool (Baggaley, 1964; Fleiss & Zubin, 1969; Fleiss, Lawlor, Platman, & Fieve, 1971; Jones, 1968; Lorr, 1966), and is not currently recommended for taxonomic applications.

Criticisms of *Q*-factor analysis include: use of correlation as the similarity measure; the fact that individuals may obtain high loadings on more than one factor; and the fact that the first factor extracts the highest proportion of variance from the correlation matrix, and thus includes more individuals with high loadings than subsequent factors.

Most clustering methods, on the other hand, can employ alternative measures of profile similarity, can identify mutually exclusive groups, and are not biased toward the construction of one large cluster followed by successively smaller and smaller clusters. Despite these criticisms and the apparent advantages of cluster analysis, *Q*-factor analysis has not been subjected to Monte Carlo tests that permit empirical comparisons with clustering methods.

Given the availability of various hierarchical, nonhierarchical, and *Q*-factoring methods for constructing taxonomies, which method should be used? *Q*-factor analysis is not currently favored as a taxometric procedure. Although they should not be entirely dismissed, nonhierarchical procedures also have several limitations. Among hierarchical methods, agglomerative procedures have been most widely used and endorsed, particularly the "linkage" procedures and Ward's method. It is important to emphasize, however, that there is considerable variation among these algorithms, and several important decisions follow the choice of a general clustering method.

Measures of Profile Similarity

For many taxometric methods, results depend on both a *similarity measure* and a *clustering rule.* Numerous measures of profile similarity are available for cluster analysis (cf. Anderberg, 1973; Cronbach & Gleser, 1953; Gregson, 1975). Euclidean distance has been the most widely used similarity measure, but it may not always be the best choice. The Euclidean distance between two profiles is obtained by calculating the difference d between scores on each scale. Euclidean distance is simply the sum of the squared distance Σd^2 and is literally a measure of how "far apart" the two profiles are in Euclidean space. One criticism of Euclidean distance is that it confounds similarity in profile *elevation, shape,* and *scatter.* Profiles identical in elevation, for example, may appear dissimilar due to differences in shape and scatter, whereas profiles identical in shape and scatter may appear dissimilar due to their difference in elevation. Euclidean distance may therefore produce clusters whose members do not share specific profile characteristics, such as shape or elevation, although they may be "close together" in distance terms.

The *Q*-correlation is an alternative measure of profile similarity that is sensitive primarily to similarity in profile *shape,* independent of the elevations of the profiles. This measure is obtained by calculating the product-moment correlation between two profiles, across their scores on all scales. Even though the *Q*-correlation is not sensitive to profile elevations, its use of profile shape to define subgroups may be an advantage for some purposes. In clinical samples, for example, patients may differ in profile elevation due to a potent *g* dimension in symptom scores. Yet it may be more useful to define clinical subgroups on the basis of their profile patterns rather than overall severity.

The *Q*-correlation has been widely criticized as a measure of profile similarity (Cronbach & Gleser, 1953; Eades, 1965; Fleiss & Zubin, 1969; Gregson, 1975), because it is not sensitive to profile elevation and because it indexes the degree of linear relationship between

Table 3. A Comparison of Similarity Measures for Two Profiles

	Scale					
	I	II	III	IV	V	Similarity measures
						Q-correlation = 1.00
Scores on Profile A	1	2	3	4	5	One-way intraclass = .34
Scores on Profile B	2	4	6	8	10	Two-way intraclass = .48

profiles rather than the degree to which profile scores are identical. For example, Table 3 portrays two profiles comprised of scores on five variables. The profiles differ with respect to elevation and shape: As scores on Profile A increase, scores on Profile B increase to a greater and greater extent. Nevertheless, the *Q*-correlation between these profiles is 1.00, which would suggest perfect similarity.

The intraclass correlations represent an alternative set of similarity measures having several desirable properties. Intraclass correlations are based on the analysis of variance of profile scores and reflect the proportion of variance shared by pairs of profile scores. (Bartko, 1976, gives computational formulas for both the one-way and two-way intraclass correlations.) An intraclass correlation of 1.00 can only be obtained if two profiles have exactly the same scores on all scales. Any differences in elevation, shape, or scatter will lower the correlation. For example, when applied to the two profiles in Table 3, the one-way intraclass correlation equals .34; whereas the two-way intraclass correlation equals .48. These values are considerably less than 1.00 because the profiles depicted in Table 3 differ with respect to both elevation and additive bias.

Monte Carlo Studies

The choice of hierarchical clustering method and similarity measure can be aided by the results of recent Monte Carlo studies (Blashfield, 1976; Edelbrock, 1979; Edelbrock & McLaughlin, 1980; Kuiper & Fisher, 1975; Mezzich, 1978; Mojena, 1977). In these studies, multivariate mixtures of several populations differing in profile parameters were generated. Clustering algorithms were then compared on their ability to recover the underlying populations. The "accuracy" of a clustering solution has been defined as agreement between obtained clusters and underlying populations. Direct comparisons among results of these studies are difficult due to the variety of data and evaluative criteria employed. In general, however, Ward's technique and the average and centroid linkage algorithms have proven to be more accurate than single and complete linkage when applied to continuous, multivariate data. Edelbrock and McLaughlin (1980), for example, evaluated the performance of Ward's technique, as well as single, complete, average, and centroid linkage, on two sets of multivariate data. The linkage algorithms were evaluated using each of four measures of similarity, including Euclidean distance, correlation, and the one-way and two-way intraclass correlations. For both data sets, the average linkage algorithm using the one-way intraclass correlation was most accurate, although Ward's technique and the centroid algorithm using the one-way intraclass correlation were also highly accurate and were not significantly worse than the most accurate algorithm.

The results of these Monte Carlo evaluations suggest which methods to consider, but they do not show one algorithm to be superior for all applications. Rational considerations are still important in choosing a clustering method. For one, clustering methods are known to differ in the nature of the clusters they produce. Single linkage tends to link profiles together in elongated chains. Ward's technique, on the other hand, tends to construct spherical clusters that minimize the within-group variance on profile scales. Depending on the application, these may or may not be desirable clustering characteristics. Second, clustering methods do not necessarily produce groups that satisfy the user's definition of a "cluster" or "type." Elongated chains or minimum variance clusters, for example, may not be satisfactory if one views a cluster as a group whose members share specific profile characteristics, such as a similar pattern or elevation of scores.

Ward's technique, as well as average and centroid linkage, currently appear to be good candidates for clustering applications in the behavioral sciences. Much more work is necessary, however, to determine which clustering algorithms are best suited to different types of data and different taxonomic tasks. New clustering algorithms and methods of measuring profile similarity are also being developed (cf. D'Andrade, 1978; Skinner, 1978).

Additional Methodological Issues

Even after we have chosen a clustering method and measure of similarity, several methodological problems and issues remain. These are addressed in the following sections.

Scaling and Standardization

Scaling of data is an important consideration in cluster analysis. Some clustering methods have been designed for data of a particular level of measurement (e.g., nominal, ordinal, interval) or distribution (e.g., binary, discrete, continuous). Thus, the nature of the data may dictate the choice of clustering method and similarity measure.

The standardization of scales can also influence clustering outcomes. Two scales may use interval levels of measurement, for example, but differ in their distribution parameters. These differences alone may bias the resulting taxonomies. Two potential biases should be noted. First, mean differences among scales may produce a "built-in" pattern of profile scores that can influence cluster formation. Such built-in patterns create an artifactual similarity among all profiles that can obscure meaningful differences among individuals and groups. Second, for many clustering methods, scales having greater variance will have more influence on cluster formation than those with less variance.

For quantitative data, biasing effects due to differences in scale means and variances can be overcome by standardizing the data. That is, each scale can be independently standardized such that means and standard deviations are equivalent (e.g., mean = 0, standard deviation = 1). Standardization reduces built-in profile patterns created by initial mean differences and can insure that scales have an unbiased opportunity to influence cluster construction.

How Many Clusters?

Many clustering methods require choices as to the number of clusters to be retained for a taxonomy. The nonhierarchical methods, for example, typically require choosing an initial set of groups as "seed" clusters. Similarly, inverse factor analysis requires a choice of factors to retain. Such choices are crucial to the nature and utility of the resulting taxonomies. In many situations, for example, the choice is between a few large clusters representing global distinctions among individuals, or several smaller clusters offering more fine-grained discriminations.

The hierarchical methods offer an advantage in this respect because they can reveal hierarchical arrangements that permit multiple levels of analysis. At low levels in the hierarchy, there are many small homogeneous clusters whose members manifest very distinctive profile characteristics. At higher levels, these clusters are combined into larger groups representing more global distinctions among individuals. Thus, hierarchical clustering methods can be used to construct hierarchical taxonomies. Such taxonomies are advantageous in research because significant differences among groups may exist at one level but not at others.

Which Clusters Are Reliable?

Measures of clustering tendency may indicate homogeneous groups within a data set, but they do not indicate which groups are reliable and which are artifacts of the clustering procedure. One way to weed out artifactual findings is to replicate clusters across samples or across methods. *Cross-method* replications should be undertaken cautiously and interpreted skeptically. Given the diversity of clustering methods, it is possible to select ones that employ such different clustering criteria that even the most distinct clusters will not replicate. Conversely, it is possible to select clustering methods that are so similar that they will replicate virtually all clusters, even when applied to random data.

The replication of clusters across independent samples of subjects, when done by the same clustering method, is evidence of cluster reliability. Although there are no universal standards for cluster replication, a general strategy and method can be recommended. This strategy involves determining whether groups identified in two or more samples manifest similar profile characteristics. *Centroid replication,* for example, involves determining if cluster centroids obtained in two or more samples are sufficiently similar to constitute replications. The cluster centroid is the "average profile" of cluster members and is obtained by computing the average score of cluster members for each scale. The centroid thus represents the common pattern of scores shared by the cluster members. Quantitative criteria, such as a correlation coefficient or other similarity measure, can be used to test for similarities between centroids obtained in different samples. Cluster centroids reaching a cutoff criterion for replication (e.g., a significance level) can be retained in the taxonomy; those that fail to reach the criterion can be rejected as unreliable or artifactual groupings.

Assigning Cases to Taxa

The goals of taxometric research often include classification of individuals not included in the original analysis. In child psychopathology, for example, the utility of empirically derived taxonomies for clinical and research purposes may depend on the ability to assign new cases to taxa. Unfortunately, most clustering methods only identify groupings and do not embody procedures for the subsequent assignment of individuals to taxa.

Several procedures are available for making assignments. The most common is linear discriminant analysis to determine the combination of profile scores that best discriminates between groups. Individual profiles are classified by entering their scores into a discriminant equation to determine the probability of membership in each group. A simpler procedure involves classifying individuals according to their profile high points. This procedure can be used to construct groups or to assign individuals to groups that have been identified in advance.

Another procedure is "nearest centroid assignment" (cf. McIntyre & Blashfield, 1980). This procedure involves determining the degree to which an individual's profile corresponds to each of the profile types, as defined by the cluster centroids. Thus, the similarity between an individual's profile and each cluster centroid can be calculated, and the individual can be assigned to the group that his or her profile most resembles.

Two important issues involve the accuracy and reliability of assignment. *Accuracy* of assignment refers to the degree to which the procedure correctly assigns individuals to groups. *Reliability* of assignment refers to the agreement obtained in assigning individuals according to scores obtained from different sources or at different times. Unfortunately, there has been little research on the accuracy and reliability of assignment procedures.

Should We Classify Everybody?

The value of any taxonomy is related to its *coverage,* which is the proportion of subjects it can classify. In the biological sciences, where many taxometric methods originated, 100% coverage is an important goal because taxonomies are intended to correspond to classifications of biological species. Such taxonomies represent groupings based on morphological, physiological, and genetic characteristics that are reliably assessed and have recognized validity as taxonomic criteria. In child psychopathology and other sciences in an earlier stage of development, we lack objective criteria on which to base empirically derived taxonomies. Extensive coverage is desirable, but classifying everybody may be unrealistic. Deviant child behavior has diverse causes and modes of expression, for example, and the available measures for deriving taxonomies are less than perfectly reliable or valid. Profiles of scores describing disturbed children may not always resemble replicable types. Should such children be classified?

It may not always be advisable to classify everybody. In most classification efforts in the behavioral sciences, there is a continuum of classifiability. At one end of this continuum are subjects who are easy to classify because they closely resemble replicable types. Moving toward the middle of the continuum, subjects become more difficult to classify because they do not resemble "pure types" or they resemble more than one type. At the opposite end of this continuum are those who cannot be classified because they do not resemble any other subjects. Trying to classify everybody may thus require the assignment of subjects who are difficult or impossible to classify. As one moves across the continuum, classifying subjects who are less and less similar to replicated types dilutes the groups and may increase their overlap. This, in turn, may dilute the predictive power of the taxonomy because differences among groups that relate to external criteria are obscured. Furthermore, moving across the continuum from "pure types" to unclassifiable subjects, the reliability of assignment decreases. Subjects resembling "pure types" can be reliably classified because slight changes in their scores do not substantially alter their similarity to the types. On the other hand, among subjects who are less similar to types, or resemble more than one type, a slight change in scores may result in a different group assignment.

Based on the continuum of classifiability, the coverage of classifications can be varied to fit the purposes of the research. In an epidemiological study, for example, the goal may be to classify as many subjects as possible, including subjects who are difficult to assign to groups. This procedure results in more heterogeneous groups and decreased reliability of assignment, but serves a major purpose of epidemiological surveys—namely, to determine the distribution of putative disorders in a population. Alternatively, evaluations of a focused treatment may require small, homogeneous groups for study. In this situation, perhaps only 10% of the subjects can be classified according to rigorous criteria, but the reliability of assignment to groups is high and the subjects represent relatively "pure types." This low level of coverage might increase the predictive power of group assignments but might decrease the generalizability of findings. That is, findings may not be generalizable to a whole population, but only that portion who resemble "pure types."

In simple terms, therefore, the question of coverage requires choices as to whether it is better to classify "some of the people some of the time," or attempt to classify everybody.

To resolve this issue, it is necessary to determine if the benefits of reduced coverage outweigh the costs. In child psychopathology research, it may be better to classify fewer individuals if the benefits are increased predictive power and reliability. Unfortunately, conventional clustering methods do not offer ready manipulation of coverage. Most methods are aimed at simply partitioning or amalgamating all subjects into groups, even if the group members differ widely. New taxometric methods are being developed, however, which address this complex issue of coverage (cf. Edelbrock & Achenbach, 1980).

Validation of Taxonomies

Most efforts to validate taxonomies in the behavioral sciences involve testing their predictive power against external criteria known to be imperfect. In psychopathology research, for example, such criteria might include measures of personality, cognitive abilities, academic achievement, neurological functioning, prognosis, and treatment response.

The ability to detect significant differences among taxa is a complex function of the number of groups, sample size, separation and homogeneity of groups, and the size of effects under study. Most empirically derived taxonomies deal with relatively few types (e.g., less than 20) and small effects. Whereas there is no absolute rule for defining "small" effect sizes, Cohen (1977) has suggested that differences accounting for less than 10% of the variance in a variable be labeled "small" effect sizes. According to Cohen's criteria, a medium effect accounts for 20–25% of the variance, and a large effect accounts for 40–50% of the variance. In the behavioral sciences, most effects are "small" due to unreliability of measurement, multidetermination of target variables, and lack of experimental control over extraneous sources of variation. This is not to say that such "small" effects are trivial. Even small group differences in prognosis or treatment response, for example, may be critical in decision making.

If samples are large relative to the number of groups and the effects under study are relatively small, the predictive power of taxonomies is largely a function of the degree to which groups are distinct from each other, yet homogeneous. Small *within-group* variance implies that group *members* are highly similar to their taxonomic type and to one another. Large *between-group* variance implies that *types* are distinct from one another on the taxonomic criteria.

A taxonomy gains predictive power by grouping subjects into homogeneous yet distinct taxa. Unfortunately, subjects do not always align themselves into stereotypical "pure types." Most taxonomies must contend with "fuzzy" groups, which overlap with respect to the taxonomic criteria. In general, as overlap among groups increases, predictive power of the taxonomy decreases. As previously mentioned, one strategy for decreasing overlap among groups is to reduce coverage of the classification. Thus, as coverage decreases, we would expect the predictive power of the taxonomy to increase. Coverage therefore affects the potential validity of taxonomies.

An Illustration of Taxometric Research on Child Psychopathology

The various methodological issues arising from taxometric methods can be illustrated in our efforts to construct taxonomies of children's behavior disorders (Edelbrock & Achenbach, 1980). Our research required methodological choices that undoubtedly influenced the resulting taxonomies. There are no absolute rules for making these choices, and they inevitably involve trade-offs. Our procedures and results, however, point up the problems and prospects of taxometric research in child psychopathology.

Our taxonomies are based on the narrow-band behavior problem syndromes of the Child Behavior Profile. This choice of instrument alone carries numerous implications regarding the source and reliability of data, the nature of the symptom scales, the age range, and so forth. Different instrumentation might yield different taxonomies. The narrow-band syndromes of the Profile were selected because they offer finer distinctions among children than broad-band syndromes do. To reflect age and sex differences in the patterning of problems, we did separate cluster analyses for boys and girls aged 6–11 and 12–16.

Clustering Procedure

We chose a hierarchical clustering method called *centroid* analysis, partly because we sought a hierarchical taxonomy wherein children could be grouped according to several low-level types manifesting specific profile characteristics, as well as higher order types representing more global distinctions. The one-way intraclass correlation was selected as the measure of profile similarity because it reflects similarities in both the patterns and elevations of scores. One reason for choosing this clustering method and similarity measure was their accurate performance in Monte Carlo evaluations (Edelbrock & McLaughlin, 1980).

The centroid clustering method was also chosen because it constructs clusters that fit our conception of a type. Specifically, this method constructs clusters comprised of individuals who are similar to the cluster centroid, which is the "average profile" of cluster members. The cluster centroid thus serves as an operational definition of the common pattern of scores, or type, represented by the group.

The centroid algorithm proceeds by first calculating the intraclass correlation between each pair of profiles in the sample. The two profiles having the highest intraclass correlation are then combined into a cluster and replaced by their centroid, which is the profile created by averaging the two subjects' scores on each scale. This newly created cluster centroid can then be treated like a profile of an individual subject. The intraclass correlations between all possible pairs of profiles are then recomputed. In each cycle, the two profiles having the highest intraclass correlation are combined into a cluster and replaced by their centroid. When a cluster is combined with another individual profile or cluster, the centroid is recomputed using scores of all members of the new cluster. As cycles proceed, larger and larger clusters are formed and combined in a hierarchical fashion. From this hierarchy, groups of children having similar profile patterns, as well as the hierarchical relations among these groups, can be identified.

The published versions of the Child Behavior Profile employ scores standardized on samples of normal children. According to these norms, however, referred children tend to have elevated scores on several scales. Moreover, scale means and variances for referred children are quite different from those for normal children. These differences in scale parameters produce a built-in pattern of scores among referred children that can bias the cluster analysis. In order to overcome such biases and differentiate maximally among referred children, we found it necessary to standardize scores within clinical samples.

For each age and sex group, the clustering algorithm was applied to two randomly drawn samples of 250 profiles each. Profile types that replicated across both samples were retained. The criterion for replication was a significant ($p < .05$) intraclass correlation between a cluster centroid obtained in one sample and a cluster centroid obtained in the other sample. A significant intraclass correlation between cluster centroids obtained in two samples indicated that a group of children in each sample shared the same profile characteristics.

Profile Types

Six reliable profile types were obtained for boys aged 6–11 and boys aged 12–16. Seven reliable profile types were obtained for girls aged 6–11 and girls aged 12–16. As an example, the profile types obtained for girls aged 6–11 are shown in Figure 1. The names assigned to these profile types simply reflect their distinguishing high points. It is important to note, however, that each profile type is defined by its entire set of scores, and not by high points alone. The hierarchical relations among profile types were also found to replicate across samples. Among girls aged 6–11, for example, three profile types were combined into a cluster representing an Internalizing pattern, as shown in Figure 2. This Internalizing cluster was characterized by high scores on the Internalizing scales and low scores on the Externalizing scales. Conversely, three profile types were combined into an Externalizing cluster characterized by high scores on the Externalizing scales and low scores on the Internalizing scales. The Sex Problems profile type did not reliably combine with either the Internalizing or Externalizing clusters, and is labeled Mixed in Figure 2.

Distribution and Correlates of Profile Types

To determine the distribution and correlates of the profile types, the profiles of clinically referred children were classified according to their similarity to the profile types obtained for their age and sex group. The "nearest centroid" assignment procedure was used. Thus, we assigned individual children to taxa by calculating the intraclass correlations between each child's profile and the centroids of the profile types. Each child was then classified according to the profile type with which his or her profile correlated most highly. A minimum cutoff point for classification can be specified, such that children whose profiles are not very similar to any of the profile types can be left unclassified. In addition, children having a total behavior problem score of 25 or less were not classified because their profile patterns were likely to be unreliable. Likewise, children with total scores of 100 or more were not classified because they tended to have extreme scores on all scales.

The distribution of 435 clinically referred girls aged 6–11 according to the profile types is shown in Figure 2. In order to classify as many girls as possible, the minimum cutoff point was set at zero. That is, to be classified, a girl's profile merely had to have an intraclass correlation greater than zero with at least one profile type. The Unclassified group shown in Figure 2 is comprised of girls who did not meet this criterion. Figure 2 also shows the percent of cases in the Internalizing, Externalizing, and Mixed profile types, as well as those not classified because their total scores were ≤ 25 or ≥ 100.

To evaluate the reliability of assignment, we compared classification of the same children based on ratings by mothers and a clinician. Averaging across age and sex groups, 74% agreement was obtained for assignments to the narrow-band profile types, whereas

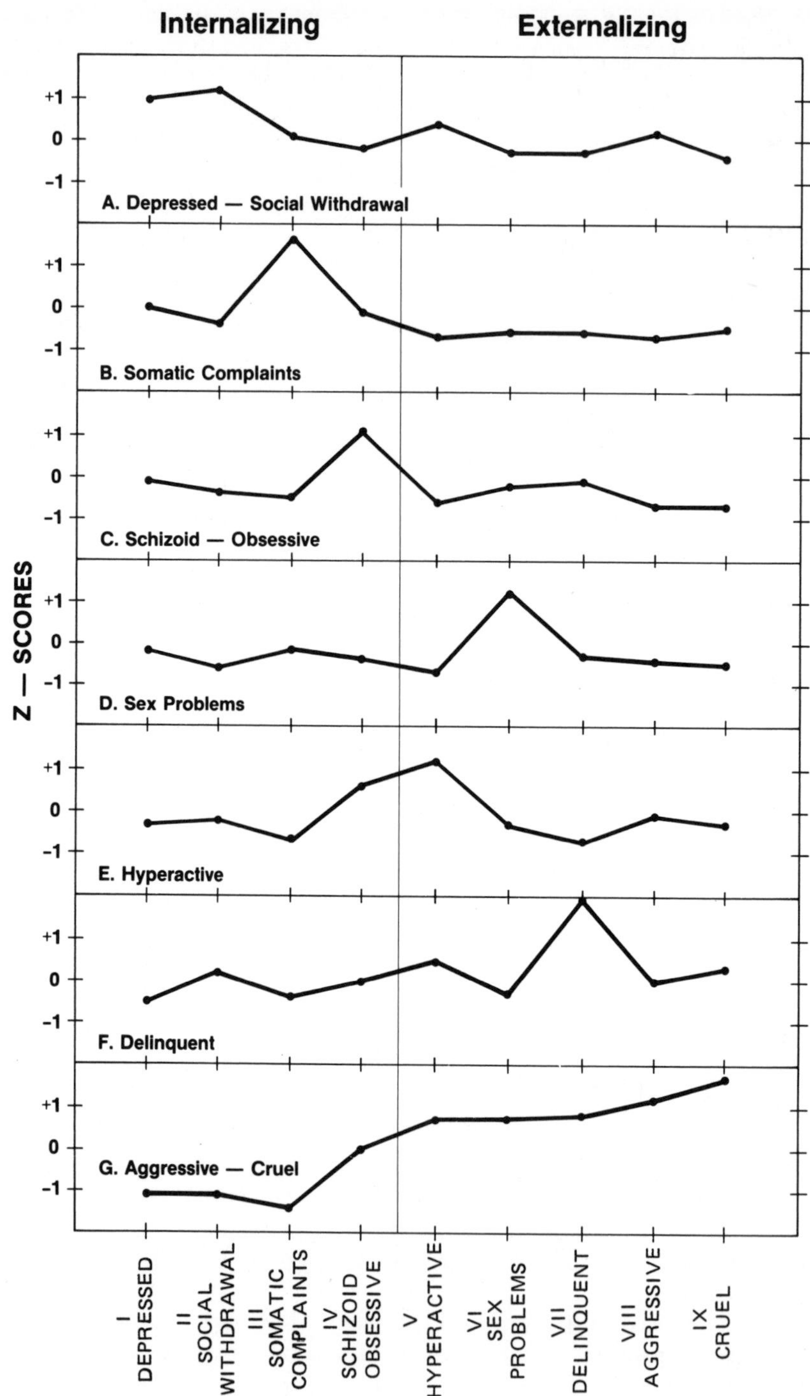

Figure 1. Child Behavior Profile types identified for girls aged 6–11.

83% agreement was obtained for assignments to the Internalizing/Externalizing dichotomy. We have also determined whether the profile types differed in demographic characteristics such as age, race, and socioeconomic status, as well as in adaptive competencies reported by parents. Among girls aged 6–11, for example, the Hyperactive group was significantly younger than other groups, contained a higher proportion of black children, and had worse school performance. Although these correlates extend the meaning and value of the taxa, further validation also depends on the predictive power of these taxonomies with respect to criteria such as etiology, prognosis, cognitive level, and treatment response.

There are several ways to explore the predictive power of these taxonomies. For one, they offer multiple ways of grouping children. Significant correlates may be detected among narrow-band profile types, for example, but not among more global groupings. Conversely, for some criteria, the Internalizing/Externalizing dichotomy may be more predictive than the narrow-band profile types. The coverage of such classifications can also be varied to optimize predictive power. That is, the choice of the minimum cutoff point for assignment permits the manipulation of coverage. A low cutoff point results in the classification of a high proportion of children into relatively heterogeneous groups, whereas a high cutoff point classifies fewer children into more distinct and homogeneous groups. The optimal cutoff point for detecting differences will depend on many factors, including sample size, distribution of children according to the profile types, and the size of effects under study. Finally, the intraclass correlations between a child's profile and the cluster centroids shows how similar he or she is to each taxon. These correlations can be used as scores in a multiple regression, for example, to determine whether particular configurations of similarities to profile types are predictive of other characteristics.

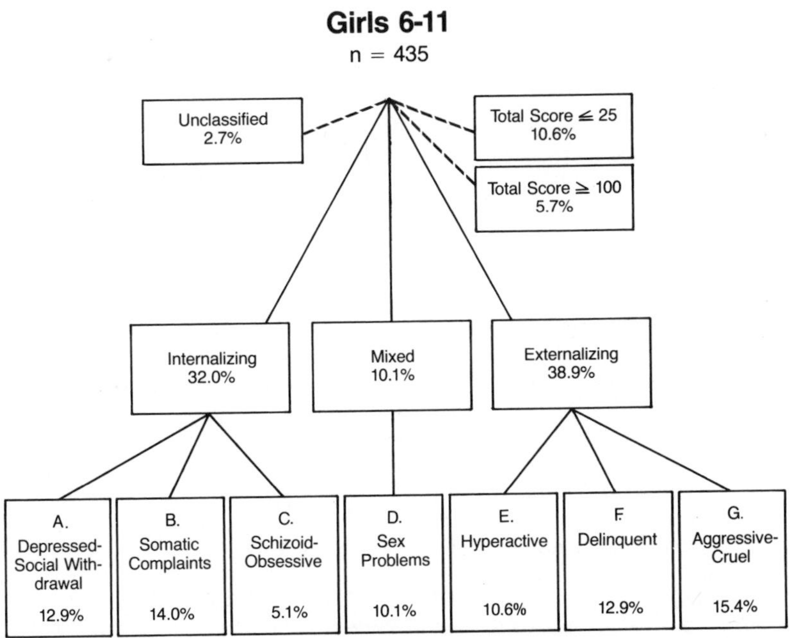

Figure 2. Hierarchical relations between Child Behavior Profile patterns identified for girls aged 6–11. Percentages indicate the proportion of clinically referred girls whose profiles fell into the indicated categories.

Summary

Although taxonomic issues may seem remote from everyday work with disturbed children, they arise in many forms: Taxonomic assumptions shape views of psychopathology, treatment and administrative decisions, professional communication, formal diagnoses, diagnostic formulations, research, epidemiology, and public policy.

Contemporary psychiatric taxonomies originated in nineteenth-century concepts of organic disease and have only recently been extended to child psychopathology in a differentiated way. Neither the extensions of traditional, adult-oriented taxonomy to child psychopathology, nor more theoretically based taxonomies designed for childhood disorders have demonstrated satisfactory reliability or validity.

As an alternative to the traditional adult-oriented taxonomy and the theoretically-based taxonomies of childhood disorders, researchers have increasingly used multivariate analyses to identify childhood syndromes. The results of numerous studies have shown convergence on a few broad-band syndromes and more plentiful narrow-band syndromes. Some of these syndromes resemble the childhood syndromes of DSM–III, while others show little correspondence to the DSM–III syndromes.

As an illustration of how multivariate findings can be put to practical use, we described our work with the Child Behavior Checklist and Child Behavior Profile. These provide quantifiable descriptions of behavioral problems and competencies at levels ranging from individual items to narrow-band syndromes, broad-band syndromes, and global total scores.

To move from multivariate description to empirically based taxonomy, we considered various *taxometric* methods such as *Q*-factor analysis and several varieties of cluster analysis. Because the application of these measures to child psychopathology is in its infancy, there are few well tested conventions or rules of thumb. We therefore reviewed methodological issues relevant to choices of procedures and their effects on resulting taxonomies. We also discussed assignment of new cases to a taxonomy and validation of empirically derived taxonomies. We illustrated the application of taxometric methods with an account of our cluster-based taxonomy of Child Behavior Profile types.

References

Achenbach, T. M. The Child Behavior Profile: I. Boys 6–11. *Journal of Consulting and Clinical Psychology,* 1978, *46,* 478–488.

Achenbach, T. M. The Child Behavior Profile: An empirically based system for assessing children's behavioral problems and competencies. *International Journal of Mental Health,* 1979, *7,* 24–42.

Achenbach, T. M. DSM–III in light of empirical research on the classification of child psychopathology. *Journal of the American Academy of Child Psychiatry,* 1980, *19,* 395–412.

Achenbach, T. M. The role of taxonomy in developmental psychopathology. In M. E. Lamb & A. L. Brown (Eds.), *Advances in developmental psychology.* Hillsdale, N.J.: Lawrence Erlbaum, 1981.

Achenbach, T. M. *Developmental psychopathology* (2nd ed.). New York: Wiley, 1982.

Achenbach, T. M., & Edelbrock, C. S. The classification of child psychopathology: A review and analysis of empirical efforts. *Psychological Bulletin,* 1978, *85,* 1275–1301.

Achenbach, T. M., & Edelbrock, C. S. The Child Behavior Profile: II. Boys aged 12–16 and girls aged 6–11 and 12–16. *Journal of Consulting and Clinical Psychology,* 1979, *47,* 223–233.

Achenbach, T. M., & Edelbrock, C. S. Behavioral problems and competencies reported by parents of normal and disturbed children aged 4 through 16. *Monographs of the Society for Research in Child Development,* 1981, *46*(1, Serial No. 188).

Ackerson, L. *Children's behavior problems: Vol. 2. Relative importance and interrelations among traits.* Chicago: University of Chicago Press, 1942.

American Psychiatric Association. *Diagnostic and statistical manual of mental disorders.* Washington, D.C.: Author, lst ed., 1952; 2nd ed., 1968; 3rd ed., 1980.

Anderberg, M. R. *Cluster analysis for applications.* New York: Academic Press, 1973.

Baggaley, A. R. *Intermediate correlational methods.* New York: Wiley, 1964.

Bailey, K. D. Cluster analysis. In D. Heise (Ed.), *Sociological methodology.* San Francisco: Jossey-Bass, 1974.

Ball, G., & Hall, D. J. A clustering procedure for summarizing multivariate data. *Behavioral Science,* 1967, *12,* 153–155.

Bartko, J. J. On various intraclass correlation reliability coefficients. *Psychological Bulletin,* 1976, *83,* 762–765.

Beitchman, J. H., Dielman, T. E., Landis, J. R., Benson, R. M., & Kemp, P. L. Reliability of the Group for the Advancement of Psychiatry diagnostic categories in child psychiatry. *Archives of General Psychiatry,* 1978, *35,* 1461–1466.

Blashfield, R. K. Mixture model tests of cluster analysis: Accuracy of four agglomerative hierarchical methods. *Psychological Bulletin,* 1976, *83,* 377–388.

Borkovec, T. D. Autonomic reactivity to sensory stimulation in psychopathic, neurotic, and normal juvenile delinquents. *Journal of Consulting and Clinical Psychology,* 1970, *35,* 217–222.

Butler, E. W., & Adams, S. W. Typologies of delinquent girls: Some alternative approaches. *Social Forces,* 1966, *44,* 401–407.

Cohen, J. *Statistical power analysis for the behavioral sciences* (Rev. ed.). New York: Academic Press, 1977.

Collins, H. A., Burger, G. K., & Taylor, G. A. An empirical typology of heroin abusers. *Journal of Clinical Psychology,* 1976, *32,* 473–476.

Cronbach, L. J., & Gleser, G. Assessing similarity between profiles. *Psychological Bulletin,* 1953, *50,* 456–473.

D'Andrade, R. G. *U*-statistic hierarchical clustering. *Psychometrika,* 1978, *43,* 59–67.

Dubes, R., & Jain, A. K. Validity studies in clustering methodologies. *Pattern Recognition,* 1979, *11,* 235–254.

Eades, D. C. The inappropriateness of the correlation coefficient as a measure of taxonomic resemblance. *Systematic Zoology,* 1965, *14,* 98–100.

Edelbrock, C. Mixture model tests of hierarchical clustering algorithms: The problem of classifying everybody. *Multivariate Behavioral Research,* 1979, *14,* 367–384.

Edelbrock, C., & Achenbach, T. M. A typology of Child Behavior Profile patterns: Distribution and correlates for disturbed children aged 6–16. *Journal of Abnormal Child Psychology,* 1980, *8,* 441–470.

Edelbrock, C., & McLaughlin, B. Hierarchical cluster analysis using intraclass correlations: A mixture model study. *Multivariate Behavioral Research,* 1980, *15,* 299–318.

Everitt, B. S. *Cluster analysis.* London: Halsted, 1974.

Fleiss, J. L., Lawlor, W., Platman, S. R., & Fieve, R. R. On the use of inverted factor analysis for generating typologies. *Journal of Abnormal Psychology,* 1971, *77,* 127–132.

Fleiss, J. L., & Zubin, J. On the methods and theory of clustering. *Multivariate Behavioral Research,* 1969, *4,* 235–250.

Freeman, M. A reliability study of psychiatric diagnosis in childhood and adolescence. *Journal of Child Psychology and Psychiatry,* 1971, *12,* 43–54.

Freud, A. *Normality and pathology in childhood.* New York: International Universities Press, 1965.

Freud, S. Inhibitions, symptoms, and anxiety. In *Standard edition of the complete psychological works of Sigmund Freud* (Vol. 20). London: Hogarth Press, 1959. (Originally published, 1926.)

Greenspan, S. I., Hatleberg, J. L., & Cullander, C. C. H. A developmental approach to systematic personality assessment: Illustrated with the case of a 6-year-old child. In S. I. Greenspan & G. Pollock (Eds.), *The course of life: Psychoanalytic contributions toward understanding personality development. Vol. 2: Latency, adolescence, and youth.* Washington, D.C.: Department of Health, Education and Welfare, 1979.

Gregson, R. *Psychometrics of similarity.* New York: Academic Press, 1975.

Griesinger, W. *Mental pathology and therapeutics* (C. L. Robertson & J. Rutherford, trans.). London: New Sydenham Society, 1867. (Originally published, 1845.)

Group for the Advancement of Psychiatry. *Psychopathological disorders in childhood: Theoretical considerations and a proposed classification,* (Report No. 62). New York: Group for the Advancement of Psychiatry, 1966.

Guze, S. B. Validating criteria for psychiatric diagnosis: The Washington University approach. In H. S. Akiskal & W. L. Webb (Eds.), *Psychiatric diagnosis: Exploration of biological predictors.* New York: Spectrum, 1978.

Hewitt, L. E., & Jenkins, R. L. *Fundamental patterns of maladjustment: The dynamics of their origin. A statistical analysis based upon five hundred case records of children examined at the Michigan Child Guidance Institute.* Springfield, Ill.: State of Illinois, 1946.

Jenkins, R. L., & Glickman, S. Common syndromes in child psychiatry: I. Deviant behavior traits. II. The schizoid child. *American Journal of Orthopsychiatry,* 1946, *16,* 244–261.

Jones, K. J. Problems of grouping individuals and the method of modality. *Behavioral Science,* 1968, *13,* 496–511.

Kanner, L. Autistic disturbances of affective contact. *Nervous Child,* 1943, *2,* 217–250.

Kraepelin, E. *Psychiatrie* (8th ed.). Leipzig: Barth, 1915. (Originally published, 1883.)

Kuiper, F. K., & Fisher, L. A Monte Carlo comparison of six clustering procedures. *Biometrics,* 1975, *31,* 777–783.

Lief, A. *The common sense psychiatry of Dr. Adolf Meyer.* New York: McGraw-Hill, 1948.

Ling, R. F. Probability theory of cluster analysis. *Journal of the American Statistical Association,* 1973, *68,* 159–164.

Ling, R. F. An exact probability distribution on the connectivity of random graphs. *Journal of Mathematical Psychology,* 1975, *12,* 90–98.

Ling, R. F., & Killough, G. S. Probability tables for cluster analysis based on a theory of random graphs. *Journal of the American Statistical Association,* 1976, *71,* 293–300.

Lorr, M. (Ed.). *Explorations in typing psychotics.* Oxford: Pergamon Press, 1966.

MacQueen, J. Some methods for classification and analysis of multivariate observations. In L. M. Lecam & J. Neyman (Eds.), *Proceedings of the fifth Berkeley Symposium on Mathematical Statistics and Probability* (Vol. 1). Berkeley: University of California Press, 1967.

Mattison, R., Cantwell, D. P., Russell, A. T., & Will, L. A comparison of DSM-II and DSM-III in the diagnosis of childhood psychiatric disorders. *Archives of General Psychiatry,* 1979, *36,* 1217–1222.

McIntyre, R. M., & Blashfield, R. K. A nearest-centroid technique for evaluating the minimum-variance clustering procedure. *Multivariate Behavioral Research,* 1980, *15,* 225–238.

McRae, D. J. MICKA: A FORTRAN IV iterative *K*-means cluster analysis program. *Behavioral Science,* 1971, *17,* 423–424.

Meehl, P. E. Theoretical risks and tabular asterisks: Sir Karl, Sir Ronald, and the slow progress of soft psychology. *Journal of Consulting and Clinical Psychology,* 1978, *46,* 806–834.

Mezzich, A. C., & Mezzich, J. E. *Diagnostic reliability of childhood and adolescence behavior disorders.* Presented at the American Psychological Association, New York, September 1979.

Mezzich, J. E. Evaluating clustering methods for psychiatric diagnosis. *Biological Psychiatry,* 1978, *13,* 265–281.

Miller, L. C. *Louisville Behavior Checklist manual.* Los Angeles: Western Psychological Services, 1977.

Milligan, G. W. An examination of the effect of six types of error perturbation on fifteen clustering algorithms. *Psychometrika,* 1980, *45,* 325–342.

Mojena, R. Hierarchical grouping methods and stopping rules: An evaluation. *Computer Journal,* 1977, *20,* 359–363.

Monro, A. B. Psychiatric types: A *Q*-technique study of 200 patients. *Journal of Mental Science,* 1955, *101,* 330–343.

Prior, M., Perry, D., & Gajzago, C. Kanner's syndrome or early onset psychosis: A taxonomic analysis of 142 cases. *Journal of Autism and Childhood Schizophrenia,* 1975, *5,* 71–80.

Quay, H. C. Classification. In H. C. Quay & J. S. Werry (Eds.), *Psychopathological disorders of childhood* (2nd ed.). New York: Wiley, 1979.

Quay, H.C., & Peterson, D. R. *Manual for the Behavior Problem Checklist.* Unpublished manuscript, University of Illinois, 1968; University of Miami, 1975.

Roth, M. Psychiatric diagnosis in clinical and scientific settings. In H. S. Akiskal & W. L. Webb (Eds.), *Psychiatric diagnosis: Exploration of biological predictors.* New York: Spectrum, 1978.

Skinner, H. A. Differentiating the contribution of elevation, scatter, and shape in profile similarity. *Educational and Psychological Measurement,* 1978, *38,* 297–308.

Sneath, P. H., & Sokal, R. R. *Numerical taxonomy: The principles and practice of numerical classification.* San Francisco: Freeman, 1973.

Spitzer, R. L., & Cantwell, D. P. The DSM-III classification of the psychiatric disorders of infancy, childhood, and adolescence. *Journal of the American Academy of Child Psychiatry,* 1980, *19,* 356–370.

Spitzer, R. L., Endicott, J., & Robins, E. Research diagnostic criteria: Rationale and reliability. *Archives of General Psychiatry,* 1978, *35,* 773–782.

Spitzer, R. L., Williams, J. B. W., & Skodol, A. E. DSM-III: The major achievements and an overview. *American Journal of Psychiatry,* 1980, *137,* 151–164.

Stephenson, W. Introduction to inverted factor analysis with some applications to studies of orexsis. *Journal of Educational Psychology,* 1936, *27,* 353–367.

Strauss, D. J. A model for clustering. *Biometrika,* 1975, *62,* 467–475.

Ward, J. H. Hierarchical grouping to optimize an objective function. *Journal of the American Statistical Association,* 1963, *58,* 236–244.

Woolf, H. B. (Ed.). *Webster's new collegiate dictionary.* Springfield, Mass.: G. & C. Merriam, 1977.

II

Specific Psychopathologies

5

Mental Retardation

ALAN C. REPP AND DIANE E. D. DEITZ

Introduction

The field of mental retardation has been in transition over the last decade as the rights of the mentally retarded have been emerging. While changes in attitudes and behavioral practices toward retarded persons used to be measured by the century, today they are measured at most by the decade and often by a few years. Some of the reasons for rapid changes are the civil rights movements of the 1960s (expanded to include handicapped persons), the intense legalism of the last two decades, and the rapid expanse of a behavioral technology that has provided countless examples of how much more achievement retarded people are capable of than we previously thought possible. These and other factors have led to a change in society's approach toward mentally retarded persons, evidenced by such movements as normalization, deinstitutionalization, least restrictive environment, least restrictive alternative, mainstreaming, and legislation such as Section 504 of P.L. 93–112 (the Rehabilitation Act), and P.L. 94–142 (the Education for all Handicapped Children Act). While, as with any concept, there is not universal agreement about the usefulness of any of these movements, there is virtually universal agreement that we are in an era of more humane, technological, and hopeful approaches toward retarded persons; such hope is evidenced by the discrepancy between historical and current definitions of mental retardation.

Definitions of Mental Retardation

Definitions of mental retardation serve many purposes, but all are intended in one way or another to fashion the approach of a portion of society toward the retarded. The

ALAN C. REPP AND DIANE E. D. DEITZ • Department of Learning and Development, Northern Illinois University, DeKalb, Illinois 60115.

two primary purposes of defining mental retardation are: (a) actuarial, whereby local and federal governments, researchers, and others can determine how many retarded persons exist, and then make plans based on these numbers; and (b) educational, whereby school agencies and personnel can provide proper staffing, curriculum, placements, and so forth, for clients. In this section, we will look at some examples of definitions as well as some historical antecedents to them.

Historical Definitions

In the early history of societies, there was no distinction between mental retardation and mental illness, and consequently there were no formal definitions. Yet we can make some inferences from the general approach of various societies. The earliest written reference to mental retardation appears to have been the Papyrus of Thebes (1552 B.C.), in which was discussed the treatment of persons whose intellectual abilities were limited. Various remains in Europe, South America, and Central America suggest that such treatment included piercing the skull, presumably to allow spirits to escape. Treatment of these individuals within Greek and Roman cultures has been characterized as the era of extermination (Kolstoe & Frey, 1965), and it was not uncommon for handicapped persons to be left to perish in open sewers (Kauffman & Payne, 1975), to be used as physician's slaves, or to be kept for the amusement of the court. In the Middle Ages, some small portions of society began to house handicapped persons (e.g., in Gheel, Belgium), while others scourged them as demonically possessed. In this period, what might have been the first working definition of mental retardation emerged when Henry II of England enacted legislation known as *de praerogitive regis,* which made "natural fools" wards of the King, and in so doing made an interesting distinction between mentally retarded and mentally ill persons; only the mentally retarded were designated as "natural fools."

The seventeenth and eighteenth century saw a break from the demonic-possession theory of retardation, while the nineteenth century provided the first systematic attempts at educating and housing the retarded. Nevertheless, there remained some rigidity in the general assumption that God, morality, and retardation were related. Howe, an eminent moralist of that time, wrote:

> [Idiocy] is not an accident, . . . it is merely the result of a violation of natural laws, . . . which, if strictly observed for two or three generations, would totally remove from any family, however strongly predisposed to insanity or idiocy, all possibility of its recurrence. (1848/1976, p. 34)

In this same paper, Howe provided one of the more lasting classifications of retardation, offering definitions of idiots ("masses of flesh and bone in human shape"), fools ("only the faintest glimmer of reason"), and simpletons ("reason enough for simple individual guidance").

Present Definitions

In the twentieth century, definitions began to be based on one or both of two concepts: (a) statistical distributions, and (b) adaptive behavior. With the development of a formal test by Binet and Simon, psychologists were first able to make extensive numerical estimates of the intellectual abilities of populations, and the facility this development gave to writing definitions of mental retardation was immediately recognized. In 1916, Terman referred to persons scoring less than 80 on the Stanford-Binet as retarded and classified them as borderline, morons, imbeciles, or idiots, depending on their scores. This system was repeated by Wechsler in 1958, and the psychometric approach is still advocated by some (e.g., Clausen, 1967, 1972), who argue that intelligence tests offer the only reliable, predictable way of assessing how well a person is functioning intellectually.

Others have argued that intellectual functioning is not the key to the definition of mental retardation. Instead, they argue, one's ability to adapt to the environment is the central point. Tredgold, for example, felt that some people who scored 90 or 100 on an intelligence test should be labeled retarded, while others scoring below 70 should not be (Sarason, 1949). He offered this definition:

> a state of incomplete mental development of such a kind and degree that the individual is incapable of adapting himself to the normal environment of his fellows in such a way as to maintain existence independently of supervision, control, or external support. (Tredgold, 1937, p. 4)

Doll, working at the Vineland Training Center, where the Vineland Social Maturity Scale was developed, also stressed the social adaptation aspects of retardation and vigorously attacked reliance on intelligence tests:

> It employs an illogical and unvalidated statistical concept without safeguarding the welfare of the individual, his family, or society. . . . It stops short at an *arbitrary* statistical gate-post and does not concern itself with the many ramifications of the conditions which if adequately explored would reveal the absurdity of its point of view. (Doll, 1947, p. 420)

Today, a reliance on adaptive behavior is still stressed by many, and is perhaps supported most definitively by Mercer (1971, 1973a,b), who argues for a sociological model in which a person is considered retarded if he/she fails to meet role expectations that a particular society has developed for him/her. According to this approach, someone with a score of 60 on an intelligence test who is functioning quite well in his/her environment would not be considered retarded, while someone with a score of 75 who is not functioning well could be labeled retarded.

While the advocates of the intelligence test and the social test approaches are often adamant in their opposition to each other, still others have sought to amalgamate the two approaches. Such an effort has been made by the American Association on Mental Deficiency (AAMD), whose definition of mental retardation is certainly the most popular today:

> Mental retardation refers to significantly subaverage general intellectual functioning existing concurrently with deficits in adaptive behavior, and manifested during the developmental period. (Grossman, 1977)

Such a definition relies quite heavily on assessment, and it does so in two areas: (a) tests of intelligence, and (b) tests of adaptive behavior. While tests of the first type have been popular in the United States for more than 60 years, they are currently under considerable criticism and have actually been precluded from use in placement of higher functioning "retarded" children in California (*Larry P.* v. *Riles,* 1972; MacMillan, Meyers, & Morrison, 1980). Tests of the second type have been in use for more than 40 years (e.g., the Vineland Social Maturity Scale); however, the more popular ones today have only recently been developed and are thus receiving expected criticisms while they continue to be revised. Hence, we have the interesting situation in which many professionals can support a definition of mental retardation, but because of test limitations, few can provide accurate predictions of how many people should be labeled retarded.

Incidence and Prevalence

Incidence and prevalence are terms that refer to the number of people in a classification, and they differ in that prevalence uses a more restrictive time base. *Incidence* refers to the number of people who might be classified at any time in their lives. *Prevalence,* on the other hand, refers to the number of people classified during a given time period (e.g., all of 1982). (For instance, if we were interested in traffic violations in a town with 10,000 drivers, we might first find how many of them violated a traffic law during the whole course of their driving history. If we found that 1,000 people had done so at least once, then we would have an incidence of traffic violations of 10%. A second question we could ask is whether the rate of traffic violations has been increasing over the years. To get the answer, we might find how many of these 10,000 people violated at least one traffic law in 1980, in 1981, and in 1982. Then we would have information on three prevalences, for example, 3.1% in 1980, 2.8% in 1981, and 3.9% in 1982.)

When we use these terms to refer to cases of mental retardation, we might first presume that the incidence and prevalence figures would be the same; after all, "once retarded, always retarded." But, regardless of the definition of retardation that we use, we may find this presumption to be untrue. If we were to use a strictly statistical model and utilize only scores on intelligence tests, we would predict that about 2.3%[1] of the population would be labeled retarded. But we know that test–retest scores are not always consistent, particularly when we are discussing a single cutoff point in the definition. Some people will score 65 on a first test and 75 a second time; others will score conversely. Thus the number of people labeled retarded at any time in their lives (incidence) would be considerably greater than the number labeled at any one point in time (prevalence). Such a statistically based classification system has been used by AAMD, which, after labeling a person by virtue of its three-part definition, then classifies that person solely by an intelligence test score.[2] Nevertheless, the incidence of people in any one classification will not be the same as the prevalence.

Other factors also lead to a discrepancy between incidence and prevalence, and the foremost factor is school. Before entering school, children who would score perhaps in the 60–70 range are generally not brought into the social system that provides the label. Only when they enroll in school, and then most often only after they have failed a grade in a normal classroom, do these children enter the system that might lead to their being labeled retarded (Mercer, 1973a). The role that schools play in the labeling process should not be underestimated, as they have often utilized a two-part definition of mental retardation: (1) intelligence test scores, and (2) school achievement. Such a system has been well underscored by Mercer (1971), who gave individual intelligence tests to a large number of children in regular classes who had never been referred to special education classes. Of 1,298 such children, Mercer found 126 who had intelligence test scores that would qualify them

[1]In actuality, there are more cases than would be predicted by the normal curve, the reason being that organicity provides a larger number of people at the lower end of the curve than would be predicted. For the sake of this example, however, we are ignoring this point.

[2]The classification system used by AAMD and the number (n) of standard deviations below the mean on the Stanford-Binet or the Wechsler are mild (2), moderate (3), severe (4), and profound (5).

for Educable Mentally Retarded (EMR) placement. The teachers, however, thought that these students could manage in a regular class (as they had apparently demonstrated), so these children had never been referred for possible testing and labeling. Thus, agencies such as schools have a great deal of influence on the prevalence rate of retardation, and as such, if we were seeking to make an estimate of the number of retarded persons, we should actually estimate the number identified by *agencies* rather than the number identified only by popular intelligence tests. Such considerations have led Mercer (1973b) and Tarjan, Wright, Eyman, and Keeran (1973) to set the prevalence rate at about 1%.

From this example and others (cf. MacMillan, 1977), we see that statistical prediction of the incidence of retardation is far different from the prevalence figures; overriding influences include the expectations and tolerances of the child's social milieu. The expectations and tolerances of schools are reflected in the fact that the retardation label is primarily assigned during the school years (hence, the term *six-hour retardate*). These persons lose their MR status when they leave school either upon graduation, by dropping out, or by being expelled. The expectations of the family must also be considered. Jones (1979) has provided interesting data from this referent, that is, the extent to which the family regards a family member as retarded. Using information from a 1976 survey of 150,000 homes by the U.S. Bureau of the Census (1977), and ignoring persons in institutions (more than 200,000), children under 3 years old, and unrelated persons under 14 years of age living in the households (e.g., foster children), Jones found a prevalence rate of .43%. Acknowledging this to be lower than the 3% and 1% estimates (and about .1% lower than the figure would be if the institutional population were included), Jones's data provide what he calls a "socially real" prevalence rate (i.e., those cases that are recognized by families). Summarizing his data, of those considered to be retarded by other household members, we find: (a) about twice as many males as females, when all ages are considered; (b) about six times as many males as females at 3 and 4 years of age, but about equal numbers at 14–17 years; (c) about half as many preschoolers as school-aged children; and (d) 70% more blacks than whites. These data point to two very strong and consistently found correlations: (a) more cases of retardation at school age, and (b) more cases of retardation in lower socioeconomic areas.

In this section, we have looked at estimates of the numbers of retarded persons. In the next section, we will look more closely at assessment procedures used in labeling the retarded.

Assessment

Assessment is a very important part of the professional field of mental retardation for many reasons, some of which are: (a) to define whether someone meets the AAMD definition of retardation, thus qualifying him/her for special services or funding; (b) to determine a particular syndrome of mental retardation, and, possibly, correlative treatment; and (c) to determine habilitative progress. In this section, we will discuss primarily the first reason; in the next section, we will discuss briefly the second reason, offering some of the ways of identifying genetic types of mental retardation.

Two of the components of the definition of mental retardation are based on assessment, and these are of course intelligence and adaptive behavior. In the first area, we will briefly describe two of the tests, the Stanford-Binet (S-B) and the Wechsler Intelligence Scale for Children—Revised (WISC-R). In the second area, we will describe two tests of adaptive behavior, the AAMD Adaptive Behavior Scale (ABS) and the Balthazar Scales of Adaptive Behavior (BSAB). Then, we will discuss another test combining some aspects of both of these types, the System of Multicultural Pluralistic Assessment (SOMPA).

Intelligence Tests

The primary intelligence tests used in the assessment of mental retardation are the S-B and the WISC-R, the properties of which are well known and discussed widely in the psychology literature. As such, only a few comments will be made about each. The S-B measures memory, perception, information, verbal ability, and logical reasoning. As the test progresses through levels of difficulty, it becomes increasingly verbal and abstract in character. When the child fails six items at one age level, the testing is concluded. The score is then converted to a mental age, which can be multiplied by 100 and then divided by the child's chronological age to provide an IQ score. Because the standard deviation of the S-B is 16, and at least two standard deviations below the mean are required in the AAMD definition, a score of 68 or less is a necessary (but not sufficient) reason for being labeled retarded. The WISC-R, instead of producing one score as the S-B does, produces two, which are then converted to an overall IQ score. These two scores, for Verbal and for Performance IQ, are derived from the scores on each of the subtests, which are Information, Similarities, Arithmetic, Vocabulary, Comprehension, and Digit Span for the Verbal IQ; and Picture Completion, Picture Arrangement, Block Design, Object Assembly, Coding, and Mazes for the Performance IQ. Because the WISC-R has a standard deviation of 15, a score less than 70 on this test is a necessary (but again not sufficient) reason for being labeled retarded.

While these two tests, and intelligence tests in general, have their critics, the critics in the field of mental retardation are at least as vituperative as any. The primary reason is a socially laden one, and therefore, an explosive one: some minorities (e.g., blacks) consistently score lower than the mean. This finding is extremely discomforting to some psychologists who argue that the tests are biased against blacks (e.g., Jackson, 1975, Williams, 1972) and should therefore be changed or abandoned. Others (e.g., Mercer, 1973a) argue that the tests were not developed with ethnic minorities in the standardization sample. Still others (e.g., Jensen, 1969) argue that the tests are reliably reporting a basic genetic difference between blacks and whites, and that typical cultural deprivation found in lower socioeconomic areas has little effect on intelligence. Whereas some take this information to mean that blacks are genetically less intelligent than whites, Kaufman (1980) has offered another interpretation: black children utilize right-hemisphere intelligence in their everyday living, while white children utilize left-hemisphere intelligence. Intelligence tests, however, measure far fewer right-hemisphere skills. Thus, one would expect lower scores from blacks. Because black children do constitute a disproportionate number of persons labeled mentally retarded, the issue is extremely controversial and has resulted in a number of court decisions (particularly in California), with two of the most important being *Diana* v. *State Board of Education* and *Larry P.* v. *Riles*. In *Diana,* an out-of-court settlement resulted in a number of mandates including: (a) testing of minority children only on test sections that do not depend on vocabulary, general information, and other such items; (b) retesting, in their native language, of Chinese-American and Mexican-American children labeled retarded; (c) norms for a new or revised test developed for Mexican-American children; and (d) a written explanation of any disproportionate number of labeled minorities in a district. The irony of this mandate has been discussed by MacMillan (1977), who noted: (a) that the supposedly biased verbal scores on the WISC are no lower than the apparently unbiased performance scores; (b) that the verbal score is still the best predictor of school success; and (c) that children are seldom tested for possible labeling until they have failed a grade. Nevertheless, the social pressures in this area have been immense, and from *Larry P.* came the mandate that mental tests could not be used in EMR placement of black children in California; this ban was then extended to all students (MacMillan *et al.,* 1980). Hence, what seemed at one time to be a theoretically arguable but pedestrianly safe test on which to base a definition of retardation is now under considerable attack, and its continued use will more likely be determined by the courts than by professionals in the field.

Adaptive Behavior

Tests of Adaptive Behavior

Inventories of adaptive behavior are simply reports of a subject's display of adaptive and maladaptive behaviors, and according to Spreat (1980), more than 300 are available. As such, there are a diverse number from which to choose; however, we will limit our discussion to the Adaptive Behavior Scale and the Balthazar Scales of Adaptive Behavior; the ABS has been adopted by AAMD, and the BSAB is one of the more well known alternatives that overcomes the primary weakness of the ABS.

The ABS (Nihira, Foster, Shellhaas, & Leland, 1974) is a two-part rating scale for mentally retarded, emotionally disturbed, and developmentally disabled persons, and is intended to provide an objective description of adaptive and maladaptive behaviors. Part One is organized to represent increasing developmental levels and covers 10 behavior domains and 21 behavior subdomains. The domains are Independent Functioning, Physical Development, Economic Activity, Language Development, Numbers and Time, Domestic Activity, Vocational Activity, Self-direction, Responsibility, and Socialization. Part Two of the ABS is not developmentally arranged, rather, it concentrates on maladaptive behavior related to social expectations placed on individuals by communities and institutions. It is comprised of 13 domains and one condition: Violent and Destructive Behavior, Antisocial Behavior, Rebellious Behavior, Untrustworthy Behavior, Withdrawal, Stereotyped Behavior and Odd Mannerisms, Inappropriate Interpersonal Manners, Unacceptable Vocal Habits, Unacceptable or Eccentric Habits, Self-abusive Behavior, Hyperactive Tendencies, Sexually Aberrant Behavior, Psychological Disturbances, and (the condition) Use of Medications.

The test is administered by an evaluator who directs questions to the person who spends the greatest number of waking hours with the individual. The ABS manual recommends three types of administrations: (a) first-person assessment, where the evaluator knows the individual well enough to personally complete each item of the scale; (b) third-person assessment, where the evaluator seeks responses to each of the items from various persons such as parents, teachers, or attendants; or (c) interview method, where the evaluator interviews someone familiar with the individual. Interestingly, the ABS manual recommends the third-party assessment because it can be completed in 20 to 30 minutes. The manual does point out, however, that data gathered from the interview method are not exactly comparable to data gathered from the other two methods. Answers to the test items are scored and then summarized by domain (there is no single score, as with intelligence tests) for comparison with norms.

The ABS manual contains a number of recommendations for best utilizing the test:

(a) as an evaluative tool to determine whether one's placement in a group is appropriate; (b) to allocate resources to particular groups with different test scores (e.g., if one school's language development score is considerably lower than another school's, language specialists could be assigned to the school with the greater need); (c) to evaluate methods of instruction (e.g., if there is an insufficient gain score when instructed by method *A*, then one could change to method *B*); and (d) to evaluate a particular program by changes between pre- and postscores.

The ABS, however, is not without its critics, some of whom maintain that: (a) it ignores the vastly different severity of the items in the maladaptive section (e.g., "talks too loudly" and "causes fights" carry equal weight in scoring—McDevitt, McDevitt, & Rosen, 1977; Taylor, Warren, & Slocumb, 1979); (b) its profiles are misleading in Part II, with small differences at the midrange of the scale resulting in large decile differences when compared to the normative sample (McDevitt *et al.*, 1977); (c) its two levels of response occurrence ("occasionally" or "frequently") are insufficient, and should have numerical ranges (Spreat & Isett, 1977); and (d) its reliability is quite low (King, Soucar, & Isett, 1980). This last criticism is significant regardless of the reason the ABS is used (i.e., for labeling, programming objectives, or measurement of progress), for if the test–retest scores vary widely, the usefulness of the test is severely impaired. Regardless of this critical problem, the ABS continues to be a widely used scale.

Many of the opponents of the ABS criticize it because of its predominant use of indirect assessment. One of the strongest critics on this point has been Balthazar (1971b), who argues that:

> Information should be provided by directly observing and studying the subject before one formally measures his performance. Accurate measures are *not* obtained by asking others what his eating and dressing behaviors are like. The only exception to this is provided by the interview procedure in the Toileting Scales (although when possible one should observe some of the individual's toilet behaviors before conducting the interview). (Part II, p. 7)

The Balthazar Scales of Adaptive Behavior for the profoundly and severely mentally retarded are organized in two sections. The Scales of Functional Independence (BSAB-I) test the ambulatory student's skills in three areas of independent functioning (Balthazar, 1971a). The *Eating Scales* cover five classes of behavior (Dependent Feeding, Finger Foods, Spoon Usage, Fork Usage, and Drinking), with each of these classes broken into 9 or 13 subclasses. In the subclasses, the behaviors are defined and scored according to how many times the individual emitted the behavior in 10 opportunities. The *Dressing Scales* cover a standard clothing list in eight categories (Shoes, Socks, Briefs, T-shirt/Undershirt, Regular Shirt or Blouse, Pants, Skirt, Dress). These categories are divided into two sections—Putting On and Taking Off—and then the behaviors necessary to complete each are listed. The behaviors are then scored on a seven-point rating scale according to the degree of independence displayed while engaging in the behavior. The *Toileting Scales* cover a number of items involved in toileting and rely on the questionnaire format. In each case, questions are phrased to occasion a numerical answer from 0 to 10 and to follow the general format, "For an average 10 times that *Johnny* . . . , how many of those times did he . . . ?"

The Scales of Social Adaptation (BSAB-II) are similarly constructed and also provide both a means for evaluating adaptive behavior and a means for programming (Balthazar, 1971b). BSAB-II is recommended for representations of the student's present level of functioning—his/her baseline skills. The scale items can then be used either as direct objectives for the student to learn, or they can continue to be used as measures of the student's progress in a training program.

SOMPA

The System of Multicultural Pluralistic Assessment (SOMPA) is an assessment battery based on the idea that American society is pluralistic, both culturally and structurally (Mercer, 1979). It accepts different scores by different ethnic groups, but it does not accept them as differences in intelligence. Rather, these differences are viewed as reflections of the child's culture; intelligence tests are viewed as achievement tests, and nothing more. SOMPA does not attempt to provide a culture-free or a culture-fair test; instead, it uses several normative frameworks so that the child's performance will only be compared with others from a similar sociocultural background.

To meet its objective, SOMPA uses three distinct assessment models, medical, social-system, and pluralistic. The medical model is directed toward organic conditions that interfere with physiological functioning, and the six tests used are Physical Dexterity Tasks, the Bender Visual Motor Gestalt Test, the Health History Inventories, Weight by Height, Visual Acuity, and Auditory Acuity. The social-system model is one in which social deviancy is regarded as a deficit in role performance rather than a deficit in the biological organism. Normal behavior, then, is that which conforms to society's expectations for that role, while deviant behavior is that which does not conform. Two assessment instruments are used in this model: the WISC-R and the Adaptive Behavior Inventory for Children (ABIC). In this social-system model, the standard norms of the WISC-R are used to represent the child's achievement in public school. In the pluralistic model, a regression equation accounting for sociocultural background is used, and the score represents a child's standing relative to his/her own sociocultural peers. The latter procedure is used for three ethnic groups—white, Hispanic, and black—and is done through the Sociocultural Scales, which produces four scores: Family Size, Family Structure, Socioeconomic Status, and Urban Acculturation.

The nine instruments in the SOMPA are administered either through Parent Interview materials or Student Assessment materials. The Parent Interview is administered in a structured interview and consists of the Sociocultural Scales, the ABIC, and the Health History Inventories. The other six measures are administered to the child and consist of the Physical Dexterity Tasks, the Bender, Weight by Height, Visual Acuity, Auditory Acuity, and the WISC-R.

Etiology

Regardless of the definition or assessment of mental retardation, it is generally considered to be a symptom of numerous diseases or conditions, some of which have identifiable etiologies or origins (Masland, 1960). Specific genetic and environmental factors which do or can cause retardation have been identified through research; additional factors which are suspected of influencing retardation are presently under investigation. Yet, even with the identification of these numerous factors, the cause of retardation is unknown in most cases. The exact percentage of retardation cases attributed to unknown etiologies differs according to various sources (e.g., 75% to 94%—Dunn, 1973; 40%—Moser & Wolf, 1971; 50%—

Stern, 1973). But even the lower figures relegate a sizeable percentage of cases to that portion of mental retardation for which the etiology remains a mystery.

Contributing to the difficulties in specifying etiologies for given cases is our tendency to attribute mental retardation to a single cause. Often, mental retardation is a consequence of the combined effects of a variety of factors. Genetic factors may interact with prenatal, perinatal, and/or postnatal environmental factors to produce the retarded development observed in a given person. The more we learn about retardation, the more we have come to view it as a problem of interacting factors.

The problem of determining etiologies in given cases is further compounded by the fact that, for many cases, definite diagnoses can be established only through autopsy. In a study reported by Polo in 1967, autopsies were performed on 123 persons who died in an institution for the mentally retarded. Correct etiological diagnoses had been made in only 24 of those cases, while entirely incorrect diagnoses had been made for 15 persons. Thus, for those cases for which etiologies have been specified, the diagnosis is often incorrect.

In this section, factors that may individually, or in combination with other factors, result in mental retardation are presented. A delineation of genetic factors (i.e., factors that modify development before and at conception) will be followed by a delineation of environmental factors (which modify development following conception).

Genetic Factors

In this section, we will only briefly describe a few of the many genetic factors related to mental retardation. For fuller descriptions, the interested reader should consult introductory texts (e.g., Robinson & Robinson, 1976), special publications on mental retardation syndromes (e.g., Gellis & Feingold, 1965), or books on genetics.

Whereas there are several fields within genetics (e.g., Mendelian genetics, population genetics), many of those in the field of mental retardation accept what has come to be called the behavioral–genetic analysis, which presumes that the number of phenotypes (i.e., observable traits) present in an individual is a function of (a) genotype (i.e., genetic composition), (b) number of environments in which the genotype operates, and (c) number of interactions among the possible genotypes and environments. In this analysis, three of the ways genetic–environmental influences can be categorized are (a) chromosomal aberrations, (b) specific dominant gene abnormalities, and (c) specific recessive gene abnormalities.

Chromosomal Aberrations

The chromosomal aberrations can be classified as those that are sex-linked and those that are not sex-linked. The latter category includes such syndromes as Edward's (Trisomy 18), Patau's (Trisomy 13), and Down's (Trisomy 21), with the latter being the most common and certainly the most well known syndrome in mental retardation. Down's syndrome is caused by the presence of an extra set of genes on the 21st chromosome, which develops in one of three ways: (a) nondisjunction (faulty chromosomal distribution, which occurs prior to conception during cell division (meiosis); (b) mosaicism (faulty chromosomal distribution, which occurs during cell division following conception); and (c) translocation (all or part of one chromosome is attached to all or part of another). The characteristics of a Down's child are quite striking and combine to make him/her quite recognizable; some of these characteristics include: (a) epicanthal folds at the inside corners of the eyes; (b) obliquely slanting eyes; (c) broad bridge of the nose; (d) protruding tongue; (e) open mouth; (f) square-shaped ears; (g) short and broad hands; and (h) congenital heart disease. Trisomy 13 typically results in a small infant, microcephalic, who does not survive the first year (Gellis & Feingold, 1965); only one adult has ever been reported (Robinson & Robinson, 1976). Trisomy 18 has many of the same manifestations, and also results in death generally before the first year.

The sex-linked aberrations include Klinefelter's and Turner's syndrome. Klinefelter's syndrome results from an extra *X* chromosome, usually of the *XXY* form but sometimes of the *XXXXXY* form. While this syndrome does not always result in retardation, when it does, it usually results in mild retardation for the *XXY* males and in more severe retardation for those with a higher number of *X* chromosomes. The syndrome is usually, but not always, associated with increased height and reduced secondary sexual characteristics, and it is apparently associated with higher rates of crime (Nielson, 1970). Turner's syndrome (female) has only 45 chromosomes (*XO*), while Turner's syndrome (male) has 46. Both are associated with absence of secondary sexual characteristics; neither, however, is always associated with mental retardation.

Specific Dominant Genes

Dominant gene disorders are generally rare and are usually inherited first through a gene mutation and then simply by direct transmission through the family. Among the disorders are: (a) Albright's hereditary osteodystrophy, which is caused by a hormone defect resulting in nervous system lesions, and which is associated with a range of intelligence from normal to severe retardation, short stature, and a stocky build; (b) Apert's syndrome, associated with a range of intelligence from normal to severe retardation, wide and lengthened head, bulging eyes, and "mitten hand" or "sock foot"; (c) neurofibromatosis, associated with a range of intelligence from normal to severe retardation, tumors of the brain, spinal cord, kidney, and heart, with the degree of retardation perhaps a function of the extent of the tumors; (d) tuberous sclerosis, associated with intelligence ranging from normal to severe retardation, frequent seizures, and tumors on the face, kidneys, heart, and lungs; and (e) Sturge-Weber, associated with intelligence ranging from normal to severe retardation, deep port-wine-like stains on the face, seizures, and possible hemoplegia.

Specific Recessive Genes

Recessive gene disorders are produced by phenotypically normal parents who produce insufficient amounts of an important enzyme. These disorders can be classified as disorders of carbohydrate metabolism, protein and amino acid metabolism, mucopolysaccharide disorders, and lipid storage disorders.

Carbohydrate Disorders. The most common carbohydrate disorder results in galactosemia, which results from an improper metabolism of the galactose derived from milk sugar. Untreated, the disorder can result in death, but a careful milk-free diet can eliminate the syndrome. The time of syndrome identification is quite important, with delayed identification increasing the probability of retardation.

Protein Disorders. Of the protein and amino acid disorders, phenylketonuria (PKU) is the most well known. It results from a deficiency in the liver enzyme phenylalanine hydroxylase, which normally would convert the amino acid phenylalanine to tryosine. The excess acts like a toxin, with resultant poisoning. Fortunately, dietary control of phenylalanine intake can reverse many of the symptoms such as hyperactivity, temper tantrums, poor motor control, eczema, insufficient pigmentation, and seizures. Unfortunately, if detection (through mandatory hospital tests) is not made soon after birth, the results can be catastrophic, with most of the children unable to talk and many unable to walk or control excretion; in these cases, there is severe retardation (Robinson & Robinson, 1976). Early detection can, however, prevent retardation.

Mucopolysaccharide Disorders. One of the functions of the body is to break down complex carbohydrates; when this does not happen, excessive amounts of mucopolysaccharides are stored. When this disorder occurs, the problem can be severe. Among the syndromes associated with this storage disease are: (a) Hurler's syndrome, characterized by severe retardation, usually by the first year, skeletal deformities, hirsutism, open mouth with large protruding tongue, hearing deficits, and respiratory infection generally causing death; (b) Hunter's syndrome, with less severe retardation than in Hurler's but with destructive and stubborn behavior problems, progressive deafness, short stature, and respiratory infections; and (c) Sanfilippo syndrome, with progressively severe retardation, deafness, and findings generally similar to but not so severe as Hurler's.

Lipid Storage Disorders. Lipid storage disorders involve fatty acids and fats, which are an important constituent of cell structure and serve as a source of fuel. These products are generally easily broken down and stored in the body, but this process sometimes results in abnormal storage resulting in no retardation in some cases (Fabry's disease) and severe retardation in other cases (Tay-Sachs disease). The latter syndrome is particularly dangerous in its most severe form, resulting in blindness, progressive motor deterioration, considerable weakness, and death by the third or fourth year. The syndrome is interesting in that it occurs with a ten-fold higher frequency among Ashkenazic Jews (Robinson & Robinson, 1976).

Environmental Factors

While genetic factors certainly influence the incidence of mental retardation, environmental factors are no less insidious. Those that influence the mental and/or physical development of a child can be classified as: (a) those that occur before birth (prenatal factors); (b) those that occur during birth (perinatal factors); and (c) those that occur following birth (postnatal factors). If the information developed through research on these factors were made readily available to the general public (perhaps through the public system of education), occurrences of mental retardation could be substantially reduced. But, even the better educated segment of our society is, for the most part, unaware of the effects of many of these factors. Hopefully, the time will soon come when more of us are aware of potential hazards posed by various environmental factors.

Prenatal Factors

MacMillan (1977) reported that according to a report issued by the National Foundation/March of Dimes in 1975, mental retardation of prenatal origin is the most common of all birth defects, affecting an estimated 1,170,000 persons in the United States under the age of 20 in 1974. The size of this figure is not surprising when one understands that many of these adverse effects occur between the time of conception and an awareness of pregnancy. The first 8 weeks of development are of vital importance.

Following conception, the growth process begins and proceeds at a rapid pace. In the first two weeks, cells divide and tissue differentiates with considerable speed. By the end of the embryonic period (i.e., the 8th week) the beginnings of all the main body organs and systems have been established. Exposure of the embryo to certain agents during this critical period of development may cause major malformations as well as mental retardation. While the formation of some organs extends beyond the embryonic period, the first 8 weeks form the time period when developmental vulnerability is at its peak.

The concept of developmental vulnerability has been derived from research in embryology. Vulnerability refers to how susceptible the organism is to being injured or altered by a traumatic incident (Chinn, Drew, & Logan, 1979). Traumatic incidents include such factors as maternal infections, toxic agents, undernourishment, and other deviations from normal sequences of developmental events. For each organ or system of the body, there is a specific time frame when that organ or system is the primary part being formed. An organ or system is most vulnerable to trauma during this time frame, and when a trauma occurs, the organs or systems primarily being formed are those most likely to be affected. According to Moore (1974), some of these critical periods are: central nervous system—weeks 3 through 5¼; arms—weeks 3½ through 7; eyes—weeks 3½ through 7½; legs—weeks 3½ through 7; ears—weeks 3¼ through 10; teeth—weeks 5¾ through 8; palate—weeks 5¾ through 9; genitalia—weeks 6¼ through 11. Most major problems result from defective formation of the neural tube during the 3rd and 4th weeks. Cell destruction in the central nervous system often produces an irreparable handicap, particularly if it occurs early in development (Robinson & Robinson, 1976).

Thus we see that a child is most vulnerable to prenatal factors during the first 2 months of development, when the mother may be unaware of its existence. In general, a child is far less vulnerable to debilitating factors during the fetal period, which extends from the beginning of the 9th week to birth. Regardless of the time period, however, prenatal factors can have considerable influence on the development of the fetus. Some of those that may have an effect are low birth weight, diabetes, maternal infections, drugs, and radiation.

Low Birth Weight. Although birth weight is not evident until birth, it is obviously determined by fetal weight gains that occur throughout pregnancy. The relationship between low birth weight and increased risk of impaired mental functioning has been well established (Drillien, 1967). This low-weight category includes low-weight, full-term children as well as low-weight, preterm children, and the effects can be considerable. For example, Rubin, Rosenblatt, and Balow (1973) found that low-birth-weight children scored lower than normal-birth-weight children on all measures of mental development, school readiness, language development, and academic achievement through the 7 years of age in which they were tested. Infants who are born with low birth weights (i.e., under 5½ pounds) are labeled "infants at risk" because low weight is the major correlate of neurological, psychological, and educational impairment (Chinn *et al.*, 1979). These infants "at risk" are also more susceptible than normals to stress after birth such as respiratory and cardiac failure and infections.

Some of the factors that cause low birth weight include malnutrition, smoking, alcohol, multiple births, maternal age, maternal parity, maternal weight gain, and maternal stress.

MALNUTRITION. Nutritional factors immediately related to a pregnancy and the antecedent reproductive years have the greatest influence on fetal growth (Naeye, Blanc, & Paul, 1973). Wigglesworth (1969) showed a correlation between the child's retarded brain development and maternal and fetal malnutrition. As malnutrition in the mother is passed on to the child, fewer brain cells than normal are developed in the child's growth process. Maternal malnutrition often creates a life-long syndrome, with poor general eating habits failing to provide important nutrients. Malnutrition is vitally significant during pregnancy, when the fetus is dependent on the mother for essential nutrients required for normal development. Faulty food habits are not restricted to mothers in low socioeconomic groups. Many persons who have access to whatever foods they want are malnourished through poor dietary habits.

Persons conducting research and/or writing on this topic do not agree about all aspects of the effects of malnutrition. While Naeye *et al.* (1973) and MacMillan (1977) stress the importance of proper diets, Moore (1974) and Robinson and Robinson (1976) write that malnutrition must be quite severe to influence mental development. Robinson and Robinson state that levels of malnutrition likely to be encountered in the world's more developed nations play a minor role in producing defects of the central nervous system and consequently mental retardation. Inconsistency is also encountered concerning the part of the prenatal period in which malnutrition most adversely affects the child. Winick (1970) has reported that malnutrition during the early prenatal period retards growth and organ size irreversibly, while malnutrition in later stages may sometimes be corrected. Naeye *et al.* (1973), on the other hand, report that maternal undernutrition before the third trimester has little or no influence on fetal body, organ, or cellular growth, while such effects are pronounced in later gestation.

Placental defects can also affect the nutritional status of a fetus. The placenta normally functions as a fetal organ and transmits nutrients to the fetus through fetal and maternal blood streams. When placental defects occur, the total surface area available for this exchange of nutrients is reduced. Regardless of any inconsistencies involved relevant to malnutrition, or, more appropriately, because of them, a mother's diet should be carefully examined and structured to provide essential nutrients throughout all stages of pregnancy.

SMOKING. Although at this time smoking has not been directly related to mental retardation, it has been directly related to low-birth-weight children. The fetal growth rate during the last 6–8 weeks of pregnancy is less for those whose mothers smoke than for those whose mothers do not smoke. Korones (1976) reported that mothers who smoke more than 20 cigarettes per day gave birth to growth-retarded children two to three times as often as nonsmoking mothers.

ALCOHOL. Pregnant, chronic alcoholics transmit some of the physical problems of their disease to their unborn children. The fetus may be born alcoholic and go through accompanying symptoms. In addition, approximately 44% of the infants born to alcoholic mothers have IQs of 80 or less (Jones, Smith, Streissguth, & Myrianthopoulos, 1974). A similar percentage of infants may be born with physical deformities. Among these children, a malformation syndrome has been identified (Jones, Smith, Ulleland, & Streissguth, 1973), which is characterized by retarded intrauterine and postnatal physical and mental development, short eye slits, microcephaly, and various limb and cardiac malformations. Corrigan (1976) has identified this fetal alcohol syndrome as the third leading recognizable cause of mental retardation in Seattle, Washington, where the syndrome was first identified. In a personal communication from Jones to Umbreit and Ostrow (1980) in 1977, Jones reported a study showing that mothers who drank one ounce of alcohol per day in their third trimester gave birth to infants weighing 150 grams less than infants of controls who did not drink. The effects also seem to be related to size, as reported by Umbreit and Ostrow (1980), who found that size deficiency is even more pronounced with regard to length of the infant than with regard to weight. The effects of alcohol on retardation are clouded by the fact that alcoholics rarely eat well and are thus undernourished, causing difficulty in isolating the effects of alcohol.

OTHER FACTORS. Additional factors that may influence low birth weight include maternal age, maternal parity, multiple births, maternal weight gain, and maternal stress during pregnancy. Mothers who are either very young or over 40 tend to give birth to premature infants who thus have low birth weights. Infants of mothers 16 years of age or less show a high incidence of developmental problems (Osofsky, 1968). Russell and Miller (1969) found significant IQ differences among offspring of mothers aged 40 or more. Maternal parity, which refers to the number of children to whom a mother has given birth, may operate in isolation or may compound the age factor in affecting birth weight. In addition to their findings relevant to older mothers, Russell and Miller also found IQ discrepancies between the children of mothers with fewer children and the children of mothers with numerous children. In addition, infants with numerous older siblings usually have lower birth weights than those siblings. Multiple births (e.g., twins or triplets) also involve risk because low birth weight often results for one or more of the infants involved (Moore, 1974). An analysis of identical twins showed the smaller of the pair to be physically and intellectually inferior (Babson & Phillips, 1973).

Another important factor relevant to infant birth weight is maternal weight gain during pregnancy. For optimal outcome, a prospective mother should gain between 24 and 27 pounds (Naeye *et al.,* 1973) or between 24 and 31 pounds (Weiss & Jackson, 1969). Not long ago, obstetricians urged women to carefully control their weight and counseled against weight gains of this amount. But Weiss and Jackson found this range of weight gain to be associated with the lowest rates of low-birth-weight infants.

A final factor that has been associated with low birth weights is prenatal stress. With nonhuman subjects, Herrenbohl (1979) and Sontag (1960) found maternal stress to be associated with low birth weight and permanent abnormal structural and/or functional development of offspring. Mitchell (1974) reported that continuing stress experienced by the mother during pregnancy resulted in lower birth weights. Researchers emphasize that only severe, continuing stress has been associated with abnormal development. No significant effects of transitory stress have been determined.

Diabetes. Whereas infants of diabetic mothers do not suffer from low birth weights, they are "at high risk" and usually exhibit excessively high birth weights. Insulin is regarded as a primary growth-regulating hormone for the fetus. Normally, no significant quantities of maternal insulin reach the fetus. Children of diabetic mothers have higher birth weights because recurring incidents of excess sugar levels in the blood stimulate hypersecretion of fetal insulin (Moore, 1974). These children run a great risk of being spontaneously aborted or dying during the birth process. Those that survive risk neurological and intellectual deficits, which are more frequent for offspring of diabetic mothers, plus respiratory problems, physical malformations, and of course diabetes itself.

Maternal Infections. In addition to low birth weight, maternal infections that occur during the prenatal period may act to cause mental retardation. An infection is a condition or disorder caused by microorganisms such as viruses or bacteria (Ingalls, 1978). Occasionally, a microorganism will attack the central nervous system, causing mental retardation. The central nervous system is at its point of highest vulnerability during weeks 3 through 5 of the embryonic period, and it is during this time that infections are most likely to cause retardation. Some infections cause only slight symptoms in the mother but profoundly affect the fetus. Infections that have been related to fetal retardation include rubella, syphilis, cytomegalic inclusion disease, toxoplasmosis, and toxemia; Rh sensitization is an associated factor.

RUBELLA. As long ago as 1914, an Australian opthamologist demonstrated the relationship between birth defects and maternal rubella (Gearheart & Litton, 1979). Rubella is a mild form of measles that can produce profound effects on the fetus. About 15% to 25% of the infants born to mothers who had rubella during their first trimester are born with malformations. To protect against this, women can develop immunity to rubella prior to conception in one of two ways: (1) by contracting the disease at an early age thus stimulating antibody production; or (2) by artificial immunization with the rubella virus, which also stimulates the production of antibodies. The importance of women developing this immunity is demonstrated by Cooper and Krugman (1966), who reported that approximately half of the infants whose mothers had not developed immunity and who contracted rubella during the first trimester of pregnancy were infected. Symptoms manifested by these infants may include deafness (the most frequent symptom), heart disease, mental retardation, blindness or lesser eye problems, and increased or decreased amounts of fluid within the skull. MacMillan (1977) reports that some states now have laws that require blood tests to determine immunity levels to rubella before a marriage license is issued. Women who show low immunity levels can then be immunized to increase their number of antibodies.

SYPHILIS. This venereal disease can be detected through blood tests that are required in most states prior to issuance of a marriage license. Of course, one can contract the disease following the blood test and prior to conception. Maternal syphilis often results in mental retardation; other symptoms include heart defects, deafness, kidney disease, bone deformities, spontaneous abortion, and stillbirth. Damage caused by the syphilis bacterium primarily occurs after the 4th month of pregnancy, so a woman who becomes aware of a syphilis infection early in pregnancy can seek treatment and possibly prevent damage to the fetus.

Although identification and treatment of syphilis have greatly improved, MacMillan (1977) cites a 1970 United States Public Health Service report that relates a 22% increase in reported cases of congenital syphilis. Carter (1975), however, suggests that this disease has decreased as a causative factor in mental retardation in the United States.

CYTOMEGALIC INCLUSION DISEASE. This disease is a viral infection of the salivary glands of the mother that is transmitted to the fetus. The cytomegalovirus infection is thought to be the most common known viral cause of mental retardation (Elek & Stern, 1974). Of pregnant women afflicted with this disease, 50% of the infants show fetal infection. Children born with this disease may evidence mental retardation, damage to the central nervous system, blindness, deafness, microcephaly, hydrocephaly, seizures, and blood abnormalities.

TOXOPLASMOSIS. Toxoplasmosis is an infection caused by a protozoan parasite that enters the mother's body through raw meat or contact with cat feces. The parasite then invades the fetus through the placenta. Symptoms in the mother may be no more serious than a common cold, but 85% of the infants who survive prenatal toxoplasmosis are mentally retarded (Robinson & Robinson, 1976). Characteristics of this infection include mental retardation, hydrocephaly, microcephaly, seizures, eye problems, and sudden rises in body temperature. To avoid this infection, women who are pregnant should (a) stay away from items or areas that may come in contact with cat feces, and (b) cook meat thoroughly.

TOXEMIA. The cause of toxemia is unknown in most cases. Mothers exhibit swelling, edema (i.e., an excess accumulation of body fluids), and high blood pressure, and the prevalence of mental retardation is higher for infants whose mothers suffer from toxemia during pregnancy.

RH SENSITIZATION. Rh factors are substances that occur in the red blood cells of the majority of people; these people are called "Rh positive," as opposed to "Rh negative." Rh factors enable us to detect what is normal for the body and what is an invader (Hutt & Gibby, 1976), and the body forms antibodies to combat invaders. When a mother with Rh negative blood carries a fetus with Rh positive blood, she develops antibodies to fight the "alien" Rh substance. Additional pregnancies increase her antibody level until the antibodies attack the blood of the latest fetus. This Rh incompatibility can have a direct effect on the neurological capacity of the fetus. In addition, the mother's destruction of the fetal Rh-positive red blood cells causes potentially fatal anemia as well as high bilirubin in the blood, which may reach toxic concentrations that produce brain damage. Rh sensitization was first treated by fetal blood transfusions prior to or at birth (depending on whether this was the first or second child). But now Rh-negative mothers who give birth to Rh-positive babies are immunized at birth by destruction of the Rh-positive blood cells before antibodies are produced.

Drugs. Drugs join birth weight and maternal infection as causes of retarded development. Most drugs freely cross the placenta to the fetus. Maternal use of hard drugs such as heroin can cause fetal drug addiction, but there are conflicting views about the effects of lesser drugs such as LSD and marijuana on embryonic development. There are some reports of limb malformation and central nervous system abnormalities from LSD and from marijuana (Moore, 1974). MacMillan (1977), however, has said that drugs such as LSD and tranquilizers are considered to be relatively safe if intake has been moderate. The most dramatic demonstration of the effects of a drug on fetal development was that evidenced by Thalidomide babies. Thalidomide was a mild tranquilizer and sedative prescribed for pregnant women, until authorities realized that about 20% of the infants born to these women had developed abnormal limbs and other body parts. An estimated 7,000 children were malformed by this drug (Moore, 1974).

The majority of women use drugs of some type. Apgar (1965) estimated that 92% of mothers use at least one drug during pregnancy, and 4% use 10 or more drugs such as aspirin, antihistamines, and tranquilizers as well as hard drugs and marijuana. Laboratory research on animals has specified over 600 drugs known to produce abnormalities. Because of the problems inherent in conducting this kind of research, less than 20 drugs have been reliably identified as causing defects in humans. Many researchers agree that, because of the uncertainty of most drug factors and the extensive list of suspected harmful drugs, *all* drugs should be avoided during pregnancy, if possible.

Radiation. The final prenatal factor to be discussed in this chapter is radiation. Excessive exposure of a pregnant woman to radiation in the first 2 months of pregnancy often results in miscarriage. If the fetus survives, mental retardation, abnormal growth of organs, and/or cancer may be manifested. Although low-level doses of radiation, such as those experienced in dental x-rays, have not been proven harmful, care is taken to protect women just in case. Most dentists cover the stomach of women patients with an apron to deflect the x-rays.

To prevent radiation damage, a bill regulating radiation equipment was passed at the federal level in 1968. Although this legislation was not implemented to any extent until 1974—and even then only newly purchased equipment was monitored—steps are being taken to reduce and, one hopes, eliminate the adverse effects of radiation.

Because infants who have developmental deficiencies from environmental factors contracted in the prenatal period are more likely to have problems during the birth process, the effects of perinatal factors are difficult to judge in isolation. The process of moving through the birth canal is one fraught with potential problems, though most deliveries are successful with no adverse effects on the infant. Among the potential hazards that may occur as part of the birth process are anoxia, mechanical injury, prematurity, and infection.

Anoxia. Anoxia, also referred to as asphyxia or hypoxia, is a condition in which inadequate amounts of oxygen reach the body tissues. If the infant is deprived of adequate oxygen for a long enough time period, damage to the central nervous system may occur; however, we do not know specifically what duration of anoxia will result in damage to the central nervous system. Infants may become unconscious or even die from deficient oxygen, and Behrman (1973) found anoxia to be the major cause of infant death for those infants born with normal birth weights. For those infants who suffer anoxia but who survive, mental impairment may result. Although anoxia infants are not all retarded, Graham and his colleagues (Graham, Ernhart, Craft, & Berman, 1963) reported significantly poorer performance on all their measures of cognitive and perceptual functioning for anoxia subjects.

Anoxia may result as a consequence of the fetus entering the birth canal in an abnormal position. Infants are dependent on the umbilical cord for oxygen. In cases of breech birth, in which the infant comes through the birth canal buttocks-first instead of head-first, the umbilical cord may either wrap around the infant's body or become detached, thus decreasing or curtailing the supply of oxygen. Excessively long labors (i.e., 24 hours or longer) may also result in oxygen deprivation. Other causes of anoxia include toxemia, placental separation, drugs (including sedatives, pain killers, and anesthesia), and maternal hemorrhaging.

Mechanical Injury. The dangers of mechanical injury are low if the infant goes through the birth canal head first. If the fetus proceeds through the birth canal in a breech or other abnormal position, the instruments and/or techniques used in delivery may cause physical trauma, which in turn may cause brain damage. In situations of incorrect positioning, doctors are increasingly using Cesarean section in which the fetus is removed from the mother's stomach, thus avoiding passage through the birth canal.

Prematurity. Premature infants are those who either are delivered prior to full term (i.e., less than 37 weeks) or weigh less than 5½ pounds. The hazards of low birth weight have already been stressed. These infants may exhibit normal development prior to early delivery, retarded development prior to early delivery, or retarded development prior to normal delivery. Research rarely discriminates among these groups and usually uses birth weight as the sole criterion for prematurity.

Premature infants are considered "at risk" because they have higher mortality rates and are more susceptible to central nervous system damage. With improved technology, many infants who would previously have perished are now kept alive. Prematurity has been correlated with low socioeconomic class, as mothers from this class tend to have infants with lower birth weights than mothers of higher classes (Drillien, 1967). Prematurity is also more prevalent in infants of black native-born mothers than in infants of white native-born mothers.

Infection. The herpes viral infection produces only mild symptoms in the mother such as fever blisters, cold sores, and vaginal inflammation. However, this virus, if transmitted to the fetus, has profound effects on development. Although the herpes virus can be transmitted to the fetus through the placenta, the more common method of fetal contact occurs through vaginal delivery. For mothers infected with herpes virus, 40% to 60% of infants who proceed through vaginal delivery are infected with the virus (Sells & Bennett, 1977). This infection carries to the brain and results in mental retardation. Cesarean section can be utilized to avoid placing the fetus in contact with the virus that has spread to the vaginal tract.

Another infection that can be contracted during labor and delivery and that may cause depressed mental functioning is bacterial meningitis. While the mortality rate for infants infected with this disease is high, those who survive often manifest retardation, among other problems.

Postnatal Factors

The period following birth is often one of anxiety for parents as they observe their offspring for signs of normal or abnormal functioning. Retardation due to prenatal and perinatal factors that is not evident at birth may become evident now. There are additional hazards that can occur in this period and cause retardation in those infants who survived previous phases. Some of these factors are the same as those that affect the fetus prior to or during birth. In most cases, the effects of a given factor are greater the earlier in the life of the embryo-fetus-child the factor occurs. Those postnatal factors that most commonly produce mental retardation include malnutrition, infection, poisons, and injury.

Malnutrition. While Robinson and Robinson (1976) write that the level of nutritional deprivation likely in the world's developed nations is not severe enough to produce irreversible central nervous system damage and consequent mental retardation, specific dietary deficiencies have been linked with specific retardation syndromes or neurological consequences. MacMillan (1977) lists the following examples:

1. Iodine deficiency can cause cretinism.
2. Protein deficiency can limit brain growth and result in the kwashiorkor syndrome.
3. Vitamin A deficiency may cause intracranial pressure.
4. Vitamin B_6 deficiency can cause seizures.
5. Vitamin B_{12} deficiency can result in mental retardation.
6. Vitamin D deficiency can cause convulsions.

While these deficiencies must be severe to result in the listed consequences, perhaps moderate deficiencies result in less observable neurological consequences. Balanced diets with all the needed nutrients are obviously desirable for normal development.

Infection. Diseases such as meningitis, roseola, and encephalitis may cause infection in the central nervous system and result in mental retardation. Encephalitis involves inflammation of the brain and may occur as a complication of common childhood diseases such as measles, chicken pox, and mumps. Contraction of rabies can also result in brain damage.

Poisons. Lead and mercury poisoning are two of the most common causes of brain damage. Although lead-based paints are no longer supposed to be produced, many children dwell in housing that still contains leaded paint. Because this paint is old, it tends to peel and flake, thus facilitating ingestion of the paint by children. Other sources of lead poisoning include some coatings on toothpaste tubes, some brands of paint on pencils, and some lead-based inks used in magazines (Lin-Fu, 1973). Automobile exhaust contributes almost all of the lead in the air (Chow & Earl, 1970). Fortunately, cars now manufactured in the United States are required to use lead-free gas.

The incidence of mercury poisoning increased with the dumping of mercury-laden wastes into rivers and lakes. The contaminated wastes are eaten by fish, which are then caught and eventually eaten by humans. Mercury poisoning often results in physical abnormalities as well as retardation. Those whose occupations bring them into contact with mercury in the air often suffer devastating consequences. Companies that have exposed persons to hazardous working conditions and/or have dumped mercury-tainted wastes that endangered the public are under scrutiny, and the government is attempting to control contamination.

Injury. Severe head injuries can result in damage to the central nervous system. The two most common causes of head injury are child abuse and automobile accidents, both of which are obviously preventable. Anoxia can also occur following birth and, depending on the severity and length of deprivation, may result in retardation. Hutt and Gibby (1976) reported a situation in which a young child suffered brain damage because the family cat climbed into the infant's crib and slept across his face, thus restricting oxygen intake.

Other Environmental Factors

There are many other postnatal environmental factors that may cause retarded development, and many of these are educational in nature. Some of these aspects have been discussed in the context of Bijou's (1966) interpretation of mental retardation. Examples of these factors include: (a) lack of reinforcement for appropriate behavior, including language development; (b) punishment of developing appropriate behavior; (c) inadequate modeling of appropriate behavior; (d) shaping of abnormal behavior such as hostility, aggression, and self-abuse; and (e) lack of materials in the home to promote learning. While these factors are extremely important, their number seems almost endless, and they are not within the scope of this chapter.

Discussion of retardation definitions, numbers, assessment, and etiologies is informative, but the reader may digest this information without forming a picture of a retarded person as an individual with his or her own personality. Interacting with retarded persons offers the best education. Following are some case studies that offer a glimpse into the lives of different children.

Case Studies

Jane spends most of the day crawling around a mat or looking between the bars of the wooden gate that restricts her to the mat area. Jane is white, 14, and weighs 58 pounds. She was born with Leprechanism. Her parents were shocked and resentful that this had happened to them. Her father is a history professor and her mother runs a travel agency. Her mother stayed home with her the first year and lost 20 pounds. She often states that losing weight was the only good thing that happened to her that year. The following year, Jane's parents hired a daytime sitter to stay with her. They argued a lot that year and discussed a divorce. Instead of getting a divorce, they placed Jane in a private home for the multihandicapped.

Jane does not walk or speak. She wears arm restraints because she hits herself on the head 80% of the time she is out of restraints. Jane learned that whenever she self-abused, she got a lot of attention from staff. Some would hold and rock her. She also learned that whenever she was told or requested to do something, if she self-abused, she escaped having to comply. While Jane now wears restraints 24 hours a day, she is still often able to hit her head because the restraints do not fit very well and she can, over time, maneuver them to allow hitting. Different programs have been attempted to decrease her self-abuse, but none of the programs have been successful due to inadequate staffing, ineffective reinforcers, or lack of commitment.

In addition to self-abuse behavior, Jane makes a whining sound much of the time. If a staff member comes into her area, Jane crawls to him and clings to his legs. If she is picked up, she wraps around the staff person and clings. When the person attempts to leave her, Jane whines and cries and attempts to self-abuse. Consequently, Jane has little interaction with others except when she is fed, bathed, dressed in the morning, and undressed and bedded at night.

Jane's parents used to visit her twice a month and take her home for holidays. Now they visit several times a year and no longer take her home for holidays, stating that they are sure she is happier with her friends.

David is an attractive, black, 11-year-old of normal appearance who is ambulatory but nonverbal. He functioned at a normal level for 9 months, at which time he drank a considerable amount of cleaning fluid, which his mother had left on the kitchen table. This resulted in damage to the central nervous system. David's family kept him at home for several years following his accident but institutionalized him at the age of 4. Because both parents have to work for the family to survive, ensuring that David always had someone with him was difficult. In addition, he had developed some bizarre behaviors with which they could not cope. The most severe of these behaviors involved a sudden thrusting of the heel of his palm into his mouth while harshly biting into the skin.

David is fortunate in that the institution in which he is housed is one of the better state institutions in the country. He lives in a cottage in which 60 other clients live. Their programming is under the supervision of a unit director who personally controls all staff who work with his clients. David's unit has 5 special education teachers, 2 music teachers, an occupational therapist, a physical therapist, a physical education teacher, a nurse, 2 social workers, a language teacher, and 45 paraprofessional staff. He is in programmed instruction or activities from 9:00 A.M. to 11:45 A.M., 1:00 P.M. to 4:00 P.M., and 6:30 P.M. to 8:30 P.M.

About 2 months ago, a new program was implemented to decrease David's biting behavior. The program is a form of overcorrection and involved guiding David to brush his teeth and gums with listerine for 5 minutes immediately following each episode of biting. He was also rewarded for periods of no biting. His behavior began to decrease within days, and within 2 weeks the behavior was occurring only occasionally. David has not had any biting episodes for the last 3 weeks. His unit director and social worker have begun working with his parents on how to maintain the elimination of biting behavior. If the behavior change maintains and the program can be successfully generalized to his home environment, his parents are anxious to have him rejoin his family. David does not realize that he may soon be going home permanently, but he always looks forward to visiting home and obviously loves his parents.

Mike finds himself going from one activity to another on Sunday nights. He often fights with his mother and brother and sisters, and has trouble sleeping. Monday morning he will be back in school. Mike has always had trouble in school, falling farther and farther behind with each day. Now he is 13 years old and in the sixth grade. Outside of school, Mike can hold his own. He swings a bat pretty well, runs fast, has a girl friend, sings all the popular songs, and dances better than most of his friends. But, in school, he has difficulty. He has trouble reading the books he is given and consequently cannot answer many questions based on their content. He also cannot do the math problems the rest of the class completes. Sometimes he is given work different from that of the others, but then they tease him for doing "sissy" work. The only part of the day to which Mike looks forward is the hour he spends in the resource room with only two other students. He was previously bothered by taunts of some of his classmates about going to the room for "dummies" and "retards," but now he looks forward to the hour away from anxieties of the regular classroom.

In the resource room, Mike is reading a story about baseball in which he knows most of the words. He is learning to measure using rulers and measuring cups and spoons, doing multiplication facts, and working on his printing. He earns points for doing well in class, but he would try just as hard even if he didn't get points. There is nothing much for which to trade the points, anyway.

Back in the regular classroom, Mike daydreams, sleeps, and draws. He has learned that his teacher does not care that he does not pay attention or respond like the rest of the kids. As long as he does not cause trouble, he is not bothered. Last year, he was in trouble all the time. He fought with some of his classmates and often did not do what his teacher told him to do. The teacher gave him special worksheets, but most of the time he did not have the skills to complete them. So he ignored the work, and when the teacher asked him for it, he would scribble all over the paper and crumple it up or hand it to her uncompleted. He was yelled at a lot and laughed at by the other kids. That is when he would say mean things or punch another kid. This year is better. At least his teacher lets him alone. But he is never happy in his classroom. He wishes he could do the same work as the others, and he cannot refrain from thinking of all the other things he could be doing during the time he sits in class doing nothing.

Steve is labeled mildly retarded and has been placed in a self-contained classroom for the retarded. Steve is a Mexican-American whose parents are migrant workers, so he has moved numerous times. His mother went back to work shortly after he was born and an older sister took care of him. His sister wanted him to be quiet and nondemanding, and she yelled at him for most behaviors other than sitting quietly. When his parents came home from work, they were tired and wanted to be left alone. He was again urged to keep quiet and out of trouble. The family's living quarters were always sparsely furnished and Steve had only a few toys, of which he had tired long ago.

When Steve was enrolled in school, his language was very low-level for his age. In addition, he did not possess the academic readiness skills that his peers exhibited. Steve was referred for evaluation and, after being given a battery of standardized tests, he was labeled as retarded and placed in a classroom for the retarded.

When Steve first went to school, he was very withdrawn and seldom interacted with anyone. Through systematic reinforcement, his teacher shaped cooperative-play behaviors and increased social responses. Steve has had the same teacher for two years. He and his mother did not travel with his father this year. This teacher feels that Steve is merely culturally retarded, and while working with her, he has made tremendous progress. She plans to mainstream Steve for half a day next year and then full time the following year. She will be extremely saddened when Steve stops coming to school one day and she learns that his family has again moved.

Pam and Lou help their father weed the garden in the summers and rake leaves in the fall. They are responsible for making their beds each morning, cleaning their rooms once a week, feeding the dog, and setting the table for dinner. Where the rest of the family go (i.e., their parents and their brother, Bob), they also go—to a restaurant for pizza once a week, to California for two weeks, on regular trips to the library, to watch Bob's basketball games. Pam and Lou are 16 and 21 years old, respectively, and they were born with Down's syndrome. Their IQs are in the high 40s. Their brother Bob is 14 and a freshman in high school, where his grades range from C to A and average a B.

After school, Bob and his friends shoot baskets at a hoop attached to the garage door. Pam and Lou are occasionally given a turn, though they seem happy just to be among the group. Most of the talk is not directed to them, but their comments are responded to courteously and pleasantly. When Bob and his friends leave on their bicycles, Pam and Lou stand looking after them, throw the basketball at the hoop a few times, and begin arguing. Their mother watches them through the kitchen window. After yelling that Lou is "retarded," Pam goes off and plays in the backyard. The mother watches Lou, again worrying about what will happen to him next year when he will be too old for the workshop. There are presently no services provided for adult, moderately retarded persons in their community.

Each morning, Lou and Pam board a small school bus that stops at their house. Lou is taken to the sheltered workshop where he works on contracts secured by the workshop staff. Today, he cuts long plastic straws, at places marked with a red line, into five parts. The parts are then put into a cup and, when all the cups in a box are filled, his trainer removes that box and presents another box with empty cups. Lou was mad at his trainer earlier today because she did not tell him that he did a good job yesterday, yet he had heard her tell both Bill and Carey that they had done good jobs, and he had watched and listened to them talk to each other much of the day. But he has since been told that he is doing well today, so he is happy. Today is Friday so he will be paid for this week's work. Tomorrow his father will take him to the bank to deposit most of his money, and on the way home he will buy his father and himself an ice-cream cone with the spending money he keeps out of his check.

While Lou is at workshop, Pam is at school where she is part of a self-contained classroom for 10 moderately retarded students. Today the class works on writing their telephone numbers, making peanut-butter sandwiches, matching clothing, counting by 5s, and reading price tags. Pam likes school except for Charlotte, who sits in front of her and rocks and makes noise all day.

Pam calls to Lou as he boards the bus that will take them home. Their mother is watching for them as their bus stops at the house. She asks questions about their day, but they are more interested in watching *Spiderman* on TV. Soon Bob will be home, and maybe he will spend time with them before he goes off with his friends.

Conclusion

The pathology of mental retardation includes persons who show a wide variety of behavioral characteristics and etiologies. While public misconceptions about the meaning of retardation persist, professionals in the field continue to disagree about definitions and the benefits of various educational placements.

In spite of these areas of inconsistency, the last decade has been one of tremendous growth for this population. The right to a free public education has been established for retarded children. Programs have been initiated to educate segments of society to increase acceptance of the retarded. The trend of deinstitutionalization has been established to move institutionalized persons into group homes or residential settings. Behavioral research has yielded techniques for teaching undeveloped behaviors and decreasing or eliminating inappropriate behavior. Embryology and genetic research has produced vast amounts of information on causes of retardation, many of which can now be prevented.

One hopes that the next decade will be a time of public education, and that society will come to see retarded persons as individuals, each with his or her own needs, much as everyone else.

References

Apgar, V. Drugs in pregnancy. *American Journal of Nursing,* 1965, *65,* 103–105.

Babson, S. G., & Phillips, D. S. Growth and development of twins dissimilar in size at birth. *New England Journal of Medicine,* 1973, *289,* 937–948.

Balthazar, E. E. *The Balthazar scales of adaptive behavior, Section I: The scales of functional independence.* Champaign, Ill.: Research Press, 1971(a).

Balthazar, E. E. *The Balthazar scales of adaptive behavior, Section II: The scales of social adaptation.* Champaign, Ill.: Research Press, 1971(b).

Behrman, R. (Ed.). *Neonatology: Diseases of the fetus and infant.* St. Louis: Mosby, 1973.

Bijou, S. W. A functional analysis of retarded development. In M. R. Ellis (Ed.), *International review of research in mental retardation* (Vol. 1). New York: Academic Press, 1966.

Carter, C. H. *Handbook of mental retardation syndromes* (3rd ed.). Springfield, Ill.: Charles C Thomas, 1975.

Chinn, P. C., Drew, C. J., & Logan, D. R. *Mental retardation—A life cycle approach.* St. Louis: Mosby, 1979.

Chow, T. J., & Earl, J. L. Lead aerosols in the atmosphere: Increasing concentration. *Science,* 1970, *169,* 577.

Clausen, J. A. Mental deficiency: Development of a concept. *American Journal of Mental Deficiency,* 1967, *71,* 727–745.

Clausen, J. A. Quo Vadis, AAMD? *Journal of Special Education,* 1972, *6,* 51–60.

Cooper, L. Z., & Krugman, S. Diagnosis and management: Congenital rubella. *Pediatrics,* 1966, *37,* 335.

Corrigan, G. E. The fetal alcohol syndrome. *Texas Medicine,* 1976, *72,* 72–74.

Diana v. *State Board of Education.* C-70-37 (RFP Dist. N. California), 1970.

Doll, E. A. Is mental deficiency curable? *American Journal of Mental Deficiency,* 1947, *51,* 420–428.

Drillien, C. M. The incidence of mental and physical handicaps in school age children of very low birth weight, II. *Pediatrics,* 1967, *39,* 238–247.

Dunn, L. M. Children with moderate and severe general learning disabilities. In L. M. Dunn (Ed.), *Exceptional children in the schools: Special education in transition* (2nd ed.). New York: Holt, Rinehart & Winston, 1973.

Elek, S. D., & Stern, H. Development of a vaccine against mental retardation caused by cytomegalovirus infection in utero. *Lancet,* 1974, *1,* 1–5.

Gearheart, B. R., & Litton, F. W. *The trainable retarded: A foundations approach.* St. Louis: Mosby, 1979.

Gellis, S. S., & Feingold, M. *Atlas of mental retardation syndromes: Visual diagnosis of facies and physical findings.* Washington, D.C.: Superintendent of Documents, 1965.

Graham, F. K., Ernhart, C. B., Craft, M., & Berman, P. W. Brain injury in the preschool child: Some developmental considerations. *Psychological Monographs,* 1963, *77,* 573–574.

Grossman, H. J. (Ed.). *Manual on terminology and classification in mental retardation.* Washington, D.C.: American Association on Mental Deficiency, 1977.

Herrenbohl, L. R. Prenatal stress reduces fertility and fecundity in female offspring. *Science,* 1979, *206,* 1097–1099.

Howe, S. G. Report of commission to inquire into the conditions of idiots of the Commonwealth of Massachusetts. In M. Rosen, G. R. Clark, & M. S. Kivitz (Eds.), *The history of mental retardation* (Vol. 1). Baltimore: University Park Press, 1976. (Originally published, 1848.)

Hutt, M. S., & Gibby, R. G. *The mentally retarded child: Development, education and treatment.* Boston: Allyn & Bacon, 1976.

Ingalls, R. P. *Mental retardation: The changing outlook.* New York: Wiley, 1978.

Jackson, G. D. Another psychological view from the Association of Black Psychologists. *American Psychologist,* 1975, *30,* 88–93.

Jensen, A. R. How much can we boost IQ and scholastic achievement? *Harvard Educational Reviews,* 1969, *39,* 1–123.

Jones, K. L., Smith, D. W., Ulleland, C. N., & Streissguth, A. P. Patterns of malformation in offspring of chronic alcoholic mothers. *Lancet,* 1973, *1,* 1267–1271.

Jones, K. L., Smith, D. W., Streissguth, A. P., & Myrianthopoulos, N. C. Outcome in offspring of chronic alcoholic women. *Lancet,* 1974, *2,* 1076–1078.

Jones, L. A. Census-based prevalence estimates for mental retardation. *Mental Retardation,* 1979, *17,* 199–201.

Kauffman, J. M., & Payne, J. S. *Mental retardation: Introduction and personal perspectives.* Columbus, Ohio: Charles E. Merrill, 1975.

Kaufman, A. S. Issues in psychological assessment: Interpreting the WISC-R intelligently. In B. B. Lahey & A. E. Kazdin (Eds.), *Advances in child clinical psychology* (Vol. 3). New York: Plenum Press, 1980.

King, T., Soucar, E., & Isett, R. An attempt to assess and predict adaptive behavior of institutionalized mentally retarded clients. *American Journal of Mental Deficiency,* 1980, *84,* 406–410.

Kolstoe, O. P., & Frey, R. M. *A high school work study program for mentally subnormal students.* Carbondale, Ill.: Southern Illinois University Press, 1965.

Korones, S. B. *High-risk newborn infants: The basis for intensive nursing care* (2nd ed.). St. Louis: Mosby, 1976.

Larry P. v. *Riles.* USLW 2033 (U.S. June 21), 1972.

Lin-Fu, J. S. Preventing lead poisoning in children. *Children Today,* 1973, *2,* 2–6.

MacMillan, D. L. *Mental retardation in school and society.* Boston: Little, Brown, 1977.

MacMillan, D. L., Meyers, C. E., & Morrison, G. M. System-identification of mildly mentally retarded children: Implications for interpreting and conducting research. *American Journal of Mental Deficiency,* 1980, *85,* 108–115.

Masland, R. L. Methodological approaches to research in etiology. *American Journal of Mental Deficiency,* 1960, *64,* 305–310.

McDevitt, S. C., McDevitt, S. C., & Rosen, M. Adaptive behavior scale, Part II: A cautionary note and suggestions for revision. *American Journal of Mental Deficiency,* 1977, *82,* 210–212.

Mercer, J. R. The meaning of mental retardation. In R. Koch & J. C. Dobson (Eds.), *The mentally retarded child and his family: A multidisciplinary handbook.* New York: Bruner/Mazel, 1971.

Mercer, J. R. *Labeling the mentally retarded.* Berkeley: University of California Press, 1973(a).

Mercer, J. R. The myth of 3% prevalence. In R. E. Eyman, C. E. Meyers, & G. Tarjan (Eds.), Sociological studies in mental retardation. *Monographs of the American Association on Mental Deficiency,* 1973(b).

Mercer, J. R. *System of multicultural pluralistic assessment.* New York: The Psychological Association, 1979.

Mitchell, S. K. *Life changes, help from others, and the outcomes of pregnancy.* Unpublished manuscript, University of Washington, 1974.

Moore, K. L. *Before we are born: Basic embryology and birth defects.* Philadelphia: W. B. Saunders Company, 1974.

Moser, H. W., & Wolf, P. A. The nosology of mental retardation birth defects. *Original Article Series* (Vol. 7). Baltimore: Williams and Williams, 1971.

Naeye, R. L., Blanc, W., & Paul, C. Effects of maternal nutrition on the human fetus. *Pediatrics,* 1973, *52,* 494–503.

National Foundation, March of Dimes. *Facts: 1975.* White Plains, N.Y.: Author, 1975.

Nielson, J. Criminality among patients with Klinefelter's syndrome and *XYY* syndrome. *British Journal of Psychiatry,* 1970, *117,* 365–369.

Nihira, K., Foster, R., Shellhaas, M., & Leland, H. *Adaptive behavior scale.* Washington, D.C.: American Association on Mental Deficiency, 1974.

Osofsky. H. J. *The pregnant teenager: A medical, educational and social analysis.* Springfield, Ill.: Charles C Thomas, 1968.

Polo, J., Lydecken, K., & Kivalo, C. Etiological aspects of mental deficiency in autopsied patients. *American Journal of Mental Deficiency,* 1967, *71,* 401–405.

Robinson, N. M., & Robinson, H. B. *The mentally retarded child: A psychological approach* (2nd ed.). New York: McGraw-Hill, 1976.

Rubin, R. A., Rosenblatt, C., & Balow, B. Psychological and educational sequelae of prematurity. *Pediatrics,* 1973, *52,* 352.

Russell, J. K., & Miller, D. G. Maternal factors and mental performance in children. In *Perinatal factors affecting human development.* Proceedings of the special session, eighth meeting of the Pan American Health Organization Advisory Committee on Medical Research, Washington, D.C., June 1969.

Sarason, S. B. *Psychological problems in mental deficiency.* New York: Harper & Brothers, 1949.

Sells, C. J., & Bennett, F. C. Prevention of mental retardation: The role of medicine. *American Journal of Mental Deficiency,* 1977, *82,* 117–129.

Sontag, L. W. The possible relationship of prenatal environment to schizophrenia. In D. D. Jackson (Ed.), *The etiology of schizophrenia.* New York: Basic Books, 1960.

Spreat, S. The adaptive behavior scale: A study of criterion validity. *American Journal of Mental Deficiency,* 1980, *85,* 61–68.

Spreat, S., & Isett, R. *Test–retest reliability of the AAMD adaptive behavior scale* (Evaluation and Research Tech. Rep. 77-4). Philadelphia: Woodhaven Center, 1977.

Stern, C. *Principles of human genetics* (3rd ed.). San Francisco: Freeman, 1973.

Tarjan, G., Wright, S. W., Eyman, R. K., & Keeran, C. K. Natural history of mental retardation: Some aspects of epidemiology. *American Journal of Mental Deficiency,* 1973, *77,* 369–379.

Taylor, R. L., Warren, S. A., & Slocumb, P. R. Categorizing behavior in terms of severity: Considerations for Part Two of the Adaptive Behavior Scale. *American Journal of Mental Deficiency,* 1979, *83,* 411–414.

Tredgold, A. F. *A textbook on mental deficiency* (6th ed.). Baltimore: William Wood, 1937.

Umbreit, J., & Ostrow, L. S. The fetal alcohol syndrome. *Mental Retardation,* 1980, *18,* 109–111.

United States Bureau of the Census. *1976 survey of income and education.* Washington, D.C.: U.S. Government Printing Office, 1977.

Weiss, W., & Jackson, C. E. Maternal factors affecting birthweight. In *Perinatal factors affecting human development* (PASBS Publication No. 185). Washington, D.C.: Pan American Health Organization, 1969.

Wigglesworth, J. S. Malnutrition and brain development. *Developmental Medicine and Child Neurology,* 1969, *11,* 792–803.

Williams, R. L. *Problem of the match and mismatch in testing black children.* Paper presented at the meeting of the American Psychological Association, Honolulu, September 1972.

Winick, M. Fetal malnutrition and growth process. *Hospital Practice,* 1970, *5,* 33–41.

6

Infantile Autism

Laura Schreibman and Jack I. Mills

Infantile autism is a relatively rare form of psychopathology in children. Yet when it does occur, the impact is indeed profound in terms of the severity and pervasiveness of its effect on the child, the family, the schools, the community, and society. Few disorders are so devastating, fascinating, and unique as the syndrome of autism. What follows is a discussion of autism, its symptoms, diagnosis, incidence, and etiology. It is hoped that from this discussion, the reader will acquire both an understanding and an appreciation for this most interesting disorder.

History of the Diagnosis

Autism was first identified in 1943 by Dr. Leo Kanner when he described the behavioral characteristics of 11 children whom he felt differed qualitatively from other recognized child clinical populations. His detailed and vivid description of the children in his initial report (1943) served as the impetus for the study of "early infantile autism," a study which has been consistently characterized by controversy, particularly over diagnosis and etiology.

Kanner (1943) described several distinct behavioral characteristics as being present in his 11 cases of autism. These characteristics included an inability to develop relationships with people (extreme aloneness), a delay in speech acquisition, the noncommunicative nature of the speech if it developed, echolalia, pronominal reversal (e.g., substituting "you" for "I"), repetitive and stereotyped play activities, a compulsive demand for the mainte-

LAURA SCHREIBMAN • Department of Psychology, Claremont McKenna College, Claremont, California 91711. JACK I. MILLS • Department of Psychology, Claremont Graduate School, Claremont, California 91711. Preparation of this chapter was supported by USPHS Research Grants 28231 and 28210 from the National Institute of Mental Health.

nance of sameness in the environment, a lack of imagination but a good rote memory, a normal physical appearance, and the appearance of abnormalities in infancy.

Following Kanner's initial report, others described children with similar characteristics (Bakwin, 1954; Bosch, 1953, 1970; Despert, 1951; van Krevelen, 1952). In addition, several earlier accounts of autistic children surfaced, although the syndrome had not yet been identified (e.g., Darr & Worden, 1951; Haslam, 1809; Itard, 1801/1964; Vaillant, 1962). Clearly the syndrome had existed for a long time before its formal recognition.

In the decades since Kanner first described the essential features of autism, much controversy and disagreement have been directed at exactly which symptoms were necessary for the diagnosis of autism. (For more detailed reviews of this literature, the reader is directed to Ritvo & Freeman, 1978; Rutter, 1966, 1968, 1971, 1978a; Rutter, Bartak, & Newman, 1971; J. K. Wing, 1976). Kanner felt that two symptoms were essential for a diagnosis of autism. These were "extreme aloneness" and "preoccupation with the preservation of sameness" (Eisenberg & Kanner, 1956). Later, however, others felt that the emphasis on these characteristics obscured the importance of some of the other symptoms. Rutter (1978a), in his review of the diagnosis of autism, makes the important point that what is needed is a systematic identification of those symptoms that are both universal among and specific to autistic children. In a research program toward this end, Rutter (1966) and Rutter and Lockyer (1967) reported that three broad groups of symptoms were found in all (or almost all) of those children diagnosed as autistic (or infantile psychotic); these symptoms were much less frequent in children with other psychiatric disorders. These symptoms were; (1) a profound and general failure to develop social relationships; (2) a delay in the acquisition of language accompanied by impaired comprehension, echolalia, and pronominal reversal; and (3) ritualistic, compulsive behaviors described by Kanner as "preservation of sameness."

As Schopler (1978) points out, the exact symptomology required for the diagnosis of autism may depend on the purpose to be served by the diagnosis. Psychologists, speech pathologists, researchers, educators, and others each may focus on different aspects of the disorder and thus emphasize certain behaviors. Indeed, from a practical point of view one can certainly make an argument for describing autism in terms of specific behaviors, and for directing research and clinical efforts toward understanding and treating these behaviors (Schreibman & Koegel, 1981).

While the controversy over the identification of the "true" combination of symptoms will doubtless continue for some time, one can nonetheless describe the symptoms most commonly associated with autism today by professionals involved in its study.

Behavioral Characteristics of Autism

Deficits in Social Behavior

One characteristic of autistic children that is unanimously emphasized involves the profound and pervasive deficits in social attachment and behavior displayed by these children. The nature of this social unresponsiveness has been studied (e.g., Bartak, Rutter, & Cox, 1975; Churchill & Bryson, 1972; Hutt & Vaizey, 1966; Sorosky, Ornitz, Brown, & Ritvo, 1968; Wing, 1969; Wolff & Chess, 1964), and some rather distinct patterns seem to emerge (Rutter, 1978a). There is a lack of attachment to others and a failure to bond with parents. For example, the children do not seem to "need" their parents. As infants they often will not cry for attention as do normal infants, they do not seek cuddling or kissing (and in fact may actively resist these overtures from others), and they do not anticipate being picked up. They are often described as "good babies" because they are content to be left alone, rarely demanding social contact. Later, they often prefer to be isolated and will wander off by themselves. They are frequently oblivious to the departures and arrivals of the parents, they do not seek out their parents for comfort when they are hurt, nor do they spontaneously express affection. In short, they show minimal affective involvement with their social environment.

This failure to develop social attachment and behavior is also evident in their lack of peer contact and cooperative play (e.g., Rutter, 1978a). Typically, autistic children avoid play situations with other children and, if in the same area as peers, engage in solitary activity. Predictably, most autistics do not show the social imitation so necessary to the acquisition of appropriate interaction with peers (e.g., Varni, Lovaas, Koegel, & Everett, 1979).

One particularly interesting feature of an autistic child's participation in his social environment is that, while true affective contact appears to be absent, social contact for other purposes may be present. For example, it is frequently reported that autistic children relate to people as "objects" rather than as people (e.g., Rimland, 1964). For example, an autistic child might stand on his mother's lap to reach a cookie jar and never look at her while doing so. The mother has served simply as a stepladder. The child may also lead people (by the hand, arm, or clothing) to something he wants them to get for him, never looking at them in the process. This lack of social eye to eye contact is often cited as another characteristic of autism (e.g., Rimland, 1964).

The profound social deficits of autism can also be noted in high-level autistics who can maintain themselves in the community (e.g., in schools with normal children). These children may display adequate academic nonsocial skills but are distinctively inept in social situations. They are typically oblivious to subtle social cues and may say or do socially inappropriate things (e.g., Rutter, 1978a) without recognition of the inappropriateness of their behavior.

Speech and Language

Frequently, parents' first suspicions that something is wrong arise when their child fails to develop speech. Kanner (1943) considered this delay or failure in the acquisition of speech to be of primary importance in autism. About 50% of autistics never develop functional speech (Rutter, 1978a). Those autistic children who do speak characteristically display abnormal speech patterns that are qualitatively different from the speech of normal children and children with other language disorders (e.g., Bartak *et al.,* 1975; Ricks & Wing, 1975; Rutter, 1965, 1966, 1978a; L. Wing, 1976).

Echolalia is quite common in speaking autistic children. Echolalia, the repetition of words or phrases spoken by others (Fay, 1969), typically occurs either immediately after the words are spoken or after a time delay (Carr, Schreibman, & Lovaas, 1975); this repetition is not used for communicative purposes. For example, in "immediate" echolalia the child parrots what has just been said. If asked "What's your name?" the child is likely to respond with "What's your name?" in "delayed" echolalia, the child repeats some verbal stimulus heard in the past, and because the situation is usually different from that of the original stimulus, the speech is contextually inappropriate (Carr *et al.,* 1975). Thus, an autistic child seated at the dinner table may suddenly start repeating commands made by her teacher hours or even days before. Sometimes the delayed echolalic response is so far removed from the original stimulus that the speech sounds quite bizarre. For example, an autistic child known to the authors was suddenly confronted by a large dog. The frightened child looked at the dog and exclaimed, "It's not a glass paperweight!" Obviously, any relationship between the original verbal stimulus and the present situation was, indeed, remote.

Echolalia, *per se,* is not peculiar to autistic children. Normal language development includes a phase of echolalia, peaking at about the age of 30 months (Van Riper, 1963; Zipf, 1949). But when this echoing persists past the age of 3 or 4 years, it is considered to be pathological (Darley, 1964; Fay, 1967; Ricks & Wing, 1975). While the variables affecting delayed echolalia are, as yet, not well understood, there is evidence indicating that immediate echolalia is related to the comprehensibility of the verbal stimulus (Carr *et al.,* 1975; Schreibman & Carr, 1978). That is, if an autistic child is presented with a verbal stimulus for which he has a response (e.g., "What's your name?"), he will give the response (e.g., "Robbie"). However, if presented with a stimulus for which he has no response (e.g., "Who's the President?"), he is likely to echo all or part of the stimulus.

Probably related to echolalia is the characteristic pronominal reversal displayed by most speaking autistics (e.g., Bartak & Rutter, 1974; Ricks & Wing, 1975; Rimland, 1964; Rutter, 1978a). Typically, the child will refer to himself as "you" or by his name. For example, an echolalic autistic child who is functioning at a level high enough to use speech somewhat communicatively may ask his mother, "Do you want a glass of milk?" or "Johnny, do you want a glass of milk?" to indicate that he would like milk.

The speech and language of autistic children are abnormal in several other respects. Their comprehension may be severely impaired (e.g., Ricks & Wing, 1975) and when they speak, it is often not for communicative purposes. They may use speech for self-stimulative purposes (e.g., Lovaas, Varni, Koegel, & Lorsch, 1977), where it seems to function only to provide the child with sensory feedback. Their use of speech for conversation is likewise quite limited and, indeed, they have great difficulty talking about anything outside of immediate situations or events (e.g., Rutter, 1978a). Thus, they do not relate past experiences or verbally anticipate future events. Even the speech of high-functioning autistics with fairly sophisticated (for an autistic individual) language, shows a certain lack of emotion, imagination, and abstraction, and a definite literalness. For example, one 22-year-old autistic man known to the authors spoke almost entirely about elevators and bridges. When asked how he *felt* about a situation, he would always answer with, "It's OK" or "I don't know." Another 12-year-old boy, when asked what kinds of television programs he enjoyed, proceeded to repeat, verbatim, an episode of *I Love Lucy* rather than responding with a more appropriate response such as "comedies."

Abnormalities in Response to the Physical Environment

Autistic children are characterized by abnormal responsiveness to sensory stimulation (Ritvo & Freeman, 1978; L. Wing, 1976). Typically, this manifests itself in under- or overreaction to various sensory events, or even to the same events. As might be expected, many autistic children have histories of suspected (but unconfirmed) deafness or blindness. They may be unresponsive to loud noises, the sound of their own name, or startle stimuli. Similarly, a child may not seem to notice salient visual features in the environment such as the comings and goings of people, approaching cars, and so forth. Yet, this unresponsiveness can be highly variable in nature (e.g., Lovaas, Schreibman, Koegel, & Rehm, 1971). The child who neither responds to her name nor to loud sounds might hear the rustle of a candy wrapper or cover her ears and scream at the turn of a newspaper page. Similarly, the child who behaves as if blind might spot a piece of candy several feet away or become fascinated by pieces of lint falling to the ground. This variable responsiveness to the environment is sometimes referred to as "apparent sensory deficit," indicating the lack of a demonstrated receptor-level sensory deficit such as deafness (Lovaas *et al.,* 1971).

This abnormal responsiveness is associated with other sensory modalities as well. In the tactile modalities, the children may be over- or undersensitive to touch, pain, or temperature (Ritvo & Freeman, 1978). In the area of vestibular functioning, the children may be over- or underresponsive to gravity stimuli and may be fascinated by spinning objects. In addition, responsiveness to gustatory stimulation is frequently unusual. They may lick or mouth inedible objects, sniff objects, eat only certain foods, and be very sensitive to different food textures (Ritvo & Freeman, 1978).

In an attempt to relate environmental responsiveness to problems autistic children have in learning new behaviors, several investigators have studied the parameters of this responsiveness. Several studies (e.g., Koegel & Wilhelm, 1973; Lovaas *et al.,* 1971b; Lovaas & Schreibman, 1971; Reynolds, Newsom, & Lovaas, 1974; Schreibman & Lovaas, 1973) have demonstrated that autistic children typically respond to only a component of the available sensory information. These researchers refer to this phenomenon as "stimulus overselectivity," indicating that when presented with simultaneous multiple cues, autistic children typically respond to only a limited portion of the cues. Because learning usually requires response to simultaneous multiple cues, it is not surprising that a failure to so respond would greatly retard learning. For example, suppose someone held a picture of a dog before an autistic child while simultaneously saying "dog." If the child heard the word "dog" but failed to respond to the picture, he would not learn the label. Similarly, learning of the label would also fail to occur if the child saw the picture but did not respond to the spoken word. (See Lovaas, Koegel, & Schreibman, 1979, and Schreibman & Koegel, in press, for reviews of the overselectivity literature.) This stimulus overselectivity has been implicated as a possible basis for many of the abnormal behaviors so characteristic of autism. For example, L. Wing (1976) speculates that overselectivity might account for the tendency of autistics to select one trivial aspect of a stimulus for attention while ignoring the rest. For example, she cites the case of a child who was fascinated by church steeples and refused to look at pictures of anything else. In addition to serving as a possible explanation of the observed variability in responsiveness, overselectivity has also been implicated as a basis for problems in acquiring new behaviors (Koegel & Covert, 1972), in generalizing new behaviors (Rincover & Koegel, 1975), in social behavior (Schreibman & Lovaas, 1973), in learning from traditional prompting procedures (Rincover, 1978a; Schreibman, 1975), and in learning through modeling (Varni *et al.,* 1979).

Demand for Sameness in Environment

One of Kanner's (1943) primary characteristics of autism was a preoccupation with the preservation of sameness in the environment (Eisenberg & Kanner, 1956; Kanner, 1943). Basically, these children are often overly sensitive to change. For example, as young children they display limited and rigid play patterns that lack variety and imagination

(Rutter, 1978a). They may endlessly line up blocks or other objects in neat rows, only to become very upset if something disturbs the pattern. They might collect certain objects such as tiny toys, rocks, pencils, or books and hold them tenaciously. They might develop strong attachments to objects and always demand them. For example, the authors recall one child who demanded to carry two pencils (one in each hand) constantly; another child would only wear a particular pair of shoes. Any attempt to take away these objects was met with severe tantrum behavior. This demand for sameness is also demonstrated by the children's intense reaction to changes in familiar furniture arrangements or in familiar routes. Often the slightest change (e.g., moving a chair a few inches) may provoke the child to attempt to return the situation to its previous state. Another child known to the authors would become extremely upset if the cereal box in the kitchen were left open, if any drawers in the house were left open, if her father's briefcase were left open, or if the reclining chair were left in the reclining position. Sometimes, the children's reactions take the appearance of fears, and the children seem to become quite frightened at stimuli and events that other people see as harmless. Take, for instance, the child who was terrified of certain doorways in his house, of the dining room drapes, and of punched computer cards.

Sometimes autistic children develop certain ritualistic preoccupations such as memorizing calendars, timetables, or patterns (Rutter, 1978a). Often they become obsessed with letters or numbers and spend large amounts of time with these rituals. One child, for example, insisted on taking her plastic letters to bed with her. These rituals also are evidenced by behaviors such as insistence on eating only particular foods, using particular eating utensils, wearing certain clothing, touching particular objects, or repeatedly asking the same questions, which must be answered in a particular fashion (Rimland, 1964; Rutter, 1978a).

Self-Stimulatory Behavior

Self-stimulation, often seen as a defining characteristic of autism (Rimland, 1964), was noted by Kanner (1943) in his original description of autism. Self-stimulation, also known as stereotypic behavior, is typically described as repetitive, persistent, stereotyped behavior that seems to have no other function than to provide the child with sensory or kinesthetic feedback (e.g., Lovaas, Litrownik, & Mann, 1971; Rincover, 1978b). At the gross motor level, these behaviors may include rhythmic body rocking, jumping, darting or pacing, head bobbing, arm or hand flapping, and posturing. At a more subtle level, the behavior may include gazing at lights, gazing or "regarding" the cupped hand, staring out of the corner of the eye, moving or rolling eyes, or tensing body muscles. Often self-stimulation involves the use of objects. The child might gaze intently at spinning objects (e.g., saucepan lids, coins, ashtrays), twirl a piece of string, or wave pencils in front of the face. Auditory and visual stimulation appear to be the focus of much of this behavior. The children sometimes stare at flickering lights (as visible when one spins a coin), wave their outstretched fingers in front of their eyes, become fascinated by shiny objects, repeat vocal patterns, tap objects in a certain sequence, and so on.

There are other defining characteristics of self-stimulatory behavior. First, many autistic children spend most of their waking hours engaged in these activities. This behavior appears to be very important to them to the extent that they engage in little else. Indeed, they resist attempts to discourage the behavior and will sometimes even risk pain or loss of food while engaging in self-stimulation (e.g., Lovaas *et al.*, 1971a). Second, self-stimulation differs in many respects from normal play behaviors associated with childhood. That is, it often looks unusual or bizarre, as when a child flaps his arms wildly while jumping repeatedly. The behavior may involve other grotesque body movements and facial grimacing. Another difference between play and self-stimulation is that self-stimulation seems to interfere with the child's responsiveness and with the acquisition of more normal behaviors (Koegel & Covert, 1972; Lovaas *et al.,* 1971a).

Elaborating on these last points, the literature is replete with discriptions of these children's unresponsivity to environmental input while engaged in self-stimulatory behavior (e.g., Kanner, 1943; Koegel & Covert, 1972; Lovaas *et al.,* 1971a; Rincover, 1978b). Indeed, it is quite striking to see an autistic child sitting alone in a corner rocking or twirling a string while the room around him bustles loudly with the activity of other children playing with toys. The autistic child is truly oblivious to the activity around him.

This resulting unresponsiveness has drawn the attention of researchers and clinicians because it seems to interfere with the acquisition of more appropriate behavior (e.g., Carr, 1977; Koegel & Covert, 1972). Indeed, in addition to anecdotal reports, there are data demonstrating that children engaged in self-stimulation are less responsive to previously learned cues (Lovaas *et al.,* 1971a) and are seriously retarded in their learning of new behaviors (Koegel & Covert, 1972). Thus, self-stimulation serves as a major obstacle to treatment.

Self-Injurious Behavior

While autistic children certainly manifest an assortment of severe behaviors, none is more dramatic than self-injurious behavior (SIB). SIB involves any behavior in which the individual inflicts physical damage to his/her own body (Tate & Baroff, 1966). The two most common forms of SIB in autistic children are head banging and self-biting of hands or wrist (Rutter & Lockyer, 1967). Other common types of self-abuse are elbow or leg banging, hair pulling or rubbing, face scratching, and self-slapping of face or sides. Sometimes the children tear their fingernails with their teeth, gouge at their eyes, and progressively bite off fingertips.

The intensity of SIB can vary, as does the level of damage incurred. Some children slap their face, bang their head, or bite themselves, leaving redness, bruises, or callouses. Other children are so intense in their abuse that they can fracture their skull, detach their retinas, break their jaw or nose, and remove large quantities of flesh from their bodies (Carr, 1977; Lovaas & Simmons, 1969). Infections are another hazard of SIB because open wounds often result from the abuse.

While the direct damages of this behavior are obvious, there are additional, more indirect damages resulting from SIB. First, with some children, the behavior is so intense and life threatening (e.g., severe head banging) that they must be physically restrained to prevent the occurrence of the behavior. Thus the child might have his hands or arms tied to the bed frame, or he might be placed in a camisole ("straitjacket"). In cases where restraint has been prolonged (e.g., periods of months or years), one can observe structural changes such as demineralization, shortening of tendons, and arrested motor development as a result of nonuse of limbs (Lovaas & Simmons, 1969). A second indirect kind of damage is that the child's behavior serves to restrict the child's psychological and educational growth. Parents and staff members dealing with such children often are reluctant to place demands on them for fear of precipitating an SIB episode (Carr, 1977). Thus, the children often miss the opportunity for productive interaction with their social and physical environment.

Treatment efforts for SIB have included the use of drugs, restraints, and reassuring affection. None of these has proven successful in alleviating SIB (e.g., Carr, 1977). More successful treatments have involved operant techniques such as extinction and punishment. For comprehensive reviews of the treatment of SIB, the reader is referred to Carr (1977), Bachman (1972), Smolev (1971), and Frankel and Simmons (1976).

SIB is certainly not peculiar to autism as it has been reported to be present in about 4–5% of psychiatric populations (Frankel & Simmons, 1976). However, many autistic children do manifest this behavior and, thanks to recent research, our ability to control this dangerous behavior has vastly improved.

Special Skills

Many autistic children display isolated areas of exceptional performance that are incongruous with their otherwise depressed level of functioning. Most frequently these abilities lie in the general areas of musical, mechanical, or mathematical behaviors (Applebaum, Egel, Koegel, & Imhoff, 1979; Rimland, 1978). Specifically, a child may be able to remember and reproduce complex melodies and song lyrics. The skill may manifest itself in the ability to assemble jigsaw puzzles (perhaps even with the picture side down) or to assemble and dismantle complicated mechanical apparatus (L. Wing, 1976). Some children become obsessed with memorizing mathematical tables, bus schedules, or random sequences of numbers. "Calendar calculation," the ability to determine what day of the week a certain day on the calendar will fall, is also seen in some children.

Kanner (1943), noting the autistic child's excellent rote memory, hypothesized the capacity for normal intelligence and saw their intellectual retardation as a consequence of the failure to establish social relationships (Rutter, 1978a). However, it is now apparent that the excellent rote memory often seen in autistic children falls in the category of isolated skill. Indeed, many of these children display exceptional performance in areas that would have little obvious utility in their environment, particularly in the absence of other, more functional behaviors. For example, the authors are familiar with a 7-year-old autistic child who was literally a musical genius. If presented with a melody, the child could reproduce it exactly on any of nine different instruments. In addition, he could instantly transpose the melody into any key and compose appropriate harmonic melodies. While this ability was indeed outstanding, its usefulness was doubtful because the boy could not say his name, was not toilet trained, and could not respond to a simple command such as "close the door."

Intellectual Functioning

The level of intellectual functioning has always been an issue in the study of autism. As mentioned, Kanner (1943) believed autistic children to be of normal intelligence. Their good rote memory, serious facial expressions, and the absence of physical abnormalities supported this hypothesis (Rutter, 1978a). The data acquired to date, however, suggest that the majority of autistic children are mentally retarded. According to Ritvo and Freeman (1978), current research estimates indicate that approximately 60% of autistic children have measured IQs below 50, 20% measure between 50 and 70, and 20% measure 70 or above. Intellectual assessment of these children is difficult because of the extreme variability of performance on the assessment instruments. The children tend to do best on tests measuring manipulative or visual–spatial skills and rote memory, and to do poorest on tasks requiring abstract thought and symbol or sequential logic (Ritvo & Freeman, 1978).

Further, the data also indicate that IQ in autistic children has the same properties as it does for other children (Rutter, 1978a). That is, it tends to remain stable throughout middle childhood and adolescence (DeMyer, Barton, Alpern, Kimberlin, Allen, Yang, & Steele, 1974; Lockyer & Rutter, 1969; Gittleman & Birch, 1967), and it tends to be somewhat predictive of future educational accomplishments (Bartak & Rutter, 1971; Lockyer & Rutter, 1969; Rutter & Bartak, 1973). Based on these facts, it appears that although autism and mental retardation are not synonymous, they frequently coexist in the same child.

Inappropriate Affect

Another feature of autistic children is their affect, which is typically noted to be flattened or inappropriate to situations (e.g., Rimland, 1964). They may have an almost constant placid expression wherein they seem to "coast" through a variety of emotional situations. Others display erratic emotional behavior ranging from a giggling and hysterical laughter to unconsolable sobbing. Often these emotional reactions seem independent of environmental events, and the child can rapidly vacillate from one to the other without apparent reason. Some of this inappropriate affect seems tied to the lack of appropriate social behavior and the failure to respond to the social cues of other people. For example, a child might laugh if another person hurts himself, or cry when others laugh.

Assessment

As discussed at the beginning of this chapter, "autism" is indeed a slippery entity when it comes to diagnosis and assessment. Professionals have found it impossible to come to agreement on exactly what symptoms are necessary for the diagnosis of autism, and there is still no consensus on the best way to assess autistic children.

Newsom and Rincover (1982) make the astute observation that autism may be the only childhood disorder where behavioral assessment has antedated more traditional cognitive assessment. Until the late 1960s, standardized intelligence tests were considered unsuitable for autistic children (Alpern, 1967). Prior to this time, some professionals (e.g., Ferster & DeMyer, 1961a,b; 1962) had already conducted research on reinforcer preferences, speed of learning, stimulus control, conceptual performance, and drug effects. Also, the middle 1960s saw other strong behavioral assessment procedures being applied to autistic children in behavioral treatment programs (e.g., Davison, 1964; Lovaas, Berberich, Perloff, & Schaeffer, 1966; Lovaas, Freitag, Gold, & Kassorla, 1965; Wolf, Risley, & Mees, 1964). These assessments, typically either automated or observational, yielded measures of presence or absence of specific behavior such as appropriate speech, psychotic speech, tantrums, play, and social behavior.

Currently, the assessment of autistic children typically involves the use of several avenues of information. One is the traditional interview and observation characteristic in clinical practice. Other instruments are also used, such as standardized intelligence tests, checklists, and direct observation techniques (Newsom & Rincover, 1982).

Of particular interest are the behavioral checklists that have been derived specifically for the assessment of autism. These checklists are of two types. One type is diagnostic and serves to distinguish an autistic child from a child with another disorder. The other type of checklist is a descriptive checklist, designed to provide information on the presence or absence of specific behaviors considered important for treatment and functioning (Newsom & Rincover, 1982).

The main diagnostic checklists used with autistic children are Rimland's Diagnostic Checklist for Behavior Disturbed Children (Rimland, 1964) and the British Working Party Diagnostic System (Creak, 1961; Lotter, 1966; O'Gorman, 1970; Polan & Spencer, 1959). The main purpose of these checklists, as mentioned, is to identify an autistic child as distinctive from other types of disordered children. These checklists have not been sufficiently validated to be used as a sole diagnostic tool, yet they can be very informative when used with other assessment instruments.

Frequently used descriptive checklists include Kozloff's (1974) Behavior Evaluation Scale (BES), the Adaptive Behavior Scale (American Association on Mental Deficiency (1975), and the Vineland Social Maturity Scale (Doll, 1965). While none of these checklists was specifically designed for use with autistic children, they can provide very relevant information concerning specific behavior characteristics, behavior deficiencies, and level of functioning. This information is, of course, very useful for assessment of needs and treatment programming.

Differential Diagnosis: Autism, Childhood Schizophrenia, Aphasia, Mental Retardation, and Environmental Deprivation

As previously discussed, experts cannot agree on exactly which behavioral characteristics are necessary for a diagnosis of autism. Adding to the difficulty in diagnosis is the heterogeneity of the autistic population. Very few children diagnosed as autistic exhibit every symptom exactly as described by Kanner (Kanner, 1969; Rimland, 1964), and not all autistic children are of the same level of severity (L. Wing, 1976).

This heterogeneity has led to confusion both in diagnosing autistic children and in choosing suitable comparison groups for research purposes. Coleman (1976) has grouped the population into three main categories: the classically autistic, childhood schizophrenics with autistic features, and neurologically impaired autistic children. Thus, it should not be surprising that one reason for this heterogeneity is that in many cases autism appears to overlap with several other childhood disorders. Sometimes this is because autism is a byproduct of a specific known pathology, such as congenital rubella or phenylketonuria (Coleman, 1976). In some instances autism coexists with another disorder such as Down's syndrome (Wakabayashi, 1979). It has also been found that many autistic children develop epileptic seizures in adolescence (Rutter, 1978a). A second source of heterogeneity follows from the fact that autism shares central features with several other handicaps. For example, impaired cognitive ability is a characteristic of both mental retardation and autism. Language deficits are characteristic of autism, mental retardation, and developmental aphasia. In this sense, the question is not whether a particular child is autistic or asphasic; the question is whether it is useful for researchers and practitioners to distinguish between autism and related developmental disorders. The evidence suggests that it is helpful to make the distinction (Rutter, 1978a). Autism can be differentiated from at least four major categories of disability, including childhood schizophrenia, developmental aphasia, mental retardation, and environmental deprivations.

Childhood Schizophrenia

Childhood schizophrenia is a broad diagnosis that has been used to describe many different types of children (Menolascino, 1971; Ornitz & Ritvo, 1976; Rutter, 1972; L. Wing, 1976). It has recently been discovered that children develop psychoses in two waves. The first wave begins to show symptoms before the age of 3 and the second between the ages of 5 and 15 (Kolvin, 1971). Children of the early-onset wave have the characteristics of autism. The late-onset wave more closely resembles schizophrenic adults. In general, autism is characterized by an early onset of symptoms (before 30 months), no history of mental illness in the family, normal or above average motor development, good physical health, but a failure to develop complex language and social skills. In contrast, childhood schizophrenia is characterized by a later onset (past 5 years), a family history of psychosis, delusions and hallucinations, poor physical health, and poor motor performance (Rimland, 1964; L. Wing, 1976).

Developmental Aphasia

Developmental aphasia is a delay in language acquisition and articulation. Aphasic children share with autistic children echolalia, pronominal reversal, sequencing problems, and difficulty understanding the meaning of words (Churchill, 1972). Aphasic children, as a consequence of impaired language ability, may also have difficulties in social relationships (Ornitz & Ritvo, 1976). However, researchers have concluded that the language difficulties of autistic children are more severe and widespread (Churchill, 1972; Rutter, Bartak, & Newman, 1971). Aphasic children are able to achieve meaningful communication through the use of gestures (L. Wing, 1976) and do exhibit emotional intent (Griffith & Ritvo, 1967) and imaginative play (L. Wing, 1976). These characteristics are not typical of autism.

Mental Retardation

Mental retardation is also a catchall diagnosis encompassing many types of disorders. Autistic and mentally retarded children share poor intellectual ability that persists throughout the lifespan (Lockyer & Rutter, 1969). In addition, some mentally retarded children exhibit autisticlike behaviors (L. Wing, 1976). However, many mentally retarded children such as those with Down's syndrome are quite sociable and communicative. On the other hand, classically autistic children nearly always have a normal physical development, while mentally retarded children do not. In general, mentally retarded children exhibit low performance in all aspects of functioning, while autistic children exhibit more severe problems in the use of meaning and concepts (Rutter, 1978a), with occasional outstanding abilities in nonlanguage related skills such as music, rote memory, mathematics, and manual performance (Rimland, 1964).

Environmental Deprivation

Maternal deprivation, anaclitic depression, and hospitalism are all characterized by developmental delays resulting from neglect, abuse, and institutionalization. The effects of such psychological trauma have been documented by Spitz (1945). Neglected children appear to be withdrawn and disinterested. They may be delayed in motor skills and speech, engage in unusual motor activity, and lack an interest in toys (Ornitz & Ritvo, 1976). However, when placed in an enriched environment, neglected children catch up on language, motor skills (Ornitz & Ritvo, 1976; Schaffer, 1965), and regain an interest in social relationships (Ornitz & Ritvo, 1976). While there are disagreements as to whether maternal deprivation or lack of environmental simtulation is the cause of the delays suffered by neglected children (Bronfenbrenner, 1979), there is consensus that autism is not a product of neglect. At no time do neglected children display the repetitious, stereotypical play, echolalia, pronominal reversal, and complete avoidance of social contact characteristic of autistic children (Ornitz & Ritvo, 1976).

Incidence

Epidemiological studies of autism vary in the way that subjects are gathered and classified. This is one reason why there are several different estimates of the prevalence of autism. With respect to the selection of subjects, investigators may study an entire population of children in a community, counting the number who exhibit autistic symptoms. For example, Lotter (1966) surveyed the entire 8- to 10-year-old population of Middlesex County in England. An alternative method of subject selection is to survey children or administrative records of children who are either referred to clinics or who are institutionalized. For example, Lotter (1978) investigated the incidence of autism occurring among children institutionalized in six countries of Africa. Surveys of exclusively institutionalized or clinic population children are not the best measure of the prevalence of autism because not all developmentally delayed children are brought to the attention of authorities (e.g., Schopler, Andrews, & Strupp, 1979), and administrative records may rely on different criteria for the diagnosis of autism. However, these types of studies are more common and can confidently be used to estimate such ratios as males/females or first borns/later borns. With respect to the classification of subjects, in some cases the incidence of childhood psychosis has been reported with no distinction made between childhood schizophrenia and autism (Kolvin, 1971). On the other hand, in his study of autism in Wisconsin, Treffert (1970) excluded children not diagnosed as autistic by a clinic and those having known organic pathology from the autism classification. One useful approach is to divide children into several groups—the classical Kanner syndrome, children with many autistic features, and nonautistic children who display some characteristics of autism—and report statistics for each group (Lotter, 1966, 1978; Treffert, 1970).

Few surveys are available that provide reliable estimates of the prevalence of autism. The existing studies have put the incidence of autism between 3.1 and 5.0 per 10,000 live births. The most often quoted statistic is Lotter's (1966) finding of 4.5 per 10,000 children in Middlesex, England, with either classical Kanner syndrome or many autistic features. This finding has also been replicated by Brask (1970) in Denmark and Wing and Gould (1979) in London. Treffert (1970) reports lower figures of .7 per 10,000 classically autistic children and 3.1 per 10,000 autistic or schizophrenic children in Wisconsin. These lower figures are probably a result of Treffert's reliance on administrative case records from institutions and clinics. When diagnostic criteria are broadened to include all children who exhibit social impairments characteristic of autism, regardless of physical or mental disability, the rate jumps to around 21 per 10,000 (Wing & Gould, 1979).

Researchers have also been interested in several other statistics pertaining to autism. Kanner (1954/1973) reported 100 cases of autism and found that almost 60% were first-born or only children. Subsequent studies have not detected this significant birth-order effect (Ando & Tsuda, 1975; Lotter, 1966, 1978; Spencer, Simmons, Brown, & Wilker, 1973; Treffert, 1970). However, investigators have consistently found a male to female ratio of around 4 to 1 (Ando & Tsuda, 1975; Kanner, 1954; Lotter, 1966, 1978; Rutt & Oxford, 1971; Spence, Simmons, Brown, & Wikler, 1973; Treffert, 1970). The incidence of autism among siblings of autistic children is consistently reported at around 2% (Coleman & Rimland, 1976; Hanson & Gottesman, 1976). This is about what would be expected by chance alone (Hanson & Gottesman, 1976). With respect to twins, both children of an identical twin pair are afflicted in 82–86% of cases, while both children of a fraternal twin pair are afflicted in about 25% of cases (Hanson & Gottesman, 1976). The last two statistics, taken together, suggest that while there may be some genetic basis for autism, there is not a simple, clear-cut genetic mechanism responsible for the condition (Hanson & Gottesman, 1976; Spence, 1976).

Etiology

While no cause of autism has yet been determined, a number of speculative theories have been advanced in the search for the etiolgy of the disorder. Researchers and theorists have focused their attentions on three fundamental mechanisms: (1) relations between autistic children and their surrounding social environment; (2) cognitive deficits and abnormalities; and (3) basic biochemical processes. Representative literature from each of these three areas is discussed in the next section.

Social Environment

Much of the early speculation concerning the causes of autism focused on apparent abnormalities in the parenting and family life experienced by autistic children. Environmental variables that might explain autism have been reviewed by Cantwell, Baker, and Rutter (1978), Cox, Rutter, Newman, and Bartak (1977), L'Abate (1972), Rimland (1964, 1972), and Ward (1970). The first evidence favoring this viewpoint is Kanner's observations (Kanner, 1943; Eisenberg & Kanner, 1956) of the parents of autistic children. Kanner described them as upper-class, well educated parents, involved in careers and intellectual pursuits, who are aloof, obsessive, and emotionally cold. Against this he contrasted another set of findings: (1) many autistic children were reported to have had impairments of social relationships from birth; (2) many parents of autistic children have also raised nonpsychotic children; and (3) many cold, aloof parents produce no autistic children. Despite representations to the contrary (Ward, 1970), Kanner does not actually believe that "refrigerator parents" are the sole cause of autism. He is not a proponent of any specific causal mechanism and concluded either that autism must be a biosocial phenomenon in which a predisposing organic condition interacts with unfavorable social conditions (Eisenberg & Kanner, 1956), or that autistic children must suffer from a more exaggerated version of a familial tendency toward social isolation (Kanner, 1954/1973).

A proliferation of theories hypothesizing relationships between family life and autism has followed Kanner's observations. Included among these factors are parental rejection, child responses to deviant parental personality characteristics, family breakup, family stress, insufficient stimulation, and faulty communication patterns (Cantwell *et al.*, 1978; Cox *et al.*, 1977; Ward, 1970). Much of the literature in this area has been of a psychoanalytic persuasion, although the same concept has also been expressed in more behavioral–ethological terms (e.g., Zaslow & Breger, 1969). Psychoanalysts favor the environmental viewpoint because they see autism, characterized by the absence of relations with physical or social objects and a preoccupation with inner stimuli, as the first stage of normal development. The shift from "primary narcissism" to object relations is seen as being accomplished through nuturing maternal acts (Spitz, 1965). Thus, a failure to progress through proper developmental stages can be attributed to a failure of mothering.

Two writers who have attempted to establish a psychodynamic mechanism that would account for autism are Bettelheim (1967) and Ruttenberg (1971). Bettelheim is the most notable proponent of this type of explanation. The essential elements of his theory are as follows. The young infant is actively engaged in exploring and reaching out to the people and objects in his environment. During several critical developmental periods, which roughly correspond with nursing, recognition of parents, and toilet training, the child may react to any number of real or imagined threats from the environment. That these threats could be imagined is also suggested by Mahler (1952), Rank (1955), and Weiland and Rudinick (1961). In response to these threats, the child begins to explore less actively. If the parents react to this withdrawal by withdrawal or evasion, the child learns that his actions do not lead to satisfying responses from the environment. This leads to chronic autistic withdrawal from the outside world. Key assumptions in this hypothesized developmental process are: (1) Children at very early ages actively interpret their experiences; (2) children who become autistic are unusually sensitive to their experiences; (3) children who become autistic have parents who are either unwilling or unable to provide satisfactory responses to their child; and (4) the children willfully immerse themselves in autism. In addition, Bettelheim doubts Kanner's claim that some children are born autistic. He believes that any autistic characteristics noted in the first weeks of life are a reaction to parenting that has already taken place.

Many criticisms have been lodged against environmental theories of autism (e.g., L'Abate, 1972; Rimland, 1964, 1972; Rutter, 1971; Schopler & Reichler, 1971; J. Wing, 1968). Chief among the criticisms is that the deviant interactions claimed to be responsible for autism have never been systematically observed. Some authors have adopted *ad hoc* theories of causality in the absence of any empirical support (e.g., Bettelheim, 1968; Zaslow & Breger, 1969). Other writers have attempted to infer parental rejections or parental deviance from self-report or projective techniques. The use of such methods is questionable given that the demand characteristics of a psychiatric interview session might prompt parents to shade their accounts of family or emotional life in the direction of the interviewer's expectancies (Orne, 1962; Yarrow, 1963). This is among the reasons why many investigators have turned to systematic observation procedures in their study of the lives of developmentally disabled children (e.g., Sackett, 1978). Additionally, it has been widely documented that children can have a strong effect on the behavior of their caretakers (Bell, 1968, 1971; Yarrow, Waxler, & Scott, 1971). Any lack of social responsiveness on the part of parents could easily be attributed to their reactions to the lack of social behavior, excessive tantrums, and bizarre behavior of their autistic children (Rimland, 1964; Rutter, 1968; Schopler & Reichler, 1971). Finally, the most damaging piece of evidence against the environmental viewpoint has come from recent, more methodologically sound studies (Cantwell *et al.*, 1978; Cox *et al.*, 1977). In studies using adequate experimental controls, parents of autistic children were found to be no different than parents of children from other clinical populations (such as developmental aphasia) on measures of personality and social interaction (Cox *et al.*, 1977; DeMyer, Pontues, Norton, Barton, Allen, & Steele, 1972; Koegel, Schreibman, O'Neill, & Burke, 1980; L'Abate, 1972; McAdoo & DeMyer, 1978; Pitfield & Oppenheim, 1964; Schopler & Loftin, 1969). There is also no evidence of a greater incidence of divorce among parents of autistic children than among parents of normal or other clinical population children (Cantwell *et al.*, 1978; Cox *et al.*, 1977).

One area of doubt still remains concerning the environment of autistic children. That is: Do autistic children come from educated, upper-middle-class families? Eisenberg and Kanner (1956) found that after 12 years and 120 families, their original finding with respect to parent socioeconomic status (SES) was maintained. A majority of parents were well educated professionals of distinction, in contrast to their normal clientele. This finding has been confirmed by other investigators (Cox *et al.*, 1977; Kolvin, 1971; Levine & Olson, 1968; Lotter, 1966; Rimland, 1964; Schopler, Andrews, & Strupp, 1979; Treffert, 1970), although at least six studies have not found unusually high SES among parents of autistic children (Schopler *et al.*, 1979). Schopler *et al.* (1979) put forth several explanations for the finding, such as: High SES individuals have more detailed information about child development, are more likely to identify their child's disability at an earlier age, maintain more detailed records of their child's developmental history, and will travel further for help. Their own study (Schopler *et al.*, 1979) confirmed these factors. Thus, Schopler and his colleagues conclude that researchers are more likely to come into contact with upper SES parents as a result of factors that systematically bias their sample. On the other hand, several of the studies reporting a higher incidence of upper SES parents of autistic children appear to be well controlled for such a bias (e.g., Cox *et al.*, 1977; Kolvin, 1971; Lotter, 1966; Treffert, 1970). At this time, it seems best to conclude that, although autistic children come from all classes and backgrounds, a moderate effect with respect to SES may exist.

Neurological Approaches

As indicated earlier, autistic children display abnormal responses to sensory stimuli. These sensory abnormalities have been conceptualized variously as: (1) a failure to maintain consistent representations of perceptual experience (Ornitz & Ritvo, 1968); (2) a failure to develop from reliance upon touch, movement, and smell to a reliance upon vision and hearing (Goldfarb, 1956; Schopler, 1965); and (3) a failure to transfer information between sensory modalities (Hermelin & O'Connor, 1970). Many have attempted to explain the sensory abnormalities of autistic children in terms of disruptions in underlying neurological mechanisms. Autistic children have literally been studied waking, sleeping, dreaming. What follows is a selective review of some of the more prominent categories of neurological investigation. For additional information on this topic, the reader is referred to Ornitz (1978) or Piggott (1979).

Reticular Activating System

The reticular activating system (RAS) is a cluster of neurons at the top of the spinal column connected to fibers from each of the sensory pathways. On the basis of information coming upward from the sensory receptors, the RAS is able to arouse the cerebral cortex. Information traveling downward from the cortex through the RAS places the body in readiness for action (Boddy, 1978). Rimland (1964) has hypothesized that a lesion in the RAS of autistic children leads to a chronic state of underarousal, thus limiting their ability to respond to external stimuli. Alternatively, Hutt, Hutt, Lee, and Ounsted (1965) suggest that a chronic overarousal of the RAS causes autistic children to defensively filter out external stimuli and avoid situations, such as changes in the environment, which might increase arousal. A third theory of RAS involvement is put forth by DesLauriers and Carlson (1969), who propose an imbalance in the relationship between the RAS and the limbic system. They believe that the limbic system, which is involved in emotion, motivation, and reinforcement, is inhibited by the RAS, rendering the autistic child unable to make associations between behavior and positive or negative rewards. While each of these positions is theoretically plausible, there is no direct evidence to support any of them. Since it has not yet been possible for investigators to observe a functioning reticular system, we must rely on indirect evidence from clinical observations or observations of children's behavior in controlled experiments (see Lovaas, Koegel, & Schreibman, 1979). At the present, however, there is no consistent evidence either that autistic children are chronically over- or underaroused or that the RAS is involved in autism (Ornitz, 1978; Rutter, 1978b). For example, abnormal arousal states may be a secondary to another factor such as environmental stimulation (Lovaas *et al.,* 1979).

Vestibular System

The vestibular system is a complex of fluid-filled canals located in the inner ear. It is responsive to the pull of gravity, aids in maintaining balance orientation in space, and has some control over the occular muscles such that vision remains stable during movement (Boddy, 1978). Ornitz (1970) reviews literature which indicates that vestibular nuclei also play a role in physiological activity occurring in rapid-eye-movement (REM) sleep. Clinical observations of autistic children and schizophrenic children with autistic tendencies (e.g., Bender & Faretra, 1972; Bergman & Escalona, 1949) indicate many unusual reactions to activities involving motion and gravity (for example, fearful reactions to being swung, being held upside down, riding in elevators or trains). These observations led Ornitz and his colleagues to conduct a series of investigations of vestibular function in autistic children (reviewed in Ornitz, 1978). Eye movements of autistic and schizophrenic children during REM sleep (Tanguay, Ornitz, Forsythe, & Ritvo, 1976), in response to vestibular stimulation during sleep (Ornitz, Forsythe, & de la Pena, 1973), and following rotations in a moving chair (Ornitz, Brown, Mason, & Putnam, 1974) have led Ornitz (1974) to conclude that a dysfunction of the vestibular system plays a possible causal role in the disturbances characteristic of autism. Ornitz (1974) speculates that since the vestibular system is involved in both visual and motor activity, these findings may indicate a fundamental dysfunction in the process of sensorimotor integration. Symptoms of autism such as language and social impairment would then be a result of this more general cognitive impairment (Ornitz, 1971). A criticism of the methods used in this line of investigation has been lodged by Yule (1978), who takes Ornitz and colleagues to task for their failure to control for mental and chronological age or to include children with other categories of disorder in their studies.

Electroencephalography

Electroencephalogram (EEG) studies of autistic children have also been used to explore the link between neurological dysfunction and autism. Reviews of this approach appear in Barnet (1979), Ornitz (1978) and in Piggott (1979). A central issue in this research is the response of brain waves to auditory or visual stimuli, although some EEGs have been performed in the absence of presented stimuli. Conclusions from this line of inquiry are difficult to make because of the enormous number of complications involved. Particular brain waves of responses are difficult to detect because they are buried in electrical activity from other parts of the brain. Autistic children are uncooperative, restless, and inattentive research participants. Slight disturbances, such as eye movements or stimuli from the external environment, easily throw off readings (Ornitz, 1978). For this reason, EEG studies are sometimes carried out while the children are sleeping.

The results of EEG studies conducted without the presentation of stimuli have shown autistic children to have EEG patterns signifcantly different from normal children of the same ages (Piggott, 1979). However, despite these differences, no unique EEG patterns characteristic of autism have been detected. One promising finding is that autistic children do not exhibit the higher voltages over one of the two brain hemispheres characteristic of normal children. This could indicate a failure to develop functional lateralization of brain hemispheres (Small, 1971). Since it is believed that language functions are carried out in specialized locations of the brain, such a finding, were it confirmed and extended, could result in a better understanding of the language impairment typical of autism (Barnet, 1979).

Those researchers studying EEG responses of autistic children to auditory and visual stimuli have also found evoked potential responses significantly different from normal, but without a pattern unique to autism (Barnet, 1979; Ornitz, 1978). Even within a given group of autistic children, evoked potential patterns are subject to a great deal of variability (Ornitz, 1978). The evoked potential abnormalities that have been found have led to various interpretations. One possible explanation is that autistic children experience a delay in neurological maturation (Ornitz, 1978). This interpretation corresponds with the finding of Tanguay *et al.* (1976) that the eye movement patterns of autistic children during REM sleep resemble those of younger normal children. The abnormalities of evoked potential responses to auditory stimuli also could be interpreted as a peripheral hearing loss (Rosenblum, Arick, Krug, Stubbs, Young, & Pelson, 1980). In general, this area of investigation is highly promising but currently in its infancy. Few investigations have been performed, fewer have been replicated, usually only small numbers of children have participated, and few comparisons have been made between autistic children and children with other types of disabilities.

Biochemistry

Biochemical approaches to etiology are yet another area of study. Within the past 20 years, numerous studies have attempted to isolate a link between neurochemical processes of the central nervous system and autistic behavior (Coleman, 1973; Piggott, 1979; Ritvo, Rabin, Yuwiler, Freeman, & Geller, 1978; Shaywitz & Cohen, 1979; Yuwiler, Geller, & Ritvo, 1976). Researchers hope to duplicate the success of Jervis's (1953) discovery of a metabolic error responsible for phenylketonuria, a form of mental retardation, which led to an effective dietary treatment regime.

A complete discussion of work in this area requires the presentation of a great deal of background information from physiology and biochemistry. A greatly simplified version will be presented here, merely to give the reader the flavor of this style of investigation. For more detailed coverage, the interested reader is encouraged to pursue the review articles listed.

Yuwiler *et al.* (1976) describe the complexity of biochemical research. Typically, the first step is an observation of different levels of a chemical substance in autistic and normal children. Next, many confounding factors must be ruled out as an explanation for the difference. For example, if the autistic children in such a study live in institutions, abnormal levels of chemical compounds may be caused by institutional diet or activity patterns. Finally, a good deal of research is needed in order to show that the chemical abnormality plays a central role in the disease.

The majority of biochemical studies have explored the workings of the biogenic amines serotonin, norepinephrine and dopamine. These chemical compounds are believed to be involved in transmissions between neurons within the central nervous system and appear to be related to emotional experience.

One hypothesis under investigation is that the autistic syndrome is the result of a failure in the metabolism of one of the biogenic amines. One piece of evidence for a metabolic error would be the presence of abnormal amounts of biogenic amines or their byproducts in the blood or urine of autistic children. The results of studies that measured naturally occurring concentrations of these substances in autistic and comparison groups of children have been inconclusive. Both abnormally high and abnormally low levels of biogenic amines have been detected in autistic populations; both differences and no differences in amine levels have been found when comparing autistic children to children of other psychiatric categories. There are even wide variations of amine concentrations among autistic children within the same experimental group (Coleman, 1973; Piggott, 1979; Shaywitz & Cohen, 1979).

Researchers have also attempted to exacerbate the hypothesized metabolic error as an alternative to measuring naturally occurring concentrations of chemical compounds. In this procedure, autistic and comparison children have been given large dosages (or "loads") of the chemical precursors from which the biogenic amines are metabolized. The results of loading research have been equivocal (Piggott, 1979; Shaywitz & Cohen, 1979) and so investigators have thus far not been successful in finding a metabolic error responsible for autism.

Another hypothesis concerning the etiologic role played by biogenic amines in autism is that the amines take on hallucinogenic properties and accumulate in the brain. In this sense, it is possible that the experience of autism would be somewhat similar to being on a permanent LSD "trip." Concentrations of a substance called bufotenin found in the urine of autistic children lend support to this notion, but it is not clear that the bufotenin originated in the brain or in some other body tissue (Shaywitz & Cohen, 1979). Similar evidence exists for schizophrenia in the form of a "pink spot" found in the urine of schizophrenics. Again, direct links between this chemical, the central nervous system, and psychosis have not been proven, and this finding remains unreplicated (Ritvo *et al.,* 1978; Shaywitz & Cohen, 1979). Loading procedures have also been used to test this hypothesis. Presumably administrations of a biogenic amine precursor over a period of time would step up the hallucinogenic effects. However, no changes in autistic behavior were observed as a result of precursor loading (Shaywitz & Cohen, 1979).

Thus we see that studies attempting to show a relationship between biochemical abnormalities and autism have produced highly tentative findings and no firm conclusions. In general, the major difficulty with neurochemical studies is that we are not able to directly observe central nervous system processes such as amine metabolism or neural transmissions. Any investigations of these processes measure rates or levels of substances several steps removed from the event of interest. Research in this area has for the most part been limited to examinations of substances occurring in the blood or urine, not the nervous system itself. Many of the substances that occur in the nervous system and that have a hypothesized relationship to psychosis also occur in other parts of the body. For example, if abnormal levels of an amine are detected in the blood, possible causes such as gastrointestinal disease and diseases of the vascular system, thyroid, and platelets must be ruled out (Coleman, 1973). It must be shown that concentrations of substances found in the body fluids must be present in the central nervous system in sufficiently excessive or depleted amounts to bear a relationship to psychotic behavior (Brown, 1976). A more fundamental problem with investigations that find too much or too little of a certain chemical in the body fluids may be the cross-sectional nature of the experimental design. Menkes (1979) points out that if a system is disturbed, measuring abnormal chemical concentrations at one point in time may be less important than monitoring the evolution of the system across time.

Shaywitz and Cohen (1979) propose animal analog experiments as one means to circumvent the inexactness of human investigations. In this procedure, rats are given chemicals that create neurological conditions hypothesized by the researcher to be responsible for autism. The animals are then observed to determine whether behavioral patterns emerge that are similar to those of brain-damaged children. However, Prensky (1979) questions the validity of such methods, given that the central features of autism such as language impairment and disturbed social relationships involve higher order abilities not possessed by rats.

Finally, neurobiological studies of autism have been plagued by an easily corrected but prevalent confound: the inclusion of children from several different clinical populations in experimental and comparison conditions. Participants in such studies have included groups labeled as psychotic, schizophrenic, hospitalized, mildly and severely retarded, as well as autistic (Coleman, 1973) Even within the category of autism alone, there are several subgroups that may have different etiologies (Coleman, 1976). In order for the results of neurobiological studies of autism to be clearly interpretable, researchers must be careful to utilize homogeneous comparison groups.

Summary Comments

As the reader has no doubt determined, nothing about autism seems to be simple. Issues regarding differential diagnosis, behavioral characteristics, etiology, and assessment continue to be addressed in the autism literature. As befitting the complex nature of its characteristics, autism has proven to be most difficult to treat and has provided many problems for all those involved in the lives of the children. While we have attempted here to provide an academic discussion of autism, perhaps it is best to present the case of an individual child to help give the flavor of the disorder. The following is that of an autistic child at the time of evaluation, with no treatment history.

Case Presentation—"Brady"

At first sight, Brady looks like he should be selling corn flakes on television commercials. He is a beautiful 4-year-old with huge brown eyes, curly brown hair, and delicate bone structure. Yet, one only needs to observe him for a few minutes until the bizarre behavior so characteristic of autism becomes evident.

Brady was adopted at the age of 6 weeks by his present parents. He has always enjoyed very good health although he is a poor eater and remains quite thin. His physical development has been unremarkable except for a delay in standing and walking. While walking was delayed, his mother reports that at age 19 months he just "stood up and walked." He never went through the toddler stage. Once walking, Brady could run, jump, and balance himself with apparent ease. He is now very agile and can, according to his mother, "run full speed on the top of a narrow fence."

Brady's mother first became concerned when the boy actively resisted affection. Typically, he would not allow anyone to hold or cuddle him and, when people made such overtures toward him, he stiffened, pushed away, and screamed. On those rare occasions when he would allow his mother to hold him, he did so passively, not holding her in return. He was like a limp rag doll.

As might be expected, Brady was a very "good" baby. He never demanded attention, did not cry for his mother, and was most content when left alone. Even now he will wander off by himself, away from the family, and remain isolated for as long as possible. He does not interact with peers and actively withdraws from social initiations to other children.

The extent of Brady's social withdrawal is further illustrated by his almost nonexistent eye contact and his failure to notice other people in his immediate environment. During the diagnostic evaluation interview with one of the authors, he at no time gave any indication that he was aware of the examiner's presence in the room. Indeed, despite numerous attempts to gain his attention (calling his name, offering toys, etc.) he never established eye contact or responded in any manner. On one occasion, when the examiner reached out and touched him, he pulled abruptly away and said "NO!" This was his only acknowledgment of the examiner in almost 2 hours.

Perhaps most disturbing to Brady's parents is his lack of any attachment to them. Not only does the child resist affection but he does not seem to "need" them. He is not upset when his mother leaves him (e.g., at preschool), nor is he happy when she returns. He frequently does not seem to even notice their presence. He does not spontaneously come to them for comfort when hurt nor at any other time. His mother sums it up by saying that she feels Brady "uses" her for the attainment of his needs and that he is not really attached to her. "If it wasn't me filling his needs," she says, "it could just as well be a stranger."

Brady did not speak until the age of 3. At first he used words such as "ma ma" and "da da" but he used them indiscriminately, apparently unable to tie them to the correct referents. As his speech increased, it was entirely echolalic. He presently engages in a great deal of immediate and delayed echolalia, all with minimal communicative intent. He can label objects and pictures, but does so in an echolalic fashion. For example, when presented with a picture of a truck, he may say "What is this, Brady? It's a truck. That's good, Brady." The truck picture triggers a delayed echolalic response. His receptive language is somewhat more advanced than his expressive language. Although he typically echoes questions and commands, he can comply to simple requests such as answer his name or sit in a chair.

Brady's parents suspected a hearing impairment might be the reason for some of his unusual behaviors. He did not speak until age 3, which might be attributed to deafness. Similarly, he neither responded to his name, loud noises, nor the voices of others. However, a hearing evaluation and the appearance of echolalia dispelled concerns about a hearing impairment. Brady's apparent sensory deficit was typically autistic in nature.

Like many other autistic children, Brady is very concerned with maintaining sameness in his environment. He notices even the most minute changes in furniture arrangements or if anything in a room is out of its usual place. On such occasions he will become quite agitated and will attempt to restore the situation to its previous state. He also remembers specific routes to places (even if he has been there only once) and resists any attempt to deviate from the route on future occasions. This resistance typically takes the form of a tantrum. As part of Brady's demand for order and sameness, he has established a number of rituals that must be performed a certain way. These include certain sequences of behavior for toileting, eating, and dressing. Again, any interruption of the ritual is met with a tantrum. Perhaps related to his attention to his environment are Brady's unusual and intense fears. His mother reports that these fears are irrational, intense, and frequently changing. For example, at the time of evaluation Brady was terrified of bread (he would eat it but not touch it), tortillas, yellow ducks, and pictures of five dogs. His reaction to these last three items took the form of screaming, crying, and violent shaking.

Brady exhibits several self-stimulatory behaviors including foot-to-foot rocking, rocking of the upper torso, jumping, gazing out of the corners of his eyes, repetitive tapping of objects, and repetitive vocalizing. He is also quite skillful at spinning and twirling objects such as coasters and saucepan lids. His parents report that while engaged in these behaviors Brady is "in another world," and that it is very difficult to "snap him out of it." His toy play is repetitive and unimaginative. He explores toys rather than plays with them and seldom uses them for their intended purpose. For example, if given a toy truck he will turn it over and spin the wheels in a self-stimulatory manner.

Several of Brady's behaviors seem inconsistent with the severe deficits so apparent in other areas of functioning. His mother describes his memory as "incredible." For example, she took him to a particular department store when he was approximately 18 months of age. He did not enter that store again until he was almost 4½, yet he remembered exactly where particular types of items were and correctly noted the absence of a counter that had been in the store 3 years earlier but was no longer there. He is fascinated by children's books and knows his own books so well that, even if the covers are separated from the contents, he can match them up immediately. The books are all very similar in content, style, and coloring, and his mother reports that it takes her over an hour to correctly sort all the covers and contents. He also learned the entire alphabet in a matter of minutes and can sing rather complex songs with perfect pitch.

On standardized intellectual assessments, Brady tests from the moderately to mildly retarded range. The variability is probably due to the different skills emphasized by particular tests. He scores highest on visual–spatial form recognition and memory tasks and scores less well on conceptual, abstract, and logic tasks.

Brady's affect is typical of many autistic children in that it seems unrelated to the environmental context. He swings from laughter to tearful sobs almost instantaneously and without apparent reason. He laughs quite frequently while staring into space and also laughs when punished. He also seems unable to understand or respond to the emotional behavior of others. Thus, he seems truly isolated from the social environment.

Acknowledgments

The authors wish to thank Karen Britten and Marjorie H. Charlop for their helpful input.

References

Alpern, G. D. Measurement of "untestable" autistic children. *Journal of Abnormal Psychology,* 1967, *72,* 478–486.

American Association on Mental Deficiency. *Adaptive Behavior Scale* (1975 revision). Washington, D.C.: Author, 1975.

Ando, H., & Tsuda, K. Intrafamilial incidence of autism, cerebral palsy, and mongolism. *Journal of Autism and Childhood Schizophrenia,* 1975, *5,* 267–274.

Applebaum, E., Egel, A. L., Koegel, R. L., & Imhoff, B. Measuring musical abilities of autistic children. *Journal of Autism and Developmental Disorders,* 1979, *9,* 279–285.

Bachman, J. A. Self-injurious behavior: A behavioral analysis. *Journal of Abnormal Psychology,* 1972, *80,* 211–224.

Bakwin, H. Early infantile autism. *Journal of Pediatrics,* 1954, *45,* 492–497.

Barnet, A. B. Sensory evoked potentials in autism. In L. A. Lockman, K. F. Swaiman, J. S. Drage, K. B. Nelson, & H. M. Marsden (Eds.), *Workshop on the neurobiological basis of autism.* Bethesda, Md.: National Institutes of Health Publication 79–1855, 1979.

Bartak, L., & Rutter, M. Educational treatment of autistic children. In M. Rutter (Ed.), *Infantile autism: Concepts, characteristics and treatment.* London: Churchill-Livingstone, 1971.

Bartak, L., & Rutter, M. Use of personal pronouns by autistic children. *Journal of Autism and Childhood Schizophrenia,* 1974, *4,* 217–222.

Bartak, L., Rutter, M., & Cox, A. A comparative study of infantile autism and specific developmental receptive language disorder. I. The children. *British Journal of Psychiatry,* 1975, *126,* 127–145.

Bell, R. Q. A reinterpretation of the direction of effects in studies of socialization. *Psychological Review,* 1968, *75,* 81–95.

Bell, R. Q. Stimulus control of parent or caretaker behavior by offspring. *Developmental Psychology,* 1971, *4,* 63–72.

Bender, L., & Faretra, G. The relationship between childhood schizophrenia and adult schiizophrenia. In A. R. Kaplan (Ed.), *Genetic Factors in "Schizophrenia."* Springfield, Ill.: Charles C Thomas, 1972.

Bergman, P., & Escalona, S. K. Unusual sensitivities in very young children. *Psychoanalytic Study of the Child,* 1949, *3–4,* 333–353.

Bettelheim, B. *The empty fortress: Infantile autism and the birth of the self.* New York: Free Press, 1967.

Boddy, J. *Brain systems and psychological concepts.* New York: Wiley, 1978.

Bosch, G. Uber primären Autismus im Kindesalter. Cited by G. Bosch in *Infantile autism.* New York: Springer-Verlag, 1970. (Originally published, 1953.)

Bosch, G. *Infantile autism.* New York: Springer-Verlag, 1970.

Brask, B. H. *A prevalence investigation of childhood psychosis.* Paper given at the 16th Scandinavian Congress of Psychiatry, 1970. Cited by L. Wing, *Early childhood autism.* Oxford: Pergamon Press, 1976.

Bronfenbrenner, U. *The ecology of human development.* Cambridge, Mass.: Harvard University Press, 1979.

Brown, W. H. *Introduction to organic and biochemistry.* Boston: Willard Grant Press, 1976.

Cantwell, D. P., Baker, L., & Rutter, M. Family factors. In M. Rutter & E. Schopler (Eds.), *Autism: A reappraisal of concepts and treatment.* New York: Plenum Press, 1978.

Carr, E. G. The motivation of self-injurious behavior: A review of some hypotheses. *Psychological Bulletin,* 1977, *84,* 800–816.

Carr, E. G., Schreibman, L., & Lovaas, O. I. Control of echolalic speech in psychotic children. *Journal of Abnormal Child Psychology,* 1975, *3,* 331–351.

Churchill, D. W. The relation of infantile autism and early childhood schizophrenia to developmental language disorders of childhood. *Journal of Autism and Childhood Schizophrenia,* 1972, *2,* 182–197.

Churchill, D. W., & Bryson, C. Q. Looking and approach behavior of psychotic and normal children as a function of adult attention and preoccupation. *Comparative Psychiatry,* 1972, *13,* 171–177.

Coleman, M. Serotonin and central nervous system syndromes of childhood: A review. *Journal of Autism and Childhood Schizophrenia,* 1973, *3,* 27–35.

Coleman, M. Introduction. In M. Coleman (Ed.), *The autistic syndromes.* New York: American Elsevier, 1976.

Coleman, M., & Rimland, B. Familial autism. In M. Coleman (Ed.), *The autistic syndromes.* New York: American Elsevier, 1976.

Cox, A., Rutter, M., Newman, S., & Bartak, L. A comparative study of infantile autism and specific developmental receptive language disorder: Parental characteristics. In S. Chess & A. Thomas (Eds.), *Annual progress in child psychiatry and child development, 1976.* New York: Brunner Mazel, 1977.

Creak, M. Schizophrenia syndrome in childhood: Progress report of a working party. *Cerebral Palsy Bulletin,* 1961, *3,* 501–504.

Darley, F. L. *Daignosis and appraisal of communication disorders.* Englewood Cliffs, N.J.: Prentice-Hall, 1964.

Darr, G. C., & Worden, F. G. Case report twenty-eight years after an infantile autistic disorder. *American Journal of Orthopsychiatry,* 1951, *21,* 559–570.

Davison, G. C. A social learning therapy programme with an autistic child. *Behaviour Research and Therapy,* 1964, *2,* 149–159.

DeMyer, M. K., Barton, S., Alpern, G. D., Kimberlin, C., Allen, J., Yang, E., & Steele, R. The measured intelligence of autistic children. *Journal of Autism and Childhood Schizophrenia,* 1974, *4,* 42–60.

DeMyer, M., Pontues, W., Norton, J., Barton, S., Allen, J., & Steele, R. Parental practices and innate activity in autistic and brain-damaged infants. *Journal of Autism and Childhood Schizophrenia,* 1972, *2,* 49–66.

DesLauriers, A. M., & Carlson, C. F. *Your child is asleep: Early infantile autism.* Homewood, Ill.: Dorsey Press, 1969.

Despert, J. L. Some considerations relating to the genesis of autistic behaviour in children. *American Journal of Orthopsychiatry,* 1951, *21,* 335–350.

Doll, E. A. *Vineland social maturity scale: Manual of directions* (Rev. ed.). Minneapolis: American Guidance Service, 1965.

Eisenberg, L., & Kanner, L. Early infantile autism 1943–55. *American Journal of Orthopsychiatry,* 1956, *26,* 556–566.

Fay, W. H. Childhood echolalia: A group study of late abatement. *Folia Phoniatrica,* 1967, *19,* 297–306.

Fay, W. H. On the basis of autistic echolalia. *Journal of Communication Disorders,* 1969, *2,* 38–47.

Ferster, C. B., & DeMyer, M. K. Increased performances of an autistic child with prochlorperizine administration. *Journal of the Experimental Analysis of Behavior,* 1961, *4,* 84. (a)

Ferster, C. B., & DeMyer, M. K. The development of performances in autistic children in an automatically controlled environment. *Journal of Chronic Diseases,* 1961, *13,* 312–345. (b)

Ferster, C. B., & DeMyer, M. K. A method for the experimental analysis of the behavior of autistic children. *American Journal of Orthopsychiatry,* 1962, *32,* 89–98.

Frankel, F., & Simmons, J. Q. Self-injurious behavior in schizophrenic and retarded children. *American Journal of Mental Deficiency,* 1976, *80,* 512–522.

Gittelman, M., & Birch, H. G. Childhood schizophrenia: Intellect, neurologic status, perinatal risk, prognosis and family pathology. *Archives of Neurological Psychology,* 1967, *17,* 16–25.

Goldfarb, W. Receptor preferences in schizophrenic children. *Archives of Neurological Psychology,* 1956, *76,* 643–652.

Griffith, R., & Ritvo, E. R. Echolalia: Concerning the dynamics of the syndrome. *Journal of the American Academy of Child Psychiatry,* 1967, *6,* 184–193.

Hanson, D. R., & Gottesman, I. I. The genetics, if any, of infantile autism and childhood schizophrenia. *Journal of Autism and Childhood Schizophrenia,* 1976, *6,* 209–234.

Haslam, J. *Observations on madness and melancholy.* London: Hayden, 1809.

Hermelin, B., & O'Connor, N. *Psychological experiments with autistic children.* Oxford: Pergamon Press, 1970.

Hutt, C., & Vaizey, M. J. Differential effects of group density on social behaviour. *Nature (London),* 1966, *209,* 1371–1372.

Hutt, S. J., Hutt, C., Lee, D., & Ounsted, C. A behavioural and electroencephalographic study of autistic children. *Journal of Psychiatric Research,* 1965, *3,* 181–197.

Itard, J. M. G. *Mémoire et rapport sur Victor de l'Aveyron.* In L. Malson, *Les enfants sauvages.* Paris: Union Generale d'Editions, 1964. (Originally published, 1801).

Jervis, G. A. Phenylpyruvic oligophrenia: Deficiency of phenylalanine oxidizing system. *Proceedings of the Society for Experimental Biology and Medicine,* 1953, *82,* 514–515.

Kanner, L. Autistic disturbances of affective contact. *Nervous Child,* 1943, *2,* 217–250.

Kanner, L. The children haven't read those books. *Acta Paedopsychiatrica,* 1969, *36,* 2–11.

Kanner, L. To what extent is early infantile autism determined by constitutional inadequacies? Reprinted in L. Kanner. *Childhood psychosis: Initial studies and new insights.* Washington, D.C.: V. H. Winston & Sons, 1973. (Originally published, 1954.)

Koegel, R. L., & Covert, A. The relationship of self-stimulation to learning in autistic children. *Journal of Applied Behavior Analysis,* 1972, *5,* 381–387.

Koegel, R. L., & Wilhelm, H. Selective responding to the components of multiple visual cues by autistic children. *Journal of Experimental Child Psychology,* 1973, *15,* 442–453.

Koegel, R. L., Schreibman, L., O'Neill, R. E., & Burke, J. C. *The personality and family interaction characteristics of parents of autistic children.* Manuscript submitted for publication, 1980.

Kolvin, I. Psychoses in childhood: A comparative study. In M. Rutter (Ed.), *Infantile autism: Concepts, characteristics and treatment.* Edinburgh: Churchill-Livingstone, 1971.

Kozloff, M. A. *Educating children with learning and behavior problems.* New York: Wiley, 1974.

L'Abate, L. Early infantile autism: A reply to Ward. *Psychological Bulletin,* 1972, *77,* 49–51.

Levine, M., & Olson, R. P. Intelligence of parents of autistic children. *Journal of Abnormal Psychology,* 1968, *73,* 215–217.

Lockyer, L., & Rutter, M. A five to fifteen year follow-up study of infantile psychosis. III. Psychological aspects. *British Journal of Psychiatry,* 1969, *115,* 865–882.

Lotter, V. Epidemiology of autistic conditions in young children. I. Prevalence. *Social Psychiatry,* 1966, *1,* 124–137.

Lotter, V. Childhood autism in Africa. *Journal of Child Psychology and Psychiatry,* 1978, *19,* 231–244.

Lovaas, O. I., & Schreibman, L. Stimulus overselectivity of autistic children in a two stimulus situation. *Behaviour Research and Therapy,* 1971, *9,* 305–310.

Lovaas, O. I., & Simmons, J. Q. Manipulation of self-destruction in three retarded children. *Journal of Applied Behavior Analysis,* 1969, *2,* 143–157.

Lovaas, O. I., Berberich, J. P., Perloff, B. F., & Schaeffer, B. Acquisition of imitative speech by schizophrenic children. *Science,* 1966, *151,* 705–707.

Lovaas, I. I., Freitag, G., Gold, V. J., & Kassorla, I. C. Experimental studies in childhood schizophrenia: Analysis of self-destructive behavior. *Journal of Experimental Child Psychology,* 1965, *2,* 67–84.

Lovaas, O. I., Litrownik, A., & Mann, R. Response latencies to auditory stimuli in autistic children engaged in self-stimulatory behavior. *Behaviour Research and Therapy,* 1971, *9,* 39–49.

Lovaas, O. I., Koegel, R. L., & Schreibman, L. Stimulus overselectivity in autism: A review of research. *Psychological Bulletin,* 1979, *86,* 1236–1254.

Lovaas, O. I., Schreibman, L., Koegel, R., & Rehm, R. Selective responding by autistic children to multiple sensory input. *Journal of Abnormal Psychology,* 1971, *77,* 211–222.

Lovaas, O. I., Varni, J., Koegel, R. L., & Lorsch, N. L. Some observations on the non-extinguishability of children's speech. *Child Development,* 1977, *48,* 1121–1127.

Mahler, M. On child psychosis and schizophrenia, autistic and symbiotic infantile psychoses. *Psychoanalytic Study of the Child,* 1952, *7,* 286–305.

McAdoo, G. W., & DeMyer, M. K. Personality characteristics of parents. In M. Rutter & E. Schopler (Eds.), *Autism: A reappraisal of concepts and treatment.* New York: Plenum Press, 1978.

Menkes, J. H. Open discussion. In L. A. Lockman, K. F. Swaiman, J. S. Drage, K. B. Nelson, & H. M. Marsden (Eds.), *Workshop in the neurobiological basis of autism.* Bethesda, Md.: National Institutes of Health Publication 79-1855, 1979.

Menolascino, F. J. The description and classification of infantile autism. In D. W. Churchill, G. D. Alpern, & M. K. DeMyer (Eds.), *Infantile autism.* Proceedings of the Indiana University Colloquim. Springfield, Ill.: Charles C Thomas, 1971.

Newsom, C. D., & Rincover, A. Behavioral assessment of autistic children. In E. J. Mash & L. G. Terdal (Eds.), *Behavioral assessment of childhood disorders.* New York: Guilford Press, 1982.

O'Gorman, G. *The nature of childhood autism.* London: Butterworths, 1970.

Orne, M. T. On the social psychology of the psychological experiment: With particular reference to demand characteristics and their implications. *American Psychologist,* 1962, *17,* 776–783.

Ornitz, E. M. Vestibular dysfunction in schizophrenia and childhood autism. *Comprehensive Psychiatry,* 1970, *11,* 159–173.

Ornitz, E. M. Childhood autism: A disorder of sensorimotor integration. In M. Rutter (Ed.), *Infantile autism: Concepts, characteristics and treatment.* London: Churchill-Livingstone, 1971.

Ornitz, E. M. The modulation of sensory input and motor output in autistic children. *Journal of Autism and Childhood Schizophrenia,* 1974, *4,* 197–215.

Ornitz, E. M. Neurophysiologic studies. In M. Rutter & E. Schopler (Eds.), *Autism: A reappraisal of concepts and treatment.* New York: Plenum Press, 1978.

Ornitz, E. M., & Ritvo, E. R. Perceptual inconstancy in early infantile autism. *Archives of General Psychiatry,* 1968, *18,* 76–98.

Ornitz, E. M., & Ritvo, E. R. Medical assessment. In E. R. Ritvo, B. J. Freeman, E. M. Ornitz, & P. T. Tanguay (Eds.), *Autism: Diagnosis, current research and management.* New York: Spectrum, 1976.

Ornitz, E. M., Forsythe, A. B., & de la Pena, A. Effect of vestibular and auditory stimulation on the REMs of REM sleep in autistic children. *Archives of General Psychiatry,* 1973, *29,* 786–791.

Ornitz, E. M., Brown, M. B., Mason, A., & Putnam, N. H. Effect of visual input on vestibular nystagmus in autistic children. *Archives of General Psychiatry,* 1974, *31,* 369–375.

Piggott, L. R. Overview of selected basic research in autism. *Journal of Autism and Developmental Disorders,* 1979, *9,* 199–218.

Pitfield, M., & Oppenheim, A. N. Child rearing attitudes of mothers of psychotic children. *Journal of Child Psychology and Psychiatry and Allied Disciplines,* 1964, *5,* 51–57.

Polan, C. C., & Spencer, B. L. Checklist of symptoms of autism in early life. *West Virginia Medical Journal,* 1959, *55,* 198–204.

Prensky, A. L. Discussion. In L. A. Lockman, K. F. Swaiman, J. S. Drage, K. B. Nelson, & H. M. Marsden (Eds.), *Workshop on the neurobiological basis of autism*. Bethesda, Md.: National Institutes of Health Publication 79-1855, 1979.

Rank, B. Intensive study and treatment of preschool children who show marked personality deviations, or "atypical development," and their parents. In G. Caplan (Ed.), *Emotional problems of early childhood*. New York: Basic Books, 1955.

Reynolds, B. S., Newsom, C. D., & Lovaas, O. I. Auditory overselectivity in autistic children. *Journal of Abnormal Child Psychology,* 1974, *2,* 253-263.

Ricks, D. M., & Wing, L. Language, communication, and the use of symbols in normal and autistic children. *Journal of Autism and Childhood Schizophrenia,* 1975, *5,* 191-222.

Rimland, B. *Infantile autism*. New York: Appleton-Century-Crofts, 1964.

Rimland, B. Comment on Ward's "early infantile autism." *Psychological Bulletin,* 1972, *77,* 52-53.

Rimland, B. Inside the mind of an autistic savant. *Psychology Today,* 1978, *12,* 68-80.

Rincover, A. Sensory extinction: A procedure for eliminating self-stimulatory behavior in autistic children. *Journal of Abnormal Child Psychology,* 1978, *6,* 299-310.

Rincover, A. Variables affecting stimulus-fading and discriminative responding in psychotic children. *Journal of Abnormal Psychology,* 1978, *87,* 541-553.

Rincover, A., & Koegel, R. L. Setting generality and stimulus control in autistic children. *Journal of Applied Behavior Analysis,* 1975, *8,* 235-246.

Ritvo, E. R., Rabin, K., Yuwiler, A., Freeman, B. J., & Geller, E. Biochemical and hematologic studies. In M. Rutter & E. Schopler (Eds.), *Autism: A reappraisal of concepts and treatment*. New York: Plenum Press, 1978.

Ritvo, E. R., Rabin, K., Yuwiler, A., Freeman, B. J., & Geller, E. Biochemical and hematologic studies. In M. Rutter & E. Schopler (Eds.), *Autism: A reappraisal of concepts and treatment*. New York: Plenum, 1978.

Rosenblum, S. M., Arick, J. R., Krug, D. A., Stubbs, E. G., Young, N. B., & Pelson, R. O. Auditory brainstem evoked responses in autistic children. *Journal of Autism and Developmental Disorders,* 1980, *10,* 215-225.

Rutt, C. N., & Oxford, D. R. Prenatal and perinatal complications in childhood schizophrenics and their siblings. *Journal of Nervous and Mental Disorders,* 1971, *152,* 324-331.

Ruttenberg, B. A psychoanalytic understanding of infantile autism and its treatment. In D. W. Churchill, G. D. Alpern, & M. K. DeMyer (Eds.), *Infantile autism*. Springfield, Ill.: Charles C Thomas, 1971.

Rutter, M. Speech disorders in a series of autistic children. In A. W. Franklin (Ed.), *Children with communication problems*. London: Pitman, 1965.

Rutter, M. Behavioural and cognitive characteristics of a series of psychotic children. In J. Wing (Ed.), *Early childhood autism*. Oxford: Pergamon, 1966.

Rutter, M. Concepts of autism: A review of research. *Journal of Child Psychology and Psychiatry,* 1968, *9,* 1-25.

Rutter, M. The description and classification of infantile autism. In D. W. Churchill, G. D. Alpern, & M. K. DeMyer (Eds.), *Infantile autism*. Springfield, Ill.: Charles C Thomas, 1971.

Rutter, M. Childhood schizophrenia reconsidered. *Journal of Autism and Childhood Schizophrenia,* 1972, *2,* 315-337.

Rutter, M. Diagnosis and definition of childhood autism. *Journal of Autism and Childhood Schizophrenia,* 1978, *8,* 139-161. (a)

Rutter, M. Etiology and treatment: Cause and cure. In M. Rutter & E. Schopler, *Autism: A reappraisal of concepts and treatment*. New York: Plenum Press, 1978. (b)

Rutter, M., & Bartak, L. Special educational treatment of autistic children: A comparative study. II. Follow-up findings and implications for services. *Journal of Child Psychology and Psychiatry,* 1973, *14,* 241-270.

Rutter, M., & Lockyer, L. A five to fifteen year follow-up study of infantile psychosis. I. Description of sample. *British Journal of Psychiatry,* 1967, *113,* 1169-1182.

Rutter, M., Bartak, L., & Newman, S. Autism—a central disorder of cognition and language? In M. Rutter (Ed.), *Infantile autism: Concepts, characteristics and treatment*. London: Churchill-Livingstone, 1971.

Sackett, G. P. (Ed.). *Observing behavior: Theory and applications in mental retardation* (Vol. 1). Baltimore: University Park Press, 1978.

Schaffer, H. R. Changes in developmental quotient under two conditions of maternal separation. *British Journal of Social and Clinical Psychology,* 1965, *4,* 39-46.

Schopler, E. Early infantile autism and the receptor processes. *Archives of General Psychiatry,* 1965, *13,* 327-335.

Schopler E. On confusion in the diagnosis of autism. *Journal of Autism and Childhood Schizophrenia,* 1978, *8,* 137-138.

Schopler, E., & Loftin, J. Thinking disorder in parents of young psychotic children. *Journal of Abnormal Psychology,* 1969, *14,* 281–287.

Schopler, E., & Reichler, R. J. Developmental therapy by parents with their own autistic child. In M. Rutter (Eds.), *Infantile autism: Concepts, characteristics and treatment.* London: Churchill-Livingstone, 1971.

Schopler, E., Andrews, C. E., & Strupp, K. Do autistic children come from upper-middle-class parents? *Journal of Autism and Developmental Disorders,* 1979, *9,* 139–152.

Schreibman, L. Effects of within-stimulus and extra-stimulus prompting on discrimination learning in autistic children. *Journal of Applied Behavior Analysis,* 1975, *8,* 91–112.

Schreibman, L., & Carr, E. G. Elimination of echolalic responding to questions through the training of a generalized verbal response. *Journal of Applied Behavior Analysis,* 1978, *11,* 453–463.

Schreibman, L., & Koegel, R. L. A guideline for planning behavior modification programs for autistic children. In S. Turner, K. Calhoun, & A. Adams (Eds.), *Handbook of clinical behavior therapy.* New York: Wiley, 1981.

Schreibman, L., & Koegel, R. L. Multiple cue responding in autistic children. In P. Karoly & J. J. Steffen (Eds.), *Advances in child behavior analysis and therapy.* New York: Lexington/D.C. Heath, in press.

Schreibman, L., & Lovaas, O. I. Overselective response to social stimuli by autistic children. *Journal of Abnormal Child Psychology,* 1973, *1,* 152–168.

Shaywitz, B. A., & Cohen, D. J. The neurochemical basis of infantile autism. In L. A. Lockman, K. F. Swaiman, J. S. Drage, K. B. Nelson, & H. M. Marsden (Eds.), *Workshop on the neurobiological basis of autism.* Bethesda, Md.: National Institutes of Health Publication 79-1855, 1979.

Smell, J. G. Sensory evoked response of autistic children. In D. W. Churchill, G. D. Alpern, & M. K. DeMyer (Eds.), *Infantile autism: Proceedings of the Indiana University Colloquium.* Springfield, Ill.: Charles C Thomas, 1971.

Smolev, S. R. Use of operant techniques for the modification of self-injurious behavior. *American Journal of Mental Deficiency,* 1971, *76,* 295–305.

Sorosky, A. D., Ornitz, E. M., Brown, N. B., & Ritvo, E. R. Systematic observations of autistic behavior. *Archives of General Psychiatgry,* 1968, *18,* 439–449.

Spence, M. A. Genetic studies. In E. R. Ritvo, B. J. Freeman, E. M. Ornitz, & P. E. Tanquay, *Autism: Diagnosis, current research and management.* New York: Spectrum, 1976.

Spence, M. A., Simmons, J. Q., Brown, N. A., & Wikler, L. Sex rating in families of autistic children. *American Journal of Mental Deficiency,* 1973, *77,* 405–407.

Spitz, R. A. Hospitalism: An inquiry into the genesis of psychiatric conditions in early childhood. *Psychoanalytic Study of the Child,* 1945, *1,* 153–172.

Spitz, R. A. *The first year of life.* New York: International Universities Press, 1965.

Tanguay, P. E., Ornitz, E. M., Forsythe, A. B., & Ritvo, E. R. Rapid eye movement (REM) activity in normal and autistic children during REM sleep. *Journal of Autism and Childhood Schizophrenia,* 1976, *6,* 275–288.

Tate, B. G., & Baroff, G. S. Aversive conrrol of self-injurious behavior in a psychotic boy. *Behaviour Research and Therapy,* 1966, *4,* 281–287.

Treffert, D. A. Epidemiology of infantile autism. *Archives of General Psychiatry,* 1970, *22,* 431–438.

Vaillant, G. E. John Haslam on early infantile autism. *American Journal of Psychiatry,* 1962, *119,* 376.

van Krevelen, D. A. Early infantile autism. *Acta Paedopsychiatrica,* 1952, *91,* 81–97.

Van Riper, C. *Speech correction.* Englewood Cliffs, N.J.: Prentice-Hall, 1963.

Varni, J., Lovaas, O. I., Koegel, R. L., & Everett, N. L. An analysis of observational learning in autistic and normal children. *Journal of Abnormal Child Psychology,* 1979, *7,* 31–43.

Wakabayashi, S. A case of infantile autism associated with Down's syndrome. *Journal of Autism and Developmental Disorders,* 1979, *9,* 31–36.

Ward, A. J. Early infantile autism: Diagnosis, etiology and treatment. *Psychological Bulletin,* 1970, *73,* 350–362.

Weiland, H., & Rudinick, R. Considerations of the development and treatment of autistic childhood psychosis. *Psychoanalytic Study of the Child,* 1961, *16,* 549–563.

Wing, J. K. Review of *The empty fortress* by B. Bettelheim. *British Journal of Psychology,* 1968, *114,* 788–791.

Wing, J. K. Kanner's syndrome: A historical introduction. In L. Wing (Ed.), *Early childhood autism: Clinical, educational and social aspects* (2nd ed.). Oxford: Pergamon Press, 1976.

Wing, L. The handicaps of autistic children—a comparative study. *Journal of Child Psychology and Psychiatry,* 1969, *10,* 1–40.

Wing, L. Diagnosis, clinical description and prognosis. In L. Wing (Ed.), *Early childhood autism: Clnical, educational and social aspects* (2nd ed.). Oxford: Pergamon Press, 1976.

Wing, L., & Gould, J. Severe impairments of social interaction and associated abnormalities in children: Epidemiology and classification. *Journal of Autism and Developmental Disorders,* 1979, *9,* 11–29.

Wolf, M. M., Risley, T. R., & Mees, H. Application of operant conditioning procedures to the behavior problems of an autistic child. *Behaviour Research and Therapy,* 1964, *1,* 305–312.

Wolff, S., & Chess, S. A behavioural study of schizophrenic children. *Acta Psychiatrica Scandinavica,* 1964, *40,* 438–466.

Yarrow, M. R. Problems of methods in parent–child research. *Child Development,* 1963, *34,* 215–226.

Yarrow, M. R., Waxler, C. Z., & Scott, P. M. Child effects on adult behavior. *Developmental Psychology,* 1971, *5,* 300–311.

Yule, W. Research methodology: What are the "correct controls?" In M. Rutter & E. Schopler, *Autism: A reappraisal of concepts and treatment.* New York: Plenum Press, 1978.

Yuwiler, A., Geller, E., & Ritvo, R. Neurobiochemical research. In E. R. Ritvo, B. J. Freeman, E. M. Ornitz, & P. E. Tanguay (Eds.). *Autism: Diagnosis, current research and management.* New York: Halsted Press, 1976.

Zaslow, R. W., & Breger, L. A theory and treatment of autism. In L. Breger (Ed.), *Clinical–cognitive psychology.* Englewood Cliffs, N.J.: Prentice-Hall, 1969.

Zipf, G. K. *Human behavior and the principle of least effort.* New York: Hafner, 1949.

7

Hyperactivity, Learning Problems, and the Attention Deficit Disorders

CAROL K. WHALEN

Introduction

Everybody probably knows at least one child considered to be hyperactive, and this child is most likely to be a school-age boy. These youngsters often behave impulsively or act before thinking, a pattern that may lead both to social friction and to academic failure. They have difficulty focusing on a single activity and often shift erratically from one task to another without finishing those projects they begin. Many of these children tend not to maintain the behaviors expected of them for more than a few minutes—whether this involves sustained attention to a task or game, patient waiting for a desired event, or modulation of spontaneous verbal and motor behaviors. They seem to have remarkably high energy levels, approaching activities with striking and sometimes formidable intensity.

A hyperactive child's mother might report that he has difficulty remembering not to trail his dirty hand along the clean wall as he runs from the front door to the kitchen. His peers may find that he spontaneously changes the rules while playing Monopoly or soccer. His teacher notes that he asks what he is supposed to do immediately after detailed instructions were presented to the entire class. He may make warbling noises or other strange sounds that inadvertently disturb anyone nearby. He may seem to have more than his share of accidents—knocking over the "tower" his classmates are erecting, spilling his cranberry juice on the linen tablecloth, or tripping over the television cord while retrieving the family cat, thereby disconnecting the set in the middle of the Superbowl game.

A hyperactive child is all too frequently "in trouble"—with his peers, his teachers, his

CAROL K. WHALEN • Program in Social Ecology, University of California, Irvine, California 92717.
Preparation of this chapter was supported, in part, by research grants from the National Institute on Drug Abuse (DA 01070) and the Spencer Foundation.

family, his community. His social *faux pas* do not seem to stem from negativism or maliciousness. In fact, he is often quite surprised when his behaviors elicit anger and rejection from others. Nor does he seem to have any basic deficits or disabilities—either in intellectual or in interpersonal spheres. He seems *almost* normal in every way, yet he has inordinate and pervasive difficulties getting along in the everyday world. This is the puzzle of hyperactivity—a puzzle that continues to perplex and intrigue child health and education specialists.

Labels, Definitions, and Diagnoses

A host of terms has been used more or less interchangeably to refer to children who exhibit the characteristics described. Common diagnostic labels include hyperactivity, hyperkinesis, hyperkinetic impulse disorder, and minimal brain dysfunction. Definitional confusion is compounded not only by a multiplicity of descriptors, but also by variations in the level of analysis or generality. The term hyperactivity may be used to denote: (a) a specific behavior or symptom (i.e., excessive locomotor activity); (b) a complex set of behavior patterns that tend to covary; or (c) a clinical syndrome or disorder in the medical sense, with a specifiable origin, symptom picture, natural history, and outcome. Some individuals use the term hyperactivity in an exclusive, categorical fashion, to refer only to children with no other serious problems; others use the term in a nonexclusive manner, including all children who receive high hyperactivity scores, regardless of their other behavior patterns (R. Glow, 1981). A third area of dissensus concerns the extensiveness of problem behavior required before the term hyperactivity is applied. Some diagnosticians rely on single-source evaluations such as parent or teacher reports; others insist that the child exhibit problem behaviors across settings and situations; and still others require that the problems be both extreme and long standing as well as transsituational.

The most recent revision of the American Psychiatric Association's Diagnostic and Statistical Manual (DSM-III) introduces the term *attention deficit disorder* (ADD) as a replacement for the diagnostic terms hyperactivity or hyperkinesis. Many children considered hyperactive do not show excessive or problematic activity levels; instead, their major problems seem to be in focusing attention and inhibiting appropriate behavior. For this reason, the new APA nomenclature recognizes two forms of ADD—with and without hyperactivity (APA, 1980). For both forms, the diagnostic criteria include at least three indicators of inattention (e.g., "Often fails to finish things he or she starts") and at least three indicators of impulsivity (e.g., "Frequently calls out in class"). In addition, the criteria for ADD *with* hyperactivity (ADD-H) include at least two indicators of excessive motor activity (e.g., "Is always 'on the go' or acts as if 'driven by a motor' ").[1]

Although the DSM-III schema is being adopted in most psychiatric settings, it remains to be seen whether these medical-psychiatric definitions will prevail among pediatricians, educators, and psychologists. DSM-III is still to be tested; there is no evidence to date of improved reliability or validity over more traditional classification systems. One promising new development is Barkley's (1981) "working set of guidelines" for the diag-

[1]Interestingly, there is some indication that children showing the characteristics of ADD without hyperactivity may actually be sluggish and underactive (Quay, 1980), a notion consistent with Denhoff's (1973) earlier suggestion that there is a hypoactive as well as a hyperactive type of minimal brain dysfunction.

nosis of hyperactivity or ADD. Building upon the empirical literature as well as the DSM-III schema, Barkley's proposal provides more precise operational definitions for both inclusionary and exclusionary criteria.

It is important to note that the diagnostic label is not (or *should* not) be applied to active and ebullient youngsters who do not have serious and enduring behavior problems. When parents or teachers are asked to evaluate school-age boys on diverse behavioral dimensions, they may rate as many as 30% to 50% of a normal sample as overactive, restless, distractible, or inattentive (Lapouse & Monk, 1958; MacFarlane, Allen, & Honzik, 1954; Werry & Quay, 1971). Such findings suggest that these "hyperactive-type" behaviors, *as perceived by parents and teachers,* may be relatively normal patterns during the early school-age years—particularly among males. In the present chapter the terms hyperactivity, hyperkinesis, and ADD-H are used synonymously, *not* to refer to a disease entity or spectrum, but rather as a descriptive convenience to refer to a large group of children who have *serious* difficulties concentrating, inhibiting inappropriate responses, and getting along in the everyday world.

Exclusionary Criteria and Relationships to other Childhood Disorders

Mental Retardation, Psychosis, and Neurological Disorders

The typical selection criteria for studies of hyperactivity include "normal IQ" and "no evidence of psychosis or gross neurological impairment." It is important to distinguish here between the diagnostic classification and the behavior patterns. Many children considered to be retarded, autistic, or brain damaged do indeed show impulsivity, poor concentration, or motor restlessness. However, it is assumed that such problem behaviors have different sources, courses, and concomitants than when they are observed in children with average intelligence and no signs of gross neurological dysfunction (Routh, 1980).

Serious Psychosocial Stressors

Children respond to external stressors in diverse ways; a parent's serious illness or sudden job loss may be followed by impulsivity, concentration problems, and motor restlessness in some youngsters. Children are not diagnosed hyperactive or ADD-H, however, when there is a clear, temporal relationship between the behavior problems and a stressful life event; the DSM-III category for such instances is *adjustment disorder.*

Conduct Disorders

There is considerable overlap between the conduct disorder and hyperactivity categories. Children given either diagnosis may show patterns of persistent lying, disobedience, inattention, impulsivity, aggression, destructiveness, or other forms of socially inappropriate behavior. In a study of consecutive admissions to a child psychiatry clinic and ward, Stewart, Cummings, Singer, and deBlois found that "three out of four children with an aggressive conduct disorder were also hyperactive, and two out of three hyperactive children also had a conduct disorder" (1981, p. 37). Numerous investigations have distinguished two broad-band dimensions of childhood disorders, one labeled "internalizing" or "over controlled," and the other labeled "externalizing" or "undercontrolled" (cf. Achenbach & Edelbrock, 1978, and Chapter 4 of this volume). There is an ongoing debate about whether hyperactivity and conduct disorder are merely different labels for the same global externalizing disorder, or whether they are relatively distinct disorders within the general externalizing rubric.

Some investigators argue that hyperactivity and conduct disorder should not be differentiated, asserting that the behaviors, etiologies, and outcomes are essentially the same (e.g., Lahey, Green, & Forehand, 1980; Quay, 1979; Sandberg, Rutter, & Taylor, 1978). Other investigators maintain that there are consequential distinctions between hyperactivity and conduct disorder, particularly in terms of concurrent behavior patterns (e.g., aggression) and long-term outcomes, and that it may even be useful to distinguish a third group of youngsters who show both patterns simultaneously (Loney & Milich, 1982; Loney, Kramer, & Milich, 1981; Milich, Loney, & Landau, in press; Offord, Sullivan, Allen, & Abrams, 1979; Paternite & Loney, 1980). This latter suggestion is consistent with the DSM-III specification that conduct disorder may coexist with ADD-H and, in such cases, both diagnoses should be given (APA, 1980). A third view is that, in addition to conduct disorder, there may be two forms of hyperactivity, an "externalizing" form that includes disorganization, impulsivity, and low frustration tolerance, and an "internalizing" form that includes immaturity and short attention span (Conners & Blouin, 1980).

The complex nature of this debate is further underscored when one attempts to examine the empirical data base underlying each set of conclusions. Cross-study comparisons are highly hazardous because the studies vary considerably on potentially critical dimensions, including sample characteristics (e.g., normal versus clinic-referred children), assessment sources (e.g., teacher or parent ratings versus professional evaluations of case history materials), and methodological features (e.g., dissimilar statistical procedures for generating factors and computing factor scores). It is not yet possible to disentangle this taxonomic muddle, but these issues have important implications for increasing our understanding of the causes of—and optimal treatments for—childhood disorders. For example, there are indications that childhood aggression is much better than hyperactivity as a predictor of some aspects of adolescent outcome (e.g., antisocial behavior and self-esteem deficits), a finding that suggests the potential value of targeting therapeutic programs specifically on aggressive behavior during childhood (Milich & Loney, 1979; Routh, 1979). The relationship between hyperactivity and conduct disorder is presently a high density research area, and it is to be hoped that ongoing assessment and intervention studies will clarify the picture within the next few years.

Learning Difficulties

Given their pervasive problems with inattention and impulsivity, it is not surprising that many hyperactive children have serious academic difficulties; they are more likely than their peers to show below average achievement rates, to earn poor grades, and to be placed in remedial or special education programs (Riddle & Rapoport, 1976; Trites, Blouin, Ferguson, & Lynch, 1981). Cantwell and Satterfield (1978) reported that approximately three-quarters of their hyperactive group were underachieving to some degree in all three subjects examined (reading, spelling, and mathematics), and that 35% were a full grade below their expected level in at least two subjects. Similarly, Conners and Taylor (1980) found that only 19% of their carefully selected hyperactive sample were free of learning problems.

Examining discrepancies between actual achievement levels and levels predicted from IQ estimates, Lambert and Sandoval (1980) concluded that 53% of a group of hyperactive youngsters were "underperforming"—even though test scores indicated average or even above average achievement levels for many of them. Two control groups were included in this study: One consisted of randomly selected classmates, and the other was comprised of children who had obtained teacher ratings that were as negative as those of the hyperactive children, yet they had not been identified as hyperactive by parents or physicians. The "underperforming" rates for these two groups were 20% and 37.5%, respectively. These findings indicate that, when disparities between ability and achievement levels are examined irrespective of actual achievement level, many children in regular classrooms are found to be performing less than optimally; the proportion is even greater within the group considered by teachers to have behavior problems, and still greater among those considered hyperactive.

It is also the case that not all hyperactive children have learning problems, and some, in fact, achieve at above average levels (Trites, 1979). Nor do all children considered learning-disabled show the behavior problems characteristic of hyperactivity. On the basis of a careful review of the literature, Safer and Allen (1976) estimated that 78% of hyperactive children have serious learning impairments, while 39% of learning-disabled children are also hyperactive.

The diagnostic complexities are reminiscent of those described for the conduct disorders. One question is whether hyperactivity and learning disability are two relatively independent behavioral dimensions or merely different manifestations of the same set of problems. Recent factor analytic research suggests that, although many children may show problems in both areas, the overlap is far from perfect, and it is both useful and valid to view the two as relatively independent behavior dimensions (Blouin, Bornstein, & Trites, 1978; Lahey, Stempniak, Robinson, & Tyroler, 1978). Some investigators are attempting to delineate distinct groups of learning-disabled versus hyperactive children, as well as a possible mixed group. Diverse family and child characteristics, treatment responses, and long-term outcomes are being examined in this enterprise (Ackerman, Elardo, & Dykman, 1979; Ackerman, Oglesby, & Dykman, 1981; Delamater, Lahey, & Drake, 1981; Singer, Stewart, & Pulaski, 1981). Douglas (1980a) maintains that hyperactive and learning-disabled children begin with distinctively different disabilities, but that the sequelae of these disabilities (e.g., failure and frustration) are similar enough to create comparable behavioral consequences. Knowledge to date is limited, however, and the fruitfulness of this differential classification approach remains to be demonstrated.

Epidemiological Patterns

Prevalence

Despite the diversity of definitions, evaluation practices, and samples, there is consensus that hyperactivity is a relatively common problem, at least among elementary school children. Of children referred for evaluation and treatment, at least 50% and often much higher proportions are diagnosed hyperactive (e.g., Stewart *et al.*, 1981). Recent epidemiological studies indicate that between 3% and 15% of school-age children in the general population may be considered hyperactive. When the focus is exclusively on youngsters diagnosed by physicians, the estimates hover at the low end of this range. The higher percentages tend to emerge in studies relying on teacher assessments (Bosco & Robin, 1980; R. Glow, 1981; Sandoval, Lambert, & Sassone, 1980; Sprague, Cohen, & Eichlseder, 1977; Trites, 1979).

Sex Differences

One exceptionally robust finding is that more boys than girls are hyperactive; typically, three to five males are identified for every female (Campbell & Redfering, 1979; Trites, 1979), and ratios as high as 9:1 or 10:1 have been reported (APA, 1980; Werry, 1968). There is some indication that increasing the stringency of the definition of hyperactivity also increases this male–female disparity; in other words, when the focus is on more severe behavior problems, the number of boys identified for each girl is even greater (R. Glow, 1981).

Little is known about hyperactive girls, who might be considered a neglected subsample (Henker & Whalen, 1980a). Most studies either restrict their samples to boys or include so few girls that statistical comparisons are precluded. There are some suggestions in the research literature that the antecedents, concomitants, and consequences of male and female hyperactivity may differ along critical dimensions. For example, hyperactive girls may engage in fewer deviant behaviors, elicit less social censure, and have more positive outcomes than hyperactive boys (Battle & Lacey, 1972; Pelham, 1980; Preis & Huessy, 1979; Prinz & Loney, 1974). Unfortunately, too little information is available at this time to allow more than intriguing speculations.

Socioeconomic Status and Family Features

Campbell and Redfering (1979) found that there was no relationship between teacher-rated hyperactivity and such environmental and demographic variables as race, birth order, number of siblings, parental age, educational level, income level, marital status, or method of child discipline. Other investigators have also failed to find meaningful relationships between hyperactivity and socioeconomic (SES) variables (e.g., Bosco & Robin, 1980; Goyette, Conners, & Ulrich, 1978), findings that are important because they discredit accusations that the diagnostic label is used often to stigmatize ethnic minority or low-income children.

These results do not imply, however, that SES variables are irrelevant to our understanding of hyperactivity. When the definition of social disadvantage is expanded beyond low-income and low-education levels to include such high-risk conditions as broken homes, overcrowding, and maternal mental distress, significant relationships between hyperactivity and social disadvantage do indeed emerge (Sandberg, Wieselberg, & Shaffer, 1980).

The SES picture is clarified further by Paternite, Loney, and Langhorne's (1976) findings that, within a group of hyperkinetic boys, low SES was related to high levels of aggressive behavior but not to high levels of hyperactive behavior. Other investigators who study more heterogeneous (not necessarily hyperactive) groups of children have found analogous relationships between SES and antisocial behavior (Robins, 1979). Thus, low-SES youngsters may be at risk for the development of antisocial behavior *whether or not* they are considered hyperactive. Following an extensive review, Robins (1979) suggested that the higher prevalence of antisocial behavior among low-SES youngsters may result from the fact that low-income families are more likely to have inadequate and socially limited parents than are middle- and high-income families. The findings that emerged from the Paternite *et al.* (1976) study of hyperkinetic boys are consistent with this view. Low- and high-SES boys differed not only in aggressive behaviors, but also in the attitudes and styles of their parents, with low-SES parents appearing more lax, easygoing, and inconsistent. It should be kept in mind, however, that the correlations are moderate at best, indicating that SES and parental characteristics are only two of many potential contributors to antisocial behavior.

Behavior Patterns and Processes

Conceptual and Methodological Issues

Before we examine specific behavioral domains, it is necessary to review some fundamental issues that constrain interpretations of the research literature. The focus here is on what might be considered the two most influential sources of variation among studies of hyperactivity: measurement modes and diagnostic (subject selection) criteria.

Measurement Modes and Muddles

Despite their inherent subjectivity, rating scales have proven remarkably useful in studies of hyperactive children. Parent and teacher checklists such as those developed by Conners (1973b) and by Werry, Weiss, and Peters (Werry, 1968) have achieved widespread use. Conners (1973b) has presented an abbreviated version of his parent and teacher checklists that contains 10 frequently endorsed items common to his two longer scales. In just a few minutes, any observer can evaluate a child on such items as "fails to finish things" and "disturbs other children." The respondent rates each item using a 4-point scale ranging from 0 = "not at all" through 3 = "very much," and then a total score is computed. Not only does this simple measure show refreshing validity, but it is also one of the few instruments for which normative data are available (e.g., Werry, Sprague, & Cohen, 1975).

A slightly reworded form has been presented by Goyette, Conners, and Ulrich (1978), and Loney and her colleagues (e.g., Loney, 1980a; Loney & Milich, in press) are currently working on a modified version that contains both a hyperactivity and an aggression factor. Their ongoing efforts to obtain independent, behavioral validation of these factors should help resolve some of the current confusions over the relationship between hyperactivity and conduct disorder.

When using child behavior checklists such as these, it is important to recognize that they are vulnerable to a practice or regression effect: Raters are likely to provide more negative assessments the first time they complete a checklist than on subsequent occasions (Achenbach & Edelbrock, 1978; Milich, Roberts, Loney, & Caputo, 1980; Werry & Sprague, 1974), a pattern that may result in spurious interpretations when treatment programs are evaluated by comparisons between single pretest and posttest scores. One way of ameliorating this problem is to obtain and then discard an initial "practice" rating before the actual pretest is administered.

A singularly bothersome aspect of rating scales is that scores obtained from two sources often fail to correspond with each other, and the literature is somewhat contradictory on this point. For example, some investigators have reported moderate relationships between parent and teacher ratings of the same children (e.g., Achenbach & Edelbrock, 1978; Goyette, Conners, & Ulrich, 1978). Others report either zero-order or weak relationships and very little overlap between the group of children identified on the basis of parent ratings and those identified from teacher ratings (R. Glow, 1981; Sandberg *et al.,* 1978). When sources disagree, it is difficult to ascertain how much of the disagreement reflects actual differences in child behaviors across settings and how much reflects such other factors as differential training, experience, or motivation of the respondents. In other words, it is difficult to separate measurement error from valid setting effects or child-by-situation interactions.

It can be concluded with some confidence that both source and situational factors play a major role in the assessment of hyperactive youngsters. Following a comprehensive analysis of a clinical sample of hyperactive boys, Langhorne, Loney, Paternite, and Bechtoldt concluded that, "measures of presumably different symptoms from a common source of information are more highly interrelated than are several alternative measures of a single symptom" (1976, p. 206). This position was substantiated by findings from an independent study of clinic-referred boys conducted by Sandberg *et al.* (1978). Examining both teacher and parent ratings as well as direct observations of overactivity and inattentiveness during psychometric testing, these investigators found that teacher ratings of hyperactivity and conduct disorder were significantly correlated ($r = .60$), as were parent ratings of these two dimensions (although to a lesser extent, $r = .34$). In addition, the five behavior observation categories were intercorrelated, with coefficients ranging between .31 and .72. There was little overlap, however, between evaluations obtained from two different information sources; parent and teacher ratings of hyperactivity were not related, nor did either of these assessments correlate significantly with direct observations of overactivity and inattention.

Analogous nonrelationships or weak relationships among sources have been reported in other assessment studies (e.g., Plomin & Foch, 1981; Schroeder, Milar, Wool, & Routh, 1980) and also in evaluations of changes following treatment (Forehand, Griest, & Wells, 1979; Gittelman-Klein & Klein, 1975). Several investigators have described what has been referred to as the "doctor's office effect"—the tendency of hyperactive children to show exemplary behavior during initial clinic or office visits (Whalen, Henker, Collins, McAuliffe, & Vaux, 1979b). Sleator and Ullman (1981) reported that 80% of the children considered hyperactive on the basis of school and home reports showed no sign of hyperactivity in the physician's office. Moreover, during a 3-year period there were no differences in classroom behaviors or treatment response between those who could and those who could not be identified as hyperactive on the basis of behavior in the office. Different sources are most likely to agree when there is considerable overlap between the contexts in which the children are observed; correlations between the ratings of two team teachers or teachers and classmates tend to be higher than those between parents and teachers or between teachers and clinicians (Achenbach & Edelbrock, 1978; R. Glow, 1981; Glow & Glow, 1980).

The multidimensionality of each behavioral domain contributes further to measurement difficulties. A child may be considered inattentive because it takes him a long time to begin an assignment, because he has difficulty attending selectively to relevant cues and ignoring distractors, or because he tends not to sustain attention over time. Analogously, a youngster characterized as having a high activity level may show excessive amounts of gross motor movement, may fidget while seated, or may tend to move in a particularly vigorous or erratic manner. Some instruments tap one type of attentional or motoric process while others tap entirely different processes, and these various components are not necessarily intercorrelated (Barkley & Ullman, 1975). In other words, "Fidgety Phil" may or may not be a perennial peripatetic, and the youngster who concentrates for only short periods of time may or may not have difficulty deploying attention to the relevant cues while ignoring the irrelevant ones.

It is also important to recognize that each assessment modality has its own advantages and pitfalls. Rating scales are global measures that are as easily influenced by the cognitive and motivational characteristics of the respondent as by the behaviors of the child. Subjectivity and bias are less likely to plague direct behavior observations, but frequency counts of target behaviors may be too specific, time limited, or reactive to provide a representative picture of the child's problematic patterns. Laboratory measures tend to be more objective than ratings, more sensitive than behavior observations, and perhaps the most comparable from study to study. However, they are often obtained under novel, artificial, and even anxiety-inducing conditions rather than in the child's natural environments. Thus their ecological validity—their relevance to everyday functioning—must be documented. Given the trade-offs involved in the selection of any single assessment approach, many investigators are now conducting multimodal evaluations that encompass diverse assessment sources and techniques.

Diagnostic Dilemmas and Sample Heterogeneity

Despite decades of active research, there is still no consensus on whether hyperactivity "really exists" as a distinct disorder (Shaffer, 1980). Sophisticated attempts to identify consistent symptom patterns or clusters repeatedly fail to support the notion of a unitary hyperactivity syndrome (Langhorne *et al.,* 1976; Routh & Roberts, 1972; Sandberg *et al.,* 1978; Werry, 1968). The pattern of dysfunctional behaviors differs from child to child, and may result from diverse and complexly interactive biological and psychological processes. In other words, the key feature is heterogeneity—in the children, the behavior patterns and concomitants, the probable causes, and the likely outcomes.

Thus it is not surprising that samples of hyperactive children selected for different studies vary markedly along diverse behavioral, familial, and physiological dimensions—some known, but many left unspecified. Two particularly influential variables are socioeconomic status and suspected (in contrast to known) neurological dysfunction. Study samples also vary along numerous other dimensions, including type and severity of problem behaviors, family stability, and treatment histories. The studies of SES and other family variables reviewed illustrate how uncontrolled variations in such factors can inadvertently result in incongruous research findings.

Cross-study diversity is further amplified by the fact that some investigators select only children who have received a clinical diagnosis, and others concentrate on children who fall at the extreme of a distribution of normal children on a particular measure, for example, teacher ratings of problem behaviors. Even with clinical samples, diagnostic criteria vary widely, with some investigators preferring more quantitative and others more global approaches to diagnosis. As illustrated in the following text, these extensive variations in sample characteristics and assessment methodologies make cross-study generalizations hazardous and make contradictory findings difficult to interpret.

Medication Studies

Important information about hyperactivity emanates not only from direct comparisons of hyperactive and normal children, but also from evaluations of psychostimulant medication effects. A large proportion of children diagnosed hyperactive is treated at some time with a stimulant drug, usually methylphenidate (Ritalin), dextroamphetamine (Dexedrine), or pemoline (Cylert). The results of one recent study indicated that "85% of those children identified as hyperactive by physicians received a prescription for medication for at least 6 months at some time during their lives" (Sandoval, Lambert, & Sassone, 1981). The majority of youngsters given optimal doses of these drugs improve markedly. With the notable exception of academic achievement, the problematic response domains that distinguish hyperactive children from their peers also tend to be the areas that show medication-related gains.[2] Indeed, many studies combine group comparisons (hyperactive versus normal children) with medication trials, and both types of research findings are sampled in the following sections.

Attention

As suggested by the new DSM-III term *attention deficit disorder,* attentional difficulties are considered by many investigators to be the fundamental problem domain for hyperactive youngsters. Diverse assessment instruments indicate that, compared to their peers, hyperactive children have considerable difficulty deploying and sustaining attention. When a simple record is kept of whether or not hyperactive children are attending to appropriate task activities in the classroom, it is found that their "on task" rates are significantly below those of their peers (Abikoff, Gittelman-Klein, & Klein, 1980; Whalen, Henker, Collins, Finck, & Dotemoto, 1979a).

Task attention is a global, undifferentiated measure that most probably subsumes several heterogeneous and interactive functions (Dykman, Ackerman, Clements, & Peters, 1971; Keogh & Margolis, 1976). One potentially important distinction is between selective and sustained attention. Selective attention involves filtering incoming stimuli, ruling out irrelevant inputs, and focusing on stimuli critical to the task at hand. Children who have difficulties in this realm are often characterized as distractible and even "stimulus-driven." Sustained attention, in contrast, involves focused and organized concentration over time. Youngsters who have problems maintaining or "protecting" attention are described as readily losing interest in an ongoing task and changing activities frequently, usually before task completion. They may be good "starters," enthusiastically and competently launching into new activities, but their attention tends to deteriorate more rapidly than that of their peers (Dykman, Ackerman, & Oglesby, 1979).

Because attentional processes are difficult to study during natural classroom activities, various laboratory games and procedures have been developed to assess specific functions. Distractibility or selective attention deficits may be assessed by measuring the child's performance as he works in a room full of colorful and interesting "distractors," by presenting extraneous sounds or sights during ongoing task performance, or by embedding irrelevant cues into the stimulus array of any given task. Studies of this type have yielded inconsistent results. Some investigators find that hyperactive children are more likely than their peers to be "seduced" and disrupted by irrelevant stimuli (Radosh & Gittelman, 1981); others

[2]Despite positive short-term changes, there are serious concerns about both physiological and psychological toxicity as well as about long-term outcomes of stimulant treatment. These issues, which are beyond the scope of the present chapter, are explored in Whalen and Henker (1980).

find either that the distractors have no detrimental effect, or that they impede the performance of normal and hyperactive children to similar degrees (Davidson & Prior, 1978; McIntyre, Blackwell, & Denton, 1978; Sykes, Douglas, Weiss, & Minde, 1971).

Attempts to reduce distracting input by having youngsters work in plain, nonstimulating cubicles do not necessarily improve performance, and there are indications that irrelevant stimuli may actually enhance the performance of hyperactive children under some conditions (Douglas & Peters, 1979). One hypothesis that is gaining support is that hyperactive children have a tendency toward sensation or stimulation seeking (Douglas, 1980b), a notion consistent with the proposition that physiological underarousal or underarousability may underly many of their problem behaviors (see p. 172). Investigators are just beginning to identify the parameters that may influence distractibility, for example, type of task, attractiveness and salience of the extraneous cues, and relationships between the distractors and the target task stimuli (Rosenthal & Allen, 1980; Steinkamp, 1980). Comprehensive reviews of these distractibility studies and of the definitional and methodological problems in this area are provided by Douglas and Peters (1979), Hallahan and Reeve (1980), and Rosenthal and Allen (1978).

In contrast to the somewhat variable and situation-specific results from studies of distractibility, evidence suggesting that hyperactive youngsters have major difficulties sustaining attention over sufficient time periods is more consistent across samples and situations, and has emerged in physiological as well as behavioral domains (Douglas, 1980b; Porges & Smith, 1980). Consider two tasks that each require fine visual discriminations: the Picture Completion subtest of the Wechsler Intelligence Scale for Children (WISC), and the Matching Familiar Figures Test (MFFT). The WISC subtest involves studying a single picture to identify the missing detail. The MFFT is a match-to-sample task in which the child must select the one of six similar drawings that is an exact match to the sample. At first glance, all six alternatives appear to be exact replicas, but all except one differ in a minor way from the sample drawing. The MFFT requires an exhaustive search consisting of detailed comparisons between each of the six alternatives and the sample stimulus. In contrast, the Picture Completion requires only a single, brief examination. Hyperactive children are likely to show performance deficits on the MFFT but not on the Picture Completion subtest, a difference that may be due to the fact that only the MFFT requires sustained attention (Douglas, 1980b).

Other tasks commonly used to assess sustained attention are adapted from those used with adults to study degradations in the detection accuracy of radar operators during a prolonged watch (Kupietz & Richardson, 1978; Mackworth, 1948). The objective of these "vigilance" or "continuous performance" tests is to detect relatively rare signals against a repetitive background of "noise." In one variant, a series of single numerals is presented on a display screen, and the individual's job is to push a button when a "4" appears, but only if it was preceded by a "6." Scores are obtained both for errors of omission (failure to push the button following a 6-4 combination) and errors of commission (pressing the button following any other numerical sequence). In a recent study using this task, Rapoport, Buchsbaum, Weingartner, Zahn, Ludlow, and Mikkelsen (1980) found that hyperactive boys made substantially more commission errors during an 8-minute session ($M = 47.7$) than did normal peers ($M = 6.7$). And this is not an isolated finding. Several other investigators have reported similar deficits on various types of continuous performance tests (Conners & Rothschild, 1968; Douglas, 1980b; Sykes *et al.*, 1971). Moreover, there is some evidence that these performance decrements may persist at least into adolescence (Hoy, Weiss, Minde, & Cohen, 1978). It should be noted, however, that high error rates on these measures do not necessarily pinpoint attentional deficits, but may result from noncompliance or a lack of involvement in the task.

These types of attention measures receive sporadic criticism because they involve monotonous routines that may have little relevance to real-life demands. Recent studies have provided some validational support for these procedures by documenting moderate correlations between continuous performance tests and other measures that have greater face validity, such as direct observations of "off task" behavior in the classroom (Kupietz & Richardson, 1978) and teacher ratings of attentional difficulties (Charles, Schain, Zelniker, & Guthrie, 1979).

Cognition and Learning Performance

As previously discussed, many hyperactive children have serious and enduring academic problems. There is some indication that such problems may not stem entirely from attentional and behavioral difficulties, but rather that these youngsters may also have cognitive limitations. Hyperactive children usually have normal IQs, by definition, but this does not necessarily mean that their general ability levels equal those of their peers. When hyperactive and comparison children are not matched on IQ, significant differences of about 7 to 10 points typically emerge in favor of the comparison groups (Campbell, Schleifer, Weiss, & Perlman, 1977; Huessy & Cohen, 1976; Satterfield, Cantwell, Lesser, & Podosin, 1972; Schroeder *et al.,* 1980; Welner, Welner, Stewart, Palkes, & Wish, 1977; Whalen *et al.,* 1979b). Pointing out that hyperactive youngsters are usually tested under advantageous conditions compared to their peers (i.e., individual versus group administration), Keogh and Barkett (1980) suggest that actual differences in general ability may be even greater than those documented. Moreover, Loney's (1974) findings indicate that an IQ gap may develop or widen as the children grow older.

Performance decrements have also been demonstrated on specific learning tasks. On one such task, children are asked to process the meanings or sounds of three-word sets. In half of the sets, two of the words are related semantically and the third one differs in meaning (e.g., "cat, book, lion"). In the other half of the sets, the relationship is acoustic: Two of the words rhyme and the third one does not (e.g., "ear, near, sky"). After the sets are presented, the children work on a 10-minute picture identification task in order to prevent rehearsal. Two recall tests are then given, the first requesting that the children remember as many of the words as possible (free recall), and the second involving prompting with one word from each pair of related words (cued recall). Hyperactive children tend to remember significantly fewer words than their normal age-mates under the free recall condition, but the groups do not differ with cued recall (Rapoport *et al.,* 1980; Weingartner, Rapoport, Buchsbaum, Bunney, Ebert, Mikkelsen, & Caine, 1980).

Although children acquire substantial amounts of information passively and almost automatically, much learning requires an active, deliberate, and organized approach. Critical ingredients are what Brown (1978) calls the "executive" functions, operations such as task analysis and strategic planning that are needed for complex problem solving. Individual tasks also require more specific competencies that children develop over the years, including strategies for efficient scanning of a visual array and for accurate recall of newly acquired information. These functions are often included under the rubric of "metacognition," perhaps most simply defined as "knowing about knowing" (Brown, 1975, 1978).

One emerging hypothesis is that hyperactive children may be deficient in the acquisition or use of some of these strategic problem-solving skills, and that these deficiencies may contribute to both their academic and interpersonal difficulties (Douglas, 1980b). Benezra (1978, as reported in Douglas, 1980a) found that hyperactive children performed well (compared to normal peers) on a paired-associates task when a "built-in" strategy was provided, that is, when the two words in each pair were associated in a meaningful way (e.g., "table–chair"). The performance of the hyperactive group diverged from their peers, however, when the task required the youngsters to produce their own strategies for remembering the associations—when the two words in each pair were unrelated (e.g., "boy–clock"). Effective problem-solving approaches under this latter condition include deliberate organization, transformation, and elaboration of the material (e.g., generating a sentence or a visual image involving a boy being awakened by an alarm clock). During postexperimental interviews, the normal youngsters reported that they had made deliberate efforts to build associations between the words in each pair, while the hyperactive children reported that they had "just listened" or had repeated the words over and over to themselves. In this context, it is noteworthy that on the paired-associates task described (Weingartner *et al.,* 1980), the hyperactive children performed as well as their peers when organization of the material was inherent in the task (cued recall), whereas differences between the groups emerged under free recall, when efficient performance required deliberate adoption of a problem-solving strategy.

Another factor that may contribute to performance deficits on cognitive tasks is atypical responsiveness to common reinforcement contingencies and practices (Cunningham & Knights, 1978). It may be that intermittent or random positive reinforcement impairs the task performance of hyperactive (but not of normal) youngsters (Firestone & Douglas, 1975; Parry, 1973). Douglas (1980b) speculates that reinforcers are unusually salient stimuli for hyperactive children and may raise their arousal to supraoptimal levels. These findings, if replicated by other investigators, have important implications for intervention programs, particularly those incorporating operant techniques.

Activity Level

Diverse procedures have been developed to assess various aspects of motoric behavior. Frequently used are teacher or parent checklists that contain such items as "acts as if driven by a motor" and "restless in the squirmy sense" (Conners & Blouin, 1980; Goyette, Conners, & Ulrich, 1978). Some investigators use mechanical recording devices such as actometers—wrist watches that have been modified to record amount of movement rather than passage of time (Rapoport *et al.,* 1980; Schulman & Reisman, 1959). Another instrument is the stabilimetric or "wiggle" cushion that records activity while the child is seated (Sprague, Barnes, & Werry, 1970). Direct observation procedures have also proven profitable, including time samples or frequency counts of specific behaviors such as fidgeting, leaving one's seat, or traversing the room (Whalen *et al.,* 1979a). An alternative observational approach involves dividing the floor of a playroom into quadrants or smaller sections and then counting the number of times the child leaves one section and enters another, that is, crosses any line on the floor (Routh, Schroeder, & O'Tuama, 1974).

Given the diversity of measurement procedures and sources, it is not surprising that the literature is somewhat contradictory, with some investigators reporting that hyperactive youngsters are more active than comparison peers (Abikoff *et al.,* 1980; Rapoport *et al.,* 1980; Routh & Schroeder, 1976), and others failing to find reliable differences (Barkley &

Cunningham, 1979). It is also common to find, within any single study, that one activity measure may distinguish hyperactive youngsters from their peers while other measures do not (Barkley & Ullman, 1975; Whalen, Collins, Henker, Alkus, Adams, & Stapp, 1978).

At this time, the most reasonable conclusion that can be drawn from the empirical literature is that many (but certainly not all) children considered hyperactive show some type of excessive motoric activity at least on some measures. Some youngsters are chronically restless and fidgety, others may show erratic bursts of particularly vigorous or rapid motor activity, and still others may just seem unable to "shut the motor off." Situational factors play an important role in activity patterns. It seems reasonable to speculate that overactive children are more likely to be distinguishable from their peers in highly structured or restrictive settings than in free play or open field settings, although this hypothesis has not yet been verified conclusively. The stylistic and contextual aspects of activity, such as intensity and situational appropriateness, are probably far more important than more easily quantified dimensions such as frequency and duration.

Longitudinal studies of normal children are yielding intriguing information about the behavioral concomitants of high activity levels. Buss, Block, and Block (1980) examined the interrelationships among actometer scores at ages 3 and 4 and various behavioral dimensions at ages 3, 4, and 7. Significant correlations (ranging between .21 and .61) emerged between actometer activity levels and several behavioral dimensions (as assessed by teachers and examiners) at all three age levels. In the interpersonal domain, for example, highly active children were more likely to be perceived as taking advantage of others, trying to be the center of attention, liking to compete, being self-assertive, being physically or verbally aggressive, and characteristically trying to stretch limits. They also tended to be seen as acting without thinking, having difficulty delaying gratification, and showing other signs of "undercontrol." These findings converge with those from other investigations to suggest that high activity levels are correlated with high levels of sociability, dominance, assertion, and aggression, and with low levels of compliance, cooperation, and inhibition (Battle & Lacey, 1972; Billman & McDevitt, 1980; Halverson & Waldrop, 1973, 1976). It should be emphasized that the correlations from studies of this type hover in the low-to-moderate range, indicating that activity level by itself is not an accurate predictor of social behavior styles. The findings do suggest, however, that youngsters who are highly active during the preschool period may be at some risk for negative encounters with their environments and for the development of problems with impulsivity and interpersonal relations.

Social Interaction and Classroom Behaviors

Many of the social transactions of hyperactive children are characterized by friction, frustration, and failure. These youngsters often have serious difficulties getting along with peers and developing enduring friendships. It is not uncommon for parents to report sadly that their hyperactive child has no friends and that other youngsters refuse to play or work with him. Sometimes the only willing playmate is a much younger child from the neighborhood. The pervasive social difficulties of many hyperactive children have been substantiated not only by parental report, but also by checklist ratings provided by parents, teachers, and peers, and even by hyperactive children's own self-evaluations (Milich & Landau, 1982; Riddle & Rapoport, 1976; Satterfield, Cantwell, & Satterfield, 1979).

School-age children are highly sensitive to the behaviors that characterize hyperactive youngsters. A recent large-scale questionnaire study yielded an unusually high correlation of .93 between peer and teacher ratings of hyperactivity (Glow & Glow, 1980). Not only do peers readily identify hyperactive behaviors, but they also respond to these behaviors with disfavor and disparagement. Klein and Young's (1979) findings from a study comparing boys whom teachers considered hyperactive to classmates considered "normal yet active" are illustrative. All children in several classrooms completed The Class Play (Bower, 1969), a sociometric instrument in which children nominate their classmates to play hypothetical positive and negative roles (e.g., "a class president" or "a mean, cruel boss"). Compared to the normal yet active youngsters, hyperactive boys were nominated more often for negative roles and were chosen less frequently for the role of "true friend." Interestingly, there were no differences between the two groups in the total number of roles for which they were nominated, suggesting similar levels of "social visibility."

A recent report by Pelham (1980) is quite consistent with these findings regarding peer perceptions. On the Pupil Evaluation Inventory, another sociometric instrument for children, hyperactive youngsters were rated as significantly different from their classmates on 32 of 35 items. An interesting sex difference also emerged: The discrepancies between hyperactive girls and their female classmates were generally smaller than those between hyperactive boys and their male classmates, suggesting that hyperactive girls are less devalued than their male counterparts.

Sociometric studies tell us that hyperactive children are salient negative stimuli for their peers, but rating scales—whether obtained from peers, teachers, or parents—do *not* tell us the specific behaviors that engender such perceptions. There is no guarantee that questionnaire responses reflect actual behaviors. High ratings on specific items such as "disturbs other children" or "uncooperative" may merely reflect a global negative halo rather than deficiencies in specific behavioral realms. To obtain precise information about what hyperactive children actually do—information that is not filtered through the child's significant others—our own research team has conducted objective assessments of social behaviors in classroom and laboratory settings. A few examples are provided.

Communication Patterns

In order to study social behavior under standardized yet relatively naturalistic conditions, we conducted special 5-week summer enrichment sessions for groups of hyperactive and comparison boys. All of the hyperactive boys had been taking methylphenidate before the research began, and our goals were to study medication effects as well as differences between unmedicated hyperactive boys and their peers. The programs were designed such that the boys participated in a series of structured assessment modules during two mornings each week and a series of classroom experiments during two other mornings each week. Following a 2-week interval designed to familiarize the boys with each other, the staff, and the settings and routines, a medication crossover was effected. During Week 3, placebos were substituted for the active medication for a randomly selected half of the hyperactive boys, while the remaining half continued taking medication. During Week 4, those who had been taking placebos returned to their usual medication, and the other half of the hyperactive group were shifted to placebo. The teacher and staff were, of course, blind as to diagnostic and medication status, nor did the boys or their parents know when placebos were used. One of the structured assessment modules is described in the following text, and summaries of some of the classroom studies are presented in a later section.

An engaging referential communication task was designed to study peer interaction patterns. The task, called "Space Flight," was presented to the children as an exercise to teach astronauts how to repair their own spaceship in case of equipment failure during an actual space mission. One boy served as "mission control" (message sender), and the other as "astronaut" (message receiver). Mission control was given a photograph of a block design, and the astronaut had a set of blocks ("equipment parts") but no information about their correct placement. The objective was for mission control to guide the astronaut in the correct placement of each block.

Each boy participated as astronaut and mission control during Week 3 and again in each role during Week 4, working with a different partner on each occasion. Several aspects of communicative style and content were analyzed, and intriguing differences between the hyperactive and comparison youngsters emerged. For example, whether taking medication or placebo, the verbal messages of the hyperactive boys were perceived as less efficient than those of the comparison boys during their first exposure to the mission control role. As can be seen in Figure 1, however, this difference disappeared during the second Space Flight session as the hyperactive boys reached the level of their comparison peers. This pattern suggests that hyperactive boys may need more time to "settle in" and "learn the ropes" in new situations. Another finding was that, while serving as astronauts, the hyperactive boys were more likely than their peers to disagree with their partners. Disagreement in this "follower" role can be viewed as situationally inappropriate: Astronauts did not have access to the block pattern and thus had no independent means of evaluating their partner's instructions or the accuracy of their own performance. We also found that the hyperactive boys showed higher rates of task-irrelevant chatter and that they were less likely to modulate their verbal messages in accord with shifting role demands, that is, when changing from mission control (leader) to astronaut (follower) status. (While these group differences appeared to be relatively independent of medication status, other behavioral dimensions such as intensity were influenced by methylphenidate. Detailed findings from this and a related study can be found in Whalen *et al.*, 1979b, and in Whalen, Henker, Dotemoto, Vaux, & McAuliffe, 1981.)

In another recent study, Ludlow, Rapoport, Bassich, and Mikkelsen (1980) compared the speech patterns of hyperactive and normal age-mates during three structured verbal activities with an adult. No differences between the two groups emerged on various measures of linguistic complexity or speech fluency. However, hyperactive boys used significantly less task-directed speech and more disruptive (nontask-directed) speech than the normal boys. In terms of total speech activity, the percentage that was self-initiated by

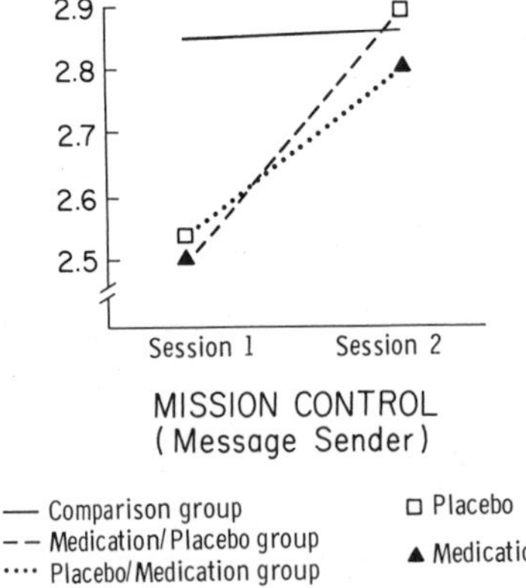

Figure 1. Mean ratings of communicative efficiency from the referential communication task "Space Flight." (From "Peer Interaction in a Structured Communication Task: Comparisons of Normal and Hyperactive Boys and of Methylphenidate (Ritalin) and Placebo Effects" by C. K. Whalen, B. Henker, B. E. Collins, S. McAuliffe, and A. Vaux, *Child Development*, 1979, *50*, 388–401. Copyright 1979 by the Society for Research in Child Development. Reprinted by permission.)

hyperactive boys (rather than responsive to the adult's comments or inquiries) was more than double the percentage self-initiated by normal boys, suggesting that hyperactive children are more likely than their peers to engage in diversionary social interactions during structured task activities.

Several additional studies indicate that hyperactive children initiate more verbal behavior than do their peers, whether in classroom, laboratory, or free-play settings (Abikoff *et al.,* 1980; Whalen *et al.,* 1979a). This difference may even be found during solitary activities when no other person is in the vicinity (Copeland, 1979).

Classroom Behaviors

As mentioned, classroom as well as laboratory studies were conducted during these summer enrichment programs for hyperactive and comparison boys. Direct behavioral observations during classroom sessions indicated that unmedicated hyperactive boys engaged in significantly higher rates of many behaviors than either medicated hyperactive boys or comparison peers. These behaviors include several that are, by definition, dysfunctional or undesirable, such as disruption and negative verbalization, and others that are often quite harmless and appropriate, such as social initiation (Whalen *et al.,* 1978, 1979a). Direct observational studies of classroom behaviors conducted by other investigators have yielded similar differences between hyperactive children and their classmates (Abikoff *et al.,* 1980; Klein & Young, 1979).

A functional understanding of the behavior patterns of hyperactive youngsters requires a simultaneous focus on the environment as well as on the child. Our classroom studies yielded some initial indications of child-by-situation interactions. Variations in the classroom dimensions of ambient noise level, task difficulty, and degree of externally imposed structure were found to amplify or diminish differences between hyperactive and normal children in rates of such behaviors as social initiation, noise-making, and disruption. Under some conditions, unmedicated hyperactive youngsters could not be distinguished from their peers. In one experiment, for example, we varied the child's control over his own work activities. In self-paced conditions, assignments were provided on individual ditto sheets and the boys could regulate their own work patterns. In other-paced conditions, task information was presented by an audiotape recorder, and successful performance required that the boys keep pace with the recorded messages. Figure 2 presents the findings for "high-energy" behaviors—acts that are perceived as particularly effortful, vigorous, intense, vehement, or loud. These results indicate that unmedicated hyperactive boys did not differ from their comparison peers under self-paced conditions, but engaged in significantly more high-

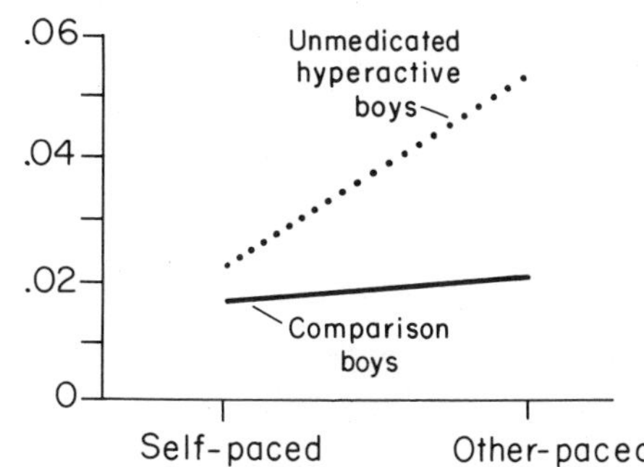

Figure 2. Probability of high energy behavior in the classroom setting.

energy behaviors when task activities were paced by an external source (Whalen *et al.*, 1978).

High energy behaviors are, of course, particularly likely to lead to interpersonal friction or rule infringement in classroom settings. Findings of this type can provide important clues about optimizing the match between classroom environments and child characteristics. However, investigators are just beginning to map the situational dimensions that are particularly relevant to hyperactive children, and replications are needed before the practical implications of these initial findings are pursued.

In this research series, two classroom studies were conducted during Week 3, when half of the hyperactive boys were taking placebos rather than their regular medication, and two additional studies were conducted during Week 4, after the medication–placebo crossover had occurred. Teacher as well as child behaviors were analyzed. Each teacher–child contact was coded as either *regular* (information-giving, small talk) or *control* (guidance, admonishments, demands for behavior change). In all four experiments, significantly more control contacts occurred between the teacher and unmedicated hyperactive children than between the teacher and either medicated hyperactive or normal comparison peers; the latter two groups did not differ from each other (see Figure 3). No consistent differences between the groups emerged for the frequency of regular contacts. The *intensity* (vigor, loudness, rapidity, or emotionality) of the teacher's behavior was also coded, and these results are presented in Figure 4. Once again, we see higher rates with the unmedicated hyperactive children and no differences between the medicated hyperactive and comparison groups. Moreover, a simple count of the number of times that the teacher identified each child by name distinguished the unmedicated hyperactive boys from the other two groups.

During these sessions, the staff also provided daily "critical incident logs" in which they described in writing any episodes that had captured their attention during the morning. From these logs, the number of discrete negative incidents was analyzed separately for each of the three groups of boys. This "social salience" measure revealed findings similar to those from analyses of teacher behaviors: Significantly higher rates of negative incidents occurred with the unmedicated hyperactive boys than with either of the other two groups, as can be seen in Figure 5. Additional details about methodologies and findings can be

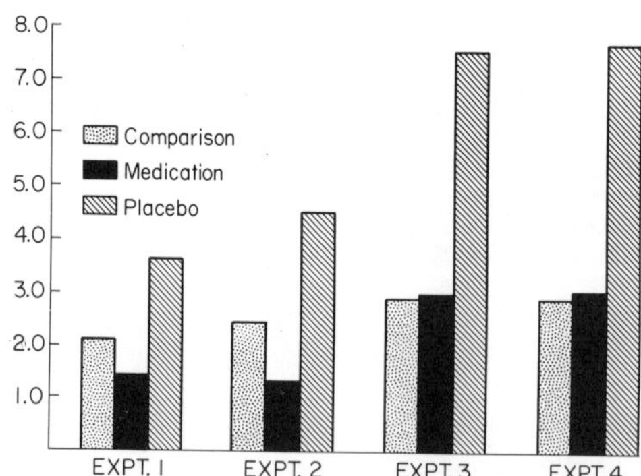

Figure 3. Frequency of control contacts by teacher toward comparison boys, hyperactive boys on medication, and hyperactive boys on placebo. (From "Teacher Response to the Methylphenidate (Ritalin) versus Placebo Status of Hyperactive Boys in the Classroom" by C. K. Whalen, B. Henker, and S. Dotemoto, *Child Development,* 1981, *52,* 1005–1014. Copyright 1981 by the Society for Research in Child Development. Reprinted by permission.)

found in Whalen, Henker, and Dotemoto (1980, 1981) and in Whalen, Henker, and Finck (1981).

Despite the decided difficulties hyperactive children have negotiating their everyday social worlds, there are no indications of deficiencies in interpersonal intelligence or social reasoning abilities. In fact, Paulauskas and Campbell (1979) reported that hyperactive children performed as well as their peers on structured tests of role taking and social understanding. When required to apply their social reasoning skills in natural settings, however, they often encounter difficulties. When asked, they know what to do, but when observed, they often are not doing it. The picture that is beginning to emerge is one of "social impulsivity"—high rates of social behaviors that are relatively impervious to the specific demands of the task or context.

Behavior Patterns: Summary and Conclusions

The four major problem domains for hyperactive children were reviewed: attention, cognition and learning, motoric activity, and social competence. Diverse assessment strategies and instruments have been developed for each of these multidimensional areas, and there is a lack of consistent evidence demonstrating covariance either within or across domains. Nevertheless, some working conclusions can be drawn at this time. Evidence supporting a pervasive distractibility deficit is equivocal, while the hypothesis that hyperactive youngsters have difficulties protecting or sustaining attention over time has survived many empirical tests. Research findings suggest that some hyperactive children may have cognitive and learning problems that are not totally attributable to attentional dysfunction. They do not seem to differ from their peers in fundamental cognitive skills such as stimulus recognition and abstraction, but they may have underdeveloped metacognitive functions, including the abilities to analyze task requirements, generate effective problem-solving strategies, and evaluate their own performance.

The evidence regarding motor dysregulation is contradictory, with results highly dependent on measurement modality and situational context. Excessive activity level, when found, may be secondary to fundamental problems with concentration and response inhibition. Stylistic aspects of activity such as intensity and appropriateness appear far more likely than the total quantity of movement to distinguish hyperactive children from their peers. Although many hyperactive children are unusually sociable and outgoing, their

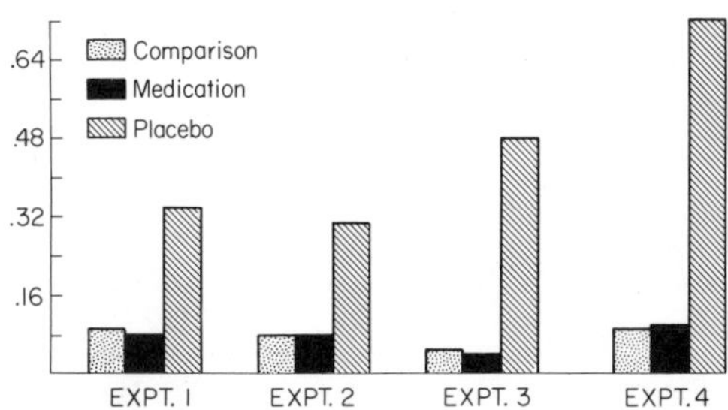

Figure 4. Frequency of teacher intensity toward comparison boys, hyperactive boys on medication, and hyperactive boys on placebo. (From "Teacher Response to the Methylphenidate (Ritalin) versus Placebo Status of Hyperactive Boys in the Classroom" by C.K. Whalen, B. Henker, and S. Dotemoto, *Child Development*, 1981, *52*, 1005–1014. Copyright 1981 by the Society for Research in Child Development. Reprinted by permission.

interpersonal competence is low and they find themselves disliked by peers and in frequent trouble with their adult supervisors.

There are few (if any) 24-hour hyperactive children. Rather, specific situations seem to provoke problem behaviors, while others tend to diminish differences between these youngsters and their peers. Hyperactive youngsters often seem somewhat out of synchrony with their environments, failing to read or respond to the subtle social and situational cues that are endemic to everyday life. There is also some indication that these youngsters respond atypically to routine reinforcement contingencies. Problems with attention, response modulation, and impulse control permeate many areas of functioning and may be at the root of the pervasive social as well as academic difficulties typically observed in hyperactive children.

Etiological Considerations

A search for the causes of hyperactivity encounters formidable methodological hurdles. Even when a potential causal agent is found to be associated reliably with hyperactivity, it appears in only a small proportion of youngsters so diagnosed. Most children considered hyperactive show normal rates or levels of any variable that has been implicated thus far. And many of the children who do have atypical family or physiological indicators do not engage in the behaviors characteristic of hyperactivity. Moreover, similar behaviors may have quite different origins, just as the source of a headache may be hypertension, a brain tumor, dietary insufficiency, and so forth. And as we have seen, the behaviors of hyperactive youngsters are not all that similar; behavioral diversity is the rule rather than the exception. Thus there is no reason to expect that a unitary etiological process will be uncovered. A more plausible perspective is the one presented by Rapoport and Quinn: "The symptoms of hyperactivity and impulsivity are most probably a final common means by which a variety of congenital, toxic, and environmental influences may be expressed" (1975, p. 41).

For communicative convenience, the discussion of etiologies is organized into three major sections (early biological influences, physical environmental influences, and psychosocial influences) with several subdivisions. It is important to keep in mind that these distinctions are somewhat arbitrary, reflecting conceptual or methodological emphases rather

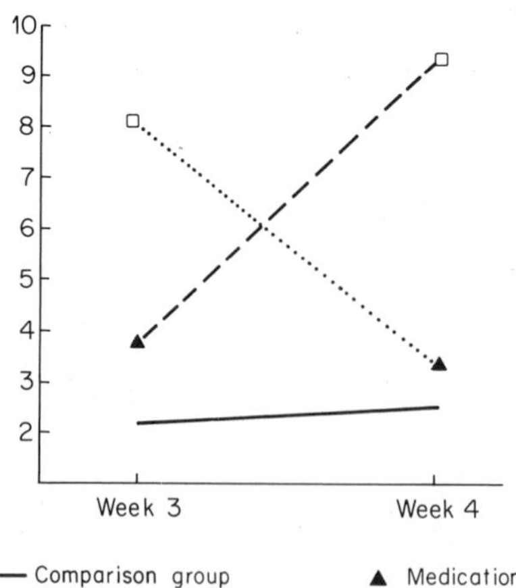

Figure 5. Frequency of negative incidents involving comparison boys, hyperactive boys taking methylphenidate Week 3 and placebo Week 4, and hyperactive boys taking placebo Week 3 and methylphenidate Week 4. (From "Medication Effects in the Classroom: Three Naturalistic Indicators" by C. K. Whalen, B. Henker, and D. Finck, *Journal of Abnormal Child Psychology,* 1981, *9,* 419–433. Copyright 1981 by Plenum Publishing Corporation. Reprinted by permission.)

than distinctive, independent processes. In reality, multiple factors interact in complex fashion. The various processes listed separately function as antecedents and consequences for each other in intricate configurations and concatenations that are still poorly understood.

Early Biological Influences

Familial–Genetic Contributions

Suggestive evidence of genetic contributions to hyperactivity has emerged from diverse family and twin studies. For example, it has been reported that: (a) A disproportionate number of parents of hyperactive children showed signs of hyperactivity during their own childhoods; (b) compared to normal peers, hyperactive boys (but, interestingly, not hyperactive girls) are more likely to have same-sex siblings who are also hyperactive; and (c) full siblings of hyperactive children are more likely than half siblings to show hyperactive behavior patterns (Cantwell, 1975; Morrison & Stewart, 1973, 1974; Safer, 1973; Stewart, 1980; Welner *et al.,* 1977). Possible links between hyperactivity in children, hysteria in biological mothers, and alcoholism or antisocial behavior in biological fathers have been suggested (Cantwell, 1978; Morrison & Stewart, 1971), and the link with antisocial parentage has been found even when the children were separated from their parents at birth (Cadoret, Cunningham, Loftus, & Edwards, 1975). Moreover, examination of the *adoptive* parents of hyperactive youngsters has indicated that the prevalence of psychiatric disturbance in these adults does not differ from the rates among parents of control children, a finding interpreted as further decreasing the likelihood that the link between childhood hyperactivity and parental psychopathology is attributable primarily to family environment or psychosocial stress rather than to genetic influence (Cantwell, 1975; Morrison & Stewart, 1973).

Interpretations of early demonstrations of links between childhood hyperactivity and parental psychopathology are constrained by the fact that the clinicians evaluating the parents were not blind as to the child's diagnosis; their judgments may have been influenced by knowledge that the child was or was not hyperactive. Moreover, the use of normal rather than psychiatric control groups makes it impossible to ascertain whether the links are specific to hyperactivity or characteristic of childhood behavioral disturbance in general. Recent studies designed to remedy these problems indicate that high proportions (perhaps between 40% and 60%) of the parents of heterogeneous groups of children referred to psychiatric clinics have diagnosable psychiatric disturbances, particularly affective disorders in mothers and antisocial patterns or alcoholism in fathers. These rates may be particularly high among parents of conduct disorder children—whether or not the youngsters are also considered hyperactive (Sandberg *et al.,* 1978; Stewart, deBlois, & Cummings, 1980).

Studies of specific behavior characteristics in twins provide additional clues. For example, several investigators have found much higher intraclass correlations for activity level in monozygotic (identical) than in dizygotic (fraternal) same-sex twins (Buss & Plomin, 1975; Matheny & Dolan, 1980; Willerman, 1973). Parental ratings of restlessness, school difficulties, and other problems also tend to be more similar for identical than for fraternal twins (O'Connor, Foch, Sherry, & Plomin, 1980). Findings emerging from temperament studies (e.g., Buss & Plomin, 1975) have prompted Kinsbourne and Swanson (1979) to speculate that hyperactive children may be quantitatively rather than qualitatively different from their peers, perhaps falling at the extreme end of one or more constitutional (and presumably congenital) dimensions of temperament such as impulsivity and activity.

Although the results of twin studies tend to be interpreted as evidence for genetic determination, such conclusions must be tempered by the fact that most parents know whether their twins are identical or fraternal. Parental ratings may be influenced by differential expectations as well as by differential observations of behavioral similarities in identical versus fraternal twin pairs. This cautionary note is underscored by Plomin and Foch's (1980) recent failure to find consistent evidence of genetic influence on some behavioral (in contrast to questionnaire) measures of attention and activity.

Unfortunately, the results of family and twin studies are far from consistent, and methodological limitations cloud our understanding of genetic contributions. Despite recent advances in technical sophistication, it is still difficult to separate genetic from environmental contributions. Children of hyperactive or antisocial fathers may not only have distinctive genetic makeups, but they are probably also exposed to atypical home environments. Identical twins are not only genetically more similar than fraternal twins, but they may also be treated more similarly. Separating cause from effect is particularly problematic. Do genetic factors associated with hyperactivity predispose relatives to hyperactivity and other forms of behavior disturbance, does the increased stress of living with a hyperactive child enhance the frequency or salience of psychological problems in family members, or are both types of processes operating simultaneously? Studies designed to help clarify questions about direction of causality (e.g., comparisons of biological versus adoptive relatives or of twins reared separately versus together) tend to have their own limitations, such as restricted sample sizes and limited knowledge about psychosocial environments.

There are some indications that a disproportionately high number of hyperactive children are adopted—perhaps 15% to 20%, in comparison to 2% in the general population (Deutsch, Swanson, Bruell, Cantwell, Weinberg, & Baren, 1982). If substantiated, this finding not only raises thought-provoking etiological questions, but may also facilitate the implementation of multidimensional comparisons between adopted and nonadopted hyperactive children and, for the former group, between biologic and adoptive relatives. The data will need to be interpreted carefully, however, as the two groups of relatives are not drawn from the same population. In general, adoptive parents are a highly selected and carefully screened group of individuals, and thus differences between adoptive and biologic parents may reflect a sampling artifact rather than (or as well as) genetic links between childhood hyperactivity and adult psychopathology.

Central Nervous System Arousal and Neurotransmitters

For many years, investigators have speculated that some hyperactive children have defects in the central nervous system (CNS) processes of arousal and inhibition. These youngsters have been characterized as suffering from overarousal, underarousal, an inhibitory deficit, an excitatory/inhibitory imbalance, or neurodevelopmental immaturity. Such theories have been buttressed by behavioral findings (e.g., patterns of inattention, impulsivity, and "sensation seeking") as well as by irregularities on diverse physiological indicators such as skin conductance levels, cardiovascular responses, clinical electroencephalograms (EEGs), and cortical evoked responses (e.g., Conners, 1975; Dykman *et al.,* 1971; Porges & Smith, 1980; Satterfield, Cantwell, & Satterfield, 1974; Zahn, Little, & Wender, 1978). Two comprehensive reviews of recent research led to similar conclusions: Those differences between hyperactive and nonhyperactive children that have emerged favor an underarousal or underarousability hypothesis (Ferguson & Pappas, 1979; Hastings & Barkley, 1978). At the present time, such hypotheses are at once tentative and global; additional conceptual and empirical specification of arousal processes will be welcome as progress continues in this active research arena.

A focus on CNS arousal processes results almost ineluctably in an exploration of biogenic amine neurotransmitters such as dopamine, norepinephrine, and serotonin. These chemicals, which act by either facilitating or inhibiting the transmission of nerve impulses, are critical to normal brain function and to a broad array of physiological and behavioral processes. Recent theoretical and technical advances have resulted in an explosion of knowledge about these chemical "messengers," and research findings are implicating irregularities of neurotransmitter metabolism in a heterogeneous array of child and adult disturbances, including unipolar and bipolar affective disorders, schizophrenias, childhood autism, epilepsies, and Gilles de la Tourette or chronic multiple tic syndrome (Axelrod, 1974; Cohen & Young, 1977).

Scattered but intriguing findings suggest that some hyperactive youngsters may also have a neurotransmitter deficit, and the most viable hypothesis at present seems to be dopaminergic depletion or underactivity (Margolin, 1978; Wender, 1978). Evidence for this view comes from diverse sources, including (a) the demonstration of links between artificially induced dopaminergic deficits and hyperactive-type behaviors in animals, and (b) lower-than-normal levels of homovanillic acid, the major dopamine metabolite, in the cerebral spinal fluid of hyperactive children (Shaywitz, Yager, & Klopper, 1976; Shaywitz, Cohen, & Shaywitz, 1978). Although reasoning from treatment to etiology is highly hazardous, the dopaminergic deficit hypothesis has been buttressed further by findings that amphetamine ameliorates problem behaviors in many hyperactive children and also increases the availability of dopamine in the brain (Cohen & Young, 1977).

It should be kept in mind that, although the hypothesis of a dopaminergic deficit in hyperactive children is scientifically appealing to many, the empirical foundation is frail and far from conclusive. Alternative hypotheses have been proposed that implicate other neurotransmitter systems, either in isolation or in combination with dopaminergic dysfunction (Glow & Glow, 1979; Lansdell, 1980).

Progress in this area has been impeded by the fact that relationships between neurotransmitters and behavior patterns are particularly elusive. In one recent study, for example, urinary norepinephrine (NE) was significantly higher for hyperactive than for normal children, but there were no reliable relationships between NE excretion and activity level or other behavioral measures (Rapoport, Mikkelsen, Ebert, Brown, Weise, & Kopin, 1978).

The familiar cause-and-effect questions are particularly problematic. Animal studies have demonstrated not only that altered neurotransmitter metabolism affects behavior patterns, but also that stress and behavior change can modify neurotransmitter metabolism (Cohen & Young, 1977). Many hyperactive children probably experience atypically high levels of stress, given repeated patterns of interpersonal friction and failure. Thus it is conceivable that neurotransmitter dysfunction may be a consequence instead of (or as well as) an antecedent of problem behaviors. And finally, the ubiquity of dopamine hypotheses to explain diverse behavioral dysfunctions raises suspicions about the specificity of causal links between dopamine and any particular type of disorder such as hyperactivity (Ferguson & Pappas, 1979).

Neurological Soft Signs

Another clinical research focus has been on what are called neurological soft signs, mild and somewhat equivocal neurological irregularities such as poor balance, impaired fine motor coordination, clumsiness, reflex asymmetries, or choreiform (irregular, jerky) limb movements. These are usually considered signs of developmental immaturity, and they tend to diminish with age (Camp, Bialer, Sverd, & Winsberg, 1978; Mikkelsen, Brown,

Minichiello, Millican, & Rapoport, 1982). Several studies have found particularly high rates of soft signs among hyperactive children. For example, McMahon and Greenberg (1977) reported that 67% of a hyperactive sample had two or more soft signs. Similarly, Werry, Minde, Guzman, Weiss, Dogan, and Hoy (1972) found that 80% of their hyperactive sample had three or more minor neurological signs, in contrast to 10% of a neurotic and 15% of a normal comparison group.

However, differences between hyperactive and other children are not uniformly found (e.g., Camp *et al.,* 1978), and the likelihood of inconsistent results is enhanced by poor interjudge reliability on individual items and by significant within-child variability from one examination to another. Moreover, the physicians conducting the neurological evaluations are not always blind as to the child's diagnostic status. Definitions and measurement procedures also vary across clinicians and settings. To ameliorate this latter problem, the Psychopharmacology Research Branch of the National Institute of Mental Health developed a standardized format for evaluating soft signs known as the PANESS, or Physical and Neurological Examination for Soft Signs (Guy, 1976), but serious questions have been raised about the clinical validity of this instrument (Camp *et al.,* 1978; Werry & Aman, 1976). It should also be noted that the measures may reflect behavioral as well as neurological differences: Children who are alert, cooperative, and motivated to succeed probably perform better on the soft sign examination than their noncompliant and less involved peers.

Perinatal Stress

Studies of early biological risk factors such as pregnancy complications and low birth weight have yielded complex, inconsistent, and contradictory findings. While the notion that perinatal stress is a major cause of hyperactivity has enjoyed some popularity, systematic studies generally fail to find reliable relationships. Following a comprehensive examination of hyperactive and normal children, Minde, Webb, and Sykes (1968) were struck more by the similarities than by the differences between the two groups in rates of problem pregnancies, complications of delivery, neonatal diseases, and so forth. One variable that should be examined carefully in future studies is maternal smoking. Nichols and Chen (1981) reported a link between maternal smoking during pregnancy and hyperkinetic-impulsive behavior in children, a finding consistent with the results of an earlier study by Denson, Nanson, and McWatters (1975). In a well known, prospective study of hundreds of multiracial youngsters on the island of Kauai in Hawaii, relationships emerged between perinatal stress and intelligence at age 10, but not between these risk factors and hyperactivity, school achievement, or hyperaggression (Werner, Bierman, & French, 1971). As discussed below, the potent influences of environmental variables such as parental adequacy and family stability must also be considered in this complex matrix (Werner, 1980). Summarizing the results of their 10-year follow-up study, Werner *et al.* concluded that "ten times more children had problems attributed to the effects of a poor environment than to the effects of serious perinatal stress" (1971, p. 134).

Minor Physical Anomalies

Another intriguing (and, as usual, puzzling) set of research findings pertains to minor physical anomalies (MPAs)—anatomical stigmata that develop during the first trimester of pregnancy, presumably as a result of genetic transmission or physical insult to the fetus. Over 35 minor physical anomalies have been identified. Examples include: a single palmar crease; steepled roof of mouth; more than one hair whorl; malformed, asymmetrical, or low-seated ears; curved fifth finger; wide gap between the first and second toes; and third toe longer than second toe. What seems to be important is not any specific anomaly or a particular constellation, but rather the total number of anomalies found in an individual (Waldrop & Halverson, 1971). Most of these anomalies occur frequently in normal populations, and it has been estimated that people with no known physiological or psychological disturbance may average between two and four MPAs (Waldrop, Bell, McLaughlin, & Halverson, 1978). Much higher numbers of anomalies are found among individuals with known biological defects such as Downs syndrome or fetal alcohol syndrome. Recent studies are also suggesting intriguing links between MPAs and hyperactivity.

In a clinical sample of hyperactive boys, Quinn and Rapoport (1974) found that those with high stigmata scores (5 or more anomalies) were more likely than those with scores below 5 to have a record of obstetrical complications, a paternal history of hyperactivity, onset of behavior problems before the age of 3, and higher teacher ratings of hyperactivity. Examining anomaly–behavior relationships in normal elementary school children, Halverson and Victor (1976) found that the total number of MPAs correlated negatively with academic achievement and positively with teacher ratings of hyperactivity, peer ratings on a "mean–noisy" factor, and actometer readings of activity level.

One of the most noteworthy findings is that MPAs at early ages are related not only to current response styles, but also to behavior patterns assessed several years later. Waldrop *et al.* (1978) found that anomaly scores obtained soon after birth were moderately correlated at age 3 with such nursery school behaviors as short attention span and peer aggression/impulsivity. In an independent longitudinal investigation of the correlates and concomitants of MPAs, Rapoport and her colleagues found that high-anomaly infants were somewhat more likely than infants with low anomaly scores to show difficult behavioral and temperamental characteristics at 1, 2, and 3 years of age (Burg, Hart, Quinn, & Rapoport, 1978; Burg, Rapoport, Bartley, Quinn, & Timmins, 1980; Rapoport, Quinn, Burg, & Bartley, 1979). However, the relationships were relatively weak, and there was little consistency across situations or over time. These longitudinal investigations are continuing as the youngsters mature, and thus more extensive data on the specificity, durability, and robustness of these relationships should be forthcoming.

Taken together, the MPA data provide further evidence of congenital contributions to hyperactive behavior patterns. Within normal as well as clinical samples, many children with high rates of hyperactive behaviors have anomaly scores higher than their peers (but still lower than those found in individuals with known biological dysfunctions). Noteworthy sex differences have emerged, with the relationships generally stronger and more consistent for males than for females (O'Donnell & van Tuinan, 1979; O'Donnell, O'Neill, & Staley, 1979; Waldrop & Halverson, 1971). It has been suggested that children with high MPA scores may be physically unattractive or "funny looking," and that their difficult behaviors may be shaped by cumulative negative responses from their social environments. It is unlikely that this type of process accounts for the bulk of the evidence, however. Most of the anomalies are minor rather than gross, and one systematic study yielded no relationship between anomaly scores and independent ratings of physical attractiveness (Rapoport & Quinn, 1975). As Kinsbourne (1979) suggested, it may be useful in subsequent studies to distinguish observable anomalies (e.g., facial characteristics) from those usually hidden by clothing.

Summary and Conclusions

The research literature on anomalies, soft signs, neurotransmitters, and other biological variables is laced with methodological problems, contradictory findings, and unsuccessful attempts at replication. Even when reliable measurements can be obtained, their meaning is ambiguous and, in most cases, it is not yet possible to separate cause from concomitant from consequence. Understanding is further clouded by the fact that the biological deviations found in subgroups of hyperactive children are also found among normal populations and in youngsters with diverse disorders that have no apparent similarity to hyperactivity. Moreover, the significant correlations that have emerged tend to be in the low-to-moderate range, indicating that the relationships are probably not spurious, but also that other factors play major roles in the complex interplay between physiology and behavior. Perhaps the best characterization at the present time is that these research enterprises are generating tantalizing and potentially consequential clues about brain-behavior relationships. The specificity, validity, and impact of such information should increase dramatically with progressive refinements in biomedical theory and technology. However, this work is still far from providing either definitive answers about the etiologies of hyperactivity, or information that has direct clinical utility for the diagnosis and treatment of hyperactive children.

Physical Environmental Influences

Numerous physical factors have been implicated as causal agents, including climate, fluorescent lighting, and even tight underwear. Such notions are highly speculative and have no empirical foundation (e.g., O'Leary, Rosenbaum, & Hughes, 1978). There are, however, two environmental substances that may be contributing to hyperactive behavior patterns in some youngsters: lead and foodstuffs. The currently available information justifies continued exploration, as discussed in the following subsections.

Environmental Lead

Child health specialists have long known that lead is a neurotoxin that can cause severe encephalopathy in children. The mortality rate is high, and those who survive severe lead intoxication or plumbism often have permanent neurological sequelae as well as cognitive and behavioral impairments (Chisolm, 1971; Needleman, 1973; Rutter, 1980). The potential relevance of lead to hyperactivity emerges not in such unambiguous instances of severe lead poisoning, but rather in more subtle cases of elevated but "subclinical" body–lead burdens. The results of several lines of research are converging to suggest that lead levels below those previously considered toxic may contribute to cognitive and behavioral problems in school-age youngsters (e.g., David, Hoffman, Sverd, Clark, & Voeller, 1976; de la Burdé & Choate, 1975).

As Chaiklin (1979) contends, lead is stubborn and pervasive in the environment. Lead wastes are disseminated by automotive exhaust, battery plants, smelters, and so on. This substance is a ubiquitous component of urban dirt, dust, and water; it contaminates the air we inhale and the nutrients we ingest (Zarkowsky, 1976). It is found in such everyday items as vegetation grown beside roads, tuna and other foods packed in lead-soldered cans, toothpaste, and printed matter, to name just a few examples (Settle & Patterson, 1980; Waldbott, 1978). Although lead-pigment paints have been banned, their use was rampant prior to the 1940s. As the newer layers of paint and plaster peel off of old, neglected buildings, the earlier layers of lead-based paint are exposed, thus creating a hazard for children with a propensity to mouth and chew inedible substances.

The human body can store significant quantities of lead for long periods of time. Concerns have been raised that large numbers of children—particularly those residing in congested urban areas—may be carrying undetected body lead burdens that produce no acute symptomatology but exert slowly evolving and long-lasting adverse effects on cognitive and behavioral processes. The concerns are accentuated by studies with rats, demonstrating that exposure to lead during the fetal or early developmental periods causes serious neurological and behavioral impairments (Silbergeld, 1977).

Lead studies are fraught with methodological problems, thus a definitive link between lead and hyperactivity (or other disorders) is difficult to demonstrate. Since random assignment of children to high- and low-lead environments is ethically (as well as logistically) untenable, much of the available evidence is necessarily indirect. Moreover, assessment is problematic. Lead levels have been measured from samples of blood, hair, or shed "baby" teeth, from x-rays of the long bones, and from urinalysis following administration of a chelating agent that causes the release of stored body lead. Each procedure has its own set of technical difficulties and sources of unreliability, and not much is known about the interrelationships among these indicators. As Rutter (1980) maintains, these measurement problems probably create underestimates of the performance differences between children with low lead levels and those with chronically elevated lead levels.

Another difficulty concerns the number of potentially confounding factors that constrain the interpretation of research findings. Children who engage in pica—the indiscriminate ingestion of inedible substances—are likely to have increased lead levels and intellectual or behavioral impairment, but it is difficult to separate cause from effect. Do elevated lead levels cause intellectual and behavioral problems? Do the behaviors of retarded and uncontrolled children increase their exposure to environmental lead? Or are both the lead levels and the performance problems caused by a third factor? The correlational studies that can be conducted with children provide only limited answers to such questions; the experimental studies conducted with infrahuman animals can answer some of these thorny "chicken-or-egg" questions, but the generalizability of the findings to human populations is unknown.

Given these conceptual and methodological problems, what can be said about lead and hyperactivity? Following an assiduous and highly critical review of the research literature, Rutter (1980) concluded that evidence supporting a link between elevated (but subclinical) lead levels and cognitive impairment is relatively robust. The documented deficits tend to be small (e.g., 3 or 4 IQ points), but such differences are statistically significant and potentially consequential. A second conclusion was that evidence supporting a link between elevated lead levels and behavior problems is more contradictory, of poorer quality, and not necessarily specific to the behavior patterns characteristic of hyperactivity.

Despite Rutter's cautious conclusions, there are enough indications of potentially unsalutary cognitive and behavioral effects to take the matter quite seriously. Perhaps the best evidence is that provided by Needleman, Gunnoe, Leviton, Reed, Peresie, Maher, and Barrett (1979) in a study of children with high and low dentine lead levels. Significant (although small) differences emerged on IQ and other measures of cognitive performance. Moreover, teachers were more likely to rate children with high-lead than with low-lead levels negatively on adjectives considered descriptive of many hyperactive youngsters, including "impulsive," "distractible," and "easily frustrated." The association is strengthened by a type of dose-response analysis: Not only were differences found between the extreme high-lead and low-lead groups (i.e., the top and bottom 10%), but when children in the middle of the distribution were examined, a gradual increase in negative teacher ratings was found with increasing lead levels.

These provocative results indicate the need not only for additional, methodologically rigorous research, but also for immediate and ongoing steps toward "environmental cleaning," since the elimination of many sources of lead contamination is now technologically possible. The issues are exceedingly complex, however. For example, the production of unleaded gas requires more oil than the production of leaded gas (Chaiklin, 1979), and it is difficult to balance various health and welfare considerations against political and economic pressures. Matters are complicated further by the methodological inadequacies of much of the research literature, the relatively subtle nature of the toxic effects demonstrated to date, and the possibility that substituting untested, lead-free ingredients in some products may have inadvertent outcomes that are even more detrimental than those attributable to lead.

Diet: Additives, Dyes, and Sugars

Most readers—even those unfamiliar with the notion of hyperactivity before turning to this chapter—have probably been exposed to media presentations highlighting a putative relationship between behavior disorders and food additives. Professionals and laymen alike are expressing increasing concerns over the potentially harmful effects of food additives; these embattled chemicals have been implicated in various forms of cancer, schizophrenia, depression, cardiovascular disease, and so forth. The possibility of a link between additives and hyperactivity was popularized in the mid 1970s when a San Francisco pediatrician proclaimed that significant proportions (perhaps 30% to 50%) of hyperactive children show dramatic improvements when food additives are excluded from their diets (Feingold, 1976).[3]

A casual scanning of labels in any supermarket demonstrates that excluding food additives from a child's daily intake must be a formidable enterprise. Many of the foodstuffs considered as "staples" by and for school-age children are forbidden—most cereals, frozen waffles, packaged drink mixes, margarine, processed cheese, and ice cream, to name just a few. To maintain such a diet, most parents must revolutionize the entire family's lifestyle. These considerations have serious research implications. One problem is ensuring compliance with the dietary restrictions; it is easy for harried or weary parents to lapse, and it is even easier for a child to obtain edible contraband from a friend. Another problem is separating the specific effects of additives from the nonspecific improvements that may attend a dramatic lifestyle change. When a child is placed on one of these restrictive diets, his life becomes more highly routinized and scrutinized, and it is also likely that he spends more time with his family, perhaps in the kitchen baking additive-free bread. (Indeed, cookbooks are now available commercially to help parents provide additive-free meals for their families.) These profound but nonspecific changes may effect marked behavioral improvements in hyperactive (as well as nonhyperactive) youngsters, and it is difficult to tell whether the dietary changes in themselves had specific ameliorative effects. Another confounding factor is that parents who place their families on such diets are certainly not blind to the treatment—nor are they free of psychological investment. Many clinical studies rely on subjective ratings by parents, measures that may reflect the parents' hopes and expectancies as well as the child's actual behavior changes.

For these reasons, the early, uncontrolled reports of diet-related improvement cannot

[3]Although Feingold's (1976) original diet excluded foods with natural salicylates (e.g., almonds, apples, and tomatoes) as well as those with additives, both the measurement and the importance of natural salicylates are controversial (Conners, 1980). Most systematic investigations of dietary effects have focused on artificial ingredients, particularly food dyes. It should also be noted that some investigators are currently examining relationships between hyperactivity and allergies to common foods such as milk, eggs, and cereals (Trites, Tryphonas, & Ferguson, 1980).

be embraced with much confidence. Because the food additive hypotheses have weighty implications for the health and well-being of all children (and perhaps adults as well), several research teams have launched ambitious attempts to conduct definitive tests, using ingenious tactics to overcome the procedural hurdles noted above (e.g., Conners, Goyette, Southwick, Lees, & Andrulonis, 1976). Detailed control diets have been developed that equal Feingold's Kaiser-Permanente (K-P) diet in preparation time, types of food restrictions, palatability, and plausibility. Laborious steps are taken to ensure dietary compliance, and food intake is monitored meticulously. In a landmark endeavor now known as the Wisconsin study, Harley and colleagues anticipated methodological snares in clever and excruciating detail. Their procedures included: (a) removing previously purchased foods from the home and delivering the family's entire food supply each week; (b) arranging weekly home visits by a dietician to monitor dietary practices and maintain motivation; (c) delivering special treats to the entire classroom for holiday and birthday parties; and (d) interpolating "pseudo-dietary manipulations and distractions," such as irrelevant changes from one week to the next, to prevent families from detecting whether they were on the experimental or the control diet (Harley, Ray, Tomasi, Eichman, Matthews, Chun, Cleeland, & Traisman, 1978). In another study conducted by Swanson and Kinsbourne (1980), children were hospitalized to ensure perfect dietary maintenance.

Two types of studies have been conducted under controlled, double-blind conditions. One procedure is to randomly assign hyperactive children to either an experimental (additive-free) or a control diet. Sometimes a separate group of children is maintained on each diet throughout the study. Or, a crossover design is used in which each child receives both diets and thus serves as his own control; half are given the experimental diet first followed by the comparison diet, and half receive the two diets in the reverse order. A second type of study involves placing children considered dye-sensitive on an elimination diet and then "challenging" them with cookies or drinks that contain specified doses of food colors. To rule out expectancy effects, placebo cookies or drinks—similar in taste and appearance—are also used.

To date, the results of these studies are both disappointing and perplexing. When the Feingold diet is initiated nonblind, striking improvements are often reported by parents, teachers, or both. The effects of the controlled, double-blind studies, however, are quite mixed, with inconsistent findings emerging even in studies conducted by the same team of researchers (Conners, 1980). It would be comforting to be able to tie the discrepancies to type of measure or response domain, but the data deter such ready resolutions. For example, negative effects of food dyes have been found on ratings but not on laboratory measures of attention and performance in some studies (Harley *et al.,* 1978; Levy, Dumbrell, Hobbes, Ryan, Wilton, & Woodhill, 1978) and on laboratory measures but not ratings in other studies (Goyette, Conners, Petti, & Curtis, 1978; Swanson & Kinsbourne, 1980). As discussed previously, some of the inconsistent findings may be attributable to differences in procedural details, child characteristics, or family attributes, but it is impossible to delineate the specific role of these and other factors at the present time. There are also unresolved methodological limitations, such as the possibility that parents may break the placebo-dye code when "challenge" cookies are used. Wender (1980) suggests that the presence of artificial colors can be detected when the cookie is moistened and then allowed to soak into an absorbent napkin or towel. It is not difficult to imagine how such "kitchen chromatography" might occur inadvertently, given the propensity young children have for dipping cookies into milk or juice.

Dosage variations may also contribute to the inconsistencies. Some investigators are concerned that the amount of food dye proposed by the Nutrition Foundation as the best estimate of children's average daily intake is in fact much too low. Swanson and Kinsbourne (1980) used quantities of food dyes more than 10 times those used by previous investigators, and did find dye-related impairments on a laboratory measure of paired-associate learning in a group of hyperactive children who had previously shown positive responses to stimulant medication. It is noteworthy that these effects did not emerge in a group of clinic-referred children who were not considered hyperactive (and who had shown adverse medication responses), nor did staff ratings of social behaviors reveal dye effects in either group of children.

One particularly puzzling finding is that children who seem to show behavioral improvements when placed on additive-free diets may *not* show deterioration when challenged with cookies loaded with food dyes (Conners, 1980; Harley & Matthews, 1980). An enigmatic sequence effect has also emerged in two controlled studies: Differential effects of an additive-free diet were found only for children who received the control diet first, followed by the experimental diet; those who received the two diets in the reverse order showed no behavioral differences (Conners *et al.,* 1976; Harley *et al.,* 1978).

Given this medley of difficulties and inconsistencies, what can be said about the relationship between food additives and hyperactivity? The most defensible interim verdict is, "not proven." Against a background of generally negative results, there are some alluring positive glimmers. A subgroup of hyperactive children may be particularly sensitive to food dyes, showing behavioral deterioration when challenged or behavioral improvement when dietary control is implemented. Conners (1980) estimates that this subgroup represents a very small proportion of hyperactive youngsters—perhaps less than 5%. Presently available data suggest that the few children who do respond are more likely to be preschool-age than elementary school-age (Harley *et al.,* 1978; Weiss, Williams, Margen, Abrams, Caan, Citron, Cox, McKibben, Ogar, & Schultz, 1980). It is also clear, however, that the etiological role of food additives has been greatly exaggerated; there are no empirical indications to date that these ingested chemicals are a major cause of hyperactivity.

Many foods replete with additives and dyes also have high sugar content, and it has been suggested that sugar may be the "offending agent," at least for hyperactive children. One recent study by Prinz, Roberts, and Hantman (1980) demonstrated a link between estimates of sugar consumption and playroom observations of destructive/aggressive and restless behaviors in young (aged 4 to 7) hyperactive children. Curiously, the results for the control group were quite different: Sugar consumption by normal youngsters was not related to either destructive/aggressive or to restless behavior but was related, instead, to locomotor activity (quadrant changes), a variable that did *not* correlate with sugar intake within the hyperactive group. One (admittedly speculative) interpretation of these findings is that there may indeed be a relationship between sugar consumption and motor behavior; normal youngsters may channel the increased activity level appropriately, by moving back and forth across the playroom, while hyperactive children react with inappropriate motoric activities such as throwing or kicking play materials. These suggestive findings indicate the need for multidimensional dose–response studies of sugar-behavior linkages in children.

Psychosocial Influences[4]

Although many people believe that hyperactivity is caused by poor parenting, social disadvantage, or artless teaching, there are no empirical indications that psychological,

[4]This discussion of psychosocial influences does not pertain to instances in which children begin showing disturbed behaviors as a result of acute environmental stressors such as a death or divorce in the family. Most knowledgeable professionals agree that a diagnosis of hyperactivity or ADD-H is inappropriate in such cases.

social, or cultural variables function as primary causal agents. What, then, is the role of the psychosocial world? Researchers are now shifting away from a "child deficit" view and toward a more ecological perspective that focuses on child-by-situation interactions (Glow & Glow, 1979; Henker & Whalen, 1980a). Here the emphasis is on identifying matches and mismatches among characteristics of the child and those of his social and physical environments (Whalen & Henker, 1977). A confluence of findings suggests that some children are born with high-risk constitutions (e.g., labile nervous systems or difficult temperaments) and that the development of behavior and learning problems depends not only on the severity of this biological load, but also on such environmental factors as family adaptability and tolerance, psychological and socioeconomic assets, and stressful life events. For example, if parents who savor peace, quiet, and orderly routines have a child who is constitutionally active, vigorous, and impulsive, problems are more likely to develop than if the same child is born to parents who tolerate and even enjoy less regularity and a more intense, disorganized, or impetuous lifestyle. A social–ecological perspective is supported not only by longitudinal studies of temperament (e.g., Thomas, Chess, & Birch, 1968), but also by evidence that social factors such as educational stimulation in the home may "make up for" early biological risk factors such as perinatal stress or low birth weight (Werner & Smith, 1977). Further support emanates from reports that family stability and quality of parenting may influence long-term outcomes for hyperactive youngsters (Loney *et al.*, 1981; Weiss, 1980).

The role of teachers must also be considered. Some teachers seem to have unusually high "detection thresholds," that is, they are relatively unlikely to perceive a child as deviant and in need of special help. At the other extreme are teachers with low thresholds who view a wide range of behaviors as changeworthy and refer many students for evaluation and remediation. These individual differences not only have an impact on day-to-day interactions in the classroom, but they may also influence the likelihood that a child is diagnosed, and even the type of treatment given. The same variations can be observed among pediatricians and other practitioners. Unfortunately, little empirical information is available about the potentially powerful role of such individual differences and person–perception processes (Henker & Whalen, 1980a).

The notion that psychosocial factors are mitigating agents is both plausible and optimistic, but the supporting data base is still inchoate. Methodological and statistical technologies have now advanced to the point where longitudinal investigations of behavioral variability, situational influences, and physiological parameters can and should be conducted at multiple sites. The large number of potential contributing factors and the complexities of their interrelationships clearly underscore the need for multivariate research strategies, a point so cogently argued by Loney and her colleagues (Loney, 1980b; Loney & Halmi, 1980). These large-scale studies are arduous and expensive, but their potential yield is sizable enough to merit the investment. Excellent models are provided by the Kauai longitudinal study and the Collaborative Perinatal Project of the National Institute of Neurological and Communicative Disorders and Stroke (Nichols & Chen, 1981; Werner, 1980).

Subgroups of Hyperactive Children

Some investigators are approaching the issues of etiological and behavioral diversity by attempting to distinguish more or less homogeneous subgroups of hyperactive children. Cognitive and behavioral characteristics, family dimensions, physiological parameters, response to stimulant medication—all have been proposed as subgrouping criteria (Conners, 1973a, 1975; Denhoff, 1973; Kinsbourne & Swanson, 1979; Kløve & Hole, 1979; Rapoport & Quinn, 1975; Satterfield, 1975). Campbell and her colleagues are comparing "true" and "situational" hyperactive children—youngsters who show disordered behaviors both at home and at school versus those whose difficulties are reported primarily in the home environment during the preschool years (Campbell, Endman, & Bernfeld, 1977).

It seems likely that many of the proposed distinctions are variations on the theme of organic versus psychosocial causation. Although the viability as well as the validity of such distinctions are still to be demonstrated, the search for nosological subgroups is a promising research strategy.

Developmental Trends, Prognoses, and Predictors

Although problem behaviors often emerge during the preschool period, many youngsters are not identified as hyperactive until they enter elementary school and are required to follow rules and routines designed to facilitate group functions rather then tailored to individual needs and preferences. Epidemiological studies based on global teacher ratings suggest that prevalence rates remain relatively constant during the elementary school grades (Sandoval *et al.,* 1980; Trites, Blouin, Ferguson, & Lynch, 1981). Studies that span broader age ranges indicate that higher rates of impulsive and hyperactive behaviors are more common in younger children (Goyette, Conners, & Ulrich, 1978). In particular, activity level excesses tend to diminish with age (Abikoff *et al.,* 1980; Minde, Weiss, & Mendelson, 1972).

Findings emerging from studies of unselected school children reveal what may be viewed as an optimistic pattern that has important implications for intervention: Children identified as hyperactive at one point in time do not necessarily continue to be perceived this way; perhaps 50% of these youngsters may move from above to below the cutoff score (on teacher ratings) during a 1-year period (Trites *et al.,* 1981).

When the focus shifts to more comprehensive clinical studies of hyperactive children, however, it is the negative rather than the positive outcomes that capture one's attention. Until recently, many child health specialists assumed that the immature and dysfunctional behaviors of hyperactive youngsters were self-limiting and would vanish with the onset of puberty, presumably as a consequence of physiological maturity. As hyperactive individuals mature, problem behaviors change in topography and often in gravity as well. For example, sedentary fidgeting is likely to replace gross motor excesses. Changes of this type tend to decrease the negative social stimulus value of these individuals and facilitate smoother problem-solving and interpersonal activities. Some hyperactive youngsters, perhaps 25% or more, show appreciable behavioral improvements and a virtual absence of serious difficulties during adolescence and adulthood. But many others continue to experience serious social and academic problems, at least during the adolescent period and perhaps throughout their lifespans.

In the course of one of the most comprehensive investigations of hyperactive children, Weiss, Hechtman, and their colleagues have aggregated a wealth of information about what happens to youngsters as they negotiate adolescence and adulthood. Hyperactive children were assessed 5 years after initial referral (during adolescence) and also 10 to 12 years after initial evaluation (during young adulthood). A major finding that emerged from the 5-year follow-up was substantial improvement in fundamental problem areas, particularly restlessness, distractibility, excitability, and antisocial behavior. However, many of these youngsters still had serious difficulties in these domains, and direct classroom observations indicated that they exhibited poorer concentration and more "organized behavior unrelated to classroom activity" than their normal classmates. Serious problems in social adjustment and self-esteem were also apparent in many instances, and poor academic functioning continued to characterize 80% of these hyperactive adolescents (Minde *et al.*, 1972; Weiss, Minde, Werry, Douglas, & Nemeth, 1971).

When 84% of the 5-year follow-up sample was reevaluated 5 or 6 years later, it was apparent that many of these young adults were still experiencing significant difficulties. Academic problems persisted, as indexed by poor grades, failed classes, negative teacher ratings, higher than average drop-out rates, and so forth. There were also indications that many were still bothered by concentration difficulties, impulsivity, restlessness, and poor self-esteem. Compared to their peers, the hyperactive group had had significantly more traffic accidents and had moved more frequently during the past 10 years (Weiss, Hechtman, Perlman, Hopkins, & Wener, 1979). Weiss noted improvement in the antisocial realm, reporting that a majority of the hyperactive adolescents who had committed delinquent acts "had gained sufficient control by the time they were young adults that they did not have significantly more court referrals than normal controls" (1980, p. 14).

To further delineate social competence, Hechtman, Weiss, and Perlman (1980) worked with a subsample of 18 each from the larger hyperactive and normal comparison groups when the youth were, on the average, 22 years of age. Hypothetical vignettes describing specific social situations were presented, and the youth were asked to describe what they would do if they actually found themselves in these situations. Two response formats were contrasted: a free response procedure, which involved oral descriptions of anticipated behaviors, and a paper-and-pencil, multiple-choice procedure. With events involving heterosocial content, the hyperactive group performed less adequately than the normal group on the open-ended (oral) measure but equally well on the multiple-choice, paper-and-pencil variant. These findings suggest that the hyperactive young adults may "know" the appropriate social responses but have difficulty producing them spontaneously—a conclusion quite reminiscent of the one reached in the prior discussion of interpersonal functioning during childhood. In addition, self-esteem measures indicated that the hyperactive group continued to have poorer self-concepts then their peers. The investigators concluded that deficits were apparent in the hyperactive youth, but that there were no signs of marked pathology.

In interpreting these findings, it is important to note that the average IQ of the hyperactive individuals participating in this study (113) was more than 10 points above the average of the larger hyperactive follow-up sample (102). This difference may limit the representativeness of the findings.

The discussion of childhood behavior patterns indicated that hyperactive youngsters do not usually experience difficulties in all situations, and that highly structured, academic settings are particularly problematic. Analogous situational differences emerge during adolescence and young adulthood. Weiss, Hechtman, and Perlman (1978) assessed current functioning of those hyperactive and comparison young adults who were attending school and also working. Teachers and employers were asked to rate these individuals on such dimensions as "completes tasks" and "gets along with classmates/co-workers." The results indicated that hyperactive youth were still perceived by teachers as having more difficulties than their peers. In contrast, they were functioning fine on the job, and no differences between the two groups emerged in the employer ratings. One interpretation of these results is that hyperactive young adults function better when they have the opportunity to select settings compatible with their own needs and proclivities. There is more diversity among occupational than among academic settings; the job market provides more options for optimizing the match between environmental demands, on the one hand, and personal skills and interests, on the other.

It was also found that the hyperactive and comparison young adults did not differ in job status or work history (Weiss *et al.,* 1979). However, other studies suggest that many adults who were hyperactive as children are not functioning optimally, even though they may be steadily employed and self-supporting. In a 20- to 25-year follow-up study, Borland and Heckman (1976) found that adults who were hyperactive as children had not achieved a socioeconomic status equal to that of their brothers or fathers. These adults were substantially older than those included in the studies by Weiss and her colleagues. Perhaps the continuing difficulties of many hyperactive individuals are not overtly disadvantageous during the early years on the job market, but have more subtle and insidious effects on long-term occupational attainment.

The findings presented by Weiss and her colleagues have been substantiated by other investigators working with different groups of hyperactive children and adults. To summarize, the forecast is neither gloomy nor particularly optimistic. Few hyperactive children become grossly disturbed (e.g., psychotic), nor do many engage in serious antisocial or criminal activity as adults. However, a large proportion continue to have marked difficulties negotiating the demands of everyday life, and signs of impulsivity, restlessness, social inadequacy, and low self-esteem endure, perhaps throughout the lifespan. Learning difficulties often persist even when many of the other problems have diminished substantially (Dykman & Ackerman, 1980; Huessy & Cohen, 1976; Loney *et al.,* 1981; Mendelson, Johnson, & Stewart, 1971; Weiss, 1980).

It is no longer uncommon to find therapy programs for hyperactive children continuing through adolescence and adulthood. In addition, some clinical investigators are now diagnosing and treating hyperactivity in adults who were not identified as hyperactive during childhood but who are currently experiencing wide-ranging problems, including impulsivity, distractibility, social inadequacy, and emotional overreactivity (Huessy, Cohen, Blair, & Rood, 1979; Wender, 1979; Wood, Reimherr, Wender, & Johnson, 1976).

The wide variability in symptomatology and outcome among individuals considered hyperactive has fueled an energetic search for predictors of long-term adjustment. Are there characteristics of the child, the family, or the environment that are related to either positive or negative long-term outcomes? A consistent pattern does seem to be emerging for antisocial behavior among hyperactive adolescents, with the best predictors being (a) aggression during childhood, and (b) family variables such as parenting style and adequacy (Loney *et al.,* 1981; Paternite & Loney, 1980; Weiss, Kruger, Danielson, & Elman, 1975). In general, however, the search for predictors has been quite disappointing: No clear prognostic indicators have emerged for such core problems as poor concentration, restlessness, social skill deficits, and low self-esteem (Weiss, 1980). Particularly noteworthy is the fact that long-term adjustment appears to be relatively independent of intervening treatment experiences such as type or duration of therapy (Blouin *et al.,* 1978; Weiss *et al.,* 1975).

Treatment

As noted previously, an exploration of treatment approaches is beyond the scope of this chapter. Suffice it to say that the major treatment modality for hyperactive children has been stimulant medication. Most youngsters given this diagnostic label receive methylphenidate, dextroamphetamine, or the newer pemoline at some time during their school years, and 60% to 90% of these youngsters show marked improvements in one or more behavioral (but not academic) domains.[5] The behavioral improvements that often attend stimulant treatment are a welcome relief for the child and his significant others. Medication helps "regularize" family interactions and classroom climates, allowing parents, peers, and teachers to get back to the normal business of living and working. In essence, medication-related changes allow the hyperactive youngster to share the spotlight rather than always being the focus of attention and concern. Hyperactive children often comment that they are not in trouble as often and that people seem to like them better since they started "taking their pills."

However, the early hopes for these "magic pills" have been curtailed by confrontation with empirical reality—that is, the disappointing outcomes emerging from long-term studies of hyperactive youngsters as they negotiate adolescence and adulthood. The oft-documented, short-term gains do not seem to translate into long-term improvements, and relationships between specific treatment experiences and ultimate outcomes are still to be demonstrated. Moreover, concerns about psychological as well as physiological toxicity have been raised.

Clinical investigators are now recognizing the need for multimodal interventions including, in particular, targeted training in academic skills and social competence. Behavioral and cognitive training programs are beginning to achieve some success, but the long-term efficacy of such approaches is still to be demonstrated, and the optimal mix of pharmacologic and nonchemical treatments still to be delineated. For illustrations and reviews of some of these nonpharmacologic treatment modalities, readers are referred to Douglas (1980b), Henker, Whalen, and Hinshaw (1980), Kauffman and Hallahan (1979), Keogh and Barkett (1980), Mash and Dalby (1979), and Routh and Mesibov (1980). The psychostimulant literature is evaluated by Campbell, Cohen, and Perry (Chapter 17 of this volume), Cantwell and Carlson (1978), Sprague and Brown (in press), and Whalen and Henker (1976, 1980).

The Children's Perspectives: Sociocognitive Sequelae of Diagnosis and Treatment

As part of our ongoing research program, we are interviewing children who have been diagnosed hyperactive and treated with stimulant medication. Our research questions focus on the message of the medication—and of the diagnosis as well. The clinical label and the daily ingestion of pills for the purpose of behavior change have an impact on a child's self-perceptions, the explanations he generates to explain events and outcomes, and the predictions he makes about future endeavors. Changes may also occur in the ways other people view and react to the child once he is diagnosed and treated. We have used the term *ema-*

[5]Although it has been argued that drug-related gains confirm a physiological dysfunction, the logical problems with such "treatment-etiology fallacies" were recently underscored by findings that normal children (and adults) show stimulant-related behavioral gains that are quite similar to those observed in hyperactive children (Rapoport *et al.,* 1980).

native effects to refer to such inadvertent and usually unrecognized treatment-related changes in cognitive constructs and causal attributions (Whalen & Henker, 1976).

The messages of the medication and the diagnosis are often quite complex, varying widely across children and families as well as across school personnel and medical practitioners. Some youngsters express wholesale rejection of the label *hyperactivity,* even though they freely discuss the fact that they take stimulant medication. In the following two excerpts, the boys not only deny they are hyperactive, but they also describe hyperactivity in highly unflattering terms.

Clyde, Age 9

CHILD: I'm not like that, no.
INTERVIEWER: You're not like that?
CHILD: Like, you know, I'm not—I might act like it sometimes, but I'm not hyper.
INTERVIEWER: What does it mean to be hyper?
CHILD: Acting stupid, you know. Don't ask me that question 'cause I already know what it is.
INTERVIEWER: What's that?
CHILD: The people are *crazy.* Why do you have to ask me that? I already know what "hyper" means, but it's hard to 'splain. I've seen a lot of hyper kids.
INTERVIEWER: It really *is* hard to explain.
(*Later*)
CHILD: They run around in circles. They act stupid. They go "dahuaah." They make stupid sounds and act like that. They're weird. I've seen a lot of 'em.

Bradley, Age 12

CHILD: Those guys are, go around saying, you know, "Oh, we have to take hyperactive pills," and that's not really what they're for.
INTERVIEWER: What *are* they for, Bradley?
CHILD: Well, we're not hyperactive, I can tell you *that.* They're just to help us calm down, and do what we're supposed to do.
INTERVIEWER: What does hyperactive really mean?
CHILD: It means, let's see, let me see if I can get a definition for it, uh, just completely wild, some kids are born, born like that, they just walk around really weird like. It's, it's that, you could say that's how they were deformed, words like that. People that were born like that, they were deformed. And I'm just glad I wasn't born like that.

In contrast, other children not only accept the diagnosis and treatment, but also develop intricate theories.

Roy, Age 9

INTERVIEWER: What's the difference between people who take Ritalin and people who don't?
CHILD: People that don't, don't have tempers—not as many—they don't—their body don't set off. People that do have that kind of problem can't stand—stand it. The body is sensitive and something not nice, or someone tells someone to start tickling them or punching them, it sets them off.
INTERVIEWER: Because they're sensitive?

CHILD: Yeah.
INTERVIEWER: Is there a word that doctors use for kids that take Ritalin?
CHILD: Yeah.
INTERVIEWER: What's that?
CHILD: Hyperkinetic. I'm on the borderline.
INTERVIEWER: You're on the borderline? What does that mean?
CHILD: That means I'm both. I can go on the Ritalin and off the Ritalin. A regular person and a hyperkinetic.
INTERVIEWER: A regular person and a hyperkinetic.
CHILD: Yes, sometimes I'm on the hyperkinetic side and sometimes I'm on the regular side.
INTERVIEWER: And what does it mean to be hyperkinetic?
CHILD: It means you are a regular person but you get very sensitive. You can't stand much of anything. . . . You can't stay in fights as long, or lunch, or play a game too long.
INTERVIEWER: Those are really good examples. Being "hyperkinetic"—is that something that a person is born with or is that a habit that somebody picks up?
CHILD: I think they're born with that.
INTERVIEWER: They're born with that. And is it something that they get over if they work on it, or is it something that they outgrow sooner or later?
CHILD: They just outgrow it.

For many youngsters and their families, attributing problems to a physiological source may be quite adaptive, serving to lift the burden of guilt: "If there's something wrong with my body, then the problems are not my fault." The welcome relief that often attends the diagnosis and prescription may allow child and family to redirect their energies toward problem solving rather than dwelling on "who did what to whom." However, explanations of problem *sources* often beget similar expectations about problem *solutions* (Henker & Whalen, 1980b; Whalen & Henker, 1976). Once they accept physiology as a cause, people may rely exclusively on physiological answers, particularly psychoactive drugs and biological maturity; they may adopt a passive "be-patient-and-wait-because-he'll-outgrow-it" stance rather than seeking needed training in academic skills, parent management strategies, and so forth.

As most children mature, their competencies increase, and their successes tend to be attributed more and more to their developing skills, while failures are blamed on lack of effort. There is a risk that diagnosis and medication may interfere with this normal developmental process. We have heard children credit their pills when they complete their schoolwork, are kind to their pets, clean their rooms, and get invited to parties. They report that the medication prevents them from acting crazy, picking fights, getting kicked out of school, and killing frogs! Analogously, forgetting to take medication is blamed for poor grades, temper tantrums, rule infractions, social squabbles, and even unrolling toilet paper down the stairs while parents are entertaining! "I can't help it—I'm hyperactive." When parents or teachers observe misbehavior, they often enhance such external, nonvolitional ascriptions by asking the child whether he forgot his medication or by suggesting that he needs an additional pill. The power often ascribed to the pill is illustrated in the following excerpts.

Lisa, Age 11

CHILD: I wasn't at all—I didn't at all have hardly any friends. I only had two, and that was it. And last year I didn't take it [the medication] in the afternoon, but the last time

I saw my doctor he said, "Why don't you have her start taking it in the afternoon?" And then since I've been doing that I've gotten about 20 more friends.

INTERVIEWER: How can you tell when you forget to take Ritalin?

CHILD: When I can tell that I'm not concentrating in school. Like she'll [the teacher] give us a half hour to do a math page, like there's about 20 problems, and I'll get about 6 done in 20 minutes, a half hour. But if I take it, I can get them all done in 10 minutes, 20 minutes, and have 10 minutes free.

INTERVIEWER: This is an "imagination" question. Let's say you stopped taking Ritalin altogether.

CHILD: Oh wow, I'd stay home from school!

INTERVIEWER: How come?

CHILD: Because I know what would be happening if I didn't. I wouldn't get my work done at all.

INTERVIEWER: How about your friends?

CHILD: Nobody would like me then, if I didn't take it. They'd think in their minds, "Gosh, she doesn't even want to play. What a baby!"

INTERVIEWER: Pretend that a friend of yours was about to start taking Ritalin and she asked you what you thought. . . .

CHILD: They'd ask me, like "What does it *do?*" I'd just tell them, "Well, it helps you concentrate, get more friends, and you want to join in the games more. And you'd be invited more places."

Roy, Age 9

INTERVIEWER: You were giving me a good example of times when you take an extra pill. Can you think back to another time?

CHILD: Yes, at Catalina. Another fishing story.

INTERVIEWER: Great, another fishing story.

CHILD: In the fishing I got bored, 'cause we couldn't catch the goldfish. There's goldfish in the ocean. . . . So we wouldn't catch them and I got bored waiting for another Catalina perch. We were bored. And I needed a pill—so I had to have another pill. And I didn't have one that morning. Then I had two. My Dad brought a case of them.

INTERVIEWER: He carries them with him?

CHILD: Yeah.

INTERVIEWER: So, how did you know you were bored and that you needed a pill?

CHILD: 'Cause my legs started kicking and my hands got all loose . . . then my feet start kicking all around and stuff. . . . My body gets all out of control and I need another pill.

Although the examples provided suggest that the diagnostic and treatment processes themselves may have negative side effects, it should be emphasized that such outcomes are not inevitable. Some of the physicians, parents, and children we talked with view hyperactivity as a handicap that people must learn to overcome. Medication is viewed as a temporary crutch that will assist but not effect problem resolution (or "cure"). Assumptions of personal responsibility for events and outcomes are maintained; child and family are perceived as actively working on problems rather than as passively receiving pills while awaiting puberty. Information is needed about how alternative cognitive contexts for intervention develop, and about the roles played by the child's family, physician, and teachers.

Another consideration is the trade-off between the potentially negative impacts of diagnosing and medicating a child, on the one hand, and failing or refusing to intervene, on the other. There is no evidence that children who escape or avoid the identification process have smoother childhoods or healthier outcomes; in fact, there are reasons to believe that the opposite occurs. The cycles of friction, failure, and frustration repeatedly experienced by hyperactive children are not the types of experiences that nourish self-perceived competence and a sense of personal causation.

A reasonable hypothesis is that youngsters taking medication who maintain or develop a strong sense of personal causation (or internal locus of control) have a more positive long-term prognosis than do those who readily attribute outcomes to the pills, thereby relinquishing personal responsibility. However, such belief–behavior linkages have not yet been demonstrated empirically. Nonpharmacologic interventions such as behavior therapy also have sociocognitive sequelae and implicit message values, and little is known about the emanative effects of these other treatment modalities (Henker *et al.*, 1980). Once the potential emanative effects of child therapies are recognized and their consequences assessed, strategies can be developed for harnessing such sociocognitive sequelae to insure that they aid rather than impede therapeutic progress.

The Mythos and Ethos of Hyperactivity: Concluding Comments

Hyperactivity is considered by many to be the most prevalent childhood behavior disorder, or at least the one most commonly identified and labeled. Diagnostic dissensus continues, as do heated debates over whether there is a distinct syndrome, a set of syndromes, or perhaps no syndrome at all. Despite these disputes, most professionals agree that serious and enduring problems with attention, impulsivity, and social relationships characterize large numbers of school-age youngsters and result in chronic confrontation and consternation, not only for the children themselves, but also for their significant others.

In previous years, it was assumed that children outgrew these behavior problems during early adolescence. It is now recognized that, for a significant proportion, difficulties negotiating the demands imposed by everyday academic, occupational, and interpersonal worlds continue through adulthood. Many hyperactive children do develop into successful adults, however, and the search is on for the behavioral, physiological, environmental, and treatment factors that portend positive outcomes.

Hyperactivity is characterized by behavioral and, most likely, etiological heterogeneity, and research findings suggest a family of hyperactive patterns rather than a unitary disorder. In terms of biological antecedents and concomitants, the pendulum is still swinging. Given repeated failures to demonstrate organic deficits, many investigators have moved away from medical models and now view the term "minimal brain dysfunction" as an unfortunate misnomer in many cases. But the findings reviewed in this chapter have provocative implications regarding potential physiological contributions, and thus we find a resurgence of interest in biomedical approaches.

It is now clear that pharmacotherapy is not a sufficient intervention for youngsters considered hyperactive. Stimulant drugs have effected heartening short-term benefits, but the improvements are limited in both scope and duration, and child health specialists are troubled by the potential for psychological as well as physiological toxicity. One current trend is toward designing and evaluating nonpharmacologic treatments—particularly behavioral and cognitive interventions—that may serve as adjuncts or alternatives to medication. Another promising trend is the identification of subgroups of hyperactive children who are more or less homogeneous with respect to core characteristics and may respond differentially to diverse treatment modalities. We are also witnessing a refreshing shift away from "child deficit" or "blame-the-victim" views toward more social ecological perspectives that recognize the potent role of environmental factors. Rather than focusing on "fixing" a defective organism, proponents of these views recognize the need to optimize the match between a child's characteristics and those of his social and physical settings. Such interactional perspectives also highlight the possibility that some of the atypical characteristics of hyperactive individuals—the qualities that often lead to friction and failure—may function as assets in certain (as yet unspecified) roles and contexts.

The complexities of hyperactivity continue to intrigue and challenge talented research investigators. Inconsistent and inconclusive findings progressively spawn more penetrating questions and more powerful research methodologies, and each new empirical wave contributes to gradual growth in our knowledge about the causes, characteristics, and optimal treatments for these baffling behavior problems.

References

Abikoff, H., Gittelman, R., & Klein, D. F. A classroom observation code for hyperactive children: A replication of validity. *Journal of Consulting and Clinical Psychology,* 1980, *48,* 555–565.

Achenbach, T. M., & Edelbrock, C. S. The classification of child psychopathology: A review and analysis of empirical efforts. *Psychological Bulletin,* 1978, *85,* 1275–1301.

Ackerman, P. T., Elardo, P. T., & Dykman, R. A. A psychosocial study of hyperactive and learning-disabled boys. *Journal of Abnormal Child Psychology,* 1979, *7,* 91–99.

Ackerman, P. T., Oglesby, D. M., & Dykman, R. A. A contrast of hyperactive, learning disabled, and hyperactive-learning disabled boys. *Journal of Clinical Child Psychology,* 1981, *10,* 168–172.

American Psychiatric Association. *Diagnostic and statistical manual of mental disorders* (3rd ed.). Washington, D.C.: Author, 1980.

Axelrod, J. Neurotransmitters. *Scientific American,* 1974, *230,* 58–66, 71.

Barkley, R. A. Specific guidelines for defining hyperactivity in children. In B. Lahey & A. Kazdin (Eds.), *Advances in child clinical psychology* (Vol. 4). New York: Plenum Press, 1981.

Barkley, R. A., & Cunningham, C. E. Stimulant drugs and activity level in hyperactive children. *American Journal of Orthopsychiatry,* 1979, *49,* 491–499.

Barkley, R. A., & Ullman, D. G. A comparison of objective measures of activity and distractibility in hyperactive and nonhyperactive children. *Journal of Abnormal Child Psychology,* 1975, *3,* 231–244.

Battle, E. S., & Lacey, B. A context for hyperactivity in children, over time. *Child Development,* 1972, *43,* 757–773.

Benezra, E. *Learning and memory in hyperactive, reading disabled, and normal children.* Unpublished manuscript, McGill University, 1978.

Billman, J., & McDevitt, S. C. Convergence of parent and observer ratings of temperament with observations of peer interaction in nursery school. *Child Development,* 1980, *51,* 395–400.

Blouin, A. G. A., Bornstein, R. A., & Trites, R. L. Teenage alcohol use among hyperactive children: A five year follow-up study. *Journal of Pediatric Psychology,* 1978, *3,* 188–194.

Borland, B. L., & Heckman, H. K. Hyperactive boys and their brothers: A 25-year follow-up study. *Archives of General Psychiatry,* 1976, *33,* 669–675.

Bosco, J., & Robin, S. Hyperkinesis: How common is it and how is it treated? In C. K. Whalen & B. Henker (Eds.), *Hyperactive children: The social ecology of identification and treatment.* New York: Academic Press, 1980.

Bower, E. *Early identification of emotionally handicapped children in school* (2nd ed.). Springfield, Ill.: Charles C Thomas, 1969.

Brown, A. L. The development of memory: Knowing, knowing about knowing, and knowing how to know. In H. W. Reese (Ed.), *Advances in child development and behavior* (Vol. 10). New York: Academic Press, 1975.

Brown, A. L. Knowing when, where, and how to remember: A problem of metacognition. In R. Glaser (Ed.), *Advances in instructional psychology*. Hillsdale, N.J.: Lawrence Erlbaum, 1978.

Burg, C., Hart, D., Quinn, P., & Rapoport, J. Newborn minor physical anomalies and prediction of infant behavior. *Journal of Autism and Childhood Schizophrenia,* 1978, *8,* 427–439.

Burg, C., Rapoport, J. L., Bartley, L. S., Quinn, P. O., & Timmins, P. Newborn minor physical anomalies and problem behavior at age three. *American Journal of Psychiatry,* 1980, *137,* 791–796.

Buss, D. M., Block, J. H., & Block, J. Preschool activity level: Personality correlates and developmental implications. *Child Development,* 1980, *51,* 401–408.

Buss, A. H., & Plomin, R. *A temperament theory of personality development.* New York: Wiley, 1975.

Cadoret, R. J., Cunningham, L., Loftus, R., & Edwards, J. Studies of adoptees from psychiatrically disturbed biologic parents. II. Temperament, hyperactive, antisocial, and developmental variables. *Journal of Pediatrics,* 1975, *87,* 301–306.

Camp, J. A., Bialer, I., Sverd, J., & Winsberg, B. G. Clinical usefulness of the NIMH physical and neurological examination for soft signs. *American Journal of Psychiatry,* 1978, *135,* 362–364.

Campbell, E. S., & Redfering, D. L. Relationship among environmental and demographic variables and teacher-rated hyperactivity. *Journal of Abnormal Child Psychology,* 1979, *7,* 77–81.

Campbell, S. B., Endman, M. W., & Bernfeld, G. A three-year follow-up of hyperactive preschoolers into elementary school. *Journal of Child Psychology and Psychiatry,* 1977, *18,* 239–249.

Campbell, S. B., Schleifer, M., Weiss, G., & Perlman, T. A two-year follow-up of hyperactive preschoolers. *American Journal of Orthopsychiatry,* 1977, *47,* 149–162.

Cantwell, D. P. Familial-genetic research with hyperactive children. In D. P. Cantwell (Ed.), *The hyperactive child. Diagnosis, management, current research.* New York: Spectrum, 1975.

Cantwell, D. P. Hyperactivity and antisocial behavior. *Journal of the American Academy of Child Psychiatry,* 1978, *17,* 252–262.

Cantwell, D. P., & Carlson, G. A. Stimulants. In J. S. Werry (Ed.), *Pediatric psychopharmacology: The use of behavior modifying drugs in children.* New York: Brunner/Mazel, 1978.

Cantwell, D. P., & Satterfield, J. H. The prevalence of academic underachievement in hyperactive children. *Journal of Pediatric Psychology,* 1978, *3,* 168–171.

Chaiklin, H. The treadmill of lead. *American Journal of Orthopsychiatry,* 1979, *49,* 571–573.

Charles, L., Schain, R. J., Zelniker, T., & Guthrie, D. Effects of methylphenidate on hyperactive children's ability to sustain attention. *Pediatrics,* 1979, *64,* 412–418.

Chisolm, J. J., Jr. Lead poisoning. *Scientific American,* 1971, *224,* 15–23.

Cohen, D. J., & Young, J. G. Neurochemistry and child psychiatry. *Journal of the American Academy of Child Psychiatry,* 1977, *16,* 353–411.

Conners, C. K. Psychological assessment of children with minimal brain dysfunction. *Annals of the New York Academy of Sciences,* 1973, *205,* 283–302. (a)

Conners, C. K. Rating scales for use in drug studies with children. *Psychopharmacology Bulletin* (Special Issue: Pharmacotherapy of children), 1973, 24–84. (b)

Conners, C. K. Minimal brain dysfunction and psychopathology in children. In A. Davids (Ed.), *Child personality and psychopathology: Current topics* (Vol. 2). New York: Wiley, 1975.

Conners, C. K. *Food additives and hyperactive children.* New York: Plenum Press, 1980.

Conners, C. K., & Blouin, A. Hyperkinetic syndrome and psychopathology in children. In B. B. Lahey (Chair), *Is there an independent syndrome of hyperactivity in children?* Symposium presented at the meeting of the American Psychological Association, Montreal, September 1980.

Conners, C. K., & Rothschild, G. H. Drugs and learning in children. In J. Hellmuth (Ed.), *Learning disorders* (Vol. 3). Seattle: Special Child Publications, 1968.

Conners, C. K., & Taylor, E. Pemoline, methylphenidate, and placebo in children with minimal brain dysfunction. *Archives of General Psychiatry,* 1980, *37,* 922–930.

Conners, C. K., Goyette, C. H., Southwick, D. A., Lees, J. M., & Andrulonis, P. A. Food additives and hyperkinesis: A controlled double-blind experiment. *Pediatrics,* 1976, *58,* 154–166.

Copeland, A. P. Types of private speech produced by hyperactive and nonhyperactive boys. *Journal of Abnormal Child Psychology,* 1979, *7,* 169–177.

Cunningham, S. J., & Knights, R. M. The performance of hyperactive and normal boys under differing reward and punishment schedules. *Journal of Pediatric Psychology,* 1978, *3,* 195–201.

David, O. J., Hoffman, S. P., Sverd, J., Clark, J., & Voeller, K. Lead and hyperactivity. Behavioral response to chelation: A pilot study. *American Journal of Psychiatry,* 1976, *133,* 1155–1158.

Davidson, E. M., & Prior, M. R. Laterality and selective attention in hyperactive children. *Journal of Abnormal Child Psychology,* 1978, *6,* 475–481.

de la Burdé, B., & Choate, M. S. Early asymptomatic lead exposure and development at school age. *Journal of Pediatrics,* 1975, *87,* 638–642.

Delamater, A. M., Lahey, B. B., & Drake, L. Toward an empirical subclassification of "learning disabilities": A psychophysiological comparison of "hyperactive" and "nonhyperactive" subgroups. *Journal of Abnormal Child Psychology,* 1981, *9,* 65–77.

Denhoff, E. The natural life history of children with minimal brain dysfunction. *Annals of the New York Academy of Sciences,* 1973, *205,* 188–205.

Denson, R., Nanson, J. L., & McWatters, M. A. Hyperkinesis and maternal smoking. *Canadian Psychiatric Association Journal,* 1975, *20,* 183–187.

Deutsch, C., Swanson, J. M., Bruell, J. A., Cantwell, D. P., Weinberg, F., & Baren, M. Overrepresentation of adoptees in children with attention deficit disorder. *Behavior Genetics,* 1982, *12,* 45–49.

Douglas, V. I. Self-control techniques. Higher mental processes in hyperactive children. Implications for training. In R. M. Knights & D. J. Bakker (Eds.), *Treatment of hyperactive and learning disordered children. Current research.* Baltimore: University Park Press, 1980. (a)

Douglas, V. I. Treatment and training approaches to hyperactivity: Establishing internal or external control? In C. K. Whalen & B. Henker (Eds.), *Hyperactive children: The social ecology of identification and treatment.* New York: Academic Press, 1980. (b)

Douglas, V. I., & Peters, K. G. Toward a clearer definition of the attentional deficit of hyperactive children. In G. A. Hale & M. Lewis (Eds.), *Attention and cognitive development.* New York: Plenum Press, 1979.

Dykman, R. A., & Ackerman, P. Long term follow-up studies of hyperactive children. In B. W. Camp (Ed.), *Advances in behavioral pediatrics* (Vol. 1). Greenwich, Conn. JAI Press, 1980.

Dykman, R. A., Ackerman, P. T., Clements, S. D., & Peters, J. E. Specific learning disabilities: An attentional deficit syndrome. In H. R. Myklebust (Ed.), *Progress in learning disabilities* (Vol. 2). New York: Grune & Stratton, 1971.

Dykman, R. A., Ackerman, P. T., & Oglesby, D. M. Selective and sustained attention in hyperactive, learning-disabled, and normal boys. *The Journal of Nervous and Mental Disease,* 1979, *167,* 288–297.

Feingold, B. F. Hyperkinesis and learning disabilities linked to the ingestion of artificial food colors and flavors. *Journal of Learning Disabilities,* 1976, *9,* 551–559.

Ferguson, H. B., & Pappas, B. A. Evaluation of psychophysiological, neurochemical, and animal models of hyperactivity. In R. L. Trites (Ed.), *Hyperactivity in children. Etiology, measurement, and treatment implications.* Baltimore: University Park Press, 1979.

Firestone, P., & Douglas, V. The effects of reward and punishment on reaction times and autonomic activity in hyperactive and normal children. *Journal of Abnormal Child Psychology,* 1975, *3,* 201–216.

Forehand, R., Griest, D. L. & Wells, K. C. Parent behavioral training: An analysis of the relationship among multiple outcome measures. *Journal of Abnormal Child Psychology,* 1979, *7,* 229–242.

Gittelman-Klein, R., & Klein, D. F. Are behavioral and psychometric changes related in methylphenidate-treated, hyperactive children? *International Journal of Mental Health,* 1975, *4,* 182–198.

Glow, P. H , & Glow, R. A. Hyperkinetic impulse disorder: A developmental defect of motivation. *Genetic Psychology Monographs,* 1979, *100,* 159–231.

Glow, R. A. Cross-validity and normative data on the Conners' Parent and Teacher Rating Scales. In K. D. Gadow & J. Loney (Eds.), *Psychosocial aspects of drug treatment for hyperactivity.* Boulder, Colo.: Westview Press, 1981.

Glow, R. A., & Glow, P. H. Peer and self rating: Children's perception of behavior relevant to hyperkinetic impulse disorder. *Journal of Abnormal Child Psychology,* 1980, *8,* 471–490.

Goyette, C. H., Conners, C. K., Petti, T. A., & Curtis, L. E. Effects of artificial colors on hyperkinetic children: A double-blind challenge study. *Psychopharmacology Bulletin,* 1978, *14,* 39–40.

Goyette, C. H., Conners, C. K., & Ulrich, R. F. Normative data on revised Conners Parent and Teacher Rating Scales. *Journal of Abnormal Child Psychology,* 1978, *6,* 221–236.

Guy, W. *ECDEU assessment manual for psychopharmacology* (Rev.) (DHEW Publication No. (ADM) 76-338). Washington, D.C.: U.S. Government Printing Office, 1976.

Hallahan, D. P., & Reeve, R. E. Selective attention and distractibility. In B. K. Keogh (Ed.), *Advances in special education* (Vol. 1). Greenwich, Conn.: JAI Press, 1980.

Halverson, C. F., Jr., & Victor, J. B. Minor physical anomalies and problem behavior in elementary school children. *Child Development,* 1976, *47,* 281–285.

Halverson, C. F., Jr., & Waldrop, M. F. The relations of mechanically recorded activity level to varieties of preschool play behavior. *Child Development,* 1973, *44,* 678–681.

Halverson, C. F., & Waldrop. M. F. Relations between preschool activity and aspects of intellectual and social behavior at age 7-½. *Journal of Developmental Psychology,* 1976, *12,* 107–112.

Harley, J. P., & Matthews, C. G. Food additives and hyperactivity in children: Experimental investigations. In R. M. Knights & D. J. Bakker (Eds.), *Treatment of hyperactive and learning disordered children. Current research.* Baltimore: University Park Press, 1980.

Harley, J. P., Ray, R. S., Tomasi, L., Eichman, P. L., Matthews, C. G., Chun, R., Cleeland, C. S., & Traisman, E. Hyperkinesis and food additives: Testing the Feingold hypothesis. *Pediatrics,* 1978, *61,* 818–828.

Hastings, J. E., & Barkley, R. A. A review of psychophysiological research with hyperkinetic children. *Journal of Abnormal Child Psychology,* 1978, *6,* 413–447.

Hechtman, L., Weiss, G., & Perlman, T. Hyperactives as young adults. *Canadian Journal of Psychiatry,* 1980, *25,* 478–483.

Hechtman, L., Weiss, G., Perlman, T., Hopkins, J., & Wener, A. Hyperactive children in young adulthood: A controlled, prospective, ten-year follow-up. *International Journal of Mental Health,* 1979, *8,* 52–66.

Henker, B., & Whalen, C. K. The changing faces of hyperactivity: Retrospect and prospect. In C. K. Whalen & B. Henker (Eds.), *Hyperactive children. The social ecology of identification and treatment.* New York: Academic Press, 1980. (a)

Henker, B., & Whalen, C. K. The many messages of medication: Hyperactive children's perceptions and attributions. In S. Salzinger, J. Antrobus, & J. Glick (Eds.), *The ecosystem of the "sick" child.* New York: Academic Press, 1980. (b)

Henker, B., Whalen, C. K., & Hinshaw, S. P. The attributional contexts of cognitive intervention strategies. *Exceptional Education Quarterly,* 1980, *1,* 17–30.

Hoy, E., Weiss, G., Minde, K., & Cohen, N. The hyperactive child at adolescence: Cognitive, emotional, and social functioning. *Journal of Abnormal Child Psychology,* 1978, *6,* 311–324.

Huessy, H. R., & Cohen, A. H. Hyperkinetic behaviors and learning disabilities followed over seven years. *Pediatrics,* 1976, *57,* 4–10.

Huessy, H. R., Cohen, S. M., Blair, C. L., & Rood, P. Clinical explorations in adult minimal brain dysfunction. In L. Bellak (Ed.), *Psychiatric aspects of minimal brain dysfunction in adults.* New York: Grune & Stratton, 1979.

Kauffman, J. M., & Hallahan, D. P. Learning disability and hyperactivity (with comments on minimal brain dysfunction). In B. B. Lahey & A. E. Kazdin (Eds.), *Advances in clinical child psychology* (Vol. 2). New York: Plenum Press, 1979.

Keogh, B. K., & Barkett, C. J. An educational analysis of hyperactive children's achievement problems. In C. K. Whalen & B. Henker (Eds.), *Hyperactive children: The social ecology of identification and treatment.* New York: Academic Press, 1980.

Keogh, B. K., & Margolis, J. S. Learn to labor and wait: Attentional problems of children with learning disorders. *Journal of Learning Disabilities,* 1976, *9,* 276–286.

Kinsbourne, M. Discussion of "Can hyperactives be identified in infancy?" In R. L. Trites (Ed.), *Hyperactivity in children. Etiology, measurement, and treatment implications.* Baltimore: University Park Press, 1979.

Kinsbourne, M., & Swanson, J. M. Models of hyperactivity. Implications for diagnosis and treatment. In R. L. Trites (Ed.), *Hyperactivity in children. Etiology, measurement, and treatment implications.* Baltimore: University Park Press, 1979.

Klein, A. R., & Young, R. D. Hyperactive boys in their classroom: Assessment of teacher and peer perceptions, interactions, and classroom behaviors. *Journal of Abnormal Child Psychology,* 1979, *7,* 425–442.

Kløve, H., and Hole, K. The hyperkinetic syndrome. Criteria for diagnosis. In R. L. Trites (Ed.), *Hyperactivity in children. Etiology, measurement, and treatment implications.* Baltimore: University Park Press, 1979.

Kupietz, S. S., & Richardson, E. Children's vigilance performance and inattentiveness in the classroom. *Journal of Child Psychology and Psychiatry,* 1978, *19,* 155–160.

Lahey, B. B., Green, K. D., & Forehand, R. On the independence of ratings of hyperactivity, conduct problems, and attention deficits in children: A multiple regression analysis. *Journal of Consulting and Clinical Psychology,* 1980, *48,* 566–574.

Lahey, B. B., Stempniak, M., Robinson, E. J., & Tyroler, M. J. Hyperactivity and learning disabilities as independent dimensions of child behavior problems. *Journal of Abnormal Psychology,* 1978, *87,* 333–340.

Lambert, N. M., & Sandoval, J. The prevalence of learning disabilities in a sample of children considered hyperactive. *Journal of Abnormal Child Psychology,* 1980, *8,* 33–50.

Langhorne, J. E., Jr., Loney, J., Paternite, C. E., & Bechtoldt, H. P. Childhood hyperkinesis: A return to the source. *Journal of Abnormal Psychology,* 1976, *85,* 201–209.

Lansdell, H. Theories of brain mechanisms in minimal brain dysfunctions. In H. E. Rie & E. D. Rie (Eds.), *Handbook of minimal brain dysfunctions. A critical view.* New York: Wiley, 1980.

Lapouse, R., & Monk, M. A. An epidemiologic study of behavior characteristics in children. *American Journal of Public Health,* 1958, *48,* 1134–1144.

Levy, F., Dumbrell, S., Hobbes, G., Ryan, M., Wilton, N., & Woodhill, J. M. Hyperkinesis and diet: A double-blind crossover trial with a tartrazine challenge. *Medical Journal of Australia,* 1978, *1,* 61–64.

Loney, J. The intellectual functioning of hyperactive elementary school boys: A cross-sectional investigation. *American Journal of Orthopsychiatry,* 1974, *44,* 754–762.

Loney, J. An abbreviated TRS scale for measuring hyperactivity and aggression. In B. B. Lahey (Chair), *Is there an independent syndrome of hyperactivity in children?* Symposium presented at the meeting of the American Psychological Association, Montreal, September 1980. (a)

Loney, J. Hyperkinesis comes of age: What do we know and where should we go? *American Journal of Orthopsychiatry,* 1980, *50,* 28–42. (b)

Loney, J., & Halmi, K. A. Clinical treatment research: Its design, execution, analysis, and interpretation, or how I stopped worrying and learned to love regressing. *Biological Psychiatry,* 1980, *15,* 147–156.

Loney, J., & Milich, R. Hyperactivity, inattention, and aggression in clinical practice. In M. Wolraich & D. K. Routh (Eds.), *Advances in behavioral pediatrics* (Vol. 2). Greenwich, Conn.: JAI Press, in press.

Loney, J., Kramer, J., & Milich, R. The hyperkinetic child grows up: Predictors of symptoms, delinquency, and achievement at follow-up. In K. D. Gadow & J. Loney (Eds.), *Psychosocial aspects of drug treatment for hyperactivity.* Boulder, Colo.: Westview Press, 1981.

Ludlow, C. L., Rapoport, J. L., Bassich, C. J., & Mikkelsen, E. G. Drug treatment. Differential effects of dextroamphetamine on language performance in hyperactive and normal boys. In R. M. Knights & D. J. Bakker (Eds.), *Treatment of hyperactive and learning disordered children. Current Research.* Baltimore: University Park Press, 1980.

MacFarlane, J. W., Allen, L., & Honzik, M. P. *A developmental study of the behavior problems of normal children between twenty-one months and fourteen years.* Berkeley and Los Angeles: University of California Press, 1954.

Mackworth, N. H. The breakdown of vigilance during prolonged visual search. *Quarterly Journal of Experimental Psychology,* 1948, *1,* 6–21.

Margolin, D. I. The hyperkinetic child syndrome and brain monoamines: Pharmacology and therapeutic implications. *Journal of Clinical Psychiatry,* 1978, *39,* 120–123; 127–130.

Mash, E. J., & Dalby, J. T. Behavioral interventions for hyperactivity. In R. L. Trites (Ed.), *Hyperactivity in children. Etiology, measurement, and treatment implications.* Baltimore: University Park Press, 1979.

Matheny, A. P., Jr., & Dolan, A. B. A twin study of personality and temperament during middle childhood. *Journal of Research in Personality,* 1980, *14,* 224–234.

McIntyre, C. W., Blackwell, S. L., & Denton, C. L. Effect of noise distractibility on the spans of apprehension of hyperactive boys. *Journal of Abnormal Child Psychology,* 1978, *6,* 483–491.

McMahon, S. A., & Greenberg, L. M. Serial neurologic examination of hyperactive children. *Pediatrics,* 1977, *59,* 584–587.

Mendelson, W., Johnson, N., & Stewart, M. A. Hyperactive children as teenagers: A follow-up study. *The Journal of Nervous and Mental Disease,* 1971, *153,* 273–279.

Mikkelsen, E. J., Brown, G. L., Minichiello, M. D., Millican, F. K., & Rapoport, J. L. Neurologic status in hyperactive, enuretic, encopretic, and normal boys. *Journal of the American Academy of Child Psychiatry,* 1982, *21,* 75–81.

Milich, R., & Landau, S. Socialization and peer relations in hyperactive children. In K. D. Gadow & I. Bialer (Eds.), *Advances in learning and behavioral disabilites* (Vol. 1). Greenwich, Conn.: JAI Press, 1982.

Milich, R., & Loney, J. The role of hyperactive and aggressive symptomatology in predicting adolescent outcome among hyperactive children. *Journal of Pediatric Psychology,* 1979, *4,* 93–112.

Milich, R., Loney, J., & Landau, S. The independent dimensions of hyperactivity and aggression: A validation with playroom observation data. *Journal of Abnormal Psychology,* 1982, *91,* 183–198.

Milich, R., Roberts, M. A., Loney, J., & Caputo, J. Differentiating practice effects and statistical regression on the Conners Hyperkinesis Index. *Journal of Abnormal Child Psychology,* 1980, *8,* 549–552.

Minde, K., Webb, G., & Sykes, D. Studies on the hyperactive child, VI. Prenatal and paranatal factors associated with hyperactivity. *Developmental Medicine and Child Neurology,* 1968, *10,* 355–363.

Minde, K., Weiss, G., & Mendelson, N. A 5-year follow-up study of 91 hyperactive school children. *Journal of the American Academy of Child Psychiatry,* 1972, *11,* 595–610.

Morrison, J. R., & Stewart, M. A. A family study of the hyperactive child syndrome. *Biological Psychiatry,* 1971, *3,* 189–195.

Morrison, J. R., & Stewart, M. A. Evidence for polygenetic inheritance in the hyperactive child syndrome. *American Journal of Psychiatry,* 1973, *130,* 791–792.

Morrison, J. R., & Stewart, M. A. Bilateral inheritance as evidence for polygenicity in the hyperactive child syndrome. *The Journal of Nervous and Mental Disease,* 1974, *158,* 226–228.

Needleman, H. L. Lead poisoning in children: Neurologic implications of widespread subclinical intoxication. In S. Walzer & P. H. Wolff (Eds.), *Minimal cerebral dysfunction in children.* New York: Grune & Stratton, 1973.

Needleman, H. L., Gunnoe, C., Leviton, A., Reed, R., Peresie, H., Maher, C., & Barrett, P. Deficits in psychologic and classroom performance of children with elevated dentine lead levels. *New England Journal of Medicine,* 1979, *300,* 689–695.

Nichols, P.L., & Chen, T. *Minimal brain dysfunction: A prospective study.* Hillsdale, N.J.: Lawrence Erlbaum, 1981.

O'Connor, M., Foch, T., Sherry, T., & Plomin, R. A twin study of specific behavioral problems of socialization as viewed by parents. *Journal of Abnormal Child Psychology,* 1980, *8,* 189–199.

O'Donnell, J.P., & van Tuinan, M. Behavior problems of preschool children: Dimensions and congenital correlates. *Journal of Abnormal Child Psychology,* 1979, *7,* 61-76.

O'Donnell, J. P., O'Neill, S., & Staley, A. Congenital correlates of distractibility. *Journal of Abnormal Child Psychology,* 1979, *7,* 465–470.

Offord, D. R., Sullivan, K., Allen, N., & Abrams, N. Delinquency and hyperactivity. *The Journal of Nervous and Mental Disease,* 1979, *167,* 734–741.

O'Leary, K. D., Rosenbaum, A., & Hughes, P. C. Fluorescent lighting: A purported source of hyperactive behavior. *Journal of Abnormal Child Psychology,* 1978, *6,* 285–289.

Parry, P. *The effect of reward on the performance of hyperactive children.* Unpublished dissertation, McGill University, Montreal, 1973.

Paternite, C. E., & Loney, J. Relationships between symptomatology and the home or family subenvironments. In C. K. Whalen & B. Henker (Eds.), *Hyperactive children: The social ecology of identification and treatment.* New York: Academic Press, 1980.

Paternite, C. E., Loney, J., & Langhorne, J. E., Jr. Relationships between symptomatology and SES-related factors in hyperkinetic/MBD boys. *American Journal of Orthopsychiatry,* 1976, *46,* 291–301.

Paulauskas, S. L., & Campbell, S. B. G. Social perspective-taking and teacher ratings of peer interaction in hyperactive boys. *Journal of Abnormal Child Psychology,* 1979, *7,* 483–493.

Pelham, W. E. Peer relationships in hyperactive children: Description and treatment effects. In R. Milich (Chair), *Peer relationships among hyperactive children.* Symposium presented at the meeting of the American Psychological Association, Montreal, September 1980.

Plomin, R., & Foch, T. T. A twin study of objectively assessed personality in childhood. *Journal of Personality and Social Psychology,* 1980, *39,* 680–688.

Plomin, R., & Foch, T. T. Pediatrician diagnoses of hyperactivity are related to parental ratings, some specific cognitive abilities, but not to laboratory measures of personality. *Journal of Abnormal Child Psychology,* 1981, *9,* 55–64.

Porges, S. W., & Smith, K. M. Defining hyperactivity: Psychophysiological and behavioral strategies. In C. K. Whalen & B. Henker (Eds.), *Hyperactive children: The social ecology of identification and treatment.* New York: Academic Press, 1980.

Preis, K., & Huessy, H. R. Hyperactive children at risk. In M. J. Cohen (Ed.), *Drugs and the special child.* New York: Gardner Press, 1979.

Prinz, R., & Loney, J. Teacher-rated hyperactive elementary school girls: An exploratory developmental study. *Child Psychiatry and Human Development,* 1974, *4,* 246–257.

Prinz, R. J., Roberts, W. A., & Hantman, E. Dietary correlates of hyperactive behavior in children. *Journal of Consulting and Clinical Psychology,* 1980, *48,* 760–769.

Quay, H. C. Classification. In H. C. Quay & J. S. Werry (Eds.), *Psychopathological disorders of childhood* (2nd ed.). New York: Wiley, 1979.

Quay, H. C. Comments on conduct disorder, attention deficit disorder and hyperactivity. In B. B. Lahey (Chair), *Is there an independent syndrome of hyperactivity in children?* Symposium presented at the meeting of the American Psychological Association, Montreal, September 1980.

Quinn, P. O., & Rapoport, J. L. Minor physical anomalies and neurologic status in hyperactive boys. *Pediatrics,* 1974, *53,* 742–747.

Radosh, A., & Gittelman, R. The effect of appealing distractors on the performance of hyperactive children. *Journal of Abnormal Child Psychology,* 1981, *9,* 179–189.

Rapoport, J. L., & Quinn, P. O. Minor physical anomalies (stigmata) and early developmental deviation: A major biologic subgroup of "hyperactive children." *International Journal of Mental Health,* 1975, *4,* 29–44.

Rapoport, J. L., Buchsbaum, M. S., Weingartner, H., Zahn, T. P., Ludlow, C., & Mikkelsen, E. J. Dextroamphetamine—its cognitive and behavioral effect in normal and hyperactive boys and normal men. *Archives of General Psychiatry,* 1980, *37,* 933–943.

Rapoport, J. L., Mikkelsen, E. J., Ebert, M. H., Brown, G. L., Weise, V. K., & Kopin, I. J. Urinary catecholamines and amphetamine excretion in hyperactive and normal boys. *The Journal of Nervous and Mental Disease,* 1978, *166,* 731–737.

Rapoport, J. L., Quinn, P. O., Burg, C., & Bartley, L. Can hyperactives be identified in infancy? In R. L. Trites (Ed.), *Hyperactivity in children. Etiology, measurement, and treatment implications.* Baltimore: University Park Press, 1979.

Riddle, K. D., & Rapoport, J. L. A 2-year follow-up of 72 hyperkinetic boys. Classroom behavior and peer acceptance. *The Journal of Nervous and Mental Disease,* 1976, *162,* 126–134.

Robins, L. N. Follow-up studies. In H. C. Quay & J. S. Werry (Eds.), *Psychopathological disorders of childhood* (2nd ed.). New York: Wiley, 1979.

Rosenthal, R. H., & Allen, T. W. An examination of attention, arousal, and learning dysfunctions of hyperkinetic children. *Psychological Bulletin,* 1978, *85,* 689–715.

Rosenthal, R. H., & Allen, T. W. Intratask distractibility in hyperkinetic and nonhyperkinetic children. *Journal of Abnormal Child Psychology,* 1980, *8,* 175–187.

Routh, D. K. Activity, attention, and aggression in learning disabled children. *Journal of Clinical Child Psychology,* 1979, *8,* 183–187.

Routh, D. K. Developmental and social aspects of hyperactivity. In C. K. Whalen & B. Henker (Eds.), *Hyperactive children: The social ecology of identification and treatment.* New York: Academic Press, 1980.

Routh, D. K., & Mesibov, G. B. Psychological and environmental intervention: Toward social competence. In H. E. Rie & E. D. Rie (Eds.), *Handbook of minimal brain dysfunctions: A critical view.* New York: Wiley, 1980.

Routh, D. K., & Roberts, R. D. Minimal brain dysfunction in children: Failure to find evidence for a behavioral syndrome. *Psychological Reports,* 1972, *31,* 307–314.

Routh, D. K., & Schroeder, C. S. Standardized playroom measures as indices of hyperactivity. *Journal of Abnormal Child Psychology,* 1976, *4,* 199–207.

Routh, D. K., Schroeder, C. S., & O'Tuama, L. A. Development of activity level in children. *Developmental Psychology,* 1974, *10,* 163–168.

Rutter, M. Raised lead levels and impaired cognitive/behavioral functioning: A review of the evidence. *Supplement to Developmental Medicine and Child Neurology,* 1980, *22,* 1–26.

Safer, D. J. A familial factor in minimal brain dysfunction. *Behavior Genetics,* 1973, *3,* 175–186.

Safer, D. J., & Allen, R. P. *Hyperactive children: Diagnosis and management.* Baltimore: University Park Press, 1976.

Sandberg, S. T., Rutter, M., & Taylor, E. Hyperkinetic disorder in psychiatric clinic attenders. *Developmental Medicine and Child Neurology,* 1978, *20,* 279–299.

Sandberg, S. T., Wieselberg, M., & Shaffer, D. Hyperkinetic and conduct problem children in a primary school population: Some epidemiological considerations. *Journal of Child Psychology and Psychiatry,* 1980, *21,* 293–311.

Sandoval, J., Lambert, N., & Sassone, D. The identification and labeling of hyperactivity in children: An interactive model. In C. K. Whalen & B. Henker (Eds.), *Hyperactive children: The social ecology of identification and treatment.* New York: Academic Press, 1980.

Satterfield, J. H. Neurophysiologic studies with hyperactive children. In D. P. Cantwell (Ed.), *The hyperactive child. Diagnosis, management, current research.* New York: Spectrum, 1975.

Satterfield, J. H., Cantwell, D. P., Lesser, L. I., & Podosin, R. L. Physiological studies of the hyperkinetic child: I. *American Journal of Psychiatry,* 1972, *128,* 1418–1424.

Satterfield, J. H., Cantwell, D. P., & Satterfield, B. T. Pathophysiology of the hyperactive child syndrome. *Archives of General Psychiatry,* 1974, *31,* 839–844.

Satterfield, J. H., Cantwell, D. P., & Satterfield, B. T. Multimodality treatment: A one-year follow-up of 84 hyperactive boys. *Archives of General Psychiatry,* 1979, *36,* 965–974.

Sandoval, J., Lambert, N. M., & Sassone, D. M. The comprehensive treatment of hyperactive children: A continuing problem. *Journal of Learning Disabilities,* 1981, *14,* 117–118.

Schroeder, S. R., Milar, C., Wool, R., & Routh, D. K. Multiple measurement, transsituational diagnosis, and the concept of generalized overactivity. *Journal of Pediatric Psychology,* 1980, *5,* 365–375.

Schulman, J. L., & Reisman, J. M. An objective measure of hyperactivity. *American Journal of Mental Deficiency,* 1959, *64,* 455–456.

Settle, D. M., & Patterson, C. C. Lead in albacore: Guide to lead pollution in Americans. *Science,* 1980, *207,* 1167–1176.

Shaffer, D. An approach to the validation of clinical syndromes in childhood. In S. Salzinger, J. Antrobus, & J. Glick (Eds.), *The ecosystem of the "sick" child.* New York: Academic Press, 1980.

Shaywitz, B. A., Yager, R. D., & Klopper, J. H. Selective brain dopamine depletion in developing rats: An experimental model of minimal brain dysfunction. *Science,* 1976, *191,* 305–308.

Shaywitz, S. E., Cohen, D. J., & Shaywitz, B. A. The biochemical basis of minimal brain dysfunction. *The Journal of Pediatrics,* 1978, *92,* 179–187.

Silbergeld, E. K. Neuropharmacology of hyperkinesis. In W. B. Essman & L. Valzelli (Eds.), *Current developments in psychopharmacology* (Vol. 4). New York: Spectrum, 1977.

Singer, S. M., Stewart, M. A., & Pulaski, L. Minimal brain dysfunction: Differences in cognitive organization in two groups of index cases and their relatives. *Journal of Learning Disabilities,* 1981, *14,* 470–473.

Sleator, E. K., & Ullmann, R. K. Can the physician diagnose hyperactivity in the office? *Pediatrics,* 1981, *67,* 13–17.

Sprague, R. L., & Brown, R. T. Behavioral pharmacology research with children. In T. Thompson & P. Dews (Eds.), *Advances in behavioral pharmacology* (Vol. 3). New York: Academic Press, in press.

Sprague, R. L., Barnes, K. R., & Werry, J. S. Methylphenidate and thioridazine: Learning, reaction time, activity, and classroom behavior in disturbed children. *American Journal of Orthopsychiatry,* 1970, *40,* 615–628.

Sprague, R. L., Cohen, M. H., & Eichlseder, W. Are there hyperactive children in Europe and the South Pacific? In R. Halliday (Chair), *The hyperactive child: Fact, fiction, and fantasy.* Symposium presented at the meeting of the American Psychological Association, San Francisco, August 1977.

Steinkamp, M. W. Relationships between environmental distractions and task performance of hyperactive and normal children. *Journal of Learning Disabilities,* 1980, *13,* 209–214.

Stewart, M. A. Genetic, perinatal, and constitutional factors in minimal brain dysfunctions. In H. E. Rie & E. D. Rie (Eds.), *Handbook of minimal brain dysfunctions. A critical view.* New York: Wiley, 1980.

Stewart, M. A., deBlois, C. S., & Cummings, C. Psychiatric disorder in the parents of hyperactive boys and those with conduct disorder. *Journal of Child Psychology and Psychiatry,* 1980, *21,* 283–292.

Stewart, M. A., Cummings, C., Singer, S., & deBlois, C. S. The overlap between hyperactive and unsocialized aggressive children. *Journal of Child Psychology and Psychiatry,* 1981, *22,* 35–45.

Swanson, J. M., & Kinsbourne, M. Food dyes impair performance of hyperactive children on a laboratory learning test. *Science,* 1980, *207,* 1485–1487.

Sykes, D. H., Douglas, V. I., Weiss, G., & Minde, K. K. Attention in hyperactive children and the effect of methylphenidate (Ritalin). *Journal of Child Psychology and Psychiatry,* 1971, *12,* 129–139.

Thomas, A., Chess, S., & Birch, H. G. *Temperament and behavior disorders in children.* New York: New York University Press, 1968.

Trites, R. L. Prevalence of hyperactivity in Ottawa, Canada. In R. L. Trites (Ed.), *Hyperactivity in children. Etiology, measurement, and treatment implications.* Baltimore: University Park Press, 1979.

Trites, R. L., Blouin, A. G., Ferguson, H. B., & Lynch, G. The Conners' teacher rating scale: An epidemiologic, inter-rater reliability and follow-up investigation. In K. D. Gadow & J. Loney (Eds.), *Psychosocial aspects of drug treatment for hyperactivity.* Boulder, Colo.: Westview Press, 1981.

Trites, R. L., Tryphonas, H., & Ferguson, H. B. Diet treatment for hyperactive children with food allergies. In R. M. Knights & D. J. Bakker (Eds.), *Treatment of hyperactive and learning disordered children. Current research.* Baltimore: University Park Press, 1980.

Waldbott, G. L. *Health effects of environmental pollutants* (2nd ed.). St. Louis, Mo.: Mosby, 1978.

Waldrop, M. F., & Halverson, C. F., Jr. Minor physical anomalies and hyperactive behavior in young children. In J. Hellmuth (Ed.), *Exceptional infant: Studies in abnormalities* (Vol. 2). New York: Brunner/Mazel, 1971.

Waldrop, M. F., Bell, R. Q., McLaughlin, B., & Halverson, C. F., Jr. Newborn minor physical anomalies predict short attention span, peer aggression, and impulsivity at age 3. *Science,* 1978, *199,* 563–565.

Weingartner, H., Rapoport, J. L., Buchsbaum, M. S., Bunney, W. E., Jr., Ebert, M. H., Mikkelsen, E. J., & Caine, E. D. Cognitive processes in normal and hyperactive children and their response to amphetamine treatment. *Journal of Abnormal Psychology*, 1980, *89*, 25–37.

Weiss, B., Williams, J. H., Margen, S., Abrams, B., Caan, B., Citron, L. J., Cox, C., McKibben, J., Ogar, D., & Schultz, S. Behavioral responses to artificial food colors. *Science*, 1980, *207*, 1487–1489.

Weiss, G. *Long-term outcome of the hyperkinetic syndrome: Empirical findings, conceptual problems, and practical implications.* Unpublished manuscript, 1980.

Weiss, G., Hechtman, L., & Perlman, T. Hyperactives as young adults: School, employer, and self-rating scales obtained during ten-year follow-up evaluation. *American Journal of Orthopsychiatry*, 1978, *48*, 438–445.

Weiss, G., Hechtman, L., Perlman, T., Hopkins, J., & Wener, A. Hyperactives as young adults. A controlled prospective ten-year follow-up of 75 children. *Archives of General Psychiatry*, 1979, *36*, 675–681.

Weiss, G., Kruger, E., Danielson, V., & Elman, M. Effects of long-term treatment of hyperactive children with methylphenidate. *Canadian Medical Association Journal*, 1975, *112*, 159–165.

Weiss, G., Minde, K., Werry, J. S., Douglas, V. I., & Nemeth, E. Studies on the hyperactive child, VIII. Five-year follow-up. *Archives of General Psychiatry*, 1971, *24*, 409–414.

Welner, Z., Welner, A., Stewart, M., Palkes, H., & Wish, E. A controlled study of siblings of hyperactive children. *The Journal of Nervous and Mental Disease*, 1977, *165*, 110–117.

Wender, E. H. New evidence on food additives and hyperkinesis: A critical analysis. *American Journal of Diseases of Children*, 1980, *134*, 1122–1124.

Wender, P. H. Minimal brain dysfunction: An overview. In M. A. Lipton, A. Dimascio, & K. F. Killam (Eds.), *Psychopharmacology: A generation of progress.* New York: Raven Press, 1978.

Wender, P. H. The concept of adult minimal brain dysfunction. In L. Bellak (Ed.), *Psychiatric aspects of minimal brain dysfunction in adults.* New York: Grune & Stratton, 1979.

Werner, E. E. Environmental interaction in minimal brain dysfunction. In H. E. Rie & E. E. Rie (Eds.), *Handbook of minimal brain dysfunctions. A critical view.* New York: Wiley, 1980.

Werner, E. E., & Smith, R. S. *Kauai's children come of age.* Honolulu: University Press of Hawaii, 1977.

Werner, E. E., Bierman, J. M., & French, F. E. *The children of Kauai: A longitudinal study from the prenatal period to age ten.* Honolulu: University Press of Hawaii, 1971.

Werry, J. S. Studies on the hyperactive child, IV. An empirical analysis of the minimal brain dysfunction syndrome. *Archives of General Psychiatry*, 1968, *19*, 9–16.

Werry, J. S., & Aman, M. G. The reliability and diagnostic validity of the physical and neurological examination for soft signs (PANESS). *Journal of Autism and Childhood Schizophrenia*, 1976, *6*, 253–262.

Werry, J. S., & Quay, H. The prevalence of behavior symptoms in younger elementary school children. *American Journal of Orthopsychiatry*. 1971, *41*, 136–143.

Werry, J. S., & Sprague, R. L. Methylphenidate in children: Effect of dosage. *Australian and New Zealand Journal of Psychiatry*, 1974, *8*, 9–19.

Werry, J. S., Minde, K., Guzman, A., Weiss, G., Dogan, K., & Hoy, E. Studies on the hyperactive child, VII: Neurological status compared with neurotic and normal children. *American Journal of Orthopsychiatry*, 1972, *42*, 441–450.

Werry, J. S., Sprague, R. L., & Cohen, M. N. Conners' Teacher Rating Scale for use in drug studies with children—An empirical study. *Journal of Abnormal Child Psychology*, 1975, *3*, 217–229.

Whalen, C. K., & Henker, B. Psychostimulants and children: A review and analysis. *Psychological Bulletin*, 1976, *83*, 1113–1130.

Whalen, C. K., & Henker, B. The pitfalls of politicization. A response to Conrad's "The discovery of hyperkinesis: Notes on the medicalization of deviant behaviors." *Social Problems*, 1977, *24*, 590–595.

Whalen, C. K., & Henker, B. The social ecology of psychostimulant treatment: A model for conceptual and empirical analysis. In C. K. Whalen & B. Henker (Eds.), *Hyperactive children: The social ecology of identification and treatment.* New York: Academic Press, 1980.

Whalen, C. K., Collins, B. E., Henker, B., Alkus, S. R., Adams, D., & Stapp, J. Behavior observations of hyperactive children and methylphenidate (Ritalin) effects in systematically structured classroom environments: Now you see them, now you don't. *Journal of Pediatric Psychology*, 1978, *3*, 177–187.

Whalen, C. K., Henker, B., Collins, B. E., Finck, D., & Dotemoto, S. A social ecology of hyperactive boys: Medication effects in structured classroom environments. *Journal of Applied Behavior Analysis*, 1979, *12*, 65–81. (a)

Whalen, C. K., Henker, B., Collins, B. E., McAuliffe, S., & Vaux, A. Peer interaction in a structured communication task: Comparisons of normal and hyperactive boys and of methylphenidate (Ritalin) and placebo effects. *Child Development*, 1979, *50*, 388–401. (b)

Whalen, C. K., Henker, B., & Dotemoto, S. Methylphenidate and hyperactivity: Effects on teacher behaviors. *Science,* 1980, *208,* 1280–1282.

Whalen, C. K., Henker, B., & Dotemoto, S. Teacher response to the methylphenidate (Ritalin) versus placebo status of hyperactive boys in the classroom. *Child Development,* 1981, *52,* 1005–1014.

Whalen, C. K., Henker, B., Dotemoto, S., Vaux, A., & McAuliffe, S. Hyperactivity and methylphenidate: Peer communication patterns. In K. D. Gadow & J. Loney (Eds.), *Psychosocial aspects of drug treatment for hyperactivity.* Boulder, Colo.: Westview Press, 1981.

Whalen, C. K., Henker, B., & Finck, D. Medication effects in the classroom: Three naturalistic indicators. *Journal of Abnormal Child Psychology,* 1981, *9,* 419–433.

Willerman, L. Social aspects of minimal brain dysfunction. *Annals of the New York Academy of Sciences,* 1973, *205,* 164–172.

Wood, D. R., Reimherr, F. W., Wender, P. H., & Johnson, G. E. Diagnosis and treatment of minimal brain dysfunction in adults. *Archives of General Psychiatry,* 1976, *33,* 1453–1460.

Zahn, T. P., Little, B. C., & Wender, P. H. Pupillary and heart rate reactivity in children with minimal brain dysfunction. *Journal of Abnormal Child Psychology,* 1978, *6,* 135–147.

Zarkowsky, H. S. The lead problem in children: Dictum and polemic. *Current Problems in Pediatrics,* 1976, *6,* 1–47.

8

Enuresis and Encopresis

DANIEL M. DOLEYS

Enuresis

Definition and Incidence

Enuresis is derived from a Greek word that roughly translates, "to make water." Enuresis is a relatively common problem among children. It appears in two forms: diurnal (daytime) wetting and nocturnal (nighttime) wetting. This behavioral disorder is further subdivided into continuous (primary) and discontinuous (secondary) types. The continuous enuretic child has never demonstrated a sustained period of continence. The discontinuous enuretic child has shown at least 6 months' continence, and has therefore shown the ability to control bladder functioning. A further differentiation relates to whether or not enuresis can be associated with organic pathology, or appears to be of a functional nature. Functional enuresis has been defined as wetting that occurs in the absence of a urologic or neurologic pathology (Doleys, 1977, 1978). Some definitions of enuresis have utilized the term "involuntary passage of urine." It is excluded from the above definition because the determination of whether the passage of urine is voluntary or involuntary is often a judgment made by the researcher or clinician. The distinction is frequently arbitrary and may not result in differential treatment. To the extent that the term "involuntary" implies underlying *organic pathology,* utilizing the latter phrase would be more descriptive. In total, there are about 90 different types of urinary incontinence (Lund, 1963). However, about 90% of cases fall into the functional category, and nearly 80% of these are the continuous (primary) type.

DANIEL M. DOLEYS • Behavioral Medicine Services, Brookwood Medical Center, Birmingham, Alabama 35209

The age at which a child can be considered enuretic continues to be a source of debate. It tends to vary within and across cultures. Most estimates fall within the range of 3–5 years of age. Muellner (1960b) noted that urinary control should be established by the age of 3. It is rare to hear of children under the age of 5 being treated for enuresis through psychological or behavioral means. The exact extent of enuresis is unknown. It has been estimated that nearly 20% of all 5-year-olds wet their beds frequently enough to be considered enuretic (Cohen, 1975; Lovibond & Coote, 1970; Oppel, Harper, & Rider, 1968). The percent of children demonstrating enuretic behavior decreases systematically with age. Approximately 5% are noted to be enuretic at 10 years and 2% or less at 12–14 years of age. Because of this decline of incidence with age, many professionals have been reluctant to treat enuresis in the younger child, taking refuge in the fact that "spontaneous remission" will occur in all probability. Although this may or may not be the case for any given child, to date, there appear to be no specific criteria by which to determine which children will become "dry" and which will continue to be "wet" into adolescence. Secondarily, this view ignores the fact that many children do not become dry "spontaneously," but are probably exposed to a variety of unsystematically applied contingencies, many of which are likely to be negative. And finally, this philosophy does not seem to consider that younger enuretic children are often much more easily and efficiently treated than older ones.

Etiology

There is considerable debate and disagreement regarding relevant etiological factors in enuresis (Doleys, 1977, 1978; Doleys, Schwartz, & Ciminero, 1981; Shaffer, 1977; Walker, 1978). Sleep has often been indited as one of the major factors associated with nocturnal enuresis. Some writers have described enuresis as an arousal disorder (Finley, 1971; Perlmutter, 1976; Ritvo, Ornitz, Gottlieb, Poussaint, Maron, Ditman, & Blinn, 1969), but recent data have not been supportive of this position (Mikkelsen, Rapoport, Nee, Gruenau, Mendelsen, & Gillin, 1980). Mikkelsen *et al.* (1980) were unable to find any systematic association between enuresis and stage of sleep. Investigations in this area have been confounded by a lack of differentiation between depth of sleep, as measured by electroencephalographic (EEG) pattern, and behavioral measures of arousability. A common supposition is that the "deeper" the child sleeps, the more difficult he/she may be to arouse. This does not appear to hold in all cases. Furthermore, data comparing enuretics to nonenuretics on the dimension of arousability are conflicting (Bostack, 1958; Boyd, 1960; Braithwaithe, 1956; Kaffman & Elizur, 1977).

The role of genetics in enuresis has also been given attention. Support for its involvement comes from data noting a higher incidence of enuresis in children from families where both parents were enuretic compared to families where one or neither parent was enuretic (77% vs. 44% vs. 15%). Additionally, higher concordance rates have been found among monozygotic as compared to dizygotic twins. As always, these findings are open to a variety of interpretations. Also, their meaningfulness regarding the selection and efficacy of treatment is debatable (Bakwin, 1973; Cohen, 1975; Faray, 1935).

Psychodynamic and psychoanalytic models have tended to suggest that enuresis is a result of underlying conflict, anxiety or emotional stress (Pierce, 1972; Sperling, 1965). Although there does appear to be some correlation between behavioral disturbance and enuresis in girls, whether or not the disturbance preceded or followed the onset of enuresis has not been demonstrated (Werry, 1967). The hypothesis put forth by this school of thought would predict "symptom substitution" in cases where only the enuresis, rather than the underlying conflict, was treated. In fact, such substitution has not been documented in studies where it has been examined (Baker, 1969; Dische, 1971; Werry & Cohrssen, 1965).

More recently a good deal of attention has been given to the role of bladder capacity in enuretic children (Esperanca & Gerrard, 1969; Starfield, 1967; Zaleski, Gerrard, & Shokeir, 1973). Some of the data show that enuretics tend to have a smaller average functional bladder capacity (ABC) than nonenuretics. This inadequate bladder capacity is hypothesized to be a result of inadequate cortical inhibition, which may be a part of a developmental delay, or indicative of an allergenic reaction whereby the bladder is maintained in spasm, preventing it from accommodating larger volumes of urine (Zaleski, Shokeir, & Gerrard, 1972). These data, however, are not consistent, and there appears to be considerable overlap in functional bladder capacities between enuretics and nonenuretics of the same age level (Rutter, 1973). Rutter speculates that the smaller bladder capacity may be a compensatory response resulting from inadequate stretching of the bladder by dilatation at night. The concern and evidence regarding bladder capacities have resulted in the frequent use of bladder expansion or retention control therapies in the treatment of enuresis, particularly of the nighttime variety.

Enuresis has also been described as a habit deficiency resulting from inadequate learning experiences and inappropriate reinforcement contingencies (Atthowe, 1973; Lovibond & Coote, 1970; Young, 1965a). This learning-behavioral model suggests that bladder fullness can be interpreted as a specific stimulus that, in the continent child, has acquired discriminative properties. Bladder fullness results in the occurrence of an inhibitory response, which delays or postpones voiding until the proper place and time. Several conditioning-based procedures have grown from this model. Perhaps the most notable has been the bell-and-pad or urine-alarm technique, originally described by Mowrer and Mowrer (1938). More recently, Azrin, Sneed, and Foxx (1973, 1974) have developed and evaluated a multifaceted approach called dry-bed training (DBT).

Assessment

As treatment techniques for daytime and nighttime enuresis continue to expand, the importance of a thorough evaluation becomes more evident. Assessment of the enuretic child should incorporate interview and behavioral data. The clinical interview should gain: (a) a history and description of the problem; (b) a family and medical history; (c) knowledge of any other problems in the family or with the child; (d) an impression of the home and family environment; and (e) information about any previous treatment attempts. The role of each of these areas of information in determining which treatment approach to take and in anticipating management problems has been discussed elsewhere (Doleys, 1978, 1979b; Doleys, Schwartz, & Ciminero, 1981). Patterns of enuretic behavior should also be examined, with the collection of relevant data on: (a) nocturnal patterns, (b) diurnal patterns, and (c) bladder capacity. By having the parents monitor the child on a regular basis during the day and intermittently during the night, accurate information can be obtained about the frequency of wetting and the magnitude of the wets. Information on maximum bladder capacity can be obtained by using a waterload procedure (Zaleski *et al.*, 1973). This waterloading can be accomplished either in the home or in the office (Harris & Purohit, 1977). A medical evaluation is strongly recommended to screen out problems that are potentially organic in nature and therefore might not be susceptible to behavioral procedures or require adaptation of standardized procedures. A general physical, urinalysis, and urine culture to rule out renal pathology and infection are usually sufficient. More intrusive procedures, such as voiding cystourethrogram, cystoscopy, or excretory urograms can generally be reserved to systematic treatment attempts (Campbell, 1970; Perlmutter, 1976). Urinary infections are much more common among females than among males and should be watched for, even though they occur in only 5–10% of cases (Jones, Gerrard, Shokeir, & Houston, 1972; Stansfeld, 1973). Recurrent urinary tract infections and unusual patterns of daytime voiding, such as frequency, inadequate retention, and abnormal stream, may be indicative of underlying pathology (Arnold & Ginsburg, 1975; Smith, 1967).

The overall evaluation and assessment period may take from 1–4 weeks. This may seem to be an unnecessary delay to the parents and/or some clinicians. Although time-consuming, this baseline period does provide data regarding the child's current functioning, assessment of the parents' and child's motivation and ability to follow directions, and a baseline against which to assess the effects of treatment. Too often, clinicians and/or researchers only casually record dry and wet nights, ignoring the fact that some children are "multiple wetters" and may wet more than once during the night. In many instances, the frequency of wetting during one single night or the size of the wet spot may be early indicators of treatment effectiveness. If these data were not collected during baseline and are not monitored during treatment, a therapeutic procedure may be abandoned prematurely on the basis that the child has not experienced a given number of consecutive *dry* nights early in treatment.

Treatment

Drugs

One of the most common approaches to the treatment of enuresis in the medical profession is the use of drugs. The most frequently used medication is a tricyclic antidepressant, imipramine hydrochloride (Tofranil). Imipramine has been found to be much more effective than other medications. The specific mechanism of action is not well understood, and the effects are often attributed to: (a) mood elevation; (b) lightening of sleep; (c) anticholinergic effects resulting in detrusor muscle relaxation and enhanced bladder capacity; and (d) increased involuntary control over urethral sphincter (Blackwell & Currah, 1973; Labay & Boyarsky, 1972; Mahony, Laferte, & Mahoney, 1973). Imipramine has been shown to be more effective than placebo when given in doses ranging from 25–75 mg, adjusted for height and weight, at nighttime. Increase in urinary control is generally observed in about 85% of the cases during the first 2 weeks of treatment (Shaffer, 1977). Total continence is achieved in only about 30% of the cases, and up to 95% have been reported to relapse following withdrawal of medication (Blackwell & Currah, 1973; Kardash, Hillman, & Werry, 1968; Shaffer, 1977; Stewart, 1975).

Bladder Expansion

The speculation that enuretic children may have a smaller functional bladder capacity than nonenuretics has led to the development of bladder expansion or retention control training (RCT). It is believed that a small functional bladder capacity is generally associated with frequent voiding, inability to inhibit voiding throughout the night, and inadequate strength of the detrusor contractions to produce arousal from sleep. The usual procedure is to have the child refrain from voiding for gradually extended periods of time. Liquid intake may be increased.

One of the earlier studies (Starfield & Mellits, 1968) found that by having children practice retaining on a daily basis, only 6 of 83 children achieved continence. Increases in bladder capacity were not always associated with changes in bedwetting. Similarly, children who showed smaller or no changes did demonstrate decreases in enuresis. Studies by Kimmel and Kimmel (1970) and Paschalis, Kimmel, and Kimmel (1972) evaluated the effects of retention control training. RCT required the child to practice retention several times during the day; 17 of 38 children exposed to this procedure reportedly became dry with treatment duration ranging from 7 to 21 days. Other studies have not been able to replicate this outcome (Allen, 1976; Harris & Purohit, 1977; Raeburn, Gemming, Lowe, & Dowrick, 1977). Retention control and bladder retention training have been shown to be less effective than the urine-alarm (Fielding, 1980) and drybed training (Doleys, Ciminero, Tollison, Williams, & Wells, 1977). Retention control training does, however, appear to be a potentially useful technique for children who demonstrate daytime enuresis (Fielding, 1980). The author has treated several daytime enuretics successfully with the combination of retention control training and overcorrection.

Although the technique of bladder expansion and retention control appears to have gained acceptance, it has not been subjected to much systematic research. One case study (Doleys & Wells, 1975) was an initial attempt to assess generalization of daytime retention training to nighttime bladder capacity. In fact, training had to be carried out for much longer than would have been anticipated by existing literature. However, there did appear to be some generalization regarding nighttime capacity. Onset of dry nights did not occur concomitantly with a significant increase in bladder capacity, but appeared later in treatment. A similar report by Franklin (unpublished manuscript) extended the procedure by developing a system that would record latency between onset of sleep and enuresis. In this study, which employed an adult enuretic, nighttime latency did increase in conjunction with bladder capacity changes that were documented during the day.

Retention control training and bladder expansion training may have some utility for the treatment of daytime enuresis. It does not, however, appear to be comparable to the urine-alarm or drybed training in the treatment of nighttime enuresis. It has been found in some cases to be helpful when used in conjunction with these other treatments.

Urine Alarm

Perhaps the most commonly used and researched procedure for the treatment of nighttime enuresis is the urine-alarm or bell-and-pad procedure. This technique makes use of a urine sensing device that rests between the child and the mattress. Ideally, any amount of urine passed onto the device triggers an alarm, which is adjusted to an intensity sufficiently strong to arouse the child. After awakening, the child toilets himself, then returns to bed. Theoretically, it is postulated that conditioning occurs such that: (a) The child will come to impose an inhibitory response upon voiding, thus sleeping through the night; or (b) bladder distention cues will acquire discriminative properties significantly strong to arouse the child from sleep so that wetting does not occur.

Early studies with the urine-alarm (Seiger, 1952) reported rates of remission up to 80%. More recent reports (Lovibond 1964; Lovibond & Coote, 1970; Turner, 1973; Yates, 1970) also describe rates of remission between 80% and 90%, with relapses approximating

35%. Doleys (1977) summarized studies conducted with the urine-alarm between 1960 and 1975. Data on over 600 subjects revealed an overall rate of remission of 75%, with treatment duration ranging 5–12 weeks. The average relapse rate was 41%. Nearly 68% of those subjects who relapsed and were exposed to retreatment became continent. The most frequently cited factors associated with relapse were noncompliance by parents or child, early withdrawal from treatment, and inconsistent application of the technique. Inadequate auditory stimulus was identified as a critical factor in rate of acquisition, but did not appear to be associated with relapse.

In spite of problems with relapse, the urine-alarm has been found to be more effective than nighttime awakening (Catalina, 1976), placebo tablets (White, 1968), no treatment (DeLeon & Mandell, 1966), verbal psychotherapy, (Novick, 1966), imipramine (McConaghy, 1969; Young, 1965b), and retention control training (Allen, 1976). Although the urine-alarm has been shown to be more effective than imipramine, little consideration has been given to combining the treatments, early in the course of therapy, for those children who tend to be long-term, recalcitrant multiple wetters. Such children have been known to respond to imipramine in a relatively short period of time, but have not shown extended periods of continence. Some immediate relief through imipramine might provide needed encouragement and motivation for parents and child to continue in therapy. Urine-alarm conditioning would then become the major mode of treatment as the medication was withdrawn. Equipment failure is a major concern in use of the urine-alarm. Equipment that produces false alarms, is insensitive to small amounts of urine, or wears out quickly can be a detriment to treatment. Many of the alarms, which are commercially available through mail-order houses, do not hold up under repeated and sustained use. There has been considerable modification in development of these devices (Finley & Smith, 1975). Modification of the devices has virtually eliminated the possibility for "buzzer ulcers."

Two recent modifications to the standard urine-alarm procedure have been introduced and are being explored as mechanisms for reducing the rate of relapse. One such modification is the use of an intermittent alarm. An intermittent alarm can be programmed to operate at a given schedule (usually 50–70%) of wets. Theoretically, it is assumed that this is analogous to a partial reinforcement schedule. Experiments in learning have shown that, although acquisition of a response may be somewhat slower under partial reinforcement, the response is much more resistent to extinction. There is some question as to the "goodness of fit" of this model to enuresis, but the data are very encouraging (Finley & Wansley, 1976; Finley, Besserman, Bennett, Clapp, & Finley, 1973; Finley, Wansley, & Blenkarn, 1977). Other attempts at the use of intermittent schedules have not been successful (Lovibond, 1963; Taylor & Turner, 1975; Turner, Young, & Rachman, 1970). Differences between these two groups of studies may lie in the schedule of alarm presentation (50% vs. 70%), degree of parental compliance to treatment regimen, and/or apparatus employed. Collectively, the Finley studies are very supportive of this procedure. Relapse rates were noted to be lower for the intermittent group (15% vs. 44%). In one study (Finley *et al.*, 1977), treatment employed a 70% intermittent variable ratio schedule with 80 enuretics. Continence (14 consecutive dry nights) was acquired by 94% of the subjects completing treatment with a mean duration of 7 weeks. Overall relapse rate was 25%. Relapses varied from 5.25% for 7- and 8-year-olds to 50% for 9- and 10-year-olds.

A second modification of the standard urine-alarm procedure is the use of "overlearning." The overlearning technique suggests that the child consume 10–32 ounces of liquid (depending upon age and weight) prior to bedtime after initial dryness has been achieved with the standard urine-alarm procedure. It is assumed (Young & Morgan, 1972) that relapses may result from absence of generalization of conditioning to a broad range of bladder fullness or degrees of bladder distention. Use of increased liquid intake tests for degree of control established under conditions of greater bladder fullness and also provides an opportunity for control to include a broader range of bladder fullness and detrusor muscle distention. Early studies in this area (Jehu, Morgan, Turner, & Jones, 1977; Taylor & Turner, 1975; (Young & Morgan, 1972) reported beneficial effects. Young and Morgan (1972), for example, showed a lower relapse rate for the overlearning versus the standard urine-alarm procedure (13% vs. 35%, respectively). Taylor and Turner (1975) found overlearning to produce lower relapse rates than continuous and intermittent alarm groups. The study by Jehu *et al.* (1977) showed that 95% of 90 children achieved continence with an average of 12 weeks of treatment; 13 of the subjects continued to be dry at a 20 month follow-up, and 4 subjects who relapsed were successfully retreated. Initial work with overlearning showed that some children who had been continent relapsed to nighttime wetting when given large amounts of liquid at night. These children were very recalcitrant to retreatment, even when nighttime liquids were removed. It is likely that the overlearning process can be applied more effectively by using gradual increases in nighttime liquids over a period of 1–2 weeks, rather than "flooding" the child.

Dry-Bed Training

Azrin *et al.* (1973, 1974) described a multifaceted program utilizing application of social contingencies as an alternative to urine-alarm conditioning. This program, referred to as dry-bed training (DBT), incorporates positive practice, positive reinforcement, retention-control training, nighttime awakening, negative reinforcement, and full cleanliness training. The initial studies conducted by Azrin and his colleagues showed the procedure to be quite effective with both normal and mentally retarded children. Azrin and Foxx (1974) developed a manual *(Toilet Training in Less than a Day)* based upon this early work. Although the manual appears to have received wide acceptance, data collected by other researchers (Butler, 1976; Matson, 1975) have noted difficulties in parental application of overcorrection and positive practice. More recently, Azrin and Besalel (1979) developed a manual to be used as a guide for parents of nonretarded, nocturnally enuretic children. A recent evaluation of this approach was undertaken by Besalel, Azrin, Thienes-Hontos, and McMorrow (1980). Thirteen parents carried out the procedure without professional assistance. Enuresis was reportedly reduced from 68% of nights during baseline to 27% at the end of 1 week, 10% at the end of 3 months, and 7% at the end of 6 months. An average of 6 wettings was recorded for the children prior to their achieving the experimental criterion of 14 consecutive dry nights. Only one child failed to achieve this criterion within 6 months.

Smith (1981) recently reported use of a modification of DBT in the treatment of mentally handicapped young adults (15–21 years). The procedure used a urine-alarm that sounded contingent upon wetting. The client was awakened and reprimanded for having wet his bed, then placed on a commode, which was stationed next to the bed. Overcorrection and positive practice were not employed. A major focus of the program was reinforcement of dry nights and toileting during the night. The use of an alarm, commode next to the bed, and sleeping in a special unit were gradually faded. Results showed a significant reduction in wetting for each of the subjects, though there was considerable between- and within-subject variability. It was interesting to note that for some subjects who relapsed after achieving initial continence, retraining took a longer time than did initial treatment.

Other attempts to replicate the original DBT procedure have yielded inconsistent results. Doleys, Ciminero, Tollison, Williams, and Wills (1977) showed DBT to be more effective than retention-control training. However, the rate of remission was not as high as that noted by Azrin. A 2-year follow-up (Williams, Doleys, & Ciminero, 1978) indicated that five of eight children that had achieved dryness through DBT continued to be continent. Bollard and Woodroffe (1977) evaluated "parent administered" DBT. The criterion for success was 14 consecutive dry nights. Treatment duration was approximately 6 weeks, with none of the children relapsing to pretreatment wetting frequency.

There is little question that DBT offers a viable alternative to urine-alarm conditioning and retention control training. The fact that replications have not always produced consistent findings implicates the need for further systematic studies on factors related to subject, therapist, technique, and parental variables that might be significant.

Dysfunctional Bladder Syndrome

Nonneurogenic. Several dysfunctional bladder syndromes have been related to abnormal voiding patterns. Urinary retention and daytime dribbling may indicate uncoordinated use of external urethral sphincter and detrusor action. Such uncoordinated action can give rise to recurrent urinary infections and bladder decompensation. This condition has been referred to as "detrusor–sphincter dyssynergia," "lazy bladder syndrome," and "nonneurogenic bladder." Such dyssnergia (uncoordinated muscle movement) may or may not be related to neurological deficits.

Two studies have examined the effects of biofeedback in treating such dyssynergia (Maizels, King, & Firlit, 1979; Wear, Wear, & Cleeland, 1979). The Maizels *et al.* (1979) study evaluated three girls, 9–13, with histories of urinary incontinence, urinary infection, and hydronephrosis (collection of urine in the kidneys). Urological evaluation revealed sphincter dyssynergia. Children were selected for treatment because they: (1) had been refractory to other treatments; (2) showed strong motivation for improvement; and (3) were able to understand the concept of biofeedback. Treatment consisted of hospitalization, during which time the patient was hydrated to increase frequency of voiding. Surface electrodes were used for EMG monitoring. Training focused on conditioning subjects how to relax external urethral sphincter during voiding. This was accomplished by their observing EMG and urine flow recordings while voiding.

One patient voided approximately every 45 minutes because of increased liquid. Each time she voided, she observed the EMG and flow rates, receiving instruction on how to relax the pelvic floor musculature and urethral sphincter. Verbal reinforcement was provided. Within 24 hours, coordinated movement was noted. Voiding became increasingly spontaneous. Urgency and diurnal incontinence diminished. Out-patient biofeedback continued, but a relapse was noted after about 2 months of treatment when the patient did not continue practicing at home. A second patient also responded well to biofeedback for dyssynergia. The third patient showed bilateral vesico-urethral reflux (backward flow or urine up the ureters). Surgery was performed, but the problem persisted, with urinary retention continuing. Although she was able to recognize sphincter dyssynergia following 2 days of biofeedback, she was unable to control it.

Hinman and Baumann (1973) described cases of functional discoordination between detrusor contraction and sphincter relaxation. The problem was characterized by failure to relax external sphincters during the time of voiding. Also, a paradixocal increase in sphincter tension was noted. Allen (1977) studied 21 such cases and described the disorder as including diurnal and/or nocturnal wetting, cramping in the lower abdomen, lack of sustained strain during voiding because of incomplete sphincter relaxation, diurnal frequency, associated bowel dysfunction, recurrent urinary infection, history of family disruption in a minority of cases, presence of residual urine, bilateral hydronephrosis, detrusor-sphincter dyssynergia as measured by either EMG recordings or the use of an anal plug or needle electrodes, and hyposensitive detrusor contractibility.

The treatment program outlined by Allen (1977) emphasized reeducation and retraining. At the time of urodynamic evaluation, the child was encouraged in the presence of the parents to relax the perineum and maintain a steady stream without straining. Through monitoring devices, the child obtained direct feedback and was reinforced for producing a sustained, uninterrupted stream. The parents were encouraged to continue practicing at home, and the child was instructed to void approximately ever 3 hours and to respond promptly to the desire to void. In addition, a sufficient time was set aside so that the child did not rush when voiding. The child was also instructed to empty the bladder completely each time voiding occurred. Continued parental encouragement, reinforcement, and maintenance of charts were employed. Residual urine was removed via catheterization at follow-up office visits. Parental understanding and support were considered essential to success; psychological consultation with the family and child was frequently carried out. Treatment frequently incorporated use of imipramine hydrochloride to reduce wetness and fecal incontinence. Bethanechol chloride aided to reduce residual urine, and stool softeners and enemas were applied as needed. Tranquilizers were occasionally used to overcome hyperactivity and anxiety. Medications were not, however, employed in place of bladder retraining, considered the cornerstone of therapy. A minimum of 6 months follow-up with close observation was considered indispensable. Data provided by Allen (1977) described the program as effective for each of the four children treated. Subjects showed a gradual but steady improvement clinically and radiographically.

It must be noted that dysfunctional voiding encompasses a broad range of disorders and is sometimes overshadowed by secondary vesico-urethral reflux. This reflux is often assumed to be the primary pathology. Under these circumstances, surgery may be carried out to correct the reflux, even though it may not be necessary.

DeLuca, Swenson, Fisher, and Loutfi (1962) described a "dysfunctional lazy bladder syndrome," wherein elevated thresholds for the initiation of bladder contractions and the ease and rapid adaptation of the bladder to inhibition of voiding were observed. They note the disorder is most prevalent among children 2–6 years of age and twice as common in females as males. The majority of cases evidence a fever of unknown origin, abdominal pains, nausea, and vomiting. Patients are sometimes referred for what appears to be an abdominal mass, but later are found to have an enlarged bladder. Infrequent voiding, incontinence, and occasionally frequency are observed in these children. The problem is created when the child does not respond to the urge to void and the contractions gradually disappear. The intravesical pressure decreases temporarily, then rises again when involuntary contractions are less effective. When voiding does occur, it is usually incomplete, and there may be a gradual elevation of intravesical pressure beyond the physiological limits of the bladder. It is hypothesized by DeLuca *et al.* that such an abnormally high threshold may develop through habitual neglect on the child's part to emptying the bladder upon sensing the urge to void. Such sustained retention may lead to the bladder yielding to subsequent enlargement. This condition is similar to what occurs with children who experience chronic constipation and no longer sense the urge to evacuate in response to normal stimuli.

Treatment in these cases begins with early management. It involves training the patient to void every 2 or 3 hours with the aim of reestablishing the urge to void at lower thresholds as an effective discriminative stimulus, thus allowing the bladder to return to normal size. The patients need to be followed regularly to treat recurrent infections. They are also instructed to practice double or triple voiding to ensure complete emptying of the bladder.

Neurogenic. Urinary dysfunction may be directly related to neurological deficits or trauma such as spinal cord lesions. These cases are referred to as "neurogenic bladder dysfunctions." Because of the underlying pathology, it has often been assumed that retraining is not likely to be effective. Two studies, however, have found retraining and biofeedback to be of use in such cases (Nergardh, von Hedenberg, Hellstrom, & Ericsson, 1974; Schneider & Westendorf, 1979). Nergardh *et al.* (1974) exposed 30 children (5–15 years of age) to a retraining program. Of these children, 18 had myelomeningocele, with deficits in the lumbar and sacral cords, and the remaining 12 had a variety of etiologies. Motivation of the parent(s) and child was a major factor in selection. Each child was noted to have a significant degree of incontinence. Treatment was conducted during an 8-week period of hospitalization. The first week was devoted to assessment and building of rapport. During the second week, liquid intake was increased and voiding was scheduled to occur each 3–4 hours. "Straining" and manual pressure on the bladder were encouraged as a means of decreasing residual urine. This regimen was carried out for the third through seventh week. Medications were used as required (bethanechol chloride to stimulate bladder contractions, ephedrine to increase bladder capacity, diazepam to relax external sphincter). Hydration and medication were discontinued during the eighth week. Two such eight-week training periods were carried out with 18 of 37 subjects. The general results showed that 16 of 30 subjects achieved "social continence" and 13 others were rated as much improved.

Schneider and Westendorf (1979) described the application of biofeedback with a 5-year-old girl who experienced spinal cord trauma and was diagnosed as having a flacid, neurogenic-type bladder. The patient had relearned to walk at the time of treatment. She also had accomplished about 40% control over bowel movements, but had no bladder control. Instrumentation was arranged to provide feedback for increased bladder pressure. Once bladder pressure was increased through sustained retention, development of voluntary voiding was shaped. Training time was noted to be about 8 days. The results showed a decrease in residual urine and spontaneous voiding, with an increase in involuntary voiding. At 18 months follow-up, continuation of "normal" functioning was observed.

Considerable work has been done in the area of sphincter electromyography (Blaivas, Labib, Bauer, & Retick, 1977; Bradley, Scott, & Timm, 1974). These data should be used in conjunction with operant and biofeedback technology to develop new therapeutic directions for patients suffering from neurogenic and functional urological disorders.

Encopresis

Definition and Incidence

The term *encopresis* began to appear in the literature of the 1920s as the fecal equivalent of enuresis. "Functional encopresis" can be defined as the passage of fecal material into the clothing or any generally unacceptable area, in the absence of organic pathology, and beyond the age of three (Doleys, 1980a). The term "fecal incontinence" or "psychogenic megacolon" have also been utilized. The term psychogenic megacolon most appropriately applies to those cases where soiling is, at least in part, a result of excessive retention, which has resulted in an enlarged colon. Unfortunately, there has been little agreement regarding the definition of encopresis (Levine, 1975; Pierce, 1975; Yates, 1970). The most common qualifying factors include age, pattern of soiling, and etiology (Fitts & Mann, 1976). There has been little agreement regarding the age at which a child can be considered encopretic. It is sometimes difficult to differentiate between the child who is encopretic and the child who has not been toilet-trained. Knowledge of the child's general developmental rate, prior attempts at toilet training, and presence of bladder control may influence the label that is applied. Generally, however, most would agree that the child should have achieved bowel control by the fourth year.

There are many types of encopresis that are not functional and result from dietary factors, allergic reactions to food and other substances, infections, diseases, or abnormalities in the anatomy and physiology. For this reason, more specific classification systems need to be developed and thorough assessment of the problem is necessary. Doleys *et al.* (1981) have attempted to describe in detail an approach to the assessment and classification of encopresis. This classification system recognizes two major factors. One factor is the degree of incontinence, which can range from very infrequent (less than weekly) to very severe (occurring daily). The second factor is the degree of constipation, which can vary on a continuum from retention for a couple of days (with defecation requiring straining and resulting in the depositing of hard stools) to severe retention up to 14 or more days (characterized by abdominal distention from impactions and a diffused, enlarged colon). The system was adopted from one presented by Levine and Bakow (1976).

The system of subclassification of functional encopresis is very much like that of enuresis. Encopresis is often divided into continuous (primary) and discontinuous (secondary) cases. The continuous encopretic has not demonstrated bowel control for at least 6 consecutive months. A further useful subdivision is that of retentive versus nonretentive (Gavanski, 1971; Walker, 1978). In the retentive type, history of constipation, infrequent bowel movements, and regular use of purgatives are found. It is also important to differentiate between children who refrain from voiding because they have a fear of defecation (a toilet phobia—Doleys, 1979a), and those who show what Berg and Jones (1964) refer to as a "pot-refusal syndrome." Smearing of feces (copraphagia) and stress incontinence also are observed (Berg & Jones, 1964). The majority of encopretics seem to have some degree of constipation or retention (Fitzgerald, 1975; Levine, 1975). Additional classification systems can be found in the writings of Woodmansey (1972), Easson (1960), and Walker (1978).

Overflow incontinence is another subcategory that demands attention. Some children will retain for prolonged periods of time. Overflow incontinence or "paradoxical diarrhea" (Davidson, 1958) refers to the leakage of fecal material about an impaction created by bowel retention or constipation. Upon casual observation, the condition mimics diarrhea and is often treated with constipating agents. This, of course, only serves to exacerbate the problem, resulting in further distention of the colon.

The estimated incidence of functional encopresis varies from 1.5% to 7.5% of children. Levine (1975) and Yates (1970) cite 3%. Bellman (1966) noted that 8.1% of 3-year-olds soiled their pants, 2.8% of 4-year-olds, and 2.2% of 5-year-olds. Newson and Newson (1968) reported figures of 2.3% for males 7–8 years of age and .7% for females of the same age. These percentages appear to drop with age such that 1.2% and .3% of males and females, respectively, in the age range 10–12 are noted to be encopretic (Rutter, Tizard, & Whitmore, 1970). Incidence of functional encopresis appears to be substantially higher in males than in females, and is often found in children who show developmental delays in other areas (Stein & Susser, 1967).

In one of the more detailed studies, Levine (1975) examined 102 encopretics; 87 were between the ages of 4 and 13, 85% were male, and 50% were incontinent during the day and night. Most denied that they could detect the urge to defecate and complained of abdominal pains, poor appetite, and lethargy. Fecal impactions were noted in 75%, and 40% were classified as continuous encopretics. Familial, marital, and behavioral pathologies were not major contributing factors. These associated problems are, however, found more often in encopresis than with enuresis (Hersov, 1977; Wolters, 1974a,b). Several studies have related quality of interaction, coerciveness of training, and ambivalence of parents as possible factors leading to development of encopresis (Anthony, 1957; Pinkerton, 1958).

Physiology

The physiology involved in fecal continence and defecation has been elaborated in a number of sources (Anthony, 1963; Gaston, 1948). Briefly, the process is reflexive in nature and is initiated by stimulation of receptors in the rectal mucosa. Defecation generally occurs in response to distention of the rectum produced by mass peristalsis of fecal material out of the colon. The filling and distention of the rectum results in: (a) increased colonic peristalsis; (b) reflexive relaxation of internal anal sphincter: and (c) a desire to defecate. Voluntary contractions of thoraxic and abdominal muscles, and relaxation of the external and sphincters bring about defecation. If defecation is voluntarily inhibited by maintenance of pressure on external anal sphincter, in the absence of thoraxic and abdominal muscle contractions, rectal receptors adapt to existing pressure and the urge to defecate diminishes. Subsequent urges may not occur until 24 hours later when mass peristalsis begins. During retention, moisture from fecal mass can be absorbed, producing a hard stool and more painful defecation.

It is easy to understand from this description how children are able to retain for extended periods of time. In addition, normal defecation is a very active and not a passive process. Muscle contractions and external anal sphincter relaxation must be a coordinated movement. External pressure during toileting can interfere with this process through anxiety or fear-mediated muscle contractions, making defecation more difficult.

Etiology

There are three major theoretical orientations that have been appealed to, collectively or individually, to account for encopresis. Psychodynamically oriented approaches discuss encopresis as a symptom of some unconscious conflict. These underlying conflicts may be in a form of lack of parental love, guilt value of feces, separation anxiety, fear of loss of feces, pregnancy wishes, aggression against a hostile world, response to familial dysfunction, and dramatic separation from the mother between oral and anal ages of psychosexual development (Lehman, 1944; Pierce, 1975; Silber, 1969). The "power struggle" that presumably develops between the parent and child during the course of toilet training has also been invoked as having etiological significance (Anthony, 1957; Hersov, 1977; Hilburn, 1968). It would seem irrefutable that the use of inappropriate or coercive training methods could contribute heavily to the development of encopresis. It does not, however, seem likely that this would result from an unconscious conflict. Such theoretical approaches have been most unproductive when applied clinically. They also appear to have very little utility when dealing with the developmentally disabled child.

A second approach to the etiology will be described as the medical-constitutional. This approach encompasses a neurodevelopmental model. Within this model, lack of neurological integrity, inappropriate functioning of a physiological mechanism involved in defecation, and anatomical malfunctions are examined. Consideration is also give to diet and constitutional factors (Davidson, 1958). This approach, of course, cannot be discarded because many cases of encopresis have an organic component. However, presence of organic pathology does not preclude application of nonmedical (i.e., behavioral) approaches in treatment. Epstein and McCoy (1977), for example, applied behavioral procedures to the treatment of a child known to have Hirschsprung's disease (Ravitch, 1958), wherein nerve intervention is inadequate for the detection or production of normal peristaltic movement (Silber, 1969). Similarly, surgical corrections of more common anatomical abnormalities such as ectopic anuses (Leape & Ramenofsky, 1978) does not always lead to the immediate resumption of normal toileting. Neurological pathology is common among the moderately and severely developmentally disabled child, yet toilet skills can be acquired. Medical personnel may sometimes be insensitive to the impact of environmental contingencies and the presence of prerequisite skills, while behavioral psychologists occasionally are too candid about the functional nature of encopresis.

A third approach is the conditioning or learning-behavioral model. This model emphasizes inadequate or inappropriate learning experiences as major etiological factors in the development and maintenance of encopresis. In the case of the primary encopretic, the learning model would evaluate presence of prerequisite skills, such as undressing, and lack of sufficient reinforcement for proper toileting. It is often assumed that cues emanating from rectal distention and internal anal sphincter relaxation have not become discriminative for temporary retention and bowel movements into the commode. Discontinuous encopresis, on the other hand, is often accounted for in terms of avoidance conditioning principles. It is postulated that pain-or fear-arousing events have been associated with onset of encopresis. Thus, retention becomes negatively reinforced by delay of pain. This behavior may persist in spite of the fact that when the child does ultimately have a bowel movement, the pain is present to a higher degree than would be the case without retention. Another view within the same model would suggest that inadvertent conditioning occurs when the child receives untimely reinforcement through parental attention following soiling.

A functional analysis is used to isolate these faulty environmental contingencies. Rearranging such contingencies is a major focus of therapy. An important consideration in the application of the conditioning model is the realization that one set of circumstances may be present and promote the development of encopresis, but a separate set of circumstances may be maintaining it. For this reason, the precise analysis of current conditions is often seen as more critical than a comprehensive understanding of the patient's early history.

Assessment

Successful treatment of the encopretic child is often preceded by a complete and thorough evaluation. It should be apparent that there are different types of encopresis. Differential application of treatment techniques is likely to result in more efficient treatment. Anthony (1957), for example, suggested that continuous encopretics should be given a steady course of basic toilet training because bowel continence had never been achieved. On the other hand, it was speculated that psychotherapy would be more appropriate for discontinuous encopretics, reasoning that regression was a result of some trauma of a psychiatric–psychological nature. Similarly, Walker (1978) recommended differential treatment of manipulative soilers, retentive encopretics, and those who demonstrated diarrhea resulting from tension or anxiety. Children with excessive bowel retention and constipation certainly require the most comprehensive attention. They may display overflow incontinence, which mimics diarrhea and has been referred to as "paradoxical diarrhea" (Davidson, 1958). If treated symptomatically with use of constipating agents, the child's status would only be worsened because a major contributing factor is the presence of impaction. Constipation, distention of the colon, and passing of stools into the pants are indicative of both "psychogenic" and "neurogenic" megacolon. A differential diagnosis is essential.

A comprehensive assessment should include a medical evaluation, clinical interview, and behavioral records (Doleys *et al.,* 1981). Medical examination often includes medical history, rectal examination, barium enema, or biopsy as required. These can help to rule out contributing organic pathology. Many encopretics display some degree of constipation. This condition can be associated with congenital hypothyroidism, anorectal anomalies (Hendren, 1978; Leape & Ramenofsky, 1978), and Hirschsprung's disease (Ravitch, 1958), particularly when seen early in life. Other factors that can contribute include: (1) a constitutional predisposition; (2) dietary intake: (3) difficulty in passing large, hard stools because of failure to provide leverage; (4) presence of pain and voluntary resistance; and (5) presence of fecal impactions (Davidson, 1958). Evidence regarding existence and degree of megacolon is also required. One must differentiate among irritable bowel syndrome and malabsorption disorders in such cases and determine what, if any, laxatives or stool softeners might be required. Medical consultation thus becomes indispensable.

The clinical interview should help the therapist to : (a) differentiate among the various types of encopresis; (b) determine related environmental contingencies and circumstances; and (c) obtain data relevant to the emotional-behavioral competencies of the parents or caregivers of the child. One must exercise caution not to cut short the assessment procedure because of the clinician's hunches about the nature of the encopresis. Care must be taken to avoid the pitfalls identified by Wright (1978) when he suggested that we (psychologists) often "tend to find what we look for." Likewise, narrowness in conceptualization and treatment of encopresis can result in all cases seeming more identical than they in fact are. As it was once noted, "If the only tool you have is a hammer, then everything around you can look like a nail."

Behavioral records can be very helpful in establishing patterns of soiling. As described in an earlier section, they can help determine parental and child motivation for treatment and ability to follow and understand directions, and they can serve as a baseline against which to assess effectiveness of treatment. Records should include recording of frequency of soiling, magnitude of each accident, when and where the episode occurred, and whether or not appropriate toileting also occurred. Unfortunately, many therapists in this area focus only on accidents and pay very little attention to whether or not the child shows any appropriate toileting behavior. Special attention needs to be given to the role of "fear." Several researchers (Ashkenazi, 1975; Doleys & Arnold, 1975; Gelber & Meyer, 1965) have documented the presence of "toilet phobias." In such cases the child is fearful of sitting on the commode or even being near the commode. Gavanski (1971) describes a "pot-refusal" syndrome, which appears to be associated with coercive toilet-training procedures and results in the child's refusing to sit on the commode. It is interesting in this regard to note that

Levine and Bakow (1976) found a significant positive relationship between parental compliance and remission soiling during treatment. It also is important to talk to the child regarding his/her sensation of the urge to defecate. Children should be asked to demonstrate how they "push" and try to "go to the bathroom." It is important to get the child's reactions, interpretations, and descriptions.

Once treatment has been undertaken, evaluation should be ongoing. Frequency of appropriate toileting, percentage of toileting that is self-initiating, frequency of accidents, degree of assistance or prompts required, situational generality of toileting skills, and frequency of laxative, stool softeners, or other medications should be monitored. If one attends only to the frequency of accidents, important aspects of treatment might be overlooked. For example, the child may reduce his frequency of soiling but accomplish this through frequent and excessive retention rather than by increasing the frequency of appropriate toileting. More specific and detailed information on assessment may be found in Doleys *et al.* (1981), Walker (1978), and Doleys (1979a, 1980a).

Treatment

Mechanical devices

Mechanical devices utilized for the treatment of encopresis are of two major types. The first type is designed to detect soiling episodes, and the second to signal that defecation has occurred while the child is sitting on the commode. Such devices allow for the immediate application of contingencies. Foxx and Azrin (1973) list many commercially available detection devices. One of these devices was modified and used by Logan and Garner (1971) in the successful treatment of a partially deaf child. A transistorized device that allows for transmission of a signal noting inappropriate elimination has been described by Van-Wagenen and Murdock (1966) and Fried (1974). Potty-chair type devices have been found useful in detecting appropriate elimination in the commode (Cheney, 1973; Watson, 1968). Hopkinson and Lightwood (1966) report on the application of an electrical device surgically implanted in the anal area that, by application of low-level electrical stimulation, maintains normal anal sphincter tone in a patient with retroprolapse (a condition resulting in nearly continual passage of feces due to the absence of appropriate anal sphincter contraction). Kohlenberg (1973) describes the application of a device for training sphincter control. The apparatus included a balloon-like structure inserted into the rectum. This assembly was attached to a tube filled with colored water in clear view of the subject. Contractions of anal sphincter resulted in a rise of the fluid level, this providing immediate feedback to the subject regarding whether or not he was applying appropriate response.

Medical Treatments

Medical treatments tend to rely on the use of purgative (laxatives and enemas) and dietary manipulations (Nisley, 1976; Ravitch, 1958; Silber, 1969). In some cases these treatments are applied without giving proper consideration to: (a) obtaining and maintaining parental and child compliance; (b) the acquisition of appropriate toileting skills; and (c) long-term maintenance of desirable behaviors once they are established. Imipramine (Tofranil) has been applied because of its antispasmatic property. It is presumed to have an inhibitory effect upon the internal anal sphincter, thus potentially reducing the frequency of bowel movement. One study (Gavanski, 1971) noted the combined use of Tofranil and psychotherapy. Case descriptions recall the successful application of this treatment in three nonretentive encopretics. Gavanski, however, cautions that imipramine: (a) should be used only for temporary relief of high-rate soiling; (b) should be applied only to nonretentive encopretics; and (c) should be used in conjunction with appropriate psychotherapy.

Berg and Jones (1964) reviewed much of the literature in this area. They noted that relief from soiling achieved through these "mechanical" methods tended to be temporary at best. One of the more successful procedures described was that of Davidson, Kugler, and Bauer (1963). These investigators describe a three-part program with 119 encopretics. The program was initiated with the use of mineral oil in an attempt to produce regular bowel movements. During the second phase of the program, laxatives were gradually withdrawn in an attempt to maintain bowel movements in a more natural fashion. The third phase employed parental counseling and monitoring of the child's behavior through periodic contacts. Of the 90 patients completing the program (75% of the total sample), 80 were identified as successfully treated (67% of the total sample and 89% of the completers). A careful reading makes it clear that counseling, feedback, self-monitoring, physician time, support, and encouragement were extensively used along with the laxatives and enemas.

Verbal Psychotherapy

Several studies have reported upon the use of various forms of verbal psychotherapy and play therapy in the treatment of encopresis (Gavanski, 1971; McTaggert & Scott, 1959; Pinkerton, 1958). The rate of remission among these studies was considerable. One review (Berg & Jones, 1964) showed that rate of remission among children receiving psychotherapy was not significantly different from those who had not received psychotherapy. The review covered some 70 cases. Similarly, Ashkenazi (1975) reported that three children who had previously failed in treatment using psychotherapy and play therapy later became continent when exposed to a behavioral program emphasizing regular potting, induced defecation, and positive reinforcement.

Pinkerton (1958) presents an illustration of the use of psychotherapy with 30 encopretic children. He postulated that bowel negativism, defiant soiling, or refusal to defecate was the basis of the disorder. These conditions were presumably exacerbated by perfectionistic or oversolicitous parents who exaggerated the noxiousness of the feces and demonstrated excessive concern regarding acquisition of toileting. Treatment was conducted through the parents and focused on abaiting parental fear and prejudices, thereby presumably permitting insight into the emotional origins of the problem and encouraging parents to become "indifferent" to the symptoms. Treatment with the child included hospitalization when parent counseling was ineffective. Play therapy was employed to

> first penetrate the child's defensive facade and establish adequate depths of contact with him; second, to define his fundamental problems for him through the medium of projective play techniques; third, to promote the working through of his difficulties with associated release during play of his pent up hostilities; and fourth, to restore his emotional stability following the resolution of these difficulties. (p. 376)

It was reported that 17 of 30 cases became continent with follow-up ranging up to 3½ years. Specific treatment duration was not given. McTaggert and Scott (1959) employed play therapy, clay modeling, and finger painting as aids in facilitating acting out of the feelings and their subjects. These techniques were combined with therapeutic counseling of the parents. Seven of twelve children presumably were cured and three were described as improved.

It is difficult to identify specifically what aspects or qualities of verbal psychotherapy are related to therapeutic outcome. These methodologies, however, have not been utilized in comparative studies against other well established procedures. The techniques often involve a variety of procedures such as self-monitoring, rewards, and laxatives. Experimental approaches focusing on a component analysis are badly needed to determine which of the factors is most closely associated with success.

Behavioral Procedures

The behavioral approaches to the treatment of functional encopresis focus on the arrangement of environmental consequences so as to encourage development and maintenance of appropriate toileting behavior. Although many of the programs share common features, treatment of the encopretic child must be individualized to take into account specific behavioral deficits. Appropriate defecation in the commode must be considered the final act in a long chain of behaviors. Unless the earlier components of the chain, such as detection of the need to defecate, ability to locate the appropriate facility, and undressing are present, accidents are likely to occur. Absence of these behavioral repertoires is most evident in mentally retarded and neurologically impaired individuals, but is certainly not restricted to these groups.

One of the foundations of behavioral procedures is the identification of target behavior(s). Target responses will need to be individualized for different children. The therapeutic focus for the continuous encopretic is likely to be the development of appropriate toileting skills, including how to disrobe and the use of appropriate muscle tension to promote defecation. Such behaviors may already be present for the child who displays excessive retention and constipation. In these instances, increased regularity of bowel movements would be the goal. Laxatives and enemas *may* have to be employed. A different approach would be called for when the major problem involves a toilet phobia wherein all prerequisite behaviors are present, but fear and anxiety interfere with desirable performance.

Doleys (1978, 1979a, 1980a), Walker (1978), and Schaefer (1979) present reviews of the behavioral treatments for encopresis. Doleys has chosen to classify the procedures into four categories: Type 1 reinforcement, Type 2 reinforcement, punishment, and Type 3 treatment. The Type 1 procedures employ positive reinforcement, which is dispensed contingently upon occurrence of appropriate bowel movements. Several studies have documented the effectiveness of this procedure (Bach & Moylan, 1975; Keehn, 1965; Neale, 1963; Plachetta, 1974; Young, 1973; Young & Goldsmith, 1972). Reinforcement in these studies was delivered when the child evidenced a bowel movement while sitting on the commode. In some cases, laxatives or enemas were used (Neale, 1963; Young, 1973).

Collectively, data on the application of Type 1 reinforcement showed that 90% of 33 subjects achieved continence, which was maintained in follow-up for over 80%. Most of the studies involved single cases, with only a few employing larger groups (Neale, 1962; Young, 1973). The study by Young utilized 24 children (4–10 years of age). Soiling was accompanied by diminished sensation resulting from dilation of the internal anal sphincter. Treatment was initiated by removal of any impaction or accumulated fecal matter. The child then began a regimen of daily toileting in the morning after consuming a warm drink or food to initiate reflexive internal bowel movement. Bowel movements on the commode were reinforced. Twenty of the 24 subjects were given Senokot (a laxative/stool softener) nightly to insure defecation in the morning. Nineteen of the subjects were treated successfully, as indicated by absence of feces in the rectum and 28 consecutive clean days. Average treatment duration was 5 months.

The Type 2 reinforcement procedure also employs positive reinforcement. In this case, reinforcement is contingent upon clean pants as opposed to appropriate toileting. Studies by Ayllon, Simon, and Wildman (1975), Pedrini and Pedrini (1971), and Logan and Garner (1971) are examples of such treatment. Logan and Garner (1971) described an interesting case wherein a pants alarm or buzzer was used with a 7-year-old, partially deaf child. The buzzer sounded contingent upon soiling, and consequently the child had to clean himself and return to his classroom. Points were awarded for each hour that the child was able to keep the buzzer silent, and the points could be exchanged for a variety of backup reinforcers.

Although the application of Type 2 reinforcement has been effective with some cases, its general utility is in question. The reinforcement of clean pants does not necessarily encourage the development of appropriate defecation habits. Children who are inclined to engage in retention may produce clean pants simply by not having a bowel movement. This, of course, complicates the problem. Procedures need to be employed where reinforcement is given for clean pants, but also for demonstration of the proper response: defecation in the commode.

A few studies have examined the application of punishment in the treatment of encopresis (Edelman, 1971; Freinden & VanHandel, 1970). In the first of these studies, a 30-minute time-out in the bedroom followed each episode of soiling with a 12-year-old female. The second study utilized cleaning of the soiled clothes and washing with strong soap and cold water as punishment. Treatment was successful in 41 and 20 weeks, respectively, for the two studies. Application of similar techniques is generally not encouraged because, in spite of periodic effectiveness with some children, there is a great potential for punishment to elicit emotional response, promote negative parent–child interactions, and lead to excessive retention. By the time a child reaches the clinician, he/she has usually already been exposed to a good deal of reprimanding, time-out, withholding of privileges, embarrassment, and spanking.

The fourth category of programs is referred to as Type 3 treatment. These techniques are comprehensive and generally involve the combined use of positive reinforcement and punishment. Laxatives, stool softeners, and enemas are employed as needed. One study (Gelber & Mayer, 1965) combined reinforcement for appropriate toileting, punishment for soiled pants, and periodic pants checks in the treatment of a 13-year-old male. Continence was achieved within 9 weeks of the onset of treatment and was maintained over a 24-week follow-up period, with only one accident occurring in the final 2 weeks of follow-up.

Ashkenazi (1975) reported on a treatment program involving 18 encopretics, 6 of whom are identified as "pot phobics." The phobic responses were treated successfully by the use of reinforcement for successive approximations to sitting on the commode. The general program involved potting of the child following the insertion of a glycerin suppository to promote bowel movements. Positive reinforcement was contingent upon defecation and the absence of soiling during the day. Use of suppositories was gradually faded over 5 consecutive days of appropriate toileting. With this regimen, 16 of 18 subjects were treated within a 9-week period, and continence was maintained through a 6-month follow-up.

Three studies (Doleys & Arnold, 1975; Doleys, Adams, & Rice, 1980; Doleys, McWhorter, Williams, & Gentry, 1977) examined use of a three-part program that included: (a) periodic pants checks; (b) full cleanliness training contingent upon soiling; and (c) positive reinforcement for appropriate toileting. Depending upon the child's age and availability, the parents were requested to check the child's pants on a regular schedule, about every hour or two. Positive verbal reinforcement was provided if the pants were clean. Younger children and encopretics who were given to excessive retention were prompted to toilet themselves or placed on the commode for a 10-minute period after a pants check. Presence of soiled clothes resulted in full cleanliness training (FCT; Foxx & Azrin, 1973). This involved: (1) parents' expression of displeasure; (2) child's washing his underpants and trousers for 20 minutes; and (3) child's taking a bath and cleaning himself for 20 minutes in cool water. Parents were instructed to be nonchalant in the execution of full cleanliness training, and to verbalize repeatedly the reason for training and how it could be avoided. Children *were not released* from FCT if they were being disruptive; this prevented parents from negatively reinforcing disruptive behavior. The third aspect of the program involved the distribution of token reinforcement in the form of stars or colored squares on a chart, contingent upon self-initiated bowel movements. Accumulation of a predetermined number of tokens resulted in the acquisition of a previously identified backup reinforcer. The reinforcers were relatively inexpensive, were selected by the child, and were maintained in the bathroom to help ensure continued motivation. The program was initially accomplished with four subjects, whose treatment duration varied from 4–10 weeks. One subject showed a relapse during follow-up as a result of parents' noncompliance to the follow-up regimen.

A recent replication of this initial study (Doleys *et al.,* 1980) utilized laxatives and suppositories when appropriate. Subjects were 20 children ranging in age from 4–12 years with a mean of 7.5 years. Fourteen children were males and six were females. Eleven were primary encopretics and nine were secondary. Nine of the children were retentive. Baseline rates of soiling ranged from 1.5 to 8 per week. Frequency of bowel movements ranged from 0 to 7 per week. Twelve children completed treatment as defined by: (1) participating in the program for 12 weeks or more; (2) following the prescribed treatment; and (3) providing data. Ten of the children were considered successfully treated, as defined by; (1) average of 1 soiling episode or less per month during follow-up (2) parental report of lack of problem; and (3) reported regular bowel movements in the commode. Analysis of the data showed that treatment duration did not vary significantly between male and female. The group of continuous encopretics was in treatment approximately 5 weeks longer than was the discontinuous group. Retentive encopretics showed the longer treatment duration. Follow-up data were available on 9 of 10 subjects considered successfully treated, and ranged from 4–36 months. Average follow-up was 17.6 months. This data showed that 8 of 9 children demonstrated a frequency of soiling of less then 2 per month on the average. Also, they continued to show bowel movements in the commode of 3 per week or greater. One child showed a relatively high frequency of intermittent soiling. These episodes were often associate with stress, such as holidays, vacations, or returning to school. It often was difficult to distinguish between retentive and nonretentive encopretics. The problem seemed to lie in the definition of a soiling episode. In most cases, any amount of fecal material passed to the underwear was considered soiling. Retentive encopretics often have very small amounts and therefore appear to be soiling at a high rate. Suppositories and laxatives were used with 3 of 4 retentive subjects. They were gradually faded out and were found to be helpful in promoting bowel movements that could then be reinforced. It was, however, discovered that prolonged use of these purgatives could establish a pattern of "passive defecation," wherein the child made no attempts on his/her own to produce a bowel movement, but simply sat passively in response to the urge. Although the use of laxatives and purgatives seemed to be helpful with retentive encopretics, they must be applied judiciously and the child's behavior monitored consistently.

Wright (1973, 1975; Wright & Walker, 1976) describes a program that employs positive reinforcement, punishment, periodic potting, enemas, and suppositories. After a thorough evaluation, parents were instructed about the program, which emphasized the need for regular evacuation and the importance of the child's accepting responsibility for his/her toileting habits. Treatment began with a thorough evaluation, usually with use of an enema. Children were potted regularly in the morning and reinforced for bowel movement. If the child did not defecate, a glycerin suppository was utilized, and a bowel movement was induced prior to the child's leaving for school. Rewards were given for artificially induced bowel movements, but the magnitude was smaller than those for self-initiated bowel movements. If a bowel movement did not occur prior to school time, an enema was used to produce evacuation of the colon. Frequency of enemas was controlled. Concern was also given to dietary manipulation. The child's clothes were checked and reinforcement was provided if no soiling occurred. Soiling was punished by application of restrictions or loss of privileges. Continued contact with parents and child occurred throughout, with emphasis on the consistent application of the program. As children began to display appropriate toileting, the investigators noted a tendency for parents to become lax regarding their compliance with the program. This often resulted in recurrence of soiling. Phasing out of the program began after 2 consecutive weeks of nonsoiling. The program was reinitiated if the child demonstrated soiling. Success was reported with 100% of 14 subjects treated, ranging in age from 3–9 years of age. Treatment duration average 16.9 weeks (range 10–38). Only 1 child was noted to relapse during a 6-month follow-up.

Direct conditioning of the anal sphincter muscles has been attempted in the treatment of fecal incontinence. Kohlenberg (1973) employed a balloon-type of apparatus inserted in the rectum and attached to a tube filled with colored water to provide feedback to the subject. Constriction of anal sphincters raised the level of the fluid and resulted in monetary reinforcement. The procedure was effective in treating a 13-year-old discontinuous encopretic who demonstrated consistent soiling due to dilated sphincters. Similar procedures have been reported by Engle, Nikoomanesh, and Schuster (1974) with 7 patients. Follow-up ranging from 6 months to 5 years revealed maintenance of the acquired continence in 5 of 7 cases.

Levine (1975) noted that about 30% of the encopretic children in his study also displayed enuresis. Some guidelines for treatment are available (Doleys *et al.*, 1981), but few studies exist in the literature. Doleys, McWhorter, Williams, and Wells (1977) and Edelman (1971) found the two problems to be functionally independent. That is, reducing the frequency of either encopresis or enuresis did not appear to affect the frequency of the other. In both instances encopresis was treated first. Epstein and McCoy (1977), however, did notice an increase in bowel movement with a 3-year-old child diagnosed as having Hirschsprung's disease following use of bladder control training for enuresis.

Summary

Although psychologists have attended to the problem of enuresis, their focus has been somewhat narrow, encompassing only nocturnal enuresis and occasionally diurnal enuresis.

Significant advances have been made in our understanding of functional nocturnal enuresis and in the development of adequate treatment techniques. Continued work is required to determine mechanisms for reducing relapse rates. Application of behavioral technology and principles is not nearly as evident in the treatment of diurnal enuresis and in cases of bladder dysfunction. Application of behavioral principles and technology to these more unusual and sometimes more difficult cases has often been spearheaded by professionals not specifically trained in behavioral psychology. Systematic investigation in these areas, employing an interdisciplinary team of knowledgeable professionals, could prove to be invaluable to those individuals experiencing the physical, psychological, and social trauma of dysfunctional bladder syndrome, whether they are shown to be neurogentic or nonneurogenic.

Encopresis continues to be somewhat ill-defined. It is frequently observed and yet has been exposed to little systematic research. Major problems appear to exist with present classification systems. The use of descriptive labels such as continuous, discontinuous, retentive, stress-induced, and manipulative encopresis is being seen with a higher degree of regularity. It seems almost a foregone conclusion that differential treatment will be required for these various types of encopresis. Similarly, the necessity to attend to the characteristics and needs of each specific child and family is strongly implicated.

Research in the area of encopresis has suffered from many inadequacies. Included among these are: (1) absence of an adequate description of the problem; (2) use of a small number of subjects; (3) lack of comparative, well controlled studies; and (4) little attention to the relationship between treatment success and characteristics of the soiling. The use of single factor treatments such as extinction, positive reinforcement, or laxatives appear to produce only temporary results at best. The more comprehensive behavioral programs show the greatest promise.

References

Allen, R. B. *Bladder capacity and awakening behavior in the treatment of enuresis.* Unpublished doctoral dissertation, University of Vermont, 1976.

Allen, T. D. The non-neurogenic neurogenic bladder. *Journal of Urology,* 1977, *117,* 232–238.

Anthony, C. P. *Textbook of anatomy and physiology* (6th ed.). St. Louis; Mosby, 1963.

Anthony, E. G. An experimental approach to the psychopathology of childhood encoprisis *British Journal of Medical Psychology,* 1957 *30,* 146–175.

Arnold, S. J., & Ginsburg, A. Understanding and managing enuresis in children. *Postgraduate Medicine,* 1975 *58,* 73–82.

Ashkenazi, Z. The treatment of encopresis using a discriminative stimulus and positive reinforcement. *Journal of Behavior Therapy and Experimental Psychiatry,* 1975, *6,* 155–157.

Atthowe, J. M. Nocturnal enuresis and behavior therapy: A functional analysis. In R. B. Rubin, J. Henderson, H. Fensterheim, & L. P. Ullmann (Eds.), *Advances in behavior therapy* (Vol. 4). New York; Academic Press, 1973.

Ayllon, T., Simon, S. J., & Wildman, R. W. Instructions and reinforcement in the elimination of encopresis: Case study. *Journal of Behavior Therapy and Experimental Psychiatry,* 1975, *6,* 235–238.

Azrin, N. H., & Besalel, V. A. *Parent's guide to bedwetting control: A step-by-step method.* New York: Simon & Schuster, 1979.

Azrin, N. H., & Foxx, R. M. *Toilet training in less than a day.* New York: Simon & Schuster, 1974.

Azrin, N. H., Sneed, T. J., & Foxx, R. M. Dry bed: A rapid method of eliminating bedwetting (enuresis) of the retarded. *Behaviour Research and Therapy,* 1973, *11,* 427–434.

Azrin, N. H., Sneed, T. J., & Foxx, R. M. Dry-bed training: Rapid elimination of childhood enuresis. *Behaviour Research and Therapy,* 1974, *12,* 147–156.

Bach, R., & Moylan, J. M. Parent-administered behavior therapy for inappropriate urination and encopresis: A case study. *Journal of Behavior Therapy and Experimental Psychiatry,* 1975, *6,* 147–156.

Baker, B. L. Symptom treattment and symptom substitution in enuresis. *Journal of Abnormal Psychology,* 1969, *74,* 42–49.

Bakwin, H. The genetics of enuresis. *Clinics in Developmental Medicine,* 1973, *48–49,* 73–77.

Bellman, M. Studies on encopresis. *Acta Paediatrica Scandinavica* (Supplement No. 70), 1966.

Berg, I., & Jones, K. V. Functional fecal incontinence in children. *Archives of Disease in Childhood,* 1964, *39,* 465–472.

Besalel, V. A., Azrin, N. H., Thienes-Hontos, P., & McMorrow, M. Evaluation of a parent's manual for training enuretic children. *Behaviour Research and Therapy,* 1980, *18,* 358–366.

Blackwell, B., & Currah, J. The pharmacology of nocturnal enuresis. In I. Kolvin, R. C. MacKeith, & S. R. Meadow (Eds.), *Bladder Control and enuresis.* Philadelphia: Saunders, 1973.

Blaivas, J. G., Labib, K. L., Bauer, S. B., & Retick, A. B. A new approach to electromyography of the external urethral sphincter. *Journal of Urology,* 1977, *117,* 773–777.

Bollard, R. J., & Woodroffe, P. The effect of parent-administered dry-bed training on nocturnal enuresis in children. *Behaviour Research and Therapy,* 1977, *15,* 159–165.

Bostack, J. Exterior gestation, primitive sleep, enuresis and asthma; A study in aetiology. *Medical Journal of Australia,* 1958, *149,* 185–192.

Boyd, M. M. The depth of sleep in enuretic school children and in non-enuretic controls. *Journal of Psychosomatic Research,* 1960, *4,* 274–281.

Bradley, W. E., Scott, F. B., & Timm, G. W. Sphincter electromyography. *Urologic Clinics of North America,* 1974, *1,* 69–80.

Braithwaithe, J. V. Some problems associated with enuresis. *Proceedings of the Royal Society of Medicine,* 1956, *49,* 33–39.

Butler, J. F. The toilet training success of parents after reading "Toilet training in less than a day." *Behavior Therapy,* 1967, *7,* 185–191.

Campbell, M. F. Neuromuscular uropathy. In M. F. Campbell & T. H. Harrison (Eds.), *Urology* (Vol. 2). Philadelphia: Saunders, 1970.

Catalina, D. A. Enuresis: The effects of parent contingent wake-up. *Dissertation Abstracts,* 1976, *37,* 28–025.

Cheney, C. D. Mechanically augmented human toilet training or the electric potty chair. In R. L. Schwitzgebel & R. H. Schwitzgebel (Eds.), *Psychotechnology: Electronic control of mind and behavior.* New York: Rinehart & Winston, 1973.

Cohen, M. W. Enuresis. *Pediatric clinics of North America,* 1975, *22,* 545–560.

Davidson, M. D. Constipation and fecal incontinence. In H. Bakwin (Ed.), *Pediatric clinics of North America.* Philadelphia: Saunders, 1958.

Davidson, M. D., Kugler, M. D., & Bauer, C. H. Diagnosis and management in children with severe and protracted constipation and obstipation. *Journal of Pediatrics.* 1963, *62,* 261–266.

DeLeon, G., & Mandell, W. A comparison of conditioning and psychotherapy in the treatment of functional enuresis. *Journal of Clinical Psychology,* 1966, *22,* 326–330.

DeLuca, F. G., Swenson, O., Fisher, J. H., & Loutfi, A. H. The dysfunctional "lazy" bladder syndrome in children. *Archives of Disease in Childhood,* 1962, *37,* 117–121.

Dische, S. Management of enuresis. *British Medical Journal,* 1971, *2,* 33–36.

Doleys, D. M. Behavioral treatments for nocturnal enuresis in children: A review of the recent literature. *Psychological Bulletin,* 1977, *84,* 30–54.

Doleys, D. M. Assessment and treatment of enuresis and encopresis in children. In M. Hersen, R. Eisler, & P. M. Miller (Eds.), *Progress in behavior modification.* New York: Academic Press, 1978.

Doleys, D. M. Assessment and treatment of childhood encopresis. In A. J. Finch & P. C. Kendall (Eds.), *Treatment and research in child psychopathology.* New York: Spectrum. 1979. (a)

Doleys, D. M. Assessment and treatment of childhood enuresis. In A. J. Finch & P. C. Kendall (Eds.), *Treatment and research in child psychopathology.* New York: Spectrum, 1979. (b)

Doleys, D. M. Enuresis. In J. Ferguson & C. B. Taylor (Eds.), *Advances in behavioral medicine.* New York: Spectrum, 1980. (a)

Doleys, D. M. Enuresis. In J. Gerguson & C. B. Taylor (Eds.), *Advances in behavioral medicine.* New York: Spectrum, 1980. (b)

Doleys, D. M., & Arnold, S. Treatment at childhood encopresis: Full cleanliness training. *Mental Retardation,* 1975, *13,* 14–16.

Doleys, D. M., & Wells, K. C. Changes in functional bladder capacity and bed-wetting during and after retention control training. *Behavior Therapy,* 1975, *6,* 685–688.

Doleys, D. M., Adams, R., & Rice, J. *Behavioral treatment of encopresis.* Paper presented at Association for Advancement of Behavior Therapy. New York, November 1980.

Doleys, D. M., Ciminero, A. R., Tollison, J. W., Williams, C. L., & Wells, K. C. Dry-bed training and retention control training: A comparison. *Behavior Therapy,* 1977, *8,* 541–548.

Doleys, D. M., McWhorter, A. Q., Williams, S. C., & Gentry, R. Encopresis: Its treatment and relation to nocturnal enuresis. *Behavior Therapy,* 1977, *8,* 77–82.

Doleys, D. M., Schwartz, M. S., & Ciminero, A. R. Elimination problems: Enuresis and encopresis. In E. J. Mash & L. G. Terdal (Eds.), *Behavioral assessment of childhood disorders.* New York: Guilford Press, 1981.

Easson, W. M. Encopresis—psychogenic soiling. *Canadian Medical Association Journal,* 1960, *82,* 624–630.

Edelman, R. F. Operant conditioning treatment of encopresis. *Journal of Behavior Therapy and Experimental Psychiatry,* 1971, *2,* 71–73.

Engle, B. I., Nikoomanesh, D., & Schuster, M. M. Operant conditioning of recto-sphincteric responses in the treatment of fecal incontinence. *New England Journal of Medicine,* 1974, *290,* 646–649.

Epstein, L. H., & McCoy, J. F. Bladder and bowel control in Hirschprung's disease. *Journal of Behavior Therapy and Experimental Psychiatry,* 1977, *8,* 97–99.

Esperanca, M., & Gerrard, J. W. Nocturnal enuresis: Comparison of the effect of imipramine and dietary restriction of bladder capacity. *The Canadian Medical Association Journal,* 1969, *101,* 721–724.

Faray, L. G. Enuresis: A genetic study. *American Journal of Diseases of Childhood,* 1935, *49,* 557–578.

Fielding, D. The response of day and night wetting children and children who wet only at night to retention control training and the enuresis alarm. *Behaviour Research and Therapy,* 1980, *18,* 305–317.

Finley, W. W. An EEG study of the sleep of enuretics at three age levels. *Clinical Electroencephalography,* 1971, *2,* 46–50.

Finley, W. W., & Smith, H. A. A long-life, inexpensive urinedetection pad for conditioning of enuresis nocturna, *Behaviour Research Methods and Instrumentation,* 1975, *7,* 273–276.

Finley, W. W., & Wansley, R. A. Use of intermittent reinforcement in a clinical-research program for the treatment of enuresis nocturna. *Journal of Pediatric Psychology,* 1976, *4,* 24–27.

Finley, W. W., Besserman, R. L., Bennett, L. F., Clapp, R. K., & Finley, P. M. The effect of continuous, intermittent, and "placebo" reinforcement on the effectiveness of the conditioning treatment for enuresis nocturna. *Behaviour Research and Therapy,* 1973, *11,* 289–297.

Finley, W. W., Wansley, R. A., & Blenkarn, M. M. Conditioning treatment of enuresis using a 70% intermittent reinforcement schedule. *Behaviour Research and Therapy,* 1977, *15,* 419–427.

Fitts, M. D., & Mann, R. A. Encopresis: An historical and behavioral perspective of definition. *Journal of Pediatric Psychology,* 1977, *4,* 31–38.

Fitzgerald, J. F. Encopresis, soiling, constipation: What's to be done? *Pediatrics.* 1975, *56,* 348–349.

Foxx, R. M., & Azrin, N. N. *Toilet training the retarded.* Champaign, Ill.: Research Press, 1973.

Franklin, J. *Retention control training in the treatment of nocturnal enuresis: A controlled case study of the generalization of changes in functional bladder capacity.* Unpublished manuscript, Prince Henry Hospital.

Freinden, W., & VanHandel, D. Elimination of soiling in an elementary school child through application of aversive technique. *Journal of School Psychology,* 1970, *8,* 267–269.

Fried, R. A device for enuresis control. *Behavior Therapy,* 1974, *5,* 682–684.

Gaston, E. A. The physiology of fecal continence. *Surgery, Gynecology, and Obstetrics,* 1948, *87,* 280–290.

Gavanski, M. The treatment of non-retentive secondary encopresis with imipramine and psychotherapy. *Canadian Medical Association Journal,* 1971, *104,* 227–231.

Gelber, H., & Meyer, V. Behavior therapy and encopresis: The complexities involved in treatment. *Behaviour Research and Therapy,* 1965, *2,* 227–231.

Harris, L. S., & Purohit, A. P. Bladder training and enuresis: A controlled trial. *Behaviour Research and Therapy,* 1977, *15,* 485–490.

Hendren, W. H. Constipation caused by anterior location of the anus and its urgical correction. *Journal of Pediatric Surgery,* 1978, *13,* 505–512.

Hersov, L. Fecal soiling. In M. Rutter & L. Hersov (Eds.), *Child psychiatry: Modern approaches.* Philadelphia: Blackwell Scientific Publications, 1977.

Hilburn, W. B. Encopresis in childhood. *Journal of Kentucky Medical Association,* 1968, *66,* 978.

Hinman, F., & Baumann, F. Vesical and ureteral damage from voiding dysfunction in boys without neurologic or obstructive disease. *The Journal of Urology,* 1973, *109,* 727–732.

Hopkinson, B. R., & Lightwood, R. Electrical treatment of anal incontinence. *The Lancet,* February 1966, 297–298.

Jehu, D., Morgan, R. T. T., Turner, R. K., & Jones, A. A controlled trial of the treatment of nocturnal enuresis in residential homes for children. *Behaviour Research and Therapy,* 1977, *15,* 1–16.

Jones, B., Gerrard, J. W., Shokeir, M. K., & Houston, C. S. Recurrent urinary infections in girls: Relation to enuresis. *Canadian Medical Association Journal,* 1972, *106,* 127–130.

Kaffman, M., & Elizur, E. Infants who become enuretic: A longitudinal study of 161 kibbutz children. *Child Development Monographs,* 1977, No. 42.

Kardash, S., Hillman, E., & Werry, J. Efficacy of imipramine in childhood enuresis: A double-blind control study with placebo. *Canadian Medical Association Journal,* 1968, *99,* 263–266.

Keehn, J. D. Brief case report: Reinforcement therapy of incontinence. *Behaviour Research and Therapy,* 1965, *2,* 239.

Kimmel, H. D., & Kimmel, E. C. An instrumental conditioning method for the treatment of enuresis. *Journal of Behavior Therapy and Experimental Psychiatry,* 1970, *1,* 121–123.

Kohlenberg, R. J. Operant conditioning of human anal sphincter pressure. *Journal of Applied Behavior Analysis,* 1973, *6,* 201–208.

Labay, P., & Boyarsky, S. The pharmacology of imipramine and its mechanism of action on enuresis. *Archives of Physical Medicine and Rehabilitation,* 1972, *53,* 584.

Leape, L. L., & Ramenofsky, M. L. Anterior ectopic anus: A common cause of constipation in children. *Journal of Pediatric Surgery.* 1978, *13,* 627–630.

Lehman, E. Psychogenic incontinence of feces (encopresis) in children. *American Journal of Diseases of Childhood,* 1944, *68,* 190–198.

Levine, M. D. Children with encopresis: A descriptive analysis. *Pediatrics.* 1975, *56,* 412–416.

Levine, M. D., & Bakow, H. Children with enopresis: A study of treatment outcome. *Pediatrics.* 1976, *58,* 845–852.

Logan, D. L., & Garner, D. G. Effective behavior modification for reducing chronic soiling. *American Annals of the Deaf,* 1971, *116,* 382–384.

Lovibond, S. H. Intermittent reinforcement in behavior therapy. *Behaviour Research and Therapy,* 1963, *1,* 127–132.

Lovibond, S. H. *Conditioning and enuresis.* Oxford, England: Pergamon Press, 1964.

Lovibond, S. H., & Coote, M. A. Enuresis. In C. G. Costello (Ed.), *Symptoms of psychopathology,* New York: Wiley, 1970.

Lund, C. J. Types of urinary incontinence. In C. J. Lund (Ed.), *Clinical obstetrics and gynecology.* New York: Harper & Row, 1963.

Mahony, D. T., Laferte, R. O., & Mahoney, J. E. Observations on sphincter-augmenting effect of imipramine in children with urinary incontinence. *Urology,* 1973, *1,* 317–323.

Maizels, M., King, L. R., & Firlit, C. F. Urodynamic biofeedback: A new approach to treat vesical sphincter dyssynergia. *Journal of Urology,* 1979, *122,* 205–209.

Matson, J. L. Some practical considerations for using the Foxx and Azrin rapid method of toilet training. *Psychological Reports,* 1975, *37,* 350.

McConaghy, N. A controlled trial of imipramine, amphetamine, pad-and bell conditioning and random waking in the treatment of nocturnal enuresis. *Medical Journal of Australia,* 1969, *2,* 237–239.

McTaggert, A., & Scott, M. A review of twelve cases of encopresis. *Jornal of Pediatrics,* 1959, *54,* 762–768.

Mikkelsen, E. J., Rapoport, J. L., Nee, L., Gruenau, C., Mendelsen, W., & Gillin, C. Childhood enuresis: I. Sleep patterns and psychopathology. *Archives of General Psychiatry,* 1980, *37,* 1139–1144.

Mower, O. G., & Mower, W. M. Enuresis—A method of its study and treatment. *American Journal of Orthopsychiatry,* 1938, *8,* 436–459.

Muellner, S. R. Development of urinary control in children: A new concept in cause prevention and treatment of primary enuresis. *Journal of Urology,* 1960, *84,* 714–716. (a)

Muellner, S. R. Development of urinary control in children. *Journal of the American Medical Association,* 1960, *172,* 1256–1261. (b)

Neale, D. H. Behavior therapy and encopresis in children. *Behaviour Research and Therapy,* 1963, *1,* 139–149.

Nergardh, A., von Hedenberg, C., Hellstrom, B., & Ericsson, N. Continence training of children with neurogenic bladder dysfunction. *Developmental Medicine and Child Neurology,* 1974, *16,* 47–52.

Newson, J., & Newson, E. *Four-year-old in the urban community.* London: Allen & Unwin, 1968.

Nisley, D. D. Medical overview of the management of encopresis. *Journal of Pediatric Psychology,* 1976, *4,* 33–34.

Novick, J. Symptomatic treatment of acquired and persistent enuresis. *Journal of Abnormal Psychology,* 1966, *71,* 363–368.

Oppel, W. C., Harper, P. A., & Rider, R. V. The age of attaining bladder control. *Pediatrics,* 1968, *42,* 614-626.

Paschalis, A. P., Kimmel, H. D., & Kimmel, E. Further study of diurnal instrumental conditioning in the treatment of enuresis nocturna. *Journal of Behavior Therapy and Experimental Psychiatry,* 1972, *3,* 253-256.

Pedrini, B. C., & Pedrini, D. T. Reinforcement procedures in the control of encopresis: A case study. *Psychological Reports,* 1971, *28,* 937-938.

Perlmutter, A. D. Enuresis. In R. Kelalis (Ed.), *Clinical pediatric urology.* Philadelphia: Saunders, 1976.

Pierce, C. M. Enuresis. In A. M. Freedman & H. I. Kaplan (Eds.), *The Child: His psychological and cultural development; Volume I.* New York: Atheneum, 1972.

Pierce, C. M. Enuresis and encopresis. In A. M. Friedman, H. I. Kaplan, & B. J. Sadock (Eds.), *Comprehensive textbook of psychiatry, II.* Baltimore: Williams & Wilkins, 1975.

Pinkerton, P. Psychogenic megacolon in children: The implications of bowel negativism. *Archives of Diseases in Childhood,* 1958, *33,* 371-380.

Plachetta, K. E. Encopresis: A case study utilizing contracting, scheduling and self-charting. *Journal of Behavior Therapy and Experimental Psychiatry,* 1974, *7,* 195-196.

Raeburn, J. M., Gemming, J. S., Lowe, B., & Dowrick, P. W. *The Kimmel and Kimmel technique for treating nocturnal enuresis: Two controlled studies.* Unpublished manuscript, University Of Auckland Medical School, Auckland, New Zealand, 1977.

Ravitch, M. M. Pseudo Hirschsprung's disease. *Annals of Surgery,* 1958, *148,* 781-795.

Ritvo, E. R., Ornitz, E. M., Gottlieb, F., Poussaint, A. F., Maron, B. J., Ditman, K. S., & Blinn, K. A. Arousal and nonarousal enuretic events. *American Journal of Psychiatry,* 1969, *126,* 115-122.

Rutter, M. Indication for research. In I. Kolvin, E. C. MacKeith, & S. R. Meadow (Eds.), *Bladder control and enuresis.* Philadelphia: Lippincott, 1973.

Rutter, M., Tizard, J., & Whitmore, K. (Eds.). *Education, health and behavior.* London: Longman, 1970.

Schaefer, C. R. *Childhood encopresis and enuresis: Causes and therapy.* New York: Van Nostrand Reinhold, 1979.

Schneider, R. D., & Westendorf, K. Adjuvant bladder pressure biofeedback in treating neurogenic bladder dysfunction: A case report. *The Behavior Therapist,* 1979, *2,* 29-31.

Seiger, H. W. Treatment of essential nocturnal enuresis. *Journal of Pediatrics,* 1952, *49,* 738-749.

Shaffer, D. Enuresis. In M. Rutter & L. Hersov (Eds.), *Child psychiatry: Modern approaches.* Philadelphia: Blackwell Scientific Publications, 1977.

Silber, D. L. Encopresis: Discussion of eitology and management. *Clinical Pediatrics,* 1969, *8,* 225-231.

Smith, E. D. Diagnosis and management of the child with setting. *Australian Paediatric Journal,* 1967, *3,* 193-205.

Smith, L. J. Training severely and profoundly mentally handicapped nocturnal enuretics. *Behaviour Research and Therapy.* 1981, *19,* 67-74.

Sperling, M. Dynamic considerations and treatment of enuresis. *Journal of the American Academy of Child Psychiatry,* 1965, *4,* 19-31.

Stansfeld, J. M. Enuresis and urinary tract infection. In I. Kolvin, R. C. MacKeith, & S. R. Meadow (Eds.), *Bladder control and enuresis.* Philadelphia: Lippincott, 1973.

Starfield, B. Functional bladder capacity in enuretic and nonenuretic children. *Journal of Pediatrics,* 1967, *70,* 777-781.

Starfield, B., & Mellits, E. D. Increase in functional bladder capacity and improvements in enuresis. *Journal of Pediatrics,* 1968, *72,* 483-487.

Steing, Z. A., & Susser, M.. The social dimensions of a symtom: A social-medical study of enuresis. *Social Science and Medicine,* 1967, *1,* 183-201.

Stewart, M. A. Treatment of bedwetting. *Journal of the American Medical Association,* 1975, *232,* 281-283.

Taylor, P. D., & Turner, R. K. A clinical trial of continuous, intermittent and overlearning "bell and pad" treatments for nocturnal enuresis. *Behaviour Research and Therapy,* 1975, *13,* 281-293.

Turner, R. K. Conditioning treatment of nocturnal enuresis: Present status. In I. Kolvin, R. C. MacKeith, & S. R. Meadow (Eds.), *Bladder control and enuresis.* Philadelphia: Lippincott, 1973.

Turner, R. K., Young, G. C., & Rachman, S. Treatment of nocturnal enuresis by conditioning techniques. *Behaviour Research and Therapy,* 1970, *8,* 368-381.

Van Wagenen, R. K., & Murdock, E. E. A transistorized signal package for the toilet training of infants. *Journal of Experimental Child Psychology,* 1966, *3,* 312-314.

Walker, C. E. Toilet training, enuresis, encopresis. In P. R. Magrad (Ed.), *Psychological management of pediatric problems* (Vol. 1). Baltimore: University Park Press, 1978.

Watson, L. S. Application of behavior shaping devices to training severely and profoundly mentally retarded children in an insitutional setting. *Mental Retardation,* 1968, *6,* 21–23.

Wear, J. B., Wear, R. B., & Cleeland, C. Biofeedback in urology using urodynamics: Preliminary observations. *Journal of Urology,* 1979, *119,* 464–468.

Werry, J. S., Enuresis—A psychosomatic entity? *Canadian Medical Association Journal,* 1967 *97,* 319–327.

Werry, J. S., & Cohrssen, J. Enuresis: An etiologic and therapeutic study. *Journal of Pediatrics,* 1965, *67,* 423–431.

White, M. A thousand consecutive cases of enuresis: Results of treatment. *The Medical Officer,* 1968, *120,* 151–155.

Williams, C. L., Doleys, D. M., & Ciminero, A. R. A two-year follow-up of enuretic children treated with dry bed training. *Journal of Behavior Therapy and Experimental Psychiatry,* 1978, *9,* 285–286.

Wolters, S. Encopresis. *Psychotherapy and Psychosomatics,* 1971, *19,* 266–287.

Wolters, W. H. G. *Kinderin mit encopresia, een psychosomatische benadering.* Utrecht: Elinhivyk, 1974. (a)

Wolters, W. H. G. A comparative study of behavioral aspects in encopretic children. *Psychotherapy and psychosomatics,* 1974, *24,* 86–79. (b)

Woodmansey, A. C. Wetting and soiling. *British Medical Journal,* 1972, *3,* 161–163.

Wright, L. Handling the encopretic child. *Professional Psychology,* 1973, *4,* 137–144.

Wright, L. Outcome of a standardized program for treating psychogenic encopresis. *Professional Psychology,* 1975, *6,* 453–456.

Wright, L. Psychogenic encopresis. *Ross Timesaver: Feelings and their Medical Significance,* 1978, *20,* 11–16.

Wright, L., & Walker, C. E. Behavioral treatment of encopresis. *Journal of Pediatric Psychology,* 1976, *4,* 35–37.

Yates, A. J. *Behaviour therapy.* New York: Wiley, 1970.

Young, G. C. The aetiology of enuresis in terms of learning theory. *The Medical Officer,* January 1965, pp. 19–23. (a)

Young, G. C. Conditioning treatment of enuresis. *Developmental Medicine and Child Neurology,* 1965, *7,* 557–562. (b)

Young, G. C. The treatment of childhood encopresis by conditioned gastroileal reflex training. *Behaviour Research and Therapy,* 1973, *2,* 499–503.

Young, G. C., & Morgan, R. T. T. Overlearning in the conditioning treatment of enuresis. *Behaviour Research and Therapy,* 1972, *10,* 419–420.

Young, I. L., & Goldsmith, A. D. Treatment of encopresis in a day treatment program. *Psychotherapy; Theory, Research and Practice,* 1972, *9,* 231–235.

Zaleski, A., Shokeir, M. K. K., & Gerrard, J. W. Enuresis: Familial incidence and relationship to allergic disorders. *Canadian Medical Association Journal,* 1972, 106, 30–31.

Zaleski, A., Gerrard, J. W., & Shokeir, M. H. K. Nocturnal enuresis: The importance of a small bladder capacity. In I. Kolvin, R. C. MacKeith, & S. R. Meadow (Eds.), *Bladder control and enuresis.* Philadelphia: Saunders, 1973.

9

Stereotypic Behaviors, Stuttering, and Elective Mutism

DUANE G. OLLENDICK AND JOHNNY L. MATSON

Introduction

The present chapter focuses upon three variances of childhood psychopathology: stereotypic behaviors, stuttering, and elective mutism. Separately, these behaviors are observed in children on a relatively infrequent basis, yet they are particularly problematic and refractory to change. Stereotypic behaviors usually develop during middle childhood years, while the two language disorders commonly occur in preschool or early school years. Within the realm of specific behavioral disorders, all three are representative of the more general category of childhood habit disorders. Stereotypic behaviors are more comprehensively reviewed in this chapter, while stuttering and elective mutism are more briefly examined.

Stereotypic Behaviors

According to the Diagnostic and Statistical Manual of the American Psychiatric Association (1980), a variety of stereotypic behaviors exist: transient and chronic motor tic disorders, Tourette's Disorder, atypical tic disorders, and atypical stereotyped movement disorders. In the first section of this chapter, issues related to the definition, incidence, assessment, and etiology of transient and chronic motor tic disorders and Tourette's Disorder will be illustrated and specifically addressed.

DUANE G. OLLENDICK • Department of Psychology, Zumbro Valley Mental Health Center, Rochester, Minnesota 55901. JOHNNY L. MATSON • Department of Learning and Development, Northern Illinois University, DeKalb, Illinois 60115.

Introduction

Tics are observed in diverse forms such as jerking of the head, twitching of the eyes, coughing, arm or shoulder jerking, nasal wheezing, facial grimaces, and rapid eye blinking. As Yates (1970) noted in his review of the literature, professional interest in tics has fluctuated markedly since their identification in the 19th century. Currently, an extensive literature is available, and various aspects of tic behavior have been examined.

An early description of tics provided by Meige and Feindel (1907) illustrates how tics were originally viewed:

> A tic is a coordinated purposive act, provoked in the first instance by some external cause or by an idea; repetition lends to its becoming habitual and finally to its involuntary reproduction without cause and for no purpose, at the same time as its form, intensity and frequency are exaggerated; it thus assumes the character of a convulsive movement, inopportune and excessive; its execution is often preceded by an irresistible impulse, its suppression associated with malaise. The effect of distraction or of volitional effort is to diminish its activity; in sleep it disappears. It occurs in predisposed individuals who usually show other indications of mental instability. (pp. 260–261)

Although this early definition of Meige and Feindel lacked clarity and comprehensiveness, it served as the basis for subsequent descriptions of tic behavior. As will be seen shortly (see "Assessment"), later clarifications have permitted greater differential diagnosis from other motor movement disorders, many of which possess similar characteristics to tics.

A variety of definitions have been put forth. Most simply, a tic can be defined as "any spasmodic movement or twitching" (*Dorland's Medical Dictionary,* 1965, p. 1583). The American Psychiatric Association defined a tic as "an intermittent, involuntary, spasmodic movement of a group of muscles, often without a demonstratable external stimulus. A tic may be an expression of an emotional conflict or the result of *neurologic* disease" (1975, p. 148). More recently, tics have been differentiated from stereotyped motor behaviors thought to have neurologic or organic bases. For example, Duffy (1974) has indicated that "tics are spasms characterized by sudden involuntary and repetitious movements of circumscribed muscle groups, not explainable on an organic basis" (p. 96); while Azrin and Nunn (1977) have noted that "a nervous tic is a compulsive and persistent muscle movement that is not organic in origin" (p. 17). Further, the American Psychiatric Association's *Diagnostic and Statistical Manual of Mental Disorders* (1980) differentiated among stereotyped movement disorders that are organically based and those that are environmentally determined.

Incidence

Little research is available on the incidence of different types of tics. In an early study, however, Paterson (1945) reported an incidence of 1% among psychiatric admissions and .02% among general hospital admissions for one type of tic, spasmodic torticollis. Similarly, Bakwin and Bakwin (1972) did not report overall incidence figures, but indicated that the "incidence is greater in boys than in girls (3:1) and in Jewish than in other children" (p. 315). In the absence of survey data, Azrin and Nunn (1977) estimated a "conservative approximation" of the incidence of tics to be about 1% in the general population. This would indicate that well over one million children exhibit tics.

At least two investigations have reported that transient tics are common in children (LaPouse & Monk, 1964; Torup, 1972). These studies reported an incidence rate of 12–

16% among children, a rate significantly higher than the general population estimate provided by Azrin and Nunn (1977). Wilson, Garron, and Klawans (1978) reviewed incidence rates of transient tics reported by a number of investigators (Boncour, 1910; Kanner, 1957; Kellmer-Pringle, Butler, & Davie, 1967; LaPouse & Monk, 1958; Standardized Micro-Data Tape Transcripts, 1976) and found estimates to range from 3% to over 20%. In one of these studies (*Standardized Micro-Data Tape Transcripts,* 1976), it was found that 4.1% of 7,091 noninstitutionalized children seen on physical examination exhibited tics or ticlike mannerisms. The children represented a United States probability sample of the National Health Examination Survey from 1963 through 1965.

An interesting area of increasing investigation involves familial incidences. For example, LaPouse and Monk (1964) found that 38% of children with transient tics have parents who also have tics. In addition, there have been an increasing number of investigations into the familial incidence of Tourette's syndrome (e.g., Dunlap, 1960; Eisenberg, Ascher, & Kanner, 1959; Friel, 1973; Frost, Freighner, & Schuckit, 1976; Lucas, 1973; Sanders, 1973). For example, Wilson *et al.* (1978) reported that 30% of children with either Tourette's syndrome or transient tics had a positive family history of tics. Further, Golden (1978) investigated a sample of Tourette children and reported that 31% of the families had another member with Tourette's syndrome and 21% of the families had another member with chronic multiple tics.

Assessment

Onset

The age of onset of tics is highly variable, although Bakwin and Bakwin (1972) reported the most frequent onset to be between 8 and 12 years of age. Duffy (1974) noted that tics were more commonly observed in children than in adults, and that they were "seldom observed in mentally deficient children or children under 5 years of age" (p. 96). Bakwin and Bakwin noted that tics were rare below age 6, with the exception of transient eye blinking, which they indicated was common in preschool children. While the onset of tics may be more prevalent in middle-age children, there are several well documented cases of onset occurring during adulthood (e.g., Barrett, 1962; Beck & Fedoravicius, 1977; O'Brien & Brennan, 1979). With Tourette's syndrome, most authors agree the onset is during childhood. Bakwin and Bakwin (1972) have stated that onset is before the age of 10, with initial symptoms being similar to motor tics. Shapiro, Shapiro, and Wayne (1973) utilized age at onset between 2 and 15 as one of their four diagnostic criteria for Tourette's syndrome. Similarly, Friedman (1980) reported a mean age of onset of 7 years, with a range of 2 to 14 years.

As noted in Meige and Feindel's (1907) original definition, tics have been viewed as "provoked in the first instance of some external cause." Bakwin and Bakwin (1972) found that a background of emotional tenseness was a common feature of children with tics. A sudden occurrence of serious home conflicts was seen as the most frequent precipitating factor; however, these authors were unable to confirm a demonstrable cause in about one-third of their cases. These findings are in agreement with those of Azrin and Nunn (1973), who viewed tics as nervous habits originating as reactions to physical injury or psychological trauma *or* starting as infrequent but normal behaviors that increase in frequency and become altered in their form (in which case there may be no "known" cause). Examples of specific psychological trauma include death of a parent (O'Brien & Brennan, 1979), employment stress (Beck & Fedoravicius, 1977), military stress (Barrett, 1962), and family illness (Ollendick, 1981). Additional onset factors and causes will be discussed in the next section regarding differential diagnosis of tics.

Differential Diagnosis

Because of potential implications for treatment, it is important to differentiate between tics that are "psychogenic" in origin and other stereotyped motor movements that resemble tics but are "neurogenic" in origin. Yates (1970) noted that ticlike movements occur in many organic conditions involving brain injury or physiologic malfunction. Bakwin and Bakwin (1972) specifically discussed how movements closely resembling those of psychogenic tics were frequently observed in chronic stages of encephalitis.

Yates (1970) reported that the principal *organic* conditions with which tics are confused are spasms, choreas, and cerebellar and cerebello-rubrospinal tremors. He further explicated the primary differentiating features, including whether the ticklike movement is subject to voluntary control, whether the motor behavior is painful, whether it occurs during sleep activity, and whether muscle atrophy is present. In addition to Yate's review, Nunn (1978) added that the "neurologically based movements and sounds also demonstrate a different clinical course and age of onset, and are often associated with specific signs of metabolic and brain dysfunction" (p. 350).

The principal *functional* conditions from which tics must be differentiated are stereotyped acts (e.g., rhythmic rocking) and psychiatric conditions such as compulsions and phobias that often involve repetitive sequences of behavior. Phobias and compulsions usually involve much more extensive and complex sequences of behavior than tics (Yates, 1970).

Tics range from jerking of the shoulders or jerking of the head to the side, to blinking of the eyes or twitching or squinting the eyes, to hand trembling. Tics can also be classified as to whether they are clonic or tonic. In the clonic type, movement is abrupt and short-lived; in the contrasting tonic type, movement is long-lasting and more or less continuous. As Yates has pointed out, most attempts to classify tics into various categories have been of little value. From both a theoretical and treatment viewpoint, however, the most important factor about a tic may be its degree of complexity, which will determine in part the degree to which an individual can accurately reproduce the movement on a voluntary basis (Yates, 1970).

Perhaps the most concern in the area of differential diagnosis is in contrasting the very rare condition of Gilles de la Tourette's syndrome and that of psychogenic tics. In the psychological and medical literature, there is an abundance of discussion, debate, and disagreement regarding the psychogenic or neurogenic basis of this syndrome, originally described by Gilles de la Tourette in 1885. Since the early work of Ascher (1948) and Mahler (1949), Tourette's syndrome has been comprehensively reviewed by Kelman (1965), Fernando (1967, 1968), and others. While Yates (1970) recognized the debate regarding etiology, he stated that Tourette's syndrome could be differentiated from other complex tics by the accompaniment of coprolalia (compulsive obscene utterances), of echolalia (repetition of other persons' words and phrases), and, more rarely, of echokinesis (repetition of other persons' actions). The involuntary utterance of words or noises is the one differentiating factor that is stressed most often and, in fact, is one of the diagnostic criteria used for this syndrome (Shapiro *et al.,* 1973). Goggin and Erickson (1979) state that, prior to 1960, Tourette's syndrome was considered psychogenic because "there was an absence of any objective or definitive pattern that indicated an organic mechanism was operative" (p. 340). However, since that time, evidence has mounted to suggest that Tourette's syndrome has a neurogenic basis. In addition to the familial patterns noted earlier, which suggest a genetic predisposition, other authors have noted effects of Haloperidol therapy (Connell, Corbett, Horne, & Mathews, 1967; Eldridge, Sweet, Lake, Ziegler, & Shapiro, 1977; Ford & Gottlieb, 1969; Healy, 1970; Maldofsky, Tullis, & Lamon, 1974; Stevens & Blackly, 1966), prevalence of "soft" neurological signs (Shapiro, Shapiro, & Clarkin, 1974; Sweet, Solomon, Wayne, Shapiro, & Shapiro, 1973), and increased prevalence of abnormal electroencephalograms (Shapiro, Shapiro, Bruun, & Sweet, 1978; Sweet *et al.*, 1973; Wayne, Shapiro, & Shapiro, 1972). Recently, even in the presence of this mounting evidence, at least one author has questioned this distinction and has suggested that "chronic multiple tics and Tourette syndrome represent different positions on the same continuum and are not distinct conditions" (Golden, 1978, pp. 147–148). However, the majority of evidence supports a view of Tourette's syndrome as being a separate entity distinct from tics. From a diagnostic viewpoint, differential diagnosis remains an important issue because of potential treatment implications.

Final discussion of differential diagnosis is directed to the nomenclature of the *Diagnostic and Statistical Manual of Mental Disorders* (American Psychiatric Association, 1980). Under the general category of Stereotyped Movement Disorders, specific categories including Transient Tic Disorder (307.21), Chronic Motor Tic Disorder (307.22), Tourette's Disorder (307.23), Atypical Tic Disorder (307.20), and Atypical Stereotyped Movement Disorder (307.30) are listed. The diagnostic criteria for Transient Tic Disorder include: (1) onset during childhood; (2) presence of recurrent, involuntary, repetitive, rapid, purposeless motor movements; (3) ability to suppress the movements voluntarily for minutes to hours; (4) variation in intensity of symptoms over weeks or months; and (5) duration of at least 1 month but not more than 1 year. The Chronic Motor Tic Disorder is differentially diagnosed by differences in duration (at least 1 year), unvarying intensity of the tics, and limitation of the tics involving no more than three muscle groups at any one time. Tourette's Disorder diagnostic criteria are different in that: (1) age at onset is specified between 2 and 15 years; (2) presence of motor movements affecting multiple muscle groups are evident; (3) multiple vocal tics are evident; (4) intensity of symptoms vary (as with the transient tic); and (5) duration is more than 1 year (as in the chronic motor tic). The presence of "multiple vocal tics" appears to be the distinguishing characteristic. Finally, the Atypical Tic Disorder is used to classify tics that do not meet the criteria of previous categories, and the Atypical Stereotyped Movement Disorder is reserved for conditions such as head banging, rocking, and repetitive hand movements, which are distinct from tics in that they cue voluntary movements and not spasmodic ones.

Assessment Techniques

Initially, behavioral observation can be used as a basic assessment tool. Yates (1970) makes specific mention of the "time-sampling" technique in which an individual is observed for a standard period of time, during which movements of a prespecified type are recorded. Observations, via a time-sampling procedure, can be done by an individual in the tiqueur's environment (e.g., parent, spouse, teacher). Reliable use of this approach has been reported across a variety of age groups, situations, and tic disorders (Yates, 1970). In addition, the use of self-monitoring is increasingly being used as an assessment technique. With self-monitoring, an individual is required to self-record his/her own tic behavior. This procedure has the advantage of increasing an individual's awareness of tic behavior and, perhaps more importantly, has been shown to alter the frequency of the tic in a therapeutic direction (Maletzky, 1974; Ollendick, 1981; Thomas, Abrams, & Johnson, 1971).

In the overall assessment of tics, other variables need to be considered as well. As mentioned previously, family history should be examined. A current medical (including neurological) examination is recommended to aid differential diagnosis from, for example, Tourette's syndrome. While coprolalia is seen as a primary difference, the medical examination may reveal "soft" neurological signs or an abnormal electroencephalogram, which may aid in total assessment. Finally, some authors (Crown, 1953; Goggin & Erickson, 1979) have suggested an assessment of personality function to help determine whether tics are a primary behavior problem or are perhaps secondary to other psychic conflicts that may also require attention and treatment along with that of the tic behavior.

Etiological Considerations

Psychoanalytic Viewpoint

Different theoretical accounts regarding the etiology and development of tics have been proposed, each of which has served as the basis for differential treatment. The first viewpoint, and perhaps the earliest, is that espoused by psychoanalytic theorists.

While Ferenczi (1921), theorized that tics represented the fixation of libido on single organs, he also postulated that a tic might arise as the result of a traumatic event. He explained that

> an unexpectedly powerful trauma can have the result in tic, as in traumatic neurosis, of an overstrong memory fixation on the attitude of the body at the moment of experience of the trauma, and that to such a degree as to provoke a perpetual or paroxysmatic reproduction of the attitude. (p. 13)

Later theorists provided additional interpretations based on the psychoanalytic viewpoint. Fenichel (1945), for example, considered the mechanism underlying Tourette's syndrome to be "conversion." He theorized that tics represented displacement of sexual and hostile impulses in an individual whose personality structure was fixated at the pregenital level of development. Similarly, Mahler and Rangell (1943) proposed that a tic was the overt manifestation of conflict between gratification of, and defense against, instinctual impulses; and later, Mahler and Luke (1946) considered tics as "erotic and aggressive impulses . . . which are continually escaping through pathological discharge" (p. 441). Other early psychoanalytic studies of tics have been described by Levy-Suhl (1937), Mahler (1944), and Gerard (1946), and reviewed by Weisman (1952). The psychoanalytic viewpoint on etiology of tics continues to receive at least minimal attention, and one recent study (e.g., Morphew & Sim, 1969) speculated that the origin of tics was due to conflicts at the anal level of development. Morphew and Sim (1969), specifically addressing the development of Tourette's syndrome, suggested that this syndrome is distinct from more general tics even from a psychodynamic viewpoint.

Perhaps what has led to the decline of psychoanalysis as a major or prominent theory of etiology has been the minimal success attained by analytically-based treatment methods. In most cases, analytic treatment consists of providing psychotherapy that "shows" the patient that his/her instinctual inpulses are the causes of the patient's problem (i.e., giving insight and teaching him/her to channel these impulses more contructively). As late as 1969, Eriksson and Persson (1969) concluded that "some patients become permanently disabled and resistant to every form of treatment" (p. 351). Other authors have also reported limited success with traditional psychotherapy. For example, Patterson and Little (1943) reported that 73% of torticollis (contraction of the neck muscles) patients were not "appreciably improved"; Paterson (1945) found traditional psychotherapy effective in only 25% of transient and chronic tic cases, and Garnett and Elbirlik (1953) found that only 33% of torticollis patients improved with psychotherapy. Finally, in a study of Tourette patients, Mahler and Luke (1946) found that 40% were only very slightly or not at all improved. Unfortunately, as is seen by a review of the literature, there are no reports on the overall efficacy of psychoanalytic treatment across the range of tic behaviors. However, limited case-study supports exists for use of analytically-oriented psychotherapy in treating multiple tics (e.g., Tiller, 1978).

Learning-Based Viewpoints

Since the early description by Meige and Feindel (1907) of tics as learned habits, learning-based theories have been employed frequently to account for the genesis and maintenance of tics. Yates (1970) delineates two learning-based models derived from general experimental psychology: The first is a *respondent* model based largely on the work of Hull (1943); the second is an *operant* model based on the work of Skinner (1938). While etiological considerations emanating from these models will be discussed separately, it is important to stress that both models regard tics as learned responses.

Respondent Model. Yates (1958) hypothesized that tics may be drive-reducing, conditioned avoidance responses, originally evoked in highly traumatic situations. He stated:

> In this situation, intense fear is aroused and a movement of withdrawal or aggression is made. If the movement produces or coincides with the cessation of the fear-inducing stimulus, it acquires strength through reinforcement. On subsequent occasions, through stimulus-generalization (including internal symbolization), conditioned fear ("anxiety") may be aroused, which is then reduced by the performance of the movement. In this way, the tic comes to be elicited by a large variety of stimulus and eventually achieves the status of a power habit. (p. 175)

It is noted that Yates's model closely parallels the two-factor theory of learning expounded by Mowrer (1950). Yates further explained:

> In terms of Hullian learning theory, the reaction potential of a tic at a given moment may be conceived as a multiplicative function of the habit strength ($s^{H}r$) of the tic (determined mainly by the number of times it has previously been evoked) and the momentary drive strength of anxiety (D), which fluctuates from time to time. Since habit strength increases as a simple negatively accelerated positive growth function and eventually reaches an asymptote, further performance of the tic cannot increase its habit strength beyond a given point. (p. 176)

In terms of this theory, a tic is viewed as a learned habit that has attained maximum habit strength. Therefore, it should be possbile to extinguish the habit by building a negative or incompatible habit of not performing the tic. To further summarize Yates's theory, if an individual is given massed practice in the tic, reactive inhibition should build rapidly. When inhibition reaches a critical point, the person will be forced to "rest" or not perform the tic. This habit of not performing the tic will be associated with drive-reduction due to dissipation of reactive inhibition, and hence will be reinforced. With repeated massed practice, therefore, a negative habit ("not doing the tic") will be built up, incompatible with the positive habit of performing the tic. Furthermore, repeated voluntary evocation of the tic should not serve to increase habit strength of the tic because it is already asymptotic and consequently not subject to strengthening by massed practice.

Treatment procedures based on this theory have generally proven effective in the elimination of tics, although a few authors have not reported success. In perhaps the earliest investigation, Dunlap (1932) reported that tics could be eliminated by having a subject repeat them "voluntarily and deliberately." Unfortunately, Dunlap provided few details of his negative practice procedure and no experimental demonstration of its empirical validity. Yates (1958) reported that the optimum condition for the growth of the negative habit ("not doing the tic") appeared to be a combination of very prolonged massed practice followed by prolonged rest. Yates (1958), and Jones (1960), who later worked with the same patient, have reported moderate success, although generalization to "real life" remained incomplete.

Successful use of massed practice was also reported by Rafi (1962), who found a significant decrease in frequency of a head jerk and facial grimace tic in one patient. Other tics that have responded to massed practice include eyebrow raising (Browning & Stover, 1971), eyeblinking (Costello, 1963; Frederick, 1971; Knepler & Sewall, 1974), mouth grimacing (Chapel, 1970; Lazarus, 1960), head jerking (Agras & Marshall, 1965; Turner, Hersen, & Alford, 1974), and, even in some cases, Tourette's syndrome (Clark, 1966; Savicki & Carlin, 1972; Tophoff, 1973). In at least two studies, supportive evidence has not been obtained. Feldman and Werry (1966) found that massed practice actually increased the frequency of tic behavior in a 13-year-old boy with multiple tics, while Hollandsworth and Bausinger (1978) obtained negligible results with an 18-year-old female with Tourette's syndrome. Feldman and Werry theorized that an increase in drive-level, produced by stress in the experimental condition, rose faster than reactive inhibition and actually served to increase frequency of tic behavior; and, Hollandsworth and Bausinger felt that perhaps "massed practice was not given a fair trial." It appears that more well controlled studies need to be completed on "optimal conditions" before routine use of massed practice can be fully endorsed.

O'Brien and Brennan (1979) classify two other treatment techniques under the respondent model: Wolpe's (1958) systematic desensitization (Thomas *et al.,* 1971) and drug-induced anxiety reduction (Connell *et al.,* 1967). Systematic desensitization has been used in conjunction with other behavioral treatments (Meares, 1973; O'Brien & Brennan, 1979) and Walton (1961, 1964) has examined the utility of employing drug-induced anxiety reduction along with massed practice.

Operant Model. The second model to be considered under learning-based viewpoints asserts that tics are learned responses that are maintained by contingent reinforcers. While Yates (1970) stated that a precise model using operant principles has yet to be worked out, he reported that "the contingencies which movements produce, either in the external environment or within the organism via internal feedback systems, are reinforcing and, therefore, strengthen and maintain the behavior" (p. 197). Discussions regarding the genesis of tics utilizing this model are notably lacking, although a great variety of operant techniques have been used in treatment. Azrin and Nunn (1973) summarized the goal of treatment in this model: "arrange for aversive stimuli for the response in order to counteract the effect of these reinforcers" (p. 619).

To this end, Barrett (1962), using white noise as an aversive stimulus, clearly demonstrated that operant schedules of reinforcement significantly affected output of involuntary tic movements. Rafi (1962) used a buzzer to reduce evocation of foot tapping; Brierley

(1967) successfully used shock for treatment of spasmodic torticollis; and Knepler and Sewall (1974) used smelling salts to reduce tics.

More recently, treatment attempts have been aimed at eliminating or at least minimizing the use of aversive stimuli, while still employing operant principles. Azrin and Nunn (1973) developed a habit-reversal method of treating tics whereby the client practices "a behavioral pattern opposite to that of the problem behavior" (p. 623). Others have used this method either alone or in conjunction with other components, and achieved success (Azrin & Nunn, 1977; Azrin, Nunn, & Frantz, 1980; Beck & Fedoravicius, 1977; O'Brien & Brennan, 1979; Ollendick, 1981). Still other investigators have employed parents to administer operant reinforcers (Cohen, & Marks, 1977; Schulman, 1974), have used relaxation training (Azrin & Nunn, 1977; Beck & Fedoravicius, 1977; O'Brien & Brennan, 1979), and have used self-monitoring techniques (Friedman, 1980; Hutzell, Platzek, & Logue, 1974; Maletzky, 1974; Ollendick, 1981; Thomas *et al.,* 1971).

Medical Viewpoint

Discussion of the genetic/neurological viewpoint concerning etiology will be brief, as these considerations are directed primarily at the development of Tourette's syndrome. Since, however, Tourette's syndrome is frequently confused with other tic disorders, the discussion is warranted. Genetic and neurological components will be discussed separately, although both emanate from the medical viewpoint and are commonly discussed together.

Genetic. The primary support for Tourette's syndrome as a genetically based disease comes from family incidence reports (Dunlap, 1960; Eisenberg *et al.,* 1959; Friel, 1973; Frost *et al.,* 1976; Lucas, 1973; Sanders, 1973). It is hypothesized that Tourette's syndrome develops because of a genetic predisposition, transmitted like other genetically based disorders such as Huntington's disease. This hypothesis is based on four observations: (1) studies of familial aggregation (Eldridge *et al.,* 1977; Feild, Corbin, Goldstein, & Klass, 1966; Fernando, 1967; Friel, 1973; Golden, 1977a, b, 1978; Maldofsky *et al.,* 1974; Sanders, 1973; Shapiro *et al.,* 1978; Shapiro, Shapiro, & Wayne, 1972; Van Woert, Jutkowitz, Rosenbaum, & Bowers, 1976; Wassman, Eldridge, Abuzzanhab, & Nee, 1978); (2) predominance of males afflicted by Tourette's syndrome (Shapiro *et al.,* 1978); (3) increased prevalance among blacks (Eldridge *et al.,* 1977; Golden, 1977b; Mahler, Luke, & Daltroff, 1945; Shapiro *et al.,* 1978; Wassman *et al.,* 1978); and (4) apparent similarities to the Lesch-Nyhan syndrome, an X-linked recessive disorder (Moldofsky *et al.,* 1974; Van Woert *et al.,* 1976).

In evaluating these observations, Wilson *et al.* (1978) note that, although multiple studies have revealed ethnic differences, sampling bias and differences in reporting of Tourette symptoms exist in these studies. Further, they report that Johnson, Pepple, Singer, and Littlefield (1977) failed to identify a similar metabolic abnormality between the Lesch-Nyhan syndrome and Tourette's syndrome, and that the "significance of the predominance of males among the afflicted is also uncertain" (p. 505). Hence, support for the genetic hypothesis, based on these indicators, is not overwhelming. However, Wilson *et al.* (1978) note that the most consistent support of a genetic hypothesis may be found in the familial aggregation studies: "The mere fact of familial aggregation might suggest some genetic influence, and the pattern of aggregation might suggest the mode of transmission" (p. 505). As will be seen in the following section, the "mode of transmission" receiving most attention involves the neurological system.

Neurological. Research has accumulated suggesting that ticlike symptoms of Tourette's syndrome result from "metabolic disturbance which causes enzyme or neurotransmitter dysfunction of the central nervous system" (Yates, 1970, p. 202). More recently, Goggin and Erickson (1979), in their discussion of Tourette's syndrome, outrightly state that "Gilles de la Tourette syndrome (TS) is a neurological disorder" (p. 339). Indeed, much research has shown how uniquely efficacious Haloperidol therapy has been in the treatment of Tourette's syndrome (Bruun, Shapiro, Shapiro, Sweet, Wayne, & Solomon, 1976; Challas & Brauer, 1963; Chapel, Brown, & Jenkins, 1964; Connel, Corbett, Horne, & Matthews, 1967; Klawans, Falk, Nausieda, & Weiner, 1978; Lucas, 1967; Pollack, Cohen, & Friedhoff, 1977; Shapiro & Shapiro, 1968; Stevens & Blachly, 1966). Perhaps some of the strongest evidence supporting the neurological basis comes from a study completed by Stevens and Blachly (1966). Although these authors were able to produce reduction of ticlike behaviors in an experimental situation using operant conditioning techniques, they were unable to obtain full control until Haloperidol was employed. Furthermore, when a placebo was administered, the symptoms quickly returned. In addition to "dysfunction of the central nervous system," further neurological evidence is provided by the prevalence of "soft" signs on neurological examination (Shapiro *et al.*, 1974; Sweet, Bruun, Shapiro, & Shapiro, 1976) and abnormal electroencephalograms (Shapiro *et al.,* 1978; Sweet *et al.,* 1976; Wayne *et al.,* 1972).

Wilson *et al.,* (1978) further speculate that Tourette's syndrome may be similar both on a clinical and biochemical basis to the heterogeneous Parkinson syndrome. These authors indicate that the pathophysiological basis of Parkinsonian symptoms is decreased dopaminergic input to the striatum, a presynaptic defect. However, in a subset of patients, indistinguishable on clincial grounds, there is a loss of striatal responsiveness to dopamine, a postsynaptic defect. These pathophysiological differences, then, are reflected in different responses to treatment. Thus, patients with the presynaptic form of the disorder respond to levadopa, while those with the postsynaptic defect typically do not. In a similar vein, it is probable that the neurological basis of Tourette's syndrome is an important consideration, and that treatment may well hinge on appropriate subclassification of the disorder.

Summary

Careful observation of children reveals the presence of stereotyped movements; tics, in their simplest form, are but a subset of these behaviors. However, other stereotypic disorders, such as Tourette's syndrome, are more complex and refractory to change. As is evident in the present review, problems of definition, assessment, differential diagnosis, and etiology remain. However, these issues are increasingly being clarified as research is accumulated.

Issues related to treatment also remain. Novel approaches to treatment are being undertaken at this time and are meeting with success. Using the complex behavioral hypothesis alluded to by Nicassio, Lieberman, Patterson, Raminez, and Sanders (1972), O'Brien and Brennan (1979) have stressed the need for multifaceted therapy. Other authors have similarly used various components in conjunction with one another. Detailed studies evaluating these individual components, such as the one by Ollendick (1981), will be required. Also, comparative studies are necessary; for example, Azrin *et al.* (1980) compared habit reversal with negative practice and found habit reversal substantially more effective. Finally, there may well be other pharmacologic, psychotherapeutic, or learning-based techniques that may prove to be effective but have not been investigated.

Case Example

The following case example illustrates the development, possible etiology, type, duration, and final treatment of a chronic tic in an 11-year-old white male, David (Ollendick, 1981).

David exhibited excessive eye-twitching since 5 years of age. His parents reported that the eye-twitching developed when David entered kindergarten and, about the same time, his mother was hospitalized for glaucoma treatments. In the summer preceding his mother's operation and David's entry into kindergarten, his mother had recurring visual problems that resulted in numerous examinations and brief hospitalizations. David, the second of three children and described as "Mommy's boy," was highly distraught by these happenings and was placed on medication. David's eye-twitching continued over the years and began to include the mouth and cheek. The only precipitating stress identified at the time of referral was David's entry into his first year of junior high school (seventh grade). It was hypothesized by Ollendick that his entry into the new school was sufficiently similar to entry into kindergarten, resulting in an intensification of the nervous tic. Reports from his elementary school revealed that he was of average intelligence, achieved at an average level, and was well-liked by his peers.

Ollendick employed a single-subject, multiple-baseline design across settings to demonstrate functional control of the treatment procedure over the tic behaviors. Treatment consisted of baseline, self-monitoring, and self-monitoring plus competing response practice, sequentially applied in the school setting and then at the home. Twenty-minute time sampling periods were employed during the 5-day baseline period by both David's teacher and his mother. David was then instructed on the use of self-monitoring, and he was supplied with a wrist counter; further, he recorded the frequency of tics during specific time periods over the 5-day self-monitoring period. David was then instructed in competing response practice, which generally consisted of extensive practice in tensing muscles antagonistic to his tic. Following this, he continued the self-monitoring and began the competing response practice, first for just 5 days in the school setting, and then also at home. David was seen for a total of eight treatment sessions and three follow-up sessions.

It was found that David's self-monitoring was highly reliable when compared to that of his teacher (.88) and his mother (.99). The results reveal that David's tics were reduced by approximately 50% following initial self-monitoring in each subsequent setting. However, the self-monitoring alone produced no further reduction. With the use of the competing response practice, the frequency was reduced to a near-zero level, and that level was maintained for the remainder of the intervention and at 1 year follow-up.

This case study highlights several points stressed in the foregoing discussion of tics. It is seen how tics appear to have developed following a traumatic and stressful event in this child. In spite of the dissipation of the trauma and stress, the tics continued until they were again exacerbated by another stressful event. Ollendick's results indicate that children are "proficient in self-monitoring their behavior and self-administering treatment procedures" and clearly show the efficacy of learning-based treatment in a relatively short period of time. As was noted, recent literature on transient and multiple tics focuses on the use of behavioral strategies, rather than the use of traditional psychotherapy or medications for treatment. Securing the child's active involvement in treatment and providing him with effective self-control techniques appears to be one of these very promising behavioral strategies.

Stuttering

Language ability is a skill specific to humans. This behavior complex emerges in infancy, and by 5 years of age, the typical child has a vocabulary of over 2,000 words. Given rapid development of speech, it is not particularly surprising that children with speech problems usually come to the attention of professionals when they enter school. It has been observed that, along with other forms of abnormal behavior, language disorders tend to be identified 3 years after school entry (Chess & Rosenberg, 1974). The present section of this chapter focuses on one such speech problem: stuttering. Again, a brief review of definitions, incidence, assessment, etiology, and treatment are provided.

Introduction

Stuttering involves speech disruptions that are chronic and that frequently become more severe in anxiety-producing situations. Stuttering can be operationally defined as a speech disruption or dysfluency that occurs when a person is speaking. There are two specific types of dysfluencies: repetition of all or part of a phrase, and silent or vocal blocks prior to onset of a word or syllable (Resnick, Wendiggensen, Ames, & Meyer, 1978). These two general types of stuttering are readily identifiable, particularly when stuttering is severe. The evaluation of whether or not a specific dysfluency is present must be conducted in a particularly careful fashion with children to insure that the speech difficulty is the cause of disruption in articulation, rather than some other inadequacy in speech related to maturational factors.

The *Diagnostic and Statistical Manual of Mental Disorders* (1980) provides additional insight into the definition of stuttering. In this manual, it is noted that "stammering" is a synonym for stuttering and that the primary aspect of the disorder is frequent repetitions or prolongations of sounds, syllables, or words, or frequent, unusual hesitations and pauses that disrupt rhythmic flow of speech. The extent of the disturbance varies from situation to situation and is most severe when there is special pressure to communicate, such as may occur when a child is asked to recite in class. Additionally, there may be periods when stuttering is completely absent. Speech may be very rapid or exceedingly slow, and there may be an inappropriate inflection or lack of variation in pitch. In moderate to severe cases, there may be avoidance of particular words, or situations in which stuttering is anticipated. Also, it is noted that a number of behaviors may occur concomitantly with stuttering, and frequency, intensity, and number of these collateral behaviors may increase with greater severity of stuttering. Behaviors frequently noted include eye blinks, tics, tremors of the lip or jaw and/or jerking of the head (behaviors addressed in the first section of this chapter).

Stuttering is generally chronic, with periods of partial remission extending for weeks or months, and exacerbations occur most frequently when there is particular pressure to verbalize. One half of children with this disorder recover without treatment; however, improved cases tend to be those that are mild.

Incidence

Stuttering occurs more frequently in boys with estimated sex ratios ranging from 3:1 to 8:1 (Bakwin & Bakwin, 1972; Jones, 1970). Persistent stuttering is found in only 1–2% of the population, while transient stuttering appears in 4% or 5% of the population (Bakwin & Bakwin, 1972; Jones, 1970). About 50% of stutterers recover without treatment by 12 years of age, and 80% have normal speech by the time they reach their late teens (Sheehan & Marlyn, 1966, 1967).

Stuttering is extremely rare in adult females and marked cultural differences in stuttering exist. Remarkably, in underdeveloped areas of the world and among American Indians, stuttering is unknown. Intelligence also seems to be a factor in rate of stuttering and other speech difficulties. It is generally agreed that the lower the intelligence level, the greater the likelihood of speech impairment (Eisenson, 1965).

A final factor contributing to the incidence of stuttering and other speech deficiencies involves parenting skills and specific speech patterns of parents. Thus, adults with poor parenting skills and/or speech difficulties tend to have children with speech difficulties. Inappropriate verbal stimulation by parents, emotional trauma, illness, birth of siblings, parental rejection, and negative parent–child interaction patterns are additional, related factors that correlate highly with incidence of stuttering (Irwin, 1969; Mysak, 1972).

Assessment

Onset

Stuttering occurs between the ages of 2 and 5 with onset rarely occurring after 8 years of age (Johnson, 1979). It is noted in the *Diagnostic and Statistical Manual of Mental Disorders* (1980) that the disturbance starts gradually with repetitions of initial consonants, whole words at the beginning of phrases, or particularly long, complex words. As the disorder progresses, repetitions become more frequent, and stuttering occurs on the most important words or phrases. The child becomes aware of the speech difficulty, and in certain situations some words and sounds become more difficult.

Differential Diagnosis

Despite clearcut definable aspects of stuttering, it is still a difficult problem to accurately identify in many situations. This problem is particularly noticeable in attempts to differentially diagnose stuttering from dysfluencies in normal speech. A second problem has been the failure to establish reliability of independent raters in the assessment of this condition. It has been reported in some cases that disagreements occur in as many as 50% of the cases observed (Perkins, 1977). It should be noted, however, that degree of reliability in many of these cases may be due to methods of training raters, defining raters, conditions under which behaviors are observed, and other related factors.

For present purposes, we will adhere to the description provided above. However, it should be noted that, as with other types of psychopathology, problems in differential diagnosis and assessment not only exist but are frequent.

Assessment Techniques

Attention to assessment problems regarding stuttering have been infrequent (Yates, 1975). Ingham and Andrews (1971, 1973) are among the few authors who have considered this issue, and it is their belief that assessment should focus particularly on altering the stutterer's attitude toward his/her speech and on the comfort she/he displays while speaking. Normal errors in speech should be considered appropriate, and assessment should be developed with this in mind. As indices of normal speech, these authors have developed a measure of percentage of syllables stuttered as an indication of speech rate. These measures, it is suggested, should be taken in situations that approximate normal social situations. The other assessments required may involve self-ratings by the stutterer, ratings by observers, and use of standardized psychometric tests. Brady (1971) and others (Resnick *et al.*, 1978; Schmitt & Cooper, 1978) have used variations of these measures.

Etiology and Treatment

A number of rival theories have been put forth concerning the development and maintenance of stuttering among children and adults. While numerous approaches have been described, our focus of attention will be on four theories discussed most frequently. These methods of describing the origins of stuttering emanate from the theoretical approach to treatment most frequently taken by therapists in these various areas. No particular significance should be given to the order in which these formulations are discussed. These approaches include: theories emphasizing an organic basis of the disorder, articulation difficulties, psychodynamic, and behavioral approaches to the problem.

The Organic Basis

One method of describing stuttering is proposed by Porfert and Rosenfield (1978). They argue for an innate predispositional approach to development of stuttering, although no rationale for the particular locus of this disorder is offered. However, the authors suggest two major pieces of evidence to support their hypothesis. First, they remark that a correlational basis between prevalence of the disorder of parents and their children is quite strong and, second, that despite increasing numbers of clinicians trained to treat this problem, there has been no appreciable decrease in incidence of stuttering. Admittedly, evidence for the organic hypothesis is weak.

Articulation Difficulties

A rival hypothesis for explaining the etiology of stuttering is that speaking difficulties arise due to problems in phonatory processes that may underlie stuttering behavior (Adams, 1975; Agnello, 1975; Schwartz, 1974). Agnello cited evidence that speaking interacts with specific superaglottal articulatory movements. Thus, he hypothesized that the primary site of difficulty for the stutterer was in the time-dependent articulatory transition from phoneme to phoneme. The relationship between stuttering and phonatory behavior has been supported in a considerable body of research (Adams & Hayden, 1974; Adams & Reis, 1971; Agnello, 1975; Allen, Peters, & Williams, 1975; Conture, McFall, & Brewer, 1974; Freeman, 1975; Freeman & Ushijima, 1974; Gautheron, Liorzon, Even, & Vallancien, 1973; Kerr & Cooper, 1976). In the Freeman and Ushijima (1974) and Kerr and Cooper (1976) studies, differences in laryngeal activity between normal speech and stuttering were noted. Thus, based on existing knowledge, articulation difficulties represent one of the best accounts of stuttering.

Psychodynamic Approach

From the psychodynamic view, stuttering is formulated as a neurotic symptom of a deeper psychic disorder (Barbara, 1954; Glauber, 1958; Travis & Sutherland, 1957). Stutterers are viewed as persons who perceive themselves as limited, inadequate, and different. In terms of expectations, a stutterer anticipates having anxieties and problems with telephone calls, with reading aloud, with in-class participation, with asking for help, and with related social situations (Freund, 1966). At a more phenomenological level, the experience of a stutterer involves not only feelings of inferiority but helplessness and immobilization (Van Riper, 1971). At this point the stutterer's system is self-limiting and relatively inflexible; therefore, the system is inefficient and absorbs effort and energy without the production of socially acceptable speech. The stutterer expends his/her energy in avoiding challenging situations with others, in sifting through words, and in holding back feelings (Sheehan, 1958). Treatment involves a psychotherapeutic approach for resolving the neurotic conflict (Kaplan & Kaplan, 1978). However, little support is currently available to affirm this approach to the problem

Behavioral Theories and Treatments

From a behavioral perspective, stuttering is viewed as a learned behavior. One behavioral view of stuttering is that the problem is related to increased anxiety about speaking. From this approach, stuttering is viewed as a complex set of cognitive, affective, and behavioral–motoric responses learned situationally by the speaker in an effort to avoid situations or to correct perceived self-deficiencies. Moreover, stutterers appear to hold certain distorted ideas, beliefs, or attitudes about speech and speaking in interpersonal situations. These irrational ideas serve as cues eliciting anxiety and speech dysfluency (Johnson, 1958; Woods & Williams, 1971). As the level of anxiety increases, so does prevalence and severity of stuttering behavior.

A second behavioral explanation for stuttering is that it is due primarily to poorly developed speech patterns. As such, this response class is nothing more than a negative habit (Dalali & Sheehan, 1974). To reverse this trend, focus on relearning speech in socially appropriate ways is required. For example, Perkins (1977) has suggested that stutterers attempt to speak at rates considerably in excess of their abilities to coordinate phonation with articulation. By doing so, coordinated speech under normal circumstances will seem relatively easy. A second approach is called Delayed Auditory Feedback (Curles & Perkins, 1969; Goldiamond, 1965). It is generally hypothesized that this behavioral method of retraining the stutterer's speaking patterns is effective because it results in a slower rate of speech (Resnick *et al.,* 1978).

Direct validation of these two behavioral formulations of the etiology of stuttering have not been directly observed. However, the treatment methods developed from these models have proven to be most effective in alleviating stuttering. Aspects of this treatment literature will now be briefly reviewed.

Treatment

Stuttering has been effectively treated in a number of ways. However, the empirical literature attests primarily to the efficacy of behavioral procedures. One behavioral method that has frequently been employed and has proven to be successful is the modification of voice rhythm whereby the stutterer's speech is paced to the beat of a metronome. Once speech has been regulated, use of the metronome is gradually decreased (Brady, 1971). A similar approach to the problem involves slowing of speech (Perkins, 1977). With both of these methods, providing performance feedback and reinforcing appropriate responses are important aspects of training.

A second tactic in treating stuttering is to emphasize the amelioration of emotional disorders hypothesized to be causing the problem. The emotional problem most frequently cited is anxiety (Moleski & Tosi, 1976). Therefore, if this problem can be decreased, the likelihood that the person's speech will improve is enhanced. This hypothesis is considered viable since incessant failure in normal speech can result in anxiety. Procedures typically employed to accomplish this task involve reinforcement, shaping, systematic desensitization, and assertion training (Dalali & Sheehan, 1974).

Conclusions

Based on the prevailing literature on stuttering, it can be concluded that the problem is not only prevalent but that it tends to be fairly long-standing. As was seen, a number of rival hypotheses exist about the etiology and treatment of stuttering. It has been found that learning-based approaches and/or speech therapies that emphasize speech articulation difficulties have been used most frequently and most efficaciously.

Elective Mutism

In this chapter's final section, the particularly difficult problem of childhood elective mutism is discussed. Again, definitions, incidences, etiology, and assessment and treatment procedures are briefly reviewed, and a case history is provided.

Introduction

Elective mutism was first described 100 years ago and was called "aphasia voluntaria." The disorder took on its current name, elective mutism, in the 1930s. Elective mutism consists of a child's speech pattern in which she/he selects only specific isolated situations or certain persons to whom she/he will speak. For instance, a child who speaks frequently with his or her family may refuse to say anything to a teacher or other children at school. For children, an additional component must be added to the definition: in situations in which the child does speak, his/her verbal behavior must be age-appropriate. This latter aspect of the definition is important because a child with extremely regressed speech patterns might be mistaken as electively mute (Sanok & Striefel, 1979).

The *Diagnostic and Statistical Manual of Mental Disorders* (1980) provides a similar definition for the disorder. In this manual, it is noted that the essential feature of elective mutism is continuous refusal to speak in almost all social situations despite ability to comprehend spoken language and to speak. The final criterion is that lack of speech is not due to another mental or physical disorder. This manual also illustrates a number of behaviors that are characteristic of the electively mute child. These include excessive shyness, social isolation and withdrawal, clinging, school refusal, oppositional behavior, and a marked ability to communicate with others through nonverbal means such as nodding and shaking the head, using arm, head, and torso gestures, facial gestures and, in some cases, grunts or utterances of words in a monotone fashion.

Incidence

Elective mutism is slightly more common in girls than in boys. The disorder is described in the *Diagnostic and Statistical Manual of Mental Disorders* (1980) as being rare since it is found in less that 1% of child guidance and social casework referrals. This view of the problem is supported further by the popular press in England, where a clear case of elective mutism was reported in a Lancashire primary school in 1961 and received head-line attention in at least one national newspaper as being a unique phenomenon (Reed, 1963). Seelfield (1950) also has presented data that corroborates this incidence rate of elective mutism, as did Morris (1953). Thus, while the disorder is not extremely frequent, it is found at a high enough rate to be problematic, and it has recieved isolated attention in the treatment literature.

Assessment

Onset

As in the case of stuttering, onset of elective mutism is generally before the age of 5, although it frequently does not come to the attention of professionals until the child enters school. In most cases, the disturbance lasts only a few weeks or months, although in some cases the disorder can linger for several years if remediation is not successful.

Differential Diagnosis

In the *Diagnostic and Statistical Manual of Mental Disorders* (1980), brief guidelines for differential diagnosis respective to other disorders are provided. It is noted that, with mental retardation and language disorders, there may be a general inability to speak; the problem may be due to articulation difficulties or physical anomalies rather than cognitive deficits. With depression, overanxiety, phobias, and oppositional behavior, there may be a general refusal to speak due to current emotional states in the child rather than to particular discriminative stimuli. Additionally, in none of these latter instances is lack of speech the predominant disturbance.

Assessment Techniques

No formalized psychometric procedures have been developed to assess elective mutism. The primary modes of assessment reported in the literature include reports of teachers, parents, and other significant persons in the child's life, and direct behavioral observations of speech. The case presented later in this section of the chapter by Matson, Esvelt-Dawson, and O'Donnell (1979) typifies these assessment methods.

Etiology

As is the case with stuttering, there are a number of formulations concerning the etiology of elective mutism. The most prominent theories that have been put forth to account for this disorder are psychodynamic theory and learning theory. Certain variations exist in specific aspects of the explanations given for etiology of the disorder, even within the theoretical frameworks to be described.

Psychodynamic Approach

Typically, the psychodynamically oriented professional classifies elective mutism as a neurotic reaction of a personality trait disturbance. The multiple causal factors often evoked include: (1) constitutional hypersensitivity to instinctive drives; (2) psychosocial trauma during one of the critical periods of language development; (3) lack of secure environment; (4) psychological fixation with mutism as a fear reduction mechanism; and (5) family issues that may involve openness and dependency. Resolving these conflicts through insight-oriented therapy is implicated as the primary mode of treatment.

Learning Theory

Behavior therapists assert that elective mutism is a learned response that is maintained by reinforcing circumstances in which the child profits from not speaking in selected situations. Particular emphasis is placed on discriminative properties that are axiomatic in the development and maintenance of the disorder. Thus, the behavior therapist constantly refers to stimulus control as a major focal point for treatment. It is generally believed that the speech patterns of electively mute children are under strong stimulus control of parents and other family members (Wulbert, Nyman, Snow, & Owen, 1973). This hypothesis is supported at least to some degree by the fact that these children tend most often to evidence mutism in public settings but not in the home.

Treatment

Following an evaluation of representative studies of this topic, it can be concluded that behavioral techniques are used most frequently (Norman & Broman, 1970). For purposes of the present review, all or even part of the studies in this area cannot be adequately covered. Thus, the purpose here is to provide examples of successful programs and techniques. Behavioral treatments in this area are significant because clinicians and researchers had believed until only recently that this condition was intractable to treatment and would persist over an extended period of time (Reed, 1963).

The first method commonly used is stimulus fading (Conrad, Delk, & Williams, 1974). With this procedure, the treatment program begins in places where the child is likely to speak, then the therapist and child gradually change the situation through successive approximations until, finally, the child responds verbally to the teacher's questions in a classroom with students present—something the child had refused to do previously. Procedures similar to this have been used by a number of researchers (e.g., Van der Kooy & Webster, 1975).

A second representative treatment for this problem, *in vivo* desensitization, is provided by Scott (1977), who based treatment on the assumption that presence of strangers aroused responses incompatible with speaking (e.g., anxiety responses such as withdrawal and quiesence). Thus, the primary mode of treatment involved *in vivo* desensitization. Although relaxation exercises are frequently an element of such a program, they were not employed here; instead, the child initially listened to her voice on a tape player without the therapist present, then with the therapist present, and, finally, through a series of graduated steps spoke to the therapist in the room.

These brief examples give some idea of methods that are acceptable and that have proven successful for treating elective mutism. What follows is a more detailed description of an electively mute child.

Case Example

In the preceding sections, forms of speech disorders, specifically those dealing with stuttering and elective mutism, have been described. One method of treating these problems has been behavior modification procedures, particularly shaping, fading, and reinforcement. The second author, along with two colleagues, recently treated a particularly reticent electively mute child with a behavior modification package (Matson *et al.,* 1979).

The boy treated was 9 years of age and had had normal speech until the age of 6. He was from a poor family in the Appalacian area of West Virginia. His school performance was average with respect to grades and standard academic achievement tests. For the previous 3 years he had not spoken to anyone, and the problem had progressed to the point that he would not initiate sounds. An example of the latter problem can be exemplified by an instance in which he was punched in the nose (making it bleed) soon after being admitted to the hospital where the study was conducted. He neither said anything to the child who had hit him nor, for that matter, did he make a sound.

Over the 3-year period during which he failed to speak, he had received a number of evaluations and treatments at local mental health centers. A consistent theme of medical assessments was that no physical abnormalities existed that precluded speech. Despite this prognosis, none of the treatments attempted had been successful—including 37 sessions of training by a speech therapist.

The therapists in this study devised a program that incorporated both reinforcement and overcorrection procedures. The treatment involved a hierarchy of responses, from "imitates lip movements of the therapist" to "imitates sounds," "imitates 'yes' and 'no,'" "imitates nouns," and finally "answers yes-or no questions." Individual sessions were held twice daily with a therapist in a room adjacent to the child's classroom. Sessions varied in length from 10 to 20 minutes, depending on the length of time required to administer treatment procedures. The patient was shown 10 pictures of animals and other objects with which he was familiar (e.g., bear, fish). While showing the child each visual stimulus, the therapist would pronounce the word and ask the child to attend to her while she showed him the behavior she wished him to imitate; then she asked him to perform the behavior. For correct responses, the therapist would give the child a penny plus a slip of paper indicating that he had earned 1 minute of time to spend with any adult on the unit he chose. In addition, verbal praise was provided by the therapist. For inappropriate resonses, the child was required to write 10 times the name of the picture that had just been shown.

In a matter of 5 weeks, treatment proved to be initially effective in the reduction of this child's mutism. A small amount of generalization was found from lip movements to sounds, but it was consistently found that the desired behaviors were under stimulus control of the treatment package. Frequency counts of words spoken in the child's ward were also kept during the study. This behavior occurred only during the latter phase of the study but, in a 7-day span, the child did say 12 words to unit staff who had not been involved in the training. Furthermore, six of the words spoken were ones that had not been specifically trained.

Summary

In the preceding section, two problematic speech-related disorders have been discussed: stuttering and elective mutism. While the former problem is a greater prevalence, both occur at a sufficient rate to warrant concerted attention in regard to etiology, diagnosis, and treatment. This situation is the case despite the fact that a large percentage of both these behaviors recover spontaneously. Clearly, development of effective means of identifying and treating recalcitrant cases is needed. In addition, all cases could benefit from management procedures that enhance the ease with which affected children can manage in their environment while these conditions are present.

References

Adams, M. R. Vocal tract dynamics in fluency and stuttering: A review and interpretation of past research. In L. M. Webster & L. C. Furst (Eds.), *Vocal tract dynamics and dysfluency.* New York: Speech and Hearing Institute, 1975.

Adams, M. R., & Hayden, P. Stutterers' and nonstutterers' ability to initiate and terminate phonation during non-speech activity. *American Speech and Hearing Association,* 1974, *16,* 521.

Adams, M. R., & Reis, R., The influence of the onset of phonation on the frequency of stuttering. *Journal of Speech and Hearing Research,* 1971, *14,* 639–644.

Agnello, J. G. Voice onset and voice termination features of stutters. In L. M. Webster & L. C. Furst (Eds.), *Vocal tract dynamics and dysfluency.* New York: Speech and Hearing Institute, 1975.

Agras, S., & Marshall, C. The application of negative practice to spasmodic torticollis. *American Journal of Psychiatry,* 1965, *122,* 579–582.

Allen, G. D., Peters, R. & Williams, C. Spectrographic study of fluent and stuttered speech. *American Speech and Hearing Association,* 1975, *17,* 664.

Ascher, E. Psychodynamic considerations in Gilles de la Tourette's disease *(maladie des tics). American Journal of Psychiatry,* 1948, *105,* 267–276.

Azrin, N. H., & Nunn, R. G. Habit reversal: A method of eliminating nervous habits and tics. *Behaviour Research and Therapy,* 1973, *11,* 619–628.

Azrin, N. H., & Nunn, R. G. *Habit control in a day.* New York: Simon and Schuster, 1977.

Azrin, N. H., Nunn, R. G., & Frantz, S. E. Habit reversal vs. negative practice treatment of nervous tics. *Behavior Therapy,* 1980, *2,* 169–178.

Bakwin, H., & Bakwin, R. M. *Behavior disorders in children* (6th ed.). Philadelphia: Saunders, 1972.

Barbara, D. *Stuttering: A psychodynamic approach to its understanding and treatment.* New York: Julian, 1954.

Barrett, B. N. Reductions in the rate of multiple tics by free operant conditioning methods. *Journal of Nervous and Mental Disease,* 1962, 135, 187–195.

Beck, S., & Fedoravicius, A. S. Self-control treatment of an eye blink tic. *Behavior Therapy,* 1977, *8,* 277–279.

Boncour, G. *Les tic chez l'ecolier et leur interpretation. Progressive Medicine,* 1910, *26,* 495–496.

Brady, J. P. Metronome-conditioned speech retraining for stuttering. *Behavior Therapy,* 1971, *2,* 129–150.

Brierley, H. The treatment of hysterical spasmodic torticollis by behavior therapy. *Behaviour Research and Therapy,* 1967, *5,* 139–142.

Browning, R. M. & Stover, D. O. *Behavior modification in child treatment.* Chicago: Aldine/Atherton, 1971.

Bruun, R., Shapiro, A., Shapiro, E., Sweet, R., Wayne, H., & Solomon, G. A follow-up of 78 patients with Gilles de la Tourette's syndrome. *American Journal of Psychiatry,* 1976, *133,* 944–947.

Challas, G., & Brauer, W. Tourette's disease: Relief of symptoms with R1625. *American Journal of Psychiatry,* 1963, *120,* 283–284.

Chapel, J. L. Behavior modification techniques with children and adolescents. *Canadian Psychiatric Association Journal,* 1970, *15,* 315–318.

Chapel, J. L., Brown, N., & Jenkins, R. L. Tourette's disease: Symptomatic relief with haloperidol. *American Journal of Psychiatry,* 1964, *121,* 608–610.

Chess, S., & Rosenberg, M. Clinical differentiation among children with initial language complaints. *Journal of Autism and Childhood Schizophrenia,* 1974, *1,* 99–109.

Clark, D. F. Behavior therapy of Gilles de la Tourette's syndrome. *British Journal of Psychiatry,* 1966, *112,* 771–778.

Cohen, D., & Marks, F. M. Gilles de la Tourette's syndrome treated by operant conditioning. *British Journal of Psychiatry,* 1977, *130,* 315.

Connell, P. H., Corbett, J. A., Horne, D. J., & Mathews, A. M. Drug treatment of adolescent tiqueurs: A double blind trial of diazepan and haloperidol. *British Journal of Psychiatry,* 1967, *113,* 375–381.

Conrad, R. D., Delk, J. L., & Williams, C. Use of stimulus fading procedures in the treatment of situation specific mutism: A case study. *Journal of Behavior Therapy and Experimental Psychiatry,* 1974, *5,* 99–100.

Conture, E. G., McFall, G., & Brewer, D. Laryngeal activity during the movement of stuttering: Some preliminary observations. *American Speech and Hearing Association,* 1974, *16,* 521.

Costello, C. G. The essentials of behavior therapy. *Canadian Psychiatric Association Journal,* 1963, *8,* 162–166.

Crown, S. An experimental inquiry into some aspects of the motor behavior and personality of tiqueurs. *Journal of Mental Science,* 1953, *99,* 84–91.

Curlee, R. F., & Perkins, W. H. Conversational rate control therapy for stuttering. *Journal of Speech and Hearing Disorders,* 1969, *34,* 245–250.

Dalali, I. D., & Sheehan, J. G. Stuttering and assertion training. *Journal of Communication Disorders,* 1974, *7,* 97–111.

Diagnostic and statistical manual of mental disorders (3rd ed.). Washington, D.C.: American Psychiatric Association, 1980.

Dorland's illustrated medical dictionary. Philadelphia: W. B. Sanders, 1965.

Duffy, J. C. (Ed.). *Child psychiatry.* Flushing, N.Y.: Medical Examination Publishing, 1974.

Dunlap, J. A case of Gilles de la Tourette's disease *(maladie des tics):* A study of the intrafamily dynamics. *Journal of Nervous Mental Disease,* 1960, *130,* 340–344.

Dunlap, K. *Habits: Their making and unmaking.* New York: Liveright, 1932.

Eisenberg, L., Ascher, E., & Kanner, L. A clinical study of Gilles de la Tourette's disease *(maladie des tics)* in children. *American Journal of Psychiatry,* 1959, *115,* 715–723.

Eisenson, J. Speech disorders. In B. B. Wolman (Ed.), *Handbook of clinical psychology.* New York: McGraw-Hill, 1965.

Eldridge, R., Sweet, R., Lake, C. R., Ziegler, M., & Shapiro, A. Gilles de la Tourette's syndrome: Clinical, genetic, psychologic, and biochemical aspects in 21 selected families. *Neurology,* 1977, *27,* 115–124.

Eriksson, B., & Persson, T. Gilles de la Tourette's syndrome. *British Journal of Psychiatry,* 1969, *115,* 351–353.

Feild, J., Corbin, K., Goldstein, N., & Klass, D. Gilles de la Tourette's syndrome. *Neurology,* 1966, *16,* 453–462.

Feldman, R. B., & Werry, J. S. An unsuccessful attempt to treat a tiqueur by massed practice. *Behaviour Research & Therapy,* 1966, *4,* 111–117.

Fenichel, O. *The psychoanalytic theory of neurosis*. New York: Norton Press, 1945.

Ferenczi, S. Psycho-analytical observations on tic. *International Journal of Psychoanalysis,* 1921, *2,* 1–30.

Fernando, S. J. M. Gilles de la Tourette's syndrome: A report on 4 cases and a review of published case reports. *British Journal of Psychiatry,* 1967, *113,* 607–617.

Fernando, S. J. M. Gilles de la Tourette's syndrome. *British Journal of Psychiatry,* 1968, *114,* 123–125.

Ford, & Gottlieb, F. An objective evaluation of haloperidol in Gilles de la Tourette's syndrome. *Diseases of the Nervous System,* 1969, *30,* 328–332.

Frederick, C. J. Treatment of a tic by systematic desensitization and massed response evocation. *Journal of Behavior Therapy and Experimental Psychiatry,* 1971, *2,* 281–283.

Freeman, F. J. Phonation and fluency. In L. M. Webster & L. C. Furst (Eds.), *Vocal tract dynamics and dysfluency*. New York: Speech and Hearing Institute, 1975.

Freeman, F. J., & Ushijima, T. An SME, Siber-optic study of laryngeal activity accompanying the moment of stuttering. *American Speech and Hearing Association,* 1974, *16,* 521.

Freund, H. *Psychopathology and the problems of stuttering*. Springfield, Ill.: Charles C Thomas, 1966.

Friedman, S. Self-control in the treatment of Gilles de la Tourette's syndrome: Case study with 18-month follow-up. *Journal of Consulting and Clinical Psychology,* 1980, *48,* 400–402.

Friel, P. Familial incidence of Gilles de la Tourette's disease, with observations on aetiology and treatment. *British Journal of Psychiatry,* 1973, *122,* 655–658.

Frost, N., Freighner, J., & Schuckit, M. A family study of Gilles de la Tourette's syndrome. *Diseases of the Nervous System,* 1976, *37,* 537–538.

Garnett, R. W., Jr., & Elbirlik, K. Torticollis. *Southern Medical Journal,* 1953, *46,* 892–898.

Gautheron, B., Liorzon, A., Even, C., & Valliancien, B. The role of the larynx in stuttering. In Y. Lebrun & R. Hoops (Eds.), *Neurolinguistic approaches to stuttering*. The Hague: Mouton, 1973.

Gerard, M. W. The psychogenic tic in ego development. In A. Freud (Ed.), *Psychoanalytic study of the child* (Vol. 2). New York: International University Press, 1946.

Glauber, I. The psychoanalysis of stuttering. In J. Eisenson (Ed.), *Stuttering: A symposium*. New York: Harper, 1958.

Goggin, J. E., & Erickson, M. Dilemmas in diagnosis and treatment of Gilles de la Tourette's syndrome. *Journal of Personality Assessment,* 1979, *43,* 339–346.

Golden, G. S. Genetic aspects of Tourette's syndrome. *Neurology,* 1977, *27,* 400. (a)

Golden, G. S. Tourette's syndrome: The pediatric perspective. *American Journal of Diseases of Children,* 1977, *131,* 531–534. (b)

Golden, G. S. Tics and Tourette's: A continuum of symptoms? *Annals of Neurology,* 1978, *4,* 145–148.

Goldiamond, I. Stuttering and fluency as manipulatable operant response classes. In L. Krasner & L. P. Ullman (Eds.), *Research in behavior modification: New development and implications*. New York: Holt, Rinehart and Winston; 1965.

Healy, C. E. Gilles de la Tourette's syndrome *(maladie des tics)*. *American Journal of Diseases of Children,* 1970, *120,* 62–63.

Hollandsworth, J. G., Jr., & Bausinger, L. Unsuccessful use of massed practice in the treatment of Gilles de la Tourette's syndrome. *Psychological Reports,* 1978, *43,* 671–677.

Hull, C. L. *Principles of behavior*. New York: Appleton Century, 1943.

Hutzell, R. R., Platzek, D., & Logue, P. E. Control of Symptoms of Gilles de la Tourette's syndrome by self-monitoring. *Journal of Behavior Therapy and Experimental Psychiatry,* 1974, *5,* 71–76.

Ingham, R. J., & Andrews, C. Stuttering: The quality of fluency after treatment. *Journal of Communication Disorders,* 1971, *4,* 279–288.

Ingham, R. J., & Andrews, G. Behavior therapy and stuttering: A review. *Journal of Speech and Hearing Disorders,* 1973, *38,* 405–441.

Irwin, O. C. Infant speech effect of systematic reading of stories. *Journal of Speech and Hearing Research,* 1969, *3,* 187–190.

Johnson, G., Pepple, J., Singer, H., & Littlefield, J. HGPRT in the Gilles de la Tourettee's syndrome. *New England Journal of Medicine,* 1977, *297,* 399.

Johnson, W. *Stuttering in children and adults*. Minneapolis: University of Minnesota Press, 1958.

Johnson, W. *The onset of stuttering*. Minneapolis: University of Minnesota Press, 1959.

Jones, H. G. Continuation of Yates: Treatment of a tiqueur. In H. G. Eysenck (Ed.), *Behavior therapy and the neuroses*. Oxford: Pergamon, 1960.

Jones, H. G. Stuttering. In G. G. Costello (Ed.), *Symptoms of psychopathology: A handbook*. New York: Wiley, 1970.

Kanner, L. *Child psychiatry.* Springfield, Ill.: Charles C Thomas, 1957.

Kaplan, N. R., & Kaplan, M. L. The Gestalt approach to stuttering. *Journal of Communication Disorders, 1978, 11,* 1–9.

Kellmer-Pringle, M., Butler, M., & Davie, R. *11,000 seven year olds.* London: National Bureau for Co-operation in Child Care, 1967.

Kelman, D. H. Gilles de la Tourette's disease in children: A review of the literature. *Journal of Child Psychology and Psychiatry,* 1965, *6,* 219–226.

Kerr, S. H., & Cooper, E. B. *Phonatory adjustment times in stutterers and nonstutterers.* Unpublished manuscript, University of Alabama, 1976.

Klawans, H. L., Falk, D. K., Nausieda, P. A., & Weiner, W. J. Gilles de la Tourette's syndrome after long-term chlorpromazine therapy. *Neurology,* 1978, *28,* 1064–1068.

Knepler, K. N., & Sewall, S. Negative practice paired with smelling salts in the treatment of a tic. *Journal of Behavior Therapy and Experimental Psychiatry,* 1974, *5,* 189–192.

LaPouse, R., & Monk, M. An epidemiologic study of behavior characteristics in children. *American Journal of Public Health,* 1958, *48,* 1134–1144.

LaPouse, R., & Monk, M. Behavior deviations in a representative sample of children: Variation by sex, age, race, social class and family size. *American Journal of Orthopsychiatry,* 1964, *34,* 436–446.

Lazarus, A. A. Objective psychotherapy in the treatment of dysphemia. *Journal of South African Logopedic Society,* 1960, *6,* 8–10.

Levy-Suhl, M. Resolution by psychoanalysis of motor disturbances in an adolescent. *Psychoanalytic Quarterly,* 1937, *6,* 336–345.

Lucas, A. R. Gilles de la Tourette's disease in children: Treatment with haloperidol. *American Journal of Psychiatry,* 1967, *124,* 147–149.

Lucas, A. R. Report of Gilles de la Tourette's disease in two succeeding generations. *Child Psychiatry and Human Development,* 1973, *3,* 231–233.

Mahler, M. S. Tics and impulsions in children: A study of motility. *Psychoanalytic Quarterly,* 1944, *17,* 430–444.

Mahler, M. S. A psychoanalytic evaluation of tic in psychopathology of children: Symptomatic and tic syndrome. In A. Freud (Ed.), *Psychoanalytic study of the child.* New York: International University Press, 1949.

Mahler, M. S., & Luke, J. A. Outcome of the tic syndrome. *Journal of Nervous and Mental Disorders,* 1946, *103,* 433–445.

Mahler, M. S., & Rangell, L. A psychosomatic study of *maladie des tics* (Gilles de la Tourette's disease). *Psychiatric Quarterly,* 1943, *17,* 579–603.

Mahler, M. S. Luke, J. A., & Daltroff, W. Clinical and follow-up study of the tic syndrome in children. *American Journal of Orthopsychiatry,* 1945, *15,* 631–647.

Maldofsky, H., Tullis, D., & Lamon, R. Multiple tic syndrome (Gilles de la Tourette's syndrome): Clinical, biological and psychosocial variables and their influence with haloperidol. *Journal of Nervous and Mental Disorders,* 1974, *159,* 282–292.

Maletzky, B. M. Behavior recording as treatment: A brief note. *Behavior Therapy,* 1974, *5,* 107–111.

Matson, J. L., Esvelt-Dawson, K., & O'Donnell, D. Overcorrection, modeling and reinforcement procedures for reinstating speech in a mute boy. *Child Behavior Therapy,* 1979, *4,* 363–371.

Meares, R. A. Behavior therapy and spasmodic torticollis. *Archives of General Psychiatry,* 1973, *28,* 104–107.

Meige, H., & Feindel, E. *Tics and their treatment.* London: Appleton, 1907.

Moleski, R., & Tosi, D. J. Comparative psychotherapy: Rational-emotive therapy versus systematic desensitization in the treatment of stuttering. *Journal of Consulting and Clinical Psychology,* 1976, *44,* 309–311.

Morphew, J., & Sim. M. Gilles de la Tourette's syndrome: A clinical and psychopathological study. *British Journal of Medical Psychology,* 1969, *42,* 293–301.

Mowrer, O. H. *Learning theory and personality dynamics.* New York: Ronald, 1950.

Mysak, E. D., & Gilbert, G. M. Child speech pathology. In B. B. Wolman (Ed.), *Manual of child psychopathology.* New York: McGraw Hill, 1972.

Nicassio, F. J., Lieberman, R. T., Patterson, R. L., Raminez, E., & Sanders, N. The treatment of tics by negative practice. *Journal of Behavior Therapy and Experimental Psychiatry,* 1972, *3,* 281–288.

Norman, A., & Broman, H. J. Volume feedback and generalization techniques in shaping speech of an electively mute boy: A case study. *Perceptual and Motor Skills,* 1970, *31,* 463–470.

Nunn, R. G. Maladaptive habits and tics. *Psychiatric Clinics of North America,* 1978, *2,* 349–361.

O'Brien, J. S., & Brennan, J. H. The elimination of a severe long term facial tic and vocal distortion with multi-facet behavior therapy. *Journal of Behavior Therapy and Experimental Psychiatry,* 1979, *10,* 257–261.

Ollendick, T. H. Self-monitoring and self-administered overcorrection: The modification of nervous tics in children. *Behavior Modification,* 1981, *5,* 75–84.

Paterson, M. T. Spasmodic torticollis: Results of psychotherapy in 21 cases. *The Lancet,* 1945, *249,* 556–559.

Patterson, R. M., & Little, S. C. Spasmodic torticollis. *Journal of Nervous and Mental Disease,* 1943, *98,* 571–599.

Perkins, W. H. *Speech pathology: An applied behavioral science* (2nd ed.). St. Louis: Mosby, 1977.

Pollack, M. A., Cohen, M. L., & Friedhoff, A. J. Gilles de la Tourette's syndrome. *Child Neurology,* 1977, *34,* 630–632.

Porfert, A. R., & Rosenfield, D. B. Prevalence of stuttering. *Journal of Neurology, Neurosurgery and Psychiatry,* 1978, *41,* 954–956.

Rafi, A. A. Learning theory and the treatment of tics. *Journal of Psychosomatic Research,* 1962, *6,* 71–76.

Reed, G. F. Elective mutism in children: A re-appraisal. *Journal of Child Psychology and Psychiatry,* 1963, *4,* 99–107.

Resneck, P. A., Wendiggensen, P., Ames, S., & Meyer, R. Systematic slowed speech: A new treatment for stuttering. *Behaviour Research and Therapy,* 1978, *16,* 161–167.

Sanders, D. Familial occurrence of Gilles de la Tourette's syndrome: Report of the syndrome occurring in a father and son. *Archives of General Psychiatry,* 1973, *28,* 326–328.

Sanok, R. L., & Striefel, S. Elective mutism: Generalization of verbal responding across people and settings. *Behavior Therapy,* 179, *10,* 357–371.

Savicki, V., & Carlin. A. S. Behavioral treatment of Gilles de la Tourette's syndrome. *International Journal of Child Psychotherapy,* 1972, *1,* 97–109.

Schmitt, L. S., & Cooper, E. B. Fundamental frequencies in the oral reading behavior of stuttering and non-stuttering male children. *Journal of Communication Disorders,* 1978, *11,* 17–23.

Schulman, M. Control of tics by maternal reinforcement. *Journal of Behavior Therapy and Experimental Psychiatry,* 1974, *5,* 95–96.

Schwartz, M. F. The core of the stuttering block. *Journal of Speech and Hearing Disorders,* 1974, *39,* 169–177.

Scott, E. A desensitization programme for the treatment of mutism in a seven year old girl: A case report. *Journal of Child Psychology and Psychiatry,* 1977, *18,* 263–270.

Seelfield, D. J. Observations on elective mutism in children. *Journal of Mental Science,* 1950, *96,* 1024–1032.

Shapiro, A. K., & Shapiro, E. Treatment of Gilles de la Tourette's syndrome with Haloperidol. *British Journal of Psychiatry,* 1968, *114,* 345–350.

Shapiro, A. K., Shapiro, E., Bruun, R., & Sweet, R. *Gilles de la Tourette's syndrome.* New York: Raven Press, 1978.

Shapiro, A. K., Shapiro, E., & Clarkin, J. Clinical psychological testing in Tourette's syndrome. *Journal of Personality Assessment,* 1974, *38,* 464–478.

Shapiro, A. K., Shapiro, E., & Wayne, H. Birth, development, and family histories and demographic information in Tourette's syndrome. *Journal of Nervous and Mental Disease,* 1972, *155,* 335–344.

Shapiro, A. K., Shapiro, E., & Wayne H. The symptomatology and diagnosis of Gilles de la Tourette's syndrome. *Journal of American Academy of Child Psychiatry,* 1973, *12,* 702–723.

Sheehan, J. G. Conflict theory of stuttering. In J. Eisenson (Ed.), *Stuttering: A symposium.* New York: Harper, 1958.

Sheehan, J. G., & Marlyn, M. M. Spontaneous recovery from stuttering. *Journal of Speech and Hearing Research,* 1966, *9,* 121–135.

Sheehan, J. G., & Marlyn, M. M. Methodology in studies of recovery from stuttering. *Journal of Speech and Hearing Research,* 1967, *10,* 396–400.

Skinner, B. F. *The behavior of organisms.* New York: Appleton-Century, 1938.

Standardized Micro-Data Tape Transcripts, publication (HRA) 76-1213, Washington, D.C.: National Center for Health Statistics, 1976.

Stevens, J. R., & Blachly, P. H. Successful treatment of the *maladie des tics. American Journal of Diseases of Children,* 1966, *112,* 541–545.

Sweet, R., Bruun, R., Shapiro, A. K., & Shapiro, E. The pharmacology of Gilles de la Tourette's syndrome (chronic multiple tic). In H. L. Klawans (Ed.), *Clinical neuropharmacology* (Vol. 1). New York: Raven Press, 1976.

Sweet, R., Solomon, G., Wayne, H., Shapiro, E., & Shapiro, A. K. Neurological features of Gilles de la Tourette's syndrome. *Journal of Neurology, Neurosurgery and Psychiatry,* 1973, *36,* 1–9.

Thomas, E. J., Abrams, K. S., & Johnson, J. B. Self-monitoring and reciprocal inhibition in the modification of multiple tics of *Gilles de la Tourette's* syndrome. *Journal of Behavior Therapy and Experimental Psychiatry,* 1971, *2,* 159–171.

Tiller, J. W. G. Brief family therapy for childhood tic syndrome. *Family Process,* 1978, *17,* 217–223.

Tophoff, M. Massed practice, relaxation and assertion training in the treatment of Gilles de la Tourette's syndrome. *Journal of Behavior Therapy and Experimental Psychiatry,* 1973, *4,* 71–73.

Torup, E: A follow-up study of children with tics. *Acta Paediatrica,* 1972, *51,* 261–268.

Travis, L., & Sutherland, L. The unspeakable feelings of people with special reference to stuttering. In L. Travis (Ed.), *Handbook of speech pathology.* New York: Appleton-Century-Crofts, 1957.

Turner, S. M., Hersen, M., & Alford, H. Effects of massed practice and meprobamate on spasmodic torticollis: An experimental analysis. *Behaviour Research and Therapy,* 1974, *12,* 259–260.

Van der Kooy, D., & Webster, C. D. A rapidly effective behavior modification program for an electively mute child. *Journal of Behavior Therapy and Experimental Psychiatry,* 1975, *6,* 149–152.

Van Riper, C. Symptomatic therapy for stuttering. In L. Travis (Ed.), *Handbook of speech pathology and audiology.* New York: Appleton-Century-Crofts, 1971.

Van Woert, M., Jutkowitz, R., Rosenbaum, D., & Bowers, M. Gilles de la Tourette's syndrome: Biochemical approaches. In M. Yahr (Ed.), *The basal ganglia.* New York: Raven Press, 1976.

Walton, D. Experimental psychology and the treatment of a tiquer. *Journal of Child Psychology and Psychiatry,* 1961, *2,* 148–155.

Walton, D. Massed practice and simultaneous reduction in drive level—further evidence of the efficacy of this approach to the treatment of tics. In H. J. Eysenck (Ed.), *Experiments in behavior therapy.* London: Pergamon, 1964.

Wassman, E., Eldridge, R., Abuzzahab, S., & Nee, L. Gilles de la Tourette's syndrome: Clinical and genetic studies in a midwestern city. *Neurology,* 1978, *28,* 304–307.

Wayne, H., Shapiro, A. K., & Shapiro, E. Gilles de la Tourette's syndrome: Electroencephalographic investigation and clinical correlation. *Clinical Electroencephalography,* 1972, *3,* 160–168.

Weisman, A. D. Nature and treatment of tics. *Archives of Neurology and Psychiatry,* 1952, *68,* 444–459.

Wilson, R. S., Garron, D. C., & Klawans, H. L. Significance of genetic factors in Gilles de la Tourette's syndrome: A review. *Behavior Genetics,* 1978, *8,* 503–510.

Wolpe, J. *Psychotherapy for reciprocal inhibition.* Stanford, Calif.: Stanford University Press, 1958.

Woods, C. L., & Williams, D. E. Speech clinicians' conceptions of boys and men who stutter. *Journal of Speech and Hearing Disorders,* 1971, *36,* 225–234.

Wulbert, M., Nyman, B. A., Snow, D., & Owen, Y. The efficacy of stimulus fading and contingency management in the treatment of elective mutism: A case study. *Journal of Applied Behavior Analysis,* 1973, *6,* 435–441.

Yates, A. J. The application of learning theory to the treatment of tics. *Journal of Abnormal and Social Psychology,* 1958, *56,* 175–182.

Yates, A. J. *Behavior therapy.* New York: Wiley, 1970.

Yates, A. J. *Theory and practice in behavior therapy.* New York: Wiley, 1975.

10

Childhood Obesity and Anorexia Nervosa

Gloria R. Leon and David Dinklage

Childhood Obesity

Introduction

Historically, moderate obesity in infants and children has been viewed as a sign of health and as an affirmation that one's mother is loving and nurtrant. In less affluent countries such as India, obesity is considered to be a demonstration that the family has enough wealth to procure food. Additional evidence also suggests that various cultures differ in the norms for body weight that are considered to be the ideal of physical attractiveness for men and women (Goldblatt, Moore, & Stunkard, 1965).

These positive conceptions of obesity are counterbalanced by the other evidence of prejudice against obese persons. William Sheldon (1954) linked the endomorphic, obese body build to temperamental characteristics such as laziness, self-indulgence, love of comfort, and being weak-willed. A marked tendency to respond to obese youngsters in a negative manner is indicated by findings that performance of obese adolescents was rated less favorably than performance of equally qualified normal-weight peers (Canning & Mayer, 1966). Further, children and adolescents in the United States and Mexico responded negatively to figures of peers with endomorphic physiques (Lerner & Pool, 1972; Lerner & Schroder, 1971), and fat children were rated as less likeable than children with recognized

GLORIA R. LEON AND DAVID DINKLAGE • Department of Psychology, University of Minnesota, Minneapolis, Minnesota 55455.

physical disabilities (Maddox, Back, & Liederman, 1968). Thus, obesity can be seen as a deviation from cultural norms for appropriate body build, just as persons with any other type of physical handicap deviate from specified norms. The effects of this deviation can be demonstrated by findings that obese children exhibit an expectation of rejection by others and that they manifest psychological characteristics similar to those that racial prejudice produces for black youngsters (G. Allport, cited in Mayer, 1975).

Diagnostic Criteria and Clinical Features

Simple obesity (whether in children or adults) is not considered a psychiatric disorder in DSM-III, the newly revised psychiatric diagnostic manual. Obesity is classified as a psychopathological problem only in the category of Psychological Factors Affecting a Physical Disorder. The rationale is that there have been no distinct psychopathological phenomena that have been demonstrated to occur in obesity. (It seems to the authors, however, that a more accurate classification for obesity problems might be Physical Disorder Affecting Psychological Factors because the attitudes and behaviors of others toward the obese youngster seem quite important in the development of psychological problems associated with obesity.) Negative mood states and behavioral problems manifested by some obese youngsters may thus be the result, rather than the cause, of their obesity.

Seltzer and Mayer (1965) have published obesity standards for male and female Caucasian Americans from ages 5 through 50, based on the measurement of triceps skinfold thickness. Skinfold thickness is used as an indirect measure of the amount of fat or adipose tissue beneath the skin. Obesity is then defined for a particular age and sex as the percentage of body fat that is one standard deviation or more above the mean of the population norms. The triceps area is considered to be roughly representative of adipose composition in other areas of the body, although some investigators use a percentage of body fat based on the mean of measurements taken from the triceps, subscapular, and gluteal areas. The measurement of adipose tissue avoids the inaccuracies inherent in using height or weight tables, and also avoids the norm problems particular to growing youngsters. The popularly used growth chart tables for children present norms for age by height, or age by weight. However, the tables do not take into account the interaction of weight and height at a particular age. For example, a child at a given age may be considered overweight according to the weight distribution, but only because his or her height is also above the norm for that particular age.

In order to increase the representativeness of the skinfold thickness norms, it would be important to develop norms for other racial populations. For research and clinical purposes, however, measurement of skinfold thickness is more accurate than any other currently available method.

Prevalence

Obesity appears to be frequent in relatively affluent countries at all ages and in both sexes. The prevalence of obesity in the United States has increased from the period of 1960–1962 to 1971–1974 (National Center for Health Statistics, 1977). Similar findings have been reported based on epidemiological studies in other developed countries.

Obesity in urban areas in the United States and Great Britain has been found to be inversely related to socioeconomic factors. Huenemann (1969) found that this inverse relationship was well established by the adolescent period; 11.6% of lower class girls were obese compared to 5.4% of upper class girls. Comparable figures for boys were 6.2% for lower class and 2.3% for upper class boys. An investigation of over 3,000 Caucasian school children from urban areas of the United States (Stunkard, d'Aquili, Fox, & Filion, 1972) demonstrated that 8% of lower SES and 0% of upper SES girls at age 6 were obese. By age 18, 32.5% of lower SES and 12% of upper SES girls were obese, indicating a greater yearly increment in the percentage of obese girls in the lower social class group. Although lower SES boys showed a greater prevalence of obesity than was found among boys of the upper class, this difference was not as marked or as consistent over the childhood and adolescent periods as was the case for girls.

Outcome

Longitudinal investigations of the stability of body weight from childhood to adulthood suggest that the majority of obese youngsters do not "outgrow" their obesity (Charney, Goodman, & McBride, 1975). Although persons with juvenile-onset obesity have been found to lose weight as readily as those with adult onset obesity, juvenile-onset obesity has proven to be a poor prognostic indicator for long-term maintenance of weight loss (Sjöström, 1978). (The issue of the permanence of obesity is discussed further in the section entitled "Constitutional Factors.")

Theoretical Formulations and Research Evidence

Childhood obesity is not a unitary phenomenon but appears to result from a complex interaction of a variety of psychological and biological factors. In understanding the etiology of obesity in a specific child, it is important to ascertain specific variables or a combination of variables that appear to be of significance for that particular child. Theoretical formulations of obesity, however, have often proceeded from an assumption that all obese individuals share a common etiology.

Genetic Factors

Studies of identical twins reared together and those reared apart indicate the influence of both genetic and environmental factors. The average percentage variations in body weight for monozygotic twins living together was found to be 1.39%; and for monozygotic twins living apart, 3.6%. The variation in body weight of dyzygotic twins is similar to that found with siblings at a comparable age (Von Verschuer, cited in Mayer, 1965c). Further, Mayer (1965a) found that 40% of youngsters with one obese parent also were obese; 80% of youngsters with two obese parents were obese; and 10% of youngsters with normal-weight parents were obese.

Somatotype appears to be another genetic factor that might predispose an individual to obesity. Studies of obese and normal-weight adolescent girls (Seltzer & Mayer, 1964) and women (Seltzer & Mayer, 1969) demonstrated that obesity was associated with an endomorphic–mesomorphic body build.

Constitutional Factors

Constitutional influences are determined by early environmental events that cause a permanent change in the physical makeup of a particular organism. For example, a difficult labor and delivery may cause brain damage to the neonate, resulting in permanent disabilities in areas of intellectual and motor functioning.

Constitutional factors in obesity are associated with formation of adipose cells. The number of these cells laid down during childhood is primarily the result of early feeding practices of the infant's caretakers, and later, eating practices engaged in by the child. The research on adipose cellularity has demonstrated that from infancy through the adolescent period, the amount of calories consumed principally affects the number of adipose cells that develop (Sjöström, 1978). After adolescence, further weight gain results primarily in an increase in the size of the adipose cells. However, recent studies by Sjöström and others indicate that in adults, weight gain can result in some increase in cell number as well as cell size.

The research findings thus far are consistent in demonstrating that once an adipose cell is laid down, this cell becomes a permanent part of the body tissue, that is, a permanent constitutional change in the individual. With weight reduction, there is a shrinking or decrease in the size of the adipose cells as lipids are drained from the cell; however, the cell itself is not lost. During weight regain, the adipose cells expand again through being refilled with lipids.

One should note that genetic factors are also important in adipose cellularity, in terms of the number of adipose cells or the amount of adipose tissue present at birth. Although animals show genetic differences in adipose cellularity, overfeeding during the preweaning period (an environmental influence) can permanently increase fat cell number in both the obese rat and its lean littermate (Johnson, Stern, Greenwood, Zucker, & Hirsch, 1973).

The relative permanence of obesity developed during childhood has been evaluated through a number of longitudinal studies. Eid (1970) conducted a follow-up of children who had manifested excessive weight gain during the first 6 months of life, and found a significant correlation between weight during infancy and at ages 6 to 8. It is important to note that rapidity of weight gain was a better predictor of weight in later childhood than was weight of the parents. Lloyd, Wolff, and Whelan (1961) found that 80% of overweight children and adolescents continued to be overweight as adults; similar findings were reported by Crisp, Douglas, Ross, and Stonehill (1970).

Psychological Factors

Imitation Learning and Reinforcement. Family environment clearly interacts with biological factors in producing an obese child. Although parents provide genes that predispose a child to obesity, they also exert an influence through modeling attitudes and behaviors in relation to food. If a parent is obese, it is likely that that person is not only overeating, but also that she/he is eating in response to emotional and environmental stimuli unrelated to cues of hunger (Leon & Chamberlain, 1973a,b). The child growing up in this particular family milieu may therefore learn through observation to overeat or to use food as a means of dealing with emotional arousal. Further, the amount of food that a child is expected to eat by a parent who eats large quantities of food may be greater than the amount of food that a child is expected to eat by a parent who eats a lesser amount. Therefore, the social approval that a child receives for the amount of food consumed will vary according to the criterion set by the parent for the appropriate amount the child should eat at meal times and between meals. A child who consumes all of the food she/he is given may receive a great deal of social reinforcement from parents and others, while failure to eat the amount expected might result in withdrawal of positive reinforcement or even punishment.

The strong orientation in our Western culture toward the expression of love through the offering of food might result in the child's learning that he or she can please mother and other caretakers through eating food offered even though one is not hungry. Over time, this social interaction, already begun through overnutrition in infancy and early childhood, results in a permanent, constitutional change—the development of a relatively large number of adipose cells, and thus an obese child. (The various social interactions involved in food consumption by the child, and particularly the attention-getting value of food refusal, will be discussed again in relation to the development of anorexia nervosa.)

Psychodynamic Theories. Traditional psychoanalytic theory has conceptualized obesity as a fixation at, or regression to, the oral stage of development (e.g., Jones, 1953). The lack of progress in psychosexual growth to a more mature level has been posited to be caused by conflicts centering on unfulfilled dependency needs (Alexander & Flagg, 1965). The outward expression of these oral conflicts is the incorporation of food.

The concept of obesity as a depressive equivalent or a symptom of an underlying state of depression has also been a common psychodynamic formulation. Based on a review of the case histories of 33 extremely obese adult patients who had undergone psychoanalytically oriented interviews, Rotman and Becker (1970) concluded that overeating was used as a defense mechanism against unconscious affects of helplessness and hopelessness arising from object loss situations.

In her theoretical formulations and treatment procedures with obese persons, Bruch has shifted from a classical psychoanalytic to a more psychodynamic approach that takes into account interpersonal relationships, particularly early mother–infant interactions (Bruch, 1958, 1973). Bruch has stated that obese youngsters have a significantly greater number of emotional problems than do normal-weight youngsters. She used the term *developmental obesity* to refer to a condition associated with severe emotional and personality disturbances, which she viewed as resembling preschizophrenic development. The etiology of this disorder was seen as due to a fundamental disturbance in the basic mother–infant relationship because of severe emotional problems on the part of the mother. This disturbance is manifested by the mother's responding to all of the child's physical and emotional needs by offering food. Thus, the child never learns to distinguish between signals of various bodily urges, and ultimately develops a feeling of not owning his or her own body. "Reactive obesity" was delineated as a less serious type of obesity that is due to stressful environmental factors. Bruch cautioned, however, that removal of the obesity symptom without dealing with the underlying cause would result in severe depression.

An investigation of obese adolescents by Hammar, Campbell, Campbell, Moores, Sareen, Gareis, and Lucas (1972) demonstrated that low self-esteem, depression, and a generally poor self-image characterized the obese population they studied. The formulations of Bruch and others, and empirical findings such as those of Hammar *et al.* have led many professionals to conclude that all obese children and adults are emotionally disturbed and may be manifesting their disturbance through their obesity. However, as pointed out previously (Leon & Roth, 1977), one should bear in mind that the obese persons described in a majority of case reports and clinical investigations are a biased sample, that is, individuals (or their parents) who have identified the obese state as a problem in need of treatment. These persons may be different on a number of psychological variables from obese persons who have not sought treatment. Therefore, emotional concomitants of obesity such as poor self-image and depression should not automatically be assumed to be present in all obese individuals. Further, emotional factors, when present, seem just as likely to be the result of, rather than the cause of the obese state.

Body Image Findings. Body image can be defined as the perception and evaluation of one's own body. The social prejudice against obese individuals (e.g., Canning & Mayer, 1966; Wooley, Wooley, & Dyrenforth, 1980) appears to be influential in the negative evaluation that many obese youngsters, particularly adolescents, have about their own bodies. Stunkard and Burt (1967) found that disturbances in body image (i.e., the attitude that one's body is ugly and loathsome) were not manifested in preadolescent obese youngsters but were seen in persons whose obesity began during the adolescent period. Obese adolescent boys and girls were found to have a less positive and more impaired body concept than nonobese youngsters to whom they were compared (Hammar *et al.,* 1972). The obese group of adolescents expressed a greater dissatisfaction with their physical characteristics and intensely disliked their bodies. Nathan (1973) found that groups of obese children (ages 7, 10, and 13) produced more immature figure drawings (i.e., more global and less differentiated) than did normal weight controls. Obese youngsters were hypothesized to be more immature in their body perceptions because of the incorporation of negative societal attitudes about obesity, resulting in denial and avoidance of bodily interest. Body image disturbances in obese adolescents in treatment were also reported by Schonfeld (1964). On the other hand, Leon, Bemis, Meland, and Nussbaum (1978) found that obese children (ages 8–13) were just as accurate as normal-weight children of the same age in the estimation of the size of various body parts. Further, there was no difference between the two groups on body image barrier and penetration responses (Fisher & Cleveland, 1968).

Comparisons of juvenile-onset and adult-onset massively obese adults suggest a greater degree of disturbance during weight reduction in those who were obese since adolescence (Grinker, 1973). Nonetheless, it does not seem warranted to conclude that there is a greater degree of psychological disturbance in all juvenile-onset obese persons. However, it is possible that if an obese adolescent develops a poor self-concept and body image, then these self-evaluations might become relatively permanent, and subsequent weight loss might not affect these feelings. An individual with adult-onset obesity might have developed a more positive body image during the formative adolescent period that is not affected so markedly by gain in weight during adulthood.

Physical Activity Influences

Studies of obese and normal-weight youngsters have demonstrated that obese persons engage in fewer physical activities and expend a lesser amount of energy in the physical activities they do engage in. Motion picture sampling of obese and normal-weight adolescent girls participating in swimming, volleyball, and tennis demonstrated a lower intensity of movement by the obese, and therefore a relatively lesser burning of calories (Bullen, Reed, & Mayer, 1964). The fact that not all obese persons consume excessive amounts of calories is demonstrated by the finding that obese adolescents in this study consumed a relatively smaller amount of food than did normal-weight campers. The physical inactivity of obese persons and their lesser caloric intake has also been demonstrated in adults (Mayer, 1965b), suggesting that for some persons physical inactivity rather than excessive caloric intake may be the most important influence determining their obesity.

Conclusions

Findings about the association between physical activity factors and obesity underscore the point that it might not be justified to assume that obesity is always the result of underlying psychopathology. There appear to be a number of types of obesity, each differing in terms of the importance of particular variables. Based on a diathesis-stress model, some children might have a greater biological predisposition for obesity than other youngsters. In some, family, cultural, and socioeconomic factors might assume a relatively greater degree of importance. The prevalence of obesity among persons of lower socioeconomic classes suggests the importance of dietary patterns, particularly the high carbohydrate "filler" diets eaten by the poor, in the development of childhood and adult obesity. Further, differences in racial and ethnic standards of ideal body weight might also be a factor in the higher average weights found among children from lower socioeconomic groups, because of the correlation between race and ethnic status and social class.

The social learning histories of some children might be instrumental in the development of a highly overlearned habit of excessive food intake. This pattern of food consumption, learned through processes of reinforcement and imitation, then generalizes over time. Eventually, a diversity of environmental and emotional stimuli unrelated to cues of hunger become signals for eating behavior (Leon & Chamberlain, 1973a). Obesity developing under these circumstances can be conceptualized as a lack of self-control or self-regulation of food consumption. These particular habit patterns are not necessarily psychopathological. However, in some subset of the obese population, it is possible that excessive food consumption could be associated with severe psychopathological disturbance.

Treatment

Individual Psychotherapy

Individual psychotherapy does not appear to be an effective method for treating obesity in children or adults (see review by Leon, 1976). It is difficult to evaluate the efficacy of these procedures because the treatment literature primarily consists of case descriptions aimed at highlighting particular psychodynamic factors that the clinician felt were important in the etiology of the disorder. Specific data about weight loss, weight loss maintenance, and changes in interpersonal functioning are often lacking. Further, follow-up evaluation has rarely been carried out or reported. The general conclusion from Bruch's writings (e.g., Bruch, 1970c) is that juvenile obesity is frequently an outward manifestation of a range of severe underlying difficulties, and that treatment of these youngsters is quite difficult and prolonged.

Dietary and Fasting Regimens

Dietary management has been of marginal success in producing lasting weight loss. Hammar, Campbell, and Woolley (1971) conducted a 1–8 year follow-up of obese adolescents treated by diet or some type of counseling. They found that 70% of the respondents were still obese. The large number of persons who did not respond to the follow-up (70.5%) precludes any conclusions about the relative effectiveness of the various types of treatment used.

Prolonged fasting or starvation involving hospitalization during the period of the fast has been used in the treatment of adolescent obesity (Nathan & Pisula, 1970). Similar to reports with adult patients, many adolescents manifested negative psychological effects during hospitalization. Further, the fasting procedure was quite ineffective: results of an 8–24 month follow-up indicated that all but two of the adolescents regained weight after leaving the hospital. Further, the majority had regained or exceeded their admission weight.

Behavior Modification Procedures

Behavior modification techniques for weight reduction that were initially used with adult populations have been adapted for programs with obese children and adolescents. The behavioral procedures used with children include reinforcement for weight loss or changing habits of food consumption, response costs to parent or child for failing to meet various program requirements such as keeping a food dairy, and instruction in stimulus control procedures (i.e., how to change the environmental stimuli associated with food intake).

Behavior modification procedures have been effectively used to produce weight loss in obese children and adolescents (Aragona, Cassady, & Drabman, 1975; Kingsley & Shapiro, 1977; Weiss, 1977) and to decrease caloric intake in a school setting (Epstein, Masek, & Marshall, 1978). Weiss's study involved a comparison of the efficacy of five different treatment conditions. The 1-year follow-up carried out in this investigation is the longest reported of the studies surveyed, and indicated that subjects in the two habit-change groups (i.e., stimulus control, and stimulus control plus conventional diet) exhibited the greatest amount of weight loss maintenance. However, a continuing problem in all of the studies cited is the relative failure for long-term weight change to occur in many of the youngsters treated.

Parental Involvement. Kingsley and Shapiro (1977) systematically evaluated the effect of involvement of the mother on the weight reduction progress of obese 10- to 11-year-old children. The treatment conditions in the behaviorally oriented groups were as follows: children and their mothers in the same group; mothers only with no child involvement; children only with no mother involvement; and a no-treatment control group. There were no significant differences in weight loss between the treatment groups at the posttreatment or at the 6- and 20-week follow-up periods. The mean posttreatment weight loss in the combined treatment groups was 3.5 lbs. This investigation does not support the notion that active parental involvement in the treatment group increases the efficacy of the child's weight loss. However, the crucial element for successful weight loss by the child might be the ability of the family as a whole to make a more general change in lifestyle. There is a need for this issue to be systematically evaluated.

Family Lifestyle Modification

It seems crucial for family factors to be taken into account in improving the treatment prognosis for significant childhood obesity. Since there is a high probability that the obese child comes from a family with other obese members, the child might justifiably feel scapegoated if he or she is the only one in the family expected to make a change in eating behavior. Modifications in food consumption patterns by the entire family seem to be the most likely approach for maintaining weight changes in any member of that family. General lifestyle changes involving increases in physical activity also might increase the efficacy of particular programs aimed at altering eating habits within the family. These modifications can be beneficial to the health of all family members, and will redefine the eating problem as a family rather than as an individual member's problem.

It is also important to ascertain particular behaviors contributing to obesity among various family members (i.e., over-eating, lack of physical activity, or a combination of these factors) so that an integrated and appropriate treatment plan can be developed. Each family member can then be encouraged to implement the particular changes that are especially pertinent to him or her.

Case Illustration

Jerry was 14 years old, 5 feet, 10 inches tall, and weighed 220 pounds at the time he was referred for psychological evaluation. Jerry was an only child, and he lived with his parents in a middle-class neighborhood. His mother was approximately 5 feet, 4 inches tall and weighed 200 pounds. She indicated that she had been overweight since childhood. Jerry's father was of normal weight, and he had never had a weight problem.

The parents both corroborated the fact that Jerry had always had a "big appetite," even as an infant, and had always eaten a great deal. Pediatric records indicated that Jerry had consistently been well above the body-weight norms for his age since early childhood.

Jerry reported that he had no friends, was teased a great deal by other students in his junior high school class, and was almost continually in trouble at school for fighting with both peers and teachers. He engaged in loud arguments with his teachers and he frequently got into fist fights with other boys when they provoked him through their teasing. He stated that the other boys were afraid of him because he was so big, and he enjoyed intimidating them to avoid their teasing and as a response to their taunts. He generally ignored the teasing he received from girls at school.

Both of Jerry's parents worked. Because he had no friends and did not engage in any extracurricular activities, Jerry went home each day after school. He watched television alone and snacked on candy, potato chips, and cookies until one of his parents arrived home. At that point, there was usually an argument about his eating behavior. Both Jerry and his father reported instances when the two of them had gotten into physical fights due to Jerry's eating something and his father's attempting to take food away from him.

Family strife was also a consistent feature of the parents' interactions with each other. The parents had separated on a number of occasions because they seemed to disagree on most issues. However, they generally reconciled after a period of time because it was easier financially to live together.

Jerry was referred for psychological evaluation by the school guidance counselor because he had punched one of his male teachers in the wake of an argument about being disruptive in class that day. Jerry agreed to be seen for individual counseling, and he was also placed on a behavior modification program for weight reduction. His parents were seen periodically in reference to Jerry's eating and behavioral problems. Very little progress was made in treatment, in part because of the enmeshment of the eating behavior in power struggles between Jerry and his parents, and between the parents themselves. Four weeks after treatment began, Jerry enrolled in karate classes, with his father's enthusiastic endorsement and contrary to the therapist's recommendation. Jerry dropped out of treatment soon after the lessons began.

Jerry initiated contact with the therapist a year later. He said that he wanted to work on his weight alone, without his parents' involvement. He did so, and was successful in gradually losing weight over the next year. His social interactions also showed moderate improvement.

Anorexia Nervosa

Introduction

The self-starvation, body emaciation, and other physical and behavioral characteristics noted primarily among female adolescents were classified according to the term "anorexia nervosa" in the late 1800s by the English physician, Sir William Gull. However, this disorder was vividly described as "nervous phthisis" by Richard Morton in 1694 when he depicted a case of an 18-year-old girl. Morton wrote:

> She was wont by her studying at Night, and continued pouring upon Books, to expose herself both Day and Night to the injuries of the Air, which was at that time cold. . . . I do not remember that I did ever in all my Practice see one, that was conversant with the Living, so much wasted with the greatest degree of a Consumption (like a Skeleton only clad with skin); yet there was no Fever, but on the contrary a coldness of the whole body. . . . Only her Appetitie was diminished, and her Digestion uneasie. (cited in Bliss & Branch, 1960)

The fundamental features of this severe eating disorder have remained unmodified over the 288 years since Morton's description. Although societal and family patterns have obviously changed over this time period, physical and behavioral aspects of anorexia nervosa continue to exhibit a marked similarity.

The term *anorexia nervosa,* literally translated, means a nervous loss of appetite, and it was commonly believed that anorexics did not experience sensations of hunger. However, clinical and research evidence indicates that this term is a misnomer, and that anorexics do indeed suffer from pangs of hunger (Garfinkel, 1974), often extremely intense in nature. (Only with food intake of less than 200 calories per day do hunger sensations generally cease.) The consistent feature of the anorexia nervosa syndrome is the relentless pursuit of thinness, that is, the phenomenon of continual dieting or food restriction to the point of self-starvation and sometimes death.

Diagnostic Criteria and Clinical Features

The refusal of food is a behavior that is associated with a number of psychopathological disorders, including schizophrenia, depression, hysteria, and hypochondriasis. It is therefore important to evaluate the problem areas or clinical features in addition to the food restriction before diagnosing the problem as anorexia nervosa.

The diagnosis of anorexia nervosa employed by Halmi and Sherman (1975) is based on an adaptation of the criteria proposed by Feighner, Robins, Guze, Woodruff, Winokur, and Munoz (1972): an onset between the ages of 10 and 30 years; weight loss of at least 25% of original body weight, resulting in the individual's being at least 15% below normal weight; and a distorted, implacable attitude and behavior toward eating, food, or weight—an attitude that overrides hunger, reassurance, or threats. For females, the criteria also include amenorrhea (absence or suppression of menstruation) of at least three months' duration, unless symptoms occur before onset of menses, with no known medical illness that could account for the amenorrhea. A further sign designated by Feighner *et al.* is no known psychiatric disorder or medical illness. (The DSM-III requirements for the diagnosis of anorexia nervosa consist of similar criteria expressed in broader terms.)

Anorexia nervosa is an eating disturbance that occurs primarily in Caucasian adolescent females of middle or upper class socioeconomic status. There is only one case on record of this disorder occurring among black persons. Clinical descriptions of the behavioral characteristics of these youngsters before onset of severe weight loss have mentioned obsessive–compulsive characteristics, shyness or timidity in peer and adult social interactions, conscientiousness, and achievement orientation (Bemis, 1978). Psychological evaluations of hospitalized anorexics have demonstrated neurotic and introverted psychometric test profiles in the patients evaluated (Crisp & Stonehill, 1972; Smart, Beumont, & George, 1976). Anorexics whose weight has been newly restored to normal have exhibited on psychological tests a high sensitivity to social interactions coupled with timidity and low self-esteem (Pillay & Crisp, 1977).

An overriding feature of anorexia nervosa is the intense desire for an extremely thin appearance. Crisp, Kalucy, Lacey, and Harding (1977) referred to the disorder in terms of a phobic avoidance centering around the pubertal weight threshold. They also discussed anorexia nervosa as a disorder of shape, with extreme anxiety manifested by the youngster as she gains weight above this pubertal weight threshold. A phobia of gaining weight and of taking in food seems to be a consistent feature in persons suffering from this disorder. Thus, a strong desire for thinness rather than a diminishment or cessation of hunger appears most characteristic of the eating disturbance.

Extreme hyperactivity of a highly ritualized nature is also commonly noted in anorexia nervosa. In individuals who are conscientious and obsessive-compulsive, it can be seen how a strong drive to exercise can take on the form of a complex daily ritual. The daily exercise activities become highly structured and rigorous and result, over the course of a 24-hour period, in the expenditure of a great number of calories. Anorexics may often carry out some of these exercise activities in the middle of the night, feeling driven to engage in these activities even though weak and exhausted from their low level of food intake. Intense physical activity along with restricted caloric intake results in a further reduction of body weight. These exercise activities may also serve as a distraction from the severe hunger pangs these youngsters often feel.

Primary or secondary amenorrhea is a characteristic symptom in female anorexics and indeed is one of the diagnostic criteria for this disorder in females. Of interest is the fact that the cessation of menstruation may occur *before* significant weight loss has occurred (Danowski, Livstone, Gonzales, Jung, & Khurana, 1972; Halmi, 1974; Halmi, Goldberg, Eckert, Casper, & Davis, 1977). Conversely, resumption of the menstrual cycle may be delayed for months or even years after attainment of the minimal weight necessary for a particular height for the menstrual cycle to be restored. Psychological stress appears to play a significant role in the amenorrhea pattern, although a review of the literature (Bemis, 1978) suggests that neither a generalized stress phenomenon nor a starvation phenomenon can be posited as the primary agent in the etiology of menstrual disturbance in anorexia nervosa.

Prevalence

Although anorexia nervosa occurs primarily in females, estimates of the prevalence of this disorder in males have varied between 5% and 15% of total anorexics (Bemis, 1978). In terms of age of onset, Halmi (1974) found that 78% of the 94 cases she surveyed had an illness onset between the ages of 10 and 25. The incidence of anorexia nervosa appears to be increasing in our culture in a proportion far greater than that which can be explained by an enhanced awareness of the symptoms of this disorder. Although previous estimates of the prevalence of anorexia nervosa suggests that it is an extremely rare disorder, more recent research contradicts this. Nylander (1971), on the basis of his research in Sweden, concluded that anorexia nervosa is present in a quite definite and severe form in 1 in every 150 adolescent females. Crisp, Palmer, and Kalucy (1976) carried out a careful prevalence study of anorexia nervosa among British school girls and included in their statistics only those cases in which an unequivocal diagnosis could be made. All the school girls classified as anorexic had lost at least 30% of their body weight over the course of the illness. The findings indicated a prevalence of 1 in 100 cases of school girls aged 16 and over, and a prevalence of approximately 1 in 200 over the surveyed age range of 15 years and under to 16 years and over. Crisp *et al.* (1976) also reported a social class factor in that the disorder was more common in Social Classes I and II.

Outcome Variables

Estimates of the death rate from anorexia nervosa have ranged from approximately 3% (Dally, 1967) to 21% (Halmi, Brodland, & Rigas, 1975). Crisp *et al.* (1977) reported that anorexics of lower socioeconomic classes have a poorer prognosis and more marked psychopathology, often of a clear sexual nature, than do anorexics of higher socioeconomic classes. Morgan and Russell (1975) conducted a follow-up of 41 patients with anorexia nervosa who had been treated primarily by nursing care aimed at rapid weight restoration. The minimum follow-up period from hospital discharge was 4 years. Approximately 39% of the patients they evaluated were categorized as manifesting a good outcome, 27% an intermediate outcome, 29% a poor outcome, and 5% had died. Among the predictors of unfavorable outcome were: a relatively late age of onset (age 30 and over); a longer duration of illness; premorbid peronality difficulties and previous admissions to psychiatric hospitals; and a disturbed relationship between the patient and other family members. Further, Halmi *et al.* (1975) found that early onset was related to a good prognosis.

Garfinkel, Moldofsky, and Garner (1977) also conducted a follow-up study of treated anorexics, and evaluated 42 patients approximately 32 months from the time of initial treatment. The method of treatment varied among patients in the group that was studied. In general, 50% of the patients were rated as doing quite well at follow-up and 19% were categorized as exhibiting a poor outcome. Among the factors related to good outcome were good premorbid educational and vocational adjustment; a poorer outcome was found among anorexics with a prehospitalization history of bulimia (food-binging or gorging) and vomiting. These latter findings confirm previous reports by Crisp, Harding, and McGuinness (1974), Selvini-Palazzoli (1971), and Theander (1970) of the pathogenic significance of and vomiting in relation to outcome.

The treatment outcome for anorexic males generally appears to be less favorable than the outcome findings reported for females. Crisp *et al.* (1977) speculated that overeating and vomiting are probably a more common feature among male than among female anorexics, and that the disorder develops in males in the context of prior massive obesity, gender identity problems, and a generally more marked psychopathological premorbid history. Crisp and Toms (1972) found that anorexia nervosa in males did not show the same preponderance in middle and upper social classes as is found in females, and further, that the prognosis was generally poor.

Theoretical Formulations

Psychoanalytic Theories

Since the dieting and self-starvation pattern of anorexia nervosa often begins at the pubertal period, psychoanalytic theorists have viewed the severe food restriction characteristic of this disorder as symbolic of severe sexual conflicts. Waller, Kaufman, and Deutsch (1940/1964) presented a formulation of anorexia nervosa as a disorder caused by food intake being symbolically linked with preganacy fantasies, and the refusal of food was seen as a symbolic denial of the infantile fantasy of oral impregnation by the father. The concern expressed by anorexic girls that their stomachs are protruding (a comment frequently made by anorexics) was therefore viewed as a fear of pregnancy psychodynamically related to psychosexual conflicts concerning the father. However, the amenorrhea associated with the disorder was seen as symbolic of being pregnant (Kaufman & Heiman, 1964), and also as a denial of feminine sexuality (Lorand, 1943/1964). Selvini-Palazzoli (1971), on the other hand, conceptualized the basic psychodynamic conflict of anorexia nervosa as occurring at puberty, when development of breasts and other secondary sexual characteristics results in the body's being experienced as the maternal object that has been incorporated within the self. Food restriction therefore functions as active aggression against, and a means of controlling, the incorporated bad object (i.e., mother).

Other Psychodynamic Theories

Hilde Bruch has written extensively about anorexia nervosa, based primarily on her clinical experience in the intensive treatment of persons with severe eating disorders. She has moved from a classical psychoanalytic perspective, in her theoretical formulations and method of treatment of anorexia nervosa, to a broader psychodynamic approach. Bruch (1970a,b) has posited that primary anorexia is the result of a very early and profound disturbance in mother–child interactions. As a result of this severe disturbance, the youngster's ego development is deficient, and this deficiency is manifested by a disturbance in body identity that includes lack of a sense of ownership of one's body. As in the case of obesity, the youngster is seen as growing up unable to discriminate between signals of various bodily urges because the mother proffered food to the child irrespective of the child's specific needs and urges. The result is a distorted body image, and a feeling that one is not in control of one's own body. It is posited that the anorexia nervosa syndrome occurs when the individual feels overpowered by reality demands in which the fragile sense of self is undermined (Bruch, 1973).

Bruch (1978) has also commented about the histories of compliance and being a model child that are typical of the anorexics she has seen in treatment. Many of these youngsters indicated that the refusal to eat gave them a sense of superiority and a feeling of being more worthwhile and a "better person" through the self-discipline required in losing weight. The anorexic, according to Bruch, lives in a continual fear of not being loved and acknowledged within the family structure. In terms of the issue of sexuality, Bruch postulated that the concern over bodily changes during puberty is related to an anxiety about being expected to act in a more independent manner. Therefore, life events that may force the adolescent to act more independently, or events that make the adolescent feel that she has little control over her life, may precipitate the self-starvation syndrome. The significance of puberty therefore lies in the implications for independent behavior and feelings of control over one's life, rather than being related to unconscious fears of impregnation or incorporation fantasies.

Family Interaction Theories

Minuchin and his colleagues have been influential in highlighting the role of family interactions in promoting and maintaining psychosomatic symptoms, including anorexia nervosa, in the children of particular families (e.g., Minuchin, Rosman, & Baker, 1978). Four characteristics of the structure of "psychosomatic families" are delineated: enmeshment (no autonomy of the individual family members); overprotectiveness; rigidity (particularly in adapting to adolescence); and lack of conflict resolution (particularly between parents). The interactions among family members are seen as a way of avoiding conflict, and the result is that various family problems are left unresolved. According to this analysis, the key factor supporting the child's symptom is his/her involvement in parental conflict. The child becomes caught in the middle between the parents or in a coalition with one parent against the other. In addition, parents may deny their own conflict by defining the sick child as the family problem. Minuchin *et al.* commented on the great degree of enmeshment in anorexic families, with family members behaving in an interpersonally intrusive manner. Concurrently, there may be a change of child–parent roles during development of the child's illness with, for example, the child communicating with the father through the mother. Nonetheless, however the family system operates, conflict avoidance appears to be a strong factor in the interpersonal dynamics of anorexic families.

Family Research. Family psychopathology in families of anorexics has been clearly demonstrated by the investigations of Crisp *et al.* (1974) and Kalucy, Crisp, and Harding (1977). Crisp *et al.* extensively evaluated parents during the period of the anorexic's weight restoration and found that they became significantly more anxious and depressed as the anorexic youngster improved. In particular, severe anxiety in mothers and significant depression in fathers was commonly noted. Further, these changes in the psychological status of the parents concurrent with improvement in their child were associated with long-standing, severely impaired marital relationships. Kalucy *et al.*, in their evaluation of 56 families of anorexics, reported that 40% of the parents indicated marked degrees of unhappiness about their sexual relationship with each other. These negative feelings were expressed in a manner suggesting dissatisfaction with the functioning of the family as a whole. The adolescent within the family is seen as attempting to cope with the family psychopathology by modifying her shape. The investigators felt that the recovering anorexic, as an adolescent, challenges the family stability in a way that does not occur when the anorexic is childlike in appearance and behavior. Other family characteristics or problems noted by Kalucy *et al.* were high achievement orientation, various difficulties with food, body weight, and shape in other family members, and a high incidence of anorexia nervosa-like symptoms in the parents' adolescent histories. It is also interesting to note that excessive alcohol use was found in 7% of the mothers and 19% of the fathers in anorexic families.

Behavioral Theories

The behavioral literature has focused on the development of effective behavior modification treatment programs and has not been as concerned with formulation of the types of social learning experiences that might be fundamental to the etiology of anorexia nervosa. Food refusal has been considered as a manifestation of avoidance behavior, and an analysis of environmental reinforcement patterns has been considered important in understanding the development of eating disturbances in a particular individual (Blinder, Freeman, & Stunkard, 1970; Leitenberg, Agras, & Thomson, 1968).

Leon (1979) proposed that in anorexia nervosa a strong learned association develops between extremely negative thoughts and images about weight gain and the behavioral act of food consumption. Over time, this learning process becomes strengthened and generalizes to an association between thoughts or images of food and feelings of revulsion and disgust. This aversive affect then also occurs in association with the actual consumption of food. Thus, a conditioned aversion to food intake becomes established and a cognitive judgment is made as well that eating will lead to weight gain. Following a two-process theory of avoidance learning (Mowrer, 1947), the reinforcer maintaining this behavioral sequence is the anxiety reduction associated with the affirmation of self-control and control over one's life through food restriction.

The distorted body image noted in persons suffering from anorexia nervosa may be conceptualized within the same self-control framework. The emaciated adolescent who looks in the mirror and says "I'm fat" may not be manifesting a severe perceptual distortion as much as an evaluation that she would like to be thinner still, the thinness again serving as an affirmation of control over one's self and over one's life in general. An initial confirmation of this hypothesis is found in the findings of Leon, Bemis, and Lucas (1980) with 18 newly hospitalized anorexics. All of the patients indicated that dieting and weight loss resulted in a feeling of self-control and willpower, and a generally greater feeling of control over their lives. In relation to the aversive conditioning hypothesis proposed in the previous paragraph, it is relevant to note that anorexic subjects indicated that food that they had found pleasant-tasting in the past and that they had previously enjoyed eating, tasted unpleasant to them.

Self-Control and Food Consumption. The issue of self-control in relation to food intake becomes highlighted still further when evaluating cognitions and behaviors of anorexics before and after clear development of the self-starvation pattern. Many persons who become anorexic have had problems with regulating their food intake well before the development of this self-starvation disorder. Crisp *et al.* (1977) found a high proportion of premorbid obesity, including massive obesity, in the anorexics they treated. Further, Halmi (1974) reported that 31% of the 94 cases of anorexia nervosa that she reviewed had a history of overweight before the age of 12. It may also be significant that Pertschuk (1977), in a follow-up of 27 anorexic patients who had undergone a behavior modification treatment program, reported that 37% developed bulimia and vomiting after treatment, although none had manifested this particular food consumption pattern prior to hospitalization. Thus, a normalization of eating patterns did not parallel a normalization of weight, and the majority of patients at follow-up continued to express an inordinate concern with food.

The issue of self-control, particularly in relation to food intake, continues to be a concern for many anorexics, including those whose weight has been restored to a normal or near-normal level. The control over food intake may consist of food restriction alternating with breakthroughs of binge eating and vomiting. On the other hand, a pattern of eating relatively normal amounts of food on a daily basis may be achieved only at the expense of a constant preoccupation with food and eating. Cognitions about food intake may also consist of continuing concerns that if one eats too much or outside of a fixed routine, then uncontrolled binging will occur that one will be powerless to prevent. Flexible control over food intake appears to be an extremely difficult goal to achieve for many persons who have experienced clinically significant manifestations of eating disorders.

In addition to severe body emaciation, persons suffering from anorexia nervosa exhibit anemia, dryness of the skin, edema, lanugo hair (a fine body-hair growth), low body temperature, low basal metabolism, a slow heart beat, and a sense of pain and coldness in their limbs (Dally, 1969). Endocrine findings in female anorexics with secondary amenorrhea typically indicate abnormalities in thyroid functioning (Bliss & Branch, 1960) and in the gonadotropins. The gonadotropin abnormalities of the anterior pituitary hormones consist of reduced secretion of luteinizing hormone (LH) and follicle-stimulating hormones (FSH), and a signifcantly higher elevation in resting morning levels of plasma growth hormone (GH) (Brown, Garfinkel, Jeuniewic, Moldofsky, & Stancer, 1977). Brown *et al.* found a significant correlation between resting levels of LH and weight loss, and no relationship between LH and present caloric intake or duration of amenorrhea. Resting GH levels, on the other hand, were related to poor caloric intake but were not related to degree of body weight loss and duration of onset of amenorrhea. These findings therefore suggest that elevated GH levels are secondary to starvation, and that GH elevation can be reversed or normalized through refeeding. In anorexic women, the LH and FSH patterns appear to resemble most closely patterns of prepubertal rather than postpubertal females.

Release of the above-mentioned anterior pituitary hormones is controlled in turn by hypothalamic hormones, and these latter hormones have been proposed to be functioning abnormally as well. The possibility of an impairment of hypothalmic receptor function was suggested by the findings of Casper, Davis, and Pandey (1977), and Mecklenburg, Loriaux, Thompson, Anderson, and Lipsett (1974). However, the direction of causality remains to be established. As Bruch (1978) and others have pointed out, the various disturbances in endocrine and higher brain functioning can be demonstrated to occur in cases of malnutrition for reasons other than self-starvation. Loss of sexual interest, depression, tension, irritability, and food preoccupations have all been manifested by persons evaluated during states of semistarvation (Schiele & Brozek, 1948). Further, cessation of menstruation is also a concomitant of malnutrition (Frisch, 1977). However, there are a number of differences between the general effects of starvation and the effects of anorexia nervosa. Amenorrhea in anorexics often occurs before significant weight loss has occurred; 37% of the patients in the Halmi *et al.* (1977) study experienced amenorrhea before an appreciable amount of weight had been lost. Further, the resumption of the menstrual cycle may not occur for a number of years after normal body weight has been restored. The extreme hyperactivity, intense mental acuity, and sleep disturbances noted in anorexics (i.e., sleeping as little as 3–4 fours a night) also is not a common feature of the semi-starvation syndrome due to famine or experimentally induced food restriction.

Treatment Efficacy

There has been an increasing interest in the implementation of behavior modification methods in the treatment of anorexia nervosa. Investigators using these particular techniques have provided some of the first careful treatment outcome studies on increasingly larger numbers of persons suffering from anorexia nervosa. Leon (1979) and Van Buskirk (1977) have reviewed the studies employing behavioral treatment methods, and Bemis (1978) has provided a review of the efficacy of a range of treatment methods used with anorexics. The behavioral treatment outcome studies initially seemed quite promising. The primary focus of these particular programs was on modification of anorexic eating patterns and on reinforcement of eating larger quantities of food (e.g., Bhanji & Thompson, 1974; Halmi, Powers, & Cunningham, 1975). However, the relative effectiveness of these particular procedures is blurred because other interventions, such as psychoactive medication in the former study and family involvement during the maintenance period in the latter study, were added to the behavioral program.

Despite the criticism by Bruch (1978) and others of the dangers of using strict behavior modification programs with anorexics, Garfinkel, Moldofsky, and Garner (1977) demonstrated that patients treated with behavior modification procedures did not show negative effects at follow-up, in comparison with patients treated with somatic or other types of treatment. However, the relatively greater efficacy of behavior modification programs primarily oriented toward changing eating patterns can be called into question by a number of recent findings. The marked success seen in the first patient treated with operant conditioning procedures (Bachrach, Erwin, & Mohr, 1965) has been documented by pictures in numerous abnormal psychology textbooks. The patient weighted 47 pounds on hospital admission and 85 pounds 2 years later. However, a 16-year follow-up by Erwin (1977) points to a markedly less favorable long-term outcome. Mrs. A's weight at follow-up had declined to 55 pounds, only 8 pounds higher than her pretreatment weight 16 years previously. It was reported, though, that there had been an enhancement in her social activities, and the ability to care for herself and her mother were considered her greatest sustained advance

A further disappointment to the thesis of the greater efficacy of behavior modification treatment approaches is the results of an extensive multicenter collaborative treatment study of 105 female patients comparing a 35-day behavior modification protocol with various combinations of drug therapy and placebo (Goldberg *et al.,* 1977; Halmi *et al.*, 1977). Halmi (1980) reported that the behavior modification program did not have any overall consistent effect on weight gain over the 35 days on that treatment regimen. Since patients gained weight in the hospital irrespective of the treatment condition they were in, there was no greater efficacy demonstrated with the behavioral program.

As Van Buskirk (1977) pointed out, treatment outcome can be evaluated from the short-term perspective of weight gain in the hospital, and from the long-term perspective of general psychological adjustment and normalization of eating patterns without undue food preoccupations. It remains to be demonstrated that behavioral approaches focusing specifically on food consumption patterns can achieve the goal of a long-term maintenance of eating behavior change or of weight restoration. The issue of long-term maintenance of weight change following release from the hospital is crucial to the ultimate success of any treatment program. However, the issue of "quality of life" is also important, and if the weight gain is maintained through social isolation, intense food preoccupations, or the development of a bulimia–vomiting pattern, then one can justifiably question whether a particular treatment program has been a success.

A promising direction in the treatment of anorexia nervosa has been the use of family therapy (Rosman, Minuchin, Baker, & Liebman, 1977) and peer group therapy in conjunction with specific behavior modification procedures. Issues of control over one's body and one's life, as well as concerns about growing up and dealing with heterosexual relationships, would also seem to be important areas to explore in individual psychotherapy. The potent attention-getting value of self-starvation in an extremely controlling and achievement-oriented family (Bruch, 1978) appears to be an important issue to deal with in treatment. The development of cognitive-restructuring techniques in relation to eating behavior also seems promising (Ollendick, 1979).

A further area in which treatment might be focused is in terms of the anorexic's body image. Goldberg *et al.* (1977) administered a body perception test (Slade & Russell, 1973) in which the subject is asked to estimate the size of various body parts. Although most individuals tend to overestimate their body dimensions (Leon *et al.*, 1979), Goldberg *et al.* found that those anorexics who at pretreatment evaluation showed the greatest tendency to overestimate their body parts exhibited a lesser weight gain in-hospital and a greater denial of their illness. Further, using a distorting photograph technique, Garner, Garfinkel, Stancer, and Moldofsky (1976) found that, for anorexics, increased body size estimate was significantly related to degree of neuroticism and absence of a feeling of self-control. These findings suggest that it might be important to incorporate discussions about feelings and perceptions in relation to one's body in treatment program for anorexics.

Case Illustration

Wendy was 16 years old when her parents insisted that she be seen by the family pediatrician because of severe weight loss. Wendy was 5 feet, 3 inches tall and weighed 78 pounds. She had been dieting for the past 2 years, since she decided, at a weight of 110 pounds, that she was too fat. Wendy had begun menstruating at age 13, but she had not had a menstrual period for the previous 1½ years. She indicated that she was not concerned that her periods had stopped, but she was extremely concerned that she was still too fat. At the time she was seen, Wendy was consuming an average of about 500 calories of food per day.

Over the course of her past 2 years' dieting efforts, Wendy had become increasingly stricter about how much she would eat, and each mealtime ended in a battle with her parents over her food intake. If possible, she tried to avoid eating meals with her parents and two older brothers, saying that she was not hungry at that time and that she would eat more if she ate alone at a later time. If her parents insisted that she eat with them, she toyed with her food, cut it up into small portions, and piled the left-over food on one part of her plate in order to make it look as if she had eaten more than she actually had. Typically, her daily food consumption consisted of an egg, a small portion of bread, a carrot stick, and some water or diet soda.

Wendy had always been a good student in school. However, both of her brothers had consistently been on the honor roll and had excelled in academic and in extracurricular activities. Wendy worked hard to get good grades, but her academic performance was taken for granted by her parents in the context of the superior achievements of her older brothers.

Wendy was described by her parents as having been an obedient child who always complied with her parents' wishes. They indicated that they were fairly structured in raising Wendy, setting limits on her outside activities, the time she went to bed each night, and who the youngsters were that she played with. Wendy was described as agreeable to this structure. Her parents were therefore amazed and helpless in dealing with her intractable stubborness in relation to eating, given her compliant behavior in all other areas since childhood.

As Wendy grew thinner, she became increasingly more preoccupied with planning how much she was going to eat each day, and how to avoid situations in which she would be pressured to eat more than she had planned to. Wendy began an exercise program at the time she started dieting, and her daily exercises, carried out in a strictly ordered routine, became lengthier and more strenuous each day. Wendy always swam a given number of laps four times a day. During the summer, she would swim these laps outdoors even if there were lightening or thunder outside. Over time, even though feeling exhausted, she added an extra swimming session at night without her parents' knowledge, jumping out of her second-story bedroom window to go outside to swim. Wendy felt extremely hungry, tired, and irritable almost all of the time. She was also preoccupied with thoughts of food and how she looked. Her weight continued to drop and her school work suffered. She stopped interacting with the few girls she talked to at school and became quite isolated from others.

Despite the efforts of her parents and her pediatrician, Wendy refused to stop dieting. She indicated that she felt extremely good about herself, knowing that she could control her bodily urges to the extent that she would not eat when hungry, and could exercise strenuously even though she felt exhausted. Eventually, Wendy was hospitalized for treatment, despite her strong objections that there was nothing wrong with her. Her weight at the time of hospitalization was 68 pounds.

General Overview

Severe eating disorders, particularly food restriction, appear to be a mark of an affluent society. In countries in which food is scarce, most persons do not have the luxury of overeating to the point of obesity, or gaining attention through refusing to eat. In countries such as India and Sri Lanka, where food is scarce and obesity has traditionally been highly valued as a sign of wealth, extremely low rates of anorexia nervosa are manifested. Both obesity and anorexia nervosa are most common in more affluent countries of the Western hemisphere.

Obesity and anorexia nervosa can be conceptualized along a continuum related to self-control over food intake. The anorexic can be viewed as exhibiting a pathological excess of self-control, while the obese youngster can be seen as manifesting a lack of self-control. The bulimia–vomiting pattern may fall somewhere in the middle of the continuum. The binge eating represents a breakdown in self-control mechanisms in relation to food, with control again being reinstituted through food restriction until the next binge episode occurs.

The frequent intractability of the various eating disorders and the devastating intra- and interpersonal consequences that can result from them point to the necessity of childhood prevention and early treatment intervention. The incidence of childhood obesity may be lessened through sound nutritional information, family lifestyle changes that incorporate physical activity as an enjoyable family experience, and implementation of alternatives for expressing affection and "proving" oneself a good parent other than through overfeeding of one's youngsters. In treating an obese child, changing family eating patterns may be a more efficient treatment strategy than one that is focused on modifying the eating patterns of a particular child while ignoring the eating behavior of other family members. Because so many of the psychological problems associated with obesity appear to be the result of, rather than the cause of the obese state, childhood prevention takes on even greater importance. On the other hand, in situations where obesity is associated with marked emotional problems, exploring alternatives for dealing with emotional arousal, other than through food intake, would also be quite beneficial.

Bruch (1973) has cited the American preoccupation with slimness as a strong etiological factor in the increasing incidence of anorexia nervosa. Further, the overwhelming female incidence of this disorder can be viewed in terms of societal definitions of physical attractiveness for women, definitions that are centered on being as slim as possible. The large proportion of adolescent females developing anorexia nervosa may also be due to the greater tendency for girls to define their self-hood and personal worth in terms of their physical appearance.

The widespread phenomenon of dieting, particularly among female adolescents and adults, provides a fertile soil for the development of eating disorders. It seems extremely important for public health education efforts to focus on the dangers of extreme thinness and indiscriminate dieting to the same extent that there has been an emphasis on the health problems associated with severe obesity.

References

Alexander, F., & Flagg, G. W. The psychosomatic approach. In B. J. Wolman (Ed.). *Handbook of clinical psychology*. New York: McGraw-Hill, 1965.

Aragona, J., Cassady, J., & Drabman, R. S. Treating overweight children through parental training and contingency contracting. *Journal of Applied Behavior Analysis,* 1975, *8,* 269–278.

Bachrach, A. J., Erwin, W. J., & Mohr, J. P. The control of eating behavior in an anorexic by operant conditioning techniques. In L. P. Ullman & L. Krasner (Eds.), *Case studies in behavior modification*. New York: Holt, Rinehart & Winston, 1965.

Bemis, K. Current apprroaches to the etiology and treatment of anorexia nervosa.*Psychological Bulletin,* 1978, *85,* 593–617.

Bhanji, S., & Thompson, J. Operant conditioning in the treatment of anorexia nervosa: A review and retrospective study of 11 cases. *British Journal of Psychiatry,* 1974, *124,* 166–172.

Blinder, B. J., Freeman, D. M. A., & Stunkard, A. J. Behavioral therapy of anorexia nervosa: Effectiveness of activity as a reinforcer of weight gain. *American Journal of Psychiatry,* 1970, *126,* 1093–1098.

Bliss, E. L., & Branch, C. H. H. *Anorexia nervosa: Its history, psychology, and biology*. New York: Paul Hoeber, 1960.

Brown, G. M., Garfinkel, P. E., Jeuniewic, N., Moldofsky, H., & Stancer, H. C. Endocrine profiles in anorexia nervosa. In R. Vigersky (Ed.), *Anorexia nervosa*. New York: Raven Press, 1977.

Bruch, H. Developmental obesity and schizophrenia. *Psychiatry,* 1958, *21,* 65–70.

Bruch, H. Eating disorders in adolescence. *Proceedings of the American Psychopathology Association,* 1970, *59,* 181–202. (a)

Bruch, H. Instinct and interpersonal experience. *Comprehensive Psychiatry,* 1970, *11,* 495–506. (b)

Bruch, H. Juvenile obesity. Its course and outcome. *International Psychiatry Clinics.,* 1970, *7,* 231–254. (c)

Bruch, H. *Eating disorders: Obesity, anorexia nervosa, and the person within*. New York: Basic Books, 1973.

Bruch, H. *The golden cage. The enigma of anorexia nervosa.* Cambridge, Mass.: Harvard University Press, 1978.

Bullen, B. A., Reed, R. B., & Mayer, J. Physical activity of obese and nonobese adolescent girls appraised by motion picture sampling. *American Journal of Clinical Nutrition,* 1964, *14,* 211–223.

Canning, H., & Mayer, J. Obesity: An influence on high school performance? *American Journal of Clinical Nutrition,* 1966, *20,* 352–354.

Casper, R. C., Davis, J. M., & Pandy, G. N. The effect of the nutritional status and weight changes on hypothalamic function tests in anorexia nervosa. In R. Vigersky (Ed.), *Anorexia nervosa.* New York: Raven Press, 1977.

Charney, E., Goodman, H. C., &McBride, M. Childhood antecedents of adult obesity: Do chubby infants become obese adults? *New England Journal of Medicine,* 1975, *295,* 6–9.

Crisp, A. H., & Stonehill, E. *Some psychological characteristics of patients with anorexia nervosa before and after treatment.* Paper read at IX European Psychosomatic Conference, Vienna, 1972.

Crisp, A. H., & Toms, D. A. Primary anorexia nervosa or weight phobia in the male: Report on 13 cases. *British Medical Journal,* 1972, *1,* 334–338.

Crisp, A. H., Douglas, J. W. B., Ross, J. M., & Stonehill, E. Some developmental aspects of disorders of weight. *Journal of Psychosomatic Research,* 1970, *14,* 313–320.

Crisp, A. H., Harding, B., & McGuinness, B. Anorexia nervosa: Psychoneurotic characteristics of parents: Relationship to prognosis. *Journal of Psycchosomatic Research,* 1974, *18,* 167–173.

Crisp, A. H., Kalucy, R. S., Lacey, J. H., & Harding, B. The long-term prognosis in anorexia nervosa: Some factors predictive of outcome. In R. A. Vigersky (Ed.), *Anorexia nervosa.* New York: Raven Press, 1977.

Crisp, A. H., Palmer, R. L., & Kalucy, R. S. How common is anorexia nervosa? A prevalence study. *British Journal of Psychiatry,* 1976, *128,* 549–554.

Dally, P. J. Anorexia nervosa: Long term follow up and effects of treatment. *Journal of Psychosomatic Research,* 1967, *11,* 151–155.

Dally, P. J. *Anorexia nervosa.* New York: Grune & Stratton, 1969.

Danowski, T. S., Livstone, E., Gonzales, A. R., Jung, Y., & Khurana, R. C. Fractional and partial hypopituitarism in anorexia nervosa. *Hormones,* 1972, *3,* 105–118.

Diagnostic and Statistical Manual (III). Washignton, D.C.: American Psychological Association, 1980.

Eid, E. E. Follow-up study of physical growth of children who had excessive weight gain in first six months of life. *British Medical Journal,* 1970, *2,* 74–76.

Epstein, L. H., Masek, B. J., & Marshall, W. R. A nutritionally based school program for control of eating in obese children. *Behavior Therapy,* 1978, *9,* 766–778.

Erwin, W. J. A 16-year follow-up of a case of severe anorexia nervosa. *Journal of Behaviour Therapy & Experimental Psychiatry,* 1977, *8* , 157–160.

Feighner, J. P., Robins, E., Guze, S. B., Woodruff, R. A., Winokur, G., & Munoz,, R. Diagnostic criteria for use in psychiatric research. *Archives of General Psychiatry,* 1972, *26,* 57–63.

Fisher, S., & Cleveland, S. E. *Body image and personality* (2nd ed.). New York: Dover Publications, 1968.

Frisch, R. Food intake, fatness, and reproductive ability. In R. A. Vigersky (Ed.), *Anorexia nervosa.* New York: Raven Press, 1977.

Garfinkel, P. E. Perception of hunger and satiety in anorexia nervosa. *Psychological Medicine,* 1974, *4,* 309–315.

Garfinkel, P. E., Moldofsky, H., & Garner, D. M. The outcome of anorexia nervosa: Significance of clinical features, body image, and behavior modification. In R. A. Vigersky (Ed.), *Anorexia nervosa.* New York: Raven Press, 1977.

Garner, D. M., Garfinkel, P. E., Stancer, H. C., & Moldofsky, H. Body image disturbances in anorexia nervosa and obesity. *Psychosomatic Medicine,* 1976, *38,* 327–336.

Goldberg, S. C., Halmi, K. A., Casper, R., Eckert, E., & Davis, J. M. Pretreatment predictors of weight change in anorexia nervosa. In R. A. Vigersky (Ed.). *Anorexia nervosa.* New York, Raven Press, 1977.

Goldblatt, P. B., Moore, M. E., & Stunkard, A. J. Social factors in obesity. *Journal of the American Medical Association,* 1965, *192,* 1039–1044.

Grinker, J. Behavioral and metabolic consequences of weight reduction. *Journal of the American Dietetic Association,* 1973, *62,* 30–34.

Halmi, K. A. Anorexia nervosa: Demographic and clinical features in 94 cases. *Psychosomatic Medicine,* 1974, *36,* 18–25.

Halmi, K. A. *Direct and interactive effects of behavior therapy in anorexia nervosa.* Paper presented at the World Congress on Behavior Therapy, Jerusalem, Israel, July 1980.

Halmi, K. A., & Sherman, B. M. Gonadotropin response to LHRH in anorexia nervosa. *Archives of General Psychiatry,* 1975, *32,* 875–878.

Halmi, K. A., Brodland, G., & Rigas, C. A follow-up study of 79 patients with anorexia nervosa: An evaluation of prognostic factors and diagnostic criteria. In R. D. Wirt, G. Winokur, & M. Roff (Eds.), *Life history research in psychopathology* (Vol. 4). Minneapolis: University of Minnesota Press, 1975.

Halmi, K. A., Goldberg, S. C., Eckert, E., Casper, R., & Davis, J. M. Pretreatment evaluation in anorexia nervosa. In R. A. Vigersky (Ed.), *Anorexia nervosa.* New York: Raven Press, 1977.

Halmi, K. A., Powers, P., & Cunningham, S. Treatment of anorexia nervosa with behavior modification. *Archives of General Psychiatry,* 1975, *32,* 93–95.

Hammar, S. L., Campbell, M. M., Campbell, V. A., Moores, N. L., Sareen, C., Gareis, F. J., & Lucas, B. An interdisciplinary study of adolescent obesity. *The Journal of Pediatrics,* 1972, *80,* 373–383.

Hammar, S. L., Campbell, V., & Woolley, J. Treating adolescent obesity. *Clinical Pediatrics,* 1971, *10,* 46–52.

Huenemann, R. L. Factors associated with teenage obesity. In N. L. Wilson (Ed.), *Obesity.* Philadelphia: F. A. Davis, 1969.

Johnson, P. R., Stern, J. S., Greenwood, M. R. C., Zucker, L. M., & Hirsch, J. Effect of early nutrition on adipose cellularity and pancreatic insulin release in the Zucker rat. *Journal of Nutrition,* 1973, *103,* 738–743.

Jones, E. *The life and work of Sigmund Freud.* New York: Basic Books, 1953.

Kalucy, R. S., Crisp, A. H., & Harding, B. A study of 56 families with anorexia nervosa. *British Journal of Medical Psychology,* 1977, *50,* 381–395.

Kaufman, M. R., & Heiman, M. (Eds.). *Evolution of psychosomatic concepts: Anorexia nervosa, a paradigm.* New York: International Universities Press, 1964.

Kingsley, R. G., & Shapiro, J. A comparison of three behavioral programs for the control of obesity in children. *Behavior Therapy,* 1977, *8,* 30–36.

Leitenberg, H., Agras, W. S., & Thomson, L. E. A sequential analysis of the effect of selective positive reinforcement in modifying anorexia nervosa. *Behaviour Research and Therapy,* 1968, *6,* 211–218.

Leon, G. R. Current directions in the treatment of obesity. *Psychological Bulletin,* 1976, *83,* 557–578.

Leon, G. R. Cognitive-behavior therapy for eating disturbances. In P. Kendall & S. Hollon (Eds.), *Cognitive-behavioral interventions: Theory, research, and procedures.* New York: Academic Press, 1979.

Leon, G. R., & Chamberlain, K. Emotional arousal, eating patterns, and body image as differential factors associated with varying success in maintaining a weight loss. *Journal of Consulting and Clinical Psychology,* 1973, *40,* 474–480. (a)

Leon, G. R., & Chamberlain, K. Comparison of daily eating habits and emotional states of persons successful or unsuccessful in maintaining a weight loss. *Journal of Consulting and Clinical Psychology,* 1973, *41,* 108–115. (b)

Leon, G. R., & Roth, L. Obesity: Psychological causes, correlations, and speculations. *Psychological Bulletin,* 1977, *84,* 117–139.

Leon, G. R., Bemis, K. M., & Lucas, A. R. *Family interactions, control, and other interpersonal factors as issues in treatment of anorexia nervosa.* Paper presented at the World Congress on Behavior Therapy, Jerusalem, Israel, July 1980.

Leon, G. R., Bemis, K. M., Meland, M., & Nussbaum, D. Aspects of body image perception in obese and normal-weight youngsters. *Journal of Abnormal Child Psychology,* 1978, *6,* 361–371.

Leon, G. R., Eckert, E. D., Teed, D., & Buchwald, H. Changes in body image and other psychological factors after intestinal bypass surgery for massive obesity. *Journal of Behavioral Medicine,* 1979, *2,* 39–59.

Lerner, R. M., & Pool, K. B. Body build stereotypes: A cross cultural comparison. *Psychological Reports,* 1972, *31,* 527–532.

Lerner, R. M., & Schroeder, C. Physique identification, preference, and aversion in kindergarten children. *Developmental Psychology,* 1971, *5,* 538.

Lloyd, J. K., Wolff, O. H., & Whelan, W. S. Childhood obesity: A long-term study of height and weight. *British Medical Journal,* 1961, *2,* 145–148.

Lorand, S. Anorexia nervosa: Report of a case. In M. R. Kaufman & M. Heiman (Eds.), *Evolution of psychosomatic concepts: Anorexia nervosa, a paradigm.* New York: International Universities Press, 1964. (Reprinted from *Psychosomatic Medicine,* 1943, *5,* 282–292).

Maddox, G. L., Back, K. W., & Liederman, V. R. Overweight as social deviance and disability. *Journal of Health & Social Behavior,* 1968, *9,* 287–298.

Mayer, J. Obesity in adolescence. *The Medical Clinics of North America,* 1965, *49,* 421–432. (a)

Mayer, J. Inactivity as a major factor in adolescent obesity. *Annals of the New York Academy of Sciences,* 1965, *131,* 502–506. (b)

Mayer, J. Genetic factors in human obesity. *Postgraduate Medicine,* 1965, *37,* A-103-A-108. (c)

Mayer, J. Obesity during childhood. In M. Winick (Ed.), *Childhood obesity.* New York: Wiley & Sons, 1975.

Mecklenburg, R. S., Loriaux, D. L., Thompson, R. H., Anderson, A. E., & Lipsett, M. B. Hypothalamic dysfunction in patients with anorexia nervosa. *Medicine,* 1974, *53,* 147–159.

Minuchin, S., Rosman, B. L., & Baker, L. *Psychosomatic families.* Cambridge, Mass.: Harvard University Press, 1978.

Morgan, H. G., & Russell, G. F. M. Value of family background and clinical features as predictors of long-term outcome in anorexia nervosa: 4 year follow-up study of 41 patients. *Psychological Medicine,* 1975, *5,* 355–372.

Mowrer, O. H. On the dual nature of learning—A reinterpretation of "conditioning" and "problem solving." *Harvard Educational Review,* 1947, *17,* 102–148.

Nathan, S. Body image in chronically obese children as reflected in figure drawings. *Journal of Personality Assessment,* 1973, *37,* 456–463.

Nathan, S., & Pisula, D. Psychological observations of obese adolescents during starvation treatment. *Journal of the American Academy of Child Psychiatry,* 1970, *9,* 722–740.

National Center for Health Statistics. Weight by height and age of adults 18–74 years: United States, 1971–1974. *Vital and health statistics advance data no. 14.* November 30, 1977.

Nylander, I. The feeling of being fat and dieting in a school population: An epidemiologic interview investigation. *Acta Sociomedica Scandinavica,* 1971, *3,* 17–26.

Ollendick, T. H. Behavioral treatment of anorexia nervosa: A five-year study. *Behavior Modification,* 1979, *3,* 124–135.

Pertschuk, M. J. Behavior therapy: Extended follow-up. In R. A. Vigersky (Ed.), *Anorexia nervosa.* New York: Raven Press, 1977.

Pillay, M., & Crisp, A. H. Some psychological characteristics of patients with anorexia nervosa whose weight has been newly restored. *British Journal of Medical Psychology,* 1977, *50,* 375–380.

Rosman, B. L., Minuchin, S., Baker, L., & Liebman, R. A family approach to anorexia nervosa: Study, treatment, and outcome. In R. A. Vigersky (Ed.), *Anorexia nervosa.* New York: Raven Press, 1977.

Rotman, M., & Becker, D. Traumatic situations in obesity. *Psychotherapy and Psychosomatics,* 1970, *18,* 372–376.

Schiele, B. C., & Brozek, J. Experimental neurosis resulting from semi-starvation in man. *Psychosomatic Medicine,* 1948, *10,* 31–50.

Schonfeld, W. A. Body-image disturbances in adolescents with inappropriate sexual development. *American Journal of Orthopsychology,* 1964, *34,* 493–502.

Seltzer, C. C., & Mayer, J. Body build and obesity—Who are the obese? *Journal of the American Medical Association,* 1964, *189,* 677–684.

Seltzer, C. C., & Mayer, J. A simple criterion of obesity. *Postgraduate Medicine,* 1965, *38,* A-101–A-107.

Seltzer, C. C., & Mayer, J. Body build (somatotype) distinctiveness in obese women. *Journal of the American Dietetic Association,* 1969, *55,* 454–458.

Selvini-Palazzoli, M. Anorexia nervosa. In S. Arieti (Ed.), *World Biennial of Psychiatry & Psychoterapy,* 1971, *1,* 197–218.

Sheldon, W. H. *Atlas of men.* New York: Harper & Row, 1954.

Sjöström, L. The contribution of fat cells to the determination of body weight. *Psychiatric Clinics of North America,* 1978, *1,* 493–521.

Slade, P. D., & Russell, G. F. M. Awareness of body dimensions in anorexia nervosa: Cross-sectional and longitudinal studies. *Psychological Medicine,* 1973, *3,* 188–199.

Smart, D. E., Beumont, P. J. V., & George, G. C. W. Some personality characteristics of patients with anorexia nervosa. *British Journal of Psychiatry,* 1976, *128,* 57–60.

Stunkard, A., & Burt, V. Obesity and the body image: I. Age at onset of disturbances in the body image. *American Journal of Psychiatry,* 1967, *123,* 1443–1447.

Stunkard, A., d'Aquili, E., Fox, S., & Filion, R. D. L. Influence of social class on obesity and thinness in children. *Journal of the American Medical Association,* 1972, *221,* 579–584.

Theander, S. Anorexia nervosa: A psychiatric investigation of 94 female patients. *Acta Psychiatrica Scandinavica,* 1970, Suppl. 214.

Van Buskirk, S. S. A two-phase perspective on the treatment of anorexia nervosa. *Psychological Bulletin,* 1977, *84,* 529–538.

Waller, J., Kaufman, M. R., & Deutsch, F. Anorexia nervosa: A psychosomatic entity. In M. R. Kaufman & M. Heiman (Eds.), *Evolution of psychosomatic concepts: Anorexia nervosa, a paradigm.* New York: International Universities Press, 1964. (Reprinted from *Psychosomatic Medicine,* 1940, *2,* 3–16.)

Weiss, A. R. A behavioral approach to the treatment of adolescent obesity. *Behavior Therapy,* 1977, *8,* 720–726.

Wooley, S. C., Wooley, O. W., & Dyrenforth, S. The case against radical interventions. *American Journal of Clinical Nutrition,* 1980, *33,* 465–471.

11

Obsessive-Compulsive and Phobic Reactions

Wallace A. Kennedy

Phobias

Introduction—Definition

Clinical descriptions of phobias, along with the obsessional behaviors frequently accompanying them, appear in earliest medical writings, dating at least from the time of Hippocrates. Marks (1969), in his insightful book on phobias, details the clinical descriptions and treatment recommendations proposed since the early Greeks. Ten years later, Graziano, DeGiovanni, and Garcia (1979), in an extensive review of the behavioral treatment of children's fears, called for research that more clearly recognized their complexity. Because of their vividness, their often sudden onset, their debilitation, and their frequentness in the population of otherwise normal persons, phobias have attracted broad attention both in the clinical and the experimental psychopathology areas of psychology.

Frequent in children, phobias diminish with age. Almost half of all children suffer from an identifiable phobia during the 6- to 12-year range. Phobias differ from fears in that: (1) they are inappropriate to the danger of the situation; (2) they are admittedly irrational; (3) they are involuntary; and (4) they are limiting in lifestyle.

This final point causes the most problems for the clinician. How does one define limitation of lifestyle? A child may be terrified of tigers and, comfortable in the knowledge that tigers will be encountered only in zoos, simply avoid zoos, an avoidance that limits lifestyle little. An equal terror of snakes, on the other hand, would limit lifestyle significantly in many areas of the United States.

WALLACE A. KENNEDY • Department of Psychology, Florida State University, Tallahassee, Florida 32306.

The subjective probability of significant encounter in one's lifespace seems to be the critical dimension. Being unable to fly in a commercial airplane may be a minor limitation; being unable to ride in an automobile can be a major limitation. The sure test of the phobia's severity, then, has to be the amount of disruption in a normal life, rather than an abstract measurement on a scale from 1 to 10 describing how frightened one is of tarantulas. That is why, of course, the phobic literature contains six times as many articles on school phobia as on any other phobia; the second most frequent is medical and dental phobias; and the third is agoraphobia. Children who do not go to school are at a high level of social disruption, as are children who do not go to doctors or dentists and children who cannot go outside their homes.

Some fears are virtually universal, instinctive, and inborn, such as fear of loud noises, fear of being dropped, and fear of hyperstimulation or stimulus flooding. In our culture, some fears are frequent in young children, such as fear of the dark, fear of strange objects and strange faces, and fear of sudden, unexpected movement. Some fears seen to be culturally determined, such as fear of snakes and spiders, both of which are unfeared, even attractive to young children. But with the passage of time, both attain high phobic value. Some predisposing factors must make conditioned fear of some objects easier than of others.

Incidence

Before looking at details of etiologies of phobias and obsessions, a word about their frequency is in order. A good argument can be made that at birth the fear responses of children are to few objects, but intense to these. Children at birth readily demonstrate intense fear responses to sudden loud noise, to loss of support, and to almost any intense stimulation. By 6 months, children develop a fear of sudden movement in the periphery and a fear of heights. In the second 6 months of life they develop fear of strangers, and after 1 year fear of novelty.

Several good inventories of children's fears are available, perhaps none better than the classic inventory of Jersild and Holmes (1935a). By 4 years of age, their study indicated, the major sources of fear reactions come from imaginary creatures, the dark, bad dreams, and being alone. Their work also indicated that animal fears and threats of danger with some reality basis, such as traffic, drowning, fire, and so forth, are moderately common. They found the signs of fear in others and warning from others seldom to be causes of fear in 4-year-olds. The fear of noise is reduced greatly by school age, as is the fear of strange people, situations, and objects.

Lapouse and Monk (1959), using an excellent sample in the city of Buffalo, interviewed mothers about their children's phobias. According to their report, the percentage of children worried about "germs" had increased markedly since the work of Jersild and Holmes; the remainder of children's fears appear much in the same order. Lapouse and Monk further indicated that girls have more fears than boys, and that children from 6 to 8 have more fears than children from 9 to 12. They also found a significant race and socioeconomic effect, with black and poorer children being more fearful. The strong contamination between the race and economic variables does not affect interpretation of the data because no causal factor was intended.

A more recent study of school children between 9 and 12 by Scherer and Nakamura (1968) reported a high incidence of fears of elevators, of being sent to the principal, of being bombed or invaded, of fire or being burned, of being hit by a truck, of being seriously ill, unable to breathe, or dying, of poor grades or failing a test, and of having parents argue. The least frequently reported fears were loud sirens, going to bed in the dark, being in a dark room or closet, mystery movies, flying, riding in cars or trains, and talking on the phone.

True phobias in children seem to relate to required performance outside the home. The literature has focused primarily on school phobia, but dental and doctor phobias and agoraphobia are the major focus of children set to clinics and practitioners. Agoraphobias frequently relate to dog phobias, with relatedness to car accidents increasing in frequency, as are stranger phobias related to crowd phobias.

Although these data on fears are reasonably representative of the general population, true phobias occur much less frequently (about 77 per 1000 in the normal adult population), with the percentage in children variously estimated at .5% to 1%, as compared to the 50% of children who report significant fears not of phobic proportion.

Assessment

Five principal methods are used to assess phobias in children, the first three of which rely on questionnaires or inventories.

Inventories for Children

Several available inventories provide rather exhaustive lists of fears or phobias. These can be group administered to children by the age of ten, or used individually with younger children. The Fear Survey Schedule for Children is an example. A particular advantage of this technique is that it can identify intense fears or phobias not a part of the initial referral but nevertheless presenting serious adjustment problems for the child. With children, fear inventories have the twin advantages of speed and cost effectiveness.

Inventories for Parents

A second, similar inventory is administered to parents rather than children. This can be identical, but usually is more complex, as, for example, the 200-item questionnaire developed by Lapouse and Monk (1959). Their inventory requires 1½ hours to administer, but is more inclusive than one administered to children. The parent inventory also has the advantage of focusing on the degree of disruption caused by the phobia in the life of the child. Obviously it is cost effective to administer inventories to both child and parent when a phobic child is brought to a clinic. This assists the clinician in determining whether the admitting phobia is a unique problem in an otherwise nonphobic child, or represents only a part of the fear complex in a panphobic child.

Phobia Hierarchy

A third method of assessing phobias is the development of a phobia hierarchy, following the procedure outlined by Wolpe (1961). The child or his parent describes for the clinician the lowest level of encounter she or he can tolerate with the phobia-producing situation. Then, step by step, a hierarchy of confrontation is built up to the most extreme dimension of the phobic situation. This method assumes that the phobia is rather specific and not a part of a panphobic child's complex personality. It is especially useful in developing a treatment program following the desensitization method.

Projective Method

The projective method, a fourth tool for assessing phobias, presents to the child a series of pictures representing situations that commonly produce phobic responses, such as the Children's Apperception Test. This method is useful in developing an understanding of the cognitive style with which the child deals with his phobia.

In Vivo Technique

The final assessment tool is the situational or *in vivo* technique, in which the child is presented with actual fear-producing situations, or with varying degrees of the single phobia-producing situation. The method, developed by Jersild and Holmes (1935b), presents to the child a series of eight common, fear-producing situations, ranging from the child's penetration into a dark hallway, through confrontation with a large dog. This technique also can be adapted to the individual phobic hierarchy of the child, such that his/her levels of tolerance can be examined.

This procedure has been used to reduce phobias by Bandura and others (Bandura, 1971; Bandura, Blanchard, & Ritter, 1969; Barlow, Agras, Leitenberg, & Wincze, 1970; Matthews, 1978; Sherman, 1972) when using a combination of modeling and desensitization. This technique is particularly useful for the practitioner when data regarding the severity of the phobia are unclear and the actual disruption of the child's life is not specific, due to different views coming from the child, parents, and teachers, as well as from other significant adults in the environment. Often, a simple walk with the child down the street to an ice cream shop tells me more about his agoraphobia and separation anxiety than an exhaustive history taken from significant adults and from the child himself.

Etiological Considerations

Issues in Acquisition and Treatment

Several issues involved in the acquisition and treatment of phobias have contributed to a vast range of theoretical formulations regarding phobias.

Professed versus Functional. The first issue, already alluded to, is that of the professed versus functional nature of phobias. Since this chapter focuses on severe and debilitating clinical phobias and obsessions in children, this issue is not simple: Children seen by clinicians must always be brought to them. That is, children seen by clinicians are prescreened by significant adults, generally their parents and teachers. Thus, the seriousness of the phobia already has been weighed subjectively by an adult, and translated into adult language and logic.

A child of divorce may display an intense fear of flying when taken to the airport by his mother to fly alone to visit his father, now 300 miles away. The fear of flying is displayed by autonomic, cognitive, and verbal behavior on the part of the child. It obviously is real enough. But quiet conversation with the child outside of the mother's presence reveals that the child is acting out his mother's concern, worry, and fear. The mother thinks that visitation by a 5-year-old 300 miles away from her is not in the best interest of her child, is dangerous, unnecessary, and simply meanness on the part of her ex-husband. The child, on the other hand, reveals a keen interest in flying with his mother to Kansas City, 600 miles in the other direction. He shows an interest in airplanes and a willingness to do things involving airplanes that a severely phobic child will not.

The problem, then, is to determine whether the professed fear, whatever it is, is translated into actual, functional practice. Even adults who profess intense fears of certain objects or situations will, in fact, deliberately encounter them when distracted, motivated, or answering a conflicting impulse. Such adults, like children, are often totally at loss to offer any explanation of this paradox.

State versus Trait. Second is the question of the state versus trait nature of the phobic response; that is, is the phobic stimulus specific or part of an underlying character trait? Although specific and intense phobias usually are the prime reason children are referred for treatment, rarely do the referred children not display other phobic responses to a lesser degree; referred children usually display panphobia.

Susceptibility. A related question has to do with susceptibility. Some children appear virtually immune to severe stimulus pairing, while others develop nearly intractable phobias in rather mild situations.

Relationship to Other Undesirable Behavior. Closely related to the trait issue is the question of the relationship between phobias and other undesirable or maladaptive behavior. In the case of school phobia, particularly in Type One school phobia, the most frequent type, there is virtually no relationship between school phobia and any other referrable condition. Kennedy (1965) and Miller, Barrett, Hampe, and Noble (1971), using large clinical studies and long-range follow-ups, found the most frequent school phobia free of other psychopathological behavior. Also, Lapouse and Monk (1959), in extensive interviews with children whose fears were remarkable but not referrable, found no correlation between the existence of fears and other emotional problems.

Classically Conditioned. Another question is whether phobias are accounted for largely, or indeed accounted for at all, in terms of classical conditioning. Some phobias appear to be set up on the basis of readily identifiable stimulus associations or easily retrievable experiences linking the object of the child's phobia with an obviously aversive situation. Yet efforts under controlled conditions to elicit classically conditioned phobic responses to certain classes of neutral objects in the environment have failed repeatedly, even when the intensity of the stimulation is quite severe (Bregman, 1934; English, 1929; Valentine, 1930). Further, Rachman (1977) and Bandura *et al.* (1969) have pointed out that, whereas classical learning theory assumes that conditioning of phobias occurs through the autonomic system and is therefore involuntary, the preponderance of evidence (including such issues as failure of severely traumatic situations oftentimes to produce phobias) indicates that some stimuli are simply ineffective as phobic stimuli.

The finding is unmistakable. Recently I examined a child who had his entire thumb burned off from placing a key in a 220 dryer outlet. On being asked how it happened, he was quite willing to stick a key in the socket in our office, which was almost identical to the one that burned off his thumb. Whole classes of objects made of wood and plastic seem almost never to meet the criterion of a phobic stimulus.

The issue of choice of symptom points to a significantly higher role for cognitive mediation. Almost all children have an excessive amount, let us say, obsessive-compulsive amount of cognitive rehearsal of their phobias (Bandura, 1969).

Also, as pointed out by Herrnstein (1969), the phobic stimulus may, after a short time, no longer be an aversive one, but may indeed be a discriminative stimulus that permits total avoidance of the aversive stimulus.

Operantly Conditioned. This latter point is related directly to the next issue concerning the acquisition and treatment of phobias, the operant nature of phobias. Basic to most psychological theory is the belief that behavior exists in the long run because it works, and phobias are no exception to this belief. Short of an infant's cry of distress, his startle or fear response generates more action for his relief on the part of significant adults in his environment than any other response in his repertoire.

This secondary gain or reinforcement of the phobic and obsessional response always has been a complicating factor in the interpretation and treatment of the disorder, particularly in young children. School phobia, for example, as Kennedy (1965) pointed out, has a massively controlling effect on the home and school environment and may, from the point of view of the child, prevent the truly noxious event, loss of the mother, from occurring. Mothers who stay home and read stories, prepare soup, rub backs, and, in addition, attend rapidly to the feeble cry of "Mommie," do something else also: They do not die, disappear, or get sick, as the child feared they would.

In addition, none of the bad things feared at school, or feeling strange at school because of having missed a few days, having a lot of hard schoolwork to make up, or having the teacher be mean because of the absence, can happen either, so long as the child is too phobic to go to school. Unquestionably, all phobic behavior exhibited in a normal household has strong reinforcement in the short run. Perhaps longitudinal studies repeatedly find remission in most phobias because they grow old to the parents and child alike and thereby lose much of their reinforcement.

As an aside, the problem is complicated somewhat by the issue of whether the phobic object may actually become a discriminative stimulus rather than a noxious stimulus. Herrnstein (1969) has pointed out that it may be the avoidance response that receives the reinforcement, which accounts for the close relationship between phobias and the obsessional behavior that frequently simply elaborates the avoidance response.

Relationship to Cognitive Development. An issue that complicates both the interpretation of the self-limiting nature of most phobias and the shift, as a function of age, in types of objects of the phobic response is the effect of cognitive development on phobias. The literature has demonstrated repeatedly, since the classic study of Jersild and Holmes (1935a), that children's fears change as a function of age. Until fairly recently, this was considered a function of changes in the child's environment and further exposure to phobia-producing stimulation as a result of the "growing up" process. Thus, children were supposed to begin life with basic reflex fear responses to loud noises, loss of support, and hyperstimulation such as being extremely hot or cold. Aside from these, about the only frightening thing that impinges on the infant's environment is finding himself alone, and newborn children do not give a fear response to that.

Accordingly, the environment expands and children become exposed to more fearful objects, such as large, aggressive animals, physical injury from accidents, and stories of ghosts and ghoulies and things that go "bump" in the night. Later, children experience separations for the first time, criticism, strict teachers, failure. Fears are seen generally as exaggerated responses to real changes in exposure, not appropriate in magnitude, but certainly tracking the real exposure.

A rival hypothesis, which has increasing support in both the behavioral and learning literature, is that not simply environmental exposure but cognitive development has a role in fear development, as suggested by Piaget (1929, 1930). Miller, Barrett, Hampe, and Noble (1972) suggest that children's fears can be described in three clusters, not unlike other factor studies conducted over the past 30 years. These three classifications of children's fears are: (1) fear of physical injury; (2) fear of psychic distress, such as embarrassment, school failure, or social ineptness; and (3) fear of natural and supernatural dangers, such as lightning, thunder, trains, witches, ghosts, and the like. The first two factors remain fairly constant over life, whereas the third factor diminishes rather rapidly during childhood. Now, given that all phobias leading to clinical referral tend to diminish with or without treatment over a 2-year span (Hampe, Noble, Miller, & Barrett, 1973), a likely cause of this spontaneous remission, in addition to the loss of significance, is a cognitive change that reduces the phobic quality.

Genetic Predisposition. We have alluded already to the possibility that some fears and phobias of children have a high frequency because of genetic predisposition. Early in the research on children's fears, several efforts failed totally to induce phobic responses to objects outside of a certain classification. Following research in behavior genetics and the concept of sign tracking, it now appears reasonable that certain types of learning are much easier than others. Children more easily develop fears of snakes, spiders, rats, cats, dogs, and other furry objects than they do of more benign or neutral objects, such as toy airplanes, toy cars, wooden furniture, and the like, suggesting an evolutionary preparedness for these fears (Marks, 1977). Also, this susceptibility may be developmental in nature and time-limited, which could account for both the onset and the remission of such behavioral problems.

Etiology

The clinic population of phobic children is rather high, compared to phobic incidence in the population as a whole. Treatment programs usually involve a combination of methods, rather than a clearly distinct method based upon probable etiology.

Sign-Learned Phobias. The number of children who appear at clinics with classical conditioning being at the root of their phobias is small but consistent. The usual cause is severe trauma. Car accidents, dog attacks, intense family arguments, or physical abuse are the most predominant causes of sign-learned phobias. In diagnosing and prescribing treatment for classically induced phobias, it is important that the therapist determine whether the phobia is based upon a correct sign, an exaggerated sign, or an erroneous sign.

Recently, a child with a severe dog phobia was referred to me by a plastic surgeon. Now a referral from a plastic surgeon probably would alert any clinician to the possible adaptive nature of the phobia. That, plus the reconstruction of the child's hand and arm, suggested to me that the dog in question had gone for the child's throat; the hand and arm had simply gotten in the way.

The first question I asked was: "Son, where is that dog now?" His answer was stupefying: "He is still there!" The dog that had so injured this lad remained behind the same, fragile, low fence in the neighbor's yard, attended only by children who frequently teased and taunted the patient by making "sic um" noises at the dog.

Now, although this lad exhibited extremely high-level phobic behavior, and although he was, in fact, terrified whenever outside in the neighborhood and out of immediate reach of the door of his own home, his intense fear was not a phobia by the first criterion. His fear was not inappropriate to the danger inherent in the situation. The task was not clinical treatment for a phobia but a lawsuit to remove the dog from the neighborhood. Since the child's behavior with other dogs was adequate, even during the risk period with the attack dog, his decision to forego treatment when the dog was shipped away was not surprising.

Even when such a cause is unlikely, it is important to consider first the possibility of correctness in the fear. Extreme bullying by a neighborhood playmate or classmate, sexual abuse, child battering, animal attacks, and parental fighting all are real hypotheses in cases of apparent classically induced phobia. Only consistent interviewing of all parties separately, sometimes accompanied by a home visit, offers significant guarantee that a correct sign will be identified. Tragic results can stem from failure of intervention as a result of overlooking such a sign and simply assuming that treatment of a phobia is in order. I have seen several severely battered children who originally were treated by school counselors for free-floating anxiety and mild agoraphobia. Had more careful follow-up been possible or practical, severe injury might have been avoided.

Far more common than a referral with a correct-sign phobia is the child referred with an exaggerated-sign phobia. In this case, some real danger exists, but not to the degree the child perceives. For example, the child has been in an automobile accident, has been hurt, and is now unable to ride in a car. Cars are dangerous, even when driven carefully and when seatbelts are in place, but their convenience and necessity far outweight their danger.

Occasionally a dog is vicious and highly dangerous, but few dogs are, and neighborhood dogs seldom are. A child who has been mauled by a dog may be unable to go outside, even when the offending dog is well penned.

Parents in the middle of a donnybrook do represent the possibility of serious risk to the happiness of the child. He might conceivably be hurt, a separation or divorce might ensue, but generally, such is not the case. The child will be all right, even in the case of divorce, and the percentage of parents who argue and yell far outnumbers the precentage who ultimately divorce. A child who panics when parents or significant adults argue is overreacting to a correct sign. In this case, it is important for the clinician to evaluate the child's environment to determine the significance of the sign. Again, a detailed history obtained independently, as well as contacts with significant adults, such as teachers and physicians, is important in identifying the significance of the sign.

Erroneous signs in classical conditioning represent contiguity of truly independent events. Erroneous signs make up the few but extremely difficult cases of pure phobia, the phobias without logical explanation unless the contiguity can be identified. Because children's memories are eidetic, they have an impressive capacity to associate images in a way extremely difficult for adults to evaluate.

A partially toilet-trained child suddenly develops an extreme phobia to the toilet. Very careful study indeed is required to discover the occasion when the child observed that his father accidently let slip a diaper he was rinsing in the toilet and the whole thing disappeared. This child, who already had an uneasy sensation hanging down over that toilet, immediately realized how easy it would be simply to disappear down that thing, never to be seen again. The toilet represents no actual danger to the child, but the child has formed an image that makes it represent extreme danger to him.

A father, who wears a strong aftershave, loses control of himself and severely spanks the child after some accidental but extreme property damage by the child. The child becomes totally panicked whenever anyone comes near him wearing aftershave lotion. Aftershave lotion has no predictive power with regard to parental violence, which has occurred only once in the child's whole life, but the smell has been associated with that once. The child is not afraid of his father, or of other men, just of the smell of aftershave.

In identifying the etiology of classically induced phobias, the history is everything. The history should focus on four elements of the phobia: contiguity, continuity, association, and termination.

Contiguity refers to the elements usually present at the time the phobia occurs and to events that always seem immediately to precede the phobic behavior. Often phobias depend upon a rather complex sequence of stimuli. A thunder phobia may depend on the absence of a favorite brother, who was not present at the traumatic experience with lightning.

Continuity concerns the events that preceded the first phobic response. Sometimes this is utterly obvious. A child who displays excessive phobic behavior when his father comes home under the influence of alcohol, even when daddy is pleasant and happy, has had previous experience when one thing led to another and a frightening fight between the parents occurred. Sometimes it is not at all obvious; the sequence leading up to the phobic behavior is just not known. At dusk in the evening, the child wants to be in the house. He wants the door closed and he wants the lights on. That it is summertime and bats are flying in the yard, sometimes coming close, that a rerun of Count Dracula was on TV last week, and that a neighborhood child has teased the child aggressively concerning bats, are all elements in a continuity that led to an extreme bat phobia in the child.

Often the stimuli that produce phobic responses are not unique or specific, but merely gradients of association. In order to extinguish or countercondition the phobic response, the associated stimuli need to be identified and included in the extinction paradigm. In the case of the child with a dog phobia, for example, the phobia may operate only in large open spaces, or only in one corner of the yard, or only on a front stoop. Going through all the associations with the child, determining what he thinks of when he thinks of dogs as dangerous, will greatly increase the precision of the treatment.

Often, treatment can take advantage of behavior on the part of the child, or of significant others around him, or of change in the situation that tends to terminate the phobic attack. Again, in the case of a dog phobia, the child may find he feels utterly secure walking to the schoolbus corner, so long as he carries a walking stick with him. He may find he can get off the bus in the evening if he can see the family car in the driveway and is thus assured that his mother is home. He may find that he can terminate or prevent the phobic attack by wearing two pairs of trousers. All of these rituals or compulsions have the distinct advantage of low-cost effectiveness and little disruption, and may well prove a bridge to eliminating the phobia. Virtually no phobia, no matter how intense, has no stimulus, or situation, or ritual that makes it more bearable. Good assessment of this lead enables the clinician to develop a treatment plan that takes advantage of the natural healing forces, which generally leads to a remission in the phobia itself.

Solution-Learned Phobias. In the majority of phobic cases seen in a clinic, the classical component of the phobia is far more easily understood and obtained from the history than the operant component. A frightened, pitiful child, a badly shaken set of parents, and a child's normal lifespace in tatters provide for difficult interpretation on the basis of reinforcement. The terror seems real enough. All the classical signs of terror are exhibited, but what happens to the child as a result of his terror is harder for the clinician to assess.

Does the night terror result in the child's sleeping between his mother and father? Does the school phobia result in tender, loving "care" and "control" over the mother and her safety? Does an agoraphobia "control" the mother, the father, and, in fact, everyone?

Does the tremendous amount of extra attention fill some significant need on the part of the child?

Because partial reinforcement plays such a strong role, determination of solution learning is sometimes extremely difficult. Parents say "never" when they mean "hardly ever," or, more precisely, about one time in seven on a fixed-interval schedule. They use the term "always" when they mean "sometimes," or "when we get around to it," or "when the child's behavior becomes intolerable." Often there is no substitute for costly, direct observation in the home or school, because the reporting behavior of parents is unreliable.

A good history usually will assess accurately the direct contingencies. The remedial efforts the parents have made to the phobia usually are recent, deliberate, and obvious. Reviewing the premorbid history, the routines, and the changes usually gives a cue to direct contingencies, such as mother's staying home and taking leave from her job, father's giving more attention and special time to the child, time taken away from sister, and the like. Often, blocking this reinforcement gives accurate cues as to its role in the phobic behavior of the child.

On the other hand, parents and the child are poor informants regarding indirect contingencies. The parents may be having a rather serious argument over a period of several days. The difference is serious, but not threatening to the marriage. Discussions over money are typical of these arguments that go on indefinitely.

The child overhears this on-going argument and begins to find it threatening. He is unable to sleep and becomes mildly frightened by seeing something at his window. He goes into his parents' room and tells them he is afraid; and he is, but not of the shadow at the window. The child is afraid that something bad is happening to the family.

After the parents get caught up in his expressed fears, and spend a good deal of time patting him, tucking him in, and reassuring him, they go back into their room and go to sleep; they do not continue the argument. The child has enjoyed the direct reinforcement of attention and patting, and he appears to be afraid of something at the window, but neither the feared object nor the reinforcement is as it appears.

There are times when the contingency is purely superstitious. A child has a fear of dying, for example, and runs in terror to his or her mother's bed to get help. Mother wakes up, speaks to him or her and he or she does not die. This superstitious contingency is the basic element of compulsive and obsessional behavior in children. Here, the fear of the child is unfounded and the behavior of the mother is ineffective, but in the child's eyes, the phobic response produces behavior that is effective.

In summary, then, in evaluating a phobia, it is critical to look carefully over the behavior of the child to determine the actual and imagined reinforcement that maintains such an otherwise aversive behavior pattern. In doing so, take into account both the positive reinforcement (the direct, functional utility of the phobia) and the negative reinforcement (what does not happen as a result of the phobic behavior) as well as the accidental reinforcement (or superstitious chaining) that occurs from the phobic behavior.

Case Presentation

Albert, a 10-year-old fourth-grader in a private school, was an "A" student, well regarded by teachers and peers, and in excellent physical health. The middle child, son of a physician and public health nurse, he was essentially asymptomatic prior to mid-year of the fourth grade, when three events occurred simultaneously.

While visiting his father in a large metropolitan hospital, where the father was a pathologist–coroner, he became lost and wandered into a treatment hall in the radiation medicine area, where a large number of litter-borne, critically ill, cancer patients were awaiting treatment. The further he went, the more confused he became, and the more circular his route became, until it appeared that he was surrounded by death.

Second, his mother went on a trip to a foreign country as a temporary medical missionary at the time of the United States embassy take-over in Iran.

Third, he was taken to a football stadium for a major game; during the opening ceremonies, the roar of the crowd and the confusion was so great that he panicked and tried to run home, but the aisles were totally blocked with in-coming crowds. His parents finally caught him and calmed him down.

He initially developed a claustrophobia that restricted his entry into most buildings, including most hotels, the hospital, his dentist's office, his barber shop, most restaurants, and his church. He as able to attend school only because the modern edifice had glass outside walls and open corridors.

He soon became excessively concerned about any absence of his mother and very frightened if left with a baby-sitter. Initially he stayed with his father, until his father was called in for an emergency while baby-sitting and had to take his son with him to the hospital.

Typical of most severely phobic children seen in our clinic, he developed the phobia bit by bit over a 4- to 6-week period, and suddenly accelerated the intensity to become almost totally claustrophobic and highly fearful of separation from his mother. Unlike many of our severe phobic cases, school attendance was never involved except at the beginning of school following a summer vacation, and by that time, an intense preventive program had been undertaken, so that he never developed into a school phobic.

The elements of both classical and operant conditioning were present in this case. The hospital scene was similar to a television movie he had seen several weeks before, after which he had been mildly upset. The initial response to being lost in the hospital was full-blown psychophysical reaction. Subsequent reactions appeared almost identical. The intensity of the phobic stimulus for the child depended on its likeness to the initial situation in the hospital.

In the initial assessment, he gave a benign history except for some apprehension regarding an impending family move to a remote homesite, some pressure from being a middle child, and some concern about the loss of a family friend who had been his favorite baby-sitter and was moving across the country. He was able to build a cognitive fear hierarchy, with the elements being strangeness, confusion in corridors, inside corridors, sick people, dizziness, and mother not coming home. His barber shop, of which he was fearful, was both inside a mall and downstairs, and had white sheets draped over people. This cognitive hierarchy was examined in the field and was quite accurate, except that the limits were exaggerated. He could tolerate situations higher on the hierarchy than he had reported.

Psychologial tests were unremarkable, except that the CAT stories were filled with emphasis on closed doors, being alone, and people being ill. The intelligence test answers in many cases carried a negative cast that emphasized dangers. His description of the essential cognitive dimension of the phobia was an intense dizziness and fear of fainting, a fear for the safety of his mother, and fear of being locked in a room where everyone was dying. He had frequent nightmares, the content of which for the most part recapitulated the phobic experience described in the assessment.

By all appearances, his older brother aggravated his phobic symptoms by taunting him and reminding him of his weakness. He was also rivaled in his mother's affection by a totally irresistible 3-year-old sister.

Treatment involved desensitization, counterconditioning, modeling, and a considerable amount of cognitive rehearsal and rational-emotive therapy, while working with the parents to follow-through on the behavioral gains made by the lad in therapy. Most of the treatment was conducted outside the clinic and was, for the most part, unremarkable, with the exception of an exacerbation of symptoms following the move and loss of the babysitter.

Obsessive-Compulsive Behaviors

Although obsessive-compulsive behavior seems high in the repertoire of young children, it rarely leads to clinical referral except when directly involved in phobic behavior. In the past 25 years of the Psychology Teaching Clinic at Florida State University, there has been no referral of an obsessive-compulsive child without other pathology as the primary referring problem. The reason for this is obvious. Repetitions, perseverations, and rhythmic behaviors are a normal delight of young children , and embedded in the memory banks of their parents. These behaviors are almost certainly instinctive in young children. Surely, no extended family has not suffered the trauma of having gone through the night with the agony of the lost "noonie" of a preschool child. And most parents have sympathy for the just-so nighttime or naptime rituals that are part of the security system of the child. There is extensive evidence of such behavior in animals and considerable anthropomorphic speculation regarding the utility of such behavior.

On the other hand, any severely phobic child who survives an encounter with his phobic object or situation almost invariably is faced with the cognitive discovery that that which was about to happen did not. At the same time, because of the high density of such obsessive behavior, he is very likely to have been engaging in some form of repetitive behavior. Thus, this repetitive behavior, in addition to its instinctive value, receives a heavy boost as a result of its operant quality in preventing, in the child's mind, the pending disaster.

Any child who fears being attacked in the dark, and who goes through a ritual at bedtime, finds double comfort in the ritual. First, he finds comfort in its natural, instinctive pleasure, and second, in its clear effectiveness. Compulsive patterns are extremely common in children, particularly phobic children, because they are both intrinsically pleasurable and tension-reductive.

Many unobstrusive rituals and compulsions continue on into adulthood to form the basis of many of our social interactions, particularly those at the most superficial level. Obsessive-compulsive behavior becomes a clinical problem only when it becomes low in cost-effectiveness.

Children who "nest" at bedtime, getting everything in order, particularly when that includes setting out shoes for tomorrow, are seldom referred for treatment. The referral usually comes only when the compulsion is time-consuming, when it is consistent with some behavior the family deems bizarre, or when any interruption in the ritual causes panic on the part of the child.

The task of the diagnostician is to determine whether the compulsive behavior is truly disruptive of the child's life. Generally these compulsive behaviors drop out in time and drop out in direct proportion to the severity of the phobia with which they deal. Assessment, then, requires close study of the seriousness of the disruption, which should be done secondary to the analysis of the phobia and its treatment.

Unless the child is very young, a cognitive-behavioral approach would seem to promise the best result, a childhood version of rational-emotive therapy. The therapist should take an uncritical approach to the ritual. He should encourage the child to explain and demonstrate the ritual in its fullest details, how it works, its key elements, how much of the ritual is absolutely necessary, and how much is nice but not necessary.

Postponing the ritual slightly, terminating the ritual a bit early, and altering the precise steps in the ritual all seem possible for most children, particularly while they are at the same time being counterconditioned and desensitized to the phobic setting. If counterconditioning can take on a ritualistic flavor itself, with precise ministeps in the treatment and overprecision in the details, the phobic child may well transfer his obsessional behavior into the counterconditioning regima.

Very mild humor induction, helping the child to develop some appreciation for the foolishness of his ritual, is effective if the first steps have been completed and if the counterphobic treatment has gotten underway. The obvious irrationality of assuming the ritual to be effective in the face of so many other children being protected by more common sense behaviors tends to reach most children.

Blocking strategies need to be used lightly, more as an interruption or delay rather than as total blocks. But even total blocking can be done, if the treatment of the phobia is well underway and the emotional credit of the therapist is high. Helping the child to recognize how many silly rituals everyone engages in for various known and unknown reasons helps to totter his now somewhat top-heavy ritual.

And finally, a few words need to be said for good old reinforcement. If the child is within striking distance of altering his compulsive behavior, if any progress can be detected, no matter how small, a somewhat gaudy reinforcement can be given, and a more gaudy one held out for the next step. Statements such as, "If you will go to bed and lie still for 10 minutes without 'doing it,' daddy will read you this special story and lie down with you awhile as you go to sleep." The following day, a gaudy reward to remind the child how he was able to break his pattern is highly suggestive to the child that, once he makes a breakthrough, once he puts the old habit off for awhile, he really "has it made." Always the underlying assumption is that the carrot gets a little further away, and the frowns get a little deeper, if he does not do what we all know now that he can do.

The major issue to remember is that we do not want to tidy up children as far as their small rituals are concerned. Most parents do well to leave these alone, with the advice that he will outgrow them. Only when the ritual is highly elaborate and expensive, as well as precarious, can it justify treatment as a clinical problem.

Summary

Clearly, fears and rituals are common in the lives of children, who have a genetic predisposition to them because, historically at least, they are functional. These are, for the most part, short-lived, self-limiting, and benign, requiring no treatment.

Phobias and obsessions also are generally self-limiting. But phobias and obsessions present the possibility of moderate to severe social and educational disruption, along with the risk of expanding problems in other areas of adjustment. The literature indicates that agoraphobia and school phobia are the most common debilitating phobias, with the most serious expanded problems caused by the disruption of school and sleep.

Early behavioral analysis of the phobic and obsessional behavioral hierarchy seems an essential prerequisite for the development of a treatment plan. Behavioral treatment, covert and overt desensitization, counterconditioning, escape blocking or ritual interruption, modeling, and reinforcement of competing responses, accompanied by rational-emotive therapy, seems the treatment of choice.

Most studies indicate that therapy is justified on the basis of its cost effectiveness, its speed-up of a natural self-limiting process, and its prevention of the development of secondary problems or gain. The prognosis for treatment is excellent. Total remission usually occurs within 6 months with any behavioral treatment. Dynamic treatment generally lasts much longer, and remission is significantly slower, particularly in the case of school phobia.

References

Bandura, A. *Principles of behavior modification.* New York: Holt, Rinehart, & Winston, 1969.

Bandura, A. Psychotherapy based upon modeling principles. In A. E. Bergin & S. L. Garfield (Eds.), *Handbook of psychotherapy and behavior change: An empirical analysis.* New York: Wiley, 1971.

Bandura, A., Blanchard, E. B., & Ritter, B. Relative efficacy of desensitization and modeling approaches for inducing behavioral, affective, and attitudinal changes. *Journal of Personality and Social Psychology,* 1969, *13,* 173–199.

Barlow, D. H., Agras, W. S., Leitenberg, H., & Wincze, J. P. An experimental analysis of the effectiveness of "shaping" in reducing maladaptive avoidance behavior: An analogue study. *Behaviour Research and Therapy,* 1970, *8,* 165–173.

Bregman, E. O. An attempt to modify the emotional attitudes of infants by the conditioned response technique. *Journal of Genetic Psychology,* 1934, *45,* 169–196.

English, H. B. Three cases of the "conditioned fear response." *Journal of Abnormal and Social Psychology,* 1929, *34,* 221–225.

Graziano, A. M., DeGiovanni, I. S., & Garcia, K. A. Behavioral treatment of children's fears: A review. *Psychological Bulletin,* 1979, *86,* 804–830.

Hampe, I. E., Noble, H., Miller, L. C., & Barrett, C. L. Phobic children one and two years posttreatment. *Journal of Abnormal Psychology,* 1973, *83,* 446–453.

Herrnstein, R. J. Method and theory in the study of avoidance. *Psychological Review,* 1969, *76,* 49–69.

Jersild, A. T., & Holmes, F. B. Children's fears. *Teachers College Child Development Monographs* (No. 20), 1935. (a)

Jersild, A. T., & Holmes, F. B. Methods of over-coming children's fears. *Journal of Psychology,* 1935, *1,* 75–104. (b)

Kennedy, W. A. School phobia: Rapid treatment of fifty cases. *Journal of Abnormal Psychology,* 1965, *70,* 285–289.

Lapouse, R., & Monk, M. A. Fears and worries in a representative sample of children. *American Journal of Orthopsychiatry,* 1959, *29,* 803–818.

Marks, I. M. *Fears and phobias.* New York: Academic Press, 1969.

Marks, I. M. Phobias and obsessions: Clinical phenomena in search of laboratory models. In J. D. Maser & M. E. P. Seligman (Eds.), *Psychopathology: Experimental models.* San Francisco: W. H. Freeman, 1977.

Matthews, A. Fear-reduction research and clinical phobias. *Psychological Bulletin,* 1978, *85,* 390–404.

Miller, L. C., Barrett, C. L., Hampe, I. E., & Noble, H. Revised anxiety scales for the Louisville Behavior Check List. *Psychological Reports,* 1971, *29,* 503–511.

Miller, L. C., Barrett, C. L., Hampe, I. E., & Noble, H. Factor structure of childhood fears. *Journal of Consulting and Clinicial Psychology,* 1972, *39,* 261–268.

Piaget, J. *The child's conception of the world.* New York: Harcourt, Brace, 1929.

Piaget, J. *The child's conception of physical causality.* New York: Harcourt, Brace & World, 1930.

Rachman, S. The conditioning theory of fear-acquisition: A critical examination. *Behaviour Research and Therapy,* 1977, *15*, 375–387.

Scherer, M. W., & Nakamura, C. Y. A fear survey schedule for children (FSS-FC): A factor analytic comparison with manifest anxiety (CMAS). *Behaviour Research and Therapy,* 1968, *6*, 173–182.

Sherman, A. R. Real-life exposure as a primary therapeutic factor in the desensitization treatment of fear. *Journal of Abnormal Psychology,* 1972, *79*, 19–28.

Valentine, C. W. The innate bases of fear. *Journal of Genetic Psychology,* 1930, *37*, 394–420.

Wolpe, J. The systematic desensitization treatment of neuroses. *Journal of Nervous and Mental Disease,* 1961, *132*, 189–203.

12

Depression and Withdrawal in Children

THEODORE A. PETTI

Introduction

In orienting oneself to this chapter, it is important that the reader be aware of several potentially confusing issues. The first is that depression and social withdrawal, though highly correlated, are distinct entities and not synonymous in children. Second, depression and withdrawal are symptoms that are manifested across all diagnostic categories of childhood psychopathology. Third, a rigorous application of scientific methodology has been sporadically applied in child psychiatry/psychology and has greatly lagged behind when compared to the adult arena. Fourth, the clinical picture for disturbed children is incessantly blurred by developmental, familial, social, cultural, and cognitive factors. Fifth, physiological and biochemical correlates to childhood psychopathology are minimally reported. Finally, and perhaps most importantly, depression in children has been referred to in several contexts in the scientific literature as a symptom, a symptom complex, a syndrome, and a specific disease entity. An attempt will be made throughout this chapter to specify the particular usage when the term is being applied.

Depression as a symptom generally implies that the child looks or complains of feeling sad, crying easily, or being dysphoric, lonely, hopeless, or pessimistic. Moodiness, irritability, and self-deprecatory ideation (with or without morbid or suicidal content) are frequently associated with the symptom complex. The significance of childhood depression as a specific disease entity regularly engenders heated discussion from professionals involved in this area. Designating a group of symptoms and signs as a syndrome suggests a morbid process, all of which, considered together, constitute a disease. Pneumonia, for instance, is

---

THEODORE A. PETTI • Department of Psychiatry, Western Psychiatric Institute and Clinic, University of Pittsburgh Medical School, Pittsburgh, Pennsylvania 15213.

a disease. Pneumococcal, streptococcal, and viral pneumonia are disease entities. As will be detailed, a significant number of children suffer from the syndrome of depression and from what some presently consider the disease entity of depression.

Any public discussion of the depressive syndrome of childhood leads to great debate and is marked by an absence of agreement. It has been generally accepted that a dysphoric mood present over time, generally more than a few weeks, and some manifestation of self-deprecatory ideation are critical to the diagnostic picture. The concept of masked depression, which has had intercurrent popularity and acceptance in general psychiatry, constitutes a global entity in which the dysphoric mood needs to be inferred by the clinician. Associated symptoms traditionally considered part of the syndrome of depression in children, such as hyperactivity, somatic complaints, difficulties in school, or school refusal all are considered to be part of the masked depression picture (Blumberg, 1978). However, though this concept remains viable in general psychiatry (Lesse, 1974), it has lost credibility for children (Cytryn, McKnew, & Bunney, 1980; Welner, 1978).

The depressive syndrome itself has been portrayed in a number of ways, as will be depicted in the following sections on epidemiology and assessment. Childhood depression as a specific entity has been described, based on their definitions of the disorder, by a number of workers. Among the most rigorous studies are those of Poznanski and Zrull (1970) and Puig-Antich, Blau, Marx, Greenhill, and Chambers (1978). The former study required that either the child be described as sad, unhappy, or depressed, or report those feelings in the interview, and that additional clinical confirmation be documented, such as excessive self-criticism, sleep difficulties, excessive concern about death, and feelings of inadequacy. They found that a negative self-image was the most frequent disturbance found in the clinical picture, but withdrawal in some form was consistently present. Puig-Antich *et al.* (1978) employed unmodified research diagnostic criteria (RDC) (Spitzer, Endicott, & Robins, 1975) in defining a specific disease entity. These criteria are as follows:

A. Dysphoric mood
B. Depressive syndrome
   1. Poor appetite
   2. Sleep disturbance
   3. Loss of energy
   4. Psychomotor agitation or retardation
   5. Loss of interest
   6. Inappropriate guilt
   7. Slowed thinking
   8. Thoughts of death or suicide
C. Duration over 2 weeks
D. Referred during the dysphoric period
E. Function is impaired
F. No signs of schizophrenia

Views concerning the syndrome of childhood depression range from the nonexistence of the entity, to rigorous definitions of a clinical picture and disease entity, to a disorder that encompasses virtually all childhood psychopathology.

On the one hand, we have the psychoanalysts (Mahler, 1961; Rie, 1966), who do not accept the concept (based primarily on psychoanalytic dogma). On the other hand, we have the work of research psychologists (Lefkowitz & Burton, 1978), suggesting that prevalence of many of the symptoms of the depressive syndrome of children is at such high rates in normal children that such symptoms may be neither statistically atypical, psychopathologic, nor long-lasting.

More toward the middle of the spectrum, Campbell (1952), Dyson and Barcai (1970), and Varsamis and MacDonald (1972) describe symptoms linked to the framework of manic-depressive illness as a specific disease entity for children. Such symptoms occur in a periodic or cyclic nature and include psychomotor retardation, school refusal, loss of interest, withdrawal in the depressed phase, and extreme mental activity, motor overactivity, and overtalkativeness in the manic or hypomanic phase.

Malmquist (1975, p. 91) has proposed a thorough delineation of depressive symptomatology into a number of categories including:

- I. Association with organic diseases
  - A. Part of pathologic process
  - B. Secondary (reactive) to a physical process
- II. Deprivation syndromes—Reality-based reactions to impoverished or nonrewarding environment
  - A. Anaclitic depressions
  - B. Affectionless character types
- III. Syndromes associated with difficulties in individuation
  - A. Problems of separation—Individuation
  - B. School phobias with depressive components
  - C. Developmental precursors of moral masochism
- IV. Latency types
  - A. Associated with object loss
  - B. Failure to meet unattainable ideals
  - C. Depressive equivalents (depression without depressive affect)
  - D. Manic-depressive states
  - E. Affectless character types (generalized anhedonia)
  - F. Obsessional character (compensated depressive)
- V. Adolescent types

Cytryn and McKnew (1972) attempt to integrate this plethora of approaches into a classification for childhood neurotic depression composed of acute, chronic, and masked depression (with the latter occurring most frequently). They conceptualize depressive illness as depressed affect of long (several months) duration and associate it with severe impairment in personal, social, and vegetative areas of functioning. In more "serious" cases, general retardation and feelings of despair and hopelessness affect the child's thinking, and suicidal thoughts are present. They postulate a masked-depressive reaction when the reaction is most pervasive and manifests itself in a spectrum of deviant behaviors. Underlying depressive mood is inferred from episodes of pure depression upon hospitalization and themes rich in depression, elicited through projective tests and fantasy materials. In the smaller groups of acute and chronic depressive reactions, the picture more clearly resembles that of adult depressive reactions. The masked and chronic varieties are differentiated from the adjustment reaction of childhood by the pervasiveness, intensity, and duration of the clinical picture, as well as a more long-lasting personality change; acute depressive reactions show little of the latter changes.

Cytryn and McKnew (1974) postulate a hierarchy of depressive development. At the basic level of fantasy, prior to verbalization or manifestation of depressed mood, depressive themes were said to predominate (as in the so-called masked depression). When a fantasy defense fails to operate and the factors causing the depression are not resolved, then depressive verbalizations occur. This, they contend, is present in most children manifesting an acute-depressive reaction or in some recovering from a chronic-depressive reaction. When, over time, the second level of defenses fail, the depression is manifested by depressive mood and behavior. This is typical of the chronic depression or early stages of acute reaction. The authors also assert that in carefully studied cases of resolving depression, the third level is first resolved, usually followed by the verbal level of manifest depression. The fantasy level is said to clear only after resolution of the depressive conflict. Petti (1978) raised serious questions about these formulations, and recent work (Cytryn *et al.*, 1980), suggests that this hypothesized developmental level may not be true for the fantasy portion.

A Canadian group led by McConville (McConville, Boag, & Purohit, 1973) has delineated three aspects of childhood depression, which they have correlated to developmental and chronological factors. This categorization consists of the following depressive subtypes: affectual, negative self-esteem, and guilt. The affectual subtype is found most frequently in 6- to 8-year-olds, the negative self-esteem in the 8- to 12-year-olds, and the rarer guilt subtypes are found in children over age 10 years. Children who were evaluated showed an increase in frequency of items in the various subtypes with increasing age, though the authors point out the frequent overlap of subtype items (McConville, 1975). Affectual subtype is depicted by such items as sadness, crying, helplessness, hopelessness, withdrawal and inner loss, separation, and nurturance concerns. The negative self-esteem items, commonly found in the 8- to 12-year-olds, include demeaned self-estimate, low estimate of self-worth to others, and negative assumption of others' estimates of the child, fear of exploitation, and assumption of continuing failure or misfortune. The third or guilt depression subtype, which is found to be uncommon (generally following a loss that began after the age of 10 years), includes items related to excessive guilt, punitive self-estimate, passive and active thoughts of self-destruction, and a desire for restitution with a lost one. Petti and Wells (1980) provide a poignant example of a child fitting this category.

Connell (1972) describes two types of childhood depression. She divides the depressed children into high- and low-neuroticism categories on the basis of a Junior Eysenck Personality Inventory score. Children of the low-neuroticism group showed a persistent fluctuating course, had a long (4 years or more) history of dysphoric mood, and generally had a family history of depression. This group of children generally required tricyclic antidepressant therapy. The high neurotic group had a shorter duration of symptomatology (a few months to two years), had symptomatology usually related to specific events, and responded to environmental manipulation or group therapy. Less than half this group had depression in the family history.

Kuhn and Kuhn (1972) studied 100 depressed children, only a few of whom could be regarded as suffering from classical melancholia, which they considered to be sadness, severe retardation and inhibition, suicidal tendencies, delusions of guilt, and the cardinal symptom of morning tiredness. Other signs and symptoms that were reported in the larger group of depressed children, in order of frequency were as follows: poor performance in school, anxiety, sleep disturbances, inhibition, diminished activity, tiredness, inability to concentrate and other disturbances of mental activity, enuresis, behavioral problems, somatic complaints, dissatisfaction, lack of enthusiasm, tendency to weep, sensitivity, irritability, aggressivity, excessive dreams, nervousness, unruly behavior at school, lack of interest and inability to derive pleasure from activity normal for age, loss of appetite, weight loss, dyslexia, and lying and stealing. These workers go on to enumerate a variety of other, less common symptoms. In essence, the whole range of psychopathology of childhood appears to be subsumed under the category of depression.

Krakowski (1970) uses the following criteria in describing depression in children. The child is exposed to a loss that may be true or imaginary. Also, there may be failure to achieve a desired goal or inability to establish a defensive dependence. Inability to establish a compensatory dependence generally results in the lowering of the child's self-esteem, which is then followed by expressions of inadequacy, despair, or symptoms such as isolation, lying, and stealing. This, then, creates a vicious cycle leading to more rejection. The overt-depressive feelings may be admitted, but are frequently denied by such children, especially when the child manifests hostile or aggressive behavior. Intellectual achievement is lowered either by the depression or by the behavioral disturbances. In a similar vein, Agras (1959) hypothesized that childhood depression accompanies a depressive family constellation. In this study, Agras noted that depression underlies many other psychiatric disorders of childhood. He evaluated seven grade-school-age children who openly expressed fear of going to school, and found depressive symptoms in six, with frequent outbursts of weeping for no apparent reason, together with unhappy, miserable whining behavior as the most common signs. Three children feared dying and wished to die, and one made several suicidal gestures. The seventh child only seemed depressed when describing his father, who had deserted the family. This child was inappropriately cheerful and had frequent attacks of hyperactive-violent behavior. Five of these children had somatic complaints and five had fears, phobias, and paranoid ideation. Six of the seven mothers showed signs of overt depression that continued for weeks. Agras felt that these cases were similar to those wherein adults manifested significant depression.

Glaser (1967) talks about the masked depressions of children, and states that the depression need not be the underlying causative pathology or even the main psychopathologic reaction, but a part of the total disturbance. He outlines behavioral, psychoneurotic, and psychophysiologic reactions. The behavioral aspects of depression include truancy, temper tantrums, disobedience, and running away. The psychoneurotic reactions include school phobia and failure to achieve in school. Psychophysiologic reactions include headaches, abdominal pains, and vomiting. Glaser states that

> depression or depressive features are understood to exist when the patient expresses feelings of inadequacy, worthlessness, low self-esteem, helplessness, hopelessness, rejection by others, isolation; yet viewed by the examiner of the patient's immediate environment these feelings do not correspond to the patient's actual life situation or are stronger than the patient's actual condition seems to warrant. (p. 566)

Murray (1970) also takes a broad view of childhood depression and states that there are eight major symptoms or symptom groups that may help to indicate the existence of the depressive syndrome. These are enumerated as depression, sleep disturbance, fears of death, social withdrawal, nonattendance in school, somatic complaints, aggression, and general anxiety. He notes that depressed children have at least four of these symptoms during their episodes and notes existence of a spectrum of symptoms with a cluster of aggressive items at one end and anxiety at the other. He states that developmental factors probably play a role because younger children, age 6 to 10 years, have anxiety as a prominent part of their disorder, while aggressive behavior for the 11- to 15-year-olds is more typically displayed.

Thus, we see the gamut of conceptualizing the syndrome of childhood depression from those who completely deny its existence, to those who delineate what they perceive as the syndrome, to those who subsume most of the important elements of child psychopathology under the rubric of this disorder.

There is far less controversy around the concept of social withdrawal. Gottman (1977) notes that social isolation is not a unitary concept and that two separate literatures based on intervention strategies exist. One group of withdrawn children has been so defined on the basis of a relatively low frequency of peer interactions (Walker & Hops, 1973). The second group has been defined on the basis of low levels of peer acceptance and high levels of peer rejection (Gottman, Gonso, & Rasmussen, 1975). However, Greenwood, Walker, and Hops (1977) suggest a definition that includes avoidance of social contact with others, particularly peers, and assumes a low frequency of peer interactions with a high frequency of other behaviors such as self-play, self stimulation, and so forth. Social isolation resulting from rejection by peers and not by the isolated child's withdrawal would not be considered to be social withdrawal. Gelfand (1978) notes the continuum between shyness and social withdrawal. Richards and Siegel (1978) comment on the overlap between anxiety states and withdrawal behaviors in children, and state that social withdrawal and avoidance behaviors are reasonably self-descriptive. School refusal or school phobia are considered in Chapter 11 of this volume.

Clusters of behaviors noted in the extensive work of Jenkins (1973) and his associates have led to the definition of groups of behaviorally disturbed children and adolescents whose disorders were more stable, internalized, and resistant to treatment than transient adjustment reactions. But they were less fixed than the neuroses, psychoses, or personality disorders. One such diagnostic group was labeled as withdrawing reaction of childhood or adolescence. The disorder was characterized by "seclusiveness, detachment, sensitivity, shyness, timidity and general inability to form close interpersonal relationships." These individuals were not to be so diagnosed if they could be classified as cases of schizophrenia or schizoid personality (American Psychiatric Association, 1968).

In the newest diagnostic manual (American Psychiatric Association, 1980), the Avoidant disorder of childhood or adolescence is a similar classification. The critical characteristic is persistent and excessive shrinking from contact with strangers to the extent that it interferes with peer relations. At the same time, these children long for affection and acceptance and have warm, satisfying relations with family and familiar people. They often show embarrassed, timid, and inarticulate behavior when faced with social situations, even while expressing interest for social relationships. They are often unassertive, lack self-confidence, fail to develop age-appropriate social skills, and have a variable clinical course.

Incidence

Incidence of depression in children depends on a number of variables, including the population studied, the age range, the definition of depression, the type of assessment instrument, and the identity of the informants. Few studies are available that use a strict definition of depressive disorders and that sample general populations.

Rutter, Tizard, and Whitemore (1970), employing a diagnosis that required predominance of sadness and misery as an indication of "pure" depression, found an incidence of .1% in boys (10 to 11 years) residing on the Isle of Wight. Kovacs, Betof, Celebre, Mansheim, Petty, and Raynak (1977), employing standardized criteria, found global ratings of mild depression in 5% of a nonpsychiatric population of children ($n = 20$) selected by door-to-door canvassing in the clinicians' neighborhoods, playgrounds, and from clinic staff families. Various depressive symptoms of a mild degree were found in 5% to 10% of the cases.

Albert and Beck (1975) studied elementary students attending a coeducational parochial school in suburban Philadelphia. There were 31 students in the seventh grade and 32 in the eighth grade. Age range was 11 to 15 years, with a median age, in the seventh grade, of 12 years, 9 months, and for the eighth grade, 13 years, 5 months. Sixty-two of the students were white and one pupil had one parent who was Oriental. Students living with both parents numbered 82%, 14% lived with one parent, and 4% lived with grandparents. Only one serious illness was reported; no children were taking medication, except one who was receiving Actifed for an allergy. One parental death and six sibling deaths were reported. Parent vocation was found to be 46% blue-collar workers and 32% white-collar workers. The remaining 12% were shopkeepers, executives, and professionals.

There data were obtained through administration of a questionnaire composed of the Beck Depression Inventory and some special additional questions. It was most interesting that 30% of the girls and 31% of the boys had no or minimal depression; 30% of the girls and 36% of the boys had mild depression. But 40% of the girls and 33% of the boys had moderate to severe depression. Comparison of mean scores showed a trend toward higher depression in the eighth grade, especially among girls. In addition, 35% of the sample acknowledged current suicidal ideation. In answering the item relevant to suicidal thoughts and wishes, 30% endorsed the statement, "I have thoughts about harming myself but would not carry them out," and 5% endorsed the statement "I feel I would be better off dead." The most serious problems perceived by students in descending order were: social, 42%; school-related, 26%; home-related, 18%; and independence or identity, 14%. It was also interesting that a comparison of the mean Beck Depression Inventory scores from this study of early adolescents to that of the adolescents in an earlier high school study revealed a significantly higher level of depression in the preadolescent group.

These data suffer from three major problems: (1) The results are not borne out by clinical experience either in regard to the total incidence or with the conclusion that 40% of normal children could be suffering from moderate to severe depression; (2) it is unlikely that a preadolescent group would be more disturbed than an adolescent group, where the figures are generally considerably higher (Mezzich & Mezzich, 1979); and (3) the instrument, even with its modifications, was inappropriate for the assigned task.

Kashani and Simonds (1979), in the best survey to date, studied 103 children selected from two sources: one a family health plan and the other from a list of those who were delivered at a University hospital. Interviews were conducted in the family homes throughout Missouri and reliability was assessed. In this "normative" sample, 17.4% of the children demonstrated clinically significant sadness or depression, but only 1.9% met DSM-III criteria for a major affective disorder. A comparison between the 18 children who demonstrated significant sadness to the 85 who did not, revealed significant differences in the following areas: "Sad" children were more overtly overactive or restless, had more somatic complaints, showed diminished self-esteem, were involved in excessive fighting, and refused to attend school.

Incidence of depression in the clinical area is dependent on the specific arena. I have arbitrarily divided this section into Clinic and Hospital, and subdivided these sections into Psychiatric and Nonpsychiatric. There have been numerous studies of the incidence of depressed children in outpatient psychiatric clinics. One of the earliest and most stringent was the retrospective study of 1,788 outpatient records by Poznanski and Zrull (1970), who found an incidence of about 1%. Cebiroglu, Sumer, and Polvan (1972) report 85 children who showed "depressive equivalent symptoms" in a group of 10,661 children referred to the University Department of Child Psychiatry in Istanbul between 1960 to 1970. Of these 85, 5 were between ages 3 to 6 years, 33 between 7 to 10 years, and 47 between 11 to 16 years. The most fascinating aspect of their short report, however, was the statement that one third of the total group of 10,661 children "did receive antidepressive treatment and psychotherapy," with the most important psychodynamic factors being fear of losing, or actual loss of, the loved object. Two of the older children suffered from intermittent attacks of manic-depressive psychosis. The remainder of the 85 children were classified as cases of neurotic or reactive depression (82%), endogenous depression (8%), and anaclitic depression (3%).

Murray (1970), on the other hand, noted that over 60% of school children aged 6 to 15 years seen in the Department of Child Psychiatry, Guys Hospital, London, and a Child and Family Guidance Clinic, Cork, showed four or more groups of symptoms that he considers to be indicative of depression. The most frequently occurring combination of such symptoms include depression, aggressive behavior, and nonattendance in school. Many of these children had a family history for depression. Kovacs *et al.* (1977) report that 3% to 14% of clinic children had moderate to severe depressive symptoms, with sadness/crying, decreased motivation, depressed demeanor, and decreased sleep and appetite most frequently rated and occurring in 11% to 14%. Severe symptoms of self-deprecation, hopelessness and pessimism, psychomotor retardation, and underproductive speech were observed in 3% to 6% of the cases. Six percent of the clinic children showed depressive symptoms of a mild degree. On global rating, 14% were substantially depressed and an additional 24% showed mild depression. In a study conducted by Pearce (1977), of 547 children aged 1 to 17 years attending a child psychiatric department, 23% had the symptoms of depression. Using a definition of a depressive disorder that included association of depression, sadness, unhappiness, misery, or tearfulness with a lowered mood persisting for 4 weeks (and representing a change from normality, with symptoms great enough to interfere with everyday social and/or cognitive functioning), 15% to 20% of children, Pearce maintains, can be expected to have a depressive disorder.

In medical and specialty clinics, incidence varies. Of children attending pediatric and dental clinics who were used as normal controls in an English study, 25.8% of the children showed depression (Rutter, 1966). Criteria for depression and reasons for referral were not specified. Children with severe headaches presenting at a clinic were studied for depression by Ling, Oftedal, and Weinberg (1970). Of the group of 25 children presenting to a private, child neurology service with a complaint of headaches (employing research criteria for depression), 10 were found to have significant depression. These children were all Caucasian between the ages of 4 and 16 years with a majority 12 years or younger. However, these workers qualified their results by pointing out that the children had headaches that were frequent, chronic, and refractory to treatment with mild sedatives or aspirin. Also, incidence of depressive disease in this group really could not be generalized to nonselective children with headaches.

In one special clinic, Gittelman-Klein and Klein (1971) reported that 12 of the 34 children referred for school refusal were rated as "quite depressed" by the examining psychiatrist. Satterfield, Satterfield, and Cantwell (1979) report a significant number of very hyperactive boys as requiring treatment for significant depression. Weinberg, Rutman, Sullivan, Penick, and Dietz (1973) report 42 of 72 children (58%) met criteria for depression in an initial examination. These children had been referred to an educational or diagnostic center for evaluation of learning and/or behavior problems noted in school. All were prepubescent or 13 years or younger. Considering suicidal thoughts as indicating severe depression, 12% fell into this group. Moderate depression in which the symptoms were incapacitating or were of major concern to the child or parents constituted 38% of the group. Mild depression, designated by symptoms that were of secondary importance to the parents and child, constituted 50% of the group.

Figures for children who are hospitalized for psychiatric reasons or in residential care are equally as high as those reported for outpatient studies. Nissen (1971) reports that 1.8% of the total number of child and adolescent patients admitted over the period of January 1942 to December 1968 as inpatients to a psychiatric unit in West Berlin were diagnosed as manifesting medium and severe grades of depressive states. Milder forms of depression were not included in the depressive category. Preschool children had to be hospitalized for a minimum of 2 to 4 months, and school-aged children and adolescents for a minimum of 8 to 12 months. Excluded from the evaluation were those with short-term depressive reactions, depressive moods with dominant neglect, depressive states that were part of the clinical picture of psychosis or infantile autism, depressive moods associated with neurologic or endocrine disorders, and depressive moods that were not distinguishable from other types of neurotic disorders. The average age at referral was 10.7 (plus or minus 3.6 years), with a definite peak for depression at ages 11 to 14.

Carlson and Cantwell (1979) report on the administration of the Children's Depression Inventory (CDI) to 210 children between the ages of 7 and 17 at the time of their admission to the inpatient and outpatient children's services at the Neuropsychiatric Institute in Los Angeles. They note that 60% of the children had symptoms of either depression, withdrawal, low self-esteem, or suicidal ideation. Furthermore, 49% of these children scored on the CDI in a range that is considered to be indicative of moderate depression. In interviewing 102 of these children and their parents in a systematic way, they found that almost 25% were rated at least moderately depressed on interview, and that 28 of the 102 had an affective disorder diagnosed. In breaking down their sample into inpatient and clinic, 16% of the outpatients and 36% of the inpatients had affective-related diagnoses. Almost a quarter of the total group had a major depression.

Petti (1978) reports 49 of 73 children (or 61% of those hospitalized on a child unit) were diagnosed as depressed by clinicians, and 59% of the children were so diagnosed utilizing the Bellevue Index of Depression (BID), a semistructured interview scale. McConville *et al.* (1973) report the prime symptoms of depression to be present in 51% of a group of children treated in an inpatient setting at Beechgrove Children's Unit in Ontario. Petti and Ulrich (1981) found that 67% of the children admitted to an acute-care child psychiatric unit met research criteria for depression (BID). However, the unit was reputed to specialize in treating depressed children, and many referrals were for that expressed purpose.

It has long been noted that children admitted to pediatric hospitals often develop or manifest unhappy behavior. Blumberg (1978) described several cases of masked depression in children hospitalized on a general pediatric service. Poznanski, Cook, and Carroll (1979) studied a sample of 30 children who were inpatients in a tertiary children's hospital. Children were between the ages of 6 and 12 years (mean age was 8.6 years), and each child was evaluated by two child psychiatrists. Of the 30 children, 8 received a global rating of moderate or severe depression by both child psychiatrists.

A recently completed study by Kashani, Barbero, and Bolander, (1980) of 100 children, aged 7 to 12, residing in a pediatric hospital unit, found 7 who met both the DSM-

III and BID criteria. Two more met BID criteria and two, who were acutely depressed, met neither BID nor DSM III criteria. Gastro-intestinal patients comprised only 14 of the 100 children studied, but made up 4 of the 7 depressed children. This is similar to findings on an adult medical ward and is particularly interesting because it was the chronic "belly-achers" who first made me aware that anxiety was not the sole cause of somatic complaints in children. Moreover, a very high percentage of children with depression also manifest somatic complaints, often referred to the gastro-intestinal system. Children with particular medical problems seen to be prone to depressive disorders (Petti, 1981a). This is especially true of diabetics, children with seizure disorders and organic brain syndromes, and perhaps children with hyperthyroidism. Boswell, Lewis, Freeman, and Clark (1967) describe 12 children who developed hyperthyroidism between the ages of 4 and 14 years and were admitted to the North Carolina Memorial Hospital. Nine were actively hyperthyroid and three were eurthyroid or had previously been treated for hyperthyroidism. They found that five of these children, who were predominantly from lower social economic classes, showed a profound chronic depression based on clinical, psychodynamic investigation. Vranjesevic, Radoljcic, Bumbasirevic, and Todorovic (1972) described children with brain tumors and cited an incidence of 32.5% of the cases with psychiatric disturbances, more than half with depression.

Incidence of depression in special populations also has been described. For instance, Welner, Welner, McCrary, and Leonard (1977), in studying the offspring of depressed individuals who had to be hospitalized, found that 7% of these children met diagnostic criteria used in the diagnosis of adult depression. McKnew, Cytryn, Efron, Gershon, and Bunney (1979) studied offspring of manic-depressive parents and found that 30% were depressed and met their Children's Affective Rating Scale (CARS) criteria while 50% met Weinberg's criteria.

Incidence of social withdrawal or isolation has been studied as an aspect of general behavior rather than as a specific disorder. In a prospective study, MacFarlane, Allen, and Honzik (1954) found that children with excessive reserve, if considered as related to withdrawal, exhibited an average incidence of about 35% across the years measured in their Berkley population of 252 children. Shepherd, Oppenheim, and Mitchell (1971), on the other hand, noted that withdrawal was found in fewer than 3% of 6,000 children residing in an English county. These children ranged in age from 5 to 15 years. Such withdrawal was not associated with age or sex. The finding that isolation as a symptom remains relatively constant with age is corroborated in the Mid-Manhattan study as well (Greene, Langer, Herson, Jameson, Eisenberg, & McCarthy, 1973).

In clinical populations, the incidence of withdrawal or social isolation, excluding children also diagnosed as psychotic or autistic, is much higher. A low incidence (6.7%) of diminished socialization was found in non-depressed children referred to a center for children with academic and behavior problems in school (Brumback, Dietz-Schmidt, & Weinberg, 1977). But, among 500 cases studied of children attending the Michigan Child Guidance Institute, 61 were selected who had at least three of the following characteristics: seclusive; shyness or timidity; absence of close friendships; apathy; underactivity; depressed or discouraged attitude. The interquartile age range was 9 to 14 years, and 21% were girls (Jenkins, 1973). In another study described by Jenkins (1973), of 1,500 cases at the Institute for Juvenile Research, 120 withdrawn schizoid children were selected who manifested at least two of the six items described above. A few were considered to be schizophrenic. The incidence of withdrawal or isolation is even higher in children with depression. Poznanski and Zrull (1970) report that withdrawal behavior, in some form, was consistently found in the case histories of the 14 depressed clinic children they studied. Kashani, Barbero, and Bolander (1981) report that diminished socialization was found in 85% of children hospitalized in a pediatric unit who met research criteria for depression. Brumback *et al.* (1977) report diminished socialization in 66.7% of the depressed children they evaluated. The prevalence of the avoidant disorder of childhood or adolescence is apparently uncommon (American Psychiatric Association, 1980).

Assessment

Historically, assessment has been a low priority in terms of specific tools for making the diagnosis of depression. This area has been reviewed previously (Petti, 1978). The early studies were predominantly anecdotal. The 1952 issue of the *Nervous Child* contained several papers dedicated to childhood depression. Papers by Campbell (1952, 1954), Kasanin (1931), Krakowski (1965, 1970), Kuhn (1963), Frommer (1967, 1968), and Cytryn and McKnew (1972, 1974) are typical of the anecdotal approach to describing children who manifest depression. With advent of DSM-III and the Research Diagnostic Criteria (Spitzer *et al.* 1975), hope for a refined approach to diagnosing and following the course of childhood depression may be around the corner. Though there may be several pitfalls in this approach by making *a priori* judgments about what depression is and is not, limiting the childhood disorder to the adult criteria, and assuming that secondary depression is similar for children and adults, the approach of using standardized criteria may be one of the most helpful innovations in child psychiatry regarding depression. As described earlier, Poznanski and Zrull (1970) used specified criteria in the assessment of depression. They followed the pioneering work of Sandler and Joffe (1965), who described features of childhood depression as including: looking sad, unhappy, or depressed; appearing withdrawn or bored; discontented or anhedonic; sense of feeling rejected; inability to accept comfort or assistance; tendency to regress to oral passivity; sleep disturbance; oral erotic or repetitive activities; and difficulties of the therapist in making sustained contact.

Cytryn and McKnew (1974) employed their Children's Affective Rating Scale which measured three categories of mood and affect: mood and behavior, talk, and fantasy. Ling *et al.* (1970) and Weinberg *et al.* (1973) employed criteria that were modified from those used in research work with depressed adults. Petti (1978) modified this scale to make it more stringent in assessing depression in children and demonstrated good correlation between clinicians' judgment of depression and that of the scale. Kovacs *et al.* (1977) have devised scales based on modifications of the Beck Depression Inventory. Puig-Antich *et al.* (1978) have modified the Schedule for Affective Disorders and Schizophrenia SADS) interview of Spitzer and Endicott for children in order to use unmodified research diagnostic criteria for depression. Herjanic (1980) has approached the field from the epidemiologic perspective and has devised a scale that correlates well with DSM-III criteria.

The following will be broken down into clinical, behavioral, and biochemical/physiological approaches. The clinical approach is represented by workers from many centers and perspectives. Weinberg *et al.* (1973) modified the scale used by Ling *et al.* (1970), in which ten categories of depressive symptomatology were arbitrarily chosen. In the modification, 40 items were subsumed under 10 headings: dysphoric mood; self-deprecatory ideation; aggressive behavior; sleep disturbance; change in school performance; diminished socialization; change in attitude towards school; somatic complaints; loss of usual energy;

and unusual changes in appetite and/or weight. To be considered depressed, a child had to manifest one item from each of the first two categories and one item from any two of the other categories. Symptoms had to be of concern to the child or his parents, represent a change from the usual self, and be present for at least 1 month. One of the difficulties with the scale is the very high sensitivity but low specificity for depression.

One modified version of the scale is that reported by Petti (1978), in which each of the 40 items is rated for absence or degree of severity on a scale from 0 (absent) to 3 (severe). Similar criteria for presence or absence of depression to the Weinberg scale was that an item from each of categories one and two be required for the diagnosis, and that each item be present for at least 1 month and considered a change in the usual self. A total score of 20 is required for a diagnosis of moderate depression on the Bellevue Index of Depression. This scale also has higher sensitivity than specificity, but is much improved over the original Weinberg. Petti (1978) has demonstrated a high correlation between ratings of depression by psychiatrists and the BID scale. A recent report documents highly significant interrater reliability for each of the 40 items on the scale for the interview of the child. Reliability based on test–retest of the paper-and-pencil parent form was also highly significant for each of the items of the BID, with the exception of appraisal for suicidal attempts, difficulty awakening in the morning, and being less friendly (Petti &Ulrich, 1981). However, only 85% of children diagnosed positive on the BID would meet research diagnostic criteria for depression. This has been borne out by two studies of Kashani (Kashani, 1980; Kashani *et al.*, 1981), as well as by Petti (1981a).

Puig-Antich, Perel, Lupatkin, Chambers, Shea, Tabrizi, and Stiller, (1979b) have employed the Kiddie-SADS as an assessment instrument to determine whether children 6 to 12 years of age meet the various types of depression diagnosable for adults. The instrument is a modification of the interview format for the widely used Schedule for Affective Disorders and Schizophrenia and is used as a structured interview. Both parents and the child are interviewed and the final score is a summary rating for each symptom. Very high interrater reliability is reported, as well as physiological correlation in the form of cortisol hypersecretion (Puig-Antich, Chambers, Halpern, Hanlon, & Sacher, 1979a).

The Interview Schedule for Children (ISC) (Kovacs *et al.* 1977) is a structured interview used for research into depression in children, ages 8 to 13 years. This assessment instrument provides comprehensive coverage of the symptoms associated with depression, including research diagnostic criteria, but does not provide a differential diagnosis. This instrument requires careful training of the interviewer, who must for appropriate use possess clinical experience. The instrument also has good interrater reliability. The Kiddie-SADS, ISC, Weinberg Scale, and BID can potentially be used to monitor clinical change. Poznanski *et al.* (1979) have also developed an instrument to assess the severity of depression: the Children's Depression Rating Scale (CDRS). The CDRS was created for use with 6- to 12-years-olds and was modeled after the Hamilton Depression Rating Scale. Each of the 15 items is rated on a graduated scale, with operational definitions for each graduation. Multiple sources of information may be used to rate any particular item. The authors cite good interrater reliability and correlation of the behavioral items with the global ratings for depression.

The earlier CARS of Cytryn and McKnew (1972) did provide a severity rating as well. Cytryn *et al.* (1980) compared the diagnostic criteria for the various depression rating scales (Weinberg, CARS, CDI, and DSM-III) and found considerable overlap and few differences.

The School Age Depression Listed Inventory (SADLI) contains 16 items: 5 observation, 11 self-report, and a global rating by the interviewer. We have developed this format to successfully assess clinical change in hospitalized children receiving various treatments (Petti & Law, 1982). In the hospital setting, parents are not available to be observers of their child's behavior or mood, hence a separate scale beyond the BID Screening Instrument was necessary. Good reliability has been obtained with this scale.

Kovacs (1980) has reviewed the more recent literature on depression rating scales. The Children's Depression Inventory (Kovacs *et al.*, 1977) is a self-report scale modified from the Beck Depression Inventory and described earlier. It has been extensively used in its earlier form (Carlson & Cantwell, 1979, 1980). The approach described by Lefkowitz and Tesiny (1980) is very comprehensive and should be helpful in epidemiologic studies. Application of their methodology to clinical populations should be attempted.

Behavioral assessment of depression in adults is being developed at a rapid rate. However, little substantial work has been accomplished in using this approach with children. This may be due to the lack of constant dysphoric mood in children that is prominent with depressed adults. Gelfand (1978) presents an interesting view of the field related to social withdrawal and negative emotional states. A number of strategies have been devised to assess for social withdrawal. Greenwood *et al.* (1977) provide a comprehensive review of such strategies and highlight the most frequent and fruitful ones: sociometric peer ratings; behavioral observation methods; and teacher ratings. The work of Lefkowitz and Tesiny (1980) addresses itself to some of the issues described by Greenwood *et al.* (1977). Later work (Bornstein, Bellack, & Hersen, 1977; Whitehill, Hersen, & Bellack, 1980) has emphasized particular aspects related to socially isolative or withdrawn behavior.

A variety of biochemical and physiologic measures described elsewhere (Petti, 1982b) and in the section below have been used to ascertain correlations with depression as a disease and depression as a syndrome. As we become more sophisticated in our assessment skills, it is probable that refinement of the biological tools of measurement may provide us with the means to assess the type of depression, degree of severity, and optimal forms of multimodal treatment. Strategies such as those employed by Lefkowitz and Tesiny (1980), if coupled with a formal clinical interview of the child or family, and physiological measures, will be critical to scientific and clinical advances in the assessment of childhood depression (Kovacs, 1977).

Assessment of social isolation, withdrawal, or avoidance has been approached from several directions. Greenwood *et al.* (1977) review the three most commonly used methods in a critical manner: those based on (a) sociometric measures by peer rating; (b) direct behavioral observation measures of frequency or duration of social interactions; and (c) teacher nomination or teacher ratings. Weinrott, Corson, and Wilchesky (1979) note that withdrawn children receive little attention from clinicians and researchers because they are infrequently identified as disruptive or as experiencing academic difficulties. They employed the following criteria in a behavior checklist to assess the disorder: (1) perceived as "a major problem requiring professional intervention" or "a minor problem worthy of a short-term treatment program"; (2) any two items of (a) rarely or never volunteers in class, (b) often or always daydreams, or (c) rarely or never initiates conversations with peers; and (3) has been referred for psychological testing, or was the subject of a teacher-initiated parent conference, or was the subject of at least one discussion between the teacher and counselor or school principal.

Lazerson (1980) employed questionable criteria for assessment of withdrawn behavior by designating two behavioral categories of the Devereaux Elementary School Behavior Rating Scale: inattentive–withdrawn and need of closeness to teacher. Whitehill *et al.*

(1980), on the other hand, were far more conservative in their assessment of children targeted for behavioral intervention for their social isolation. First, three sociometric questionnaires were given to several classrooms of children ($N = 95$) to identify children perceived by their peers as isolated. These children ($N = 23$) received fewer than three nominations on the positive peer nomination scale, fewer than five negative nominations, and a roster and rating average of less than three. Second, these 23 children were given a conversational skills role-playing test, and eight showed at least three deficient conversational skills. Third, the children needed to be identified as having trouble with group activities as rated with the abbreviated Conner's Teacher Questionnaire. Five children were so selected. Fourth, classroom observers noted free-play activity and identified five children who spent a disproportionate amount of time alone. Finally, the naturalistic classroom data were compared with teacher ratings, and four children were identified by both.

This approach by Whitehill *et al.* (1980) is certainly comprehensive, though one must wonder about excluding the children identified sociometrically as withdrawn because they had reasonable conversation skills. The review by Greenwood *et al.* (1977) should prove helpful to those interested in further pursuing the assessment of social withdrawal.

Etiology

There is a cluster of hypothesized etiologies for the development of depression in children. One way of organizing the various approaches to describing the roots of this disorder is by employing the integration of 10 conceptual models of depression proposed by Akiskal and McKinney (1975) for adult depressive disorders. It is important to note that even though Harms (1952) complained that a single volume of the *Nervous Child* dedicated to depression in children was likely to raise untold criticism of the editors, and that depression was said to be a trivial matter in childhood, a number of proposed etiologies have been posited for children. Akiskal and McKinney broke the models of depression into five major schools: psychoanalytic, behavioral, sociological, existential, and biological. These workers then described depressive illness as a final, common, psychobiological pathway that is dependent on the interaction of several factors, including: genetic vulnerability, developmental events, psychosocial events, physiological stressors, and personality traits.

The psychoanalytic school emphasizes the Abraham–Freud model of retroflexed anger (i.e., the inward turning of the aggressive instinct caused by the loss of an ambivalently-loved object). This aggressive instinct is then converted into depressive affect. The object loss model, described by Spitz and later by Bowlby, involved separation and disruption of the attachment bond. The ego-psychological model, described by Bibring, views depression as an affect, independent of the aggressive drive but said to be related to the ego's awareness of its helplessness. This in turn leads to collapse of self-esteem, which ultimately ends up as depression. This model is very similar to Karen Horney's concept of basic anxiety. Horney (1950) describes basic anxiety as a feeling of hopelessness and helplessness as well as abandonment. She conceives all psychopathology as evolving from this basic sense of feeling overwhelmed.

Beck's (1967) model of depression, which espouses the concept of the negative cognitive triad, is considered by some to be a bridge between psychoanalytic and behavioral models. The negative triad consists of a negative view of the self, the environment, and the future. The individual feels helpless to overcome the vicissitudes of life and hopeless in controlling his or her destiny.

The behavioral school is predominantly made up of two models: the learned helplessness model of Seligman, (1973), which is related to the individual's inability to escape from aversive conditions; and the loss of reinforcement model of Lewinsohn and associates (Lewinsohn, Weinstein, & Shaw, 1968), which describes the rewards of the sick role as substituting for lost sources of positive reinforcement.

The sociological school consists of a model that is predominantly concerned with the breakdown of the individual's self-esteem, including objective and subjective symbolic losses. The existential model is similar to the sociological one in that the depression results from a loss of the meaning of existence. The biological model is predominantly confined to the Biogenic Amine Theory in which impaired monoaminergic neurotransmission is seen as the basis for depression. In the neurophysiological model, various mechanisms are hypothesized, including cholinergic dominance, hyperarousal that is secondary to intraneuronal sodium accumulation, and reversible functional derangement of diencephalic mechanisms of reinforcement. Akiskal and McKinney (1975) thus provide tentative bridges between the various models of depression and the many hypotheses generated from observations made with children and also provide a theoretical framework for future research.

The following constructs make up the behavioral model of depression: (1) learned helplessness; (2) loss of reinforcement, chronic frustration, and lack of control over interpersonal relationships; and (3) negative cognitive set, hopelessness, and helplessness. The learned helplessness model (Seligman & Maier, 1967) was derived from observations of animals who were repeatedly subjected to an inescapable aversive stimulus. When these experimental animals had the opportunity to escape, they continued to allow themselves to be subjected to punishment. Seligman (1979) has noted that multiple studies have correlated learned helplessness and depression and that when both are found, motivation is impaired, as is cognition. Lowered self-esteem occurs as individuals feel responsible for their ineffectiveness; aggression or assertive deficits, as well as appetitive and physiological deficits, subsequently occur. Although the majority of evidence for this model has been found with adults, there is substantiating support for a similar model for children.

Dweck (Dweck, 1975; Dweck & Reppucci, 1973) demonstrates that children experience helplessness and negative cognitions after failing in a task. Helplessness is defined by Dweck as the perception by the involved individual that the aversive event means that she or he has no control over that event and subsequent events and that unpleasant results will persist even when she or he tries to control them. Dweck (1977) asserts that helplessness probably plays a major role in mood disorders of child psychopathology. She has found that helpless children become incapable of solving problems that they may have just completed successfully. Also, demoralization and passivity will follow. Even though as competent as the nonhelpless control children in experimental conditions, helpless children perceive their failure as attributable to their own lack of confidence or to external noncontrollable sources.

Moyal (1977) conducted a similar study in which the relationship between depressive symptoms, self-esteem, locus of control, and stimulus appraisal was investigated in a group of fifth- and sixth-grade Toronto school children who had not been referred for psychiatric problems. Employing standardized scales such as the Piers–Harris Children's Self-Concept Scale, the Nowicki–Strickland Children's Locus of Control Scale, and her own stimulus appraisal scale, Moyal found a strong negative correlation between self-esteem and depression. There was also a negative correlation between external locus of control (a cognitive style associated with perceived helplessness over one's situation) with self-esteem and with choice of adaptive responses. The external locus of control or perceived helplessness did correlate positively with a depression score and the choice of helplessness and self-blaming or externalized blaming responses.

Similar support for this concept of learned helplessness, an external locus of control (the feeling that one's destiny is controlled by external forces, a roll of the dice, luck, the side of the bed one gets up on, etc.), and depression is found in an extensive study by Lefkowitz and Tesiny (1980). They employed a peer-nominating inventory of depression, the Children's Depression Inventory of Kovacs, a modified self-rating depression scale, the Coopersmith Self Esteem Inventory, the Nowicki–Strickland Locus of Control Scale, a human figure drawing, teacher rating scale, and academic records. The results demonstrated highly significant correlations between high-peer nominations for depression, poor social behavior, depressed intellectual functioning, and external locus of control, apathy, and self-ratings of depression.

Thus, if one is willing to accept the potential relationship between an external locus of control and helplessness, then the evidence generally suggests that learned helplessness plays a major role in depressive symptomatology in children. There is no direct study that correlates a diagnosable depressive syndrome or depressive disorder with either learned helplessness or locus of control in children. Albert (cited in Kovacs & Beck, 1977) found a very strong correlation between grades and depression. From the study described earlier (Albert & Beck, 1975), students who had low modified Beck Depression Inventory scores were rated as excellent by their teachers regarding school performance, and conversely those students who were rated as poor performers had high depression scores.

The learned helplessness model in some way relates to the loss of reinforcement model of the behavioral school. Ferster (1973) notes that "adversively motivated behavior," such as crying, irritability, and complaints, occurs more frequently in depressed individuals, while behaviors that would make the individual feel good and be positively reinforced are decreased in frequency. Lewinsohn *et al.* (1968) systematically applied behavioral assessment to depression. They found that the historical antecedents of depressive behavior could be considered to be a deficient rate of response-contingent positive rewards of reinforcement. The general absence of available reinforcers in the environment or the inability of the individual to access himself to those reinforcers because of a lack of appropriate social skills were seen as possible factors in this deficit of rate of response-contingent positive reinforcers.

Petti (1981a) suggests examples of this relationship (such as the child living in a ghetto neighborhood with alcoholic parents) as conducive to the general absence of available reinforcers. Children who lack basic friendship-building skills are representative of those unable to obtain reinforcers. Three ways (Lewinsohn, 1975) in which the reduced rate of response-contingent positive reinforcement might occur include: diminished capacity of reinforcer effectiveness; lack of available reinforcing events; and lack of the necessary social behaviors to attain the available reinforcers. These conditions are equally important for depressed children and for withdrawn children. The best example may be that of the depressed hyperactive child so poignantly described by Satterfield, Satterfield, and Cantwell (1979). These were extremely hyperactive children who required anti-depressant therapy and multimodal approaches in dealing with their many deficits, including social and academic skills. Children with learning disabilities are also vulnerable to being unable to derive positive reinforcements from their school environment. As a group they are, in terms of this model, particularly vulnerable to depression or isolation.

One of the earliest descriptions of affective disorders in children (Kasanin, 1931) noted that constitutional factors seemed of greater importance than environmental issues. Kuhn (1963) elaborated on this concept. The anaclitic depression described by Spitz and Wolf (1946) of infants going through protest, despair, and detachment phases was later applied to older children (Bowlby, 1960; McConville *et al.,* 1973). It has been demonstrated to have an animal analog that responds to biological treatment (Suomi, Seamon, Lewis, DeLizio, & McKinney, 1978). Frommer (1968), Connell (1972), Ossofsky (1974), Weinberg *et al.* (1973), and Puig-Antich *et al.* (1978) strongly suggest that a biologic component is a major factor in depressive disease, disorder, or endogenous depression of children. Dyson and Barcai (1970) imply that a psychophysiologic disorder operates in the offspring of parents who have responded to lithium medication, if the children show symptoms of mixed hypomania and depression.

A limited number of studies have attempted to demonstrate an underlying physiologic dysfunction in depressed children. McKnew and Cytryn (1979) have reported their study of urinary metabolites in depressed children. Only 3-methoxy-4-hydroxyphenylethylene (MHPG) showed a significant difference between normal controls, hospitalized orthopedic patients, and chronically depressed children, with the control group having the greatest MHPG excretion followed by the depressed and finally the orthopedic children. These workers postulate that orthopedic patients may have been experiencing an "emotional defensive detachment" analogous to Bowlby's detachment phase in abandonment or anaclitic depression. This would then explain why their urinary MHPG excretion was lower than that of the chronically depressed children. These results are similar to those reported in depressed adults and are hypothesized as mediated through a suppression of the general arousal system of the nervous system.

Pugi-Antich *et al.* (1979a) also report preliminary neuroendocrine data supporting the hypothesis that adult and child depressive disorders may be the same disease. Plasma cortisol levels were measured before treatment and after clinical recovery in four prepubertal children who met unmodified Research Diagnostic Criteria (RDC) for major depressive disorder, endogenous type. In two of the four children, cortisol hypersecretion was present during the illness and cleared upon clinical recovery—a pattern analogous to that found in 50% of adults with a major depressive disorder.

The work of the Pittsburgh group (Kane, Coble, Conners, & Kupfer, 1977; Kupfer, Coble, Kane, Petti, & Conners, 1979; Petti, Law, Coble, & Kupfer, 1982; Taska, Kupfer, Coble, Klecha, Petti, & Matson, 1980) also forges a link between physiologic findings in adult and childhood depression through the means of all-night EEG sleep analysis. A shortened Rapid Eye Movement Latency (REML) is found in adults with primary depression and in many depressed children. REML is the time that elapses between the onset of sleep and the beginning of the first REM period. Moreover, both adults and children who show a positive response to tricyclic antidepressant therapy show a marked prolongation of the REML.

Although far from sufficient to demonstrate that many depressions of children have a significant biological component, the number of open studies (Petti, 1981a,c) demonstrated that childhood depression and symptoms commonly associated with the syndrome do show dramatic improvement in many targeted symptoms with tricyclic antidepressants. Another inconclusive line of evidence supporting the biologic contribution to childhood depression emanates from the pediatric literature that has been noted. Although it is possible that such disorders as hyperthyroidism (Boswell *et al.,* 1967), hypothyroidism and thyrotoxicosis (Morillo & Gardner, 1979), hypopituitary shortness of stature (Rotnem, Genel, Nintz, &

Cohen, 1977), diabetes (Blumberg, 1978; Petti, 1981c), brain tumors (O'Keeffe, 1969; Vranjesevic *et al.* 1972;), and neurological disorders (Petti, 1981b,c; 1982a) may be secondary to the precursors related to depression, it is equally possible that such disorders are the physiologic strata that make children susceptible to depression.

The psychoanalytic literature is surprisingly rich, given a dogma that insisted that a depressive disorder in childhood could not exist. There have been a number of reviews that posit the disorder as arising from a variety of roots. Malmquist (1975) presents a very satisfactory summary of "infantile" depressions and the early psychodynamic formulations of Freud, Abraham, and Gero, and a description of attachment, bonding, dependency, and object relations as they apply to childhood depression. French and Berlin (1979) have edited a work in which a number of contributors present psychodynamic and psychoanalytic formulations regarding the etiology of depression in childhood. Phillips (1979) provides a developmental chart of childhood depression and emphasizes psychological interactions, such as parental disability (depression, rejection, abuse/neglect, separation, and chronic illness) that interferes with the parent–child interaction and impairs development of the relationship needed by the child to develop to innate potential.

Krakowski (1970) takes a similar approach to depicting the development of exogenous depression in childhood and adolescence. Parental loss is described as the most frequent cause, followed by depression in a parent, and finally by parental rejection. The threat of a real or perceived loss of love is responded to with hostility by the child, which in turn leads to feelings of guilt. These, then, result in a move toward independence by the child and a sense of ambivalence. Finally, unless the environment becomes supportive and protective, the child becomes depressed and has a profound decrease in self-esteem due to this inability to establish a compensatory defensive dependence. In this model, the child expresses insecurity, helplessness, and hopelessness by becoming isolative, or by developing other symptoms that cause further rejection and intensification of a depressive cycle.

Symonds (1968a, 1970) argues that the parental climate is crucial for development of chronic depression in children. He notes that the climate formed by "defeated, cynical, sarcastic, hypercritical and rejecting parents" leads directly to a profoundly pessimistic outlook on life and severe resignation. Like Krakowski (1970), he believes that depression results from the inability of such a child to attain what Bowlby has described as the fourth phase of grief and mourning in infancy and early childhood (i.e., reorganization of behavior toward a new object). Such thwarting of achieving resolution of the problems may often be due to indulgent, masochistic mothering. In my personal experience, depression is more prominent in children from lower socioeconomic families. Symonds (1968a) offers an explanation for this by noting that when the predominant parental climate leads to overwhelming effects on development, hopelessness finds poverty to be the most nurturant base.

It has become clear that depressive symptoms and syndromes in childhood have multiple roots, that several factors play a role in the development of this disorder, and that strategies for treating the depression must be based on an assessment that attempts to delineate the relevance of each factor. Frequently, the family influences the development, course, and intensity of the depression, possibly as genetic vulnerability, modeling of depressive, helpless behavior, or through constant thwarting, separations, and psychological abandonment and rejection.

The child plays a major role in this process, and the outcome seems to depend on genetic vulnerability, individual temperamental factors, intellectual level, internal physiologic changes, and adaptation to chronic stress. The type of cognitive organization maintained by the child may be crucial in determining how the depressive process progresses and to what extent. The ego ideal, or set of goals set by the child for attainment, is also very important. McConville *et al.* (1973), among others (Cytryn & McKnew, 1974; Malmquist, 1975; Phillips, 1979) note that the developmental level is also critical. For instance, they report that younger children predominantly express sadness and helplessness, seemingly as related to perceptions of loneliness, emptiness, and alienation from parents or peers. This in part stems from the younger child's dependence on feeling states rather than organized thought. Issues of separation and nurturance are paramount to such young children.

In older children, "thought-feelings" are predominant, and the youngsters are capable of developing fixed negative ideas of low self-esteem, which seem to set the depression more firmly in place. This picture is often seen in middle-latency children who have experienced repetitive loss and separations from loved ones. A third or guilt type of depression found in older children occurs when they may be first able to enter into abstract thinking and when

> the sudden increase in drive strength at the beginning of puberty may give rise to considerable loosening of certain aspects of ego functioning, permitting the eruption of both sexual and aggressive impulses which would be turned against the self. (McConville *et al.,* 1973, p. 134)

McConville and Boag (1976) studied the etiologic factors in 73 children who had clinically significant depression based on a rating scale score. Their previous study (McConville *et al.,* 1973) had found that acute loss was of great importance in the guilt type of depression, and more chronic losses were important in the affectual, negative self-esteem, and mixed depressive types. Their 1976 paper found that loss of parent(s) or siblings was found in 100% of the affectual Type 1 depressed children and 83% of guilt Type 3 children. They report that 63% of the mixed affective/negative self-esteem and only 36% of the negative self-esteem children experienced such a loss. All four of the groups had suffered rejection short of placement away from home, at the rate of about 50%. Incidence of chronic depressions in the family, predominantly neurotic, occurred in 10% of the guilt type depressions, 67% of the affectual, 58% of the mixed affectual/negative self-esteem, and only 3% of the negative self-esteem types. An important aspect of this paper relates to the observation that acute onset depressions were uncommon except in the guilt type, but that associated family rejection and scapegoating were common in those families. These same workers (McConville, Boag, & Purohit, 1972) report that loss of parenting figures is handled by "normal" children through an intense mourning process that lasted about 6 weeks.

In a very succinct manner, Nissen (1978) charts out and discusses the multifactorial causes of depression in children. The continuum stretches from the psychogenic–sociogenic or socialization-related depressions in children to the endogenous somatogenic types. Within the former fall anaclitic depression (infancy), separation and induced depressions (late infancy, toddlerhood), "school" depression (due to excessive demands and occurring during the school-age years), and neurotic depressions (prepuberty and early adolescence). All are said to be related predominantly to family, environmental, or societal influences, which include the unwanted or unaccepted child, separations from the family, pathogenic attitudes of the parents, changing adult attitudes toward children, communication of a mother's depressive mood, and the overtaxing expectations set for the child in school.

In the middle of the continuum fall the milieu-reactive and constitutionally determined depressions, which include the neurotic depressions of a purely constitutional nature, such as endogenous phasic depression (bipolar, major depression). At the somatogenic or symptomatic end of the spectrum fall the depressions associated with epilepsy, endocrine disorders, infections, head injuries, and convalescence. However, Nissen notes that there is much overlap on both ends of the continuum.

Hypotheses have been generated concerning the etiology of social isolation or withdrawal. Gottman (1977) notes that many low-peer interaction children may be anxious to make friends, and that we know little about their actual behavior. He suggests that some might not know how to go about making friends. Ross (1980) suggests that fears of being ignored, ridiculed, or attacked by others may be another reason that children do not interact. A number of single case and group studies (O'Connor, 1969, 1972; Ross, 1980; Weinrott *et al.*, 1979) have employed interventions directed to the lack of appropriate social skills. Reinforcement and attention by adults toward the "shy" child and the development and maintenance of withdrawn behavior by the actions and behaviors of significant adults is reviewed by Ross (1980).

Jenkins (1973) summarizes his vast experience in a very philosophical chapter on "The Withdrawing Reaction (leave me alone)." He notes that the critical and depreciative maternal attitude toward such children seems contributory and much less wholesome than that of the average clinic mother. Mothers with chronic illness, disability, or a mental health problem, or those from an alcoholic household, were disproportionately represented in the withdrawal group of children. The latter had an overrepresentation of intellectually slow children compared to the rest of the clinic population. Jenkins conceptualizes the disorder as secondary to an abnormally protective barrier around the surface of the personality. This barrier does not allow external stimuli to be perceived or internal impulses to become external actions. Many of the withdrawn schizoid children from the Institute for Juvenile Research study would probably fit into the category of borderline conditions, and the hypothesized etiologies of these disorders have been described elsewhere (Petti & Law, 1982; Petti & Unis, 1981). No known etiology is ascribed for the avoidant disorder of childhood and adolescence at this time (American Psychiatric Association, 1980).

Case Report

This is a 7-year-old Caucasian male, referred for in-patient evaluation and treatment of "severe emotional and behavioral difficulties" and a "possible thought disorder." The parents first noted difficulties with George when he entered kindergarten at age 5 years, although he had always been noted to be immature for his age. Behavior in school, which had led to previous mental health evaluations, consisted of several episodes in which George placed straight pins into the coat sleeves, cuffs, and hats hanging in the cloakroom that belonged to "model" students in his class. He was involved in sexual preoccupation and frequent self-stimulation. George often became violent and would scream, yell, and become combatant with other children when they separated from him or when he was frustrated at home. Incessant whining and complaining were noted at home, school, and with peers. He often expressed wishes to play with other children, but they would taunt and tease him instead. His activity level was reported as high, but he could easily attend to entire television programs without being distracted. The parents also described an excessively rich fantasy life, which was composed of tall tales regarding fires, violent accidents, and death. They also reported several accidents and accident-prone behavior, stealing behavior, verbalizations of being "a bad boy" and being "dumb," and on one occasion telling his parents that he wished to die. Two periods lasting several months also were reported in which his appetite decreased, and he had lost 5–10 lbs over the previous year. George had been in a class for socially and emotionally disturbed children over the past year, but failed to demonstrate significant improvement. He was evaluated by a child psychiatrist who entertained the possibility of a schizophrenic process versus a severely "compromised" ego. His birth and past medical history were relatively unremarkable.

On admission, his physical examination was within normal limits, except for multiple nonfocal neurological signs and evidence of maturational lag. He presented as a well-developed, tall, thin, well groomed child who appeared somewhat older than his stated age. He was cooperative and appeared calm when relating to the examiner. His affect was bright but then became sad when he spoke of his "problems" at school and at home. Thought content was generally appropriate, and he was able to follow instructions and demonstrate that he was oriented to time, place, and person. He did make inappropriate comments regarding his desire to have his blood drawn, and that his blood was yellow in color. He related that he was a "bad boy."

His Bellevue Index of Depression was positive for a moderate dysphoric episode. Positive items for moderate depression reported by the parents included sad, lonely, unhappy feelings, irritability, easy crying, persecutory ideation, early morning awakening, loss of usual effort in school, drop in school performance, decreased participation with groups of children, lack of enjoyment of school and desire not to attend, being too tired to think, play, or work, and a decreased appetite. George minimized his difficulties but did report that sadness, loneliness, and irritability were problems, and that trouble falling asleep and awakening early, incomplete school work, headaches, muscle aches, and decreased appetite were of moderate or severe intensity.

The following modalities were employed during this child's hospitalization: milieu therapy, dynamically oriented psychotherapy, psychoeducational therapy in a small classroom setting, social skills training, behavioral programing, and parent work and training. After his discharge from the hospital, the child continued his individual psychotherapy with the same therapist, was begun on pharmacotherapy, and parent work continued.

During the first two weeks of hospitalization, George continued to be involved in the production of tall tales with themes related to fires, accidents, and feats of unusual physical prowess. He demonstrated the capacity to differentiate fantasy from reality, and verbalized a willingness to cease this behavior. He was also evaluated for appropriate social skills and was found to have a high-level capacity for social interactions. However, it was noted that he often engaged in behaviors that indicated poor timing in his approach to interactions with peers and demonstrated behavior that was contrary to his capacities. For instance, he tended to irritate peers because of his inappropriate overtures to them. Another major difficulty noted was his immature and silly behavior. This often resulted from his being a follower rather than an instigator or institutor of such behavior, and when not exposed to peers who were provocative and instigating, his behavior appeared much more organized and mature, particularly around activities of daily living. In the structured milieu setting, he often demonstrated a decrease in his whining and silliness. Tremendous difficulty with separation from his parents during visitation periods was marked. He would become teary, whine, and utter threats to his parents about leaving. He often verbalized his concerns about "their difficulties and problems." He also demonstrated a previously reported stuttering problem on the unit and in the school setting. Stuttering occurred when he was excited about something or when he became anxious. He did not evince stuttering in structured reading exercises.

During the first two weeks, there was no evidence of suicidal ideation, sexual preoccupation, self-stimulation and provoking sexual activity, or discussions from his peers. His appetite was good, and he did not lose any weight. In the classroom, his on-task behavior was 47%, mean disruptive behavior was 3%, and neutral behavior was 50%. In a free-play setting, his mean adaptive peer interactions was 54%, mean maladaptive peer interactions 7%, mean solitary play rate 32%, and mean rate of interacting with staff 6%. His gross motor rate was 42%. His Teacher Affect Rating scores in the classroom averaged 24 during the first week and 18.5 in the second week. On the Pittsburgh Activities of Living Scale (PALS) (Petti & Unis, 1981), his mean activities of daily living subscale score was 73%, mean mealtime score was 81%, mean appropriate peer interaction score was 65%, and mean compliance score was 83%.

The Child Behavior Profile (Achenbach, 1978) indicated that schizoid behavior was one and one-third standard deviations above the mean; uncommunicativeness was one and a half standard deviations above the mean; obsessive/compulsive behavior was one standard deviation above the mean; and social withdrawal was one standard deviation above the mean. His Children's Depression Inventory score was 23, with several statements relating to poor self-image as well as self-derogatory ideation. The School Age Depression Listed Inventory (SADLI) was scored by both observers to fall within the moderate depressive range.

Psychoeducational testing in the past had demonstrated an average IQ with a full-scale IQ of 97. Testing in the hospital revealed a full-scale IQ of 101, with high scores obtained on Picture Arrangement and Picture Completion, and low scores on Block Design, Digit Span, and Coding. He seemed to have difficulty with immediate recall of auditory information, nonverbal concept formation, the ability to reproduce abstract designs, and flexibility in new and varying situations. His Bender Gestalt suggested organicity or immaturity. A speech, hearing, and language evaluation was performed and was well within normal limits, as was an EEG. However, the child was noted to be 1 year behind academically. In our classroom setting, he was very compliant to rules and seemed to be motivated to perform well. The diagnosis at the end of the first 2-week period of time was "mixed emotional and behavioral disorder of childhood, with depressive features, moderate childhood depression, speech articulation difficulties under stress, and probable specific learning disability with auditory processing deficits."

The designated treatment for the depression involved obtaining a self-derogatory baseline, with the provision then made to provide opportunities for success in activities, as well as provisions for reinforcement for adaptive behaviors. A reinforcement program was devised for his adaptive peer interactions and mealtime social interactions (Petti & Unis, 1981). Also, he was programmed to be involved in activities with a staff member and a peer as frequently as possible. Weekly weight checks were to be maintained, and individual therapy, milieu therapy, and positive reinforcement for tasks attempted were part of his treatment program. An accident base line was also instituted. To deal with his poor impulse control, he was to be reinforced for PALS compliance performance. Appropriate means for expressing anger were to be modeled, and a locked, quiet room was to be used for extremely aggressive behavior. Since lying was felt to be a form of poor impulse control, a base line to observe and record all instances of lying and categories of lying, such as avoidance lies, denial lies, and tall tales, was instituted. He was to receive positive reinforcement for truthfulness, and consideration was to be given for a lying program, if so indicated. Social skills training was considered for his poor impulse control. Involvement in small-group activity with peers was another form of treatment to allow him the opportunity to gain success when he was able to show good impulse control. The parents were evaluated and found to require parent management skills. Training was instituted to teach them to be more consistent with regard to appropriate forms of punishment and positive reinforcement.

After two weeks of intensive treatment, his affect was reported as frequently depressed; he seemed to be seeking punishment. No accidents were observed on the unit but one was reported on a short visit outside the hospital with his parents. Impulse control remained problematic but he eliminated his telling of tall tales. He was completing 80% of his work in school but continued to show auditory processing and perceptual-motor problems. His parents were actively involved in the parenting skills training, learning to ignore attention-seeking negative behavior. Father was encouraged to spend more time with him; conversely, mother was expected to spend less time with him.

Although he had shown a high level of tested social skills, his scores on formal assessment revealed the following changes, as defined elsewhere (Matson, Esvelt-Dawson, Andrasik, Ollendick, Petti, & Hersen, 1980; Petti, 1981d).

The number of single words in response to 10 test scenes: Pre = 27; Post = 185.

Intonation scored as 1 = flat, unemotional tone to 5 = full and/or lively tone with emotional expressiveness: Pre = 15/50; Post = 31/50.

Appropriate verbal responses that match the scene being role-played: Pre = 7/10; Post = 9/10.

This demonstrated significant improvement in already satisfactory social skills.

At discharge, after 6 weeks of hospital assessment and treatment, the following observations and impressions were obtained. His parents successfully completed the training program, seemed highly motivated and pleased with the changes in their own behaviors, and were to become involved in out-patient supportive work focusing on parenting. George completed his social skills training. He continued to show academic progress in the school setting as demonstrated by mid-first-grade level functioning, a high level of work completion, and absence of disruptive behaviors. His SADLI dropped from 63 at 2 weeks to 46 on discharge (still in the depressive range); his CDI dropped from 23 to 19. There was some regression during the last week of hospitalization, which included suicidal ideation, self-concentration on negative behaviors, involvement in several accidents, and verbalized concerns about his parents. It was generally felt that he had made progress, but his estimated impairment at the time of discharge was felt to be severe in relation to perception of self, and moderate in regard to school functioning, family relationships, and peer relations at both school and play. Individual psychotherapy for George, a special program for learning disabled children in the school, and parent counseling were recommended.

His outpatient work initially progressed well, with his parents concertedly applying what they had learned. George was having difficulty with a peer but was able to be appropriately assertive. When his father was pressured at work and had little time to spend with George, a recurrence of depressive behavior ensued. This was marked by destructive and self-aggressive behavior and ideation, sleep problems, and regression in general levels of functioning. It was felt that little could be done with the family situation because his school system was on strike. Therefore, no positive reinforcement in a structured setting could be expected. Because the themes of therapy were repetitive, self-defacing, aggressive, negative, and seemingly becoming deeply ingrained, a trial of antidepressant medication was considered.

Results of imipramine treatment were dramatic. On the maximum dose of medication (5 mg/kg/day in 3 divided doses and with careful monitoring), George began experiencing a change in his depressed affect. In therapy sessions his play began to reflect the disruptions and conflicts in his family, and he talked about the need the entire family had for "a foster home." His father began to spend time more constructively with him. All the vegetative functions improved, his themes in individual therapy became more constructive, and he was able to begin to deal with the problems his parents were experiencing. At home his moodiness and irritability cleared and his negative complaints and accidents ceased. However, the parents were unable to accept George's verbalization of anything that expressed disappointment or anger.

With divorce looming for his parents, and with his father's consistently negative behavior and absences, George manifested swings in his behavior, particularly at home. At school, on the other hand, he was described as "the best kid in the class." However, after the father was reminded of his family obligations and received a job promotion, the home atmosphere improved and so did George. In his individual sessions, George was much less negative and began showing more positive affect and positive themes. Following 2 weeks of missed sessions, his mother reported that he was regressing once again. The therapist felt this was related to the father's removal of attention from George, since earlier themes related to the father's neglect (dare-devil antics, accidents, aggression, sadism, and magical solutions) reappeared in therapy hours. After an intermittent number of missed sessions, his parents called to say they were terminating therapy. They reported that George was doing well. They had brought George to a Pentecostal service and he had been "saved."

Overall, this case demonstrates a number of principles regarding the etiology and treatment of depression in children. The bottom line, of course, for children, is that they are dependent on their environment for positive reinforcers, that the developmental level of a young child dictates the manner in which the depression is manifested, and that a multimodal approach is necessary for comprehensive, effective treatment.

Summary

Depression and social withdrawal as symptoms are found in a number of the psychiatric disorders of childhood and adolescence. The two are also disorders in their own right and at times coexist as symptoms, behaviors (Lefkowitz & Burton, 1978), or disease entities. Depression in children has been portrayed in a number of ways and from a variety of theoretical perspectives; the literature increases yearly. Social withdrawal, in contrast, has a more limited and predominantly behaviorally oriented literature.

The etiology has not been established for either disorder, though a number of hypotheses have been entertained for both. Childhood depression, because of the difficulty in achieving consensus about its definition, diagnosis, and assessment, is a real challenge to clinicians and researchers. Whether it is considered a symptom, syndrome, or disease does not alter the need to understand the depression, to determine its etiology, and to devise strategems for its treatment and prevention. Incidence of depressive symptomatology is high, particularly in clinical populations.

This chapter presented the variety of perspectives from which depression and social withdrawal in children have been viewed. A number of promising approaches for assessing these disorders have been described. Greater attention has been given to depression because it has been of greater concern to a larger number of clinicians and researchers, and because it has a greater incidence, particularly in clinic populations. Social withdrawal or isolation should become the focus of increased attention in the future because it is a relatively stable behavior, is associated with poor or marginal social functioning in adult life, and is frequently found in depressive disorders throughout the life span. The new Diagnostic and Statistical Manual of Mental Disorders of the American Psychiatric Association (1980) should facilitate the diagnostic task of the clinician regarding depression and social withdrawal in children.

References

Achenbach, T. M. The child behavior profile: I. Boys aged 6–11. *Journal of Consulting and Clinical Psychology*, 1978, *46*, 478–488.

Agras, S. The relationship of school phobia to childhood depression. *American Journal of Psychiatry*, 1959, *116*, 533–536.

Akiskal, H. S., & McKinney, W. T. Overview of recent research in depression. *Archives of General Psychiatry*, 1975, *32*, 285–305.

Albert, N., & Beck, A. T. Incidence of depression in early adolescence: A preliminary study. *Journal of Youth and Adolescence*, 1975, *4*, 301–307.

American Psychiatric Association. *Diagnostic and statistical manual of mental disorders* (3rd ed.). Washington, D.C.: American Psychiatric Convention, 1980.

Beck, A. *Depression: Clinical, experimental and theoretical aspects.* New York: Harper & Row, 1967.

Blumberg, M. L. Depression in children on a general pediatric service. *American Journal of Psychotherapy*, 1978, *32*, 20–32.

Bornstein, M. R., Bellack, A. S., & Hersen, M. Social skills training for unassertive children: A multiple-baseline analysis. *Journal of Applied Behavior Analysis*, 1977, *10*, 183–195.

Boswell, J. I., Lewis, C. P., Freeman, D. F., & Clark, K. M. Hyperthyroid children: Individual and family dynamics: A study of twelve cases. *Journal of the American Academy of Child Psychiatry*, 1967, *6*, 64–85.

Bowlby, J. Grief and mourning in infancy and early childhood. *Psychoanalytic Study of the Child*, 1960, *15*, 9–52.

Brumback, R. A., Dietz-Schmidt, S. G., & Weinberg, W. A. Depression in children referred to an educational diagnostic center: Diagnosis and treatment and analysis of criteria and literature review. *Diseases of the Nervous System*, 1977, *38*, 529–535.

Campbell, J. D. Manic-depressive psychosis in children: Report of 18 cases. *Journal of Nervous Mental Disorders*, 1952, *116*, 424–439.

Campbell, J. D. Manic-depressive disease in children. *Journal of the American Medical Association*, 1954, *148*, 154–157.

Carlson, G. A., & Cantwell, D. P. Depressive symptoms in a child psychiatric population: Interview data. *Journal of the American Academy of Child Psychiatry*, 1979, *18*, 587–599.

Carlson, G. A., & Cantwell, D. P. Unmasking masked depression in children and adolescents. *American Journal of Psychiatry*, 1980, *137*, 445–449.

Cebiroglu, R., Sumer, E., & Polvan, O. Etiology and pathogenesis of depression in Turkish children. In A. Annell (Ed.), *Depressive states in childhood and adolescence.* New York: Halstead Press, 1972.

Connell, H. M. Depression in childhood. *Child Psychiatry and Human Development*, 1972, *4*, 71–85.

Cytryn, L., & McKnew, D. H., Jr. Proposed classification of childhood depression. *American Journal of Psychiatry*, 1972, *129*, 149–155.

Cytryn, L., & McKnew, D. H., Jr. Factors influencing the changing clinical expression of the depressive process in children. *American Journal of Psychiatry*, 1974, *131*, 879–881.

Cytryn, L., McKnew, D. H., Jr., & Bunney, E. Diagnosis of depression in children: Reassessment. *American Journal of Psychiatry*, 1980, *137*, 22–25.

Dweck, C. S. The role of expectations and attributions in the alleviation of learned helplessness. *Journal of Personality and Social Psychology*, 1975, *31*, 674–685.

Dweck, C. S. Learned helplessness: A developmental approach. In J. G. Schulterbrandt & A. Raskin (Eds.), *Depression in childhood.* New York: Raven Press, 1977.

Dweck, C. S., & Reppucci, N. D. Learned helplessness and reinforcement responsibility in children. *Journal of Personality and Social Psychology*, 1973, *25*, 109–116.

Dyson, W. L., & Barcai, A. Treatment of children of lithium-responding parents. *Current Therapeutic Research*, 1970, *12*, 286–290.

Ferster, C. B. A functional analysis of depression. *American Psychologist,* 1973, *28,* 857–870.

French, A., & Berlin, I. *Depression in children and adolescents.* New York: Human Sciences Press, 1979.

Frommer, E. A. Treatment of childhood depression with antidepressant drugs. *British Medical Journal,* 1967, *1,* 729–732.

Frommer, E. A. Depressive illness in childhood. *British Journal of Psychiatry Special Publications,* 1968, *2,* 117–136.

Gelfand, D. M. Social withdrawal and negative emotional states: Behavior therapy. In B. B. Wolman, J. Egan, & A. O. Ross (Eds.), *Handbook of treatment of mental disorders in childhood and adolescence.* Englewood Cliffs, New Jersey: Prentice Hall, 1978.

Gittelman-Klein, R., & Klein, D. F. Controlled imipramine treatment of school phobia. *Archives of General Psychiatry,* 1971, *25,* 204–207.

Glaser, K. Masked depression in children and adolescents. *American Journal of Psychotherapy,* 1967, *21,* 565–574.

Gottman, J. M. Toward a definition of social isolation in children. *Child Development,* 1977, *48,* 513–517.

Gottman, J. M., Gonso, J., & Rasmussen, B. Social interaction, social competence, and friendship in children. *Child Development,* 1975, *46,* 709–718.

Greene, E. L., Langner, T. S., Herson, J. H., Jameson, J. D., Eisenberg, J. G., & McCarthy, E. D. Some methods of evaluating behavioral variations in children 6 to 18. *Journal of the American Academy of Child Psychiatry,* 1973, *12,* 531–553.

Greenwood, C. R., Walker, H. M., & Hops, H. Issues in social interaction/withdrawal assessment. *Exceptional Children,* 1977, *43,* 490–499.

Harms, E. The problem of depressive and manic sickness in childhood. *Nervous Child,* 1952, *9,* 310–316.

Herjanic, B. Personal communication, 1980.

Horney, K. *Neurosis and human growth: The struggle toward self realization.* New York: W. W. Norton, 1950.

Jenkins, R. L. *Behavior disorders of childhood and adolescence.* Springfield, Ill.: Charles C Thomas, 1973.

Kane, J., Coble, P., Conners, C. K., & Kupfer, D. J. EEG sleep in a child with severe depression. *American Journal of Psychiatry,* 1977, *134,* 813–814.

Kasanin, J. The affective psychosis in children. *American Journal of Psychiatry,* 1931, *10,* 897–926.

Kashani, J. Personal communication, 1980.

Kashani, J. H., Barbero, G. J., & Bolander, F. D. Depression in hospitalized pediatric patients. *Journal of the American Academy of Child Psychiatry,* 1981, *20,* 123–134.

Kashani, J., & Simonds, J. F. The incidence of depression in children. *American Journal of Psychiatry,* 1979, *136,* 1203–1205.

Kovacs, M. Conclusions and recommendations of the subcommittee on assessment. In J. G. Schullerbrandt & A. Raskin (Eds.), *Depression in childhood: Diagnosis, treatment and conceptual models.* New York: Raven Press, 1977.

Kovacs, M. Rating scales to assess depression in school aged children. *Acta Paedopsychiatry,* 1980-1981, *46,* 305–315.

Kovacs, M., & Beck, A. T. An empirical clinical approach toward a definition of childhood depression. In J. G. Schulterbrandt & A. Raskin (Eds.), *Depression in childhood: Diagnosis, treatment, and conceptual models.* New York: Raven Press, 1977.

Kovacs, M., Betof, N. G., Celebre, J. E., Mansheim, P. A., Petty, L. K., & Raynak, J. T. *Childhood depression: Myth or clinical syndrome?* Unpublished manuscript, 1977.

Krakowski, A. J. Outpatient treatment of the emotionally ill child: A comparison of two psychotropic agents. *Psychosomatics,* 1965, *6,* 402–409.

Krakowski, A. J. Depressive reactions of childhood and adolescence. *Psychosomatics,* 1970, *11,* 429–433.

Kuhn, R. The occurrence and treatment of endogenous depression in children. *Schweizerische Medizinische Wochenschrift,* 1963, *93,* 86–90.

Kuhn, V., & Kuhn, R. Drug therapy for depression in children. Indications and methods. In A. Annell (Ed.), *Depressive states in childhood and adolescence.* New York: Halsted Press, 1972.

Kupfer, D., Coble, P., Kane, J., Petti, T. A., & Conners, C. K. Imipramine and EEG sleep in children with depressive symptoms. *Psychopharmacology,* 1979, *60,* 117–123.

Lazerson, D. B. "I must be good if I can teach!" Peer tutoring with aggressive and withdrawn children. *Journal of Learning Disabilities,* 1980, *13,* 43–48.

Lefkowitz, M. M., & Burton, N. Childhood depression: A critique of the concept. *Psychology Bulletin,* 1978, *85,* 716–726.

Lefkowitz, M. M. & Tesiny, E. P. Assessment of childhood depression. *Journal of Consulting and Clinical Psychology,* 1980, *87,* 43–50.
Lesse, S. Depression masked by acting out behavior. *American Journal of Psychotherapy,* 1974, *28,* 352–361.
Lewinsohn, P. M. Behavioral study and treatment of depression. In M. Hersen, R. M. Eisler, & P. M. Miller (Eds.), *Progress in behavior modification* (Vol. 1). New York: Academic Press, 1975.
Lewinsohn, P. M., Weinstein, M. & Shaw, D. Depression: A clinical research approach. In R. D. Rubin & C. M. Franks (Eds.), *Advances in behavior therapy.* New York: Academic Press, 1968.
Ling, W., Oftedal, G. & Weinberg, W. Depressive illness in childhood presenting as severe headache. *American Journal of Diseases of Children,* 1970, *120,* 122–124.
MacFarlane, J. N., Allen, L., & Honzik, M. P., *A developmental study of the behavior problems of normal children between 21 months and 14 years.* Berkeley: University of California Press, 1954.
Mahler, M. S. On sadness and grief in infancy and childhood: Loss and restoration of the symbiotic love object. *Psychoanalytic Study of the Child,* 1961, *16,* 332–351.
Malmquist, C. P. Depression in childhood. In F. F. Flach & S. C. Draghi (Eds.), *The nature and treatment of depression.* New York: Wiley, 1975.
Matson, J. L., Esvelt-Dawson, K., Andrasik, F., Ollendick, T. H., Petti, T. A., & Hersen, M. Observation and generalization effects of social skills training with emotionally disturbed children. *Behavior Therapy,* 1980, *11,* 522–531.
McConville, B. J. Personal Communication, 1975.
McConville, B. J., & Boag, L. C. *Therapeutic approaches in childhood depression.* Paper presented at the American Academy of Child Psychiatry 23rd Annual Meeting, Toronto, October 1976.
McConville, B. J., Boag, L. C., & Purohit, A. P. Mourning depressive responses of children in residence following sudden death of parent figures. *Journal of Child Psychiatry,* 1972, *11,* 341–364.
McConville, B. J., Boag, L. C., & Purohit, A. P. Three types of childhood depression. *Canadian Psychiatric Association Journal,* 1973, *18,* 133–137.
McKnew, D. H., & Cytryn, L. Urinary metabolites in chronically depressed children. *Journal of the American Academy of Child Psychiatry,* 1979, *18,* 608–615.
McKnew, D. H., Cytryn, L., Efron, A. M., Gershon, E. S., & Bunney, W. E. Offspring of patients with affective disorders. *British Journal of Psychiatry,* 1979, *134,* 148–152.
Mezzich, A. C., & Mezzich, J. E. A date-based typology of depressed adolescents. *Journal of Personality Assessment,* 1979, *43,* 238–246.
Morillo, E., & Gardner, L. I. Bereavement as an antecedent factor in thyrotoxicosis of childhood: Four case studies with survey of possible metabolic pathways. *Psychosomatic Medicine,* 1979, *41,* 545–555.
Moyal, B. R. Locus of control, self-esteem, stimulus appraisal, and depressive symptoms in children. *Journal of Consulting and Clinical Psychology,* 1977, *45,* 951–952.
Murray, P. A. The clinical picture of depression in schoolchildren. *Journal of the Irish Medical Association,* 1970, *63,* 53–56.
Nissen, G. *Depressive syndrome in kindes-und Jugendalter.* Berlin: Springer-Verlag, 1971.
Nissen, G. The depressive child. In F. Freyhan (Ed.), *Social aspects of depression.* Switzerland: Geigy, 1978.
O'Connor, R. D. Modification of social withdrawal through symbolic modeling. *Journal of Applied Behavior Analysis,* 1969, *2,* 15–22.
O'Connor, R. D. Relative efficacy of modeling, shaping and the combined procedures for modification of social withdrawal. *Journal of Abnormal Psychology,* 1972, *79,* 327–334.
O'Keeffe, K. A. Depression in a child after neurosurgery. *Developmental Medicine and Child Neurology,* 1969, *11,* 799–801.
Ossofsky, H. J. Endogenous depression in infancy and childhood. *Comprehensive Psychiatry,* 1974, *15,* 19–25.
Pearce, J. Depressive disorder in childhood. *Journal of Child Psychology and Psychiatry,* 1977, *18,* 79–82.
Petti, T. A. Depression in hospitalized child psychiatry patients: Approaches to measuring depression. *Journal of the American Academy of Child Psychiatry,* 1978, *17,* 49–59.
Petti, T. A. *A comparison of the Bellevue Index of Depression and DSM III criteria in diagnosing childhood depression.* Unpublished data, 1981. (a)
Petti, T. A. Depression of children—Behavioral and other treatment strategies. In J. F. Clarkin & H. Glazer (Eds.), *Depression: Behavioral and directive treatment strategies.* New York: Garland Press, 1981. (b)
Petti, T. A. Depression in children—A significant disorder. *Psychosomatics.* 1981, *22,* 444–447. (c)
Petti, T. A. Behavioral approaches in the treatment of depressed children. In D. Cantwell & G. Carlson (Eds.), *Childhood depression.* New York: Spectrum Publications, 1982. (a)

Petti, T. A. Imipramine in the treatment of depressed children. In D. Cantwell & G. Carlson (Eds.), *Childhood depression*. New York: Spectrum Publications, 1982. (b)

Petti, T. A., & Law, W. Borderline psychotic behavior in hospitalized children: Approaches to assessment and treatment. *Journal of the American Academy of Child Psychiatry*, 1982, *21*, 197–202.

Petti, T. A., & Ulrich, M. S. *Depression in hospitalized child psychiatry patients, II: Reliability assessment and incidence*. Unpublished data, 1981.

Petti, T. A., & Unis, A. Treating the borderline child with imipramine: A controlled study. *American Journal of Psychiatry*, 1981, *138*, 515–518.

Petti, T. A., & Wells, K. Crisis treatment of a preadolescent who accidentally killed his twin. *American Journal of Psychotherapy*, 1980, *34*, 434–443.

Petti, T. A., Law, W., Coble, P., & Kupfer, D. *Longitudinal psychiatric and polysomnographic EEG monitoring of a depressed child treated with imipramine*. Submitted for publication, 1982.

Phillips, I. Childhood depression: Interpersonal interactions and depressive phenomenon. *American Journal of Psychiatry*, 1979, *136*, 511–515.

Poznanski, E. O., Cook, S. C., & Carroll, B. J. A depression rating scale for children. *Pediatrics*, 1979, *64*, 442–450.

Poznanski, E. O., & Zrull, J. P. Childhood depression: Clinical characteristics of overtly depressed children. *Archives of General Psychiatry*, 1970, *23*, 8–15.

Puig-Antich, J., Blau, S., Marx, N., Greenhill, L., & Chambers, W. Prepubertal major depressive disorder: A pilot study. *Journal of the American Academy of Child Psychiatry*, 1978, *17*, 695–707.

Puig-Antich, J., Chambers, W., Halpern, F., Hanlon, C., & Sachar, E. J. Cortisol hypersecretion in prepubertal depressive illness: A preliminary report. *Psychoneuroendocrinology*, 1979, *4*, 191–197. (a)

Puig-Antich, J., Perel, J. M., Lupatkin, W., Chambers, W. J., Shea, C., Tabrizi, M. A., Stiller, R. L. Plasma levels of imipramine (IMI) and desmethylimipramine (DMI) and clinical response in prepubertal major depressive disorder. A preliminary report. *Journal of the American Academy of Child Psychiatry*, 1979, *18*, 616–627. (b)

Richards, C. S., & Siegel, L. J. Behavioral treatment of anxiety states and avoidance behaviors in children. In D. Marholin, II (Ed.), *Child behavior therapy*. New York: Gardner Press, 1978.

Rie, H. E. Depression in childhood: A survey of some pertinent contributions. *Journal of the American Academy of Child Psychiatry*, 1966, *5*, 653–685.

Ross, A. O. *Psychological disorders of children: A behavioral approach to theory, research and therapy*. New York: McGraw-Hill, 1980.

Rotnem, D., Genel, M., Nintz, R., & Cohen, D. Personality development in children with growth hormone deficiency. *Journal of the American Academy of Child Psychiatry*, 1977, *16*, 412–426.

Rutter, M. *Children of sick parents: An environmental and psychiatric study*. London: Oxford University Press, 1966.

Rutter, M., Tizzard, J., & Whitmore, K. (Eds.). *Education, health and behavior*. London: Longmans, 1970.

Sandler, J., & Joffe, W. G. Notes on childhood depression. *International Journal of Psychoanalysis*, 1965, *46*, 88–96.

Satterfield, J. H., Satterfield, B. T., & Cantwell, D. P. Multimodality treatment of hyperactive children. In N. A. Reatig (Ed.), *Proceedings of the N.I.M.H. Workshop on the Hyperkinetic Behavior Syndrome*. Washington, D.C.: U.S. Government Printing Office, 1979.

Seligman, M. E. P. Fall into learned helplessness. *Psychology Today*, 1973, *7*, 43–49.

Seligman, M. E. P. *Learned helplessness*. Paper presented at the University of Pittsburgh, Pittsburgh, Pennsylvania, October 29, 1979.

Seligman, M. E. P., & Maier, S. Failure to escape traumatic shock. *Journal of Experimental Psychology*, 1967, *74*, 1–9.

Shepherd, M., Oppenheim, B., & Mitchell, S. *Childhood behavior and mental health*. London: University of London Press, 1971.

Spitz, R., & Wolf, K. M. Anaclitic depression: An inquiry into the genesis of psychiatric conditions in early childhood. *Psychoanalytic Study of the Child*, 1946, *2*, 313–342.

Spitzer, R. L., Endicott, J., Robins, E. Research diagnostic criteria. *Psychopharmacology Bulletin*, 1975, *11*, 22–25.

Suomi, S. J., Seamon, S. F., Lewis, J. K., DeLizio, R. D., & McKinney, W. T. Effects of imipramine treatment of separation induced social disorders in Rhesus monkeys. *Archives of General Psychiatry*, 1978, *35*, 321–325.

Symonds, M. The depressions in childhood and adolescence. *American Journal of Psychoanalysis,* 1968, *28,* 189–195. (a)

Symonds, M. Our youth: Apathy, rebellion and growth. A symposium. Disadvantaged children growing in a climate of hopelessness and despair. *American Journal of Psychoanalysis,* 1968, *28,* 15–22. (b)

Symonds, M. Depression in adolescence. *Science and Psychoanalysis,* 1970, *17,* 66–74.

Taska, B. A., Kupfer, D. J., Coble, P. A., Klecha, P., Petti, T. A., & Matson, J. L. *EEG sleep in depressed children: Changes during inpatient treatment.* Presented at the Annual Meeting of the American Psychophysiological Study of Sleep, Mexico City, March 1980.

Varsamis, J., & MacDonald, S. M. Manic depressive disease in childhood: A case report. *Canadian Psychiatric Association Journal,* 1972, *17,* 279–281.

Vranjesevic, D., Radoljcic, B., Bumbasirevic, S., & Todorovic, S. Depressive manifestations in children with intracranial tumors. In A. Annell (Ed.), *Depressive states in childhood and adolescence.* New York: Halsted Press, 1972.

Walker, H. M., & Hops, H. The use of group and individual reinforcement contingencies in the modification of social withdrawal. In L. A. Hamerlynck, L. C. Handy, & E. J. Mash (Eds.), *Behavior change: Methodology, concepts and practice.* Champaign, Ill.: Research Press, 1973.

Weinberg, W. A., Rutman, J., Sullivan, L., Penick, E. C., & Dietz, S. G. Depression in children referred to an educational diagnostic center: Diagnosis and treatment. *Pediatrics,* 1973, *83,* 1065–1072.

Weinrott, R., Corson, J. A., & Wilchesky, M. Teacher-mediated treatment of social withdrawal. *Behavior Therapy,* 1979, *10,* 281–294.

Welner, Z. Childhood depression: An overview. *Journal of Nervous and Mental Disease,* 1978, *166,* 588–593.

Welner, Z., Welner, A., McCrary, M. D., & Leonard, M. A. Psychopathology of children of inpatients with depression: A controlled study. *Journal of Nervous Mental Disorders,* 1977, *164,* 408–413.

Whitehill, M. B., Hersen, M., & Bellack, A. S. Conversation skills training for socially isolated children. *Behaviour Research and Therapy,* 1980, *18,* 217–225.

13

Aggressive and Oppositional Behavior

LARRY A. DOKE AND JOSEPH R. FLIPPO

Introduction

The results of uninterrupted childhood aggression and oppositional behavior appear in daily media reports of homicides, arson, armed robberies, and an alarming variety of other offenses. In 1975, even though youth in the 13–17 age range comprised only 10% of the U.S. population, this group was involved in 43% of all arrests for property crimes and violent crimes, as classified by the FBI (Strasberg, 1978). Strasberg also reported that juvenile arrests for violent crimes climbed 293% between 1960 and 1975.

Surveys for 1980 showed that 30% of American households were touched by a serious crime, and that violent crimes during 1980 were 10% higher than the year before (Public Broadcasting System, 1981). In some families, ineffective parents have succumbed to batterings and violent threats by their children, abdicating authority to the extent that the children are finally in charge (Harbin & Madden, 1979). In some severely disorganized or catastrophically stressed families, attacks by adolescents on their parents are even fatal (Tanay, 1973).

It may be that youth are involved in problems of this magnitude, because patterns of aggression and opposition are not identified before they emerge in the form of crime. In fact, it has been shown that aggression and oppositional behavior comprise approximately one-third of mental health clinic referrals from parents and teachers (Wiltz & Patterson, 1974). Longitudinal studies of aggressive children identified in mental health clinics further

LARRY A. DOKE • Center for Adolescent Rehabilitation and Education, New Mexico State Hospital, Las Vegas, New Mexico 87701. JOSEPH R. FLIPPO • Department of Behavioral Sciences, New Mexico Highlands University, Las Vegas, New Mexico 87701. The preparation of this manuscript was partially supported by Grant 2 S06 RR08066-10 from the Division of Research Resources and the National Institute of Mental Health.

suggest that such aggression is related to criminal behavior, alcoholism, and psychosis in adulthood (Robins, 1966).

In addition, according to a U.S. Senate Subcommittee report on February 1, 1977, at least 600 million dollars are spent annually as a result of school vandalism, and a growing number of teachers (and students) are more concerned with self-preservation than with education (Tygart, 1980). School rules are violated to the extent that many classrooms are out of control; youth are openly selling and using illegal drugs; and episodes of physical violence at school are common. During 1976, 70,000 serious assaults were reported on teachers and hundreds of thousands of assaults on students were cited (Tygart, 1980).

The magnitude of such problems has prompted increasing numbers of studies of childhood aggression and oppositional behavior. Fundamental to such studies is a perspective on these behavior categories in terms of definition, systems of classification, theoretical formulations, assessment and measurement methods, and etiology. These topics constitute the outline for this chapter. At the end of the chapter, an illustrative case of childhood aggression and opposition will be presented.

Definitions

Childhood aggression and opposition take many different forms: one youngster curses another, then shoves the other to the ground; a 3-year-old responds to an instruction from his mother by saying "No," then walking away; a 10-year-old kicks at her older brother in response to his teasing; an adolescent boy informs his therapist of an intense wish to tear his mother's underwear into shreads; a child subject in an experiment punches an inflated clown after having viewed a 10-minute film; a young girl threatens to take her own life. What is the level of consensus regarding which of these episodes represent aggression or opposition? What about the child who "accidentally" injures another or the one who fights to defend himself or a friend? Are there degrees of aggression and opposition, or are these "all-or-not-at-all" phenomena? Answers to such questions (i.e., the task of defining aggression and opposition) require attention to the multiple components of the labeling process, also to methods of classification and assessment.

Aggression

Bandura (1973) has formulated one of the most useful conceptual systems for defining aggression. His analysis of aggression successfully resolves some of the problems with definitions that focus primarily either upon the topography of the act or upon the intent of the perpetrator. Bandura's analysis also accommodates exceptions to definitions of aggression purely in terms of the consequences of an act (i.e., physical or psychological injury or property damage).

According to Bandura, designation of an act as "aggressive" is a function of multiple components of a social labeling process, which considers each of the following in determining whether a sample of behavior qualifies as aggression: (1) *Topography or quality of the behavior.* Is the act in question one that is likely to result in some physical or psychological injury or damage? (2) *Intensity of the behavior.* Is the magnitude of the act in question such that it could be judged to be potentially painful or damaging? (3) *Observed effects of the behavior.* Does the act result in some violation of the basic rights of others, expression of pain, observable injury to the victim, or damage to property? (4) *Inference about the performer's intentions.* Based on information about the social context, the performer's role, antecendent conditions (particularly earlier provocations), and the observer's liking for the performer, is the performer's intent inferred to be premeditated, evil, or vengeful? (5) *Characteristics of the labeler.* As a function of socioeconomic status, sex, ethnic background, education, occupation, personal tendencies toward aggressive behavior, and so forth, is the *labeler* sensitized (or desensitized) to aggression? Are there experiential variables that make some individuals more inclined to attribute hostile intent to others and to label as "aggressive" actions that others would regard as benign? (6) *Characteristics of the performer.* Is the identification of an act as "aggressive" based to some extent on existing information about the cultural background, age, sex, religion, ethnicity, occupation, social status, and so on of the person being observed?

In view of the complexity of the social labeling process, it should come as no surprise that consensus regarding identification of aggressive children is rarely perfect. Not only is it important for those involved in labeling to observe the same components of the event to be labeled, but it may also be necessary that the labelers be relatively similar to each other with respect to their sensitivity or set toward aggression. Finally, it may be necessary for each labeler to have a common base of information about the target child. Rarely would all these conditions be met under normal circumstances.

As a result, while some disputes over the identification of aggression might be resolved by systematically considering the various components of the social labeling process, it seems very unlikely that definitional agreement will always be perfect. Furthermore, the variations in judgments that are possible within each component of the social labeling process would indicate that wide differences in "aggressiveness" are possible across behaviors and individuals. Finally, a given episode of behavior (e.g., an accidental shooting) may be aggressive in some ways but nonaggressive in other respects.

Oppositional Behavior

Most of the foregoing social labeling considerations also apply to the definition of oppositional behavior. However, for this category of behavior, a few specific definitional criteria may be specified. Oppositional behavior includes aggressive and nonaggressive violations of rules or laws, as well as actions that are opposite to behaviors specified in a directive (e.g., spitting on the floor after a specific instruction not to spit on the floor).

Oppositional behavior may be viewed as a subclass of noncompliant behavior. However, not all noncompliant behaviors are oppositional. The factor that distinguishes oppositional and nonoppositional forms of noncompliance is competence (i.e., whether the child has the ability—has learned—to do, or to stop doing, whatever is specified in a directive). One child walking along a sidewalk may plod straight into an area marked "Wet Cement," in spite of the fact that he has read the sign and has been taught to avoid walking on wet cement: an example of oppositional behavior. The same action performed by a second child who has never experienced wet cement would qualify as noncompliance, but not as oppositional behavior. Similarly, to use an extreme example, a retarded child's failure to comply with an instruction to explain Einstein's theory of relativity would be defined, for purposes of this chapter, as noncompliance, but not as oppositional behavior.

Difficulties in establishing the incidence of childhood aggression and oppositional behavior are largely due to differences in definitional criteria across surveys, precluding data comparisons. Incidence studies are also often impeded by the use of unreliable or invalid methods of assessment (Graham, 1979). Finally, labeler bias with respect to socioeconomic status often results in the spurious underrepresentation of certain groups of children in incidence surveys.

Systems of Classification

In spite of the complexities and persistent ambiguities in defining aggression and oppositional behavior, formal systems have been developed for classifying children who exhibit these behaviors. As will be seen, some of these systems are better than others in accommodating aggressive and oppositional children. One of the purposes of these classification systems is to facilitate statistical record keeping and incidence studies. However, most would probably agree that classification and diagnostic systems are of little value unless they also serve some prescriptive function. That is, having properly classified a child and having examined results of studies on children similarly classified, it should be possible to make useful statements regarding future behavior, unexamined aspects of the child's performance, environment, or history, and types of treatment that are likely to benefit the child. Following is a review of provisions for classifying aggressive and oppositional children within clinically-derived systems, systems based upon mutivariate statistical analyses, and the legal classification system.

Clinically-Derived Systems

The most widely used systems of classification in psychology and psychiatry have evolved from clinicians' daily observations. After noting the regularity with which certain behaviors occur together across cases, clinicians gradually conceptualize common symptom clusters as diagnostic entities. A degree of consensus can often be reached regarding the composition of diagnostic categories. However, questions regarding reliability or validity have not weighed heavily in the development of clinically-derived classification systems.

The most popular example of such a system is the *Diagnostic and Statistical Manual of Mental Disorders,* or DSM-III (American Psychiatric Association, 1980). Compared to earlier editions of this manual, DSM-III offers a wider range of categories appropriate to aggressive and oppositional children. Most such children, if they are not psychotic or retarded, will carry a DSM-III (Axis I) diagnosis of Conduct Disorder or Oppositional Disorder. The Conduct Disorder category includes Aggressive and Nonaggressive subtypes. A child classified as Aggressive shows a repetitive and persistent pattern of behavior that violates the rights of others by either physical violence against persons (e.g., rape, mugging, assault, homicide) or thefts outside the home involving confrontation with a victim (e.g., extortion, holdups, purse-snatching). In contrast, the Nonaggressive Conduct Disorder applies to behaviors such as truancy, substance abuse, repeated running away, persistent lying, and stealing, which do not involve confrontation with the victim.

DSM-III also subdivides Conduct Disorders into Socialized and Undersocialized. This distinction is made on the basis of the child's assessed feelings of guilt over wrongdoing and involvement with or commitment to others, particularly peers, over at least 6 months.

DSM-III provides specific criteria for making this determination. Aggressive or oppositional children who do not qualify for the Conduct Disorders classification may meet the criteria for Oppositional Disorder. This category, for children over age 3, requires at least 6 months of persistent oppositional behavior, including at least two of the following: violations of minor rules, temper tantrums, arguments, provocative behavior, and stubbornness.

Much greater specificity is found in DSM-III than in its predecessors. This same trend has been evident across revisions of another clinically derived classification system, the *Manual of the International Statistical Classification of Diseases, Injuries, and Causes of Death* (Commission on Professional and Hospital Activities, 1978; World Health Organization, 1969). Due to space limitations, provisions for aggressive and oppositional children in this system will not be discussed.

Empirically-Derived Classification Systems

Paralleling the development of clinically-derived classification systems, numerous investigations have applied multivariate statistical techniques to identifying behaviors that are interrelated. This empirical, factor-analytic approach to child behavior classification has recently been reviewed by Quay (1979), who concludes from a "factor matching" analysis of 37 factor-analytic studies that there are four major factors that account for most of the variance in scores on various behavioral checklists. He has labeled these major dimensions: Conduct Disorder, Anxiety-Withdrawal, Immaturity, and Socialized-Aggressive Disorder.

From the 37 studies Quay examined, lists of characteristics defining each factor were constructed. Table I presents lists of characteristics that cluster together to define the two factors most relevant to this chapter: Conduct Disorder and Socialized-Aggressive Disorder. The characteristics defining these two factors appear (in Table I) in order of the number of studies in which they were found to be statistically related to other characteristics in each list.

Numerous studies have examined the reliability of assigning children to categories that have emerged from multivariate statistical approaches to classification. Results have been favorable with respect to internal consistency (Quay & Parsons, 1971), interrater reliability (Behar & Stringfield, 1974), and rate–rerate reliability (Evans, 1975). In addition, favorable outcomes have resulted from studies on the validity of various factors comprising these classification systems (Jenkins, 1973; Quay, 1979). Besides the fact that empirically-derived classification systems have generated considerable research, their reliance on quantitative methods typically makes it possible not only to assign a child to a dimension, but also to determine the degree to which the child represents the dimension (i.e., the child's level of deviance).

The Legal System of Classification

More serious forms of childhood aggression and oppositional behavior are defined and classified by law. Therefore, it is appropriate to review the system commonly used by the courts in classifying juvenile offenses.

One of the least serious categories, Status Offenses, includes violations that would not be crimes if committed by an adult: offenses such as truancy, runaway, and incorrigibility. A second general category, Index Offenses, consists of Violent (Personal) Crimes such as homicide, assault, forcible rape, and robbery, and Property Crimes such as larceny, burglary, auto theft, embezzlement, extortion, arson, and vandalism. A third general category is commonly labeled Non-Index Offenses. Examples of offenses in this category are: illegal possession or use of weapons, receipt of stolen property, commercial sex, incest, public indecency, offenses involving narcotics, passing bad checks, violations of liquor laws, intoxication, disorderly conduct, vagrancy, obscene phone calling, perjury, and trespassing.

Discussion

Quay (1979) contends that the ideal classification system should meet several criteria: It should provide operational definitions of characteristics defining each category or dimension. Definitions should be clear enough to permit reliable categorizations. Secondly, the system should be complete (i.e., with respect to the limited topic of this chapter, it should provide categories appropriate to all possible forms of childhood aggression and oppositional behavior). Thirdly, the system should be parsimonious (i.e., it should have no more categories than are necessary to produce reliable, valid, and mutually exclusive classifications). Finally, the system should consist of categories that have an already demonstrated relationship to etiology, prognosis, or treatment.

The types of classification systems that have been reviewed satisfy these criteria to differing degrees. With respect to reliability of classification, appropriate studies have been done only with systems derived from a multivariate statistical approach. Although the definitions of categories are relatively clear in the latest clinically-derived system (DSM-III)

Table 1. The Dimensions of Conduct Disorder and Socialized Aggressive Disorder [a]

Conduct disorder	
1. Fighting	9. Restlessness; inability to sit still
2. Temper tantrums	10. Boisterousness; rowdiness
3. Disobedience; difficulty in disciplinary control	11. Irritability; hot tempered; easily aroused to anger
4. Destructiveness in regard to his own and/or other's property	12. Attention seeking, "show-off" behavior
5. Impertinence; sauciness	13. Hyperactivity; "always on the go"
6. Uncooperativeness in group situations	14. Profane language; swearing; cursing
7. Disruptiveness; tendency to annoy and bother others	15. Jealousy over attention paid over children
8. Negativism; tendency to do the opposite of what is requested	16. Irresponsibility; undependability
	17. Dislike for school

Socialized-aggressive disorder
1. Has bad companions
2. Steals in company with others
3. Loyal to delinquent friends
4. Belongs to a gang
5. Stays out late at night
6. Truancy from school

[a]From the *Manual for the Behavior Problem Checklist* (Quay & Peterson, 1975).

and in the legal classification system, no formal reliability studies have been performed with these systems.

Both the clinically-derived and the empirically-derived systems appear to be relatively complete. DSM-III presents three major categories for classifying patterns of aggression: Socialized and Undersocialized Aggressive Conduct Disorders and Oppositional Disorder.[1] In comparison, the empirically derived system provides only two first-order factors in which aggression is involved. One of these, Socialized Aggressive Disorder, finds a remarkably similar counterpart in DSM-III. The other factor, Conduct Disorder, seems to subsume characteristics defining the two DSM-III categories of Undersocialized Aggressive Conduct Disorder and Oppositional Disorder. However, subclusters or second-order factors corresponding to these DSM-III categories have been described in extended analyses of the empirically-derived factor labeled Conduct Disorder (Dreger, 1980).

The legal classification system is, of course, complete only in regard to aggressive and oppositional behaviors that are of general concern to society. Although the category of Status Offenses includes some behaviors that are of more limited concern (i.e., to parents or to school personnel), this category is much less "complete" than are the classes pertaining to aggressive and oppositional behavior in the clinically-derived or empirically-derived systems.

It would be very difficult at this point to determine the extent to which each type of classification system meets Quay's criterion of parsimony. Clearly, more research is needed on the reliability and validity of categories that comprise the various systems.

Although research in the right direction has started with the empirically-derived systems, much more work is needed before firm conclusions can be reached with respect to the relationship of each classification category to etiology, prognosis, or treatment. Whereas three or four categories might suffice for statistical, demographic, or record-keeping purposes, narrower and more finely graduated categories may have to be specified before accurate predictions or prescriptions regarding treatment or progress assessment can be made. Notably absent in the current formal classifications system are criteria for categorizing aggression and oppositional behaviors with respect to strength or frequency, setting or situational considerations, or coexisting aggressive or nonaggressive behaviors. It is recommended that future research aim at determining the relationship of variables such as these to etiology, prognosis, and treatment.

Finally, it appears that the clinical utility of classification systems will hinge on the reliability, validity, and sensitivity of the measures upon which classifications are based. For this reason, it is predicted that future systems for classifying childhood aggression will be based upon more direct quantitative measures of very specific behaviors. Such measures could, of course, be employed in any of the three types of classification systems that have been described.

Theoretical Perspectives

At least three theoretical viewpoints regarding aggression have been identified (Baron, 1977). They include aggression as: (1) instinctive behavior; (2) an elicited drive; and (3) learned social behavior.

[1]It should be noted that the Antisocial Personality Disorder applies only to persons aged 18 and older.

The two major approaches to aggression as instinctive behavior are the psychoanalytic approach and the ethological approach. Sigmund Freud, the major proponent of the psychoanalytic approach, proposed late in his career that all human behavior is generated from the complex interaction between *eros*—the life instinct directed toward prolonging life—and *thanatos*—the death instinct directed toward terminating life. Freud further proposed that aggression resulted from the redirection of the self-destructive death instinct away from the individual and outward toward others. Konrad Lorenz, the major proponent of the ethological approach, suggested that aggression is generated by an innate fighting instinct that *homo sapiens* shares with other animals.

A second theoretical position is that aggression in humans is generated by various environmental conditions that lead to the arousal of a drive or motivation to injure or harm others. Perhaps the most prominent statement of this theoretical position is the frustration–aggression hypothesis advanced by Dollard, Doob, Miller, Mowrer, and Sears (1939). These authors proposed that frustration brings out an instigation to aggression (an aggression drive), which then leads to the performance of aggressive actions. When aggression does not always follow frustration, it is usually due to the inhibiting influence of threat of punishment. However, inasmuch as the motivation to aggress is still intact, displacement is thought to occur; aggression is directed at persons other than the frustrater who are associated with weaker threats of punishment. Miller (1948) provided an elaborate model to account for displaced aggression. The most recent revision of the aggression-as-an-elicited-drive theory is by Berkowitz (1973), who disagrees with the Dollard *et al.* (1939) position that frustration is the only factor producing aggression.

Finally, an increasingly popular view of aggressive behavior is that it is primarily a function of social learning. One of its major proponents is Bandura (1973), who argued that a careful analysis of aggression requires that we examine: (1) how it is acquired; (2) what factors instigate its performance; and (3) what factors maintain its performance. Operant conditioning and social modeling are emphasized in Bandura's account of the acquisition of aggressive behavior. A number of different factors are identified as influential in instigating aggression, while several variables (e.g., social and material reinforcers) are assumed to be involved in the maintenance phase.

Baron's (1977) critical review of these three theoretical positions concluded that, of the three, the social learning theories have the most substantial empirical backing. He further contended that they are the most optimistic regarding potential prevention and control of aggression.

Methods of Assessment and Measurement

The Interview

The interview has been termed the universal method of data collection (O'Leary & Johnson, 1979) because this method is used widely by clinicians who differ markedly in theoretical orientation and treatment bias. A systematically conducted interview can yield information about aggressive and oppositional behavior that often cannot be obtained through other means. However, the quantity and quality of interview data depend upon several basic considerations, which require careful attention.

Early in the interview an effort should be made to develop rapport and to reconcile any misconceptions or apprehensions parents might have about the examination. It is generally found that the validity of parent reports and the level of cooperation in later phases of assessment and treatment are largely a function of the interviewer's skill in gaining the parents' trust. Therefore, the interviewer should begin by assuring parents of his or her desire to help. Any concerns the parents have about the referral, assessment, or later treatment of their child should be addressed. It is also advisable to spend some time discussing confidentiality, particularly with cases that might involve court action (e.g., delinquency, custody, or abuse/neglect petitions). In general, the interviewer should attempt to make parents feel comfortable by keeping the tone of the interview light and by avoiding accusatory comments.

Interviews with parents may be conducted with or without the child. However, in cases involving aggressive or oppositional children, a separate interview with the parents may avoid possible disruptive interactions, increase the amount of information the parents give, and prevent some parents from feeling embarrassed or inhibited (as a result of fears of later retaliation on the part of their child). It is preferable to interview both parents together, in order to assess their styles of interaction and discrepancies in their perceptions, attitudes, or motivation. Interviewing both parents together may also increase their truthfulness, curb any tendencies they might have toward exaggerating, and increase their later cooperation in treatment.

Once some degree of rapport has been established, the parents should be asked why the child was referred and what they see as the child's major problems or deficits. The interviewer should then attend to the level of agreement between parents and to their precision in describing the child's problems (e.g., whether they say anything about behavior frequencies or settings in which the problems occur). Patterson and his colleagues (Patterson, Reid, Jones, & Conger, 1975), in their work with families of aggressive children, take steps during the intake interview to increase parents' precision by presenting definitions and examples of numerous categories of child behavior, then asking the parents to indicate contexts or settings in which the behaviors occur. Such effort appears to be warranted, since it has been noted (O'Leary & Johnson, 1979) that the validity of interview data is greater when the behavior of interest is easily quantified (e.g., shouting threats) than when the interviewer settles for global judgments (e.g., the child is edgy or deviant).

The interviewer should invite the parents to discuss what they perceive to be causes of their child's aggression and opposition, noting the extent to which they attribute the problem behaviors to genetic or organic, as opposed to environmental, factors. Usually this can be done in the context of a history which not only focuses on physical and psychological development, but which also identifies major changes in the child's family and environment (e.g., family moves, deaths of significant figures, separations, divorce, births of siblings, etc.) and the child's reactions to these changes.

Parents should be asked to describe what they have tried previously in managing the child's aggression and oppositional behaviors. Attention should be given to types of interventions used, how long each intervention was in effect, consistency with which each intervention was applied, and identity of the disciplinarian. It is also very appropriate to determine what typically happens *now* when aggressive or oppositional behaviors occur.

Finally, an attempt should be made to learn something about the affective or emotional climate of the home. How do parents feel toward the target child? How do members of the family express their feelings toward each other? Do parents experience any guilt because of the child's behavior? How do parents compare the target child to his siblings? Do parents feel that the child should atone for his misbehavior? Do parents defend the child, sheltering him from the consequences of his behavior? Questions should also be suited to determining whether other family members exhibit aggressive or oppositional behavior.

Another purpose of the interview is to identify parents' capabilities to participate later in the child's treatment. The interviewer should determine whether parents have control over potential reinforcers and whether there might be economic or domestic obstacles to the consistent implementation of a treatment program (e.g., income, family size, parents' work hours, interferences in family affairs, etc.). In further exploring the feasibility of home-based intervention, the interviewer should obtain a description of household routines and physical features (e.g., crowding, noise levels, privacy, traffic in and out of the home, recreational provisions, etc.). Some assessment should also be made of family "insularity" in view of indications of a relationship between oppositional child behavior and mothers' social activities outside the home (Wahler, 1980).

Interviewing the Child

One might expect children to be apprehensive in clinic interviews; they are usually aware that they have been brought to the clinic because of some problem. Suspecting that the examiner is working for parents or the court, many children are likely to resist attempts by the interviewer to verify what the parents or courts claim to be wrong with them. Therefore, rapport building is as important with children as it is with parents.

Patterson *et al.* (1975) recommend, as in the parent interviews, that a friendly or light affective tone be maintained and that the interviewer be flexible. These workers suggest first asking the child to say why he is at the clinic, then inviting him to talk about his family, particularly about things in the family that he would like to change. They recommend comments such as: "I have a hunch that things get pretty uncomfortable for you sometimes, people yelling at you, scolding you. . . . I'd like to understand better how things work in your family and what changes you'd like to see made." In addition, Simmons (1974) advises interviewers of children to avoid prying, appearing judgmental, showing irritation or anger, or talking too much. However, he also cautions that for some children prolonged silences can be anxiety-producing.

Some aggressive and oppositional children, particularly younger children, may resist questioning and formal testing, but may show interest in playing with toys or games. In such cases it is important to have plenty of materials for dramatic and creative play, as well as for fine and gross motor activity. Most examiners find it easier to interview younger children while they are involved in play, posing questions to fit the child's activity. Having toys available also makes it possible for the examiner to assign things for the parents to do with the child, while the examiner stands aside and observes their interactions.

Although flexibility is recommended, the interview with the child should have some degree of structure. Herjanic, Herjanic, Brown, and Wheatt (1975), using a relatively structured interview technique focusing on present (rather than past) events, obtained 80% agreement between mothers and children when they answered comparable interview questions. Simmons (1974) has suggested that the examiner systematically attempt to collect data on the following topics in interviews with children: (1) the child's reasons for coming to the interview; (2) recreational patterns and interests; (3) perception of social, cultural, and ethnic influences; (4) peer relationships; (5) plans for the future; (6) roles and relationships among members of the child's family; (7) presenting problems; (8) health and physical status; (9) fantasies and fears; and (10) social awareness (compliance with social rules and expectations).

With respect to each of these topics, aggressive/oppositional material might be elicited. For example, the child may admit to having successfully resisted coming to be examined on several previous occasions; he may report primarily on recreational activities in which players are often injured, or may play in settings where fights are frequent; the child may rebuke many of the common practices in his neighborhood, ethnic group, school or church; he may deny having close friends and may admit to fighting as the primary means of settling disagreements with peers. In interviews with communicative children, it is suggested that the examiner keep either a tally record or a log of comments that might subsequently be related to aggressive or oppositional behavior. Later, of course, the examiner will need to determine whether the child's comments are, in fact, related to his behavior outside the clinic. As noted by O'Leary and Johnson (1979), a young child may be delightful in an interview but a hellion at home.

However, even in these cases the interview can be of value. The examiner should be able to directly observe the child's physical appearance and general demeanor; how he interacts with parents (eye contact, polite gestures, touching, threatening, sulking, talking back, etc.); and how he responds to requests and instructions from the parents and the examiner.

Still, as Hetherington and Martin (1979) note, interviews and observations during interviews often yield data that are distorted and unstable. For this reason, and in view of the volume of information that is needed in assessing aggressive and oppositional children, other more efficient and standardized procedures have been developed for use in conjunction with the interview.

Personality Inventories

Numerous tests, typically paper-and-pencil and self-report questionnaires, have been developed for the purpose of assessing children's emotional, motivational, interpersonal, and attitudinal characteristics, as distinguished from abilities. Some of these "personality tests" yield scores that research has related to patterns of aggressive and oppositional behavior.

For example, Cattell and his colleagues used factor-analytic techniques to develop three personality questionnaires for use with 6- to 8-year-olds, 8- to 12-year-olds, and 12- to 17-year-olds. With these questionnaires, score profiles have been described for aggressive and oppositional children on 14 source factors of personality. On the High School Personality Questionnaire (Cattell & Cattell, 1973), aggressive delinquents have scored higher on factors related to sensitivity and irresponsibility, dominance, and temperamental individuality, and lower on factors related to intelligence, excitability, guiltproneness, and self-sufficiency. Young delinquents have scored lower than nondelinquent controls on the factor related to superego; however, older and more hardened delinquents have tended to score *higher* on this factor, as well as on the factor related to ego strength (Cattell & Cattell, 1975).

Among other personality inventories that have been field-tested with aggressive and oppositional children is the 180-item California Test of Personality (Thorpe, Clark, &

Tiegs, 1953), which yields a score for Social Adjustment. This score is based on responses to six subgroups of 15 items, many of which refer to aggressive and oppositional behavior.

Research employing the 550-item Minnesota Multiphasic Personality Inventory (MMPI) (Hathaway & McKinley, 1943) with deviant and nondeviant adolescents has identified a high-point code pattern (F-4-9) that correlates with a history of delinquency (Huesman, Lefkowitz, & Eron, 1978). Whereas males tend to score higher on these delinquency-associated MMPI scales in *normal* samples, females score higher than males on these scales in delinquent samples.

Another personality test applicable to the assessment of childhood aggression and opposition is the Jessness Inventory (Jessness, 1966). This 155-item questionnaire yields 10 trait scores and an Asocial Index, which relates closely to delinquent behavior (Simonds & Kashani, 1979). Norms for this instrument are available for delinquent and nondelinquent boys and girls, including youth from lower and lower-middle socioeconomic classes.

Caution is advised in using personality inventories like these to assess or to predict aggression. A child or adolescent who is able to read and mark his responses on the inventory may malinger (i.e., fake good or fake bad). Indeed, one should be alert to the possibility that, for the truly aggressive child, testing conditions are often conducive to faking. Although some inventories include special scoring keys to detect deliberate malingering and response sets, this procedure is only partly successful.

Children may also give inaccurate answers because they are unable to discriminate statements that are self-descriptive. In other words, scores that are obtained may be misleading because the child is not skilled at labeling his own behavior.

Another disadvantage to personality inventories is that their validity is often questionable. Scale scores or score profiles that are determined in group correlational studies to be related to aggressive or oppositional behavior may not be predictive with respect to the single case. Also, because validation studies typically look at populations with well-established patterns of aggression and oppositional behavior, the clinician may be unwarranted in assuming that the "aggression scores" for these populations predict a pattern of aggression for the child who is presently not acting out seriously. It may be that predictive scores or profiles are very different from those that correlate with extant patterns of chronic delinquency.

Projective Methods

Attempts are often made to measure or predict aggression by presenting the child with relatively unstructured stimuli; then asking the child to describe, tell a story about, complete, or respond to the stimuli in some other way. It has been theorized that the child's responses will "project" the psychic forces that also underly or determine his/her responses to similar uncontrived situations away from the testing situation. To some clinicians, aggression or opposition in the content of the child's responses is taken as a "manifestation" of *internal* aggression or opposition. Others simply regard projective methods as simulations in which observed aggressive or oppositional responses may or may not represent more generalized patterns of response. Examiners in this latter group usually avoid inference concerning underlying psychic predispositions.

The most popular of projective methods, the Rorschach Inkblot Test (Rorschach, 1942), is often used with children and adolescents to predict aggressive or antisocial tendencies. Ten cards, each featuring one bilaterally symmetrical black-and-white or colored inkblot, are presented in sequence. The child is directed to tell what she or he sees or to describe everything that might be represented in each inkblot. From the content of individual responses, and on the basis of ratios computed from counts of responses scored in various categories, conclusions are drawn about the child's aggression, mental ability, emotionality, school readiness, imagination, and numerous additional characteristics.

Despite the length of time required in administering and scoring the Rorschach, and despite the fact that among thousands of publications concerning the Rorschach, the test has not fared very well in reliability and validity studies (Aiken, 1971). Even so, large numbers of clinical psychologists and psychiatrists continue to rely on the Rorschach for "in-depth" analysis of child and adolescent personality. For many who are more skeptical of generalizations derived from the Rorschach, the test remains a valuable tool for identifying questions and topics to be pursued in the interview and in subsequent evaluation sessions.

The Thematic Apperception Test (TAT) (Murray, 1943) and a modification of this test for children, the Children's Apperception Test (Bellak & Bellak, 1949), and for adolescents, the Symonds Picture-Story Test (Symonds, 1949), also represent projective methods that have been used in screening for patterns of aggression and opposition. More structured than the Rorschach, these thematic apperception methods involve directing the child to tell stories about a sequence of pictures, depicting people or animals in various ambiguous situations. With a similar technique, the Hand Test (Wagner & Medvedeff, 1963), an aggression score is obtained from records of children's interpretations of nine drawings of a hand in various ambiguous poses. Coding of responses on these instruments is generally subjective and impressionistic. In fact, hostile content on the TAT has been found to be inversely related to data from more direct assessments of adolescent aggression (Matranga, 1976).

A similar projective method, the Picture-Frustration (P-F) Study (Rosenzweig, 1953), was specifically designed for use in assessing aggression. This test consists of 24 cartoon sketches, each showing two people in a situation that is clearly frustrating for one of them. A caption on each sketch shows what one of the characters is saying. The child is requested to provide the other character's reply to the frustration that is represented. Responses are classified according to the direction of expressed aggression (extrapunitive vs. intropunitive). A children's form of the P-F Study is available for use with 4- to 13-year-olds. Although the scoring procedures for the P-F Study are more objective than for other projectives, reliability figures have been low (.50 to .75).

Yet another type of projective method asks the child to complete partially worded sentences. One example of this technique is the Rotter Incomplete Sentences Blank (ISB) (Rotter, 1950), which consists of 40 sentence beginnings such as "I regret . . .," "What pains me . . .," "I secretly . . .," and so forth. Sentence completions are scored by assigning to each response a scale value from 0 to 6. The total of these scores is an index of maladjustment. Each response may also be assessed with respect to aggressive or oppositional content. Interscorer reliabilities approximating .90 have been reported with this technique. The Rotter ISB has been shown to be moderately successful in differentiating youth classified as "maladjusted" and "adjusted." In addition to the high school form of the Rotter ISB, sentence completion blanks for younger children are available.

As was noted with respect to validation of personality inventories, it is not yet clear that projective tests have utility in detecting pre- or subclinical deviance (i.e., in finding children who are likely *later* to be overtly aggressive or oppositional). Aside from questions regarding reliability and validity of projective methods, one must also consider their clinical efficiency. Because they take a relatively long time to administer and score, one must ask whether any new information they provide might have been obtained more simply or in less time. It is often found that material from lengthy formal projective testing could have been obtained more conveniently via a well-conducted interview of the child and/or the child's family.

Behavioral Checklists

Other methods for assessing or measuring childhood aggression and opposition are more valid than personality inventories and considerably more objective, reliable, and valid than projective instruments. Persons familiar with the child can be asked to respond to checklists of specific problem behaviors or descriptive adjectives. These informants can be asked to indicate which descriptors apply to the child and/or to rate the frequency, intensity, or severity of problems. Typically, behavioral checklists call for the informant to respond on the basis of observations of the child over a relatively short specified period of time (a few days to a few months).

Behavioral checklists can be especially valuable in assessing youth who are uncooperative or who tend to fake responses on personality inventories and projective tests. In addition, data from behavioral checklists tend to be more reliable because the informant is asked only to respond according to what he/she has observed. Subjective interpretations of responses and guesses about the relationship between the child's score and his/her overt behavior are not required in summarizing checklist data. Also, because many checklists are reliable and relatively convenient to readminister, they are well suited to the assessment of *changes* in aggression or oppositional behavior over time.

One of the most widely used behavioral checklists is the Behavior Problem Checklist (BPC) (Quay & Peterson, 1975). Typically filled out by parents or teachers, this instrument is a three-point rating scale for 55 problem behaviors. As noted earlier in this chapter, factor analyses of data from child guidance clinic records have identified four primary dimensions on the BPC, two of which, Conduct Disorder and Socialized-Aggressive Disorder, are most descriptive of aggressive and oppositional children (see Table 1).

Validity studies have shown that the BPC not only has value in determining how similar a given child is to normal versus deviant groups (Speer, 1971; Victor & Halverson, 1976), but that it also differentiates between high- and low-anxious delinquents (Borkovec, 1970; Skrzypek, 1969). Studies involving informants who have comparable levels of contact with the target child have generally shown BPC ratings to be reliable (Quay, 1977). The same reviewer has reported even higher test–retest reliabilities (.82 to .93).

Among other behavioral checklists derived through factor analysis are the Devereux Elementary School Behavior Rating (DESB) (Spivack & Swift, 1967) and modifications of this instrument for older children. The DESB consists of 47 items defining 11 behavioral factors. Each item is rated on a five-point frequency scale. Interrater reliabilities for the DESB have ranged from .61 to .87 with a mean of .80, and test–retest reliabilities have ranged from .49 to .86 with medians in the low .70's (O'Leary & Johnson, 1979).

A study by Proger, Mann, Green, Bayuk, and Burger (1975) found that seven of the DESB factors (Classroom Disturbance, Impatience, Disrespect–Defiance, External Blame, Irrelevant Responsiveness, Unable to Change, and Quits) correlated significantly with the

Conduct Disorder subscale of the BPC. Two of these DESB factors, Classroom Disturbance and Disrespect–Defiance, correlated significantly with the Socialized Aggressive Disorder factor from the BPC. Further research with the DESB must be done before conclusions can be drawn regarding this instrument's predictive validity with respect to aggressive and oppositional behavior. However, a study by Forbes (1978), using one of the other Devereux scales, demonstrated the instrument's utility in differentiating hyperactive from matched emotionally disturbed (mostly aggressive and oppositional) children between the ages of 5 years, 4 months and 10 years, 4 months.

Three additional child behavior checklists deserve mention because of the number of aggressive/oppositional items that are included in each and because of their widespread use by investigators who are generating norms for deviant and nondeviant groups. Two of these checklists, the Telephone Interview Report on Social Aggression and the Taplin Checklist (Patterson *et al.*, 1975), are routinely used in many treatment and research programs based on the Oregon Research Institute's social learning model of intervention in families with aggressive children. The Walker Problem Behavior Identification Checklist (Walker, 1970) has also been widely applied over the past decade, particularly in screening and assessment for special education programs. On this instrument the informant simply marks which of 50 statements apply to the target child, based upon observations of the child's behavior over the preceding months. Of the five derived scale scores on the Walker Checklist, one scale labeled Acting-Out is defined by 14 items that are particularly relevant to aggressive and oppositional children.

Although data from many behavioral checklists have been found to be reliable, one should not lose sight of the fact that information from these instruments can be contaminated by human error or bias. A mother who objects to the possibility of residential treatment for her son may produce a behavioral checklist that makes the son look better controlled than he actually is. Similarly, the informant may not accurately recall what the child has done. A checklist that asks the rater to respond on the basis of observations over a relatively short period of time (a day) may yield more reliable and valid data than the checklist that is completed on the basis of observations over a longer period (1 or 2 months). The latter checklist may reflect recent events, to the exclusion of events that the rater no longer recalls. Finally, there may be raters who do not understand behavioral descriptors such as "meticulous," "impertinent," and so on, or who misunderstand instructions for completing checklists.

As noted by Walls, Werner, Bacon, and Zane (1977), checklists vary greatly in their *objectivity*. Reliability of checklists may be largely determined by whether the checklist consists of objectively worded items specifying observable behaviors, standards of performance, and conditions of performance, as opposed to vague and general items (e.g., respect, guilt, impertinence, etc.).

Because informants on behavioral checklists may be inaccurate or biased, and because checklists themselves may be vague or may require too much of the informant, it is advisable to routinely have more than one person complete each checklist. To the extent that each informant's exposure to the child is similar, reliability of the checklist can be established. Routine reliability checks, while feasible with behavioral checklists, would be more difficult for most personality inventories and projective tests, due to the time that is required in administering these latter methods.

Aside from reliability of behavioral checklists, questions may be raised regarding their sensitivity to changes in aggressive or oppositional behaviors. Although, as noted earlier, some behavioral checklists have been shown to differentiate delinquent and nondelinquent populations, it has not yet been determined whether aggression scores on currently used checklists correspond to quantitative aggression data from direct and more continuous observational records (see the section that follows). The efficiency with which checklists can be repeatedly administered recommends their use in evaluating the aggressive or oppositional child's response to treatment. Ultimately, however, it is the sensitivity of checklists to independently measured changes in aggressive and oppositional behavior that will determine the clinical utility of these techniques.

Direct Observational Methods

Instead of assessing aggressive or oppositional behavior on the basis of what people say or what is inferred about the child's behavior, one may choose to measure aggressive and oppositional behavior directly. Direct observational methods suited to this purpose will now be discussed.

Children who are generally regarded as "nonaggressive" and "obedient" can sometimes be seen doing the same things that aggressive and oppositional children do. Often what distinguishes these two groups is the frequency of misbehaviors. Therefore, one way to assess aggressive and oppositional behavior is to simply count episodes of such behavior. Frequency records may be generated by anyone who spends time with the target child, a professional examiner or therapist, a parent, a teacher, a peer, or the target child himself.

These frequency records may be segmented into standard units of time (minutes, hours, days, weeks, etc.) for the purpose of examining changes over time. The "best" unit of time for use in monitoring changes in frequency may vary from one behavior to the next. Consider, for instance, two different forms of self-injury. For a retarded child who moves quickly around the room, butting his head repeatedly against rigid objects, a response-per-minute analysis of head-banging might be most appropriate. For an adolescent girl who runs away from home intermittently, a summary across weeks or months might be most appropriate, for only across these longer blocks of time would changes in the frequency of runaways be viewed as significant.

Sometimes it is not possible to record behavioral frequencies over standard periods of time (e.g., during treatment sessions that vary in duration). So long as differences in the length of observation sessions remain relatively small, the session frequency count may be divided by the observation time, yielding a response rate (responses per minute, hour, etc.) which may be compared from one session to the next.

With certain forms of aggression or oppositional behavior, direct timing measures may be applicable. For example, consider the child who occasionally throws long, screaming tantrums. This form of oppositional behavior might be quantified by timing the duration of each tantrum. When treating such a child, a duration measure might be the most suitable initial measure in that the duration of tantrums might be affected by treatment earlier than might the probability (or frequency) of tantrums.

Another method for assessing aggressive and oppositional behavior is to time intervals between episodes of misconduct (i.e., interresponse times). This assessment procedure is particularly applicable to the child who not only "acts out" more frequently but who seems to have difficulty in refraining from acting out for any significant period of time. Where precision is desired, an interresponse time measure would be necessary both in identifying such a child and in later gauging that child's progress in behaving appropriately for progressively longer intervals.

When lengthy or continuous observations are precluded, it may be possible to quantify some forms of aggressive and oppositional behavior by spot-checking. Spot-checks are very brief, intermittent observations of behavior. At predetermined intervals (fixed or variable), the observer glances at the target child or watches for a short period of time, then makes a record of behaviors exhibited during the observation period. After several spot-checks, one may describe the "level" of aggression or opposition in terms of the proportion of spot-checks in which behaviors in these categories were recorded.

Because most episodes of aggressive or oppositional behavior occur infrequently and last only a short period of time, spot-checking may not be the procedure of choice for recording these behaviors. However, when it is necessary to record aggressive or oppositional behavior by spot-checking, measurement sensitivity may be enhanced by increasing the frequency of spot-checks and the length of each observation period.

Another form of intermittent recording, interval time sampling, may lend itself better (than brief spotchecks) to the measurement of children's aggression and opposition. This method requires that the observer first identify optimal times for observing the child. For example, it may be that a child only exhibits aggressive behavior during 20-minute school recess periods; therefore, these periods present optimal times for measuring the child's aggression. Once an observation period is determined, the period is divided into smaller time segments (e.g., 10-, 15-, 30-second intervals). Then, during actual observations, records are made of the occurrence/nonoccurrence of aggressive or oppositional behaviors in each interval. Once the entire observation period is over, the "level" of aggression may be calculated and expressed in terms of the proportion of composite intervals in which aggression was observed to occur. So long as observation procedures remain standard, the derived aggression proportions may be compared form one observation period to the next.

Yet another direct method for measuring aggression and oppositional behavior involves the use of aggression content checklists concurrent with or shortly following episodes of aggression. For example, it might be determined that a given child's aggressive outbursts consist of a variety of discrete aggressive behaviors over which the child has little control, and/or that during aggressive outbursts, specific prosocial behaviors are typically absent. The aggressive episode may consist of an increase in voice amplitude, verbal threats, insulting remarks or gestures, damage to objects, physical threats, glaring, and so forth. Concurrently, certain other behaviors, such as comments describing something positive about the other person, requests for clarification of issues in the conflict, or relaxation, may not be present. A checklist featuring these specific aggression components and skill deficits might be completed by an observer after each aggressive incident for the purpose of assessing the child's progress over time in controlling part, if not all, of his/her aggression. In some cases, changes may be detected with aggression content checklists before any changes are seen in the frequency or duration of aggressive outbursts.

Some aspects of childhood aggression and oppositional behavior (e.g., sarcasm, voice control, muscle tension, etc.) may be quantified most efficiently via rating scales. Many discussions of behavioral measurement have eschewed use of ratings because they often are unreliable. However, they need not be, as evidenced by agreement levels in the scoring of gymnastic events and diving performance. By pairing observable behavioral criteria with points on an aggression rating scale and by training observers who will apply ratings, it is possible to quantify components of aggression and oppositional behavior that could not otherwise be measured. Of course, the greater subjectivity of rating methods would require very frequent assessments of interrater agreement.

To the extent that aggressive behaviors are accompanied by increments in voice volume, heart rate, respiration, perspiration, muscle tension, rate of hormone production, and so forth, it may be feasible to directly measure aggression with instruments. Factors such as the bulkiness and expense of current instruments suited to the measurement of aggression components largely preclude their use in open settings. However, instrumentation may provide very useful data on aggression in laboratories and clinics where attempts are made to alter some of the responses that are collateral to aggression. Technological advances leading to increased instrument portability and lowered costs may bring instrumentation into greater prominence, particularly if it should be established that certain of the processes being measured invariably precede or are functionally related to aggression.

None of the direct recording methods discussed above have to be used independently. Indeed, it may be that in some cases the most useful aggression index will be the one derived from a combination of recording methods. For example, by recording both frequency and duration of aggressive episodes, an index of duration-per-occurrence may be obtained. Aggression ratings and aggression content checklists may be used in conjunction to obtain information on the quality as well as the probability of aggressive responses. Interval sampling records and repeated measures of aggression frequency and duration may take the form of spot-checks conducted aperiodically or at fixed intervals. The ideal single behavioral measure or combination of measures will be that which yields the greatest volume of reliable and useful information, at the same time minimizing expenditures of time, money, and effort.

To conclude, it may very well be that one of the most valuable methods for assessing aggression and noncompliance focuses not on the child's behavior, but upon the settings in which aggression and noncompliance occur. Because aggressive and oppositional behaviors are often only exhibited under certain circumstances or stimulus conditions, it becomes very important to identify these conditions. Thus, whenever aggression or opposition occurs, it is advisable to log the environmental events immediately antecedent and consequent to these behaviors.

With information regarding the conditions under which aggressive or oppositional behavior is most likely to occur, steps may be taken to deliberately set the occasion for such behavior for purposes of further assessment. This possibility of arranging "probes" for aggressive and oppositional behavior can provide a shortcut in the assessment process by removing the need to wait for these behaviors to occur.

Etiology

Age, Race, and Sex

Hartup (1974) gathered observational data suggesting that older children are less aggressive than younger children. Hartup also found that older black children were significantly more aggressive than older white subjects. Numerous studies have documented that males are more aggressive than females (e.g., Hoffman, 1977). Such findings are typically explained in terms of differential socialization mediated by learning mechanisms such as operant conditioning, modeling, and frustration-aggression (Maccoby & Jacklin, 1980). A second factor involved in sex differences in aggression is the male hormone, androgen. Eme (1979) has recently reviewed the research on humans and animals that supports the role of androgen in childhood aggression.

Organic Factors

Quay's (1979) review of multivariate studies of classification revealed that evidence for the independence of Hyperactivity as a classification category separate from Conduct Disorder (a category that includes aggressive and oppositional children) is dubious at best. For that reason, Werry (1979), in his review of the role or organic factors in childhood psychopathology, argued that statements from studies of hyperactivity may be taken to be equally true of conduct disorders. Werry concluded that a majority of studies have found an association between conduct disorders and certain pre- and perinatal neurological, EEG, cognitive, and physical abnormalities. However, Werry and others (Ross & Ross, 1976) agree that the relationship between conduct disorders and brain functioning is not clear. In fact, Ross and Ross (1976) argue that there is growing evidence against the hypothesis that brain damage is present in most Hyperactive/Conduct-Disordered children. In summary, the role of organic factors in the etiology of conduct disorders is, as of now, not clearly understood and will remain unclear until more methodologically rigorous studies are conducted.

Diet

An intriguing hypothesis is that diet may influence aggressive behavior in children. If one accepts Werry's (1979) position that statements from studies investigating hyperactivity may be applied equally well to conduct disorders, then studies examining dietary correlates of hyperactivity warrant attention. From observational data, Prinz, Roberts, and Hantman (1980) determined that amount of sugar products consumed, ratio of sugar products to nutritional foods, and ratio of carbohydrates to protein were all significantly associated with levels of destructive-aggressive and restless behaviors during free play. Although Prinz *et al.* (1980) did not find a relationship between food additives (e.g., food coloring) and hyperkinetic behaviors, other studies suggest that food additives may be functionally related (Rose, 1978).

Family Variables

Important in the acquisition and maintenance of aggressive behavior in children are family variables that have been examined in a comprehensive review by Hetherington and Martin (1979). The following discussion conforms to the outline they provided.

Parental Characteristics and Interactions

A review of the research literature shows that deviant children are often the offspring of deviant parents. Bandura and Walters (1963) have suggested that much of aggressive behavior in children may be due to imitation of aggressive models, including parents. In this regard, Sandberg, Weiselberg, and Shaffer (1980) found a significant relationship between childhood conduct disorder and maternal mental distress. Becker, Peterson, Hellmer, Shoemaker, and Quay (1959) also found that parents of conduct-disordered children were maladjusted, inconsistent, arbitrary, and given to explosive expressions of anger. These findings parallel those of McCord and McCord (1958), who found that children with cold mothers and criminal fathers in combination were most likely to become delinquent, particularly if the fathers were also cruel and neglecting. Parent influence is further demonstrated by research describing unhappy marital relationships and interparental conflict in families of delinquent or conduct-disordered children (Johnson & Lobitz, 1974).

Actually, it appears that children with behavior problems not only have parents who are deviant but are, in fact, part of a larger family system that is not functioning properly. Patterson (1976) collected home observational data that demonstrated that both mothers and siblings of aggressive children emit higher rates of aggressive behaviors than do mothers and siblings of normal children. In a related finding, behavioral intervention programs often produce a reduction in antisocial behavior, not only in the treated child but in untreated siblings as well (Arnold, Levine, & Patterson, 1975). Additional evidence of deviance in family systems comes from the finding that relationships and patterns of communication among members of families with a delinquent adolescent are defensive, whereas they are supportive in families with a nondeliquent adolescent (Alexander, 1973).

Parent–Child Interactions

Another critical factor in the development of aggression in children is the parents' style of interaction with the child. The research literature suggests that parents who employ either extremely restrictive or permissive controlling strategies have sons who are appropriately assertive, but that either too much or too little control by the parent is associated with aggressive behavior. Bandura and Walters (1959) demonstrated that aggressive nondelinquent adolescents have mothers who are extremely lax in discipline, whereas the fathers employ overly rigid restrictive discipline. Other studies (e.g., Baumrind, 1967) suggest that moderate levels of parental warmth alone are not sufficient to prevent aggression in children, and that more active parental control is required.

In addition to the restrictiveness or permissiveness of parental control, types of consequences provided for children are related to aggressive behavior. Laboratory work by Hayes, Rincover, and Volosin (1980) suggests that modeling (discussed more fully later in this chapter) primarily influences the initial acquisition of aggressive behaviors, whereas sensory (proprioceptive, visual, auditory) consequences are more effective in maintaining aggression.

Aversive consequences also have an effect inasmuch as reported aggression in the home and in the school is positively related to severity of parental punishment (Sears, Maccoby, & Levin, 1957). Studies that have collected observational data have determined that parents of aggressive children are in practice more rejecting of their children (Bugental, Love, Kaswan, & April, 1971). These parents are not only more rejecting, but the manner in which they go about disapproving is different from parents of normal children. They give more commands (Terdal, Jackson, & Garner, 1976) and they punish deviant behavior more often (Sallows, 1973). However, the proportion of deviant behaviors punished does not differ from that of nonclinic populations, for aggressive children emit higher absolute frequencies of deviant behavior (Patterson, 1976). Even though parents of aggressive children punish their children in proportions equal to parents of normal children and use the same forms of "punishment," such as scolding, nagging, threatening, yelling, or spanking, it only makes matters worse. When parents use these forms of discipline, it increases the likelihood that the aggressive child will repeat his aggressive behavior, whereas such discipline with the normal child typically suppresses aggressive behavior. Similar effects have been seen in aggressive children's responses to differential parent attention (Herbert, Pinkston, Hayden, Sajwaj, Pinkston, Cordua, & Jackson, 1973).

The paradox of supposed punishment increasing inappropriate behavior may be related to the inconsistent application of consequences by parents of aggressive children. Laboratory studies by Sawin and Parke (1979) demonstrated that aggressive responding in young boys, when followed by inconsistent discipline (approval from one agent and disapproval from the other), is greater than when followed by consistent disapproval. Further, they found that aggression during consistent disapproval was most frequent following a period of inconsistent discipline and least frequent following a period of consistent ignoring.

In addition, although parents of aggressive children may possess normal parenting skills (Green, Forehand, & McMahon, 1979), they are more likely to respond positively to deviant child behavior (Sallows, 1973) and negatively to nondeviant behavior (Lobitz & Johnson, 1975). The problem appears to be that parents of deviant children use appropriate parenting skills less often than do parents of normal children.

Due to their inconsistency, mothers of aggressive children may inadvertently accelerate their children's coercive behaviors. This situation can lead such mothers to feel helpless, powerless, and inept as parents. Hence, it is not surprising to learn that mothers of clinic-referred, behavior-problem children are significantly more depressed than mothers of nonclinic children (Griest, Forehand, Wells, & McMahon, 1980).

The relationship between parental mood and aggressive child behavior can be better understood by considering recent work by Wahler and his associates, who have examined not only intrafamily functioning but also the interactions of the family, especially the parents, with the community. Wahler (1980) has identified two kinds of families: insular and noninsular. Insular families typically have the following characteristics: (1) extremely low income, (2) one parent who is poorly educated, and (3) few social contacts, most of which are negative. Leske, Afton, Rogers, and Wahler (1978) found that, as a mother's frequency of self-initiated positive outside contacts increases, so too does the pleasant nature of intrafamily interactions. Further, these investigators found that oppositional behavior varies as a function of daily unpleasant contacts in the community by the mother. As a result, they determined that standard contingency-management programs can and do product short-term improvements in insular family functioning and oppositional child behavior, but these improvements do not persist over time.

The insular mother appears to be functioning in an environment well suited to depression. Lewinsohn (1974) proposed that a low rate of response-contingent positive reinforcement is a sufficient explanation for the depressed person's low rate of behavior and for many of the cognitive and somatic components of the disorder (including feelings of dysphoria and guilt, fatigue, loss of appetite, etc.). Also pertinent is recent work by Seligman (1975), who has drawn a parallel between learned helplessness in animals exposed to inescapable shock and the depressed person's perceived inability to control environmental events. Functioning in an environment that provides a low rate of response-contingent reinforcement and nearly inescapable aversive situations, the insular parent is a good candidate for becoming depressed.

The work of Forehand and his colleagues, who have intensively examined the interactions between mothers and noncompliant children, provides additional information regarding the relationship between parental mood and child aggression. They have found that mothers of noncompliant children give more vague, unclear commands and fewer rewards than mothers of compliant children (Forehand, Wells, & Sturgis, 1978; Peed, Roberts, & Forehand, 1977). However, the best predictors of a child's referral for treatment of noncompliant behavior are the mother's perception of the child and her tolerance or psychological adjustment to the child's behavior (Griest *et al.,* 1980). Griest, Wells, and Forehand (1979) further determined that the parents' perceptions of their clinic-referred children were best predicted by maternal depression, whereas mothers of nonclinic children appear to base their perceptions solely on their children's actual behavior. This finding parallels that of Wahler and Afton (1980), whose study suggests that how mothers describe their oppositional children's behavior is a critical factor in determining long-term treatment success. The insular mother gives global, blame-oriented descriptions of her child's behavior, whereas noninsular mothers give detailed descriptions that are not blame-oriented. Wahler and Afton (1980) relate this difference to difficulty on the part of insular mothers in attending to their children's behavior, a problem that the authors relate further to failures in maintaining improvements after parent training. Findings from the two laboratories of Wahler and Forehand suggest that the way parents perceive and describe their oppositional child, the parents' mood, and the parents' community contacts may all have an important influence on the child's oppositional behavior, referral to treatment, and response to treatment.

Disciplinary inconsistency in families of conduct-disordered children, as described, may be either interparental (Read, 1945) or intraparental in nature (Hetherington, Cox, & Cox, 1977b). Inconsistency is sometimes seen as a discrepancy between vocal intonation and the approving or disapproving content of a parent's communication. This type of inconsistency has been related to behavior problems in children (Bugental & Love, 1975). Research has also shown parental inconsistency to be correlated with family disorganization (Hetherington, Cox, & Cox, 1977a) and abuse of children by parents (Parke & Collmer, 1975).

Parental Absence

The effects of both paternal and maternal absence have been related to conduct disorders. Goldfarb (1945) found that institutionalized children, compared to noninstitutionalized children, engaged in more temper tantrums, lying, and stealing, made more demands for affection and attention from adults, and exhibited greater unpredictable cruelty and aggression to peers, adults, and animals.

The effects of part-time maternal absence by working mothers on the development of behavior problems in children are not yet known. Results of a number of studies have not been consistent. Even so, the studies to date suggest that if family relations are positive and stable, and supervision is adequate, children of working mothers are not harmed.

Broken homes are often implicated in the development of conduct disorders (Hetherington *et al.,* 1977b; Shinn, 1978). Children with conduct disorders more frequently come from homes that have been disrupted by divorce, death, desertion, or father absence than do nondeviant children. Inasmuch as methodological difficulties plague nearly every study of single-parent families, it is difficult to determine whether conduct disorders in children result from the effects of father absence, *per se,* or from the stress and conflicts that precede and accompany disruption or loss of father.

Nevertheless, studies of both clinic and nonclinic samples of children demonstrate that children of divorced parents are more likely to be conduct-disordered, whereas children whose fathers have died are more likely to show depression, anxiety, or habit disturbances (Santrock, 1975). Again, boys are more likely to respond in an antisocial, aggressive way to divorce than are girls (Hetherington *et al.,* 1977b).

Peer Influences

Older children and adolescents who perform delinquent acts (including aggression) tend to have friends who approve of and also perform these acts (Haney & Gold, 1973). Haney and Gold (1973) also found that a large majority of delinquent acts occurred in the company of friends. Many older children and adolescents belong to gangs, especially in lower-class ghettos. In contrast to gangs of the past, today's gangs are likely to be small, loosely organized groups of only about 12 members, and today's gangs are increasingly more likely to victimize ordinary citizens instead of rival gang members (Miller, 1977). Although gangs are alike in a number of respects, the most common similarity is their tendency toward violent behavior (Friedman, Mann, & Friedman, 1975).

Cognitive Variables

Recently, attention has been focused on identifying cognitive characteristics of aggressive children. Little and Kendall (1979) have reviewed evidence that juvenile delinquents have skill deficits in the following cognitive areas: (1) problem-solving, a complex of abilities needed to solve interpersonal problems; (2) role-taking, ability to take the perspective of the other person; and (3) self-control, language-based internal mechanisms for inhibiting impulses. Research by Nasby, Hayden, and DePaulo (1980) provides support for the possibility that, under certain conditions, boys who tend to react in an aggressive manner mistakenly attribute their hostility to surrounding social stimuli to a far greater extent than their less aggressive counterparts.

Mass Media Influences

An hypothesis that has received considerable attention is that observation of television violence by children instigates aggressive behavior either through a process of modeling or through a process of disinhibition (desensitization). Support for this hypothesis came originally from Bandura and his colleagues (Bandura, Ross, & Ross, 1963), who brought children into the laboratory and exposed them to films of adult models engaging in novel aggressive acts directed at other adults and at inanimate objects. Although the children did imitate the novel aggressive acts with inanimate objects, no attempt was made to determine if the children would imitate aggressive acts directed at human victims. Subsequently, Hanratty, Liebert, Morris, and Fernandez (1969) exposed one-half of a group of 4- and 5-year-old boys to a short film in which an adult model aggressed against a human clown. The aggressive acts included verbal insults, shooting with a toy gun, and beating with a plastic mallet. The other half of the group saw no film. Afterwards, the investigators permitted the children to play in a room either with a human clown or with a plastic, inflated clown doll. They found that those children who had observed the aggressive film emitted significantly more aggressive acts against the plastic doll and the human clown than did the children who had seen no film. These findings were replicated with girls (Hanratty, 1969) and with older boys (Hanratty, O'Neal, & Sulzer, 1972).

Correlational studies have shown a relationship between the amount of violence a child observes and the amount of aggressive behavior displayed in naturalistic situations. This relationship has been found for both elementary (Dominick & Greenberg, 1972) and high school youth (McLeod, Atkin, & Chaffee, 1972). Lefkowitz, Eron, Walder, and Huesmann (1972) conducted an even more ambitious 10-year longitudinal study of over 900 children in a New York rural county. Consistent with other investigators, they found a significant relationship between the amount of television violence observed at age 9 and independently assessed peer ratings of how aggressive the children were at the time. Ten years later, Lefkowitz *et al.* found that the best and most highly significant predictor of peer-related aggression at age 19 was the amount of television violence viewed at age 9.

Although correlational studies are highly supportive of the hypothesis that watching television violence can produce aggressive behavior, naturalistic field experiments have been required to put the hypothesis to a more demanding test. Such a study was conducted by Stein and Friedrich (1972), who systematically exposed nursery-school children to either aggressive cartoons (*Batman* and *Superman*), neutral television programs (e.g., children working on the farm), or prosocial television programs *(Mister Roger's Neighborhood)*. Children who were already above average in aggression were observed to emit significantly greater interpersonal aggressive behaviors after exposure to the aggressive programming.

In summary, empirical and corrrelational studies conducted in the laboratory and in the field have provided evidence supporting a relationship between television violence and children's aggressive behavior. However, more research needs to be directed at determining conditions under which such mass media influence may be weakened.

Case Study: Maria

Maria, a 15-year-old girl from a city in the southwestern United States, had been in residential treatment for about a year, pursuant to civil commitment orders. Reasons for her commitment were chronic aggressive and destructive behavior, running away, use of illegal drugs, and poor school performance. She was physically healthy and well developed; however, her personal hygiene was poor, and she was slightly overweight (weight 132 lbs, height 5 ft. 1¼ in.).

History

Maria's natural parents, both Hispanic, had histories of intravenous drug abuse with heroin. Although Maria's mother had been addicted to heroin during her pregnancy with Maria, she recalled having experienced no health problems at the time. The only recorded neonatal problems had been those associated with drug withdrawal. Maria's birth weight was normal. All early developmental milestones were reached within normal limits, and there was no history of difficulty with mobility, feeding, sleeping, or bowel or bladder control.

However, Maria's mother did report that Maria "always" experienced difficulty relating to other children and making and keeping friends. As a young child, she was irritable, temperamental, and easily angered. In early elementary school, she also was identified as a slow learner, and had since been assigned to C-level special education programs.

When Maria was 5, her natural father was killed in a violent, drug-related incident. Her mother remarried a year or two later. According to Maria and her mother, the stepfather was an alcoholic who was physically abusive to everyone in the family. This stepfather has been separated from the family for the past 3 years.

Though Maria's mother has recently been participating in a community drug-abuse program, her life has been chaotic, including at least a year in jail, brief episodes of depression, chronic unemployment and economic difficulty, periodic physical illness, marital problems, and preoccupation with drugs. (However, there is no known family history of psychosis.) Maria's mother's social contacts are very limited. She feels that her only present source of emotional support is from her sister, who lives in the same community.

Economic problems in the family have been compounded by the presence of three children besides Maria; a full sister (now age 22), a half sister (age 7), and a half brother (age 4). Supervision at home has been lacking. Maria herself remembers walking the streets without supervision when she was only 5 or 6. Although Maria sometimes wants to return home and help her mother, she feels that the situation there is too difficult for her.

Maria's mother reported that sometime in early childhood Maria began having "mental lapses," accompanied by twitching and tenseness of the arms and legs. A Generalized Seizure Disorder was diagnosed and successfully treated with anticonvulsant medication. This medication was discontinued nearly 3 years ago, and Maria has experienced no seizure episodes since.

Around the time that the anticonvulsants were discontinued, perhaps a few months earlier, Maria reportedly became more belligerent, disruptive, and unpredictable. Her mother recalled that Maria also began exhibiting bizarre behaviors such as inappropriate laughing and smiling, increased anxiety and fearfulness, and difficulty sleeping (including walking around the house at night). Maria also occasionally reported hearing voices speaking to her when no one was present. Concurrent with these problems, Maria's school performance worsened. Her teachers found her to be more "defiant" and "oppositional," noting greater difficulty in attending to her work. Fights at school increased in frequency.

For several months prior to Maria's admission to residential treatment, she reportedly exhibited increasing oppositional behavior: leaving home without permission; stealing; using alcohol, cigarettes, marijuana, and inhalants; and engaging in sexual intercourse. Maria's mother finally sought an alternative placement, at the time feeling totally unable to control her daughter. Within a 3-month period, Maria moved through three different placements: a group foster home, a "runaway" center, and a court-administered detention home. In each setting she was described as disruptive, aggressive with peers, agitated, and intent on using drugs. During this time, reports of occasional inappropriate emotional behavior and disorganized thinking continued. It was in this context that Maria was first committed to residential treatment.

The first children's residential treatment center that served Maria was located in her home community. In this center, Maria was diagnosed Schizophrenic, Paranoid Type, and given neuroleptic medication for a few months. Under these conditions, she no longer reported hallucinations, and episodes of inappropriate emotional behavior (e.g., bizarre laughter) decreased in frequency. However, she continued to argue and fight with peers (several times a week), she frequently refused to comply with rules and with direct instructions from staff, she continued to withdraw from group interactions and recreational activities, and she continued to evince violent temper tantrums (striking out at peers and staff, calling out insults and threats, pulling away, etc.). In view of these continuing problems, after 7 months in the first treatment center, Maria was judged to have reached "optimum benefit." Thereupon, she was transferred out of her home community to a hospital-based residential treatment program for adolescents. It was in this setting that the following direct assessments were conducted.

Current Status

Different examiners in Maria's second residential treatment program have independently described her as "surly," "belligerent," and "defensive." Maria's eye contact has often been read as "suspicious" (she tends to glare or stare at other people out of the corners of her eyes). Although most examiners have found her to become more cooperative over time, Maria has continued to avoid giving data about her history or presenting problems. Most of the information in the preceding section was, of necessity, obtained entirely from Maria's mother or from caseworkers.

Results of intelligence testing placed Maria well below average (WISC-R VIQ = 68, PIQ = 72, and FSIQ = 68). Consistent with these results, Maria's performance on the Peabody Individual Achievement Test was at the middle or upper third-grade level across academic content areas. Results of screening for neurological impairment were negative.[2]

In view of Maria's intellectual limitations, the High School Personality Questionnaire (HSPQ) (Cattell & Cattell, 1973), one of the personality inventories discussed earlier, was administered. Questions and response choices were read aloud to Maria by the examiner. Maria's profile of scores on the 14 HSPQ source traits showed elevations (Stens of 7 and higher) on Factors C, G, and H. Low scores (Stens of 4 or lower) were derived on Factors B, I, and O. Although many of the traits suggested by these results are consistent with Maria's past and present behavior (e.g., persistence, aloofness from peers, thick-skinned, impulsive, low intelligence, hardness), an overwhelming number of her HSPQ traits are *not consistent* (e.g., emotional discipline and maturity, restraint, good organization of thinking, domination by a sense of duty, freely participating in group situations, eagerness to meet other people, self-confidence, cheerfulness). Therefore, Maria's results on the HSPQ were not accepted as valid.

Another instrument, the Measurement of Depression Rating Scale (Zung, 1967), was used to screen Maria for depression. Zung's scale is similar to personality inventories, but it is briefer, consisting of only 20 self-report items that pertain only to symptoms of depression. Maria's score of 63 falls outside the range for normal controls, but does not compare well to scores obtained with hospitalized depressed patients. Her score falls more clearly within the range for depressed outpatients or for clients with primary diagnoses of Anxiety Disorder, Personality Disorder, or Transient Situational Adjustment Reaction. Specific responses on Zung's scale indicate that Maria has crying spells, feels that her heart beats faster than usual, often gets tired for no reason and feels more irritable than usual. She does not feel that her life is full, nor is she very hopeful about the future. Overall, Maria's responses indicate that she is moderately depressed and anxious.

Two of the projective techniques discussed earlier were administered: the Rotter Incomplete Sentences Blank (ISB) (Rotter, 1950) and the Rorschach Inkblot Test (Rorschach, 1942). Maria's total ISB score of 108 falls below the mean score for "adjusted" adolescent girls. Of her total ISB responses, 20 were scored "positive" and only 14 were

[2]However, an impulsive response pattern was reported with respect to Maria's reproduction of figures on neuropsychological exams.

scored "conflict." The coefficient of agreement between raters on Maria's total ISB score was .98 (.75 on an item-by-item analysis).

Regarding the content of ISB items, only two of Maria's 14 conflict responses referred to aggression: "The best . . . wepon i have ever used is a gun" and "My father . . . is mean to me." Most of her 20 positive responses (e.g., "The future . . . is good," "People . . . are good to me," "I am very . . . happie prson") seem incongruous with her behavioral history.

The authors asked another clinical psychologist,[3] who was blind to Maria's history and presenting problems, to administer and interpret her Rorschach Inkblot Test. This examiner's observations during the testing session identified several instances of oppositional behavior, (e.g., saying to the examiner, "I can't finish it. You finish it," refusing to give more than one response on all but the first three cards, and walking out of the testing room before the end of the session).

Following is part of the interpretation of Maria's responses on the Rorschach:

> It is noteworthy that she shows signs of a great deal of hostility which may emerge when she releases her emotions. Many of her responses have aggressive connotations. Thus she saw "vampires," "Frankenstein," "a dragon," and "two rats eating Count Dracula" . . . it is significant that this type of response emerged as frequently as it did.

In addition, the examiner concluded that Maria "lacks a firmly developed response style and is likely to vacillate in coping situations." Her performance on the Rorschach suggested further that when Maria displays affect, "it probably tends to get out of control." Becoming "overwhelmed by her emotions . . . , she shows some tendency to withdraw from affectively-ladened situations." It was also noted that "she lacks the resources to handle failure very well" and she "appears to have some anxieties concerning interpersonal relations. This may result in a tendency to avoid and/or disregard others in her thinking." While Maria's Rorschach responses showed some reality *distortions,* it was observed that "she does not appear to have any type of psychotic disorder."

It was noted further that Maria showed an "ability to perceive conventional ways of behaving, even though she may resist such guidelines." This tendency to "choose"to engage in unconventional behavior seems consistent with Maria's history of oppositional conduct. In fact, the interpretation of Maria's Rorschach appears generally to be very descriptive of her, except with respect to indications of schizophrenia in her history.

Behavioral checklists were also used in evaluating Maria. The first of these was the Behavior Problem Checklist (BPC) (Quay & Peterson, 1975). The BPC was completed independently by a nurse and a hospital attendant who were both in close daily contact with Maria. These raters agreed on 71% of the BPC items, and their agreement coefficient across scale scores averaged .72 (range, .67 to .75). In comparison to norms for institutionalized delinquent adolescent females, Maria was shown by both raters to score higher on both the Conduct-Disorder and Immaturity-Inadequacy scales and lower on the Anxiety-Withdrawal (Personality-Disorder) scale (although nine of the 14 items in this latter scale were identified by both raters as problems for Maira). Maria also scored relatively higher on the Socialized Aggressive Disorder scale (norms for which are limited). In summary, the BPC results for Maria, based upon current observations of her behavior, were consistent with her recent history.

The next behavioral checklist, the Walker Problem Behavior Identification Checklist (Walker, 1970), was independently completed by a nurse and two hospital attendants.

[3]The authors extend their appreciation to Dr. John Clark for his gracious and very skillful assistance.

Interrater reliability on this checklist was poor. However, all three Walker checklists did show elevated scores for Maria on the Acting Out and Withdrawal scales.

Finally, the Nurses' Observation Scale for Inpatient Evaluation (NOSIE-30) (Honigfeld & Klett, 1965) was administered. On this instrument, 30 short behavioral descriptors are rated on the basis of observations over the last 3 days of contact with the targeted individual. A nurse and two attendants evaluated Maria using the NOSIE-30. As with the Walker checklist, interrater agreement was poor. However, the results of all three ratings placed Maria above the 85th percentile on the Irritability scale and below the 50th percentile on the Social Competence and Neatness scales.

Considered together, data from the behavioral checklists appeared to be valid with respect to Maria's major problems. However, caution is advised in the use and interpretation of these checklists, in view of the findings that absolute scores on some of the checklists were not very reliable.

Direct observational data from Maria's chart showed that after 22 weeks in her second residential treatment program, her presenting problems were relatively unchanged. Counts of the most reliable entries in her chart over a 22-week period showed 23 occurrences of runaway (unauthorized leave), 23 instances in which seculusion or physical restraints were ordered, and 9 episodes of physical aggression toward staff (the last 3 of which had resulted in physical injury). These problems were occurring as frequently at the end as at the beginning of the 22-month period. Similarly, no change was evident in records of other problem behaviors (e.g., verbal and physical aggression toward peers, verbal opposition and aggression with staff, intoxication following runaway episodes, forging points on the group motivational system, shoplifting during periods of unauthorized leave, etc.) In the most recent two months, notes in her chart described Maria's behavior as "sarcastic, secretive, demanding, and sneaky." Although she would often laugh or smile inappropriately (particularly after an episode of misbehavior), Maria's behavior was not psychotic.

During her first week in the present residential treatment program, Maria ran away. She was returned by the police, who reported that she had stabbed a man who had met Maria at a bar and had taken her home. The police had found Maria with this man when they responded to a call and found the man lying in his own bed with a stab wound. The victim recovered, and no charges were filed against Maria.

As the final draft of this chapter was being typed, Maria ran away from the treatment center and the same day was again returned by the police. On this occasion, she appeared to be intoxicated. She had been apprehended after having broken into a private residence, threatening the occupants with a bloody knife.

The following day, she was charged with the murder of a man who lived alone in a house that was linked by a trail of blood to the residence where Maria had been found the evening before. The victim, found lying in his own bed, had suffered head injuries and brutal knife multilations. Maria is presently detained in jail while she undergoes forensic evaluation.

Discussion

This case study illustrates the application of the interview, personality inventories, projective methods, behavioral checklists, and direct observation in assessing an adolescent girl with oppositional and aggressive behavior. Among these assessment methods, the greatest volume of reliable information came from interview and direct-observational records.

Scores from Maria's behavioral checklists and inferences from projectives were consistent with interview and direct-observational data. However, the checklists and projectives provided very little in the way of *new* information about Maria. The personality test that was used in this case was time-consuming and yielded essentially invalid results. Indeed, the best predictor of the tragic event that subsequently resulted in Maria's arrest was the direct-observational record, or baseline, of her repeated episodes of oppositional and aggressive behavior.

That Maria is an appropriate case example for this chapter is evidenced in her wide range of oppositional behaviors (breaking rules at home and school, running away, using illegal drugs, insulting and arguing with others, refusing to participate in activities with peers, etc.) and aggressive behaviors (fighting, threatening harm to others, etc.). Based upon the information obtained, the most fitting diagnosis for Maria is Conduct Disorder, Undersocialized Aggressive Type, with below-average intelligence and achievement, disturbed family relationships, and anxiety and withdrawal.

Etiologically, few conclusions may be drawn, although Maria's case certainly presents many of the conditions that this chapter has discussed as being related to aggressive and oppositional behavior: maternal depression and insularity, family disorganization and economic deprivation, death of the natural father, physical and verbal abuse, loose supervision, etc.) In addition, questions may be raised concerning the extent to which Maria's aggressive and oppositional patterns were related to her mother's history of drug use or to her early seizures, low intelligence, or learning problems.

Summary

A fixed definition of aggressive and oppositional behavior is precluded by the complexities of the social labeling process. Therefore, less than perfect definitional agreement should be expected, particularly regarding acts that are less extreme or that are in some way justifiable.

This chapter has reviewed major systems for classifying childhood aggression and oppositional behavior: clinically-derived systems; empirically-derived systems based upon multivariate statistical techniques; and the legal system of classification. Similarities exist in the categories that comprise the first two systems. In comparison, the legal system is less complete. Within the empirically-derived system, small beginnings have been made in researching the relationship of classification to etiology, prognosis, and treatment. It is suggested that future research in this direction consider the strength of aggressive/oppositional behaviors, setting or situational variables, and response–response relationships.

Three theoretical viewpoints on aggression were discussed. Aggression was examined from psychoanalytic and ethological perspectives, from a perspective that views it as an elicited drive, and from a social-learning perspective. It was concluded that social-learning accounts have the strongest empirical support and the greatest potential for prevention and control.

Methods for assessing and/or measuring aggressive and oppositional behavior were reviewed. Specific suggestions were offered for planning and conducting interviews with children and their parents. Examples of personality inventories, projective methods, and behavioral checklists were selected with respect to applicability to aggressive/oppositional children. Suggestions were given for measuring aggressive and oppositional behaviors via a variety of direct observational techniques. With each assessment strategy, attention was given to measurement reliability, validity, and economy.

Etiological factors pertaining to aggressive and oppositional behavior were also examined. Studies were reviewed describing relationships between aggressive/oppositional behavior and age, race, sex, organic (neurological) factors, diet, and family variables, peer influences, cognitive variables, and mass media influences. Considerably greater attention was given to studies of the relationship between parent characteristics/parent–child interactions and childhood aggression and opposition.

Finally, a representative case study of an oppositional and aggressive adolescent female was presented to illustrate material discussed in preceding sections. As the chapter was being typed, the young girl selected for study was charged with a brutal murder in the face of persuasive evidence against her.

Acknowledgments

The authors wish to thank the following individuals for their assistance in this project: John Clark, Paul Cruz, Stephanie Garduno, Rosario Novalis, Jeff Rothweiler, and Esther Ruiz.

References

Aiken, L. R. *Psychological and educational testing.* Boston: Allyn & Bacon, 1971.

Alexander, J. F. Defensive and supportive communications in normal and deviant families. *Journal of Consulting,* 1973, *40,* 223–231.

American Psychiatric Association, *Diagnostic and statistical manual of mental disorders* (3rd ed., DSM-III). Washington, D.C.: American Psychiatric Association, 1980.

Arnold, J. E., Levine, A. G., & Patterson, G. R. Changes in sibling behavior following family intervention. *Journal of Consulting and Clinical Psychology,* 1975, *43,* 683–688.

Bandura, A. *Aggression: A social learning analysis.* Englewood Cliffs, N.J.: Prentice-Hall, 1973.

Bandura, A., Ross, D., & Ross, S. A. Imitation of film-mediated aggressive models. *Journal of Abnormal and Social Psychology,* 1963, *66,* 3–11.

Bandura, A., & Walters, R. H. *Adolescent aggression.* New York: Ronald, 1959.

Bandura, A., & Walters, R. H. Aggression. In H. W. Stevenson, J. Kagan, & C. Spiker (Eds.), *Child psychology: The sixty-second yearbook of the National Society for the Study of Education.* Chicago: University of Chicago Press, 1963.

Baron, R. A. *Human aggression.* New York: Plenum Press, 1977.

Baumrind, D. Child care practices anteceding three patterns of pre-school behavior. *Genetic Psychology Monographs,* 1967, *75,* 43–88.

Becker, W. C., Peterson, D. R., Hellmer, L. A., Shoemaker, D. J., & Quay, H. C. Factors in parental behavior and personality as related to problem behavior in children. *Journal of Consulting Psychology,* 1959, *23,* 107–118.

Behar, L., & Stringfield, S. A. A behavior rating scale for the preschool child. *Developmental Psychology,* 1974, *10,* 601–610.

Bellak, L., & Bellak, S. *Children's apperception test.* New York: Psychological Corporation, 1949.

Berkowitz, L. Control of aggression. In B. M. Caldwell & H. M. Ricciutti (Eds.), *Review of child development research (Vol. 3).* Chicago: University of Chicago Press, 1973.

Borkovec, T. D. Autonomic reactivity to sensory stimulation in psychopathic, neurotic, and normal juvenile delinquents. *Journal of Consulting and Clinical Psychology,* 1970, *35,* 217–222.

Bugental, D. B., & Love, L. Nonassertive expression of parental approval and disapproval and its relationship to child disturbance. *Child Development,* 1975, *46,* 747–752.

Bugental, D. B., Love, L. R., Kaswan, J. J., & April, C. Verbal–nonverbal conflict in parental messages to normal and disturbed children. *Journal of Abnormal Psychology,* 1971, *77,* 6–10.

Cattell, R. B., & Cattell, M. D. L. *Manual for the high school personality questionnaire.* Champaign, Ill.: Institute for Personality and Ability Testing, 1973.

Cattell, R. B., & Cattell, M. D. L. *Handbook for the high school personality questionnaire* (2nd ed.). Champaign, Ill.: Institute for Personality and Ability Testing, 1975.

Commission on Professional and Hospital Activities: *The international classification of diseases* (9th rev., clinical modification). Ann Arbor, Mich.: Commission on Professional and Hospital Activities, 1978.

Dollard, J., Doob, L. W., Miller, N. E., Mowrer, O.H., & Sears, R. R. *Frustration and aggression.* New Haven, Conn.: Yale University Press, 1939.

Dominick, J. R., & Greenberg, B. S. Attitudes toward violence: The interaction of television exposure, family attitudes, and social class. In G. A. Comstock & E. A. Rubinstein (Eds.), *Television and social behavior, Vol. III. Television and adolescent aggressiveness,* Washington, D.C.: U.S. Government Printing Office, 1972.

Dreger, R. M. The initial standardization of the Adolescent Behavioral Classification Project Instrument. *Journal of Abnormal Child Psychology,* 1980, *8,* 297–322.

Eme, R. F. Sex differences in childhood psychopathology, *Psychological Bulletin,* 1979, *86,* 574–595.

Evans, W. R. The Behavior Problem Checklist: Data from an inner-city population. *Psychology in the Schools,* 1975, *12,* 301–303.

Forbes, G. B. Comparison of hyperactive and emotionally-behaviorally disturbed children on the Devereux Child Behavior Rating Scale: A potential aid in diagnosis. *Journal of Clinical Psychology,* 1978, *34,* 68–71.

Forehand, R., Wells, K. C., & Sturgis, E. T. Predictors of child noncompliance in the home. *Journal of Consulting and Clinical Psychology,* 1978, *46,* 179.

Friedman, C. J., Mann, F., & Friedman, A. S. A profile of juvenile street gang members. *Adolescence,* 1975, *10,* 563–607.

Goldfarb, W. Psychological privation in infancy and subsequent adjustment. *American Journal of Orthopsychiatry,* 1945, *15,* 247–255.

Graham, P. Epidemiological studies. In H. C. Quay & J. S. Werry (Eds.), *Psychopathological disorders of childhood* (2nd ed.). New York: Wiley, 1979.

Green, K. D., Forehand, R., & McMahon, R. J. Parental manipulation of compliance and noncompliance in normal and deviant children. *Behavior Modification,* 1979, *3,* 245–266.

Griest, D. L., Forehand, R., Wells, K. C., & McMahon, R. J. An examination of differences between nonclinic and behavior problem clinic-referred children and their mothers. *Journal of Abnormal Psychology,* 1980, *89,* 497–500.

Griest, D., Wells, K. C., & Forehand, R. An examination of predictors of maternal perceptions of maladjustment in clinic-referred children. *Journal of Abnormal Psychology,* 1979, *88,* 277–281.

Haney, B., & Gold, M. The juvenile delinquent nobody knows. *Psychology Today,* September 1973, 49–52; 55.

Hanratty, M. A. *Imitation of film-mediated aggression against live and inanimate victims.* Unpublished masters thesis, Vanderbilt University, 1969.

Hanratty, M. A., Liebert, R. M., Morris, L. W., & Fernandez, L. E. Imitation of film-mediated aggression against live and inanimate victims, *Proceedings of the 77th Annual Convention of the American Psychological Association,* Washington, D.C.: American Psychological Association, 1969.

Hanratty, M. A., O'Neal, E., & Sulzer, J. L. The effect of frustration upon imitation of aggression. *Journal of Personality and Social Psychology,* 1972, *21,* 30–34.

Harbin, H. T., & Madden, D. J. Battered parents: A new syndrome. *American Journal of Psychiatry,* 1979, *136,* 1288–1291.

Hartup, W. W. Aggression in children. *American Psychologist,* 1974, *29,* 335–341.

Hathaway, S. R., & McKinley, J. C. *Manual for the Minnesota multiphasic personality inventory.* New York: Psychological Corporation, 1943.

Hayes, S. C., Rincover, A., & Volosin, D. Variables influencing the acquisition and maintenance of aggressive behavior: Modeling versus sensory reinforcement. *Journal of Abnormal Psychology,* 1980, *89,* 254–262.

Herbert, E. W., Pinkston, E. M., Hayden, M. L., Sajwaj, T. E., Pinkston, S., Cordua, G., & Jackson, C. Adverse effects of differential parental attention. *Journal of Applied Behavior Analysis,* 1973, *6,* 15–30.

Herjanic, B., Herjanic, M., Brown, F., & Wheatt, T. Are children reliable reporters? *Journal of Abnormal Child Psychology,* 1975, *3,* 41–48.

Hetherington, E. M., & Martin, B. Family interaction. In H. C. Quay & J. S. Werry (Eds.), *Psychopathological disorders of childhood.* New York: Wiley, 1979.

Hetherington, E. M., Cox, M., & Cox, R. The aftermath of divorce. In J. H. Stevens & M. Mathews (Eds.), *Mother–child, father–child behaviors.* Washington, D.C.: N.A.F.Y.C., 1977. (a)

Hetherington, E. M., Cox, M., & Cox R. *The development of children in mother-headed families.* Paper presented at Conference on Families in Contemporary America, George Washington University, June 1977. (b)

Hoffman, L. W. Changes in family roles, socialization and sex differences. *American Psychologist,* 1977, *32,* 644–657.

Honigfeld, G., & Klett, C. J. The Nurses' Observation Scale for Inpatient Evaluation. *Journal of Clinical Psychology,* 1965, *21,* 65–71.

Huesmann, L. R., Lefkowitz, M. M., & Eron, L. D. Sum of MMPI scales F, 4, and 9 as a measure of aggression. *Journal of Consulting and Clinical Psychology,* 1978, *45,* 1071–1078.

Jenkins, R. L. *Behavior disorders of childhood and adolescence.* Springfield, Ill.: Charles C Thomas, 1973.

Jessness, C. F. *The Jessness inventory.* Palo Alto, Calif.: Consulting Psychologists Press, 1966.

Johnson, S. M., & Lobitz, G. R. The personal and marital status of parents as related to observed child deviance and parenting behaviors. *Journal of Abnormal Child Psychology,* 1974, *3,* 193–208.

Lefkowitz, M. M., Eron, L. D., Walder, L. O., & Huesmann, L. R. Television violence and child aggression: A follow-up study. In G. A. Comstock & E. A. Rubinstein (Eds.), *Television and social behavior, Vol. III: Television and adolescent aggressiveness.* Washington, D.C.: U.S. Government Printing Office, 1972.

Leske, G., Afton, A., Rogers, E. S., & Wahler, R. G. The interpersonal functioning of insular and non-insular families: Factors related to treatment success and failures. In B. B. Lahey & A. E. Kazdin (Eds.), *Advances in clinical child psychology (Vol. 2).* New York: Plenum Press, 1978.

Lewinsohn, P. M. A behavioral approach to depression. In R. J. Friedman & M. M. Katz (Eds.), *The psychology of depression: Contemporary theory and research.* New York: Wiley, 1974.

Little, V. L., & Kendall, P. C. Cognitive-behavioral interventions with delinquents: Problem solving, role-taking, and self-control. In P. C. Kendall & S. D. Hollon (Eds.), *Cognitive-behavioral interventions: Theory, research, and procedures.* New York: Academic Press, 1979.

Lobitz, G. R., & Johnson, S. M. Normal versus deviant children: A multimethod comparison. *Journal of Abnormal Psychology,* 1975, *3,* 353–374.

Maccoby, E. E., & Jacklin, C. N. Sex differences in aggression: A rejoinder. *Child Development,* 1980, *51,* 964–980.

Matranga, J. T. The relationship between behavioral indices of aggression and hostile content on the TAT. *Journal of Personality Assessment,* 1976, *40,* 130–134.

McCord, J., & McCord, W. The effects of parental role model of criminality. *Journal of Social Issues,* 1958, *14,* 66–75.

McLeod, J. M., Atkin, C. K., & Chaffee, S. H. Adolescents, parents and television use: Adolescent self-report measures from Maryland and Wisconsin samples. In G. A. Comstock & E. A. Rubinstein (Eds.), *Television and social behavior, Vol. III: Television and adolescent aggressiveness.* Washington, D.C.: U.S. Government Printing Office, 1972.

Miller, N. E. Theory and experiment relating psychoanalytic displacement to stimulus–response generalization. *Journal of Abnormal and Social Psychology,* 1948, *43,* 155–178.

Miller, W. The rumble this time. *Psychology Today,* May 1977, 52–59: 88.

Murray, H. A. *Thematic apperception test.* New York: Psychological Corporation, 1943.

Nasby, W., Hayden, B., & DePaulo, B. M. Attirbutional bias among aggressive boys to interpret unambiguous social stimuli as displays of hostility. *Journal of Abnormal Psychology,* 1980, *89,* 459–468.

O'Leary, K. D., & Johnson, S. B. *Psychological assessment.* In H. C. Quay & J. S. Werry (Eds.), *Psychopathological disorders of childhood* (2nd ed.). New York: Wiley, 1979.

Parke, R. D., & Collmer, W. C. Child abuse: An interdisciplinary analysis. In E. M. Hetherington (Ed.), *Review of child development research* (Vol. 5). Chicago: University of Chicago Press, 1975.

Patterson, G. R. The aggressive child: Victim and architect of a coercive system. In E. J. Mash, L. A. Hamerlynck, & L. C. Handy (Eds.), *Behavior modification and families.* New York: Brunner/Mazel, 1976.

Patterson, G. R., Reid, J. B., Jones, R. R., & Conger, R. E. *A social learning approach to family intervention: Families with aggressive children* (Vol. 1). Eugene, Ore.: Castalia Publishing, 1975.

Peed, S., Roberts, M., & Forehand, R. Evaluation of the effectiveness of a standardized parent training program in altering the interaction of mothers and their noncompliant children. *Behavior Modification,* 1977, *1,* 323–350.

Prinz, R. J., Roberts, W. A., & Hantman, E. Dietary correlates of hyperactive behavior in children. *Journal of Consulting and Clinical Psychology,* 1980, *48,* 760–769.

Proger, B. B., Mann, L., Green, P. A., Bayuk, R. J., & Burger, R. M. Discriminators of clinically defined emotional maladjustment: Predictive validity of the Behavior Problem Checklist and Devereux Scale. *Journal of Abnormal Child Psychology,* 1975, *3,* 71–82.

Public Broadcasting System, *MacNeil, Lehrer Report,* March 5, 1981.

Quay, H. C. Measuring dimensions of deviant behavior: The Behavior Problem Checklist. *Journal of Abnormal Child Psychology,* 1977, *5,* 277–289.

Quay, H. C. Classification. In H. C. Quay & J. S. Werry (Eds.), *Psychopathological disorders of childhood.* New York: Wiley, 1979.

Quay, H. C., & Parsons, L. B. *The differential behavioral classification of the juvenile offender* (2nd ed.). Washington, D.C.: U.S. Bureau of Prisons, 1971.

Quay, H. C., & Peterson, D. R. *Manual for the Behavior Problem Checklist.* Unpublished, 1975. (Available from H. C. Quay, University of Miami, P. O. Box 248074, Coral Gables, FL 33124).

Read, R. H. Parents' expressed attitudes and children's behavior. *Journal of Consulting Psychology,* 1945, *9,* 95–100.

Robins, L. N. *Deviant children grown up.* Baltimore: Williams & Wilkins, 1966. Reprinted and published by Robert E. Krieger Publishing Co., Huntington, New York, 1974.

Rorschach, H. *Psychodiagnostics: A diagnostic test based on perception.* (P. Lemkan & B. Kronenburg, trans.). Berne: Huber, 1942. (1st German ed., 1921; U.S. distr., Grune & Stratton).

Rose, T. L. The functional relationship between artificial food colors and hyperactivity. *Journal of Applied Behavior Analysis,* 1978, *11,* 56–62.

Rosenzweig, S. Rosenzweig picture-frustration study. In A. Weider (Ed.), *Constributions toward medical psychology: Theory and psychodiagnostic methods* (Vol. 2). New York: Ronald, 1953.

Ross, D., & Ross, S. *Hyperactivity: Research, theory, action.* New York: Wiley, 1976.

Rotter, J. B. *Incomplete sentences blank—High school form.* New York: Psychological Corporation, 1950.

Sallows, G. *Responsiveness of deviant and normal children to naturally occurring parental consequences.* Paper presented at the Midwestern Psychological Association Convention, Chicago, Illinois, 1973.

Sandberg, S. T., Weiselberg, M., & Shaffer, D. Hyperkinetic and conduct problem children in a primary school population: Some spidemiological considerations. *Journal of Child Psychology and Psychiatry,* 1980, *21,* 293–311.

Santrock, J. W. Father absence, perceived maternal behavior and moral development in boys. *Child Development,* 1975, *46,* 753–757.

Sawin, D. B., & Parke, R. D. Inconsistent discipline of aggression in young boys. *Journal of Experimental Child Psychology,* 1979, *28,* 525–538.

Sears, R. R., Maccoby, E. E., & Levin, H. *Patterns of child rearing.* Evanston, Ill.: Row and Peterson, 1957.

Seligman, M. E. P. *Helplessness.* San Francisco: W. H. Freeman, 1975.

Shinn, M. Father absence and children's cognitive development. *Psychological Bulletin,* 1978, *85,* 295–324.

Simmons, J. E. *Psychiatric examination of children* (2nd ed.). Philadelphia: Lea & Febiger, 1974.

Simonds, J. F., & Kashani, J. Drug abuse and criminal behavior in delinquent boys committed to a training school. *American Journal of Psychiatry,* 1979, *136,* 1444–1448.

Skrzypek, G. J. Effect of perceptual isolation and arousal on anxiety, complexity preference, and novelty preference in psychopathic and neurotic delinquents. *Journal of Abnormal Psychology,* 1969, *74,* 321–329.

Speer, D. C. The Behavior Problem Checklist (Peterson-Quay): Baseline data from parents of child guidance and non-clinic children. *Journal of Consulting and Clinical Psychology,* 1971, *36,* 221–228.

Spivack, J., & Swift, M. *Devereux elementary school behavior rating scale manual.* Devon: The Devereux Foundation, 1967.

Stein, A. H., & Friedrich, L. K. Television content and young children's behavior. In J. P. Murray, E. A. Rubinstein, & G. A. Comstock (Eds.), *Television and social behavior, Vol. II: Television and social learning.* Washington, D.C.: U. S. Government Printing Office, 1972.

Strasberg, P. A. *Violent delinquents: A report to the Ford Foundation from the Vera Institute of Justice.* New York: Monarch, 1978.

Symonds, P. M. *Adolescent fantasy: An investigation of the picture-story method of personality study.* New York: Columbia University Press, 1949.

Tanay, E. Adolescents who kill parents—Reactive parricide. *Australian and New Zealand Journal of Psychiatry,* 1973, *7,* 263–277.

Terdal, L., Jackson, R., & Garner, A. Mother-child interactions: A comparison between normal and developmentally delayed groups. In E. J. Mash, L. A. Hamerlynck, & L. C. Handy (Eds.), *Behavior Modification and families.* New York: Brunner/Mazel, 1976.

Thorpe, L. P., Clark, W. W., & Tiegs, E. W. *California test of personality.* Los Angeles: California Test Bureau, 1953.

Tygart, C. E. Student social structures and/or subcultures as factors in school crime: Toward a paradigm. *Adolescence,* 1980, *15,* 13–22.

Victor, J. B., & Halverson, C. F. Behavior problems in elementary school children: A follow-up study. *Journal of Abnormal Child Psychology,* 1976, *4,* 17–29.

Wagner, E. E., & Medvedeff, E. Differentiation of aggressive behavior of institutionalized schizophrenics with the Hand Test. *Journal of Projective Techniques,* 1963, *27,* 111–113.

Wahler, R. G. The insular mother: Her problems in parent–child treatment. *Journal of Applied Behavior Analysis,* 1980, *13,* 207–219.

Wahler, R. G., & Afton, A. D., Attentional processes in insular and noninsular mothers. *Child Behavior Therapy,* 1980, *2,* 25–41.

Walker, H. M. *Walker problem behavior identification checklist.* Los Angeles: Western Psychological Services, 1970.

Walls, R. T., Werner, T. J., Bacon, A., & Zane, T. Behavior checklists. In J. D. Cone & R. P. Hawkins (Eds.), *Behavioral assessment: New directions in clinical psychology.* New York: Brunner/Mazel, 1977.

Werry, J. S. Organic factors. In H. C. Quay & J. S. Werry (Eds.), *Psychopathological disorders of childhood.* New York: Wiley, 1979.

Wiltz, N. A., & Patterson, G. R. An evaluation of parent training procedures designed to alter inappropriate aggressive behavior of boys. *Behavior Therapy,* 1974, *5,* 515–521.

World Health Organization. *Manual of the international statistical classification of diseases, injuries, and causes of death* (Vol. 1, 8th rev.). Geneva: World Health Organization, 1969.

Zung, W. W. K. *The measurement of depression.* Milwaukee, Wisc.: Lakeside Laboratories, 1967.

14

Juvenile Delinquency

DENNIS R. MOORE AND JUDY L. ARTHUR

Introduction

Juvenile delinquency has garnered the attention of social scientists for well over half a century. Unlike most other forms of child psychopathology, this attention has not come exclusively nor even in majority from the mainstream of psychological inquiry. Instead, delinquency has been viewed primarily as a "social problem" of interest to sociologists or as an adolescent transition period evoking psychoanalytic interpretations. This emphasis is reflected in the accumulated delinquency literature. Theoretical formulations on delinquency have generally been either of a sociological (cf. Elliott, Ageton, & Canter, 1979) or a psychoanalytic (cf. review by Gold & Petronio, 1980) perspective. Major treatment studies have been guided by social work strategies (Powers & Witmer, 1951) or psychoanalytic principles (Redl & Wineman, 1951). In addition, the majority of etiological studies of delinquency have been large-scale sociological investigations (McCord & McCord, 1959; Nye, 1958; Wadsworth, 1979; West & Farrington, 1973, 1977; Wolfgang, Figlio, & Sellin, 1972). While these approaches have added immensely to our knowledge of delinquent behavior, they have generally pictured delinquency as being the product of global social and economic conditions or as demonstrating transitory adjustment difficulties during adolescence. This has left juvenile delinquency in a somewhat awkward position of straddling the fence between sociological and psychological disciplines. In turn, this places a discussion of the *psychopathology* of delinquency in a similar position. It is the goal of this chapter to recognize the sociological heritage of delinquency but to gently coax delinquency off the fence into the investigative domain of current behavioral psychology.

Several overriding assumptions concerning delinquency will guide the approach taken in this chapter. The first of these is that delinquency is not comprised of homogenous behav-

---

DENNIS R. MOORE AND JUDY L. ARTHUR • Moore/Arthur Associates, 191 Crest Drive, Eugene, Oregon 97405. This chapter was written while the authors were supported by NIMH grants MH-29757 and MH-29786 from the Center for Studies of Crime and Delinquency.

ior patterns, nor does it always represent psychological disturbance. Within the broad range of delinquent children lies a group whose behavior signals a high probability of lifespan maladjustment. This group will be of central importance to the following discussion. Second, delinquent behavior indicative of psychopathology represents a developmental problem that is tied to preadolescent patterns of child rearing and socialization. Although a majority of delinquent behavior occurs during adolescence, onset of delinquency during this period is less predictive of continued maladjustment than preadolescent onset. Third, given that problem delinquency is the result of developmental processes, then these processes must be elucidated in order to understand the problem. This indicates that delinquent patterns of behavior comprise one of many potential developmental outcomes that range from social competence to life-span maladjustment. Adequate explanation of one outcome (delinquency) rests on adequate explanation of more general social development processes.

Defining Juvenile Delinquency

Juvenile delinquency is historically rooted in legal–judicial conceptualizations and definitions. However, it does not represent an area readily defined. This is because of the variety of delinquent behaviors, with their concomitant variance in social and psychological importance, and because of the range of definitions currently in use. To place a definition of delinquency-as-psychopathology in proper perspective, several descriptions of delinquency are offered, beginning with "delinquent behavior." The reader should keep in mind that these descriptions are not mutually exclusive.

Delinquent behavior covers all acts having legal constraints on their occurrence. For juvenile offenders, delinquent behaviors comprise two groups of acts. One group consists of behaviors that are illegal only because of the offender's age. The other consists of those that would be illegal if committed by any individual. The age-related offenses are termed *status offenses,* and are illegal until the age of majority. Status offenses include acts such as school truancy, running away from home, alcohol consumption and possession, sexual promiscuity, and more ambiguous generic offenses such as "incorrigible" or "beyond parental control." Nonstatus offenses, or *index crimes,* cover the standard range of illegal behavior from misdemeanors to first-degree murder. Common juvenile infractions include vandalism, shop lifting, auto theft, minor assault, burglary, and unarmed robbery. Less frequent are the more serious offenses such as armed robbery, assault causing bodily harm, rape, and homicide. Delinquent behavior represents the least-common-denominator definition of delinquency upon which more selective definitions are based.

A second commonly used definition is termed *official delinquency.* Official delinquency indicates that community agents or agencies have identified individuals who have engaged in delinquent behavior. This usually takes the form of police or juvenile court records. The present use of official delinquency will refer to court adjudicated offenses because this implies an impartial determination of guilt. Official delinquency represents a selective subset of delinquent behavior. First, it indicates that the offender was caught. Many offenders and offenses go undetected. Second, it implies that the offense was severe enough to warrant official involvement. Many delinquent behaviors, especially status offenses, would not result in arrest even if authorities were aware of their occurrence. Generally, adjudication results from the occurrence of an index crime or multiple status offenses that lead authorities to believe that the child cannot be controlled by parents or guardians.

The simple occurrence of delinquent behavior or official delinquency cannot be equated with child psychopathology. The problem becomes one of differentiating between delinquent children who are at-risk for continued severe maladjustment and those who are engaging in relatively common, similar behaviors that do not reflect major disorder. For the present, two additional dimensions of delinquency will aid in defining delinquent acts performed. Children who demonstrate delinquent behavior at an early age (i.e., 12 years or younger) and who commit numerous, varied delinquent acts are considered to be high-risk candidates for debilitating adult maladjustment. They are also likely to be identified as recidivistic offical delinquents during adolescence. These children comprise the core of those considered to demonstrate child psychopathology and will be referred to as *preadolescent delinquents.* Children who initiate delinquent behavior during adolescence do not carry the same risk potential, although rate and severity of delinquent acts is still of importance in this group. These children will be referred to as *adolescent delinquents.*

At this point, these definitions intentionally provide a flat, unidimensional portrayal of delinquency. The following sections provide the data to construct a more accurate, multidimensional representation of delinquent disorders.

Incidence

Sex Differences

Juvenile delinquency is generally viewed as a male disorder. This assumption is evidenced in the vast predominance of "male subjects only" studies in the delinquency literature. The meager evidence that is available on females provides support for this perspective. Survey studies measuring the occurrence of delinquent behavior have reported much higher occurrences for males (Gold & Petronio, 1980). Referrals to mental health facilities for child conduct disorders typically show at least a 3:1 male-to-female ratio (Cass & Thomas, 1979; Robins, 1966). The rate of official delinquency among a normative sample of females has been reported to be 2% (Wadsworth, 1979), approximately one-tenth the male rate. Finally, occurrence of delinquency in females does not appear to carry the negative long-term prognosis that it does in males (Robins, 1966).

Numerous rationales have been offered for these differences. For example, Rutter (1979b) proposed that female children were naturally more impervious to life stress and deprivation than were their male counterparts. Gold and Petronio (1980) suggested that females lacked peer group support for engaging in antisocial behavior. Regardless of the validity or cause of sex differences in delinquency, further clarification must await additional investigation. Thus, due to the scarcity of reliable information on female delinquency, data presented in the remainder of this chapter will refer to male delinquency only.

Self-Reported and Official Delinquency

As mentioned earlier, many delinquent behaviors go unnoticed by the authorities, and therefore are not accounted for on official records. Thus, many researchers have measured delinquent behavior by using interviews or questionnaires that ask a youth to report on his involvement in delinquent activity. These self-report measures have demonstrated that 80–90% of surveyed children have engaged in delinquent behavior (Gold & Petronio, 1980;

West & Farrington, 1973). Most self-report data indicate that delinquency is not related to the race or social class of the offender (Gold & Petronio, 1980). The results of self-report studies are in sharp contrast to those studies using official delinquency data.

The rate of official delinquency in both Great Britain and the United States is 20% (± 2%) of all male children (Polk, 1975; Wadsworth, 1979; West & Farrington, 1973). Official delinquency is generally highly related to social class and race, with inordinant numbers of delinquents coming from lower class families (West & Farrington, 1973) and minority groups (Wolfgang *et al.*, 1972). The discrepancy between official and self-reported delinquency has generated heated discussion and theoretical exposition among sociologists. Generally, explanations hypothesize that police and juvenile justice authorities exercise a negative bias in apprehending and adjudicating lower class and minority delinquents. Recent data argue against such interpretations. West and Farrington (1973) defined children as delinquent if they had reported 21 or more delinquent acts. These high-rate offenders were indistinguishable from the official delinquents on a host of child and family measures. Of the self-report delinquents, 51% were also official delinquents. These data indicated that authorities were apprehending appropriate juvenile offenders, although a high percentage (49%) was undetected at the time.

A thorough evaluation of self-report studies by Hindelang, Hirschi, and Weis (1979) also clarified the nature of "hidden" delinquency. These authors reported that self-report measures have historically tapped delinquent behaviors that are not of concern to juvenile authorities. The delinquent behavior measured by self-report is real but would typically not result in arrest of the offender. Hindelang *et al.* concluded that official delinquency provided a valid measure of the demographic distribution of criminal behavior. Elliott and Ageton (1980) documented this conclusion by analyzing data from a new self-report measure that accurately reflected the rate and severity of delinquent behavior. Race and social class were related to self-reported, severe delinquent offenses in the same manner as official delinquent records.

Taken together, these studies appear to resolve the discrepancy between self-reported and official delinquency. Delinquent behavior is widespread and common, but the majority is not of concern to juvenile justice authorities. Populations that engage in higher rates of more severe delinquent behaviors are overly represented by children from lower social classes and minority groups. These types of offenses are of concern to community agents and would lead to adjudication if the offender were caught. Because number and severity of delinquent acts are implicit to the definition of delinquency-as-psychopathology, official records of delinquency constitute the best current source of data with which to investigate this area.

Recidivism

Numerous studies have reported that 45–55% of official delinquents commit only one adjudicated offense prior to adulthood (Polk, 1975; West & Farrington, 1977; Wolfgang *et al.*, 1972). Children who commit more than one official offense (i.e., recidivist delinquents) show an increasing probability of continued offending. Wolfgang *et al.* (1972) reported that 54% of first offenders committed a second offense, 65% of two-time offenders committed a third offense, and 72% of three-time offenders committed a fourth offense. By the fourth offense, a youth has established a chronic and enduring pattern of criminal, antisocial behavior. Of such chronic delinquents, 93% committed additional criminal offenses as adults (West & Farrington, 1977).

As might be expected, recidivist delinquents account for an inordinant amount of total juvenile offenses. The recidivists in Wolfgang *et al.* (1972) comprised 18.7% of the total sample of youths and committed 84% of all recorded offenses (using police contact, not court adjudication, as the delinquency criterion). Chronic offenders, comprising only 6.3% of the total sample, committed 52% of all offenses. It is clear that a small minority of youths are responsible for the majority of social costs that accrue to juvenile misconduct.

Two other logical but important points are known about recidivists. They begin their delinquent careers earlier, and they commit more serious offenses (Osborn & West, 1979; Wadsworth, 1979; West & Farrington, 1977; Wolfgang *et al.,* 1972). Wadsworth (1979) reported that the average child's age at the point of first offense was 15.5. However, the average age for first offenses among recidivist delinquents was 13.5. Wolfgang *et al.* (1972) reported similar findings. Children who engaged in preadolescent delinquent acts at age 7 averaged 7.5 recorded offenses through adolescence; those who started at age 17 averaged 1.2 offenses. Number of police contacts correlated −.99 with age of first offense! The seriousness of offenses was also inversely correlated with age of onset (−.57). The highest seriousness-of-offense score was obtained for preadolescent delinquents who recorded their first offense at age 12.

Taken together, these data demonstrate that the recidivist delinquent tends to engage in more severe and numerous offenses, to start offending in pre- or early adolescence, and to establish a pattern of antisocial behavior that continues into adulthood. Portions of this group meet the definition of preadolescent delinquency and are high-risk candidates for severe maladjustment. It is difficult, however, to restrict maladjustment to this group or to imply that all recidivist delinquents exhibit psychopathology. The designation of "officially delinquent" is the result of apprehension by authorities. Undoubtedly, some children fitting the behavioral definition of preadolescent delinquent would not be apprehended by authorities or would not be caught on multiple occasions. Similarly, chronic antisocial behavior patterns are not restricted to adolescence, so studies measuring recidivism only during this period underestimate recidivism. For example, 56% of West and Farrington's (1973) sample were one-time offenders as juveniles. By age 21, only 26% were single-offense delinquents, and the base rate of conviction had risen from 21% to 30% of all male youths (West & Farrington, 1977). Taking chronic delinquents as a conservative estimate of children meeting the preadolescent delinquency criteria of maladjustment, then approximately 6.5% of the male population demonstrates high-risk characteristics. Since the present chapter does not equate psychopathology with delinquency, the next issue becomes "high-risk for what"?

Delinquency Prognosis

One of the first studies to report on the long-term adjustment of antisocial children was by Morris, Escoll, and Wexler (1956). These researchers followed-up a sample of children referred to a clinic for conduct disorders prior to age 15. As adults, 79% of the sample suffered from inadequate social adjustment. Surprisingly, in addition to a prevalence of criminal activity, 20% of the sample were classified psychotic. The finding that antisocial children were at-risk for a range of debilitating adult problems, including psychiatric disorders, was prescient of results that were to come from ensuing studies.

Probably the best known and documented of these was the follow-up study by Robins (1966). This study collected life adjustment data on nearly 500 individuals 30 years after they had been referred to a community mental health center. Approximately 60% of the sample had been referred for antisocial behavior, 23% for other child psychiatric problems, and 17% comprised a nonproblem comparison group. Of the antisocial children, 71% experienced later arrest, and 50% had multiple arrests and were incarcerated. Antisocial children were more likely to experience a broad range of life adjustment difficulties than were other children. These difficulties included marital conflict, unemployment, alcoholism, and overriding inadequacy in social relationships. Of the antisocial referrals, 28% were diagnosed as having sociopathic personality patterns. This rate was seven times higher than other clinic referred children and 14 times higher than the control group. Closer examination of the sociopathic adults showed that they tended to initiate antisocial behavior at a young age (i.e., 8–10) and committed multiple, diverse delinquent acts. Nearly 50% of the children who exhibited 10 or more antisocial symptoms became sociopathic adults. Equally as important, no adult was diagnosed as sociopathic without a juvenile record of severe delinquent activity. Thus, the absence of severe antisocial characteristics in childhood was 100% predictive of the absence of sociopathic personalities in adulthood. The presence of these characteristics in childhood was approximately 50% accurate in predicting adult sociopathic deviance. Adults with childhood histories of antisocial behavior who did not meet the criteria for classification as sociopathic personalities suffered in other ways. Only 16% of this group were considered to be free of psychological disturbance. Others evidenced symptoms of psychosis, alcoholism, and incapacitating social inadequacy.

More recent studies (Gersten, Langner, & Simcha-Fagan, 1979; McCord, 1978, 1979; Robins, 1978) have continued to document the bleak adult outcome of children meeting the description of preadolescent delinquents. The early onset, diversity, and severity of the delinquent behavior in these children reflects an inability to function within the constraints of normal society. Although such patterns of behavior might not fit most conceptualizations of psychopathology, they underlie adult outcomes that span the breadth of psychiatric nosology.

Assessment

Delinquency is typically perceived as a behavioral rather than a psychological problem. Thus it is not surprising that, clinically, delinquency does not always require psychological testing for diagnosis. The primary means of diagnosis comes from the reports of parents and/or community agents (e.g., schools, juvenile court), who indicate that a child is engaging in delinquent behaviors. In addition to these reports, some agencies/clinicians administer standardized instruments to provide ancillary information regarding a child's personality and/or behavioral profile. These instruments include self-esteem and attitudinal measures as well as standardized behavioral checklists.

Predictive Assessment

These methods of diagnosis are relatively accurate at identifying youth who engage in delinquent behaviors. Although the effects of these behaviors on the environment provide appropriate rationales for parental concern and therapeutic intervention, of greater importance is the predictive validity of these behaviors for later child and adult pathology. Although many studies have demonstrated certain long-range risk characteristics of samples of severely delinquent children, none has accurately predicted high-risk populations using these characteristics. As mentioned earlier, Robins (1966) reported that 50% of her sample who demonstrated the most severe antisocial behavior (e.g., truancy, theft, drug and alcohol abuse) in childhood did not exhibit sociopathic personalities as adults. Other studies that have attempted to predict severe adolescent delinquency have tended to correctly predict only 40–50% of children exhibiting the risk characteristic of concern (cf. West & Farrington, 1973, 1977). An exception to this was a study by Moore, Chamberlain, and Mukai (1979) in which they correctly discriminated 80% of their sample. Parental report of stealing by the child at age 6 to 10 was highly predictive of recidivistic adolescent delinquency. While results of this study require replication, they suggest that certain behaviors evidenced at an early stage may prove to be marker variables for later psychopathology. Some data exist that suggest the need for even more in-depth investigation of factors regarding delinquent behaviors. The location (e.g., home, community) of the committed act and the adults involved (e.g., parent, teachers, police) have been reported to be important by Robins (1966). Wadsworth (1979) suggests that severity of the behavior (as measured by social acceptability, value, etc.) may be indicative of continued child or adult maladjustment.

Characteristics other than a child's past or current behavioral repertoire are also important to attend to when attempting to discern the long-term prognosis of children. These include such factors as parental conflict, social isolation of the family, parenting styles, and family demographic variables. These factors will be discussed in greater detail later in this chapter.

Treatment Decisions

At the point when children are referred for treatment, it is not possible to accurately predict who will accrue multiple offenses in the future and who will not. Without such information, determining who should receive treatment and what treatment methods should be used remain largely unanswerable questions. Given these uncertainties, three approaches could be taken by clinicians for determining who to treat, and what techniques to employ. First, because the majority of juvenile offenses are committed by a minority of juvenile offenders (Wolfgang *et al.*, 1972), clinicians might choose to treat only those youth who have committed multiple offenses. However, there are problems with this approach. Historically, chronic juvenile offenders have either not benefited from treatment or have not maintained treatment gains. In addition, the service mandates of most public mental health service organizations would not allow for such stringent screening of clients. Given that chronic delinquents are generally considered untreatable and that most agencies are unable to screen and treat only this select population, a second treatment strategy might be taken. This approach would focus on the early identification of children who engage in delinquent behavior. Targets of such a strategy would include those children referred at an early age or who have committed a first offense. While this approach seems logical from an early intervention standpoint, there is mounting evidence to suggest that psychological interventions on these populations may have detrimental effects on later adjustment. Given the implications that such evidence has for the treatment of delinquents, these findings will be reviewed in some detail.

McCord (1978) reported on the adjustment patterns of over 500 men who had taken part in the Cambridge–Somerville Youth Study 30 years earlier. This group was comprised of men who had been treated during the course of the study and a matched, nontreated control group. Questionnaire responses concerning current life status were received from

54% of the treatment group and 60% of the control group. Official records on criminal activity were available for the entire original sample. McCord reported no difference in the occurrence of criminal activity in either minor or severe categories between the two groups. The only statistically significant difference was that criminals from the treatment group were slightly more likely to commit more than one crime than were criminals from the control group. The criminal record data indicated that treatment had failed to alter either adolescent or adult criminal behavior. In other spheres of adult adjustment, there were either no differences between groups or the treatment group tended to fare worse. Men who had been in the treatment program were more likely to be alcoholic, to show signs of serious mental illness, to die younger, to evidence stress-related diseases, to be employed in lower status occupations, and to report dissatisfaction with their employment. Even though the treated group evidenced multiple signs of adjustment difficulties in adulthood, the majority still perceived the treatment program as beneficial. McCord (1978) interpreted the increased adjustment problems in the treated group as resulting directly from the treatment experience and cautioned that "intervention programs risk damaging the individuals they are designed to assist" (p. 289).

Gersten *et al.* (1979) followed up approximately 70% of the 1,034 families in their original study, and grouped the children into those who had never been referred for treatment and those who had. The type and severity of problem behaviors exhibited in the first study by the referred-for-treatment group were matched with children from the never-referred group. This provided two samples with similar adjustment problems at Time One, which differed as to whether they had been referred or not referred for treatment. Gersten *et al.* reported that the never-referred group showed the lowest rates of disturbance across all ages and across all problem behaviors. The mean pathology for the never-referred group at Time Two was 18%. This compared with the pathology rate of 38% in the referred group at Time Two. The finding that the referred group had a higher incidence of pathology was strongest for children exhibiting delinquent behaviors. Preadolescent children referred for delinquent behavior had "the highest rate of future disturbance (64%) noted for any age referred for any other type of disturbance" (p. 139).

A carefully designed and executed prospective study by Cass and Thomas (1979) reported similar findings. This study followed up 200 children seen at a child guidance clinic for a variety of referral problems when they were approximately 9½ years of age. At the time of follow-up contact, the sample averaged 21 years of age. At the time of original clinic referral, all children had gone through extensive psychiatric evaluation and all children were judged maladjusted enough to warrant treatment. Approximately 25% of the sample refused treatment after the intake evaluation. This provided the study with a group of clinic-treated children and a group of children never treated who had identical problem symptoms at intake. Those adults who had received treatment as children demonstrated more severe social maladjustment than those who had refused treatment.

The results of these three studies are clear. Treatment not only did not appear to benefit recipients, but it consistently was associated with increased maladjustment. Although the results are consistent, explanations of these findings vary. It might well be that those children whose families accepted treatment were more seriously disturbed than those not referred or those who refused treatment. This is not evident from data collected on the families. However, the possibility exists that the behavioral and psychiatric assessment procedures were not sensitive to the appropriate differences. A second explanation concerns the sensitivity of the parents to the problem behavior of the child. Given similar behavior problems, some parents may be overanxious concerning the problems that resulted in clinic referral. The combination of behavior problem and anxious parent may result in continued amplification of the problem, thus accounting for differences in treated and non-nontreated groups. Neither of these two explanations is applicable to McCord's (1978) outcome data because these children were assigned social workers and were not self-selected clinic referrals. A third explanation concerns labeling effects that emanate from treatment status. An individual identified as being in need of psychological treatment may suffer adverse side effects due to real or perceived negative sanctions from family and community members. A fourth explanation is that treatment produces direct effects that are detrimental to the adjustment of the child. This could result from failure of the treatment program to alter referral problems, leaving families resigned to their continuance.

The reports of negative effects accruing to children who have received psychological treatment illustrate the need for clinicians to exercise caution when applying interventions. This calls attention to the third possible approach to deal with delinquency. This approach would deemphasize psychological treatment of youth referred for committing delinquent behavior, and instead promote innocuous educative programs directed at both the youth and other important persons within their environment (e.g., parents, teachers, peers, etc.). The emphasis of such programs would be to provide information (e.g., legal, employment, social service), skills training (e.g., child management techniques for parents and teachers, tutoring or communication skills for youth), and opportunities for these people to form mutual support groups. Such endeavors would be oriented toward the probable causal factors behind preadolescent delinquency that are detailed in the following sections.

Etiological Considerations

Thus far, the chapter has described delinquency in terms of patterns of child behavior. These patterns represent the outcome of developmental histories that encompass a multitude of influential variables and events. An etiological investigation of delinquent behavior is confronted with compiling relevant variables and then attempting to determine those with apparent causal relationships with behavior development, those with correlative relationships, or those without discernable systematic relationships. In an arena as complex as the development of behavior, such a task becomes exceedingly difficult. The difficulty is not one of compiling sufficient variables, but one of sorting through the myriad associated variables to arrive at a comprehensible model of behavior development that still reflects the complexity of behavioral outcomes. In the present etiological discussion of delinquency, a few theoretical assumptions and perspectives have aided in deriving the core of probable causal factors described and in integrating them into a mode of behavior development. Since these perspectives have been influential guides in constructing this section, it is necessary to briefly describe them.

The first of these is a social learning perspective on the development of behavior. Social learning indicates that children develop social behavior according to their experiences and interactions within their environment. Such experiential learning instills basic competencies that direct the course of later behavior. Environments and interactive variables can be grouped according to the probable level of their influence on child development. In the current case, primary variables are considered to be those that stem from the parent–child relationship. The primacy, continuity, and intensity of this relationship equip it to have unparalleled influence on child behavior, especially prior to adolescence. Secondary variables include aspects of the family environment that affect the parent–child relationship and child experiences in settings outside the home. Bronfenbrenner (1979a,b) and Hartup (1979) have both described primary influences as providing basic learning experiences that are then practiced and modified in secondary settings. Thus, the social learning perspective aids the etiological investigation by directing attention to environmental conditions and circumstances and by providing an initial framework for sorting the probable magnitude of variable influence.

The second theoretical assumption concerns the manner in which influences on behavior function within and across settings. It is assumed that variables and settings affect behavior in a complex, fully interactive fashion. This indicates that behavioral influences and developmental patterns are reciprocal. Methods used by a parent to socialize a child are affected by child behavior (and vice versa), and both child and parent behaviors develop and change over time. Likewise, the impact of settings (e.g., school, church, neighborhood) on child behavior is determined by specific reciprocal events that take place within the setting and by secondary influences resulting from intersetting networks and linkages. Such an interactive model of behavior development not only predicts complex channels of behavioral influence but reduces the expectation of simple linear or additive effects on behavior from identified causal variables. Bronfenbrenner (1979b), in his detailed elaboration on the ecology of human development, states, *"in ecological research, the principal main effects are likely to be interactions"* (p. 38). Thus, an etiological description of delinquency development can be expected to derive a set of probable causal factors that operate in a complex fashion in which the effects of any given variable must be examined in relationship to all other variables.

The third assumption is that the acquisition and use of social behavior follows a basic developmental process. This process is assumed to be the same for both adjusted and maladjusted individuals. Differences in outcome result from differential experiences during stages of development. Elucidation of the specifics of this process requires that data be examined from studies of both socially maladjusted (in this case delinquent) and socially adjusted children. This avoids a common error in etiological descriptions of deviancy. There is a tendency to offer causal explanations based on factors that are observed to occur in problem families without determining the likelihood of the occurrence of these factors in the general population. A high rate of occurrence of "causal" factors in the general population would question their status as causal agents in delinquency. Equally as important, primary causes of maladjustment may stem from factors that *fail* to occur in problem families. Maladjustment resulting from nonoccurrence of critical factors would not be discovered unless factors leading to normative adjustment were also studied. In the following section major variables associated with delinquency will be presented, and these will then be contrasted with findings from research on normative development.

The final guideline concerns the selection of studies and findings presented in the discussion of delinquency etiology. The previous perspectives help narrow a broad, multidisciplinary field to studies examining family functioning, family–community factors, and developmental aspects of social competence. Within these general areas an attempt was made to apply a selection criterion of "nonsystematic" replication. Findings that repeatedly occurred across diverse disciplines, data sources, and study objectives were included. This diversity, especially across sociological and psychological disciplines, demanded a loose conceptualization of replication. However, the generalizability of the discussion was aided by this process.

As stated previously, the parent–child relationship is viewed as the primary force that shapes the course of behavior development in children. Children are presumed to emerge from this lengthy, intense relationship equipped with sufficient skills to function and develop within adult social arenas. It is clear that this does not always occur. Three areas of parent–child functioning have been identified as having etiological significance for differential child outcomes. These are: (1) the quality of the parent–child affiliative relationship; (2) the style and consistency of parental supervision; and (3) the quality of parental socialization of the child. Data to support the importance of these areas are presented from studies of delinquency development and more normative investigations of social competence. Social competence represents a complex construct not readily defined or measured (cf. Zigler & Trickett, 1979). It refers to the ability of a child to function in a wide range of social arenas (family, school, peer groups) at a level meeting or exceeding normative social expectations. As a construct, social competence reflects the integration of the cognitive, affective, and behavioral skills of the individual. It also offers the advantage of providing a continuous measure of social adjustment across the maladjustment–adjustment range. Because of its predominance in the delinquency literature, parental supervision is discussed first.

Style and Consistency of Parental Supervision of the Child

Methods of parental discipline have consistently been related to child adjustment. Glueck and Glueck (1950) reported that fathers using erratic, overly strict, or physically punitive disciplinary techniques had a high probability of having delinquent sons. Similarly, McCord and McCord (1959) showed that, among families of similar social circumstance, those exhibiting lax or erratic discipline techniques had a high probability of having a delinquent child, while those using strict or love-oriented techniques did not. Numerous other studies of delinquent and normative populations have reported that hostile, permissive, or overly strict parental discipline was associated with antisocial behavior in children (Robins, 1966; Suh & Carlson, 1977; West & Farrington, 1973). In a study of violent juvenile delinquents, Lewis, Shanok, Pincus, and Glaser (1979) reported that the most violent offenders were much more likely to have experienced physically abusive punishment than were their less violent counterparts. Although most of these studies used different descriptions for styles of parental discipline, they all indicated that specific techniques of discipline have an important impact on child adjustment. It would appear that physically punitive, lax, and erratic disciplinary styles are most closely associated with delinquent behavior patterns in children.

The consistency with which a particular style of parental discipline is applied has also been repeatedly associated with child adjustment. McCord and McCord (1959) concluded that "the *consistency* of parental behavior is more important than the methods parents use for enforcing their demands" (p. 78). Consistent application of any of the disciplinary styles described by the McCords decreased the likelihood of delinquent behavior in the child. Disciplinary style and consistency of application interacted in a logical fashion of severity. For example, punitive discipline, as defined by the McCords, was associated with decreased delinquency when it was consistently applied. However, inconsistent, punitive discipline was associated with high rates of delinquency and proved to be more detrimental than inconsistent, love-oriented discipline. More recently, McCord (1979) demonstrated the power of specific parental characteristics to account for variance in adult adjustment. This study classified the family environment of over 200 adolescents according to style of parental discipline, style of parent interaction (e.g., aggressive, affectionate), and family social status. The criminal records and life-adjustment of the former adolescents were determined 30 years later. The family factors were then used in a multiple-regression analysis to account for adult criminal behavior. McCord found that 39% of the variance in adult outcome was accounted for by style and consistency of child supervision (26%), style of interaction (7%), and social status (6%). A discriminate function alaysis using the family environment variables correctly identified 74% of all men according to their criminal record (i.e., both criminal and noncriminal). These results clearly point to the importance of styles of parental supervision in determining life-course adjustment patterns.

These delinquency studies demonstrate that parental supervision and discipline are important variables associated with child and adult adjustment patterns. This importance is bolstered by laboratory studies demonstrating the effects of inconsistent, erratic punishment on behavior. Warren and Cairns (1972) showed that children experiencing noncontingent consequences for behavior tended not to alter their behavior in situations where consequences were contingently applied. It is reasonable to assume that children who naturally establish maladjusted behavior patterns under these conditions will be resistant to changing their behavior by the application of consistent discipline strategies. Sawin and Parke (1979) showed, in addition, that the application of inconsistent punishment resulted in more aggressive responses on the part of children than did a condition of consistent punishment. Children experiencing inconsistent punishment again demonstrated greater resistance to change under both an extinction and punishment condition (Deur & Parke, 1971). Taken together, these studies demonstrate that application of erratic, noncontingent, aversive behavior results in aggressive response patterns that are highly resistant to change even when subjected to consistent, contingent punishment.

Similar indications of the importance of parental discipline have been reported from child development research. Prominent in this area has been the programmatic research of Baumrind (1968, 1971, 1973, 1975, 1978). This research has focused on specific styles of parental discipline in child rearing and the affects of these styles on later social competence of children. Three major styles of parenting were differentiated. The first of these was termed "authoritarian" and was typified by the use of forceful methods in a superordinate/subordinate parent–child relationship. The second type was "permissive," characterized by a benign stance toward the child in which the parents acted as resources but not as active child-control agents. The third type was "authoritative," characterized by consistent use of power and reason in directing the child's behavior. Children raised by both authoritarian and permissive parents were more likely to demonstrate antisocial behavior problems. Authoritative parents were associated with the highest level of social competence in children. It is interesting to note that these parents altered their supervisory techniques as the child matured. In early childhood, authoritative parents used consistent, contingent social approval and disapproval. After their child reached 6 years of age, these parents increasingly provided rationales, consistent punishment, and used empathic role taking and argumentive discourse when interacting with their child. Argumentive discourse, as defined in this study, did not reflect angry confrontation but the opportunity for the child to question and contradict the parent. Baumrind summarized the benefits of authoritative parenting styles as stemming from the consistency of parental control, the use of reasoning, and the increasing maturity demands to the child. These benefits were elaborated by Lamb and Baumrind (1978). They attributed the beneficial effects of authoritative parents to the use of direct teaching methods, consistent restraints on behavior, and parental attention to and involvement with differential stages and temperaments of the child. This latter quality stresses the changing, interactive nature of the parent–child relationship over time. Several additional specific points were also summarized. Social competence in children was associated with consistent parental punishment, even corporal punishment, when it was administered immediately following transgressions and coupled with appropriate rationales for the action. Parental warmth was seen as beneficial, although not necessary when coupled with firm parental control. In contrast, parental use of inconsistent, repressive, or hostile punishment was associated with antisocial behavior, especially in male children.

Zahn-Waxler, Radke-Yarrow, and King (1979) also reported differential parental responsiveness to child's transgressions as being related to differential social competence in children. Mothers who responded to misbehavior with high intensity and with cognitive and affective clarity had children who were highly competent. The maternal responses to these children were often emotionally laden and, at times, harshly enforced. These authors implicated the use of appropriate but widely divergent emotional affect on the part of the mothers as being a key characteristic in promoting competence. It appeared that these mothers displayed a wide range of emotion, punitiveness, and consequences for varying child misbehavior. Grusec and Kuczynski (1980) reported that mothers of normal children responded on the basis of the particular child transgression when determining the appropriate discipline. As opposed to favoring a specific discipline style, these mothers chose what was deemed appropriate according to the behavior of the child, demonstrating again the interactive nature of parent–child relationships.

Studies conducted from both the delinquency and child development perspectives point to the importance of style and consistency of parental discipline on the development of behavior patterns in children. More importantly, similarity was found across studies in specific methods that promoted or hindered social adjustment. Consistent, contingent parental disciplinary practices that were accompanied by rationales and appropriate affective demeanor appeared to provide clear benefits for child development. Conversely, inconsistent, permissive, or physically punitive discipline was related to delinquency in children.

Parent–Child Affiliative Relationship

Affiliative aspects of the parent–child relationship comprise a second dimension that has been related to adjustment patterns in children. McCord and McCord (1959) characterized families as being: (1) cohesive; (2) quarrelsome but affectionate; or (3) quarrelsome and neglecting. They showed that quarrelsome, neglecting homes exhibited the highest rates of delinquency as measured by both child conviction and incarceration. This dimension interacted with disciplinary techniques. Love-oriented, consistent disciplinary techniques mitigated the negative affects of quarrelsome homes, while inconsistent and physically punitive disciplinary techniques amplified those effects. Although the samples were very small, families having a combination of inappropriate disciplinary techniques and poor affiliative relationships exhibited delinquency rates of 75–100%. McCord and McCord (1959) differentiated child effects according to parent. Nonaffectionate fathers were associated with families having the highest rates of delinquency. This was especially true when nonaffectionate fathers and erratic discipline were combined. Nonaffectionate mothers and indifferent mothers were both associated with high rates of delinquency. More recent longitudinal studies have continued to demonstrate the importance of affective variables in the family. West and Farrington (1973) reported that boys of parents rated as lacking affection, neglectful, or indifferent, frequently became delinquent. Similarly, Wadsworth (1979) indicated that parents rated as having low concern for their child were more likely to have delinquent children.

Direct observation of parent–child interaction also supports affiliative differences among families. Reid and Hendricks (1979) reported that families with delinquent children tended to have rates of aversive behaviors intermediate to those families with young, acting-out children or nonproblem children. However, these families had the lowest rates of positive social interaction of the groups studied. These families exhibited a restricted range of affect, especially in the direction of affectionate behavior. It is interesting to note the similarity to previously cited studies (Zahn-Waxler *et al.,* 1979) stressing the importance of appropriate use of a full range of affect on the part of the parent in promoting social competence in children.

Affiliative aspects of the parent–child relationship, primarily those of the mother and infant, have received considerable attention within the child development field. Primary within this area has been the work of Ainsworth and her associates (Ainsworth, 1979; Ainsworth & Bell, 1974; Ainsworth, Blehar, Waters, & Wall, 1978). These researchers developed the "strange situation" procedure that entails observing child behavior before, during, and after a brief period of separation from the mother, as a measure of mother–infant attachment.

Data from this procedure were used to classify mother–infant dyads into three groups according to the quality of the attachment bond. In two of these groups the infant was described as insecurely or anxiously attached. The third was described as securely attached. Securely attached infants were characterized as using mother as a base from which to explore novel surroundings. On separation from mother, they expressed distress, as evidence by a reduction in exploration and in some cases crying. On reunion with mother, these infants sought close bodily contact or at least interaction with their mothers prior to resuming exploration. Of the two groups of insecure, anxiously attached infants, one demonstrated distress throughout the exploratory and separation phases and showed ambivalence in seeking proximity to mother during the reunion phase. The second group showed stress during the separation phase and mixed approach and avoidance behaviors during the reunion phase.

Studies of parent–child interaction in the home later demonstrated that children who were securely attached had mothers who were responsive, sensitive, and provided consistent expectatons (Ainsworth, 1979). In contrast, anxiously attached children had mothers who tended to avoid close physical contact, were more rejecting and angry, demonstrated a restricted affective range, and failed to provide consistent patterns of parenting. Differences in the social competence of differentially attached children were investigated in a study by Matas, Arend, and Sroufe (1978). In this study, infants were classified using the strange-situation procedure at age 1 and were then observed in a preschool setting years later. Children who were identified at age 1 as securely attached, were found to be more cooperative, less aggressive, and better problem solvers as preschool children than their anxiously attached peers. They also appeared to be more socially competent and demonstrated more empathic behavior. Children from the insecure and anxiously attached groups were aggressive, noncompliant, less competent, and less persistent in problem-solving situations.

These data indicated that both mother and child behaviors can differentiate levels of attachment in young infants. In turn, differences in the mother–child attachment bond were associated with behavior patterns in early school years indicating different levels of social competence. It would appear that a secure mother–child relationship (or at least guardian–

child relationship) is a necessary ingredient for promoting adjustment in children. However, other aspects of attachment indicate that this is a complex concept that interacts with additional variables. It should be noted that Ainsworth (1979) does not view the early attachment as corresponding to a "critical period." Instead, she contends that importance of the attachment stems from the continuity of environmental factors associated with it. The importance of this continuity was demonstrated in a study by Vaughn, Egeland, and Sroufe (1979). This study reported that familial instability resulting from life change situations such as parental disorganization and frequent moves was associated with insecure children. Changes from insecure to secure attachment in these children took place during periods in which the family's instability was significantly reduced. This indicated that the attachment bond was sensitive to disruptive influences but apparently could be reestablished, given favorable change.

Rutter (1979a), while not arguing in support of the concept of critical periods in attachment, discussed age limitations on acquiring potentially protective benetifts of this bond. Citing data from Tizard and Rees (1975) and Tizard and Tizard (1971), Rutter reported that children adopted after the age of 4 developed apparently deep attachments with adoptive parents. However, these late adopted children showed behavioral and attentional problems in school that were identical to children that had remained institutionalized and had not established an attachment bond. These data suggest that selective attachment must occur in early childhood (i.e., prior to 4 years of age) in order to prevent potential socialization problems in middle childhood. The research of Kennell, Voos, and Klaus (1979) indicates that a critical period for optimal parent–child bonding exists within the first few hours following birth. Their research showed affective and behavioral differences in mother–infant pairs dependent on whether the mother had received the child for close bodily contact immediately following delivery or did not receive the child for the first time until 12 hours following birth. Although not relating this early bonding experience to antisocial behavior, follow-up studies reported differences in social competence at 2 years of age between these groups, with the early-contact mothers engaging their children in greater social interaction.

A final point on attachment in children was discussed by Sroufe (1979). Sroufe noted that attachment should not be viewed as a specific behavior but rather as a construct indicating a constellation and integration of behaviors. This is evidenced from the fact that attachment differences are not reflected in the specific rate or duration of individual child behaviors (e.g., all children might cry during the strange-situation procedure). Instead, differences emanate from the organization of patterns of behavior that are engaged in under specific conditions. The distinction that knowledge of organization or patterning aspects of behavior provide more functional information than a simplistic occurrence/nonoccurrence dimension of behavior is an important conceptual point when viewing behavior from an interactional perspective.

Both delinquency and child development research indicate an association between the parent–child affiliative relationship and child behavior patterns. The two bodies of literature were not as comparable as those from the discussion of disciplinary practices because of the nonoverlapping age ranges studied. If one were to assume that a comparatively cold, detached parent–child relationship evidenced from infancy through preschool would continue throughout childhood, then the results could be viewed as similar. Poor affiliative relationships were descriptive of preschool children who tended to be aggressive and noncompliant. They also were associated with, and appeared to amplify, delinquency problems during adolescence. Conversely, loving, affiliative relationships were associated with socially competent preschool children and appeared to lessen the impact of other adverse qualities of the parent–child relationship in adolescence.

Parental Socialization of the Child

Socialization effects refer to interactive processes that educate the child as to "appropriate" behavior and social expectations on behavior. "Appropriate" would be defined by the specific social setting and might or might not conform to broader social norms and values. Parental role modeling and the quality of parent–child interaction have emerged as influential variables in child socialization. These factors obviously overlap and interact with the previous areas mentioned. However, unlike the previous areas, socialization effects cannot be circumscribed by the programmatic research of a few investigators. It is a more elusive area that currently has a weaker empirical basis than the other aspects of the parent–child relationship. This does not indicate that child socialization is a less important variable in behavior development, rather that this is a relatively new area of research with an emerging data base.

Behavior patterns modeled and promoted by parents have long been associated with development of similar patterns of behavior in children. Both fathers and mothers whose life styles are counter to normal social expectations (e.g., criminal, promiscuous, alcoholic) increase the probability of having delinquent sons (McCord & McCord, 1959). A positive relationship between paternal criminality and child delinquency has been repeatedly reported (Glueck & Glueck, 1950; Osborn & West, 1979; West & Farrington, 1977). However, this probably reflects more of an adherence to deviant values by the father than direct modeling of criminal behavior. Parental modeling of aggressive or violent behavior appears to have a stronger direct relationship to child aggression. The research of Straus, Gelles, and Steinmetz (1980) demonstrated that use of physical violence during family conflict increased use of violent behavior by children. These same children as adults were also more likely to use violent methods during family conflict. Lewis *et al.* (1979) studied a group of violent and nonviolent delinquents. They concluded that the major differentiating factors were that the violent delinquents had witnessed an extreme violent incidence and/or had been the victims of a violent attack (e.g., child abuse). Use of severe physical punishment for child transgressions also characterized the upbringing of the aggressive delinquents studied by Welsh (1976). Indirect support for modeling effects also comes from direct observation studies, showing that children with aggressive behavior problems were immersed in a family system in which nearly all family members engaged in similar styles of aversive behavior (Moore, 1975; Patterson, 1976). Finally, the laboratory research of Bandura (1977) has long supported modeling effects on the development of aggressive behavior in children.

Socializing influences leading to social competence in children appear to be related to both parental modeling and specific aspects of parent–child interaction. Zahn-Waxler *et al.* (1979) reported that mothers of competent children modeled altruistic behaviors and used empathic care-giving techniques. Their children, in turn, also demonstrated higher rates of these behaviors in settings outside the home. As mentioned earlier, Baumrind (1978) reported that authoritative parents engaged in empathic role taking and encouraged and promoted argumentive discourse in parent–child interactions. Wilton and Barbour (1978) noted that mothers of low-risk children (i.e., high competence) engaged in direct didactic teaching, encouraged the child to engage in activities, and were more successful in controlling their children than were mothers of high-risk children. These findings stand in bold contrast to observational studies of delinquent children that indicate low levels of parent–child interaction and detached autonomous functioning of each member of the family (Reid & Hendricks, 1973).

Experimental evidence on the importance of specific styles of adult–child interaction on child behavior has come from the research of Shure and Spivack (1979a,b, 1980). These investigators trained teachers to systematically engage preschool and kindergarten children in interactions designed to promote the child's thinking about alternative solutions to problems and about consequences of behavior (Shure & Spivack, 1979a, 1980). Children receiving this training demonstrated reduced impulsivity and aggressiveness and increased problem-solving abilities. The same program was instituted in the home setting by training low-income mothers in the interactive techniques (Shure & Spivack, 1979b). This training resulted in improved problem-solving skills on the part of the mothers and the children. In addition, the children showed improved behavior in the school setting following the training that took place in the home. A similar line of research has been carried out by Sigel and his associates (McGillicuddy-DeLisi & Sigel, 1980; McGillicuddy-DeLisi, Sigel, & Johnson, 1979; Sigel, 1979). This research related the use of "distancing strategies" by parents to increased cognitive development and representation in children. "Distancing strategies" were open ended questions and thought-provoking statements made by parents (e.g., "What can you tell me about the boy in the story?" = good distancing strategy; versus, "What was the boy's name?" = poor distancing strategy). Sigel (1979) reported differential ability to respond to distancing questions between low-income, disadvantaged children and normal children. This difficulty was overcome through subsequent exposure to good distancing strategies. McGillicuddy-DeLisi *et al.* (1979) observed mother–child interaction in a laboratory situation. They found that lower class, high-risk families engaged in fewer distancing behaviors than low-risk families. The mothers who used more distancing strategies in the laboratory tests had children who performed significantly better on social-cognitive tasks.

The research on child socialization within the family points to an important although understudied area. It appeared that parents who actively engaged their children in interactions that demonstrated appropriate affective behavior, that promoted the child to think about behavioral consequences, and that promoted problem-solving skills were fostering development of socially competent children. This stands in contrast to data describing families with delinquent children as having low levels of parent–child interaction that tended to be of an aversive quality when it occurred. Given that social competence requires a high level of integration of emotive, cognitive, and behavioral skills, a lengthy childhood period characterized by increasing integrative demands from parents could be hypothesized to be responsible for competent behavioral outcomes.

Integration of Parent–Child Relationship Variables

Data from both an adjustment and maladjustment perspective have indicated that similar specific areas of the parent–child relationship were related to the level of social adjustment in children. This similarity, based on research having different objectives, designs, and measures, provides a firm basis for projecting data robustness and generalizability. In addition, this convergence supports the concept of a single developmental process leading to adjusted or maladjusted patterns of behavior in children. Overlaying a developmental perspective on the three aspects of parent–child relationship discussed permits the construction of a simplistic conceptualization of how this process might function. Developmentally, onset of the three aspects of the parent–child relationship would occur in the order of: (1) affiliative relationship; (2) consistency and style of parental discipline; and (3) parental socialization of the child. These factors are viewed as functioning in accumulative, sequential fashion in which the effects accrued from one aspect provide a necessary foundation for realizing the benefits of following aspects. Parent–child attachment represents the first formulation of the relationship between parent and child. It carries obvious importance for the early care and nurturance of the child. In addition, it is viewed as creating an affective power base that the parent draws on to initiate behavior control over a young child. A strong affiliative relationship facilitates acquisition of control, while a weak relationship hinders such acquisition.

The second factor is the method used by parents to control child behavior. Effective control requires clearly delineated limits on behavior that are consistently and contingently enforced. The use of inconsistent or permissive styles of discipline would lead to difficult-to-control children regardless of the attachment relationship. The use of consistent and contingent control techniques would undoubtedly acquire an appropriate level of control over an insecurely attached child. However, it is assumed that this would occur only at the cost of increased parental attention and disciplinary efforts. Once an appropriate level of control is achieved, then increased use of rationales and indirect control methods are viewed as increasing child competence by avoiding demanding confrontations and by setting up situations that require the child to think about behavior and its consequences.

The final factor, parental socialization of the child, would be predicated on adequate child management. Without appropriate levels of control, parent–child interaction tends to be dominated by conflict and ineffectual attempts at enforcing control. Interaction of this type precludes use of the positive socialization techniques described in previous sections. In turn, effective child management does not assure positive socialization. However, given a lack of parent–child conflict and a positive, affiliative relationship, the likelihood of extended parent–child interaction would be increased. It is hypothesized that socially competent behavior in adolescence results from consistent, repeated, and lengthy exposure to normative socializing influences throughout the childhood period. Children experiencing erratic, inappropriate socialization and inconsistent control throughout this period would be expected to lack high levels of emotive, cognitive, and behavioral integration, and thus be high-risk candidates for delinquency disorders.

The quality of these parental influences would be affected in an interactive fashion by specific child characteristics such as temperament and responsiveness. Stable patterns of child behavior, whether adjusted or maladjusted, would result from chronic exposure to specific combinations of parenting variables. It is assumed that the lengthy childhood socialization process allows for considerable disruption of positive influences as long as the disruptions are of short duration or do not occur at potentially critical developmental phases.

Secondary Influences: Contributory Factors

Although the parent–child relationship has been described as the primary force shaping child adjustment, this relationship itself is immersed within a realm of influences. An inadequate or inappropriate parental role in child rearing could result directly from lack of knowledge or socialization on the part of the parent. In addition, however, numerous environmental factors could have a direct impact on the parent's behavior, thus affecting the quality and stability of the parent–child relationship. Children also experience the direct socializing influences of encounters outside the home in community and school settings. These influences may, in turn, affect the parent–child relationship due to the reciprocal nature of such influences. These secondary variables are considered in the following discussions.

Family and Community Environment

A myriad of social and environmental factors impinge on family systems. While the majority of these factors may not directly confront the child, innumerable indirect effects can accrue due to the impact these factors have on other family members. Many family environmental factors have been found to be associated with delinquent patterns of behavior in children. Probably the most salient of these factors is the quality of the marital relationship. Numerous studies have reported increased incidence of delinquency in families characterized by high levels of parental conflict (McCord, 1979; Schwarz, 1979; Rutter, 1979b; Wadsworth, 1979). Heatherington (1979) reported that during the first two years following parental divorce, boys were especially prone to show developmental deviations such as aggression, noncompliance, and dependence. However, it appeared that maintenance of the family in the face of continued marital conflict provided a higher-risk environment than parental separation, a finding also reported by Rutter (1979b). Although the single-parent family potentially presented a healthier environment than the conflict-ridden nuclear family, the long-term outcome was highly dependent on whether disruption continued within the single-parent family (Heatherington, 1979). Parental separation and divorce has a differential impact on child behavior according to the age of the child. Children under the age of 5 who experienced divorce were more prone to develop problem behavior patterns than were older children (Heatherington, 1979; Wadsworth, 1979).

Other forms of family trauma and crisis have been associated with delinquency in children. These factors include early separation and hospitalization of the subsequent problem child (Douglas, 1966; Wadsworth, 1979), death of an immediate family member (Jones, Offord, & Abrams, 1980), and parental unemployment (Tonge, James, & Hillam, 1975; West & Farrington, 1973). Such factors provide increasing stress to the family system. Rutter (1979b) reported that accumulation of stress factors operated in a multiplicative as opposed to an additive fashion. Thus, four or more stressors accumulated by a family had an adverse effect on child behavior that was three times the effect of three or less factors. The reduction or elimination of family stressors has become the major focus of preventive programs in child deviance (*Report of The Task Panel on Prevention,* 1978).

Isolation from normal community imput and sanctions has been associated with numerous types of family disturbance and deviance. Social isolation was shown to be characteristic of families with child-abusing parents (Garbarino, 1977; Young, 1964), families with delinquency-prone children (Wahler, 1980), and families with diverse psychopathology (Tonge *et al.,* 1975). Tonge *et al.* (1975) showed that problem families had fewer contacts with relatives and neighbors and participated less in normal social activities than did normal control families living under similar environmental circumstances. These authors related social isolation to marital conflict and sociopathic or psychiatric disturbance in the parents as well as antisocial behavior problems in the children. Wahler (1980) showed that rates of parent–child aversive interaction covaried inversely with the number and quality of mothers' daily friendship contacts. In other words, days with high friendship contacts were associated with low rates of parent–child conflict, and days with low friendship contacts were associated with high rates. Wahler also reported a basic difference in the quantity and quality of out-of-home contacts according to social status of families with conduct problem children. Middle-income mothers were reported to have nearly four times the number of positive daily contacts than were lower income families. The majority of low-income mothers had outside contacts only with relatives or helping agencies, and generally reported such contacts as having an aversive quality. Previous research had reported drastic differences in the maintenance of treatment effects between similar low-income isolated families and middle-income families tied to community networks (Wahler & Moore, 1975). Wahler (1980) interpreted the failure of the isolated families to maintain treatment gains as resulting from the lack of community support mechanisms for appropriate child management skills learned during treatment. Recently, Hughey and Wahler (1980) reported a difference in social isolation between problem families whose children were referred for stealing versus those referred for other conduct problems (e.g., disobedience, whining). Families having children who stole tended to have fewer friendship contacts and more aversive extended family contacts than did families having children with other types of conduct disorders. This appeared to indicate that children from isolated families who engage in covert, asocial behavior may themselves also be removed from normalizing social influences of the broader community.

A similar view of community influences was reported by McCord and McCord (1959). They found that lack of family cohesiveness was highly predictive of delinquency only when the families lived in socially and physically deteriorated neighborhoods. The supportive influences of good neighborhoods supposedly mitigated the negative effects of poor family cohesiveness. It is interesting to note that children from good neighborhoods who became delinquent were more likely to "reform" as adults than were delinquents from poor neighborhoods. This indicated that potentially positive effects of living in a supportive community environment may have more impact on adult behavior than on adolescent behavior.

In addition to family crisis and social isolation variables, numerous studies have established the importance of specific family demographic characteristics in increasing the risk of delinquency in children. Characteristics that have consistently been related to such risk include lower socioeconomic status, poor housing conditions, and large families. While these and other factors appear to contribute to delinquency, their interactive nature makes it impossible to isolate a specific causal relationship. For example, lower socioeconomic levels have disproportionately added to delinquency, but this has been variously interpreted as a reflection of parental criminality (Robins, 1966), poor, overcrowded living conditions (West & Farrington, 1973), and mental or physical incapacitation of the working adults (Tonge *et al.*, 1975). Although existance of any one or a combination of demographic variables is neither necessary nor sufficient for the development of delinquency, certain variables have consistently shown strong relationships to increased risk and severity of delinquent acts. Low socioeconomic status has been shown to be strongly associated with both chronic delinquent populations and with those committing the most severe offenses (Johnson, 1980; Robins, 1966; Suh & Carlson, 1977; West & Farrington, 1973). Similarly, although poor, overcrowded housing conditions interact with social status, this factor has demonstrated an independent relationship with recidivistic delinquency (Robins, 1966; West & Farrington, 1973). Within a relatively homogenous lower class population, Tonge *et al.* (1975) reported that the most severe problem children were likely to come from families living in the worst housing conditions. Family size and risk of child deviance have also shown a consistent relationship. Large families were positively correlated with increased rates of aggression and stealing (Rutter, Tizard, & Whitmore, 1970) and general delinquency (Douglas, 1966). West and Farrington (1973) controlled for other covarying factors such as family income and still demonstrated an increased risk for delinquency for children coming from large families. Wadsworth (1979) noted that increased risk for delinquency was especially prominent in families with four or more children. This relationship was obtained even after factors such as social standing, quality of the home environment, and mother's management of the home were covaried.

Peer Influences

While the child is quite young, a majority of environmental factors have primary impact on parents. As children grow older, however, and expand their interactive sphere to broader social environments such as the school and community, they become more directly affected by influences in those settings. Of these social and environmental influences, the major focus of previous study has been the impact of peer influences on child behavior. In a recent review of sociological perspectives of delinquency, Elliott *et al.* (1979) stressed the importance of involvement in delinquent peer culture, regardless of the theoretical framework used to explain delinquent behavior (e.g., strain theory, control theory). Generally, peer influences are thought to interact with other important dimensions. For example, Hirschi (1969) indicated that the greater the youth's stake in social conformity, the less the impact delinquent peers would have on the child's behavior. Similarly, Polk and Halferty (1966) and Elliott and Voss (1974) hypothesized that adverse effects of delinquent peers are strongest under conditions where the youth is failing to achieve normative goals. Although little direct data are available to test specific aspects of peer influences, in general, studies support peer involvement in delinquent activities. West and Farrington (1973) reported that the majority of delinquent offenses were committed by groups of two or more juveniles. In addition, they reported a delinquency rate of approximately 45% among juveniles who indicated that their friends had committed high rates of delinquent acts. Poole and Regoli (1979) note that the children in their study who had highly delinquent friends committed more frequent, more varied, and more serious delinquent acts.

Although peer influences unquestionably affect child social behavior, very little direct research has investigated the developmental impact of peer interaction variables (Hartup, 1979). This is an area, however, that is beginning to receive major research focus so that peer influences may soon be explicated.

Integrative Summary

The many factors affecting the development of social behavior in children are viewed as being fully interactive. This indicates reciprocal impact from the interface of any two variables or groups of variables and produces increasingly complex influences on behavior. The simplest form of interactive effects takes place in dyadic interaction such as between parent and child. Within a dyadic exchange, both participants are assumed to directly influence the other's behavior. By expanding influences beyond the dyad to include all family members, influences become more complex and include both direct and indirect effects from multiple family members. For example, marital conflict between parents could alter mother's behavior when interacting with the child. Thus, the direct effects of mother–child interaction are indirectly altered as a result of marital conflict. By again expanding the field of reference, the family can be viewed as an interactive system imbedded within a host of additional influences that include neighbors, employers, schools, and community agencies. The behavioral influences operating at this level become exceedingly complex. A child's behavior may be influenced directly through interactions with peers and community adults outside the home. When the child returns to the family, these interactive experiences may indirectly affect other family members. In addition, innumerable indirect effects can accrue to the child from the direct community contact of other family members. A father's job difficulties may alter his behavior at home, which in turn may alter both the father–child relationship and the marital relationship.

In normal development, it is assumed that this expanding sphere of reference provides a diversity of socializing experiences to equip a child with an appropriate diversity of social skills. As the child becomes further removed from the direct influence of the family, the family becomes less effective in directly altering the child's behavior. However, new environments provide a proving ground for the concepts and behaviors learned in the child's primary environment, the family. Delinquent children can be viewed as being less well equipped to encounter positive socializing experiences in new environments. Instead, these arenas potentially increase adverse effects by overtly or covertly excluding the problem child from normalizing social influences.

It is clear that a fully interactive model of behavioral influences, expanding from a dyad to interactive community systems, results in exceedingly complex relationships between variables. The task becomes one of reducing complexity within the system without losing or altering potentially real relationships between factors. The strategy taken to reduce complexity was to conceptualize influences as having primary or secondary impact. Primary influences are critical to understanding the development of behavior patterns. Secondary influences aid in understanding variability in the quality and consistency of primary influences and may be critical to the maintenance of behavior patterns. For example, assume that the primary variable of consistent child management was necessary to prevent delinquency in children. Consistent parenting skills could be disrupted for a variety of reasons. Parents might simply lack appropriate skills or interest in child management. In this case, the effects would be expected to be long-term and relatively uninfluenced by secondary factors (i.e., secondary influences would not disrupt an already disrupted primary relationship). Other parents might abdicate the parental role as a result of an acute crisis such as severe financial strain or marital conflict. In such a case, detrimental impact on the child would be expected to be of short duration, given that the family returned to normal functioning following the crisis. Families of a social circumstance prone to experiencing chronic multiple-crisis situations such as unemployment, poor housing, and social isolation would be immersed in environmental conditions that severely restrict parents' ability to engage in adequate, consistent child management. Families more prone to experiencing such conditions would be expected to have a higher incidence of delinquent children. While such secondary variables increase the base rate of delinquency, they do not assure this outcome. Individual parental differences in responsiveness to environmental stress would provide wide variance in disruption of the parent–child relationship, thus accounting for the low predictive efficacy of secondary variables. It is clear that primary and secondary levels of influence covary, but primary components of the parent–child relationship are viewed as causal variables, especially in the production of preadolescent delinquent patterns in children.

The etiological discussion illuminated variables associated with delinquent patterns of behavior and presented the complex interplay of these variables within a developmental process. However, two points have not yet been explicitly examined. These are how the variables relate to the forms of delinquency defined at the outset, and, in turn, how specific patterns of delinquency relate to psychopathology while others do not.

To begin with, the unusually long maturation period (i.e., childhood) common to the human species must be assumed to fill a purposeful function other than physical growth. The assumption presented here is that the lengthy childhood period is required so that each child will repeatedly encounter a broad range of social expectations and experiences. This process of socialization provides the integrative force leading to social competence. Given an adequate level of competence, then, a young adult would be expected to adapt and cope adequately to the novel, complex, and demanding situations experienced during the adult life span. Because the stress of adult roles takes a psychological toll on adults ostensibly viewed as "competent," adequate social competence becomes a necessary but not sufficient condition for adult adjustment. It should be reiterated that "social competence" reflects a complex concept and should not be equated with "social skills," which tend to be viewed as directly measurable and trainable behaviors. As Sroufe (1979) implied about the affiliative bond, social competence as a concept adheres to the Gestalt principle of part–whole relationships. It represents the level of development and integration of emotional, cognitive, and behavioral aspects of an individual. Yet, the manifestation of social competence appears greater than the sum of its parts and is highly responsive to interactive setting variables. Thus, it is assumed that the development of social competence requires the varied, progressive, and lengthy exposure to socializing influences that comes during the childhood period.

In most cases a child's involvement in delinquent behavior represents no more than experimentation with novel experiences. Attainment of official delinquent status, which usually coincides with adolescent onset of delinquent behavior, is also not viewed as reflecting serious behavioral or psychological disorder. Data are sufficient to demonstrate that the majority of these youngsters cease their delinquent activities during adolescence and lead productive adult lives. The perspective presented in this chapter would also predict that these adolescents experienced strong normative socializing influences from their families and/or communities during childhood. These children developed a level of social competence adequate to function in adult roles even though behavioral aberrations occurred during adolescence.

Preadolescent onset of delinquent behavior, especially official delinquency, raises greater cause for concern. These children have an increased probability of becoming chronic adolescent delinquents, of continuing criminal behavior into adulthood, and of experiencing lifespan adjustment difficulties, including major psychopathology. They are also more likely to have come from emotionally and behaviorally impoverished families and to have experienced exclusion from normalizing community influences. It is the basic premise of this chapter that delinquency in children who have experienced grossly inadequate socialization represents a failure on the part of the child to appropriately interpret and act on information obtained from internal and external sources. Delinquent behavior in these cases reflects true psychopathology.

As children, these individuals may experience a bleak existence, but their basic needs (e.g., housing, food, clothing) are met by the family or society. As adults this situation changes. Attainment of adult goals requires, to a large degree, the ability to maintain employment, friendships, and love relationships. Failure of socially incompetent individuals to function in the majority of adult roles results in the marginal or sociopathic personalities described by Robins (1966) and in the high rate of criminal and psychiatric incarceration of these individuals.

Case Presentation

Family Characteristics

At the time of referral, this family was comprised of a single parent named Donna, age 28, and her two sons Mark, age 8, and Shawn, age 10. They lived in a suburban community on the outskirts of a small metropolitan city. They had moved from out of state approximately 3 years earlier. Donna described her reasons for moving as "getting as far away from my ex-husband as possible" and wanting to be closer to her relatives. The history of this family was very tumultuous. Donna was pregnant with Shawn when she married at age 18. Her husband was a welder by trade but was frequently out of work. Donna described him as being quick-tempered and a heavy drinker during such layoffs. She said they fought often and that on several occasions he had physically assaulted her. Two years after they were married, she had their second child, Mark. During the next few years there was continued conflict between Donna and her husband, which resulted in two separations and finally a divorce. The children were ages 3 and 5 at the time. Since moving to her current community, Donna has worked full-time in a variety of unskilled jobs, primarily waitressing. She recently took a job as a teacher's aid.

Since moving to this state, Donna and her boys have relocated three times. The duplex that they were living in was rented, as were most dwellings in their neighborhood. Donna did not know many of her neighbors because the turnover rate for tenants was high. In fact, her family was one of the oldest in the neighborhood, and they had lived there just over 1 year. She did did get along well with most of the adults she had met from her neighborhood, primarily because Mark and Shawn fought with the neighborhood children. Donna had no long-term friends and, although she had moved to be closer to her relatives, her contacts with her parents had resulted in arguments over her life-style and child rearing. Contacts, therefore, now were very infrequent.

Description of Child Behavior Problems

Donna was encouraged to seek professional advice regarding Mark's behavior by the vice-principal of his school. This suggestion came after Mark reportedly pushed a classmate off of a high piece of playground equipment. Mark had a history of behavior problems in school prior to that incident, including not staying in his seat, swearing, having temper tantrums, and occasionally fighting with classmates. Academically, Mark was considered a bright child, but when placed in a class for gifted children he became so disruptive that he was removed.

Mark's behavior problems were not limited to his school environment. His mother admitted that she had experienced problems with his stealing, lying, and wetting his pants. Donna also reported having similar problems with her oldest boy, Shawn, particularly with vandalism, stealing, lying, bullying other kids, and smoking. Both boys had been stopped on two occasions by city police for theft and vandalism. These incidents were handled informally without juvenile court action. In school Shawn reportedly had few friends, regularly turned in incomplete assignments, and frequently complained of minor physical ailments. Donna had sought professional assistance to deal with Shawn's problems several years earlier but discontinued treatment after three weeks. Her stated reasons for stopping treatment were that it was difficult to get transportation to sessions and that Shawn had disliked the therapist.

The discipline techniques Donna described using most often were restricting privileges, threatening, and yelling. However, she did not consider any of these methods effective. She told of spanking the boys when they were younger, but reportedly had refrained from doing so since the police had investigated her one year earlier on an alleged child-abuse complaint.

Additional observations were made about the family by their therapist. Early in treatment, the therapist noted that Donna generally used a very cold tone of voice when talking to the boys. With adults, however, she often came across as pleasant and engaging. Physical contact of an affectionate nature was not witnessed between Donna and either of her sons. Of particular interest to the therapist was the overall low level of interaction between all family members. Both during office sessions and visits to their home, each appeared to function autonomously. Little in the way of shared activities or extended conversations occurred. Those that did occur most often resulted in an argument.

In summary, both Mark and Shawn had histories of engaging in high rates of antisocial behavior both at home and at school. Additionally, each engaged in various covert activities in the community at large, primarily stealing. Each boy also exhibited minor physical symptoms (i.e., Mark wet his pants and Shawn had recurring stomach ailments) that were not linked to any medical problems by their physician. Donna was an ineffectual disciplinarian and appeared to have a poor affiliative relationship with both children. As a family, their interaction was infrequent and often aversive in nature.

Treatment

Although Mark was the original cause of the referral, it was clear from information gathered during the intake interview that Shawn was also displaying problem behaviors that needed immediate attention. Therefore, Donna requested that her therapist assist her in dealing with both boys' behavior problems. Because both Mark and Shawn were exhibiting extensive problems at home and school, Donna and her therapist felt that interventions would be warranted in both settings. A home intervention was developed first.

The therapist worked with Donna to improve her child management skills. Because Donna was ineffective at controlling either boy's behavior, the therapist began by teaching her nonphysical disciplinary techniques. Initially, Donna had difficulty applying discipline. Her attempts resulted in the boys yelling, throwing temper tantrums, running out of the house, or successfully engaging her in an argument. Her threats of discipline became more frequent than her actual use of it. Donna was eventually able to effectively discipline the boys after receiving increased instruction, role-playing, and support from her therapist. She reported that both boys' behavior then dramatically improved at home, and all family members stated that they were getting along better. "Better" to this family meant not arguing as frequently. Although the therapist regarded their decrease in arguments as a sign of treatment progress, it was noted that their rate of interaction remained very low and neutral in quality. Conversations were short and centered around information gathering and sending (e.g., "What time is it?" "I'll be home at 6:00." "Did you wash my jeans?"). Pleasant ongoing conversations and positive physical contact remained almost nonexistent. To increase the positive interaction between Donna and her boys, the therapist decided that the next step should be to teach them communication skills. Donna expressed an interest in increasing the family's communication but felt that such training should be postponed. She was still receiving complaints from the boys' schools, Mark's in particular, and felt that their immediate attention should be concentrated on the school problems. The therapist agreed and an attempt was made to arrange a school intervention for Mark. To do so required the cooperation of both Mark's teacher and Donna. This proved extremely difficult to do because Donna repeatedly missed or cancelled mettings at the last minute. By the time Mark's teacher, the therapist, and Donna were able to meet, the teacher was not cooperative and insisted that it was Donna's responsibility to remedy the situation. An appeal to the school's principal was made, but the principal made it clear that she would support whatever decisions Mark's teacher made. The therapist then arranged a meeting for him and Donna to develop an alternative strategy to deal with Mark's school problems. Once again, Donna missed the appointment.

The therapist was unable to contact Donna for over a month. On reaching her, another appointment was arranged. During that session, Donna said she had lost her job and that she and the boys would be moving because she could no longer afford her rent payments. Donna reported that complaints from Mark's school were still frequent, that her boys had been caught stealing a neighbor's bicycle a week earlier, and that the incident was pending review by the juvenile court. Probes from her therapist revealed that Donna was no longer consistently disciplining the boys for misbehavior. She recognized that their misbehavior was once again on the rise and expressed an interest in reentering treatment. She felt, however, that she would wait until they were resettled.

Approximately one month after that meeting, the therapist received a call from a child protective services caseworker. The caseworker explained that Mark and Shawn had been removed from their home and placed in substitute care, and that Donna was being investigated for child abuse. The circumstance was that Mark had called his father and complained that Donna beat him after an occasion when he had wet the bed. The boys were returned to their mother 3 weeks later with the stipulation that the family continue to receive treatment.

Outcome and Prognosis

Although Donna reentered treatment, she frequently cancelled or failed to appear for sessions. Approximately 2 months after her sons were returned to her, she moved her family to another town.

The likelihood that Mark and Shawn will continue to exhibit behavior problems in school, be out of their mother's control at home, and commit covert activities (stealing, vandalism) in the community is high. Their poor performance in these environments will undoubtedly result in one or both of the boys obtaining multiple official delinquent records. Given repeated juvenile court contact and their mother's inability to control their behavior, incarceration (e.g., a state training school or reformatory) is also a probable outcome. Thus, by the time the boys are 18, they will most likely have spent additional time in foster homes, adolescent group homes, or juvenile training facilities. Given such a background, their prognosis for adult adjustment is bleak.

Summary

Juvenile delinquency has been presented as a heterogeneous compilation of individuals engaging in antisocial behavior. The meaning and prognosis of these behaviors were also shown to be highly variable. A core of delinquent children is known to be at-risk for lifespan maladjustment, while others will experience social and legal difficulties only during adolescence. However, the majority of children who engage in delinquent behavior suffer no adverse social or psychological consequences and can be viewed as participating within a normative range of behavioral experimentation.

Those children at-risk for continued maladjustment were characterized as reflecting "delinquency-as-psychopathology" and became the focus of this chapter. While these children previously have not accurately been identified at an early age, several findings have consistently been associated with their pattern of delinquency. They tend to initiate delinquent behavior at an early age and to be identified as an official delinquent prior to adolescence. Not surprisingly, these children engage in a variety of delinquent activities in numerous community settings and are likely to be recognized as chronic recidivists. Unlike the majority of delinquent children, this antisocial pattern of behavior does not end with adolescence. As adults, former preadolescent delinquents have a bleak psychological prognosis. They are more likely to commit adult crimes and to experience criminal incarceration. They are also more likely to experience incapacitating psychological disorders ranging from sociopathic personality to psychosis. Most of the individuals who escape these outcomes demonstrate multiple symptoms of marginal adjustment such as alcoholism, drug dependence, marital conflict, and repeated unemployment.

The etiological discussion approached delinquency from a social development perspective and identified primary and secondary variables that held probable causal relationships to delinquency. Primary variables were aspects of the parent–child relationship that promoted or hindered the acquisition of social competence by the child. Data-based variables were: (1) quality of parent–child attachment; (2) style and consistency of parental discipline; and (3) quality of parental socialization of the child. Secondary variables relating to the social competence of the child included indirect influences that impacted the parent–child relationship and direct influences from the child's encounters outside the family environment. Indirect influences were stresses on the family such as marital conflict, unemployment, and social isolation. These variables were depicted as being counterproductive to the maintenance of an appropriate parent–child relationship due to their disruptive effect on the parent. Direct secondary influences included the child's experiences with peers and adults in school and community settings. All the influences on child behavior were viewed as operating in a fully interactive manner with the complexity of effects increasing as the focus of interaction expanded from the dyad, to all family members, to the family within the community.

The primary variables were hypothesized to operate in a cumulative developmental sequence. A strong affiliative parent–child bond provides a power base for the parent to exert control over child behavior. The use of consistent and contingent discipline maintains control and reduces parent–child conflict. These two points set the stage for the level of positive parent–child interaction that is necessary for adequate child socialization. Nonloving family environments, harsh, inconsistent parental disipline and low levels of positive parent–child interaction were characteristic of the upbringing of chronic delinquents. Such an environment fails to provide the experiences necessary to develop and integrate the emotional, cognitive, and behavioral aspects of the individual. These children then enter secondary settings without appropriate social competencies and are overtly or covertly excluded from normalizing opportunities. Preadolescent patterns of severe antisocial behavior represent a logical attempt to acquire social needs from a basically incomprehensible world. Children exhibiting such behavior patterns with a history of poor socialization are high-risk candidates for life-span psychopathology. The complexity of the socialization deficit also provides insight into the difficulty of altering chronic delinquent behavior through therapeutic intervention.

ACKNOWLEDGMENT

Appreciation is extended to Kay McClure for her excellent manuscript preparation.

References

Ainsworth, M. D. Infant/mother attachment. *American Psychologist,* 1979, *34,* 932–937.

Ainsworth, M. D. S., & Bell, S. M. Mother–infant interaction and the development of competence. In K. J. Connolly & J. Bruner (Eds.), *The growth of competence.* New York: Academic Press, 1974.

Ainsworth, M. D. S., Blehar, M. C., Waters, E., & Wall, S. *Patterns of attachment. A psychological study of the strange situation.* Hillsdale, N.J.: Lawrence Erlbaum, 1978.

Bandura, A. (Ed.). *Social learning theory.* Englewood Cliffs, N.J.: Prentice-Hall, 1977.

Baumrind, D. Authoritarian vs. authoritative parental control. *Adolescence,* 1968, *3,* 255–272.

Baumrind, D. Current patterns of parental authority. *Developmental Psychology Monographs,* 1971, *4.*

Baumrind, D. The development of instrumental competence through socialization. In A. Pick (Ed.), *Minnesota symposium on child development,* Minneapolis: University of Minnesota Press, 1973.

Baumrind, D. The contributions of the family to the development of competence in children. *Schizophrenia Bulletin,* 1975, *14,* 12–37.

Baumrind, D. Parental disciplinary patterns and social competence in children. *Youth and Society,* 1978, *9,* 239–276.

Bronfenbrenner, U. Contexts of child rearing: Problems and prospects. *American Psychologist,* 1979, *34,* 844–850. (a)

Bronfenbrenner, U. *The ecology of human development.* Cambridge, Mass.: Harvard University Press, 1979. (b)

Cass, L. K., & Thomas, C. B. *Childhood pathology and later adjustment: The Question of prediction.* New York: Wiley, 1979.

Deur, J. L., & Parke, R. D. Effects of inconsistent punishment on aggression in children. *Developmental Psychology,* 1971, *77,* 245–255.

Douglas, J. W. B. The school progress of nervous and troublesome children. *British Journal of Psychiatry,* 1966, *112,* 1115–1116.

Elliott, D. S., & Ageton, S. S. Reconciling race and class differences in self-reported and official estimates of delinquency. *American Sociological Review,* 1980, *45,* 45–110.

Elliott, D. S., & Voss, H. *Delinquency and dropout.* Lexington, Mass.: D. C. Heath, 1974.

Elliott, D. S., Ageton, S. S., & Canter, R. J. An integrated theoretical perspective on delinquent behavior. *Journal of Research in Crime and Delinquency,* 1979, *16,* 3–27.

Garbarino, J. The human ecology of child maltreatment: A conceptual model for research. *Journal of Marriage and the Family,* 1977, *November,* 721–735.

Gersten, J. C., Langner, T. S., & Simcha-Fagan, O. Developmental patterns of types of behavioral disturbances and secondary prevention. *International Journal of Mental Health,* 1979, *7,* 132–149.

Glueck, S., & Glueck, E. *Unraveling juvenile delinquency.* Cambridge, Mass.: Harvard University Press, 1950.

Gold, M., & Petronio, R. J. Delinquent behavior in adolescence. In J. Adelson (Ed.), *Handbook of adolescent psychology.* New York: Wiley, 1980.

Grusec, J. E., & Kuczynski, L. Direction of effect in socialization: A comparison of the parent's versus the child's behavior as determinants of disciplinary techniques. *Developmental Psychology,* 1980, *16,* 1–9.

Hartup, W. W. The social worlds of childhood. *American Psychologist,* 1979, *34,* 944–950.

Hetherington, E. M. Divorce—A child's perspective. *American Psychologist,* 1979, *34,* 851–858.

Hindelang, M. J., Hirschi, T., & Weis, J. G. Correlates of delinquency: The illusion of discrepancy between self-report and official measures. *American Sociological Review,* 1979, *44,* 995–1014.

Hirschi, T. *Causes of delinquency.* Berkeley: University of California Press, 1969.

Hughey, J. B., & Wahler, R. G. *Parent insularity and child stealing problems: Some obtained results.* Paper presented at the annual meeting of the Southeastern Psychological Association, 1980.

Johnson, R. E. Social class and delinquent behavior: A new test. *Criminology,* 1980, *18,* 86–93.

Jones, M. B., Offord, D. R., & Abrams, N. Brothers, sisters, and antisocial behavior. *British Journal of Psychiatry,* 1980, *136,* 139–145.

Kennell, J. H., Voos, D. K., & Klaus, M. H. Parent-infant bonding. In J. D. Osofsky (Ed.), *Handbook of infant development.* New York: Wiley, 1979.

Lamb, M. E., & Baumrind, D. M. Socialization and personality development in the preschool years. In M. E. Lamb (Ed.), *Scoiopersonality development.* New York: Holt, Rinehart & Winston, 1978.

Lewis, D. O., Shanok, S.S., Pincus, J. H., & Glaser, G. H. Violent juvenile delinquents: Psychiatric, neurological, psychological, and abuse factors. *American Journal of Child Psychiatry,* 1979, *18,* 307–319.

Matas, L., Arend, R. A., & Sroufe, L. A. Continuity of adaptation in the second year: The relationship between quality of attachment and later competence. *Child Development,* 1978, *49,* 547–556.

McCord, J. A thirty-year follow-up of treatment effects. *American Psychologist,* 1978, *33,* 284–289.

McCord, J. Some child-rearing antecedents of criminal behavior in adult men. *Journal of Personality and Social Psychology,* 1979, *37,* 1477–1486.

McCord, W., & McCord, J. *Origins of crime. A new evaluation of the Cambridge–Somerville Youth Study.* New York; Columbia University Press, 1959.

McGillicuddy-DeLisi, A. V., & Sigel, I. E. *Parental constructs of child development, teaching strategies, and children's development.* Paper presented at the sixth Vermont Conference on Primary Prevention of Psychopathology, Burlington, Vermont, June 1980.

McGillicuddy-DeLisi, A. V., Sigel, I. E., & Johnson, J. E. The family as a system of mutual influences: Parental beliefs, distancing behaviors, and children's representational thinking. In M. Lewis & L. A. Rosenbloom (Eds.), *The child and its family.* New York: Plenum Press, 1979.

Moore, D. R. *Determinants of deviancy: A behavioral comparison of normal and deviant children in multiple settings.* Unpublished doctoral dissertation, University of Tennessee, 1975.

Moore, D. R., Chamberlain, P., & Mukai, L. H. Children at risk for delinquency: A follow-up comparison of aggressive children and children who steal. *Journal of Abnormal Child Psychology,* 1979, *7,* 345–355.

Morris, H. H., Escoll, P. S., & Wexler, R. Aggressive behavior disorders of childhood: A follow-up study. *American Journal of Psychiatry,* 1956, *112,* 991–997.

Nye, F. I. *Family relationships and delinquent behavior.* New York: Wiley, 1958.

Osborn, S. G., & West, D. J. Conviction records of fathers and sons compared. *British Journal of Criminology,* 1979, *19,* 120–133.

Patterson, G. R. The aggressive child: Victim and architect of a coercive system. In L. A. Hamerlynck, L. C. Handy, & E. J. Mash (Eds.), *Behavior modification and families. I. Theory and research. II. Applications and developments.* New York: Brunner/Mazell, 1976.

Polk, K. *Teenage delinquency in small town America.* Research Report 5. Center for Studies in Crime and delinquency, National Institute of Mental Health, Washington, D.C., 1975.

Polk, K., & Halferty, D. S. Adolescence, commitment and delinquency. *Journal of Research in Crime and-Delinquency,* 1966, *July,* 82–96.

Poole, E. D., & Regoli, R. M. *Parental support, delinquent friends, and delinquency: Test of interaction effects.* Unpublished manual, 1979.

Powers, E., & Witmer, H. *An experiment in the prevention of delinquency: The Cambridge–Somerville Youth Study.* New York: Columbia University Press, 1951.

Redl, F., & Wineman, D. *Children who hate.* New York: Free Press, 1951.

Reid, J. B., & Hendricks. A. F. A preliminary analysis of the effectiveness of direct home intervention for treatment of pre-delinquent boys. In L. A. Hamerlynchk, L. C. Handy, & E. J. Mash (Eds.), *Behavior therapy: Methodology concepts and practice.* Champaign, Ill.: Research Press, 1973.

Report of the Task Panel on Prevention. Submitted to the President's Commission on Mental Health, 1978.

Robins, L. N. *Deviant children grown up. A sociological and psychiatric study of sociopathic personality.* Baltimore: Williams & Wilkins, 1966.

Robins, L. N. Sturdy childhood predictors of adult antisocial behavior: Replications from longitudinal studies. *Psychological Medicine,* 1978, *8,* 611–622.

Rutter, M. Maternal deprivation, 1972–1978: New findings, new concepts, new approaches. *Child Development,* 1979, *50,* 283–305. (a)

Rutter, M. Protective factors in children's responses to stress and disadvantage. In M. W. Kent & J. E. Rolf (Eds.), *Primary prevention of psychopathology, vol. 3. Social competence in children.* Hanover, N.H.: University Press of New England, 1979. (b)

Rutter, M., Tizard, J., & Whitmore, K. *Education, health and behavior.* New York: Wiley, 1970.

Sawin, D. B., & Parke, R. D.Inconsistent discipline of aggression in young boys. *Journal of Experimental Child Psychology,* 1979, *25,* 525–538.

Schwartz, J. C. Childhood origins of psychopathology. *American Psychologist,* 1979, *34,* 879–885.

Shure, M. B., & Spivack, G. Interpersonal cognitive problem solving and primary prevention: Programming for preschool and kindergarten children. *Journal of Clinical Child Psychology,* 1979, *2,* 89–94. (a)

Shure, M. B., & Spivack, G. Interpersonal problem-solving thinking and adjustment in the mother–child dyad. In M. Kent & J. Rolf (Eds.), *Primary prevention of psychopathology, vol. 3. Social competence in children.* Hanover, N.H.: University Press of New England, 1979. (b)

Shure, M. B., & Spivack, G. Interpersonal problem solving as a mediator of behavioral adjustment in preschool and kindergarten children. *Journal of Applied Developmental Psychology,* 1980, *1,* 29–44.

Sigel, I. E. Consciousness-raising of individual competence in problem solving. In M. Kent & J. Rolf (Eds.), *Primary prevention of psychopathology, vol. 3. Social competence in children.* Hanover, N.H.: University Press of New England, 1979.

Sroufe, A. L. Socioemotional development. In J. Osofsky (Ed.), *Handbook of Infant Development.* New York: Wiley, 1979.

Straus, M. A., Gelles, R. J., & Steinmetz, S. K. *Behind closed doors.* Garden City, N.Y.: Anchor Books, 1980.

Suh, M., & Carlson, R. Childhood behavior disorder . . . A family typology: An epidemiological study to determine correlation between childrearing methods and behavior disorder in children. *Psychiatric Journal of the University of Ottawa,* 1977, *2,* 84–88.

Tizard, B., & Rees, J. The effect of early institutional rearing on the behavior problems and affectional relationships of four-year old children. *Journal of Child Psychology and Psychiatry,* 1975, *16,* 61–74.

Tizard, J., & Tizard, B. The social development of two year old children in residential nuseries. In H. E. Schaffer (Ed.), *The origins of human social relations.* London: Academic Press, 1971.

Tonge, W. L., James, D. S., & Hillam, S. M. *Familes without hope. A controlled study of 33 problem families.* Great Britain: Headley Brothers, 1975.

Vaughn, B., Egeland, B., & Sroufe, L. A. Individual differences in infant–mother attachment at twelve and eighteen months: Stability and change in families under stress. *Child Development,* 1979, *50,* 971–975.

Wadsworth, M. *Roots of delinquency: Infancy, adolescence and crime.* New York: Barnes & Noble, 1979.

Wahler, R. G. The insular mother: Her problems in parent–child treatment. *Journal of Applied Behavior Analysis,* 1980: *13,* 207–219.

Wahler, R. G., & Moore, D. R. School–home behavior change procedures in a "high-risk community. In *Child behavior modification in the community: A progress update.* Symposium presented at the meeting of the American Association for the Advancement of Behavior Therapy, San Francisco, December 1975.

Warren, V., & Cairns, R. Social reinforcement satiation: An outcome of frequency of ambiguity. *Journal of Exceptional Child Psychology,* 1972, *13,* 249–260.

Welsh, R. S. Severe parental punishment and delinquency: A developmental theory. *Journal of Clinical Child Psychology,* 1976, *5,* 17–21.

West, D. J., & Farrington, D. P. *Who becomes delinquent?* London: Heinemann Educational Books, 1973.

West, D. J., & Farrington, D. P. *The delinquent way of life.* New York: Crane Russak, 1977.

Wilton, K., & Barbour, A. Mother–child interaction in high-risk and contrast preschoolers of low socioeconomic status. *Child Development,* 1978, *49,* 1136–1145.

Wolfgang, M. E., Figlio, R. M., & Sellin, T. *Delinquency in a birth cohort.* The University of Chicago Press, 1972.

Young, L. Wednesday's children: A study of child neglect and abuse. New York: McGraw-Hill, 1964.

Zahn-Waxler, C., Radke-Yarrow, M., & King, R. S. Child rearing and children's pro-social initiation toward victims of distress. *Child Development,* 1979, *50,* 319–330.

Zigler, E., & Trickett, P. K. The role of national social policy in promoting social competence in children. In M. Kent & J. Rolf (Eds.), *Primary prevention of psychopathology, vol. 3. Social competence in children.* Hanover, N.H.: University Press of New England, 1979.

III

Prevention and Treatment

15

Traditional Therapies with Children

JUNE M. TUMA AND KAREN R. SOBOTKA

This chapter will review traditional psychotherapeutic procedures for children who manifest emotional problems. These approaches include psychoanalytic, psychoanalytically-oriented, relationship, structured, and client-centered therapies. The development of individual therapy with children will be traced from the work of early psychoanalysts, outlining the philosophical theories of psychotherapy and focusing on differences and commonalities of differing viewpoints. The most accepted technical considerations will then be developed in order to illustrate major trends in present psychotherapeutic practice. The present status of individual therapy with children will then be appraised through an analysis of research.

Theory and Technique

Psychotherapy with children technically dates to the case of Little Hans, reported by Sigmund Freud in 1909 (Freud, 1959). Freud did not actually treat Little Hans, rather, the boy was treated by his father under Freud's direction. Freud's interest in Little Hans was to test out the theory of infantile sexuality and mental conflicts that had been closely constructed out of work with neurotic adults, but the case opened the way for child psychoanalysis. Freud's analysis established the complicated nature of symptom formation even in young children, and showed that children could respond to interpretation. Most importantly, however, the case revealed the potential use of fantasy and play as a substitute for free association used in adult analysis (Jones, 1953).

Melanie Klein and Anna Freud are the two people best known for the development and application of the psychoanalytic approach to understanding and treatment of children.

JUNE M. TUMA AND KAREN R. SOBOTKA • Department of Psychology, Louisiana State University, Baton Rouge, Louisiana 70803.

Anna Freud explicated her views on technique and theory of child psychoanalysis in a series of lectures delivered at the Vienna Institute of Psychoanalysis in 1926 and 1927, and in books published in 1928 and 1946. Melanie Klein, at about the same time (1932), described her method of psychoanalytic treatment of children in England.

In presenting her approach of child psychoanalysis, Melanie Klein's theory included abnormal phases in every child's development, and advocated psychoanalysis for all children. According to Klein, the individual experience of the child does not alter production of neurosis, nor is speech essential in treatment. She considered the child's play to be the equivalent of free association in adults (1955) and interpreted play continuously. Klein's method is often referred to as the "English school" of child psychoanalysis.

Anna Freud's method, referred to as the "Vienna school," is different from Klein's in many ways. She advocated treatment only for a restricted range of children, and considered work with the family and the educational role of the analyst to be much more important than did Klein. In Freud's approach, interpretation of play and unconscious conflicts is much more conservative, more attention is given to ego defenses, and the child's participation is much greater.

Klein's approach, because it did not mesh with findings about the importance of experience and maturation in child development, has never been widely accepted in the United States, although it has remained popular in England. Both Klein and Anna Freud were influential in directing professional attention to "play" as an expression of unconscious impulses and fantasies in psychotherapy with children (Gerard, 1952).

The psychoanalytic approach to understanding and treating children had an immense impact on prevailing attitudes toward behavior disorders in childhood and methods of treatment. By the end of the 1930s the psychoanalytic position was widely accepted in the United States and England as an explanation for psychological disturbance, juvenile delinquency, and a variety of other behaviors. As noted in Chapter 1 of this volume, professionals emphasis shifted from remedial tutoring or training to psychotherapy as the treatment of choice.

Psychotherapeutic approaches other than analysis also developed quickly and enlisted enthusiastic supporters. Some of the prominent theories were those of Frederick Allen and the relationship theorists, David Levy and the structured theorists, and Virginia Axline and the client-centered (or nondirective) theorists. These developed during the 1930s and 1940s.

During the 1960s traditional approaches to the treatment of emotionally disturbed children were challenged by behavioral therapies. These techniques were based on the application of learning principles to modification of behavior problems of children. Such an application possibility dates to 1924, when Mary Cover Jones (Jones, 1924) described how fear of rabbits and other furry objects in a 3-year-old boy, Peter, was extinguished by pairing the noxious stimulus (caged rabbit) with pleasurable stimuli and responses (food and eating), so that only the latter were elicited.

Professional response to Peter was slow in comparison to the enthusiastic reception of psychoanalytic concepts. However, with the disquieting appraisals of psychotherapy with children (Eysenck, 1961; Hood-Williams, 1960; Levitt, 1957, 1960), interest in psychoanalytically influenced psychotherapy with children declined while interest in learning theory approaches increased. A new generation of professionals actively developed strategies of conditioning and behavior modification (Gelfand, 1969; Staats, 1971) as alternatives to traditional approaches to treating children. However, Levitt's methodology has been criticized (Barrett, Hampe, & Miller, 1978; Halpern, 1968; Heinicke & Goldman, 1960) such that psychotherapy with children, as with adults, is being researched in a more sophisticated manner. These analyses are more positive, and psychotherapy in the traditional sense is once more being considered a legitimate activity.

Concurrently, the behavior therapists are beginning to find that their techniques do not differ entirely from traditional approaches in certain areas, for example, general factors thought to influence behavior change (empathy, warmth, genuineness) (Sloane, Staples, Cristol, Yorkston, & Whipple, 1975). Cognitive factors are also being incorporated into behavioral approaches. Thus, it appears that future research will bring traditional therapy and behavior therapy within a more integrated framework much like earlier attempts by Dollard and Miller (1950) and Mowrer (1939).

The 1950s and 1960s also ushered in another treatment modality for children that was to gain clinical and research importance, that of family therapy. Its development is complicated, and its more detailed historical trends are beyond the scope of this chapter. The popularity of this modality, like the behavior therapies, owes much to the critical appraisals of individual psychotherapy mentioned earlier. Child therapists, rather than increasing research efforts like their cohorts who worked with adults, flocked to other modalities and abandoned individual psychotherapy with children. However, because family treatment has tended to be integrated into broader programs using a variety of methods and settings for helping children, it has not been viewed as a panacea for all children's problems.

Approaches to Psychotherapy with Children

Clinicians working with children, like their counterparts working with adults, have developed many different theories or schools of psychotherapy. These theories are based on diverse views of the origins of psychological disturbance and the therapist's role in helping to alleviate it. Although each theory was initially presented as a radical departure from all previous views and although each incorporated changes in therapeutic procedures, most theoretical positions share common threads in the goals they pursue and the methods they employ.

The following discussion summarizes several prominent theories of psychotherapy with children and comments on their historical significance. The reader is referred to more extensive and detailed discussion of systems of psychotherapy with children, such as those presented by Schaefer (1979) and Wolman (1972a, b).

Relationship Therapy

Relationship therapy, often referred to as the "Philadelphia school," evolved from the psychoanalytic philosophy of Otto Rank at about the same time as techniques of Melanie Klein and Anna Freud evolved from Sigmund Freud's psychoanalytic philosophy. The term "relationship therapy" was coined by John Levy in 1938, and was espoused mainly by Allen (1942) and Moustakas (1953, 1959), after exploratory work on the process and procedure by Jessie Taft (1933).

Taft (1933) wrote the first book on child psychotherapy in the United States, and Allen (1942) wrote the second. Influential in both accounts is Rank's theory that all people share the common trauma of birth, leaving them with a permanent fear of "individuation." This emphasis on the beginnings of life eliminated the need for uncovering and interpreting the past in their psychotherapy. Rather, the therapist focused on the present situation and the patient's relationship to the therapist, not in terms of transference from parent figures but as new experiences. Taft states, "He does not want a father or a mother, but he does want someone who will permit him ultimately to find himself apart from parent identifications without interference or domination; someone who will not be fooled, someone strong enough not to retaliate" (Taft, 1933, p. 9).

In relationship therapy, the therapist does not focus on symbolism in child's play as she would in the psychoanalytic tradition, rather on the child's experiencing of the self. Empathy and the capacity to see each play situation as a unique experience that enables the child's natural expression are required of the therapist. The therapist's emphasis is on being there, interacting with the child by observing, listening, and making statements of recognition (Moustakas & Schalock, 1955). In this approach, the concept of self is central (Moustakas, 1955), and self-alienation is the primary characteristic of the disturbed child. The therapeutic relationship helps the child achieve a sense of personal worth. In a climate of understanding and acceptance, the child is freed from damaging effects of his/her hostility and anxiety and begins to experience the self as a unique individual, free to venture into new experiences and relationships.

Miyamoto (1960) reported similarities between relationship therapy and Zen, and in a more recent book Moustakas (1966) also refers to his approach as experiential or existential child therapy. He advanced the notion that the experiential therapist is atheoretical and "is committed to spontaneous, flowing, human processes and potentialities that are engendered and sparked in the communion of a significant relationship."

The relationship between therapist and client continues to be a major focus of psychotherapy with children as more contemporary researchers attempt to characterize the process during psychotherapy (Alexander, 1966; Seeman, 1966). One of the major influences of the "Philadelphia school" was to direct attention to significant elements of psychotherapy (Seeman, 1966) and, because of its disinterest in a genetic approach and in interpretive communications, to place the client in the center of psychotherapeutic focus. In this regard, it bears a close resemblance to the nondirective (subsequently called client-centered) approach of Carl Rogers and its adaptations for children by Virginia Axline (1947b).

Structured Play Therapy

Some writers stress the child's "play" as the important element in working with children, as opposed to the "relationship" between child and therapist. Perhaps a better way of categorizing this difference would be to speak of the "relative directiveness" versus the "nondirectiveness" of the procedures. The structured therapists direct the play activities to focus the sessions on conflict areas. It must be noted that both viewpoints involve play as the expressive situation for the child. The relationship therapists, however, view play as the language that brings the child into a communicating relationship with others and the world, whereas the structured play therapists use purposeful play to set the stage for abreaction and catharsis around specific situations thought to be the source of the child's fear or other difficulty. Play, then, is incidental to the relationship theorist but is *the* important element in resolving difficulties in the structural approach, and thus, the relationship is incidental.

Conn (1939) discussed play as a *method* of understanding children. J. C. Solomon, however, was the first to publish articles dealing with play as a *technique* of treatment (1938). Structured play therapy is described by Hambridge (1955) as a technique in which the therapist designs a series of specific situations that the child plays out. This type of therapy has been referred to by David Levy (1938) and J. Levy (1938) as "release therapy," by Solomon (1938, 1940, 1948, 1955) as "active play therapy," and by Conn (1948, 1941, 1955) as "the play interview."

Structured play therapy developed as an "offshoot" of psychoanalytic play therapy. Freud's thesis was that if the appropriate reaction to a traumatic situation was originally suppressed, the affect that remains undischarged maintains control of the subconscious. Freud thought that language could be a substitute for action and that a suppressed emotion could be talked out. The structured play therapists applied this concept of cathartic abreaction to children by substituting the medium of play for the medium of language.

Like psychoanalysts, structured play therapists assume major responsibility for the therapeutic experience. The assumption is that therapists are more aware of the child's needs than is the child. With their knowledge of the child's difficulties, based on psychoanalytic theory of development, therapists justify controlling direction of the therapeutic hour to encourage specific abreaction. The therapists contend that catharsis allows mastery of missed developmental tasks and reinstatement of the normal developmental sequence.

The development of this technique had far-reaching effects not only in psychotherapy with children. In addition, parents and teachers often became advocates of catharsis as a key to mental health (Baruck, 1949). Catharsis, the concept of releasing unexpressed feelings, became linked to the philosophy of permissiveness in child rearing. Over time, however, the use of catharsis in child rearing and in therapy has been criticized because of the danger of maintaining immaturity in the child (Kessler, 1966). Further, due to applicability only to children who had sustained specific trauma, structured play therapy is currently considered to be a part-technique rather than a general mode of psychotherapy (Rosenblatt, 1971).

Client-Centered Psychotherapy

Client-centered therapy, as formulated by Carl Rogers (1942, 1951, 1961), rests on the premise that all people have inborn capacities for purposive, goal-directed behavior, and if free from disadvantageous learning conditions, will develop into kind, friendly, self-accepting and socialized human beings. Client-centered therapy aims to correct such faulty learning by providing the client with opportunities to expand self-awareness and positive self-regard.

Virginia Axline (1947b) has adapted client-centered therapy for use with children, and her formulations have been further elaborated by Elaine Dorfman (1955). This approach neither plans the play in advance, as the structured play therapists do, nor is it symbolically interpreted, as it is by psychoanalysts. The client-centered approach with children is similar to relationship therapy in consideration of the relationship that is created between therapist and child as the deciding factor in the success or failure of therapy. However, as Moustakas (1959) points out, client-centered therapy is different from relationship therapy because

> the focus is not on the relationship itself but on the therapist and child as separate individuals with the therapist making reflections and clarifications, conveying emphatic understanding and having unconditioned [sic] regard for the client.(Moustakas, 1959, p. xiv)

The influence of Freud and Rank are prominent in the development of the client-centered approach to therapy with children. Dorfman states:

> It is apparent that from the Freudians have been retained the concepts of meaningfulness of apparently unmotivated behavior, of permissiveness and catharsis, of repression, and of play as being the natural language of the child. From the Rankians have come the relatively ahistorical approach, the lessening of authoritative position of the therapist, the emphasis on response to expressed feelings rather than to a particular content, and the permitting of the child to use the hours as he chooses. From these concepts client-centered play therapy has gone on to develop in terms of its own experiences. (Dorfman, 1951, p. 237)

Axline believes that the well adjusted child is able to achieve self-realization by directing behavior selectively toward the environment. Conversely, the maladjusted child has not been successful in efforts to gain necessary satisfaction of needs, and thus, devious methods are learned for this purpose. However, the inner struggle for growth in the child continues, but the child is constantly blocked in efforts by the environment (e.g., criticism and domination by adults). This causes incongruence within the self, and the child eventually departs from reality both in perceptions and in experiencing (Axline, 1955).

The basic premise of client-centered psychotherapy with children is that the therapeutic experience should be different from any other experience the child has had (Axline, 1955). The playroom, the relationship, the total experience of self within this new context allows the process of reintegration to occur (Axline, 1947a). When the conditions are different than those that contributed to the disorganization, the child is able to make a new synthesis and continue forward movement in a well adjusted manner (Axline, 1964).

Play, as communication from the child, is important to this approach. When the child is allowed natural expression through play, feelings surface. The child, within the acceptance and permissiveness of the playroom, is provided the safety of a nonconditional relationship. The child is thus enabled to realize possession of power, which permits independent thinking and decision making, which in turn promote psychological maturity and development. The child, then, does not have to practice devious methods to fill needs, and the real self is allowed to unfold and have full expression (Axline, 1964).

Unlike other approaches (Freud, 1965; D. Levy, 1938; J. Levy, 1938; Reisman, 1973), Axline does not believe it necessary for the child to be aware of problems; therefore, no diagnostic interviews are required, and interpretations of the child's play are ruled out. Despite her view that the child's interaction with dominating and critical adults thwarts actualization, Axline does not advocate work with parents.

This method of psychotherapy is appropriate for mild developmental disturbances (Kessler, 1966). The research in support of the success of Axline's approach has been based on data collected during comparatively brief contacts with supposedly normal children (Woltmann, 1952). Kessler (1966) questions that the therapeutic powers of acceptance and the natural drive for growth are sufficient to help the majority of emotionally disturbed children referred for treatment. The influence of the client-centered approach to child psychotherapy is immense, however. This approach has focused attention on relationship variables rather than on technique. The approach, thus, appears to rely mostly on general factors of promoting behavior change rather than on specific factors (Strupp, 1970, 1972, 1973; Weiner, 1976).

Child Analysis and Analytically Oriented Psychotherapy

Analytical psychotherapy is the prototype for the most commonly used therapy in child treatment settings. In this approach, the relationship between child and analyst (therapist) is a means through which the goal of psychoanalysis is achieved. The goal is for the child to understand his/her troubled feelings and defenses in order to deal with them directly (known as insight). Insight is achieved by the technique of interpretation. In the process of achieving insight, the unconscious is made conscious. Anna Freud compares this task to adult psychoanalysis:

> To undo the various repressions, distortions, displacements, condensations, etc., which had been brought about by the neurotic defense mechanisms, until, with the active help of the child, the unconscious content of the material is laid bare. (1946, p. 71)

Child psychoanalysts work on the past, with the goal of resolving conflicts that interfere with future development.

The therapeutic alliance with children requires more attention than it does with adults. Anna Freud's introductory phase is designed to induce readiness and willingness for treatment. Therapists of other orientations have also noted that children do not acknowledge the presence of problems (Axline, 1947b; Reisman, 1973); some advocate special techniques to develop willingness (Reisman, 1973), as does Freud (1965). Freud's method utilizes numerous ingenious techniques to help the child gain insight into problems and to increase motivation to change. Reisman (1973) gives detailed coverage to this topic, as does Anna Freud in her own writings (1965).

As in adult psychoanalysis, analysis with children requires frequent sessions (three, four or five times per week). It is believed that this frequency promotes an intense relationship and a continuity of material. Further, it prevents the need to master anxiety aroused by treatment alone by erecting defenses against that anxiety. Recent research (Heinicke & Strassman, 1975) seems to bear out some advantages for greater frequency of sessions.

The techniques of psychoanalytic therapists vary with age and ability of the child, with nature of the symptoms, and with the child's general character. The techniques developed for adults are modified for use with children. Thus, daydreams are substituted for nightdreams in interpreting and understanding problems, and communication is through play rather than through verbalizations of problems. The child thus may show conflicts between wishes and conscience through themes enacted in play. The links between these and daily life situations are then tentatively made, and after the conflicts are worked out with toys (e.g., puppets), they are then directed to the real child. In therapeutic work with children, the child often appears to react as if the outcome has to be known before conflicts can be related to the child's situation. This "working through" of the conflicts depicted by themes and scenes in play often take several months before the conflict is mastered and the child is enabled to move to other concerns.

The provision of a setting for the child includes having a variety of play materials available. Children make varying choices among toys. Some prefer puppets while others reject their use and instead use doll families, trucks, and cars; others prefer nebulous materials such as Play Doh, drawings, or blocks. Children use toys in ways other than intended by their design, such that blocks can become cars, trains, birds or fences, and so forth. Most therapists furnish the playroom with specific toys as well as nebulous materials to permit creativity of children.

In the analytic situation, the child selects the actual materials used, but it is permissible for the psychoanalyst to enter into play. The analyst makes comments to direct and guide the child toward areas of conflict. Interpretations, when made, are sometimes made in the guise of a puppet or doll, when the child has asked the analyst to assume these roles. Drawings, when used, often express specific conflicts and general personality difficulties. It is significant when an 8-year-old draws tiny figures and objects, or, on the other hand, when the child draws exaggerated, large figures. Other children reveal a great deal when they draw violence and explosions, while others will focus on drawings of robots. The directions that the child gives the therapist also provide information about the child's concerns (e.g., the 11-year-old boy who instructed the therapist to draw a burning, torpedoed pirate ship that was about to sink, while he himself drew an architectural sketch-like drawing of a modern ship). These are the communications of the child, and they are as expressive and as clear as the spoken word of the adult. The actual words of the child about these productions as well as the events of everyday life are also used by the analyst in work with the child. Parental reports usually provide the latter and augment information obtained from the child.

The stage of analysis determines the manner in which this material is handled. Early in the process, only reflections, similar to what Rogers describes, and labeling, which consists of giving the child names for feelings and permission to have these feelings, are given. Other activities include pointing out differences between fantasy and reality or between thought and action. There may be an educative function as well, when the analyst tries to explain behavior of people or things. Reassurances that the child is not as bad, damaged, or stupid as the child presupposes, are also appropriate in early stages.

During more advanced stages in the process of analysis, interpretations, the distinguishing features of psychoanalysis, are offered. Interpretations consist of making connections for the child where the child sees none. The connections are usually between the past and the present, or between defense and feeling, or between fantasy and feeling. The rationale on which any specific interpretation is based depends on the context of the total case material as it emerges and develops. The timing, working, and reasons for the interpretations involves skills that cannot be briefly communicated.

Anna Freud (1965) suggested that within psychoanalysis and play therapy there is a movement from surface to depth, from the interpretation of ego resistances or defenses to the interpretation of unconscious impulses, wishes, and fears, or id content. She notes that as the "hidden" becomes accessible to conscious thought and reason through therapist communication of understanding, the client's level of anxiety or tension decreases.

Psychoanalysis is not appropriate for every disturbed child. The technique was designed for neurotic clients and involves interpreting repressions that were created by unrealistic anxiety stimulated by the parents' attitudes or the child's fantasies (Kessler, 1966). Children who can benefit from psychoanalysis have been described in Eysenck's terms as those with "surplus conditioned responses" rather than those with "deficient conditioned responses" (Eysenck, 1960, p. 17; cf. Kessler, 1966). Thus, the technique is not appropriate for the child who is living under intolerable conditions or the child who has a weak or defective ego. Anna Freud (1965) herself states that psychoanalysis should be used sparingly, only for those children whose development is arrested because of neurotic conflict and for whom hope of spontaneous recovery is slight.

Psychoanalytically Oriented Psychotherapy

The goal of psychoanalytically oriented psychotherapy is less ambitious than that of psychoanalysis (Arthur, 1952). While the basic theory is the same, the psychoanalyst primarily tries to relieve the child of *symptoms* that cause difficulties. Frequency is only once or twice a week, the therapist is more active in directing activity during the hour, and the child's feelings and defenses are more frequently pointed out. The analyst's comments are more selective and some material is disregarded. The objectives of psychoanalysts include interpretation of the origins of overwhelming anxiety in an area of conflict, whereas the objective of analytically oriented therapists is to interpret behavior as defenses against anxiety with the purpose of ending the behavior. Thus, psychoanalysis and psychoanalytically oriented approaches can be regarded as different in degree rather than kind of psychotherapy. The level of therapy depends on the child's needs and on what the child's ego can tolerate. The complexity and structure of the emotional illness dictates whether psychoanalysis or psychoanalytically oriented psychotherapy is more appropriate for a particular child.

Child psychoanalysis, particularly as developed by Anna Freud, has been the most influential approach in the United States. Besides advocating a lucid theory of personality development and psychopathology of children, it provides the most comprehensive and detailed approach to child psychotherapy. It incorporates techniques of fostering a therapeutic relationship as well as techniques for increasing self-awareness and resolution of conflicts. As can be gleened from the earlier summaries of other child therapy approaches, it has influenced, to greater or lesser degree, all of them.

Comparison of Theories of Child Psychotherapy

The psychotherapy approaches presented above can be classified on two major dimensions: passive versus active role of the therapist, and relationship versus technique as the agent of change. Adult therapies have been differentiated in this manner (Weiner, 1976), and the same kind of analysis applies to techniques with children.

The psychoanalytic and psychoanalytically oriented approaches fall within the therapist-passive and technique-oriented dimension, whereas the client-centered and relationship approaches are considered therapist-active and relationship-oriented. The structured approach is therapist-active and technique-oriented. In many ways, this classification is ambiguous, however. In the psychoanalytic techniques, interpretations are intrusive in an active manner (Weiner, 1976), and the unstructured opportunities for personal growth provided in the client-centered and relationship approaches constitute a passive, nonintrusive therapist stance. More importantly, Weiner points out, even the technique-oriented therapists stress the importance of an open and trusting patient–therapist relationship. Conversely, relationship-oriented therapists devote much attention to techniques for establishing and sustaining treatment relationships.

These comments reflect current views of psychotherapy. When attention shifts from terminology and theories to aims and methods in treatment, approaches to psychotherapy begin to converge. The common concerns of all approaches include: (1) reliance on both technique and relationship variables to promote progress toward the aim of exerting beneficial influence; (2) the aim of bringing the client into more effective contact with both thoughts and feelings; and (3) the aim to expand the client's self-awareness, to increase capacity to understand and control behavior, and to promote ability to find a rewarding and self-fulfilling life (Weiner, 1976).

Research supports Weiner's (1976) observations by illustrating that experienced therapists of different persuasions have similar treatment tactics, that is, in what they actually say to their clients. This has been observed with children as early as 1946 (Witmer) and more recently in adult psychotherapy research by Fiedler (1950), Strupp (1955a, b, 1958), and Wrenn (1960). With children, Witmer (1946) noted that most therapists draw from more than one source, and none of the therapists use "text book" patterns. Therapists typically respond sensitively to children's needs as they perceive them, and apply their knowledge in such diverse ways that the influence of "schools" seems transcended by principles that are common to all psychotherapy. She further notes that there are

> no magic words, no formulae by which the psychotherapy of children is accomplished. The phrases that are so often used in describing treatment techniques ("interpret the transference," "make the unconscious conscious," "get out the aggression," etc.) seem almost inapplicable, so remote are they from the reality of the therapist and patient working together on a problem. (Witmer, 1946, p. 442)

She concludes that there are rules to the game, but each therapist has to find his own way of using them. Consequently, there is no justification for proposing one method of psychotherapy as being better than another.

To this point, we have considered the development of various theories of psychotherapy with children. With the purpose of investigating the nature of psychotherapy with children, and to elucidate more clearly processes of that procedure, the remaining sections will be concerned with an analysis of definitions and factors thought to be responsible for behavior change in child psychotherapy.

The Definition of Psychotherapy

Reisman (1971) critiqued conflicting definitions of psychotherapy and proposed an integrated definition that is both more precise and more comprehensive than its predecessors. Weiner (1976) further elaborated and clarified Reisman's concepts and, in 1973, Reisman applied his earlier formulation to psychotherapy with children. His formulation is not based on a theoretical orientation, and as such, appears to reflect current practice and research with adults and children (i.e., it concentrates on elements common to all approaches to psychotherapy with children rather than on unique aspects delimited by a theoretical position).

Reisman reduced the prevailing definitions of psychotherapy into those defined by: (1) its goals, (2) its procedures, (3) its practitioners, and (4) the relationship. These four definitions, each deficient alone (see Weiner, 1976), taken together identify several characteristics common to all instances of what is usually regarded as psychotherapy. These include: (1) the use of psychological measures to assist people who are experiencing emotional problems in living; (2) the wish of the therapist to be of help to the patient; (3) an attitude of respect by the therapist for the personal integrity of the patient; and (4) the reliance on an understanding of the patient to guide conduct of treatment.

Combining these common elements, Reisman (1971) defines psychotherapy as "the communication of person-related understanding, respect, and a wish to be of help" (pp. 135–136). This definition clarifies two important issues, the distinction between psychotherapy and what may be psychotherapeutic, and the bearing of a professional relationship on the likelihood that psychotherapy will occur (Weiner, 1976, p. 336).

Distinguishing Psychotherapy from What May Be Psychotherapeutic

Reisman's definition includes treatment approaches in which the therapist attempts to enhance the patient's understanding of himself (group therapy, family therapy, individual therapy). It excludes methods in which the therapist seeks to do something to or for his patient rather than engage him in a quest for increased self-understanding (drug therapy, electric shock, directed recreational activities, sound advice, etc.). Although these latter activities may be psychotherapeutic by relieving the patient's emotional distress or increasing his life satisfaction, they do not constitute psychotherapy.

Likewise, Weiner (1976) excludes behavior modification in its traditional forms of systematic desensitization, operant conditioning, and aversive training, from the definition of psychotherapy because even though it has considerable potential for promoting behavior change and is based on some understanding of the patient's needs and problems, it does not utilize *explicit communication* of this understanding as the central feature of the method.

Weiner (1976) believes that distinction between psychotherapy and what is psychotherapeutic can contribute to advances in practice and research. The definition enables the clinician to recognize when psychotherapy is provided and when it is not, and enables the researcher to precisely define and replicate clinical interactions. Weiner believes that neither clinical nor experimental findings can systematically shape knowledge about psychotherapy without such distinctions.

The Bearing of a Professional Relationship on the Likelihood That Psychotherapy Will Occur

Reisman's definition does not exclude the possibility that psychotherapy will occur in many kinds of interpersonal relationships, but it is more likely to occur in the context of a professional relationship designed to provide psychotherapy. The reasons for this are several: (1) Understanding, respect, and the wish to be of help communicated in a relationship between two people are enchanced if one of those people is professionally trained in the understanding of human behavior and manifests conscious intent on application of this training for the benefit of the other. (2) A professional psychotherapy relationship is designed primarily for the benefit of the patient in an asymetrical arrangement. (3) A professional psychotherapy relationship is more systematic because of the provision of regularly scheduled meetings for a specified period of time without disruption. The reader is referred to Weiner (1976) for a complete development of these implications for the practice and research of psychotherapy.

Goals of Psychotherapy with Children

Children are brought to the attention of the therapist, not because they express a need or wish to be seen, but because someone is complaining about, or is disturbed by, their behavior. Parents are the usual referral source, disturbed by the child‘s aggressiveness, withdrawal, or expressions of poor self-esteem. However, often school personnel are also concerned with child behaviors such as failure despite good intelligence and disruptive or inappropriate behavior.

Therapists treating children set two general goals for psychotherapy: increased client self-understanding and behavior change. As in adult psychotherapy, if behavior change (symptom relief, problem resolution, or progress toward a less chaotic existence) does not occur, psychotherapy has not achieved its goals. Whenever the desired behavior changes do not occur despite increased understanding, further or more incisive treatment is indicated, often requiring a reassessment of parent–child interactions.

How much change should be expected as a result of psychotherapy? The child's life is dependent on others, and thus there are limitations on how much change can be tolerated by others. In addition, the factors that contribute to the child's problems in the first place probably have not been altered very much, even if the parents are being counseled concurrently. Traumatic experiences may continue to occur (e.g., birth of a sibling, a divorce, a move, a death, etc.). Another more perplexing problem is the rapid development that the child undergoes which continually causes the therapist to change patterns of adaptation.

Thus, the goals of psychotherapy do not include effecting complete or perfect resolutions, nor do they guarantee that no future psychological difficulties will occur. Psychotherapy is a helping procedure but it is not a curative one. It is a means of progress toward desired behavior change, but does not effect total and permanent change. The usual indication for termination is when substantial progress is made toward achieving goals for which treatment was entered, made when the child approximates functioning at the appropriate developmental level, and when any further progress that would justify the time, effort, and expense that such progress would require is unlikely.

General and Specific Factors Promoting Change in Psychotherapy

It is generally recognized that behavior change in psychotherapy is attributed to general and specific factors in treatment with adults. Although not actively researched, the same factors are important in psychotherapy with children, as indicated from the earlier discussion. There are differences with regard to these factors, however, that are peculiar to the age of the child.

General factors refer to aspects of the psychotherapy relationship, whereas *specific factors* refer to technical procedures employed within this relationship. As Weiner (1976) points out, these two factors are intertwined such that

> A helpful psychotherapy relationship comes into being only when the therapist employs adequate procedures for establishing it, and technical procedures promote progress only when they are employed in the context of a good treatment relationship. (p. 355)

General Factors Promoting Change

There are four general factors: (1) opportunity for catharsis, (2) expectation of change, (3) attention from the therapist, and (4) reinforcement effects.

Opportunity for Catharsis

In his early writings Freud emphasized catharsis as the primary means of alleviating his patients' symptoms. Techniques were used to allow the patient to find relief by talking about difficulties. In time, however, Freud abandoned catharsis in favor of free association and interpretive methods of psychoanalysis because people were limited in ability to report difficulties and thereby to find relief. Catharsis does, however, contribute to the helping process in psychotherapy. Research to support his notion includes such findings as the beneficial effects people receive from talking into a tape recorder regularly without a therapist even being present (Stollak & Guerney, 1964).

In psychotherapy with children, the same effects can be observed. The communication medium, is, of course, oftentimes play, through which the child expresses views of conflictual or traumatic events and masters them by graded repetitions. Some therapists, for example, David Levy (1938) and J. Levy (1938), viewed catharsis as the major goal of release therapy with children. While few psychotherapists today would endorse catharsis as the essence of psychotherapy with children, most recognize its value.

Expectation of Change

In psychotherapy, preconceived notions, professional status or reputation of the therapist, information from the therapist regarding the potential of psychotherapy, the promise of good results implicit in recommendations of psychotherapy, and anticipation of future gains caused by initial gains all serve to produce an expectation of change in the client. Research on expectancy effects (Frank, 1959, 1961; Goldstein, 1960, 1962a, b) documents that patients who receive instructions intended to instill high expectancy of gain are more likely to continue and to benefit from psychotherapy than those with low-expectancy instructions. There have even been suggestions (although there are questions of adequate research design) that simply explaining how psychotherapy works, what the patient's role in it will be, and what the patient expects from the therapist, contributes to subsequent improvements (Heilburn, 1972; Hohen-Sarick, Frank, Imber, Mansh, Stone, & Battle, 1964; and Sloane, Cristol, Pepernik, & Staples, 1970).

With children, sources of expectations for change are indirect, deriving from what parents say about the therapist and his/her procedures, and from parental attitudes. However, therapists who follow Reisman's (1973) suggestion of a thorough discussion with the child about goals, procedures, and expectations of psychotherapy, should observe a similar influence of expectation of change.

Attention from the Therapist

In psychotherapy, arrangements are made to provide a client with an opportunity to meet regularly with another person who listens to what the client says, shows respect, and conscientiously attempts to understand and be helpful. This contributes greatly to a person's feeling better about present difficulties and what the future holds. This is true with children as well as with adults, and is, in fact, probably the most powerful factor in psychotherapy with children.

It has often been noted that in the psychotherapeutic arrangement, the child is allowed undivided attention from an adult, which is different from any other situation in the child's life. Here, the child does not have to compete for attention with siblings, or to demand attention from the busy mother who has more on her mind than attending constantly to a child. The relationship with mother is also different because of the socialization training she is concerned with. Attendant to this purpose, the interactions with mother are punctuated with injunctions for the child to mind manners, to do certain things and avoid doing others.

The reaction of the child to psychotherapy is very much a positive one, especially since the young are prone to think they are the center of the universe, anyway, and the therapist's attention affirms that fact. With the strong relationship that is built based on this attitude of respect and acceptance, the child is enabled to accept interpretations and confrontations.

Rogers (1942, 1951), in his formulation of client-centered therapy, was the first to elaborate on the significant role of the therapist's attention to his clients in promoting behavior change. Much research has been stimulated by Rogers's views on the treatment relationship. The therapist's attention to his patient has been translated into measures of *empathy, warmth,* and *genuineness.*

Empathy communicates an interest and understanding of the client. It consists of accurate comments on the specific hopes, fears, conflicts, and concerns of the client. Reisman (1973) considers empathic statements one of the major and definitive tasks of the child psychotherapist, and empathic statements have been described as the cornerstone of psychotherapy (Truax & Carkhuff, 1967). In psychotherapy with children, it is especially important to communicate empathy because the child is often without verbalizations; empathic statements help bring to the awareness of the child relevant communications, even if expressed only through play and facial and behavioral means.

Children are noted for changing their play, verbalizations, and attention quite rapidly, and once they move on, the moment is hard to recapture. Even if the therapist has no idea of the meaning of the child's behavior, if empathic comments are made, the child will comprehend that the therapist is attentive and accepting of feelings. The therapist might, for example, simply acknowledge the difficulty a child uncharacteristically shows in relating a particularly embarassing event rather than press for details.

Warmth is the means by which the therapist creates an atmosphere in which the client can feel safe, secure, and respected as a person. Warmth is communicated by an accepting, nonjudgmental attitude expressed in a manner that conveys caring and receptivity of all client communications and actions. Thus, the child who comes in with a confession of wrongdoing with the comment, "My mother told me to tell you, or she said she was going to," and who shows shyness and anxiety by behavior, eye contact, and hesitancy in verbalization, is following orders under protest and fear. A therapist might comment simply, "Maybe you expect me to be angry with you about what you did, like your mother is." The child may be surprised by such a nonpunitive attitude, but will then be able to tell the therapist more about the situation without having to deny responsibility and make excuses for behavior or attempt to blame misdeeds on another child.

Children often engage in behaviors that cannot be permitted in the therapy room, such as hitting the therapist, destroying toys or aspects of the therapy room, engaging in self-injury. These situations require limit-setting by the therapist. These limits should be stated in such a way as to impose the limit without judgments concerning the goodness or badness of the behavior. Thus, the therapist might say, "I know you are angry at me, but I cannot allow you to hit me." During this episode, the child is often unable to stop with such a simple admonition. At this point, it is a useful technique to deflect the child's attention to a BoBo doll or other doll in the room, with statements such as, "Perhaps you can pretend the BoBo is me and you can show me and tell me how angry you are with me by dealing with BoBo!" Thus, the feelings and thoughts are accepted without subjecting the child to resultant guilt reactions due to hitting the therapist.

Genuineness enables a client to talk in an open, truthful, nondefensive manner. Weiner describes it as "engaging the client in a direct personal encounter in which the therapist is a truthful and authentic person who says only what he believes and does only what is comfortable and natural for him to do" (1976, p. 359). With a child, genuineness is especially important, and tends to be another area in which the therapeutic arrangement differs from experiences with adults. The therapist responds in an open and honest manner to the child's questions, accusations, and oppositional behavior while still communicating acceptance of the child. The child begins to accept the role of equal partner in the endeavor to achieve understanding of the child's behavior, and begins to view the therapist as a helpful and real person.

Accumulating research evidence points to a positive relationship between successful outcome in psychotherapy and the extent to which therapist empathy, warmth, and genuineness characterizes the treatment relationship (see summaries by Swenson, 1971; Truax & Carkhuff, 1967; Truax & Mitchell, 1971). While not much research has been attempted with children, similar relationships would be expected.

Reinforcement Effects

A whole range of possible responses by the therapist, including postural changes, facial expressions, brief utterances such as "Mm-hmm," "Uh-huh," and "I see," as well as substantive comments or questions have been pointed out by Weiner (1976) as reinforcing. In work with children, some other items must be listed. Since the child frequently moves around the room, sometimes wants to throw a ball back and forth, and otherwise invites the therapist to engage in play, the child therapist has a greater range of behaviors to use for reinforcing effects. Generally stated, if the therapist follows the child physically and responds to any reasonable request to participate in the child's activity, the therapist communicates interest and belief that the child's "productions" are important.

In regard to verbalizations in child psychotherapy, reinforcement effects usually include more than brief utterances utilized with adults. Instead of the "I see" comments, effective with adults, the child therapist may have to verbalize more (e.g., "I see, the little car is in danger of falling off the cliff"). Because the child, especially the preschool child, may not yet have learned to designate nuances of feeling and to assign words to actions, the therapist often finds it necessary to verbalize the child's play and other behavior (e.g., "You want to see what toys are in the room," and "The car is now going really fast"). Comments chosen by the therapist depend on the behavior of the child and serve to encourage further elaboration and clarification of the meaning of the play or verbalization.

The Interaction of General and Specific Factors Promoting Change

It is obvious from the preceding discussion that general factors associated with the psychotherapy relationship contribute to an atmosphere wherein the client feels safe and respected. However, in spite of benefits accrued from catharsis, expectancy, therapist attention, and reinforcement, additional progress can be made through techniques designed to increase the client's understanding of problems and alternative ways of resolving them. Thus, psychotherapy should aim to provide the opportunity "to profit not only from the generally beneficial aspects of the treatment relationship but also from specific information provided to him by the therapist about his problems" (Weiner, 1976, p. 362).

The provision of specific information to the child requires skill in communicating useful information to the child about him or herself. These skills include the translation of interpersonal skills into communications that are timed, phrased, and modulated as needed. The more experienced and skilled the therapist, the more likely is a systematic response to the child made in a manner designed to expand self-knowledge and to sustain the treatment relationship. The central role of communication in understanding problems and their possible solutions has recently been affirmed by those therapists who focus on relationship factors (Frank, 1971; Rogers, 1974; Schofield, 1964, 1970).

Specific Factors Promoting Change

Specific factors, as used here, refer to technical procedures derived from Freud's psychoanalytic methods of free association and interpretation. These technical procedures foster continued participation in psychotherapy and increase the child's ability to understand and control future behavior.

Effective psychotherapy is dependent on the communication process, verbal and nonverbal. The skills of the therapist must include ability to obtain information from the child; because sparse verbalizations often characterize the child, this skill necessitates ability to understand child's play and to use it for communication purposes. Some children, regardless of age, will play and not talk at all, others will talk to themselves with toys while they play, and yet others will be able to converse with the therapist while play materials are used as an aide or adjunct to conversation. Thus, child's play with a particular toy or activity may be regarded as communication; when the child changes to another toy or activity, it may be viewed as either a deepening of the "conversation" or an effort to avoid or change the topic. The more skilled the therapist in helping the child communicate, the more information will become available to pursue goals of treatment.

In the therapist's quest for achieving an understanding of the child, a range of responses in addition to interpretation are useful. Weiner (1976) lists five kinds of therapist responses: questions, clarifications, exclamations, confrontations, and interpretations.

Questions

Questioning elicits information and helps a child continue to converse. Weiner (1976) points out that questions communicate little new information and, thus, have minimal impact on progress in treatment. Moreover, utilization of questions with children is tricky. With preschool children, communication should be without use of the "wh" phrases (what, when, where, who, why) which are poorly understood by young children. Furthermore, promiscuous use of the "wh" forms is interpreted by young and latency-age children as an accusation, especially use of the word *why.* This is because parents often have said, "Why did you do that?" or "What did you do?" following a minor misdemeanor. Thus, the therapist, instead of saying, "Why did you hit your brother," may wish to say, "I wonder if you might have been angry with your brother," or "Maybe you were angry at your brother." With the preschooler, a statement such as "Johnny was angry at Tommy" is preferable, in accordance with language ability in a child of this age.

Declarative statements, expressed with tentative beginnings such as "Maybe," "I wonder," and "Sometimes," request information or confirmation of the statement, much as a question would, but are not as intrusive or demanding as when the same statements are phrased as questions. It only takes a few episodes of questioning a child and getting ignored, or receiving a denial of fault, a shrug of the shoulders, or a flat "I don't know," to convince a beginning child therapist that questions are not productive with children. On the other hand, tentative declarative statements often elicit further play or verbalization. Likewise, children are loyal to parents and skittish about admission of absolutes. Thus, when the child appears to be playing out or verbalizing anger toward a parent, statements such as "*Maybe* you *sometimes* get a *little* angry with mother" are more acceptable to the child and more likely to elicit information than statements such as "Why did you get angry with mother?" It must be remembered that the child is dependent for well-being and survival on his or her parents, and any indication that the therapist views the parents negatively or that the child is being accused of negative affect toward them will elicit denial, anxiety, or flat rejection of the therapist.

Clarifications

Clarifications convey possible significance of certain matters by directing the child's attention to them or by restating his/her remarks. Weiner (1976) believes clarifications are helpful because they emphasize important areas, even though they do not present new ideas or possibilities about the client.

Clarifications with children often take the form of verbalizing play activity or repeating what the child has just said. Thus, as the young child repeatedly bumps the little car with a larger car, the therapist may say, "The *big* car is bumping the *little* car. The little car must not like that." If the child intends some aggression, he might respond, "Yeah, he pushes him right off the road!" and alternatively, if helpfulness is implied, he might respond "No! The big car is trying to help the little car get started." The child is able to either agree with or disagree with the therapist's understanding of his/her statement and elaborate with further detail.

Exclamations

Exclamations include various noncommittal therapist utterances intended to facilitate the child's talking, such as "Mm-hmm" or "I see." They can have potent reinforcement effects and influence areas of likely change, but like questions and clarifications, they neither provide substantive information nor specifically influence content of the client's self-reflections (Weiner, 1976). As noted previously in the discussion of reinforcement effects, the child psychotherapist may need to use more verbalization than the simple utterances typically used with adults.

Confrontations

Confrontations are statements that call the child's attention to factual aspects of behavior that the child did not notice. Confrontations *do* present information the child was not fully aware of. Unlike interpretations, they refer to obvious facts rather than to hypotheses or alternatives, and their accuracy requires no documentation (Weiner, 1976). Confrontations may be addressed to what the client is saying ("You said you got your report card, but you didn't say what it was like"), or to what he/she is doing ("You started pouring water on the floor while you were telling me about the accident you had at Disneyland"). This kind of response represents a significant step in making what seems private, public, or what seems magical and isolated, social.

Interpretations

Interpretations suggest some previously unrecognized meaning of, or connection between, a child's thoughts and feelings. Because they constitute possibilities or alternative hypotheses for exploration, they should be phrased as conjecture and probability. Interpretations communicate new self-knowledge to the child, enabling restructuring of self-perceptions and self-feelings and permitting the child to find more rewarding and self-fulfilling ways of behaving (Weiner, 1976). Thus, an interpretation for an 11-year-old boy who finds it hard to make decisions might be, "It seems that you try to collect the opinions of all your friends and all the grown-ups you know before you decide what to do to make sure that you are not wrong."

Questions, clarifications, exclamations, and confrontations prepare the way for the interpetive process. The use of words and grammatical structures should always coincide with the child's general cognitive abilities and the actual lexicon that the child uses (Shapiro, 1979). Typically, early comments by the therapist are centered on empathic and accepting comments and may simply consist of naming and describing behaviors and expressions of the child that the therapist has observed. Later, as certain areas are pursued, questions (or their equivalent) and clarifications are used to gain a fuller understanding of the child's feelings and attitudes. Once they are understood, then confrontations are used, and, finally, when the child appears ready to accept them, interpretations are offered.

The Course of Psychotherapy with Children

Psychotherapy is usually considered to have three continuous but distinct phases. The *initial* phase consists of evaluating the client, assessing the need for psychotherapy, and making arrangements for psychotherapy. The *middle* phase of psychotherapy, the longest and most demanding, involves communication of understanding through interpretation and resolution of resistance, transference, and countertransference. The *final* phase of psychotherapy, termination, includes the task of consolidating gains made in treatment and resolving issues pertaining to termination. This overview summarizes the typical course of psychotherapy with children and provides basic guidelines for the therapist.

The Initial Phase: Evaluation, Assessment, and the Treatment Contract

A series of interviews is arranged for the purpose of achieving three tasks: (1) evaluation of the child's personality functioning and the nature of the referral problems; (2) assessment of the child's capability for participating in, and benefiting from, psychotherapy and of the parents' ability to support treatment by cooperation and motivation to seek change in their child; and (3) arrangement of a treatment contract with both child and parents where an agreement is reached concerning the means and objectives of psychotherapy.

Evaluating the Client

Evaluation of the child consists of ascertaining the nature and background of the child's presenting problem, evaluating surrounding issues such as parental adjustment, and arriving at an understanding of the child as a person. In addition, the child's coping style with parents, school, and peers should be determined. The purpose of this evaluation is to establish *clinical* and *dynamic* working formulations of the child and his or her needs. The clinical formulation consists of primary symptoms (e.g., oppositional behavior), characterological style (e.g., passive-aggressive personality), and an assessment of personality assets and liabilities. The dynamic formulation includes major sources of conflict and concerns that are related to the child's difficulties. This also includes an evaluation of the parents' relationship to the child, the quality of their parenting skills, their motivation for treatment, and their perception of the problem.

Evaluation may be conducted by the use of interview alone, but it often includes developmental history forms that parents fill out, pscyhological evaluations of intelligence and personality characteristics as revealed by objective and projective techniques, parent and school inventories, and school observations. The information yielded in this phase enables the therapist to determine which child needs psychotherapy and which does not. The evaluation should contain sufficient information to support tentative formulations about the appropriateness of psychotherapy.

Assessing the Appropriateness of Psychotherapy

Psychological problems experienced by most children exist in varying degrees and are tolerated and dealt with differently by different people. Presence or absence of difficulties is not the primary factor in determining whether psychotherapy for children is sought and received. A number of factors are involved: (1) severity of the disorder; (2) child and parent attitudes toward psychological services and psychotherapists; (3) parents' and significant others' attitudes toward the child's problems, and their assessment of the degree of their interference with the child's development; and (4) availability of services.

The dependency of children on adults complicates decisions about psychotherapy because it is adults who seek help for their children. Some children are denied professional attention even though they might desire and need it. On the other hand, some children are brought for psychotherapy by their parents despite their active opposition to this help.

Psychotherapy is rarely the treatment of choice for severely disturbed children (i.e., childhood schizophrenia and early infantile autism) because use of the area most impaired in these disorders (communication skills) is necessary in psychotherapy. Psychotherapy is most appropriate for comparatively mild to moderate problems of childhood and, with these disorders, it is associated with favorable changes in attitudes and behaviors.

Parental attitudes, particularly mother's, are important. It appears that mothers who are unable to tolerate their children's problems and who are depressed or anxious are more prone to initiate and continue children in treatment than are those who are more casual about disturbed behaviors in their offspring (Shepherd, Oppenheim, & Mitchell, 1966). The degree of interference in the development of the child, cognitively, psychologically, and intellectually, is also an important consideration because lost accomplishment during periods of disturbance (e.g., impaired school work, difficult parent–child interaction, poor peer relationships) may lead to further problems and poor self-concept. Psychotherapists emphasize that (1) some relief from great distress is experienced immediately by clients simply by entering psychotherapy, and (2) alleviation of pain and discomfort when the person feels the need for it is valuable even though the difficulties may not be appreciably altered (Weiner, 1976).

Although mild to moderate difficulties in adjustment of children may merit professional assistance, not every psychological problem requires psychotherapy or responds well to this mode of treatment. The professional therapist must take into account not only his/her own assessment of the situation, but also the assessment of the child, the parents, and often other involved parties, such as school personnel, the family physician, and foster parents (Reisman, 1973).

Arranging the Treatment Contract

On completion of evaluation and assessment, feedback and recommendations should be given to both the child and parents. The therapist's impressions are presented to parents with specific recommendations for psychotherapy and an explanation of how psychotherapy works to accomplish its aim. Because the child is the client, the child should also either be included in the feedback interview or be seen separately where the same impresssions, recommendations, and explanation of procedures are given in terms appropriate to his or her age and ability to understand.

Following agreement to undertake psychotherapy, the second step is to discuss the goals of therapy and the procedures to be employed in more detail. Again, the child should be included in goal-setting. Although there may be differences between parent and child goals, they are not necessarily at counterpurposes. Thus, while parents may be concerned with aggressive behavior in their son, the child may express concern about his parents "not letting him grow up."

Even if the child does not admit to any problems or denies them in the face of behavior during the interview to indicate otherwise, the therapist must explain his/her understanding of the child's problems and how therapy will proceed. The child is given an opportunity to respond to the therapist's delineation of the problem behaviors. If this opportunity is denied, explicit permission is given to do so later.

A thorough discussion about the role of the child and the role of the therapist is appropriate in a discussion of procedures. Both parents and child must understand what the therapist does, how goals are accomplished, and the role of the child. This is especially important with parents because they often do not undertsand how "play" can help. The therapist should explain the purpose of play and point out that play used in therapy differs from the usual conception of the activity.

The third step in formulating a treatment contract includes the making of specific arrangements for the time, place, frequency, and fees for sessions. These arrangements are made with the parents, for they bring the child, but often the child is consulted as well, especially if the time of appointment may interfere with school or if the child is an adolescent.

The Middle Phase: Interpretation, Resistance, Transference, and Countertransference

The middle phase is the longest and most important phase in achieving the goals of psychotherapy. Sometimes there are changes as a result of the evaluation phase, such that the child's behavior improves. This is due to the relationship. Technical procedures for the communication of understanding begin only when the treatment or middle phase occurs.

The major technique for communication of understanding is interpretation. *Resistance* in one or more of its forms almost invariably occurs in reaction to interpretations. Resistance interferes with the communication process and must be relieved or circumvented if treatment is to progress. The third feature of the middle phase is the development of irrational feelings and attitudes that the client and therapist form toward one another, called *transference* and *countertransference*. These aspects of the treatment relationship require resolution to permit successful therapy.

Interpretation

As defined earlier, interpretations are statements that bring to the child's attention aspects about the child and his or her behavior that the child had not previously been aware of. For interpretations to be successful, the therapist must make decisions about *what* to interpret, *when* to interpret it, and *how* to deliver the interpretive sequence.

Interpretations should be addressed to features of the child's thoughts, feelings and actions that seem distressing, or that reflect distorted, unrealistic, inconsistent, or ineffective means of coping (Weiner, 1976). Interpretations are only appropriate for what appears to be causing difficulties in life, and therefore, are selectively focused.

In regard to *when* to interpret, Anna Freud's (1965) recommendations should be considered: Material near the surface of the client's awareness should be interpreted; deeply unconscious concerns should not be interpreted until the uncovering effects of treatment have brought them close to awareness. The child can sense the plausbility of interpretations if given when the connections or relationships are close to awareness. On the other hand, if they are addressed to aspects of thoughts, feelings, and actions of which awareness is not even remote, disruptive effects that may cause anxiety are the result.

Good *timing* and *dosage* are important. The best *time* to give an interpretation is when the child is approaching awareness of the particular connection or explanation it suggests, and also when the child seems open to new ideas and is enthusiastic about treatment (Weiner, 1976). The therapist should be reasonably sure of their accuracy and be able to document interpretations. *Dosage* is determined by the child's ability to think them through, for they are new information and they require reflection. Giving interpretations too fast and too frequently may overstimulate the child.

The interpretive *sequence* involves using a graded series of interventions to prepare the way for each interpretation to be made. Thus, the therapist may begin with a clarification ("You got through drawing on that piece of paper and want another one"), continue with a confrontation ("It seems as if every time you need a piece of paper, you ask for another one even though you know you don't have to"), and conclude with an interpretation ("Maybe you are afraid that I would not approve of what you want and you have to make sure each time").

This illustration points up several features of the interpretive process. It adheres to the data, and it is phrased in conjecture ("Maybe you . . ."). The sequence allows the child to deny, make excuses for, or accept the behavior at every point, indicating the child's readiness for the interpretation, Then, when the interpretation is given, it gives the child the opportunity to confirm it. Later on, interpretation can be used as confrontation, leading to interpretation concerning other situations. This procedure is a tedious one, taking many sessions, and sessions may occur where interpretations are not possible and the therapist must rely on clarifications and confrontations for most of the communication.

Resistance

Resistance refers to the temporary inability or unwillingness of the child to adhere to terms of the treatment contract. Weiner (1976) lists four kinds of motivation that run counter to the client's conscious wish to participate in, and benefit from, psychotherapy: resistance to change, resistance to content, characterological resistance, and transference resistance. The four kinds of resistance, respectively, refer to: reluctance to give up present life patterns; avoidance of painful, depressing, or embarrassing confrontations; holding onto preferred styles of coping with cognitive and affective experiences; and developing thoughts and feelings about the therapist.

In psychotherapy with children, the therapist must also deal with another set of resistances, those of the parents that create difficulty for therapy. Thus, parents may become remiss by cancelling, skipping, or coming late for sessions. The child's resistance is shown by resisting the therapist's efforts to deal with the child's problems and by engaging in play or meaningless conversation, ignoring the therapist. As in psychotherapy with adults, sometimes the child will seek to make the therapist more of a personal friend than a helping professional, or may tenaciously insist that no problems exist.

Resistance interferes with communication in psychotherapy and may lead to premature termination, especially if the resistance resides with parents. However, if interpretations are timed to the circumstances of the resistances and the manner in which they are expressed, they can also help the child learn more about him/herself, and the interference can be minimized.

Transference

There are three concurrent levels of interaction between the client and therapist. First, there is the *real* relationship between them, influenced by the client's factual knowledge about his therapist (sex, age, physical characteristics, manner of dress). Second, there is the *working alliance,* which consists of commitment to the treatment contract and the roles it prescribes. This relationship has been distinguished from the real relationship by virtue of the asymmetry of the client's expressing him/herself without restraint and the therapist's listening and commenting (Weiner, 1976). Third, the child develops a *transference* relationship to the therapist, consisting of positive and negative feelings and attitudes originating toward other people (usually parents) and now transferred inappropriately to the therapist. This is often expressed in subtle ways by the child when attempts are made for closer physical proximity and contact, expressions of the wish for longer and more frequent contacts, and even contacts outside the treatment situation.

More direct expressions of transference are favorable or unfavorable comments about the therapist's profession, the office, the toys, or his/her person. Typical of children is the expression of love and the wish to live with the therapist, which may begin with questions about marital status, children, other children she/he might see, and so forth. These feelings always have more to do with how the child has felt or feels about others than with the real relationship between therapist and child.

Transference in child treatment has been a subject of some debate. Some have contended that it cannot occur in children, while others have thought that it exists in altered and different form from that manifested by adults. Early in her writings, Anna Freud (1946) advocated establishment of a strong attachment of the child to the therapist through the "introductory phase." She states that "the affectionate attachment, the positive transference, as it is called in analytical terminology, is the prerequisite for all later work" (Freud, 1946, p. 31). She thought that the child would only participate in psychotherapy for a loved person, and viewed negative transference toward the analyst as essentially inconvenient. But she distinguished between becoming the object toward which the child's friendly or hostile impulses are directed and a transference neurosis. This is true because parents are still real and present as love-objects, and gratifications and disappointments still in reality depend on them. Later, she revised her position to include the repetition of behaviors and positive and negative reactions to the analyst from other (parental) relationships, in addition to treating the analyst as a new object (Freud, 1965).

Countertransference

Therapists also have inappropriate reactions to child clients or parents during the treatment relationship. This is known as countertransference and can result from a generalized reaction toward certain kinds of children (e.g., enjoyment of the bright, verbal child, or limited tolerance for an aggressive, hyperactive child), or are related to areas of unresolved personal conflicts. Either positive or negative countertransference undermines the working alliance with the child if it is not recognized and controlled. Countertransference reactions to the parents emanate from unrealistic attitudes about parents in general, which also reflect unresolved conflict with the therapist's parents. This may also lead to taking sides with the child against the parents and is always counterproductive for the therapeutic goal.

Countertransference can be manifested either directly or indirectly. The treatment contract requires the therapist to respect the child and not to judge. Thus, for example, when the therapist corrects the child's behavior when the child begins swearing and hitting toys during treatment, though justifiable in a parental relationship to a child, it is not appropriate to the treatment situation and represents countertransference. The therapist's task is to understand, and to help the child understand the angry expression, not to correct the behavior as parents would.

The therapist's personal feelings may be useful by promoting understanding of the effect of the child's behavior on others, as, for example, an angry feeling in response to provocative behavior. These personal values and feelings should not divert the therapist from his task of meeting the child's needs rather than his own, however.

There are also less overt manifestations of countertransference. For example, the therapist may have positive or negative expectations about future meetings, find that attention to the child is deficient, or become reluctant to enter into play when invited to do so by the child. Also, interpretations may become too frequent and otherwise not well timed, or they may be withheld to spare the child's feelings. During off hours, the therapist may think about or dream of the child in either a pleasant or unpleasant context. The therapist should be alert to the presence of these thoughts and modify his or her actions accordingly.

The Final Phase: Termination

The therapist negotiates termination with the child when it is believed that advantages of ending the meetings outweigh what may be gained by their continuance. There is considerable variation among therapists concerning the determination of termination. Some therapists judge the relief of symptoms alone as sufficient justification for ending treatment, while others hold on to more rigorous and less easily attained goals (Reisman, 1971). Some think of termination as a kind of wrap-up, during which little more can be accomplished except to relieve the child's anxieties about functioning alone. Other therapists, such as Allen (1942), see termination as a potentially constructive experience and a representation of a crucial human conflict. For such therapists, termination is not the culmination of their efforts, but perhaps the most taxing and rewarding phase of psychotherapy.

Regardless of the view of tasks in this phase, termination should be introduced to the child without rejection. When the child agrees to it, a date should be set. Whenever possible, Reisman (1973) believes that the child should select the date, but in actual practice it is usually a decision reached between parents and therapist, with the child often not consulted. When the child is consulted, possible protestations are considered secondary to the adults' assessment of indications for termination.

Ordinarily, four to six sessions are allowed for the termination phase, but sometimes more time is allowed. However, sometimes termination is precipitously imposed. The child may be removed from psychotherapy by a parent who cannot tolerate expression of certain feelings, by parents' move to another community, by mother's pregnancy, or by family crises that are given precedence over needs of the child. Sometimes summer vacations, family trips, departures for camps, or disruptions in staff hasten termination for many children. If it is at all possible under such circumstances, the therapist should try to convince parents to allow at least one or two sessions, or ideally, up to five, for the termination phase. An explanation about unsettled feelings, including outbursts of anger and sadness often seen in children about to terminate after a series of sessions, should aid in convincing parents to comply with the request. This, however, is not always possible because it often happens that parents do not bring the child for treatment after return from vacation or camp. Also, when parents are displeased with changes in the child's behavior, the therapist's pleas for more time are rejected.

Involvement of Parents

As can be gleaned from the preceding discussion, parents are a crucial force in psychotherapy with children. It is, therefore, necessary to involve parents on some level, if only for information and feedback about the effects of the therapeutic contact. In most cases, the aim is also to involve them in a process whereby parent–child interactions can improve. The two major methods of involving parents are through parental counseling, which involves a professional meeting frequently (once a week) or infrequently (once a month), and family therapy, in which the total family is seen on a frequent and regular basis. An overview of each of these two areas will be presented. For more detailed coverage of the process of working with the parents of emotionally disturbed children, the reader is referred to Reisman (1973).

Parental Counseling

Except in rare instances, professional involvement with parents is expected when a child is seen in individual psychotherapy. However, there is disagreement about the role that parents should play in treatment of their child and the role the therapist should play with parents. One view is that parents are responsible adults who can provide reliable information about their child and can implement advice and recommendations. Another view is that parents are probably more disturbed than the child and need psychotherapy themselves. These parents sabotage and frustrate treatment and perpetuate the pathology. A third view is that parents are a heterogeneous group with varying strengths and weaknesses who nonetheless are interested in obtaining help for their child. In some cases, however, this interest is negligible and is secondary to fears and concerns. The therapist must assess the extent to which parents are able to help in treatment of their child.

Sometimes assessment reveals that parents require a psychotherapy relationship for themselves. Psychotherapy for parents may or may not be offered in the same facility in which the child is being seen, and may or may not be administered by the same therapist, if it is permitted. Often an outside referral is deemed the most expeditious arrangement for providing psychotherapy for parents.

Alfred Adler, writing in the 1930s, was influential in providing guidelines for working with parents. He presented five recommendations, which included: (1) to remember not to reproach or censure parents for the child's pathology; (2) to remember that parents are not entirely responsible for the child's behavior; (3) to avoid dwelling on what parents do that is wrong and concentrate on what they might do that would be constructive and helpful; (4) to enlist parents' cooperation despite their imperfections; and (5) to avoid being authoritarian in giving advice or recommendations through the use of qualifiers like "perhaps" or "maybe" (Ansbacher & Ansbacher, 1956, pp. 395–396). Most therapists today agree with these guidelines.

The roles of the therapist and parent as they work together can be best conceptualized as those of consultant and consultee (Reisman, 1973). The conceptualization of this approach recognizes that parents have a problem with their child, for which they seek help from a specialist in child psychotherapy. The problem is usually presented as a problem of the child, not of the parent ("Why does he do that?" "What can be wrong with her?"). The parents expect to receive suggestions but reserve the right to reject them. They also maintain responsibility for the child and believe they have more knowledge about the child than does the therapist.

The task of the therapist is to build on the strengths of parents. This is accomplished by determining the nature of the problem with the parents and then, together, considering alternative ways of dealing with the problem. Simply hearing that certain problems are not atypical can alleviate parents' concern. Parents are often perplexed by their child's behavior and their own contributions to it. In the task of consulting with parents, the therapist is helping the parents in their problems of work (i.e., those of child rearing). The task is presently beyond the parents' skills but not outside their realm of potential competence. It is in the area of helping parents improve their child-rearing skills that most assistance can be given to parents.

It should be noted that when the child is seen in psychotherapy and the parents are seen in a consultant–consultee arrangement, parents often report help for themselves although psychotherapy has not been directly offered to them. For example, Reisman and Kissel (1968) found that increased understanding about behavior of their child was sufficient for mothers of treated children, even without noticeable change in the behavior of their offspring.

It is impossible here to give more than a cursory view of working with parents in psychotherapy. Work with parents is as intricate as work with children and has been considered in detail elsewhere. The reader is referred to Kessler (1966), Reisman (1973),

Moustakas (1959), and Smirnoff (1968) for discussions of the intricacies of evaluation and engagement in counseling with parents to support treatment of the child.

Family Therapy

The practice of family therapy developed largely from a "recognition that the patient does not get sick alone, nor does he get well alone" (Jackson & Satir, 1961, p. 42). While therapists of all persuasions have long recognized the major role of the family in development and maintenance of child psychopathology, the importance of the family's role in the therapeutic process has often been minimized, if not overlooked. Although suggested as early as 1890, family therapy did not become popular until the mid 1950s.

When working with children, it often becomes clear that the treatment of choice is to involve the total family, either as the only intervention strategy or in conjunction with individual therapy with the child. Family therapy, thus, often replaces parental counseling, particularly when familial communication and interactional patterns perpetuate pathology in the identified patient and/or other family members. Family therapy is especially indicated in families that are in crisis (Korchin, 1976), have a chaotic structure (Scherz, 1962), exhibit a severe deficit or breakdown in communication (Geist & Gerber, 1960; Scherz, 1962; Wynne, 1965), or exhibit family conflicts along value or generational lines (Korchin, 1976). Family therapy is also recommended after a course of individual therapy when the patient's improvement results in symptoms developing in other family members (Clower & Brody, 1964; Glick & Kessler, 1974; Schomer, 1978), when a parent sabotages the child's therapy (Clower & Brody, 1964), when a parent is neurotic or hostile-dependent ties exist between child and parent (Scherz, 1962), or when the child's symptoms relate to high levels of family tension and inconsistent parental attitudes (Clower & Brody, 1964). Other kinds of indications that have been advanced include control or manipulation of the family by the child's symptoms (Avallone, Aron, Starr, & Breetz, 1973; Clower & Brody, 1964), as, for example, in adolescent acting-out behavior (Ackerman, 1966; Alexander & Parsons, 1973; Anthony, 1978; Beck, 1975) and in adolescent separation problems (Ackerman, 1966; Korchin, 1976; Wynne, 1965), and in situations where major conflicts are not predominantly intrapsychic or of a longstanding nature (Ackerman, 1963), or when the client cannot tolerate the demands for extensive verbal communication (Clower & Brody, 1964) or the one-to-one relationship of individual therapy (Scherz, 1964).

There are situations, however, in which family therapy would not be recommended. Contraindications include separation or divorce with little or no desire for reconciliation (Ackerman, 1966) or when one or more members of the defined functional social system is not available or not willing to participate (Clarkin, Frahces, & Moodie, 1979). Other issues that contraindicate family therapy are family prejudice against psychological intervention (Ackerman, 1966), lack of trust in the family therapist by the identified patient (Clarkin *et al.*, 1979; Scherz, 1962), family insistence on privacy (Ackerman, 1966; Korchin, 1976), or when individuation of a family member might be compromised (Glick & Kessler, 1974).

Family therapy is broadly defined here as any type of therapeutic intervention that focuses on the family system, seeking to produce beneficial changes in the structure, function, and interaction of a family unit. Although certain aspects of the personality of an individual may change as a result of family therapy, it is not the primary goal of most family therapists to change "underlying personality structure in isolation from its relationship to the family context" (Glick & Kessler, 1974, p. 5). The family system, however, is an interdependent organization in which the behavior and expression of each member influences and is influenced by all others. Thus, the positive changes in the family unit as a whole are expected to also result in benefits for each member.

Most family therapists agree that the overall goal of family therapy must be change in the family interactional pattern such that members relate in new and different ways. The underlying assumption is that if the interactional patterns change, then the individual family members will change.

Family therapy consists of three major types: adjunct, conjoint, and network family therapy. These types can be further divided into two broad theoretical groups: psychoanalytic and systems theory. For discussion of the differences in the theories and techniques of family therapy, the reader is referred to several excellent texts, including Beels and Ferber (1972), Foley (1974), Guerin and Pendagast (1976), Haley (1971), Masten (1979), and Minuchin (1974).

Trends in Child Psychotherapy Research

In comparison to research in adult psychotherapy, the number of research articles in child psychotherapy is few. The relatively meager amount is reflected in the few pages devoted to child psychotherapy research in the *Annual Review of Psychology,* as noted by Levitt (1971). Also, attempts to identify the issues of psychotherapy research with children have been sparse. For example, child psychotherapy research was excluded from review by Strupp and Bergin (1969), and also from discussion of factors influencing psychotherapy by Lubrosky, Chandler, Auerbach, Cohen, and Bachrach (1971). Barrett *et al.* (1978) assess that child psychotherapy research continues to be what Gardner (1953) described it to be almost 30 years ago: "the product of evening, weekend and vacation period labor" tacked onto service and training.

The meager state of child psychotherapy research has been attributed to the fact that only recently has there been increased programmatic development of services to children (e.g., mental health centers, early intervention programs, primary prevention, child advocacy, and public policy). Further, there has been a general lack of response to criticisms advanced by the work of Levitt (1957). During this time period, a significant drop of interest in the specific variables that cause and ameliorate emotional disorders has also been in evidence (Barrett *et al.,* 1978).

Despite this diminished interest in individual psychotherapy as a research activity, there has been steady application in clinical settings. This fact is highlighted by the results of a recent survey (Tuma & Cawunder, in press) in which it was found that a great proportion of clinical child psychologists profess a dynamic theoretical orientation and utilize dynamic techniques of intervention. Of 594 respondents, 30% listed a dynamic orientation (20% psychoanalytic or psychoanalytically oriented, 10% humanistic) as their major theoretical orientation. The major group (55%), however, claimed an eclectic orientation. Of these respondents, 48% indicated a psychoanalytic orientation as the first component of this eclecticism, and approximately 6% claimed a humanistic orientation. As their second component, 17% listed a psychoanalytic orientation and 28% listed a humanistic orientation. These respondents further indicated that play therapy and individual therapy were the most frequently used techniques with preschool and latency age children, at a frequency of almost two-to-one to those using behavioral techniques for this age group. Frequency of family therapy was also high, being second to dynamic applications. This survey did not include other professionals (e.g., psychiatrists and social workers) who provide treatment for children. It is conceivable that even a higher percentage of other mental health professionals adhere to a dynamic orientation to treatment of children, for behavioral techniques have not been as popular with them.

Recent activities of child clinicians point to increased interest and progress in conceptualizing child psychotherapy research, however. Comprehensive bibliographies of this research are presented by Klein (1973) and Berlin (1976), and Barrett *et al.* (1978) present an evaluative research review. These reviews serve to highlight the status of psychotherapy research and attempt to point out methodological requirements for future research. The present review presents an overview of these recommendations.

From the 1920s through the 1960s there were numerous research attempts by many investigators to study effects of child therapy, parent counseling, or a combination of both. From the 1960s to the present, relatively little outcome research has been reported. Research activity notably dropped after Levitt's (1957, 1963; Levitt, Beiser, & Robertson, 1959) conclusion that the effectiveness of child psychotherapy had not been demonstrated despite a 75% improvement rate of treated children in the several studies he reviewed. The absence of the mobilization effect of these reports on research efforts is in direct contrast to the response of adult clinicians toward the similar work of Eysenck (1961). As a result of efforts to design and execute quality outcome research, evidence for effectiveness of psychotherapy and other interventions with adults is much better than it was (Malan, 1973; Meltzoff & Kornreich, 1970; Sloane *et al.*, 1975).

There were several attempts to reanalyze Levitt's data and to suggest alternative conclusions (Barrett *et al.,* 1978; Halpern, 1968; Heinicke & Goldman, 1960; Hood-Williams, 1960) but higher quality research was not forthcoming. Some child clinicians turned their interests, instead, to other modalities, such as behavior modification and family therapy, and to building the institutions and programs mentioned earlier. Thus, the effect of Levitt's work was to push child clinicians toward alternatives and was not instrumental in encouraging more quality research.

It has been suggested that emphasis on institutions is declining and that a resurgence of interest in individuals is again increasing (cf. Hogan, DeSoto, & Solano, 1977). Renewed interest in child psychotherapy research is expected by some (Barrett *et al.,* 1978) who warn that if the same mistakes of combining variables (e.g., combining all kinds of diagnostic categories, patients being seen by therapists with wide variety of personal styles, each therapist making all kinds of interventions, and then assessing outcome in some gross fashion like "improved—partially improved—unimproved"), research with child psychotherapy will not advance from the present state of demonstrating that 70% of disturbed children improve with psychotherapy *or* with time alone.

A refinement of technique is suggested by many (Barrett *et al.,* 1978; Halpern, 1968; Heinicke & Goldman, 1960; Heinicke & Strassman, 1975). Areas identified as needing refinement include (1) the child and his or her disorder, (2) the therapist and his or her personality, (3) the intervention techniques, and (4) outcome measures.

The Child and the Disorder

Four factors have been mentioned as the minimum factors that need to be controlled: age, intelligence, type of onset, and severity of disorder. Correcting age in a more sophisticated manner to determine the developmental status of the child along the lines suggested by Anna Freud (1962) has been advocated by Heinicke and Strassman (1975). Intelligence is relatively easy to assess, but chronicity of the condition is difficult. This is because some problems emerge for a time and disappear, only to resurface and disappear again several times at varying time intervals in the same child. Standardized methods of quantification of chronicity are imperative for cross-study comparisons. Barrett *et al.* (1978) suggest that the Onset of Symptomatology Scale (Gossett, Meeks, Barnhart, & Phillips, 1976) is a potentially useful instrument.

Severity of illness has traditionally been a difficult area to assess, and imprecise matching of children according to this dimension is responsible for many criticisms of psychotherapy research with children, including Levitt's (1957) original review. The absence of any standard way to measure severity of disturbance makes comparisons across outcome studies meaningless. Studies in the past have rated severity unidimentionally (e.g., mildly disturbed, moderately disturbed, severely disturbed) with the rating points left unreferenced. It has been shown that clinicians can make reliable judgments on severity of disturbance (Coddington & Offord, 1967), and there has been at least one attempt to improve these judgments in research with children (Miller, Barrett, Hampe, & Noble, 1972). These investigators defined severity as the product of the intensity of the child's distress and the extensity of the phobia's (the disturbance under investigation) effect on the child's life. Using a referenced seven-point scale, they obtained high interrater reliability in the ratings. Community tolerance for the problem has also been suggested as another dimension of severity (McConville & Purohit, 1973). Barrett *et al.* (1978) suggest a fourth dimension of severity, that of treatability of the disorder. A severe disorder, using these dimensions together, would then be a disorder (1) that is subjectively distressing, (2) that invades many facets of a child's life, (3) that is not tolerated by the community, and (4) that is resistant to treatment.

The Therapist and His or Her Personality

In studies on the relationship of therapist characteristics and outcome of psychotherapy with adults, there is reasonable consensus that warmth, genuineness, empathy, level of experience, and freedom of from neurotic difficulties promote successful outcome, while the discipline of the therapist and the therapist's history of personal therapy are unrelated to outcome. More variability has been obtained in the contributions to outcome of therapist age, gender, race, religion, and social class, but there is an emerging belief that there is a curvilinear relationship between these variables and outcome. Thus, the best therapeutic results are obtained between people who are neither too much alike nor too different from each other (Carson & Heiner, 1962).

Because of the importance of warm, genuine, and empathic communications of the child therapist in developing a therapeutic alliance, it is inconceivable that these same characteristics would not be also be related to outcome measures of child psychotherapy. Research on these characteristics with children in psychotherapy has not received the attention it has in adult psychotherapy. However, Ricks, Thomas, and Roff (1974) made some attempt to answer a part of this question in research on characteristics of two therapists, the effective one now known as "Supershrink."

The Intervention Techniques

In research comparing different types of therapy, for example, reciprocal inhibition therapy and play therapy (Miller *et al.,* 1972), it has been found that there were no differences between the two approaches. In fact, Miller *et al.* propose that one treatment *was* the other. However, claims are being made about inherent differences and the superior effectiveness of one treatment modality or approach over another. Barrett *et al.* (1978) suggest that the first step in finding distinguishing features of different kinds of interventions is to discover and describe those procedures that are common to nearly all child treatments and to assess their impact. The next step would then be to determine if the maneuvers that are exclusive to one type of therapy add anything beyond the general variables.

The Measurement of Outcome

The one thing all researchers in child and adult psychotherapy agree to is that the unstructured, unidimentional judgments of "improved—partially improved—unimproved" made by the patient's therapist will not produce meaningful data. Strupp and Hadley (1977) tackle the problem of assessing outcome with a comprehensive and relativistic approach, taking into account the vantage points of those who evaluate change and the values of those who occupy each vantage point. Their three main "interested parties" are (1) society (including significant persons in the patient's life), (2) the individual patient, and (3) the mental health professional. Because society is primarily concerned with the maintenance of an orderly world, society and its representatives define mental health in terms of behavioral stability, predictability, and conformity to the social code. The individual is more likely to focus on a subjective sense of well-being. In use with children, this facet needs extra attention because many children who are brought for treatment claim they are subjectively comfortable.

The mental health professionals typically view an individual's functioning in terms of structure and dynamics of the child's personality. They are interested in variables such as richness of the child's ego structure, balance between drives and defenses, and the child's generalized orientation toward self and others.

Using these three vantage points, Strupp and Hadley state:

> the same individual may simultaneously be judged as mentally healthy or mentally ill and, correspondingly, his therapeutic experience may be judged as positive or negative depending on who is evaluating the patient. (1977, p. 196)

The criteria for each perspective is different, and therefore they cannot be compared. Strupp and Hadley note that:

> a truly adequate, comprehensive picture of an individual's mental health is possible only if the three facets of functioning—behavior, affect and inferred psychological structure—are evaluated and integrated. (1977, p. 196)

Barrett *et al.* (1978) advocate the use of an instrument or set of instruments that can be used by the patient, by the therapist, and by significant representatives of society (peers, parents, teachers). Such an "instrument should tap behavior, affect and psychological functioning in all of its normal and deviant varieties" (Barrett *et al.,* 1978, p. 432). The reason for this proposal is that none of the three viewpoints has exclusive use of its principal viewpoint. Society in part wishes the client a sense of well-being and a solid personality structure, while it is also concerned with stability, responsibility, and conformity. Patients want an integrated personality and a moderate ability to respect society's conventions as well as a sense of well-being, and therapists also want their patients to have a sense of well-being and an ability to behave in moderately conforming, responsible, and courageous fashion as well as to value intrapsychic integrity.

This kind of evaluation for child psychotherapy is more complex and demanding than it is for adult psychotherapy due to the vast differences related to the age and maturity of the child. Thus, instruments would have to be tailored to the child's developmental level and would involve scales for differing age groups. Barrett *et al.* (1978), while recognizing the enormous task this would entail, nevertheless conceives of it as a worthwhile criterion.

Several methodological issues have been addressed in the outcome work of adult psychotherapy researchers. Those researchers committed to quality outcome research for effectiveness of psychotherapy with children thus have a great deal of the spadework already done for them. It will, however, take some ingenuity to work out the knotty problems of applying some of the research designs to developmentally immature human beings. This aspect represents the unique contribution possible for child researchers; it should not be considered an impossible task, and is, of course, a worthwhile endeavor. The ethical responsibility of the child psychotherapist is to keep abreast of research in the area of practice and, by implication, to contribute to that research. Now that more is being published about the dearth of research on child psychotherapy, perhaps some of those child psychotherapists will become challenged by the possibilities of this area of endeavor.

Summary

Psychotherapy with children began with Sigmund Freud's treatment of Little Hans, reported in 1909. The most significant development of theory and technique, however, is attributed to Melanie Klein and Anna Freud. However, only Anna Freud's technique has been popular in the United States because Klein's approach did not mesh with findings in child development. Although psychoanalytically oriented psychotherapy is the prototype of the most commonly practiced psychotherapy in child treatment settings, many theories and techniques of psychotherapy with children have been developed. The important approaches in the United States are relationship therapy, structured play therapy, client-centered therapy, and of course psychoanalytic and psychoanalytically oriented psychotherapy. These approaches differ along two major dimensions: active versus passive stance of the therapist, and emphasis on relationship versus technique as the agent of change.

The most parsimonious definition of psychotherapy was developed by Reisman. He defines psychotherapy as "the communication of person-related understanding, respect, and a wish to be of help." This definition, more than any other, permits clear distinctions between what is psychotherapy and what is psychotherapeutic, and highlights the importance of the professional relationship to therapeutic results.

Both general and specific factors are attributes of all psychotherapy. General factors refer to aspects of the psychotherapy relationship (catharsis, expectation of change, therapist attention, and reinforcement effects). Specific factors refer to technical procedures employed by the therapist within that relationship. These procedures (questions, clarifications, exclamations, confrontations, and interpretations) derive from Sigmund Freud's psychoanalytic methods of free association and interpretation, and are designed to increase the client's understanding of problems and possible alternative resolutions.

Child psychotherapy consists of three distinct phases: the initial phase, the middle phase, and the final (or termination) phase. The initial phase consists of evaluation of the child, assessment of appropriateness of psychotherapy, and arrangement of the treatment contract. The middle phase is the longest and most important phase in achieving the goals of psychotherapy and is characterized by interpretation. Also important to successful psychotherapy are recognition and resolution of resistance, transference, and countertransference. The communication process between child and therapist can proceed only when these disruptive effects are adequately handled. The final stage is entered when the therapist believes that advantages of ending the meetings outweigh what may be gained by their continuance.

When working with children, parental involvement is extremely important. Parental involvement is most frequently accomplished either by parental counseling to support the child's treatment, or by family therapy, which also involves other family members but focuses on the manner in which maladjustments are perpetuated by interaction and communication between family members.

Child psychotherapy research does not compare well with adult psychotherapy research. This has been attributed to child therapists' devoting attention to programmatic development during the past 15 years as well as a general lack of response to criticism leveled at the efficacy of child psychotherapy by Levitt. Child therapists, during this period, also began utilization of alternative techniques, notably behavior therapy and family therapy. With the recent decline of emphasis on institutional development, however, there is evidence of a resurgence of interest in individual psychotherapy, and increased activity in child psychotherapy research is expected. Most critics call for a refinement of research techniques. Especially needed in child psychotherapy research are refined definition and control of factors concerning (1) the child and his or her disorder, (2) the therapist and his or her personality, (3) intervention techniques, and (4) outcome measures. The complexity of child psychotherapy research makes direct analogy to adult psychotherapy research difficult, but many of the advances made by researchers in the adult area can be adapted for child psychotherapy research.

References

Ackerman, N. Family therapy. In *Encyclopedia of Mental Health* (Vol. 2). New York: Franklin Watts, 1963.

Ackerman, N. *Treating the troubled family.* New York: Basic Books, 1966.

Alexander, E. D. An hour's journey with Cindy. *Psychotherapy: Theory, Research, and Practice*, 1966, *3*, 88–90.

Alexander, J. F., & Parsons, H. V. Short term behavioral intervention with delinquent families: Impact on family process and recidivism. *Journal of Abnormal Psychology,* 1973, *81,* 219–225.

Allen, F. H. *Psychotherapy with children.* New York: Norton, 1942.

Ansbacher, H. L., & Ansbacher, R. R. *The individual psychology of Alfred Adler.* New York: Basic Books, 1956.

Anthony, E. J. Is child psychopathology always family psychopathology? Yes, no, and neither: The views from Freud to Laing. In J. Brady & H. Brodie (Eds.), *Controversies in psychiatry.* Philadelphia: Saunders, 1978.

Arthur, H. A comparison of the technique employed in psychotherapy and psychoanalysis of children. *American Journal of Orthopsychiatry,* 1952, *22,* 484–499.

Avallone, S., Aron, R., Starr, P., & Breetz, S. How therapists assign families to treatment modalities: The development of the treatment method choice set. *American Journal of Orthopsychiatry,* 1973, *43,* 767–773.

Axline, V. M. Nondirective therapy for poor readers. *Journal of Consulting Psychology,* 1947, *11,* 61–69. (a)

Axline, V. M. *Play therapy.* Boston: Houghton Mifflin, 1947. (b)

Axline, V. M. Play therapy procedures and results. *American Journal of Orthopsychiatry,* 1955, *25,* 618–626.

Axline, V. M. Nondirective play therapy. In M. R. Haworth (Ed.), *Child psychotherapy: Practice and theory.* New York: Basic Books, 1964.

Barrett, C. L., Hampe, I. E., & Miller, L. C. Research on child psychotherapy. In S. L. Garfield & A. E. Bergin (Eds.), *Handbook of psychotherapy and behavior change: An empirical analysis.* New York: Wiley, 1978.

Baruck, D. *New ways in discipline.* New York: McGraw-Hill, 1949.

Beck, D. F. Research findings on the outcomes of marital counseling. *Social Casework,* 1975, *56,* 153–181.

Beels, C., & Ferber, A. What family therapists do. In A. Ferber, M. Mendelsohn, & A. Napier (Eds.), *The book of family therapy.* New York: Science House, 1972.

Berlin, I. N. *Bibliography of child psychiatry.* New York: Human Sciences Press, 1976.

Carson, R. C., & Heiner, R. W. Similarity and success in therapeutic dyads. *Journal of Consulting Psychology,* 1962, *26,* 38–43.

Clarkin, J. F., Frances, A. J., & Moodie, J. L. Selection criteria for family therapy. *Family Process,* 1979, *18,* 391–403.

Clower, C., & Brody, L. Conjoint family therapy in outpatient practice. *American Journal of Orthopsychiatry,* 1964, *18,* 670–677.

Coddington, R. D., & Offord, D. R. Psychiatrists' reliability in judging ego function. *Archives of General Psychiatry,* 1967, *16,* 48–55.

Conn, J. H. The child reveals himself through play: The method of the play interview. *Mental Hygiene,* 1939, *33,* 46–49.

Conn, J. H. The timid, dependent child. *Journal of Pediatrics,* 1941, *19,* 91–102.

Conn, J. H. The play interview was an investigative and therapeutic procedure. *Nervous Child,* 1948, *7,* 257–286.

Conn, J. H. Play interview therapy of castration fear. *American Journal of Orthopsychiatry,* 1955, *25,* 747–754.

Dollard, J., & Miller, N. *Personality and psychotherapy.* New York: McGraw-Hill, 1950.

Dorfman, E. Play therapy. In C. R. Rogers (Ed.), *Client-centered therapy.* Boston: Houghton Mifflin, 1951.

Eysenck, H. J. Learning theory and behavior therapy. In H. J. Eysenck (Ed.), *Behavior therapy and the neuroses.* London: Pergamon Press, 1960.

Eysenck, H. J. The effects of psychotherapy. In H. J. Eysenck (Ed.), *Handbook of abnormal psychology.* New York: Basic Books, 1961.

Fiedler, F. E. A comparison of therapeutic relationship in psychoanalytic, nondirective and Adlerian therapy. *Journal of Consulting Psychology,* 1950, *14,* 436–445.

Foley, V. D. *An introduction to family therapy.* New York: Grune and Stratton, 1974.

Frank, J. D. The dynamics of the psychotherapeutic relationship. *Psychiatry,* 1959, *22,* 17–39.

Frank, J. D. *Persuasion and healing.* Baltimore: Johns Hopkins University Press, 1961.

Frank, J. D. Therapeutic factors in psychotherapy. *American Journal of Psychotherapy,* 1971, *25,* 350–361.

Freud, A. *The Psycho-analytic treatment of children.* New York: International Universities Press, 1946.

Freud, A. Assessment of childhood disturbances. *Psychoanalytic Study of the Child,* 1962, *17,* 150.

Freud, A. *Normality and pathology in childhood.* New York: International Universities Press, 1965.

Freud, S. Analysis of a phobia in a five-year-old boy. In *Collected papers* (Vol. 3). New York: Basic Books, 1959.

Gardner, G. Evaluation of therapeutic results in child guidance programs. *Association for Research in Nervous Diseases,* 1953, *31,* 131–150.

Geist, J., & Gerber, N. Joint interviewing: A treatment technique with marital partners. *Social Casework,* 1960, *41,* 76–88.

Gelfand, D. M. (Ed.). *Social learning in childhood: Readings in theory and application.* Belmont, Calif.: Brooks/Cole, 1969.

Gerard, M. W. Emotional disorders of childhood. In F. Alexander & H. Ross (Eds.), *Dynamic psychiatry.* Chicago: University of Chicago Press, 1952.

Glick, I. D., & Kessler, D. R. *Marital and Family Therapy.* New York: Grune and Stratton, 1974.

Goldstein, A. P. Patient's expectancies and non-specific therapy as a basis for (un)-spontaneous remission. *Journal of Clinical Psychology,* 1960, *16,* 399–403.

Goldstein, A. P. Patient expectancies in psychotherapy. *Psychiatry,* 1962, *25,* 72–79. (a)

Goldstein, A. P. *Therapist-patient expectancies in psychotherapy.* New York: Pergamon Press, 1962. (b)

Gossett, J. T., Meeks, J. E., Barnhart, F. D., & Phillips, V. A. Follow-up of adolescents treated in a psychiatric hospital: The onset of symptomatology scale. *Adolescence,* 1976, *11,* 195–211.

Guerin, P. J. Family therapy: The first twenty-five years. In P. J. Guerin (Ed.), *Family therapy: Theory and practice.* New York: Gardner Press, 1976.

Guerin, P. J., & Pendagast, E. G. Evaluation of a family system and genogram. In P. J. Guerin (Ed.), *Family therapy: Theory and practice.* New York: Gardner Press, 1976.

Haley, J. A review of the family therapy field. In J. Haley (Ed.), *Changing families: A family therapy reader.* New York: Grune and Stratton, 1971.

Halpern, W. I. Do children benefit from psychotherapy? A review of the literature on follow-up studies. *Bulletin of the Rochester Mental Health Center,* 1968, *1,* 4–12.

Hambridge, G. Structured play therapy. *American Journal of Orthopsychiatry,* 1955, *25,* 601–617.

Heilburn, A. B. Effects of briefing upon client satisfaction with the initial counseling contact. *Journal of Consulting and Clinical Psychology,* 1972, *38,* 50–56.

Heinicke, C. M., & Goldman, A. Research on psychotherapy with children: A review and suggestions for further study. *American Journal of Orthopsychiatry,* 1960, *30,* 483–493.

Heinicke, C. M., & Strassman, L. H. Toward more effective research on child psychotherapy. *American Academy of Child Psychiatry,* 1975, *45,* 561–588.

Hogan, R., DeSoto, C., & Solano, C. Traits, tests and personality research. *American Psychologist,* 1977, *32,* 255–264.

Hohen-Sarick, R., Frank, J. D., Imber, S. D., Mansh, E. H., Stone, A. R., & Battle, C. C. Systematic preparation of patients for psychotherapy. I. Effects on therapy behavior and outcome. *Journal of Psychiatric Research,* 1964, *2,* 267–281.

Hood-Williams, J. The results of psychotherapy with children: A reevaluation. *Journal of Consulting Psychology,* 1960, *24,* 84–88.

Jackson, D. D., & Satir, V. A review of psychiatric developments in family diagnosis and family therapy. In N. Ackerman (Ed.), *Exploring the base for family therapy.* New York: Family Service Association of America, 1961.

Jones, E. *The life and work of Sigmund Freud.* New York: Basic Books, 1953.

Jones, M. C. A laboratory study of fear: The case of Peter. *Pedagogical Seminary,* 1924, *31,* 308–315.

Kessler, J. W. *Psychopathology of childhood.* Englewood Cliffs, N.J.: Prentice-Hall, 1966.

Klein, M. *The Psycho-analysis of children.* New York: Norton, 1932.

Klein, M. The psychoanalytic play technique. *American Journal of Orthopsychiatry,* 1955, *25,* 223–238.

Klein, Z. E. *Research in the child psychiatric and guidance clinics: Supplementary bibliography II (1972).* Department of Psychiatry: University of Chicago, 1973. (Includes Series 1971, 1923–1970; 1972 through 1971).

Korchin, S. J. *Modern clinical psychology: Principles of intervention in the clinic and community.* New York: Basic Books, 1976.

Levitt, E. E. The results of psychotherapy with children: An evaluation. *Journal of Consulting Psychology,* 1957, *21,* 189–196.

Levitt, E. E. Reply to Hood-Williams. *Journal of Consulting Psychology,* 1960, *24,* 89–91.

Levitt, E. E. Psychotherapy with children: A further evaluation. *Behaviour Research and Therapy,* 1963, *60,* 326–329.

Levitt, E. E. Research on psychotherapy with children. In A. E. Bergin & S. Garfield (Eds.), *Handbook of psychotherapy and behavior change.* New York: Wiley, 1971.

Levitt, E. E., Beiser, H. R., & Robertson, R. E. A follow-up evaluation of cases treated at a community child guidance clinic. *American Journal of Psychiatry,* 1959, *29,* 337–347.

Levy, D. Release therapy in young children. *Psychiatry,* 1938, *1,* 387–389.

Levy, J. Relationship therapy. *American Journal of Orthopsychiatry,* 1938, *8,* 64–69.

Lubrosky, L., Chandler, M., Auerbach, A. H., Cohen, J., & Bachrach, H. M. Factors influencing the outcome of psychotherapy: A review of quantitative research. *Psychological Bulletin,* 1971, *75,* 145–185.

Malan, D. H. The outcome problem in psychotherapy research: A historical review. *Archives of General Psychiatry,* 1973, *29,* 719–729.

Masten, A. S. Family therapy as a treatment for children: A critical review of outcome research. *Family Process,* 1979, *18,* 323–335.

McConville, B. J., & Purohit, A. P. Classifying confusion: A study of results in a multidisciplinary children's center. *American Journal of Orthopsychiatry,* 1973, *43,* 411–417.

Meltzoff, J., & Kornreich, M. *Research on psychotherapy.* New York: Atherton, 1970.

Miller, L. C., Barrett, C. L., Hampe, E., & Noble, H. Comparison of reciprocal inhibition, psychotherapy and waiting list control for phobic children. *Journal of Abnormal Psychology,* 1972, *79,* 269–279.

Minuchin, S. *Families and family therapy*. Cambridge, Mass.: Harvard University Press, 1974.

Miyamoto, M. Zen in play therapy. *Psychologia,* 1960, *3,* 197–207.

Moustakas, C. E. Emotional adjustment and the play therapy process. *Journal of Genetic Psychology,* 1955, *86,* 79–99.

Moustakas, C. E. *Psychotherapy with children: The living relationship*. New York: Harper & Row, 1959.

Moustakas, C. E. (Ed.), *Existential child therapy*. New York: Basic Books, 1966.

Moustakas, C. E., & Schalock, H. D. An analysis of therapist–child interaction in play therapy. *Child Development,* 1955, *26,* 143–157.

Mowrer, O. H. A stimulus–response analysis of anxiety and its role as a reinforcing agent. *Psychological Review,* 1939, *46,* 553–565.

Reisman, J. M. *Toward the integration of psychotherapy*. New York: Wiley-Interscience, 1971.

Reisman, J. M. *Principles of psychotherapy with children*. New York: Wiley-Interscience, 1973.

Reisman, J. M., & Kissel, S. Mothers' evaluation of long-term clinic services. *Bulletin of the Rochester Mental Health Center,* 1968, *1,* 13–17.

Ricks, D., Thomas, A., & Roff, M. (Eds.). *Life history research in psychopathology* (Vol. 3). Minneapolis: The University of Minnesota Press, 1974.

Rogers, C. R. *Counseling and psychotherapy*. Boston: Houghton-Mifflin, 1942.

Rogers, C. R. *Client-centered therapy*. Boston: Houghton-Mifflin, 1951.

Rogers, C. R. *On becoming a person: A therapist's view of pscyhotherapy*. Boston: Houghton-Mifflin, 1961.

Rogers, C. R. In retrospect: Forty-six years. *American Psychologist,* 1974, *29,* 115–123.

Rosenblatt, B. Historical perspectives of treatment modes. In H. E. Rie (Ed.), *Perspectives in child psychopathology*. New York: Aldine Atherton, 1971.

Schaefer, C. E. *Therapeutic use of child's play*. New York: Jason Aronson, 1979.

Scherz, F. H. Multiple client interviewing: Treatment implications. *Social Casework,* 1962, *42,* 120–125.

Scherz, F. H. Exploring the use of family interviews in diagnosis. *Social Casework,* 1964, *45,* 209–215.

Schofield, W. *Psychotherapy: The purchase of friendship*. Englewood Cliffs, N.J.: Prentice-Hall, 1964.

Schofield, W. The psychotherapist as friend. *Humanitas,* 1970, *6,* 221–223.

Schomer, J. Family therapy. In B. Wolman, J. Egan, & A. Ross (Eds.), *Handbook of treatment of mental disorders in childhood and adolescence*. Englewood Cliffs, N.J.: Prentice-Hall, 1978.

Seeman, J. Perspectives in client-centered therapy. In B. B. Wolman (Ed.), *Handbook of clinical psychology*. New York: McGraw-Hill, 1966.

Shapiro. T. *Clinical psycholinguistics*. New York: Plenum Press, 1979.

Shepherd, M., Oppenheim, A. N., & Mithcell, S. Childhood behavior disorders and the child-guidance clinic. *Journal of Child Psychology and Psychiatry,* 1966, *7,* 39–52.

Sloane, R. B., Cristol, A. H., Pepernik, M. C., & Staples, F. R. Role preparation and expectation of improvement in psychotherapy. *Journal of Nervous and Mental Disease,* 1970, *150,* 18–26.

Sloane, R. B., Staples, F. R., Cristol, A. H., Yorkston, N. J., & Whipple, K. *Psychotherapy versus behavior therapy*. Cambridge, Mass.: Harvard University Press, 1975.

Smirnoff, V. *The scope of child analysis*. New York: International Universities Press, 1968.

Solomon, J. C. Active play therapy. *American Journal of Orthopsychiatry,* 1938, *8,* 479–497.

Solomon, J. C. Active play therapy: Further experiences. *American Journal of Orthopsychiatry,* 1940, *10,* 763–781.

Solomon, J. C. Play technique. *American Journal of Orthopsychiatry,* 1948, *18,* 402–413.

Solomon, J. C. Play technique and the integrative process. *American Journal of Orthopsychiatry,* 1955, *25,* 591–600.

Staats, A. W. *Child learning, intelligence, and personality: Principles of a behavioral interaction approach*. New York: Harper & Row, 1971.

Stollak, G. E., & Guerney, B., Jr. Exploration of personal problems by juvenile delinquents under conditions of minimal reinforcement. *Journal of Clinical Psychology,* 1964, *20,* 279–283.

Strupp, H. H. An objective comparison of Rogerian and psychoanalytic techniques. *Journal of Consulting Psychology,* 1955, *19,* 1–7. (a)

Strupp, H. H. Psychotherepeutic techniques, professional affiliation and experience level. *Journal of Consulting Psychology,* 1955, *19,* 97–102. (b)

Strupp, H. H. The performance of psychoanalytic and client-centered pscyhotherapists in an initial interview. *Journal of Consulting Psychology,* 1958, *14,* 219–226.

Strupp, H. H. Specific vs. nonspecific factors in psychotherapy and the problem of control. *Archives of General Psychiatry,* 1970, *23,* 393–401.

Strupp, H. H. On the technology of psychotherapy. *Archives of General Psychiatry,* 1972, *26,* 270–278.

Strupp, H. H. On the basic ingredients of psychotherapy. *Journal of Consulting and Clinical Psychology,* 1973, *41,* 1–8.

Strupp, H. H., & Bergin, A. È. Some empirical and conceptual bases for coordinate & research in psychotherapy. *International Journal of Psychiatry,* 1969, *7,* 18–90.

Strupp, H. H., & Hadley, S. W. A tripartite model of mental health and therapeutic outcomes: With special reference to negative effects in psychotherapy. *American Psychologist,* 1977, *32,* 187–196.

Swenson, C. H. Commitment and the personality of the successful therapist. *Psychotherapy: Theory, Research and Practice,* 1971, *8,* 31–36.

Taft, J. *The dynamics of therapy in a controlled relationship.* New York: Macmillan, 1933.

Truax, C. F., & Carkhuff, R. R. *Toward effective counseling and psychotherapy.* Chicago: Aldine, 1967.

Truax, C. F., & Mitchell, K. M. Research on certain therapist interpersonal skills in relation to process and outcome. In A. E. Bergin & S. L. Garfield (Eds.), *Handbook of psychotherapy and behavior change.* New York: Wiley, 1971.

Tuma, J. M., & Cawunder, P. Similarities and differences in training experiences of active clinical child psychologists: A survey. In press.

Weiner, I. B. Individual psychotherapy. In I. B. Weiner (Ed.), *Clinical methods in psychology.* New York: Wiley, 1976.

Witmer, H. L. *Psychiatric interviews with children.* New York: Commonwealth Fund, 1946.

Wolman, B. B. (Ed.). *Handbook of child psychoanalysis.* New York: Van Nostrand Reinhold Company, 1972. (a)

Wolman, B. B. (Ed.). *Manual of child psychopathology.* New York: McGraw-Hill, 1972. (b)

Woltmann, A. G. Play and related techniques. In D. Brower & L. E. Abt (Eds.), *Progress in clinical psychology.* New York: Grune & Stratton, 1952.

Wrenn, R. L. Counselor orientation: Theoretical or situational. *Journal of Counseling Psychology,* 1960, *7,* 40–45.

Wynne, L. Some indications and contraindications for exploratory family therapy. In I. Boszormenyi-Nagy & J. Framo (Eds.), *Intensive family therapy.* New York: Harper & Row, 1965.

16

Behavioral Treatment

STEVEN A. HOBBS AND BENJAMIN B. LAHEY

Introduction

Over the past two decades, a dramatic increase in the use of behavioral treatment methods has been observed in child psychopathology. From its modest infancy, associated with development of applied behavior analysis in the early 1960s, the area of child behavior therapy has demonstrated phenomenal growth. Not only are there a large number of textbooks (e.g., Gelfand & Hartmann, 1975; Graziano, 1971, 1975; Graziano & Mooney, 1981; Marholin, 1978; Ross, 1981; Sulzer-Azaroff & Mayer, 1977) and journal publications (e.g., *Child Behavior Therapy*) devoted to the general area of behavioral approaches to child problems, but we are beginning to see the emergence of complete books as well, each focusing on behavioral treatment of a specific child population (e.g., Creer, 1979; Forehand & McMahon, 1981; Lahey, 1979; Ross, 1976).

In general, behavioral treatment departs from other therapeutic approaches to child psychopathology in that reduced emphasis is placed upon etiological considerations. Rather than speculating primarily upon causal factors in the historical sense, emphasis is placed on the child's current response deficits and excesses as well as conditions that are associated with problem responses. These may include antecedent stimulus conditions, organismic variables, contingencies, and reinforcing consequences (i.e., the S-O-R-K-C model of Kanfer & Saslow, 1969). The emphasis on present conditions stems not from the view that past events are unimportant, rather from the notion that conditions responsible for the initial development of disordered behavior may not be the same as those currently maintaining the problem. In addition, efforts to alter past events should be considered futile, for only present and future events are amenable to change.

STEVEN A. HOBBS • Center for Behavioral Medicine, Oklahoma College of Osteopathic Medicine and Surgery, P.O. Box 2280, Tulsa, Oklahoma 74101. BENJAMIN B. LAHEY • Clinical Training Program, Department of Psychology, University of Georgia, Athens, Georgia 30602.

In this approach, behavior *per se* is regarded as the only proper object of change efforts. Behavior therapists point out that, since the child's behavior is what disturbs significant other persons (peer, family, teachers) or the child him/herself, the most logical and parsimonious intervention approach involves a direct focus on altering that behavior. The notion that when current behavior is directly modified, the underlying cause will manifest itself in some other deviant behavior (i.e., the hypothesis of symptom substitution) has been refuted in a number of studies (see Mahoney, Kazdin, & Lesswing, 1974).

The advantages of focusing on behavior in the therapeutic context can also be readily seen from an empirical, scientific perspective. When childhood disorders are analyzed in a manner that specifies frequency, intensity, or duration of a target behavior, observers are able to conduct a precise and objective assessment of the problem. Similarly, within this framework, the therapist and significant others are able to objectively evaluate the efficacy of treatment. While this approach may seem confining relative to the range of behaviors that may be treated, behavior therapists are limited only by their ability to operationally define relevant problem areas. For example, O'Leary and O'Leary (1977) point out that behaviorally oriented investigators have successfully modified conceptually complex behaviors such as information seeking (Krumboltz & Thoreson, 1964) and creativity (Goetz & Baer, 1973; Reese & Parnes, 1970).

From this brief overview, it should be apparent that behavior therapy is an approach to psychopathology based on the use of empirical methodology. Although many definitions of behavior therapy emphasize application of techniques based on learning theory, this approach often involves application of knowledge from many of the areas of psychology. In the child area, findings from developmental psychology are particularly important because identification of relevant targets for change in children must be moderated by maturational factors.

Behavioral Techniques

Because of its ties with the experimental method and the development of empirical knowledge in the field of psychology, child behavior therapy should not simply be characterized as a specific set of treatment techniques. However, it is worthwhile to describe some of the behavioral procedures most commonly used in treating child psychopathology prior to discussing their specific application to various problems.

Modeling

The term *modeling* refers to vicarious learning procedures that have the common objective of teaching the client to imitate the behavior of a stimulus person whom the client observes. In more simple terms, observing certain target behaviors exhibited by another person may increase the likelihood that the same behaviors will be performed by the observer. According to Bandura (1969, 1971, 1977), who has made extensive contributions to the study of modeling and its impact on social behavior, observational learning involves two stages. First, the individual acquires the response by attending to and perceiving the important aspects of the model's behavior. Second, performance of the response occurs when the individual is capable of initiating actions previously observed, and sufficient incentive is provided for him/her to imitate the response. From this perspective, the presence of reinforcing or punishing consequences to the model is of considerable importance because these consequences can affect both the attention of the observer to the model and the observer's motivation to perform the modeled response. In clinical applications, modeling has been used primarily: (a) in acquisition and performance of new skills (e.g., speech building); (b) to inhibit inappropriate responses (e.g., aggression or avoidance responses); and (c) to disinhibit behaviors that are in the client's repertoire but are currently being inhibited (e.g., increased peer interaction).

Shaping

In cases in which the desired behavior is not fully in the child's repertoire, modeling techniques may be augmented by shaping procedures. In this approach, the child may be guided through the desired response by assisting him/her in the actual physical motions involved. Approximations to such responses on the child's part are then rewarded in such a manner as to produce behaviors that more and more closely approximate the desired response. For example, Lovaas (1977) describes procedures by which imitation was shaped in autistic children by first providing food reinforcers contingent on emission of any vocal response, then for any vocal response that followed within a few seconds of a vocalization by the therapist, and subsequently for vocal responses from the child similiar in sound to the therapist's vocalization. In this study, the trainer also held the child's mouth in a manner so as to increase the probability of an imitative response. Once imitation of sounds was mastered, vocalizations were then combined (chained) to shape complete words. This example illustrates the use of physical guidance, verbal prompts (i.e., the modeled vocalization), and increased response requirements through successive approximation and chaining in order to shape desired responses.

Differential Attention

One of the earliest behavioral treatment methods reported in the literature involved the systematic use of adult attention to alter child behavior. In the context of preschool settings, Bijou and Baer (1963) noted the high frequency with which adults paid attention to children following their performance of inappropriate and disruptive behavior. This observation led the investigators to speculate that adult attention may serve to act as reinforcement for such misbehavior. By varying the types of behavior for which adult attention was provided, several studies by Bijou and Baer (e.g., Bijou, 1965; Bijou & Baer, 1963) documented the relationship between adult attention and child behavior on which such attention was made contingent. That is, behaviors followed by attention were found to increase, while those ignored were found to decrease. Use of adult praise and attention contingent on desirable behavior combined with the ignoring of misbehavior has long been used successfully with individual children in both homes (e.g., Williams, 1959) and classrooms (e.g., Becker, Madsen, Arnold, & Thomas, 1967). Hersen and Barlow (1976) illustrate the widespread effectiveness of this method by citing over 50 studies in which differential attention was employed to modify child behaviors during the period of 1962 to 1972.

Token Reinforcement

While use of differential attention may be extremely effective in modifying many child behaviors, social reinforcement procedures alone involving positive expression in the form of words or gestures may not be sufficient, especially with older children. In these instances, tangible reinforcement may be incorporated in a token economy program. Several important features have been identified as common elements in token programs (O'Leary & O'Leary, 1977). First, a set of instructions specifies for the child desirable behaviors that will be rewarded. Second, backup reinforcers such as prizes or privileges are established as rewards that may be earned contingent upon the performance of appropriate behaviors. Third, tokens themselves (e.g., points, stars, checkmarks) that symbolize performance of the desirable behaviors at a specified level or frequency are selected, and rules governing how they are dispensed and exchanged for back-up reinforcers are established. Tokens serve as potentially reinforcing stimuli that provide the child with feedback about appropriate behavior. This approach has the advantage of teaching the child to work for symbolic rewards, to delay gratification, and to work on an intermittent schedule (Drabman, 1976). While its most widespread use has been in a classroom setting (O'Leary & Drabman, 1971), parents also have been trained to formulate and apply token programs to manage child behaviors in the home (e.g., Christophersen, Arnold, Hill, & Quilitch, 1972).

Response Cost

Within the structure of token reinforcement programs, a response cost procedure involving loss or fines often may be implemented. More technically, response cost can be defined as a form of punishment in which previously acquired reinforcers are removed contingent upon misbehavior. In research conducted on response cost, these procedures do not appear to be associated with the undesirable side effects often observed with the use of punishment (Kazdin, 1972). Similarly, relative to token reinforcement conditions, response cost procedures have been found to be equally effective as well as equally preferred by children in a comparative study (Iwata & Bailey, 1974). In most clinical applications, however, response cost is recommended for use in the context of an ongoing reinforcement program aimed at increasing appropriate behaviors.

Timeout

Methods that involve withdrawal of opportunities to obtain positive reinforcement, a set of procedures collectively termed *timeout from positive reinforcement,* frequently have been employed to decrease child problem behaviors. In general, timeout procedures consist of placing the child in a somewhat restricted environment contingent upon misbehavior. This may entail withdrawing stimulus materials (Barton, Guess, Garcia, & Baer, 1970), withdrawing adult attention (Forehand, Roberts, Doleys, Hobbs, & Resick, 1976), or isolating the subject in an area devoid of persons or objects (Hobbs, Forehand, & Murray, 1978; Lahey, McNees, & McNees, 1973) for a specified brief period of time. Timeout appears to be particularly effective in the treatment of disruptive and aggressive child behaviors that may be elicited and/or reinforced by the actions of either peers or adults. Use of timeout procedures involving isolation has been prohibited with some populations (e.g., institutionalized retardates) due to inhumane applications involving extreme deprivation and lengthy periods of isolation that preclude opportunities for learning. However, when applied with an understanding of the important parameters governing its effectiveness (Hobbs & Forehand, 1977), timeout may be used in a manner that does not evoke the fear and avoidance often associated with punishment techniques. Of particular note in this regard is the recent development of "nonexclusionary" timeout procedures, which withdraw opportunity for reinforcement but still allow the disruptive child to remain in the learning environment to observe or participate in educational activities (Foxx & Shapiro, 1978; Porterfield, Herbert-Jackson, & Risley, 1976).

Overcorrection

A relatively recent addition to the area of behavioral treatment procedures is a method of overcorrection developed by Foxx and Azrin (1972). Initially formulated as an approach for reducing aggressive and stereotyped behaviors of retarded and autistic individuals, overcorrection procedures also have been applied to child problems such as nervous habits, tics, enuresis, and toilet training in otherwise normal children (for reviews, see Marholin, Luiselli, & Townsend, 1980; Ollendick & Matson, 1978). Two methods of overcorrection, restitution and positive practice (Foxx & Azrin, 1972, 1973), both involve the idea that the child should be required to overcorrect the consequences of misbehavior. This may involve restoring one's own person or the environment to an improved state, or intensively practicing forms of correct behavior related to the inappropriate act. In both restitutional and positive practice overcorrection procedures, an adult may guide the child through the required responses. For example, oral hygiene restitution that involves having the child clean teeth, gums, and mouth with a toothbrush and washcloth dipped in mouthwash has been employed to reduce repetitive mouthing (Foxx & Azrin, 1973). Similarly, a positive practice component in programs treating enuresis involves a large number of trials in which the child arises from bed, hurries to the toilet, and attempts to urinate (e.g., Azrin, Sneed, & Foxx, 1974). Because overcorrection procedures consist of responses topographically similar to the misbehavior, this method is thought to have the advantage of incorporating an educational component within a punishment procedure.

Relaxation and Systematic Desensitization

As illustrated in previous sections, one approach to treating inappropriate child behavior is to increase occurrence of desirable responses that are incompatible with the problem behavior. Reinforcing appropriate behavior or having the child intensively practice positive forms of behavior may be a useful means of accomplishing this. An alternate method of teaching responses incompatible with certain negative emotional states may involve training in relaxation. Variations of relaxation procedures developed by Jacobsen (1938) for use with adults have met with some success in treating childhood anxiety and aggression (e.g., Linden, 1973; Robin, Schneider, & Dolnick, 1976). Progressive relaxation techniques would also appear to hold similiar promise for treatment of frustration, anger, and agitation in children as well as a treatment component of systematic desensitization in efforts to treat childhood fears (Lazarus, 1960; Lazarus, Davison, & Polefka, 1965).

Behavioral treatment of child conduct disorders in the home has primarily emphasized the importance of dealing with the family as a unit. Within this framework the child is not viewed as being solely responsible for the problem, nor is the blame placed upon the parents. Instead, such difficulties are perceived as problems in parent–child interaction. The validity of this interactive approach can be readily seen in investigations that have examined the behavioral patterns of conduct problem children and their parents, and compared the behavior of this population with that observed in nonreferred or normal children and their parents (Delfini, Bernal, & Rosen, 1976; Forehand, King, Peed, & Yoder, 1975; Lobitz & Johnson, 1975). Although significant differences between clinic-referred and nonreferred children have been found with regard to frequency of several classes of noxious child behaviors (e.g., noncompliance, negativism, yelling), considerably overlap between these groups has generally been observed. That is, the behavior of some of the children who were labeled as deviant was not measurably different from normals (Delfini, Bernal, & Rosen, 1976; Lobitz & Johnson, 1975).

Thus, in cases of child conduct disorders in the home, factors in addition to child behavior may contribute to labeling the child as deviant and to the subsequent referral process. Indeed, several investigations suggest that parental behavior may be of considerable importance in this regard. Greater frequency of negative parental behaviors (e.g., use of aversive consequences, commands, criticisms) has been shown to differentiate parents of clinic-referred from parents of nonreferred children (Delfini *et al.,* 1976; Forehand *et al.,* 1975; Lobitz & Johnson, 1975). In terms of their noxious quality, these parental responses appear to be similar to the previously described pattern of aversive child behaviors that has been observed by the cited investigators as well as by Patterson (1976).

Formulations of Problems in Parent–Child Interaction

In line with these observations, some rather sophisticated accounts of the development of child behavior problems have been formulated. One of the most elaborate formulations of this type is the "coercion hypothesis" of Gerald Patterson and his associates at the Oregon Research Institute. Patterson's model describes a pattern of interaction in which both parents and children attempt to control the behavior of each other by means of aversive acts. Children engage in behaviors that are aversive to parents, and parents in turn attempt to deal with such negative child behaviors through use of similarly noxious responses (e.g., yelling, scolding). Use of these aversive acts then escalates until one family member (either parent or child) terminates his/her noxious behavior. When one member terminates the aversive response on his/her own part, negative reinforcement is provided for the other member's use of coercion. In addition to negative reinforcement being provided for such noxious behaviors, parents model for the child use of coercion as means of coping with interpersonal conflicts (Patterson, 1976; Patterson & Reid, 1970).

This analysis nicely illustrates the importance of assessing both child and parent behavior in cases of child problems in the home. It also points to a triadic model involving child, parents, and the professional as the most efficient means of facilitating behavior change. Focus of treatment is on the professional's teaching parents to change their behavior toward the child. In this manner, treatment may be conducted in the setting in which the problem occurs and by the persons who have the greatest amount of contact with the child. Thus, behaviors of both parents and child are viewed as target responses to be modified; parents are viewed as potential mediators of behavior change; and the professional is viewed essentially as a consultant within this approach to intervention (Tharp & Wetzel, 1969).

Parent-Training Programs

Within this framework, several researchers (including Patterson) have conducted and evaluated large-scale parent-training programs aimed at dealing with child problems in the home. Forehand and his associates have developed a clinic-based parent-training program for families of noncompliant children, which emphasizes changing both parent and child behavior. The two-stage format involves, first, teaching parents to increase verbal attending and following while decreasing questions, commands, and criticisms. Parental attention in the form of positive verbal behavior (attending and praise) is then applied contingent on desirable child behavior. A second stage involves teaching the parent how to reduce the occurrence of child noncompliance, not only by rewarding compliance but by providing clear and direct commands specifying what behaviors are expected of the child. In addition, parents are trained to implement a timeout procedure following instances of child noncompliance. Outcome evaluations on the effectiveness of the program indicate positive changes in both child and parent behaviors as well as improved parental perceptions of child problems (Forehand & King, 1974; Peed, Roberts, & Forehand, 1977). Several studies also suggest that such change is maintained at a 1-year follow-up period and is associated with beneficial effects on the behavior of untreated siblings (Forehand, Sturgis, McMahon, Aguar, Green, Wells, & Breiner, 1979; Humphreys, Forehand, McMahon, & Roberts; 1978).

Patterson's approach has involved familiarizing parents with concepts of social learning theory through use of a programmed text (Patterson 1971; Patterson & Gullion, 1968), training parents to specify and track both positive and negative child behaviors and to establish a token system whereby the child earns points for positive behaviors. The points (paired with use of praise) are exchanged for backup reinforcers on a daily basis, and additional techniques (e.g., timeout, response cost) are taught for use in dealing with misbehavior in the home or school.

Outcome studies examining efficacy of the approach with families of aggressive children have demonstrated significant improvement in treated families relative to waiting list or attention controls on parent reports and/or global perceptions of child behavior. While changes in deviant child behavior in the home (as measured by trained observers) have not always been evident in replications by other investigators (Eyberg & Johnson, 1974; Ferber, Keeley, & Shemberg, 1974), results of several studies suggest that beneficial treatment effects are relatively durable and may generalize to interactions among other family members (see Patterson & Fleishman, 1979, for a review).

Use of procedures such as differential attention, token reinforcement, timeout, and response cost represent important features of numerous clinic-based behavioral parent-training programs (e.g., Bernal, Klinnet, & Schultz, 1980; Kent & O'Leary, 1976; Wahler, 1976). However, work of Christophersen and his colleagues departs somewhat from these programs in its emphasis on home-based training. These investigators (Chistophersen, Arnold, Hill, & Quilitch, 1972; Christophersen, Barnard, Ford, & Wolf, 1976) have taught parents to implement point systems similiar to that used by Patterson during home visits made by the professional. This approach is essentially a variation of the token economy implemented in residential treatment programs for predelinquent youths at Achievement Place (Phillips, Phillips, Fixsen, & Wolf, 1973; Willner, Braukmann, Kirigan, & Wolf, 1978). Christophersen and his coinvestigators suggest that an approach involving training in the natural environment rather than the clinic may enhance treatment effectiveness, particularly with regard to parental adherence to specific techniques prescribed for use in the program.

Behavioral Contracting

While token programs of this type, in effect, constitute behavioral contracts between parents and child in which child behaviors and their consequences are explicitly specified, the contract is primarily formulated by parents and professionals with little child input. However, work with adolescents has focused on behavioral contracts that enable the child to assume a more active role in negotiating privileges contingent on performance of certain behaviors, as well as to some extent selecting child and parental behaviors for change. In this manner, exchange of positive behaviors between the parents and adolescent is conducted on a reciprocal basis (Stuart, 1971). Early efforts at evaluating the use of behavioral contracting alone (Stuart & Tripodi, 1973; Stuart, Tripodi, Jayaratne, & Camburn, 1976) or combined with training in communication and negotiation skills (Alexander & Parsons, 1973) in families of predelinquent and delinquent adolescents have produced positive results on several measures of home, school, and community functioning. In the Alexander and Parsons study, substantially lower recidivism rates were observed for adolescents receiving behavioral treatment in contrast to client-centered, psychodynamic therapy, or no-treatment conditions. Similar attempts at training problem-solving and conflict-resolution skills in problem families have generally produced increases in communication and behaviors requisite for formulating successful behavioral contracts in the clinic and the home (e.g., Blechman, Olson, & Hellman, 1976; Blechman, Olson, Schornagel, Halsdorf, & Turner, 1976; Robin, Kent, O'Leary, Foster, & Prinz, 1977). While use of behavioral contracting skills has not been subjected to the same critical evaluation as parent-training programs, these approaches represent a promising direction in family treatment.

Classroom Intervention

Methods somewhat similiar to those described for use by parents in treating child behavior problems in the home also have been employed in the modification of classroom behavior. In general, behavioral intervention in the classroom has focused on two major areas of change: increasing task-relevant behavior while concurrently decreasing disruption, and enhancing academic performance.

On-Task and Disruptive Behavior

Early intervention studies focused primarily on attention to classroom tasks and deportment within the school setting. For example, Ward and Baker (1968) found that teacher praise applied contingently on appropriate classroom behavior produced substantial increases in task-related behavior and decreases in disruption. No negative effects were observed with regard to other aspects of the functioning of targeted children or nontargeted students in the classroom. Sibley, Abbott, and Cooper (1969) present a similiar example of the use of social reinforcement combined with timeout procedures in reducing the assaultive behavior of a kindergarten-age child. The effectiveness of classroom token reinforcement programs in controlling disruption and on-task behavior has been clearly documented (O'Leary & Drabman, 1971). Broden, Hall, Dunlap, and Clark (1970) demonstrated superiority of a token program over differential teacher attention in increasing study behavior in junior high school students.

While the vast majority of these intervention efforts have involved teacher-administered consequences, in several studies peer attention has been employed to reinforce behaviors such as working on assignments, talking appropriately, and remaining seated (Solomon & Wahler, 1973; Surrat, Ulrich, & Hawkins, 1969). Token reinforcement programs have also involved peers in the evaluation of performance and administration of reinforcement contingencies (Drabman, 1973; Winnett, Richards, & Krasner, 1971). Such an approach not only appears to be more practical, but has been demonstrated to be as effective as teacher-administered programs (Drabman, 1973; Frederickson & Frederickson, 1975).

Another practical alternative to the standard token reinforcement program involves design of a program that rewards classroom peers as well as target children. A "group contingency" approach sets a criterion for reinforcement that relates to the group as a whole, rather than establishing individual contingencies for each student. Within this framework a variety of options exist, depending on whether the criterion for group reinforcement depends on performance of a single child, performance of some subset of children selected from the entire class, or composite performance of the class as a whole (Litow & Pumroy, 1975; O'Leary & O'Leary, 1976). Regardless of the variation employed, results of group contingencies appear to be comparable, if not superior, to individual contingency procedures (Jones & Kazdin, 1981).

Academic Performance

Many of the previously cited studies aimed at increasing attention and decreasing disruption did not evaluate the effects on academic performance. Until recently, the notion was generally held that the behaviors altered in such treatment programs were responses that were incompatible with successful academic performance. The assumed relationship between classroom deportment and academic learning has recently been subjected to empirical tests. Studies (e.g., Ferritor, Buckholdt, Hamblin, & Smith, 1972; Hay, Hay, & Nelson, 1977) have demonstrated that reinforcement of attending behavior may produce increased attention and less disruption, but that such changes impact little on the quality of academic work. Instead, enhanced academic performance has been found only in instances when reinforcement has been made contingent on improvement in academic work (Ferritor *et al.*, 1972).

These findings have led to a change in thinking regarding the selection of appropriate target responses for classroom intervention. That is, if a child demonstrates deficits in academic performance, target responses for modification should not be attention, concentration, or interest per se, but academic performance that requires those elements for successful completion (Ayllon & Rosenbaum, 1977). This conceptualization, labeled by Lahey,

Hobbs, Kupfer, and Delamater (1978) as a paradigm shift, involves an emphasis on correct academic responding (i.e., accuracy on academic tasks) as the terminal response in a behavioral chain. Behaviors in the chain that are prerequisite to correct academic performance (e.g., sitting down, listening, looking at task materials) are indirectly modified by reinforcing correct performance. In this way, responses that are necessary for accurate academic performance are strengthened, and responses that are incompatible with accurate academic work will be eliminated.

Although behavioral treatment programs have often included academic skills such as reading (Lahey, McNees, & Brown, 1973; Wadsworth, 1971; Wilson & McReynolds, 1973) arithmetic (Greenwood, Sloane, & Baskin, 1974; Johnson & Bailey, 1974), vocabulary (Corey & Shamow 1972; Lahey & Drabman, 1974), handwriting (Hopkins, Schutte, & Garton, 1971; Lahey, Busemeyer, O'Hara, & Beggs, 1977), and phonics (Lahey, Weller, & Brown, 1973), behavior modifiers have been criticized for attempting to produce children who are "still, docile, and quiet" in classroom settings (Winett & Winkler, 1972). However, by eliminating only responses that are truly incompatible with academic learning, behaviorists have departed from the position that could be interpreted as encouraging educators to create unnecessarily regimented and controlled classrooms. While teachers may still find it necessary to deal with a few serious instances of misbehavior on the part of some children (e.g., aggressive behavior or behavior that disrupts the academic progress of others), this approach has been demonstrated to be effective with disruptive children (Ayllon & Roberts, 1974), underachieving emotionally disturbed children (Marholin, Steinman, McInnis, & Heads, 1975), educable mentally retarded children (Aaron & Bostow, 1978), and children with attention problems in remedial classes (Broughton & Lahey, 1978). In these studies, direct reinforcement of academic performance has produced academic improvement as well as improvement in attention and disruptive behaviors.

Hyperactivity and Learning Disabilities

At present, applicability of behavioral techniques across a wide range of problems in both regular and special education classes is rather well documented. However, only within the past 10 years have such procedures been extensively applied to the populations of learning-disabled and hyperactive children. Previously, labels of hyperactivity and learning-disabled were used almost exclusively to refer to medical-model disease entities involving underlying neurological, perceptual, or psycholinguistic dysfunctions (Gearheart, 1973). In contrast, in the early 1970s investigators began describing hyperactivity and learning disabilities as broad patterns of behavior that, like any other set of behaviors, may be subject to modification. With these populations, the critical problem involves determining the "proper behaviors" to target for change. Early behavioral interventions with these children paralleled efforts to modify attention deficits in other children who presented classroom problems. While several studies demonstrated considerable change in attention deficits of learning-disabled children (Drass & Jones, 1971; McKenzie, Clark, Wolf, Kothera, & Benson, 1968; Novy, Burnett, Powers, & Sulzer-Azaroff, 1973), increased academic performance was not produced as a result of these changes in attention (e.g., Wagner & Guyer, 1971). With these children, similiar efforts have been made to modify activity level as well as impulsivity, a behavior pattern of both hyperactive and learning-disabled children defined as the tendency to respond hastily to stimuli before considering alternative responses

(Kagan, 1966). Like attempts to modify disordered perceptual and cognitive processes in these children, such efforts have been neither particularly successful nor do they appear necessary to facilitate performance on academic tasks in the classroom (Lahey, Delamater, & Kupfer, 1981).

More recently, methods similiar to those employed to modify terminal academic behaviors in the classroom have been successful in treating populations of hyperactive and learning-disabled children. A study by Ayllon, Layman, and Kandel (1975) nicely illustrates the efficacy of reinforcing terminal academic responses with these children. Use of token reinforcement contingent upon correct workbook responses produced substantial increases in reading and mathematics performance in three elementary-school children labeled as both hyperactive and learning-disabled. Although their activity level had been controlled through medication (methylphenidate), students' academic performance prior to behavioral intervention had been extremely poor. Withdrawal of medication produced dramatic increases in activity, but academic performance remained unchanged. In contrast, introduction of the reinforcement contingency first for mathematics and then for reading performance resulted in dramatic changes in accuracy of responding as well as decreased activity levels in the absence of medication. Findings of this and other investigations (e.g., Pelham, 1977; Rosenbaum, O'Leary, & Jacob, 1975) indicate that high levels of activity in hyperactive or learning-disabled children may be controlled without medication. Moreover, such results confirm that academic performance in such children may be modified without directly focusing on attention problems, perceptual deficits, or activity level (Haring & Hauck, 1969; Kirby & Shields, 1972; Wadsworth, 1971).

Parents also may be employed to enhance the academic performance of learning-disabled students. Based on the idea that more effective reinforcers may exist in the home environment of these children, some investigators have attempted to link home and school together by establishing home-based reinforcement programs to modify academic performance. In this approach, teachers have completed "daily report cards," abbreviated reports that inform parents of the child's classroom performance each day. Privileges and praise are administered by the parents contingent on receipt of a good report (see Atkeson & Forehand, 1979, for a review). Although home-based programs have not generally focused on the terminal academic behavior of accuracy on classroom tasks, Schumaker, Howell, and Sherman (1977) targeted time spent and grades on assignments as well as general deportment in a program for learning-disabled adolescents. Substantial improvements were observed in semester grades, deportment, and general teacher satisfaction. Home-based programs may possess similiar promise for the control of hyperactivity in the classroom (Pelham, 1977).

Outside of the school setting, parent-training programs such as those outlined in the previous section (Behavior Problems in the Home) have been employed successfully with hyperactive children (O'Leary & Pelham, 1977; O'Leary, Pelham, Rosenbaum, & Price, 1976). These results appear to support the notion that, similar to child conduct disorders, hyperactivity is primarily characterized by high levels of inappropriate behavior (Lahey, Green, & Forehand, 1980).

Thus, despite the apparent complexity of the problems of hyperactive and learning-disabled children, approaches described suggest that the behavioral characteristics of these populations may not be uniquely different from those of other problem children. Behavior changes in both learning-disabled and hyperactive children can be achieved by focusing on the use of behavioral methods for modifying target responses similiar to those altered in populations of non-learning-disabled or nonhyperactive children.

It has been generally recognized that nearly all children experience some degree of fear or anxiety during their development (MacFarlane, Allen, & Honzik, 1954). Most childhood fears appear to be (a) age specific, (b) of mild severity, and (c) transitory in nature (Jersild & Holmes, 1935; Miller, Barrett, & Hampe, 1974). Fears that are classified as phobias, however, do not meet these criteria and require therapeutic intervention. In the following sections, behavioral treatments for childhood fears, as well as the social withdrawal that may stem from such states, are described. Major emphasis is placed on conditions involving phobias of natural events and social fears.

Fear Related to Natural Events

The largest number of investigations of fear reduction techniques have focused on treatment of fears of natural events such as contact with animals or fear of the dark. Several studies describe the application of counterconditioning in treating such problems. The earliest use of counterconditioning was reported by Mary Cover Jones (1924b) in her treatment of a 3-year-old child, Peter, who was fearful of furry objects. The procedure involved moving a rabbit closer to Peter in a gradual fashion at the same time that the child was eating. The child's fear was thought to have been weakened by pairing the feared stimulus with eating, a response incompatible with anxiety.

In current practice, a similar approach to that described by Jones (1924b) involves the use of systematic desensitization. As a counterconditioning procedure, systematic desensitization is characterized by the pairing of a response that inhibits anxiety with a gradual presentation of the feared stimuli. Stimuli are presented either through imagery or *in vivo* in order from those that elicit the least to those that elicit the most fear. Applications of systematic desensitization with adults have generally involved the use of deep muscle relaxation as the fear-inhibiting response. However, in variations of this method with children, responses other then relaxation have been employed as counterconditioning agents.

Studies focusing on children's fear of animals illustrate the use of counterconditioning as well as several other treatment procedures. Lazarus and Abramovitz (1962) used a procedure involving emotive imagery in the treatment of a 14-year-old boy who demonstrated a strong fear of dogs. While the child was encouraged to imagine his favorite heroes and goals, the therapist gradually introduced anxiety-producing scenes involving dogs into the fantasy. Similarly, Kissel (1972) used the security of the therapeutic relationship as a counterconditioning agent to decrease the avoidance behavior of an 11-year-old girl toward dogs. In a larger study, Obler and Terwilliger (1970) used a combination of procedures that included gradual exposure, therapist presence, and reinforcement for approach behavior in the treatment of 15 phobic children who demonstrated fears of dogs or riding on public buses. Following treatment, it was reported that all treated children were able to ride a bus or touch a dog, either alone or with the help of another person.

In addition to her pioneering work using counterconditioning, Jones (1924a) successfully employed social imitation (modeling) among several procedures in treating phobic children. Subsequently, Bandura and his colleagues (e.g., Bandura & Menlove, 1968; Bandura, Grusec, & Menlove, 1967; Ritter, 1968) conducted a series of studies examining the efficacy of modeling in the treatment of children's fears of animals. Following observation of live or filmed peer models who approached and made contact with the feared object, avoidance in volunteer children having demonstrable fear of dogs was successfully decreased (Bandura *et al.,* 1967; Bandura & Menlove, 1968). In subsequent investigations, use of multiple models as well as peer models has been shown to enhance treatment effectiveness (Bandura & Menlove, 1968; Kornhaber & Schroeder, 1975). In addition, direct participant contact with the feared stimulus appears to produce even further reductions in avoidance (Ritter, 1968).

Social Fears

School phobias constitute the common fear for which children are referred to mental health and guidance clinics. Coolidge, Hahn, and Peck (1957) and Kennedy (1965) have identified two distinct patterns of school phobia: Type I, or "true phobic reaction," marked by an acute onset in a younger child, as opposed to Type II, or "way-of-life phobia," typified by more gradual, chronic nonattendance in older children. Kennedy (1965) reported on the effectiveness of a rapid treatment program for Type I school phobias. The program, consisting primarily of forced school attendance, ignoring of somatic complaints and phobic behaviors, and social reinforcement for increased school attendance, was judged to be successful for all 50 cases treated over an 8-year period.

Other studies have tended to focus almost exclusively on the treatment of Type I school phobias using methods similiar to those of Kennedy (1965). Mothers of school-phobic children and classroom personnel have been taught to ignore responses such as crying and complaining about school and to reward appropriate school-related behaviors, including shaping increasingly longer periods of time spent in the classroom (e.g., Ayllon, Smith, & Rogers, 1970; Hersen, 1971). Several case studies and one large study report the use of systematic desensitization alone or in combination with operant techniques (Lazarus, 1960; Lazarus *et al.,* 1965; Miller, Barrett, Hampe, & Noble, 1972). Miller *et al.* (1972) treated 67 phobic children (69% of whom were school phobics) with either (a) imaginal systematic desensitization involving relaxation; or (b) "psychotherapy" in part aimed at having the child express hopes, fears, and dependency needs and formulate coping strategies. In addition, parents in both groups were taught to restructure contingencies that might have served to reinforce the child's fears. Outcome evaluations based on parental report and clinician impressions indicated that both desensitization and the somewhat behaviorally-oriented psychotherapy treatment were associated with rapid improvement. However, improvement was only slightly better than for waiting list controls. At 2 year follow-up, after many of the failures and waiting list controls had received extended treatment, 80% of the subjects were greatly improved or demonstrated no phobia, while only 7% still were severly phobic (Hampe, Noble, Miller, & Barrett, 1973).

Other fears that are primarily social in nature, such as test anxiety and separation anxiety, have also been successfully treated with procedures involving either imaginal or *in vivo* systematic desensitization (Barabasz, 1973, 1975; Mann & Rosenthal, 1969; Montenegro, 1968). In a comparative investigation, Kondas (1967) found use of relaxation alone to be moderately effective, but of less benefit than systematic desensitization in treating test anxiety. However, sufficient data are not available to draw conclusions regarding the general efficacy of relaxation in treatment of child anxiety conditions. In addition, the relative absence of controlled group investigations or treatment comparision studies somewhat limits the conclusions that may be drawn regarding the general efficacy of fear reduction techniques such as systematic desensitization (Ollendick, 1979).

Social Withdrawal

Social withdrawal, commonly defined in terms of infrequent interaction with peers, has been the focus of a number of treatment investigations primarily due to the link between social isolation in childhood and adjustment problems in adolescence and adulthood (Cowen, Pederson, Babijian, Izzo, & Trost, 1973; Kagan & Moss, 1962; Roff, 1961; Roff, Sells, & Golden, 1972; Ullmann, 1957). Modeling procedures typically have been employed to increase interaction with peers in withdrawn children. O'Connor (1969, 1972), selecting children who demonstrated low frequencies of peer interaction, had them observe a modeling film depicting peer models engaging in a number of social activities with other children. Modeling not only produced increases in interactions that were maintained at follow-up, but was found to be superior to adult reinforcement of social interactions (Evers & Schwartz, 1973; O'Connor, 1972). However, Gottman (1977a) was unable to demonstrate any beneficial effect resulting from a modeling procedure similar to that of O'Connor (1969, 1972); and in a subsequent study, Keller and Carlson (1974) failed to observe maintenance of behavior change at follow-up.

Gottman (1977a) has suggested that the relationship between simple frequency of interaction and adjustment problems has not been demonstrated. That is, children who do not interact at the same rate as their peers may neither suffer current maladjustment nor be at-risk for later difficulties in social adjustment. The fact that Keller and Carlson (1974) did not observe pretreatment differences between isolate and nonisolate children in their rate of peer reinforcement suggests the need to assess behavioral dimensions other than simple frequency of positive interaction (e.g., Gottman, 1977b; Gottman, Gonso, & Rasmussen, 1975). Consequently, an increased number of studies are beginning to make use of peers to identify withdrawn children, to determine social responses for training, and to evaluate treatment in both the assessment and treatment process (e.g., Hobbs, Walle, Murray, Genoff, Wadley, & Conley, 1981; Oden & Asher, 1977; Whitehill, Hersen, & Bellack, 1980).

Autism and Childhood Schizophrenia

Distinctions are often made between infantile autism and childhood schizophrenia from the perspective of etiology and prognosis (Lovaas, Young, & Newsom, 1978; O'Leary & Wilson, 1975). However, in terms of clinical intervention with these children, such a differentiation does not appear to be of considerable importance. In general, treatment has addressed behavioral excesses and deficits common to these populations. Targets for modification have included reductions in self-injurious, aggressive, and self-stimulatory behaviors and acquisition of social behaviors, including self-help and speech and language skills (Lovaas, 1977; Lovaas *et al.,* 1978).

A number of investigators have presented data indicating effectiveness of extinction and timeout (in the form of isolation) for reducing aggressive behavior and self-mutilating acts such as head banging, self-hitting, and self-biting (e.g., Lovaas & Simmons, 1969; Lovaas, Freitag, Gold, & Kassorla, 1965; Wolf, Risley, & Mees, 1964). However, since these procedures produce gradual rather than immediate reductions in responding, they do not constitute the treatment of choice for self-injurious behaviors that threaten the child's safety. In such cases, use of response-contingent physical punishment (usually in the form of brief but painful electric shock) has produced sharp decreases or elimination of self-injury (Lovaas & Simmons, 1969; Lovaas, Schaeffer, & Simmons, 1965; Merbaum, 1973; Tate, 1972).

Lovaas *et al.* (1978) emphasize that physical punishment should be used as a last resort, subject to established guidelines regarding informed consent and proper administration (May, McAllister, Risley, Twardosz, & Cox, 1974). Available data on side effects stemming from contingent punishment of self-mutilation indicate that proper application of these procedures has facilitated increases in social behavior such as eye contact and physical contact as well as decreased inappropriate responses such as whining and isolation (Bachman, 1972; Hamilton, Stephens, & Allen, 1967; Lovaas & Simmons, 1969; Lovaas, Schaeffer, & Simmons 1965; Risley, 1968).

Decreasing Self-Stimulation

In conjuction with administration of punishment contingencies for self-injury, some investigators have observed decreases in stereotyped, repetitive responses such as rocking, spinning, hand-flapping, and head-rolling (Lovaas *et al.,* 1978). These self-stimulatory behaviors appear to provide the child with sensory input but have no observable effect on the social environment. Self-stimulatory responses are of considerable importance for treatment because they often interfere with the acquisition of appropriate behavior (Koegel & Covert, 1972; Lovaas, Litrownik, & Mann, 1971). For example, Koegel, Firestone, Kramme, and Dunlap (1974) observed a marked increase in appropriate toy play concurrent with successful reduction of self-stimulation. Thus, suppression of self-stimulatory responding may be a necessary prerequisite to teaching adaptive skills to autistic and schizophrenic children. Fortunately, several reviews of procedures involving shaping and reinforcement of appropriate responses incompatible with self-stimulation, use of positive practice overcorrection, and contingent punishment (Baumeister & Forehand, 1973; Hobbs, 1976; Hobbs & Goswick, 1977) indicate the potential utility of these approaches in reducing stereotyped responding.

Skill Acquisition

Subsequent to the reduction of self-injurious, self-stimulatory, and aggressive responses, operant procedures have been used primarily to teach adaptive behaviors (e.g., Lovaas, 1977; Wolf, Risley, Johnston, Harris, & Allen, 1967; Wolf, Risley, & Mees, 1964). Once eye contact has been established, the focus of treatment programs typically has involved training of nonverbal and verbal imitative behaviors and following of directions. For example, Metz (1965) taught generalized imitation to schizophrenic children by guiding the child through various motor tasks while providing immediate reinforcement. Physical guidance was then gradually reduced and eliminated, and new imitative tasks were interspersed with those that had already been acquired. Training simple motor responses (e.g., arm raising or hand clapping) may serve as the foundation for teaching more complex behaviors involved in the areas of self-help and social or intellectual skills. Considerable emphasis may be placed on progressing from imitation of simple sounds to complete words (e.g., Lovaas, Berberich, Perloff, & Schaeffer, 1966) for mute children or on decreasing echolalia (Carr, Schreibman, & Lovaas, 1975) in other subjects. Emphasis is then typically shifted from imitative responding to receptive language in the form of following commands. Use of modeling and feedback (i.e., exaggerated approval for correct responses and disapproval for incorrect responses) is often emphasized in efforts to teach these children self-help skills, proper affect, and appropriate play (Hemsley, Howlin, Berger, Hersov, Holbrook, Rutter, & Yule, 1978; Kent, 1974; Lovaas, 1977).

Treatment Outcome

While treatment procedures have primarily involved administration by trained professionals, both parents and teachers have been trained to become primary therapists for autistic and schizophrenic children (e.g., Craighead, O'Leary, & Allen, 1973; Nordquist & Wahler, 1973). In classroom settings, O'Leary and his colleagues (Kaufman & O'Leary, 1972; O'Leary, Drabman, & Kass, 1973; Santogrossi, O'Leary, Romanczyk, & Kaufman, 1973) have demonstrated the utility of token reinforcement programs in modifying the disruptive behavior of schizophrenic children. Koegel and Rincover (1974) and Rincover and Koegel (1977) have investigated training methods to extend these changes to include increased classroom skills by providing economical individualized instruction for autistic children.

Substantial improvements (i.e., reductions in self-stimulation and echolalia, increases in appropriate play and social and verbal behavior) have been observed for participants in Lovaas' comprehensive clinic intervention (e.g., Lovaas, Koegel, & Schreibman, 1973). In one study, autistic children who were returned to the home after 12 to 14 months of treatment maintained gains achieved during training or improved further. In contrast, children who were returned to an institution lost many of the gains they had made (Lovaas, Koegel, Simmons, & Long, 1973). The inescapable conclusion reached by these authors is that only when parents are willing to commit a major portion of their lives to training their child, to managing the child's behavior with strong consequences, and to keeping the child from playing a "sick role," will moderate success be achieved in establishing adaptive responses in this population (Lovaas, Koegel, Simmons, & Long, 1973).

Somatic Disorders

In the past decade, there has been increased work in the application of behavioral methods for children's somatic disorders. Siegel and Richards (1978) indicate that these treatment efforts generally have focused on modification of overt somatic, autonomic, or visceral responses primarily through the alteration of social and environmental contingencies. Several representative examples from the respiratory, gastrointestinal, genitourinary, and nervous systems are included in the following sections.

Asthma

Behavioral techniques have been employed in reducing both frequency and severity of asthmatic responding as well as in enhancing pulmonary functioning in children. Several studies have focused on the use of operant techniques in modifying the duration of asthmatic episodes and frequency and length of hospitalization for asthma attacks. Neisworth and Moore (1972) reduced duration of bedtime coughing and wheezing in a 7-year-old child through use of parental ignoring of these responses combined with tangible rewards contingent on decreases in coughing. Asthmatic episodes previously not amenable to medical treatment decreased to under 5 minutes in duration per evening during treatment and follow-up. Use of timeout procedures also has been reported by Creer (1970) and Creer, Weinberg, and Molk (1974) to modify the malingering of asthmatic children. Unwarranted admissions to the hospital (i.e., those that were intentionally induced or were the result of not complying with medical advice) resulted in the child's being placed in a private room without access to entertainment and extratherapeutic contact with staff. These procedures reduced both the number and duration of hospitalizations in several cases.

Pulmonary functioning in asthmatic children has been modified with use of relaxation techniques. In a well designed series of studies, investigators at the National Asthma Center have documented the efficacy of progressive relaxation alone and in combination with EMG biofeedback or autogenic training. These investigators have generally demonstrated significant improvement in peak expiratory flow rates (Alexander, 1972; Alexander, Miklich, & Hershkoff, 1972: Davis, Saunders, Creer, & Chai, 1973) as well as in air pathways resistance (Alexander, Cropp, & Chai, 1979) and forced expiration volume measures of pulmonary functioning (Tal & Miklich, 1976) following treatment. Although preliminary fundings indicated similar benefits from use of EMG biofeedback (Feldman, 1976; Kotses, Glaus, Crawford, Edwards, & Scherr, 1976), mixed results have been associated with training in systematic desensitization (Miklich, Renne, Creer, Alexander, Chai, Davis, Hoffman, & Danker-Brown, 1977; Moore, 1965) and reinforcement of increased flow rates (Danker, Miklich, Pratt, & Creer, 1975; Kahn, Staerk, & Bork, 1973).

Enuresis

Persistent bed-wetting during nighttime hours constitutes perhaps the most thoroughly investigated somatic disorder in children. Three general approaches to the treatment of this problem can be readily identified from the behavioral literature. The first approach is the use of a urine alarm, or bell-and-pad device (Mowrer & Mowrer, 1938), that involves a moisture-sensitive pad that activates a buzzer or bell when urination occurs. When the alarm sounds, the child must turn it off and then finish urinating in the bathroom. Face-washing is encouraged to assure that the child is awake, the sheets are then changed, the alarm is reset, and the child returns to bed. Comparisons of this procedure with psychotherapy, nighttime awakenings, medication, and placebo control conditions demonstrate its relative effectiveness. In addition, success rates of from 70–90%, as well as the absence of negative side effects, have generally been demonstrated (see Doleys, 1977, for a review). Relapse rates of 30–40% have been greatly reduced by the addition of intermittent rather than continuous scheduling of the alarm (Finley & Wansley, 1976; Finley, Besserman, Bennett, Clapp, & Finley, 1973; Finley, Wansley, & Blenkarn, 1977) or an overlearning procedure requiring the child to consume up to a quart of liquid before bedtime after dryness has been achieved (Jehu, Morgan, Turner, & Jones, 1977; Taylor & Turner, 1975).

An alternate treatment approach, based on the findings that bladder capacity of enuretics is less than that of normals (Starfield & Mellitis, 1968), involves the use of daytime training emphasizing bladder expansion. Starfield (1972) had enuretics refrain from voiding until the point of discomfort was reached while concurrently drinking large amounts of fluid during one trial per day. Children also kept daily records of the number of ounces urinated per trial as well as the number of dry nights over the 6-month program. Treatment reportedly resulted in dry nights for one-third of the children. A similar procedure, retention control training, involves intake of large amounts of fluid followed by reinforcement for gradually increasing retention intervals up to 30–45 minutes. In treatment periods of 7–20 days, nearly one-half of the enuretics whose parents were trained to implement this procedure achieved nighttime dryness (Kimmel & Kimmel, 1970; Paschalis, Kimmel, & Kimmel, 1972). However, subsequent studies have not replicated these findings and have brought into question the relationship between bladder capacity and dryness (e.g., Doleys & Wells, 1975; Doleys, Ciminero, Tollison, Williams, & Wells, 1977; Hunsaker, 1976).

Probably the most elaborate method of treating enuresis is the dry bed training program of Azrin *et al.* (1974), a method administered by a trained therapist during a single nighttime session. The program includes: increased fluid intake prior to bedtime; hourly awakenings in which the child is encouraged either to urinate or inhibit urination for a 1-hour period (depending on the child's age); reinforcement for appropriate voiding and having a dry bed; use of urine alarm; positive practice trials that consist of arising from bed and hurrying to the bathroom; and cleanliness training involving changing of bedding, clothes, and cleaning oneself following accidents. Research on this comprehensive program has indicated improvement or elimination of wetting for as long as 6-month follow-ups (Azrin *et al.*, 1974) as well as its superiority over retention control (Doleys *et al.*, 1977) and bell-and-pad training (Azrin & Thienes, 1978). In addition, the procedures have been adapted to include afternoon and evening training components (Azrin & Thienes, 1978) and to allow implementation by parents after a single session of office counseling (Azrin, Hontos, & Besalel-Azrin, 1979).

Encopresis

Methods employed in the elimination of childhood encopresis have generally involved use of response-contingent positive reinforcement, extinction or punishment, and a combination of these techniques with enemas or laxatives (Doleys, 1977). In a large number of case studies, reinforcement has been delivered contingent on the child's defecating in the toilet (e.g., Bach & Moylan, 1975; Planchetta, 1976) or contingent on both appropriate bowel movements and clean pants (e.g., Ayllon, Simon, & Wildman, 1975). Unlike most home-based treatments, Logan and Garner (1971) reported the classroom use of reinforcement for clean pants combined with a pants alarm to signal the occurrence of soiling. Points exchangeable for back-up reinforcers were awarded the 7-year-old subject and his classroom peers contingent upon the absence of soiling. When soiling occurred, the child was to leave the classroom at the sound of the buzzer and clean himself prior to returning.

Removal of parental attention for soiling, thus requiring the child to clean him/herself (Balson, 1973; Conger, 1970), as well as punishment contingencies involving timeout (Edelman, 1971) or cleaning of soiled clothes and washing with strong soap and cold water (Freinden & Van Handel, 1970) have been employed, albeit infrequently, in eliminating encopresis. Punishment in the form of a 40-minute sequence of cleanliness training (Azrin & Foxx, 1971) involving washing clothing and taking a bath in cool water, token reinforcement for appropriate defecating, and periodic pants checks were successfully employed in a comprehensive program reported by Doleys and his associates (Doleys & Arnold, 1975; Doleys, McWhorter, Williams, & Gentry, 1977). Wright and Walker (1976, 1978) report a success rate of virtually 100% in their application of a similarly comprehensive approach that involves scheduled toileting, use of suppositories and enemas to induce defecation, and rewards for appropriate defecation and remaining unsoiled. However, well controlled investigations of this approach have not as yet been undertaken, nor has its effectiveness been compared with that of other approaches.

Seizure Disorders

Both organic and psychogenic seizures have been demonstrated to be amenable to behavioral intervention (primarily in single-case studies). Differential reinforcement has been employed in several instances to modify seizure activity. Gardner (1967) reported use of parental ignoring of seizures and reinforcement for nonseizure activity in eliminating nonorganic seizures of a 10-year-old girl. Similarly, Balaschak (1976) demonstrated environmental control over seizure activity in an epileptic child through administration of reinforcement contingent on the absence of seizures. Frequency of seizures was decreased by two-thirds under the reinforcement contingency, but increased to baseline levels after reinforcement was discontinued.

Siegel and Richards (1978) note that the primary focus of treatment for seizure disorders has been on antecedent events that precede seizure onset. Along these lines, Zlutnick, Mayville, and Moffat (1975) reduced seizures of five children by interrupting sequences of behaviors (e.g., body tensing and arm raising) that preceded seizure activity. Yelling "No!" and vigorously shaking the child produced dramatic reductions in seizure activity in four cases. In a fifth case, reinforcement provided for behaviors incompatible with preseizure responses nearly eliminated the child's seizures.

Response-contingent electric shock (Wright, 1973a, b) and self-control procedures also have been used in case studies of seizure disorders in children. The innovative self-control procedure described by Ince (1976) involved systematic desensitization followed by a cue-controlled relaxation procedure. The child, who demonstrated both *grand mal* and *petit mal* seizures, was instructed to repeat a cue word that had been associated with relaxation whenever he experienced a preseizure aura. Seizure activity was reported to have been eliminated during treatment and 11-month follow-up. Recent developments of similar promise have involved biofeedback techniques to produce brain wave patterns incompatible with seizure EEG activity (Finley, Smith, & Etherton, 1975) or increases in sensorimotor rhythm that appear to inhibit seizure activity (Lubar & Shouse, 1977; Sterman, 1973; Sterman, MacDonald, & Stone, 1974)

Other Problems

Approaches not unlike those described for treatment of childhood asthma, enuresis, encopresis, and seizure disorders have been employed in therapeutic efforts with other somatic disorders. Differential reinforcement and aversive techniques have been used with cases of vomiting and rumination (e.g., Alford, Blanchard, & Buckley, 1972; Lang & Melamed, 1969; Sajwaj, Libet, & Agras, 1974). Shaping, self-monitoring, response cost, and contingent reinforcement have been applied in comprehensive programs focusing on eating problems such as anorexia and obesity (e.g., Agras, Barlow, Chapin, Abel, & Leitenberg, 1974; Argona, Cassady, & Drabman, 1975; Azerrad & Stafford, 1969; Epstein, Masek, & Marshall, 1978; Wheeler & Hess, 1976). Taken collectively, findings of these studies suggest considerable promise for the efficacy of behavioral procedures as a therapeutic intervention in this area.

Recent Advances

Behavioral treatment procedures thus far described, in some instances, have been examined and refined in investigations covering a period of at least 20 years. In more recent research, a number of important developments also have emerged. Among the most notable contributions are work in behavioral pediatrics, self-control, social skills training, and nonprescriptive therapies; these are advances that have provided considerable breadth and direction to the field.

Behavioral Pediatrics

The preliminary success achieved in the treatment of childhood somatic problems by means of behavioral techniques has prompted a trend toward a practice referred to as "behavioral pediatrics." In general, this area may be broadly viewed as involving application of behavioral methods to a wide range of pediatric problems, or as a marriage of sorts between pediatricians and child behavior therapists (Christophersen & Rapoff, 1979). While early effort in this area has tended to focus on intervention with disorders that affect a single organ system (Siegel & Richards, 1978), comprehensive behavioral approaches to the assessment and management of chronic disorders that impact upon multiple systems (e.g., juvenile diabetes) are beginning to emerge (Epstein, Coburn, Beck, & Figueroa, in press; Johnson, 1980; Melamed & Johnson, 1981).

Treatment of common behavior problems, such as difficulty at meals or bedtime, dressing difficulties, minor tantrums, and fears, also have been included within the domain of behavioral pediatrics by some authors (Christophersen & Rapoff, 1980), apparently under the rationale that these concerns are often brought to the attention of the pediatrician.

While child behavior therapists have demonstrated considerable success in treating such problems, intervention has generally occurred in mental health and psychiatric medical settings. A noteworthy exception in this regard is the work of Melamed and her associates (Melamed & Siegel, 1975; Melamed, Hawes, Heiby, & Glick, 1975; Melamed, Yurcheson, Fleece, Hutcherson, & Hawes, 1978) in adapting modeling techniques to treat children's fears in medical and dental settings. Therefore, while many of the procedures used by behavior therapists appear to be adaptable to pediatric practice (e.g., Azrin *et al.*, 1979), development of a technology for implementation of such methods represents a considerable challenge for the future.

Self-Control

Behavioral procedures described in this chapter have often involved programs formulated and implemented by professionals or significant others in the child's environment. In many cases, however, children have contributed to the intervention program by applying therapeutic procedures to modify their own behavior. These self-control procedures have involved children contributing to the determination of goals or reinforcement standards, monitoring their own behavior and evaluating it relative to such standards, and providing self-reward for appropriate performance.

Numerous studies, many of them conducted in classroom settings, have documented that self-control interventions can be effective, particularly in maintaining change previously produced by external control procedures (Bolstadt & Johnson, 1972; Felixbrod & O'Leary, 1973; Turkewitz, O'Leary, & Ironsmith, 1975). For example, Drabman, Spitalnik, and O'Leary (1973) taught emotionally disturbed children to self-evaluate their behavior by providing token reinforcement contingent upon evaluated performance as well as accuracy of evaluation. As a result, changes in disruption were observed under both token and nontoken (generalization) conditions. In a recent innovation, Wells, Griest, and Forehand (1980) incorporated self-control procedures (self-monitoring, self-evaluation, and self-reinforcement) for parental use within a standard parent training program to enhance durability of change in child behavior.

Similar interest has been generated in the application of self-control procedures that involve children's use of cognitive strategies for managing their behavior. Cognitive-behavior therapy techniques present children with a strategy for adopting alternative methods of responding to cope with problematic situations (i.e., problem solving), often via modeling (Goodwin & Mahoney, 1975) or training in self-instruction (Meichenbaum & Goodman, 1971). The latter procedure consists of teaching children verbal coping strategies that guide appropriate behavior (e.g., "If I keep working, I will be a good boy") in relevant contexts.

Based on the assumption that training in cognitive mediating strategies will produce enhanced generalization, these procedures have been used in the treatment of hyperactivity and impulsivity (e.g., Douglas, Parry, Marton, & Garson, 1976; Kendall & Finch, 1976, 1978), classroom behavior (e.g., Bornstein & Quevillon, 1976); aggressive behavior (e.g., Robin *et al.*, 1976), social interaction (Jakibchuk & Smeriglio, 1976), and fear of the dark (Kanfer, Karoly, & Newman, 1975). In a review of this literature, Hobbs, Moguin, Tyroler, and Lahey (1980) have noted that rather impressive benefits have been associated with cognitive-behavioral techniques in some studies. Nevertheless, methodological difficulties limit conclusions that can be drawn regarding the general efficacy of this approach.

Whereas child problems relating to social withdrawal have received greater attention in terms of treatment efforts (e.g., O'Connor, 1969, 1972), the relevance of children's interpersonal skills to a wide variety of problems has been recognized (Combs & Slaby, 1977). Hersen, Bellack, and their associates (Bornstein, Bellack, & Hersen, 1977; Bornstein, Bellack, & Hersen, 1980; Matson, Esveldt-Dawson, Andrasik, Ollendick, Petti, & Hersen, 1980; Ollendick & Hersen, 1979; Whitehill *et al.,* 1980) have used social skills training procedures consisting of modeling, role-playing and direct feedback in the successful treatment of aggressive, emotionally disturbed, delinquent, and unassertive children and adolescents. Skills such as establishing eye contact, making requests, and initiating conversations have been included in these treatment packages. Several related investigations have focused on friendship-making (e.g., Oden & Ashner, 1977), positive peer interaction (e.g., Gresham & Nagel, 1980; La Greca & Santogrossi, 1980), and conversational skills (e.g., Minkin, Braukmann, Minkin, Timbers, Timbers, Fixsen, Phillips, & Wolf, 1976).

In general, these programs have tended to produce changes in targeted behaviors on role-play tests (Bornstein *et al.,* 1977) and global ratings of social skill (evaluated by trained observers or significant adults) (Bornstein *et al.,* 1977, 1980; Matson *et al.,* 1980; Minkin *et al.,* 1976). Improvement on measures of behavior in the natural environment (Gresham & Nagel, 1980; La Greca & Santogrossi, 1980; Whitehill *et al.,* 1980) or on perceptions of target children by peers (Gresham & Nagel, 1980; Oden & Asher, 1977;) have been observed less frequently. Although the impact of such training in effecting generalized behavior change and enhanced interpersonal functioning from the perspective of a child's peers has not been firmly established, social skills training approaches appear to have considerable therapeutic promise.

Non-Prescriptive Therapies

Numerous programs written for parents who wish to alter their children's behavior have emerged within the framework of "self-help behavior therapy" (Bernal & North, 1980; Glasgow & Rosen, 1978; Rosen, 1976). These "nonprescriptive" approaches, which may be totally self-administered or may involve minimal therapist contact, have focused on modifying a wide range of child behaviors such as toilet training (Azrin & Foxx, 1974), misbehavior during shopping trips (Clark, Greene, MacRae, McNees, Davis, & Risley, 1977; Green, Clark, & Risley, 1977), inappropriate mealtime behaviors (McMahon & Forehand, 1978), self-help behaviors (Baker, Heifetz, & Brightman, 1972), as well as teaching general parenting skills (Patterson & Gullion, 1968).

While such programs may constitute an effective means of extending professional services to greater numbers of clients and of providing alternate therapeutic modalities, few parent training guides have been subjected to evaluation, and only two such manuals (Azrin & Foxx,1974; Patterson & Gullion, 1968) have been subjected to multiple evaluation. As reviewed by McMahon and Forehand (1980), preliminary data from evaluation of such programs indicate that narrow-focused parenting manuals (which emphasize a single therapeutic technique or one target behavior for modification) may be effective with minimal (e.g., Clark *et al.,* 1977) or no therapist contact (McMahon & Forehand, 1978). Use of broad-focused guides for teaching general parenting skills (e.g., Patterson & Gullion, 1968) also appears to produce modest results (Christenson, Johnson, Phillips, & Glasgow, 1980;

Patterson & Reid, 1973). However, the need for more extensive evaluation of nonprescriptive methods to include consideration of cost effectiveness (e.g., Christensen *et al.*, 1980) prior to their commercial availability must be emphasized.

Summary

As demonstrated by the increasing research literature in this area, rather impressive advances in therapeutic intervention with childhood disorders have been associated with the growth of child behavior therapy. The most notable successes appear to have occurred in the treatment of varied child behavior problems in the home and school. With these problems, large-scale investigations have documented effectiveness of behavioral methods relative to alternate treatment and control conditions. In addition, various behavioral interventions have been compared with one another in an effort to determine their relative efficacy in treating certain child problems or populations.

While similar large-scale evaluations have yet to be conducted with some of the problems surveyed (e.g., hyperactivity and learning disabilities), sufficient numbers of well-controlled single-subject research studies indicate the potential efficacy of behavioral methods. However, documentation of widespread applicability to certain child problems (e.g., childhood fears) requires additional investigations of sufficient experimental rigor that extend therapeutic procedures from treatment of analogue subjects (i.e., nonclinic subjects who volunteer for treatment) to actual clinical cases. Coupled with this is the need for demonstration of generalization of treatment effects across settings and behaviors as well as over time (Forehand & Atkeson, 1977).

As the complexity of problems treated within the behavioral framework increases, there must be comparable advances in methods of assessing treatment targets as well as evaluating treatment outcome. In this regard, use of multiple outcome measures has recently received considerable emphasis in child behavior therapy (Atkeson & Forehand, 1978). Most studies in the area have relied on measures collected by independent observers as the primary index of success of behavioral treatment. However, such measures should be supported by data on relevant behaviors collected by the child and/or significant others in the natural environment and subjective evaluations from these individuals, as well as physiological measures (e.g., Van Hasselt, Hersen, Bellack, Rosenblum, & Lamparski, 1979) for certain problems (e.g., somatic disorders, phobias). Although relatively few outcome investigations meet these criteria, such data are important for demonstrating that socially valid target behaviors have been selected for modification. Changes in relevant targets should produce more favorable subjective evaluations from the social environment and/or behavior that falls within the normal range when social comparisons are made between the performance of treated children and their nondeviant peers (Kazdin, 1977). By the inclusion of generalization and social validity data of this type, the progress of child behavior therapy in promoting clinically useful procedures and socially meaningful changes in child functioning should be greatly enhanced.

Acknowledgment

The authors wish to extend their appreciation to Carolyn Gill for her valuable assistance in the preparation of this manuscript.

Aaron, B. A., & Bostow, D. E. Indirect facilitation of on-task behavior produced by contingent free time for academic productivity. *Journal of Applied Behavior Analysis,* 1978, *11,* 197.

Agras, W. S., Barlow, D. H., Chapin, H. N., Abel, G. G., & Leitenberg, H. Behavior modification of anorexia nervosa. *Archives of General Psychiatry,* 1974, *30,* 279–286.

Alexander, A. B. Systematic relaxation and flow rates in asthmatic children: Relationship to emotional precipitants and anxiety. *Journal of Psychosomatic Research,* 1972, *16,* 405–410.

Alexander, A. B., Cropp, G. J. A., & Chai, H. Effects of relaxation training on pulmonary mechanics in children with asthma. *Journal of Applied Behavior Analysis,* 1979, *12,* 27–35.

Alexander, A. B., Miklich, D. R., & Hershkoff, H. The immediate effects of systematic relaxation training on peak expiratory flow rates in asthmatic children. *Psychosomatic Medicine,* 1972, *34,* 388–394.

Alexander, J. F., & Parsons, B. V. Short-term behavioral intervention with delinquent families: Impact on family process and recidivism. *Journal of Abnormal Psychology,* 1973, *81,* 219–225.

Alford, G. S., Blanchard, E. B., & Buckley, T. M. Treatment of hysterical vomiting by modification of social contingencies: A case study. *Journal of Behavior Therapy and Experimental Psychiatry,* 1972, *3,* 209–212.

Argona, J., Cassady, J., & Drabman, R. S. Treating overweight children through parental training and contingency contracting. *Journal of Applied Behavior Analysis,* 1975, *8,* 269–278.

Atkeson, B. M., & Forehand, R. Parent behavioral training for problem children: An examination of studies using multiple outcome measures. *Journal of Abnormal Child Psychology,* 1978, *6,* 449–460.

Atkeson, B. M., & Forehand, R. Home-based reinforcement programs designed to modify classroom behavior: A review and methodological evaluation. *Psychological Bulletin,* 1979, *86,* 1298–1308.

Ayllon, T., & Roberts, M. Eliminating discipline problems by strengthening academic performance. *Journal of Applied Behavior Analysis,* 1974, *7,* 71–76.

Ayllon, T., & Rosenbaum, M. S. The behavioral treatment of disruption and hyperactivity in school settings. In B. B. Lahey & A. E., Kazdin (Eds.), *Advances in clinical child psychology* (Vol. 1). New York: Plenum Press, 1977.

Ayllon, T., Layman, D., & Kandel, H. J. A behavioral–educational alternative to drug control of hyperactive children. *Journal of Applied Behavior Analysis,* 1975, *8,* 137–146.

Ayllon, T., Simon, S. J., & Wildman, R. W. Instructions and reinforcement in the elimination of encopresis: A case study. *Journal of Behavior Therapy and Experimental Psychiatry,* 1975, *6,* 235–238.

Ayllon, T., Smith, D., & Rogers, M. Behavioral management of school phobia. *Journal of Behavior Therapy and Experimental Psychiatry,* 1970, *1,* 125–138.

Azerrad, J., & Stafford, R. L. Restoration of eating behavior in anorexia nervosa through operant conditioning and environmental manipulation. *Behaviour Research and Therapy,* 1969, *7,* 165–171.

Azrin, N. H., & Foxx, R. M. A rapid method of toilet training the retarded. *Journal of Applied Behavior Analysis,* 1971, *4,* 89–99.

Azrin, N. H., & Foxx, R. M. *Toilet training in less than a day.* New York: Simon & Shuster, 1974.

Azrin, N. H., & Thienes, P. M. Rapid elimination of enuresis by intensive learning without a conditioning apparatus. *Behavior Therapy,* 1978, *9,* 342–354.

Azrin, N. H., Hontos, P. T., & Besalel-Azrin, V. Elimination of enuresis without a conditioning apparatus: An extension by office instruction of the child and parents. *Behavior Therapy,* 1979, *10,* 14–19.

Azrin, N. H., Sneed, T. J., & Foxx, R. M. Dry bed: Rapid elimination of childhood enuresis. *Behaviour Research and Therapy,* 1974, *12,* 147–156.

Bach, R., & Moylan, J. J. Parents administer behavior therapy for inappropriate urination and encopresis: A case study. *Journal of Behavior Therapy and Experimental Psychiatry,* 1975, *6,* 239–241.

Bachman, J. A. Self-injurious behavior: A behavioral analysis. *Journal of Abnormal Psychology,* 1972, *80,* 211–224.

Baker, B. L., Heifetz, L. J., & Brightman, A. J. *Parents as teachers: Manuals for behavior modification of the retarded child.* Cambridge, Mass: Behavioral Educations Projects, 1972.

Balaschak, B. A. Teacher-implemented behavior modification in a case of organically based epilepsy. *Journal of Consulting and Clinical Psychology,* 1976, *44,* 218–223.

Balson, P. M. Case study: Encopresis: A case with symptom substitution? *Behavior Therapy,* 1973, *4,* 134–136.

Bandura, A. *Principles of behavior modification.* New York: Holt, Rinehart, & Winston, 1969.

Bandura, A. *Psychological modeling: Conflicting theories.* Chicago: Aldine-Atherton, 1971.

Bandura, A. *Social learning theory.* Englewood Cliffs, N.J.: Prentice-Hall, 1977.

Bandura, A., & Menlove, F. L. Factors determining vicarious extinction of avoidance behavior through symbolic modeling. *Journal of Personality and Social Psychology,* 1968, *8,* 98–108.

Bandura, A., Grusec, E., & Menlove, F. L. Vicarious extinction of avoidance behavior. *Journal of Personality and Social Psychology,* 1967, *5,* 16–23.

Barabasz, A. F. Group desensitization of test anxiety in elementary school. *Journal of Psychology,* 1973, *83,* 295–301.

Barabasz, A. F. Classroom teachers are paraprofessional therapists in group systematic desensitization of test anxiety. *Psychiatry,* 1975, *38,* 388–392.

Barton, E. S., Guess, D., Garcia, E., & Baer, D. M. Improvements of retardates' mealtime behaviors by timeout procedures using multiple baseline techniques. *Journal of Applied Behavior Analysis,* 1970, *3,* 77–84.

Baumeister, A. A., & Forehand, R. Stereotyped acts. In N. R. Ellis (Ed.), *International review of research in mental retardation* (Vol. 6). New York: Academic Press, 1973.

Becker, W. C., Madsen, C. H., Arnold, C. R., & Thomas, D. R. The contingent use of teacher attention and praising in reducing classroom behavior problems. *Journal of Special Education,* 1967, *1,* 287–307.

Bernal, M. E., & North, J. A. A survey of parent training manuals. *Journal of Applied Behavior Analysis,* 1980, *11,* 533–544.

Bernal, M. E., Klinnet, M. D., & Schultz, L. A. Outcome evaluation of behavioral parent training and client-centered parent counseling for children with conduct problems. *Journal of Applied Behavior Analysis,* 1980, *13,* 669–676.

Bijou, S. W. Experimental studies of child behavior, normal and deviant. In L. Krasner & L. P. Ullmann, (Eds.), *Research in behavior modification.* New York: Holt, Rinehart & Winston, 1965.

Bijou, S. W., & Baer, D. M. Some methodological contributions from a functional analysis of child development. In L. F. Lipsett & C. S. Spiker (Eds.)., *Advances in child development and behavior* (Vol. 1). New York: Academic Press, 1963.

Blechman, E. A., Olson, D. H. L., & Hellman, I. D. Stimulus control over family problem-solving behavior: The family contract game. *Behavior Therapy,* 1976, *7,* 686–692.

Blechman, E. A., Olson, D. H. L., Schornagel, C. Y., Halsdorf, M., & Turner, A. J. The family contract game: Technique and case study. *Journal of Consulting and Clinical Psychology,* 1976, *44,* 449–455.

Bolstadt, O., & Johnson, S. Self-regulation in the modification of disruptive classroom behavior. *Journal of Applied Behavior Analysis,* 1972, *5,* 448–454.

Bornstein, M. R., Bellack, A. S., & Hersen, M. Social skills training for unassertive children: A multiple-baseline analysis. *Journal of Applied Behavior Analysis,* 1977, *10,* 183–195.

Bornstein, M. R., Bellack, A. S., & Hersen, M. Social skills training for highly aggressive children in an impatient psychiatric setting. *Behavior Modification,* 1980, *4,* 173–186.

Bornstein, P. H., & Quevillon, R. P. The effects of a self-instructional package on overactive preschool boys. *Journal of Applied Behavior Analysis,* 1976, *9,* 179–188.

Broden, M., Hall, R. V., Dunlap, A., & Clark, R. Effects of teacher attention and a token reinforcement system in a junior-high special education class. *Exceptional Children,* 1970, *36,* 341–349.

Broughton, S. F., & Lahey, B. B. Direct and collateral effects of positive reinforcement, response code, and mixed contingencies for academic performance. *Journal of School Psychology,* 1978, *16,* 126–136.

Carr, E. G., Schreibman, L., & Lovaas, O. I. Control of echolalic speech in psychotic children. *Journal of Abnormal Child Psychology,* 1975, *3,* 331–351.

Christensen, A., Johnson, S. M., Phillips, S., & Glasgow, R. E. Cost effectiveness in behavioral family therapy. *Behavior Therapy,* 1980, *11,* 208–226

Christophersen, E. R., & Rapoff, M. A. Behavioral pediatrics. In O. F. Pomerleau & J. P. Brady (Eds.), *Behavioral medicine: Theory and practice.* Baltimore: Williams and Wilkins, 1979.

Christophersen, E. R., & Rapoff, M. A. Pediatric psychology: An appraisal. In B. B. Lahey & A. E. Kazdin (Eds.), *Advances in clinical child psychology* (Vol. 3). New York: Plenum Press, 1980.

Christophersen, E. R., Arnold, C. M., Hill, D. W., & Quilitch, H. R. The home point system: Token reinforcement procedures for application by parents of children with behavior problems. *Journal of Applied Behavior Analysis,* 1972, *5,* 485–497.

Christophersen, E. R., Barnard, J. D., Ford, D., & Wolf, M. M. The family training program: Improving parent–child interaction patterns. In E. J. Mash, L. C. Handy, & L. A. Hamerlynck (Eds.), *Behavior modification approaches to parenting.* New York: Brunner/Mazel, 1976.

Clark, H. B., Greene, B. F., Macrae, J. W., McNees, M. P., Davis, J. L., & Risley, T. R. A parent advice package for family shopping trips: Development and evaluation. *Journal of Applied Behavior Analysis,* 1977, *10,* 605–624.

Combs, M. F., & Slaby, D. A. Social skills training with children. In B. B. Lahey & A. E. Kazdin (Eds.), *Advances in clinical child psychology* (Vol. 1). New York: Plenum Press, 1977.

Conger, J. C. The treatment of encopresis by the management of social consequences. *Behavior Therapy,* 1970, *41,* 667–682.

Coolidge, J. C., Hahn, P. B., & Peck, A. L. School phobia: Neurotic crisis or way of life. *American Journal of Orthopsychiatry,* 1957, *27,* 296–306.

Corey, J. R., & Shamow, J. The effects of fading on the acquisition and retention of oral reading. *Journal of Applied Behavior Analysis,* 1972, *5,* 311–313.

Cowen, E. L., Pederson, A., Babijian, H., Izzo, L. D., & Trost, M. A. Long term follow-up of early detected vulnerable children. *Journal of Consulting and Clinical Psychology,* 1973, *41,* 438–446.

Craighead, W. E., O'Leary, K. D., & Allen, J. S. Teaching and generalization of instruction-following in an autistic child. *Journal of Behavior Therapy and Experimental Psychiatry,* 1973, *4,* 171–176.

Creer, T. L. The use of time-out from positive reinforcement procedure with asthmatic children. *Journal of Psychosomatic Research,* 1970, *14,* 117–120.

Creer, T. L. *Asthma therapy.* New York: Springer, 1979.

Creer, T. L., Weinberg, E., & Molk, L. Managing a hospital behavior problem: Malingering. *Journal of Behavior Therapy and Experimental Psychiatry,* 1974, *5,* 259–262.

Danker, P. S., Miklich, D. R., Pratt, C., & Creer, T. L. An unsuccessful attempt to instrumentally condition peak expiratory flow rates in asthmatic children. *Journal of Psychosomatic Research,* 1975, *19,* 209.

Davis, M. H., Saunders, D. R., Creer, T. L., & Chai, H. Relaxation training facilitated by biofeedback apparatus as a supplemental treatment in bronchial asthma. *Journal of Psychosomatic Research,* 1973, *17,* 121–218.

Delfini, L. F., Bernal, M. E., & Rosen, P. M. Comparison of deviant and normal boys in home settings. In E. J. Mash, L. A. Hammerlynck, & L. C. Handy (Eds.), *Behavior modification and families.* New York: Brunner/Mazel, 1976.

Doleys, D. M. Assessment and treatment of enuresis and encopresis in children. In M. Hersen, R. M. Eisler, & P. M. Miller (Eds.), *Progress in behavior modification* (Vol. 6). New York: Academic Press, 1977.

Doleys, D. M., & Arnold, S. Treatment of childhood encopresis: Full cleanliness training. *Mental Retardation,* 1975, *13,* 14–16.

Doleys, D. M., & Wells, K. C. Changes in functional bladder capacity and bedwetting during and after retention control training. *Behavior Therapy,* 1975, *6,* 685–688.

Doleys, D. M., Ciminero, A. R., Tollison, J. W., Williams, C. L., & Wells, K. C. Dry bed training and retention control training: A comparison. *Behavior Therapy,* 1977, *8,* 541–548.

Doleys, D. M., McWhorter, A. Q., Williams, S. C., & Gentry, W. R. Encopresis: Its treatment and relation to nocturnal enuresis. *Behavior Therapy,* 1977, *8,* 77–82.

Douglas, V., Parry, P., Marton, P., & Garson, C. Assessment of a cognitive training program for hyperactive children. *Journal of Abnormal Child Psychology,* 1976, *4,* 389–410.

Drabman, R. S. Child versus teacher administered token programs in a psychiatric hospital school. *Journal of Abnormal Child Psychology,* 1973, *1,* 68–87.

Drabman, R. S. Behavior modification in the classroom. In W. E. Craighead, A. E. Kazdin, & M. J. Mahoney (Eds.), *Behavior modification: Principles, issues, and applications.* Boston: Houghton Mifflin, 1976.

Drabman, R. S., Spitalinik, R., & O'Leary, K. D. Teaching self-control to disruptive children. *Journal of Abnormal Psychology,* 1972, *82,* 10–16.

Drass, S. D., & Jones, R. L. Learning disabled children as behavior modifiers. *Journal of Learning Disabilities,* 1971, *4,* 418–425.

Edelman, R. I. Operant conditioning treatment of encopresis. *Journal of Behavior Therapy and Experimental Psychiatry,* 1971, *2,* 71–73.

Epstein, L. H., Coburn, P. C., Beck, S., & Figueroa, J. A behavioral approach to juvenile diabetes. In T. J. Coates (Ed.), *Behavioral medicine; A practical handbook,* Champaign, Ill.: Research Press, in press.

Epstein, L. H., Masek, B. J., & Marshall, W. R. A nutritionally based school program for control of eating in obese children. *Behavior Therapy,* 1978, *9,* 766–778.

Evers, W. L., & Schwartz, J. C. Modifying social withdrawal in preschoolers: The effects of filmed modeling and teacher praise. *Journal of Child Psychology,* 1973, *1,* 248–256.

Eyberg, S. M., & Johnson, S. M. Multiple assessment of behavior modification with families: Effects of contingency contracting and order of treated problems. *Journal of Consulting and Clinical Psychology,* 1974, *42,* 594–606.

Feldman, G. M. The effects of biofeedback training on respiratory resistance of asthmatic children. *Psychosomatic Medicine,* 1976, *38,* 27–34.

Felixbrod, J., & O'Leary, K. D. Effects of reinforcement on children's academic behavior as a function of self-determined and externally imposed contingencies. *Journal of Applied Behavior Analysis,* 1973, *6,* 241–250.

Ferber, H., Keeley, S. M., & Shemberg, K. M. Training parents in behavior modification: Outcome of and problems encountered in a program after Patterson's work. *Behavior Therapy,* 1974, *5,* 415–419.

Ferritor, D. E., Buckholdt, D., Hamblin, R. L., & Smith, L. The noneffects of contingent reinforcement for attending behavior on work accomplished. *Journal of Applied Behavior Analysis,* 1972, *5,* 7–17.

Finley, W. W., & Wansley, R. A. Use of intermittent reinforcement in a clinical-research program for the treatment of enuresis nocturna. *Journal of Pediatric Psychology,* 1976, *4,* 24–27.

Finley, W. W., Besserman, R. L., Bennett, L. F., Clapp, R. K., & Finley, P. M. The effect of continuous, intermittent, and "placebo" reinforcement on the effectiveness of the conditioning treatment for enuresis nocturna. *Behaviour Research and Therapy,* 1973, *11,* 289–297.

Finley, W. W., Smith, H. A., & Etherton, M. D. Reduction of seizures and normalization of the EEG in a severe epileptic following sensorimotor biofeedback training: A preliminary study. *Biological Psychology,* 1975, *2,* 189–203.

Finley, W. W., Wansley, R. A., & Blenkarn, M. M. Conditioning treatment of enuresis using a 70% intermittent reinforcement schedule. *Behaviour Research and Therapy,* 1977, *15,* 419–427.

Forehand, R., & Atkeson, B. M. Generality of treatment effects with parents as therapists: A review of assessment and implementation procedures. *Behavior Therapy,* 1977, *8,* 575–593.

Forehand, R., & King, H. E. Preschool children's noncompliance: Effects of short-term therapy. *Journal of Community Psychology,* 1974, *2,* 42–44.

Forehand, R., & McMahon, R. J. *Parent training for child noncompliance.* New York: Guilford, 1981.

Forehand, R., King, H. E., Peed, S., & Yoder, P. Mother–child interactions: Comparison of a noncompliant clinic group and a nonclinic group.

Forehand, R., Roberts, M., Doleys, D., Hobbs, S., & Resick, P. An examination of disciplinary procedures with children. *Journal of Experimental Child Psychology,* 1976, *21,* 109–120.

Forehand, R., Sturgis, E. T., McMahon, R., Aguar, D., Green, K., Wells, K. C., & Breiner, J. Parent behavioral training to modify child noncompliance: Treatment generalization across time and from home to school. *Behavior Modification,* 1979, *3,* 3–25.

Foxx, R. M., & Azrin, N. H. Restitution: A method of eliminating aggressive-descriptive behavior of mentally retarded and brain damaged patients. *Behaviour Research and Therapy,* 1972, *10,* 15–27.

Foxx, R. M. & Azrin, N. H. The elimination of self-stimulatory behavior of autistic and retarded children by overcorrection. *Journal of Applied Behavior Analysis,* 1973, *6,* 1–14.

Foxx, R. M., & Shapiro, S. T. The timeout ribbon: A non-exclusionary timeout procedure. *Journal of Applied Behavior Analysis,* 1978, *11,* 125–136.

Frederikson, L. W., & Frederikson, C. B. Teacher-determined and self-determined token reinforcement in a special education classroom. *Behavior Therapy,* 1975, *6,* 310–314.

Freinden, W., & Van Handel, D. Elimination of soiling in an elementary school child through application of aversive technique. *Journal of School Psychology,* 1970, *8,* 267–269.

Gardner, J. E. Behavior therapy treatment approach to a psychogenic seizure case. *Journal of Consulting Psychology,* 1967, *31,* 209–212.

Gearheart, B. R. *Learning disabilities: Educational strategies.* Saint Louis: C. V. Mosby, 1973.

Gelfand, D. M., & Hartmann, D. P. *Child behavior analysis and therapy.* New York: Pergamon, 1975.

Glasgow, R. E., & Rosen, G. M. Behavioral bibliotherapy: A review of self-help behavior therapy manuals. *Psychological Bulletin,* 1978, *85,* 1–23.

Goetz, E. M., & Baer, D. M. Descriptive social reinforcement of creative block building by young children. *Journal of Applied Behavior Analysis,* 1973, *6,* 209–218.

Goodwin, S. E., & Mahoney, M. J. Modification of aggression through modeling: An experimental probe. *Journal of Behavior Therapy and Experimental Psychiatry,* 1975, *6,* 200–202.

Gottman, J. M. The effects of a modeling film on social isolation in preschool children: A methodological investigation. *Journal of Abnormal Child Psychology,* 1977, *5,* 69–78. (a)

Gottman, J. M. Toward a definition of social isolation in children. *Child Development,* 1977, *48,* 513–517. (b)

Gottman, J. M., Gonso, J., & Rasmussen, B. Social interaction, social competence, and friendship in children. *Child Development,* 1975, *46,* 709–718.

Graziano, A. M. *Behavior therapy with children* (Vol. 1). Chicago: Aldine, 1971.

Graziano, A. M. *Behavior therapy with children* (Vol. 2). Chicago: Aldine, 1975.

Graziano, A. M., & Mooney, K. *Behavior therapy with children* (Vol. 3). Chicago: Aldine, 1981.

Greene, B. F., Clark, H. B., & Risley, T. R. *Shopping with children.* San Rafael, Calif.: Academic Therapy, 1977.

Greenwood, C. R., Sloane, H. N., & Baskin, A. Training elementary aged peer-behavioral managers to control small group programmed mathematics. *Journal of Applied Behavior Analysis,* 1974, *7,* 103–114.

Gresham, F. M., & Nagle, R. J. Social skills training with children: Responsiveness to modeling and coaching as a function of peer orientation. *Journal of Consulting and Clinical Psychology,* 1980, *48,* 718–729.

Hamilton, J., Stephens, L., & Allen, P. Controlling aggressive and destructive behavior in severely retarded institutionalized residents. *American Journal of Mental Deficiency,* 1967, *71,* 852–856.

Hampe, E., Noble, H., Miller, L. C., & Barrett, C. L. Phobic children one and two years post-treatment. *Journal of Abnormal Psychology,* 1973, *82,* 446–453.

Haring, N. G., & Hauck, M. A. Improved learning conditions in the establishment of reading skills with disabled readers. *Exceptional Children,* 1969, *35,* 341–351.

Hay, W. M., Hay, L. R., & Nelson, R. O. Direct and collateral changes in on-task and academic behavior resulting from on-task versus academic contingencies. *Behavior Therapy,* 1977, *8,* 431–441.

Hemsley, R., Howlin, P., Berger, M., Hersov, L., Holbrook, D., Rutter, M., & Yule, W. Treating autistic children in a family context. In M. Rutter & E. Schopler (Eds.), *Autism: A reappraisal of concepts & treatments.* New York: Plenum Press, 1978.

Hersen, M. The behavioral treatment of school phobia. *Journal of Nervous and Mental Disease,* 1971, *153,* 99–107.

Hersen, M., & Barlow, D. H. *Single case experimental designs: Strategies for studying behavior change.* New York: Pergamon, 1976.

Hobbs, S. Modifying stereotyped behavior by overcorrection: A critical review. *Rehabilitation Psychology,* 1976, *23,* 1–11.

Hobbs, S., & Forehand, R. Important parameters in the use of timeout with children: A re-examination. *Journal of Behavior Therapy and Experimental Psychiatry,* 1977, *8,* 365–370.

Hobbs, S., & Goswick, R. Behavioral treatment of self-stimulation: An examination of alternatives to physical punishment. *Journal of Clinical Child Psychology,* 1977, *6,* 20–23.

Hobbs, S., & Lahey, B. The behavioral approach to "learning disabled" children. *Journal of Clinical Child Psychology,* 1977, *6,* 10–14.

Hobbs, S., Forehand, R., & Murray, R. Effects of various durations of timeout on the non-compliant behavior of children. *Behavior Therapy,* 1978, *9,* 652–656.

Hobbs, S., Moguin, L., Tyroler, M., & Lahey, B. Cognitive behavior therapy with children: Has clinical utility been demonstrated? *Psychological Bulletin,* 1980, *87,* 147–165.

Hobbs, S., Walle, D., Murray, R., Genoff, T., Wadley, D., & Conley, C. *Social validation of a behavioral assertiveness test for children.* Paper presented at Southeastern Psychological Association, Atlanta, 1981.

Hopkins, B. L., Schutte, R. C., & Garton, K. L. The effects of access to a playroom on the rate and quality of printing and writing of first- and second-grade students. *Journal of Applied Behavior Analysis,* 1971, *4,* 77–87.

Humphreys, L., Forehand, R., McMahon, R., & Roberts, M. Parent behavioral training to modify child noncompliance: Effects on untreated siblings. *Journal of Behavior Therapy and Experimental Psychiatry,* 1978, *9,* 235–238.

Hunsaker, J. H. A two-piece approach to nocturnal enuresis: Preliminary results. *Behavior Therapy,* 1976, *6,* 560–561.

Ince, L. P. The use of relaxation training and a conditioned stimulus in the elimination of epileptic seizures in a child: A case study. *Journal of Behavior Therapy and Experimental Psychiatry,* 1976, *7,* 39–42.

Iwata, B. A., & Bailey, J. S. Reward versus cost token systems: An analysis of the effects on students and teacher. *Journal of Applied Behavior Analysis,* 1974, *7,* 567–576.

Jacobsen, E. *Progressive relaxation.* Chicago: University at Chicago Press, 1938.

Jakibchuk, Z., & Smeriglio, V. L. The influence of symbolic modeling on the social behavior of preschool children with low levels of social responsiveness. *Child Development,* 1976, *47,* 838–841.

Jehu, D., Morgan, T., Turner, R., & Jones, A. A controlled trial of the treatment of nocturnal enuresis in residential homes for children. *Behaviour Research and Therapy,* 1977, *15,* 1–16.

Jersild, A. T., & Holmes, F. B. Children's fears. *Child Development Monographs,* 1935, No. 20.

Johnson, M., & Bailey, J. S. Cross-age tutoring: Fifth graders as arithmetic tutors for kindergarten children. *Journal of Applied Behavior Analysis,* 1974, *7,* 223–232.

Johnson, S. B. Psychosocial factors in juvenile diabetes: A review. *Journal of Behavioral Medicine,* 1980, *3,* 95–116.

Jones, M. C. The elimination of children's fears. *Journal of Experimental Psychology,* 1924, *7,* 382–390. (a)

Jones, M. C. A laboratory study of fear: the case of Peter. *Journal of Genetic Psychology,* 1924, *31,* 308–315. (b)

Jones, R. T., & Kazdin, A. E. Childhood behavior problems in the school. In S. M. Turner, K. S. Calhoun, & H. E. Adams (Eds.), *Handbook of clinical behavior therapy.* New York: Wiley, 1981.

Kagan, J. Reflection impulsivity: The generality and dynamics of conceptual tempo. *Journal of Abnormal Psychology,* 1966, *71,* 17–24.

Kagan, J., & Moss, H. A. *Birth of maturity: A study in psychological development.* New York: Wiley, 1962.

Kahn, A. U., Staerk, M., & Bonk, C. Role of counter-conditioning in the treatment of asthma. *Journal of Psychosomatic Research,* 1973, *17,* 389–392.

Kanfer, F., Karoly, P., & Newman, A. Reduction of children's fear of the dark by competence-related and situational threat-related verbal cues. *Journal of Consulting and Clinical Psychology,* 1975, *43,* 251–258.

Kanfer, F., & Saslow, G. Behavioral diagnosis. In C. M. Franks (Ed.), *Behavior therapy: Appraisal and status.* New York: McGraw Hill, 1969.

Kaufman, K. F., & O'Leary, K. D. Reward, cost, and self-evaluation procedures for disruptive adolescents in a psychiatric hospital. *Journal of Applied Behavior Analysis,* 1972, *5,* 293–309.

Kazdin, A. E. Response cost: The removal of conditioned reinforcers for therapeutic change. *Behavior Therapy,* 1972, *3,* 533–546.

Kazdin, A. E. Assessing the clinical or applied importance of behavior change through social validation. *Behavior Modification,* 1977, *1,* 427–451.

Keller, M. F., & Carlson, P. M. The use of symbolic modeling to promote social skills in preschool children with low levels of social responsiveness. *Child Development,* 1974, *45,* 912–919.

Kendall, P. C., & Finch, A. J. A cognitive behavioral treatment for impulse control: A case study. *Journal of Consulting and Clinical Psychology,* 1976, *44,* 852–857.

Kendall, P. C., & Finch, A. J. A cognitive behavioral treatment for impulsivity: A group comparison study. *Journal of Consulting and Clinical Psychology,* 1978, *46,* 110–118.

Kennedy, W. A. School phobia: Rapid treatment of fifty cases. *Journal of Abnormal and Social Psychology,* 1965, *70,* 285–289.

Kent, L. R. *Language acquisition program for the severely retarded.* Champaign, Ill.: Research Press, 1974.

Kent, R. N., & O'Leary, K. D. A controlled evaluation of behavior modification with conduct problem children. *Journal of Consulting and Clinical Psychology,* 1976, *44,* 586–596.

Kimmel, H. D., & Kimmel, E. An instrumental conditioning method for the treatment of enuresis. *Journal of Behavior Therapy and Experimental Psychiatry,* 1970, *1,* 121–123.

Kirby, F. D., & Shields, F. Modification of arithmetic response rate and attending behavior in a seventh grade student. *Journal of Applied Behavior Analysis,* 1972, *5,* 79–84.

Kissel, S. Systematic desensitization therapy with children: A case study and some suggested modifications. *Professional Psychology,* 1972, *3,* 164–169.

Koegel, R. L., & Covert, A. The relationship of self-stimulation to learning in autistic children. *Journal of Applied Behavior Analysis,* 1972, *5,* 381–387.

Koegel, R. L., & Rincover, A. Treatment of psychotic children in a classroom environment. I. Learning in a large group. *Journal of Applied Behavior Analysis,* 1974, *7,* 45–59.

Koegel, R. L., Firestone, P. B., Kramme, K. W., & Dunlap G. Increasing spontaneous play by suppressing self-stimulation in autistic children. *Journal of Applied Behavior Analysis,* 1974, *7,* 521–528.

Kondas, O. Reduction of examination anxiety and stage fright by group desensitization and relaxation. *Behaviour Research and Therapy,* 1967, *5,* 275–281.

Kornhaber, R. C., & Schroeder, H. E. Importance of model similarity on extinction of avoidance behavior in children. *Journal of Consulting and Clinical Psychology,* 1975, *5,* 601–607.

Kotses, H., Glaus, K. D., Crawford, P. L., Edwards, J. E., & Scherr, M. S. Operant reduction of frontalis EMG activity in the treatment of asthma in children. *Journal of Psychosomatic Research,* 1976, *20,* 453–459.

Krumboltz, J. D., & Thoresen, C. E. The effect of behavioral counseling in group and individual settings on information-seeking behavior. *Journal of Counseling Psychology,* 1964, *11,* 324–333.

La Greca, A. M., & Santogrossi, D. A. Social skills training with elementary school students: A behavioral group approach. *Journal of Consulting and Clinical Psychology,* 1980, *48,* 220–227.

Lahey, B. B. *Behavior therapy with hyperactive and learning disabled children.* New York: Oxford University Press, 1979.

Lahey, B. B., & Drabman, R. S. Facilitation of the acquisition and retention of sight word vocabulary through token reinforcement. *Journal of Applied Behavior Analysis,* 1974, *7,* 307–312.

Lahey, B. B., Busemeyer, M. K., O'Hara, C., & Beggs, V. E. Treatment of severe perceptual-motor disorders in children diagnosed as learning disabled. *Behavior Modification.* 1977, *1,* 123–140.

Lahey, B. B., Delamater, A., & Kupfer, D. Intervention strategies with hyperactive and learning disabled children. In S. M. Turner, K. S. Calhoun, & H. E. Adams (Eds.), *Handbook of clinical behavior therapy.* New York: Wiley, 1981.

Lahey, B. B., Green, K. D., & Forehand, R. L. On the independence of ratings of hyperactivity, conduct problems, and attention deficits: A multiple-regression analysis. *Journal of Consulting and Clinical Psychology,* 1980, *48,* 566–574.

Lahey, B. B., Hobbs, S. A., Kupfer, D., & Delamater, A. Current perspectives on hyperactivity and learning disabilities. In B. B. Lahey (Ed.), *Behavior therapy with hyperactive and learning disabled children.* New York: Oxford, 1979.

Lahey, B. B., McNees, M. P., & Brown, C. C. Modification of deficits in reading for comprehension. *Journal of Applied Behavioral Analysis,* 1973, *6,* 475–480.

Lahey, B. B., McNees, M. P., & McNees, M. C. Control of an obscene "verbal tic" through time-out in an elementary school classroom. *Journal of Applied Behavior Analysis,* 1973, *6,* 101–104.

Lahey, B. B., Weller, D. R., & Brown, W. R. The behavior analysis approach to reading: Phonics discriminations. *Journal of Reading Behavior,* 1973, *5,* 200–206

Lang, P. J., & Melamed, B. G. Avoidance conditioning therapy of an infant with chronic ruminative vomiting. *Journal of Abnormal Psychology,* 1969, *74,* 1–8.

Lazarus, A. A. The elimination of children's phobias by deconditioning. In H. J. Eysenck (Ed.), *Behaviour therapy and the neuroses.* New York: Pergamon, 1960.

Lazarus, A. A., & Abramovitz, A. The use of "emotive imagery" in the treatment of children's phobias. *Journal of Mental Science,* 1962, *108,* 191–195.

Lazarus, A. A., Davison, G. C., & Polefka, D. A. Classical and operant factors in the treatment of school phobia. *Journal of Abnormal and Social Psychology,* 1965, *70,* 225–229.

Linden, W. Practicing of meditation by school children and their levels of field dependence–independence, test anxiety, and reading achievement. *Journal of Consulting and Clinical Psychology,* 1973, *41,* 139–143.

Litow, L., & Pumroy, D. K. A brief review of classroom group-oriented contingencies. *Journal of Applied Behavior Analysis,* 1975, *8,* 341–347.

Lobitz, G. K., & Johnson, S. M. Normal versus deviant children: A multimethod comparison. *Journal of Abnormal Child Psychology,* 1975, *3,* 353–374.

Logan, D. L., & Garner, D. G. Effective behavior modification for reducing chronic soiling. *American Annals of the Deaf,* 1971, *116,* 382–384.

Lovaas, O. I. *The autistic child: Language development through behavior modification.* New York: Irvington Publishers. 1977.

Lovaas, O. I., & Simmons, J. Q. Manipulation of self-destruction in three retarded children. *Journal of Applied Behavior Analysis.* 1969, *2,* 143–157.

Lovaas, O. I., Freitag, G., Gold, V. J., & Kassorla, I. C. Experimental studies in childhood schizophrenia: Analysis of self-destructive behavior. *Journal of Experimental Child Psychology,* 1965, *2,* 67–84.

Lovaas, O. I., Schaeffer, B., & Simmons, J. W. Experimental studies in childhood schizophrenia: Building social behavior in autistic children by use of electric shock. *Journal of Experimental Research in Personality,* 1965, *1,* 99–109.

Lovaas, O. I., Berberich, J. P., Perloff, B. F., & Schaeffer, B. Acquisition of imitative speech by schizophrenic children. *Science,* 1966, *151,* 705–707.

Lovaas, I. O., Litrownik, A., & Mann, R. Response latencies to auditory stimuli in autistic children engaged in self-stimulatory behavior. *Behaviour Research and Therapy,* 1971, *9,* 39–49.

Lovaas, O. I., Loegel, R. L., & Schreibman, L. *Experimental studies in child schizophrenia* (Research Project MH-11440-07). Washington, D.C.: National Institute of Mental Health, 1973.

Lovaas, O. I., Koegel, R. L., Simmons, J. Q., & Long, J. S. Some generalization and follow-up measures on autistic children in behavior therapy. *Journal of Applied Behavior Analysis,* 1973, *6,* 131–65.

Lovaas, O. I., Young, D. B., & Newsom, C. D. Childhood psychosis: Behavioral treatment. In B. B. Wolman, J. Egan, & A. D. Ross (Eds.), *Handbook of treatment of mental disorders in childhood and adolescence.* Englewood Cliffs, N.J.: Prentice-Hall, 1978.

Lubar, J., & Shouse, M. Use of biofeedback in the treatment of seizure disorders and hyperactivity. In B. B.

Lahey & A. E. Kazdin (Eds.), *Advances in clinical child psychology* (Vol. 1). New York: Plenum Press, 1977.

MacFarlane, J. W., Allen, L., & Honzik, M. P. *A Development study of the behavior problems of normal children between 21 months and 14 years.* Berkely: University of California Press, 1954.

Mahoney, M. J., Kazdin, A. E., & Lesswing, W. J. Behavior modification: Delusion or deliverance? In C. M. Franks & G. T. Wilson (Eds.), *Annual review of behavior therapy: Theory and practice* (Vol. 2). New York: Brunner/Mazel, 1974.

Mann, J., & Rosenthal, T. L. Vicarious and direct counterconditioning of test anxiety through individual and group desensitization. *Behaviour Research and Therapy,* 1969, *7,* 359–367.

Marholin, D. *Child behavior therapy.* New York, Gardner Press, 1978.

Marholin, D., Luiselli, J. K., & Townsend, N. M. Overcorrection: An examination of its rationale and treatment effectiveness. In M. Hersen, R. M. Eisler, & P. M. Miller (Eds.), *Progress in behavior modification* (Vol. 9). New York: Academic Press, 1980.

Marholin, D., Steinman, W. M., McInnis, E. T., & Heads, T. B. The effect of a teacher's presence on the classroom behavior of conduct problem children. *Journal of Abnormal Child Psychology,* 1975, *3,* 11–25.

Matson, J. L., Esveldt-Dawson, K., Andrasik, F., Ollendick, T. H., Petti, T., & Hersen, M. Direct, observational, and generalization effects of social skills training with emotionally disturbed children. *Behavior Therapy,* 1980, *11,* 522–531.

May, J. G., McAllister, J., Risley, T., Twardosz, S., Cox, C. H. *Florida guidelines for the use of behavioral procedures in state programs for the retarded.* Joint Task Force assembled by the Florida Division of Retardation and the Department of Psychology of the Florida State University, 1974.

McKenzie, H., Clarke, M., Wolf, M., Kothera, R., & Benson, C. Behavior modification of children with learning disabilities using grades as tokens and allowances as back-up reinforcers. *Excptional Children,* 1968, *34,* 745–752.

McMahon, R. J., & Forehand, R. Nonprescription behavior therapy: Effectiveness of a brochure in teaching mothers to correct their children's inappropriate mealtime behaviors. *Behavior Therapy,* 1978, *9,* 814–820.

McMahon, R. J., & Forehand, R. Self-help behavior therapies in parent training. In B. B. Lahey & A. E. Kazdin (Eds.), *Advances in clinical child psychology* (Vol. 3). New York: Plenum Press, 1980.

Meichenbaum, D., & Goodman, J. Training impulsive children to talk to themselves: Means of developing self-contol. *Journal of Abnormal Psychology,* 1971, *77,* 115–126.

Melamed, B. G., & Johnson, S. B. Chronic illness: Asthma and juvenile diabetes. In E. J. Mash & L. Terdal (Eds.), *Behavioral assessment of childhood disorders.* New York: Guilford, 1981.

Melamed, B. G., & Siegel, L. J. Reduction of anxiety in children facing hospitalization and surgery by use of film modeling. *Journal of Consulting and Clinical Psychology,* 1975, *43,* 511–521.

Melamed, B. G., Hawes, R., Heiby, E., & Glick, J. The use of film modeling to reduce uncooperative behavior of children during dental treatment. *Journal of Dental Research,* 1975, *54,* 797–801.

Melamed, B. G., Yurcheson, R., Fleece, E., Hutcherson, S. & Hawes, R. Effects of film modeling on the reduction of anxiety-related behaviors in individuals varying in level of previous experience in the stress situation. *Journal of Consulting and Clinical Psychology,* 1978, *46,* 1357–1367.

Merbaum, M. The modification of self-destructive behavior by a mother–therapist using aversive stimulation. *Behavior Therapy,* 1973, *4,* 442–447.

Metz, J. R. Conditioning generalized imitation in autistic children. *Journal of Experimental Child Psychology,* 1965, *2,* 389–399.

Miklich, D. R., Renne, C. M., Creer, T. L., Alexander, A. B., Chai, H., Davis, M. H., Hoffman, A., & Danker-Brown, P. The clinical utility of behavior therapy as an adjunctive treatment for asthma. *Journal of Allergy and Clinical Immunology,* 1977, *5,* 285–294.

Miller, L. C., Barrett, C. L., & Hampe, E. Phobias of childhood in a prescientific era. In A. Davids (Eds.), *Child personality and psychopathology: Current topics.* New York: Wiley, 1974.

Miller, L. C., Barrett, C. L., Hampe, E., & Noble, H. Comparison of reciprocal inhibition, psychotherapy, and waiting list control for phobic children. *Journal of Abnormal Psychology,* 1972, *79,* 269–279.

Minkin, N., Braukmann, C. J., Minkin, B. L., Timbers, G. D., Timbers, F. J., Fixen, D. L., Phillips, E. L., & Wolf, M. M. The social validation and training of conversation skills. *Jouranl of Applied Behavior Analysis,* 1976, *9,* 127–140.

Montenegro, H. Severe separation anxiety in two preschool children: Successfully treated by reciprocal inhibition. *Journal of Child Psychology and Psychiatry,* 1968, *9,* 93–103.

Moore, N. Behavior therapy in bronchial asthma: A controlled study. *Journal of Psychosomatic Research,* 1965, *9,* 257–276.

Mowrer, O. H., & Mowrer, W. M. Enuresis: A method for its study and treatment. *American Journal of Orthopsychiatry,* 1938, *8,* 436–459.

Neisworth, J. T., & Moore, F. Operant treatment of asthmatic responding with the parent as therapist. *Behavior Therapy,* 1972, *3,* 95–101.

Nordquist, V. M., & Wahler, R. G. Naturalistic treatment of an autistic child. *Journal of Applied Behavior Analysis,* 1973, *6,* 79–87.

Novy, P., Burnett, J., Powers, M., & Sulzer-Azaroff, B. Modifying attending to-work behavior of a learning disabled child. *Journal of Learning Disabilities,* 1973, *6,* 217–221.

Obler, M., & Terwilliger, R. F. Pilot study on the effectiveness of systematic desensitization with neurologically impaired children with phobic disorders. *Journal of Consulting and Clinical Psychology,* 1970, *34,* 314–318.

O'Connor, R. D. Modification of social withdrawal through symbolic modeling. *Journal of Applied Behavior Analysis,* 1979, *2,* 15–22.

O'Connor, R. D. Relative efficacy of modeling, shaping and the combined procedures for modification of social withdrawal. *Journal of Abnormal Psychology,* 1972, *79,* 327–334.

Oden, S., & Asher, S. R. Coaching children in social skills for friendship making. *Child Development,* 1977, *48,* 495–506.

O'Leary, K. D., & Drabman, R. Token reinforcement in the classroom: A review. *Psychological Bulletin,* 1971, *75,* 379–398.

O'Leary, K. D., & O'Leary, S. G. *Classroom management: The successful use of behavior modification.* New York: Pergamon, 1977.

O'Leary, S. G., & O'Leary, K. D. Behavior modification in the school. In H. Leitenberg (Ed.), *Handbook of behavior modification and therapy.* Englewood Cliffs, N.J.: Prentice-Hall, 1976.

O'Leary, S. G., & Pelham, W. E. Behavior therapy and withdrawal of stimulant medication in hyperactive children. *Pediatrics,* 1977, *61,* 211–217.

O'Leary, K. D., & Wilson, G. T. *Behavior therapy: Application and outcome.* Englewood Cliffs, N.J.: Prentice-Hall, 1975.

O'Leary, K. D., Drabman, R., & Kass, R. E. Maintenance of appropriate behavior in a token program. *Journal of Abnormal Child Psychology,* 1973, *1,* 127–138.

O'Leary, K. D., Pelham, W. E., Rosenbaum, A., & Price, G. H. Behavioral treatment of hyperkinetic children. *Clinical Pediatrics,* 1976, *15,* 510–515.

Ollendick, T. H. Fear reduction techniques with children. In M. Hersen, R. M. Eisler, & P. M. Miller (Eds.), *Progress in behavior modification* (Vol. 8). New York: Academic Press, 1979.

Ollendick, T. H., & Hersen, M. Social skills training for juvenile delinquents. *Behaviour Research and Therapy,* 1979, *17,* 547–554.

Ollendick, T. H., & Matson, J. L. Overcorrection: An overview. *Behavior Therapy,* 1978, *9,* 830–842.

Paschalis, A., Kimmel, H. D., & Kimmel, E. Further study of diurnal instrumental conditioning in the treatment of enuresis nocturna. *Journal of Behavior Therapy and Experimental Psychiatry,* 1972, *3,* 253–256.

Patterson, G. R. *Families: Applications of social learning to family life.* Champaign, Ill.: Research Press, 1971.

Patterson, G. R. The aggressive child: Victim and architect or a coercive system. In E. J. Mash, L. A. Hamerlynck, & L. C. Handy (Eds.). *Behavior modification and families.* New York: Brunner/Mazel, 1976.

Patterson, G. R., & Fleishman, M. J. Maintenance of treatment effects: Some considerations concerning family systems and follow-up data. *Behavior Therapy,* 1979, *1,* 168–185.

Patterson, G. R., & Gullion, M. E. *Living with children.* Champaign, Ill.: Research Press, 1968.

Patterson, G. R., & Reid, J. B. Reciprocity and coercion: Two facets of social systems. In C. Neuringer & J. Michaels (Eds.), *Behavior modification in clinical psychology.* New York: Appleton-Century-Crofts, 1970.

Patterson, G. R., & Reid, J. B. Intervention for families of aggressive boys: A replication study. *Behaviour Research and Therapy,* 1973, *11,* 383–394.

Peed, S., Roberts, M., & Forehand, R. Evaluation of the effectiveness of a standardized parent training program in altering the interaction of mothers and their noncompliant children. *Behavior Modification,* 1977, *1,* 323–350.

Pelham, W. E. Withdrawal of a stimulant drug and concurrent behavioral intervention in the treatment of a hyperactive child. *Behavior Therapy,* 1977, *8,* 473–479.

Phillips, E. L., Phillips, E. A., Fixsen, D. L., & Wolf, M. W. Behavior shaping works for delinquents. *Psychology Today,* June 1973, 75–79.

Plachetta, K. E. Encopresis: A case study utilizing contracting, scheduling, and self-charting. *Journal of Behavior Therapy and Experimental Psychiatry,* 1976, *7,* 195–196.

Porterfield, J. K., Herbert-Jackson, E., & Risley, T. Contingent observation: An effective and acceptable procedure for reducing disruptive behavior of young children in a group setting. *Journal of Applied Behavior Analysis,* 1976, *9,* 55–64.

Reese, H. W., & Parnes, S. J. Programming creative behavior. *Child Development,* 1970, *41,* 413–423.

Rincover, A., & Koegel, R. L. Classroom treatment of autistic children: II. Individualized instruction in a group. *Journal of Abnormal Child Psychology,* 1977, *5,* 113–126.

Ritter, B. The group desensitization of childrens' snake phobias using vicarious and contact desensitization procedures. *Behaviour Research and Therapy,* 1968, *6,* 1–6.

Robin, A. L., Kent, R., O'Leary, K. D., Foster, S., & Prinz, R. An approach to teaching parents and adolescents problem-solving communication skills: A preliminary report. *Behavior Therapy,* 1977, *8,* 639–643.

Robin, A. L., Schneider, M., & Dolnick, M. The turtle technique: An extended case study of self-control in the classroom. *Psychology in the Schools,* 1976, *73,* 449–453.

Roff, M. Childhood social interactions and young adult bad conduct. *Journal of Abnormal and Social Psychology,* 1961, *63,* 333–337.

Roff, M., Sells, B., & Golden, M. M. *Social adjustment and personality development in children.* Minneapolis: University of Minnesota Press, 1972.

Rosen, G. M. The development and use of nonprescriptive behavior therapies. *American Psychologist,* 1976, *31,* 139–141.

Rosenbaum, A., O'Leary, K. D., & Jacob, R. Behavioral intervention with hyperactive children: Group consequences as a supplement to individual contingencies. *Behavior Therapy,* 1975, *6,* 315–324.

Ross, A. O. *Psychological aspects of learning disabilities and reading disorders.* New York: Wiley, 1976.

Ross, A. O. *Child behavior therapy.* New York: Wiley, 1981.

Sajwaj, T., Libet, J., & Agras, S. Lemon-juice therapy: The control of life threatening rumination in a six-month-old infant. *Journal of Applied Behavior Analysis,* 1974, *7,* 557–563.

Santogrossi, D. A., O'Leary, K. D., Romanczyk, R. G., & Kaufman, K. F. Self-evaluation by adolescents in a psychiatric hospital school token program. *Journal of Applied Behavior Analysis,* 1973, *6,* 277–287.

Shumaker, J. B., Howell, M. F., & Sherman, J. A. An analysis of daily report cards and parent-managed privileges in the improvement of adolescents' classroom performance. *Journal of Applied Analysis,* 1977, *10,* 449–464.

Sibley, S., Abbott, M., & Cooper, B. Modification of the classroom behavior of a "disadvantaged" kindergarten boy by social reinforcement and isolation. *Journal of Experimental Child Psychology,* 1969, *4,* 281–287.

Siegel, L. J., & Richards, C. S. Behavioral intervention with somatic disorders in children. In D. Marholin (Ed.), *Child behavior therapy.* New York: Gardner Press, 1978.

Solomon, R. W., & Wahler, R. G. Peer reinforcement control of classroom problem behavior. *Journal of Applied Behavior Analysis,* 1973, *6,* 49–56.

Starfield, B. Enuresis: Its pathogenesis and treatment. *Clinical Pediatrics,* 1972, *11,* 343–349.

Starfield, B., & Mellitis, E. D. Increase in functional bladder capacity and improvements in enuresis. *Journal of Pediatrics,* 1968, *72,* 483–487.

Sterman, M. B. Neurophysiological clinical studies of sensorimotor EEG biofeedback training: Some effects on epilepsy. *Seminars in Psychiatry,* 1973, *5,* 507–525.

Sterman, M. B., MacDonald, L. R., & Stone, R. K. Biofeedback training of the sensorimotor electroencephalogram rhythm in man: Effects on epilepsy. *Epilepsia,* 1974, *15,* 395–416.

Stuart, R. B. Behavioral contracting within the families of delinquents. *Journal of Behavior Therapy and Experimental Psychiatry,* 1971, *2,* 1–11.

Stuart, R. B., & Tripodi, T. Experimental evaluation of three-time constrained behavioral treatments for pre-delinquents and delinquents. In R. D. Rubin, J. P. Brady, & J. D. Henderson (Eds.), *Advances in behavior therapy.* New York: Academic Press, 1973.

Stuart, R. B., Tripodi, T., Jayaratne, S., & Camburn, D. An experiment in social engineering in serving the families of pre-delinquents. *Journal of Abnormal Child Psychology,* 1976, *4,* 243–261.

Sulzer-Axaroff, B., & Mayer, G. R. *Applying behavior analysis procedures with children and youth.* New York: Holt, Rinehart, & Winston, 1977.

Surrat, P. R., Ulrich, R. E., & Hawkins, R. P. An elementary student as a behavioral engineer. *Journal of Applied Behavior Analysis,* 1969, *2,* 85–92.

Tal, A., & Miklich, D. R. Emotionally induced decreases in pulmonary flow rates in asthmatic children. *Psychomatic Medicine,* 1976, *38,* 190–200.

Tate, B. G. Case study: Control of chronic self-injurious behavior by conditioning procedures. *Behavior Therapy,* 1972, *3,* 72–83.

Taylor, P. D., & Turner, R. K. A clinical trial of continuous, intermittent, and over learning "bell-and-pad" treatments for nocturnal enuresis. *Behaviour Research and Therapy,* 1975, *13,* 281–293.

Tharp, R. G., & Wetzel, R. J. *Behavior modification in the natural environment.* New York: Academic Press, 1969.

Turkewitz, H., O'Leary, K. D., & Ironsmith, M. Producing generalization of appropriate behavior through self-control. *Journal of Consulting and Clinical Psychology,* 1975, *43,* 577–583.

Ullmann, C. A. Teachers, peers, and tests as predictors of adjustment. *Journal of Educational Psychology,* 1957, *48,* 257–267.

Van Hasselt, V. B., Hersen, M., Bellack, A. S., Rosenblum, N., & Lamparski, D. Tripartite assessment of the effects of systematic desensitization in a multi-phobic child: An experimental analysis. *Journal of Behavior Therapy and Experimental Psychiatry,* 1979, *10,* 51–56.

Wadsworth, H. G. A motivational approach toward the remediation of learning disabled boys. *Exceptional Children,* 1971, *38,* 32.

Wagner, R. F., & Guyer, B. P. Maintenance of discipline through increasing children's span of attending by means of a token economy. *Psychology in the Schools,* 1971, *8,* 285–289.

Wahler, R. G. Deviant child behavior within the family: Developmental speculations and behavior change strategies. In H. Leitenberg (Ed.), *Handbook of behavior modification and behavior therapy.* Englewood Cliffs, N.J.: Prentice-Hall, 1976.

Ward, M. H., & Baker, B. L. Reinforcement therapy in the classroom. *Journal of Applied Behavior Analysis,* 1968, *1,* 323-328.

Wells, K. C., Griest, D. L., & Forehand, R. The use of a self-control package to enhance temporal generality of a parent training program. *Behaviour Research and Therapy,* 1980, *18,* 347–354.

Wheeler, M. E., & Hess, K. W. Treatment of juvenile obesity by successive approximation control of eating. *Journal of Behavior Therapy and Experimental Psychiatry,* 1976, *7,* 235–241.

Whitehill, M. B., Hersen, M., & Bellack, A. S. Conversation skills training for socially isolated children. *Behaviour Research Therapy,* 1980, *18,* 217–225.

Williams, C. D. Case report: The elimination of tantrum behavior by extinction procedures. *Journal of Abnormal and Social Psychology,* 1959, *59,* 269.

Willner, A. G., Braukmann, C. J., Kirigan, K. A., & Wolf, M. M. Achievement Place: A community treatment model for youths in trouble. In D. Marholin (Ed.), *Child behavior therapy.* New York: Gardner Press, 1978.

Wilson, M. D., & McReynolds, L. U. A procedure for increasing oral reading rate in hard of hearing children. *Journal of Applied Behavior Analysis.* 1973, *6,* 231–239.

Winett, R. A., & Winkler, R. C. Current behavior modification in the classroom: Be still, be quiet, be docile. *Journal of Applied Behavior Analysis,* 1972, *5,* 499–504.

Winett, R. A., Richards, C. S., & Krasner, L. Child-monitored token reading program. *Psychology in the Schools,* 1971, *8,* 259–262.

Wolf, M. M., Risley, T., Johnston, M., Harris, F., & Allen, E. Application of operant conditioning procedures to the behavior problems of an autistic child: A follow-up and extension. *Behaviour Research Therapy,* 1967, *5,* 103–112.

Wolf, M. M., Risley, T., & Mees, H. Application of operant conditioning procedures to the behavior problems of an autistic child. *Behaviour Research and Therapy,* 1964, *1,* 305–312.

Wright, L. Aversive conditioning of self-induced seizures. *Behavior Therapy,* 1973, *4,* 712–713. (a)

Wright, L. Handling the encopretic child. *Professional Psychology,* 1973, *4,* 137–144. (b)

Wright, L., & Walker, C. E. Behavioral treatment of encopresis. *Journal of Pediatric Psychology,* 1976, *4,* 35–37.

Wright, L., & Walker, C. E. A simple behavioral treatment program for psychogenic encopresis. *Behaviour Research and Therapy,* 1978, *16,* 209-212.

Zlutnick, S., Mayville, W. J., & Moffat, S. Modification of seizure disorders: The interruption of behavioral chains. *Journal of Applied Behavior Analysis,* 1975, *8,* 1–12.

17

Psychopharmacological Treatment

MAGDA CAMPBELL, IRA L. COHEN, AND RICHARD PERRY

Introduction

Pharmacotherapy, at the present state of our knowledge, is viewed only as an adjunct to psychosocial and other treatments in certain disturbed children. It has been said that, even in adults, the only lasting effect of a drug is indirect; a result of the changed interaction between the patient and his/her environment due to concurrent psychosocial treatment(s) (Irwin, 1968). The nondrug treatments in children include individual psychotherapy, behavior modification, remedial work, and parental counseling. It is expected that a therapeutically effective drug will make the disturbed child more amenable to these treatments, or enhance (interact with) them.

The actual therapeutic efficacy of psychoactive drugs in various disorders of childhood is difficult to assess and measure for at least two reasons.

First, with the exception of research in attention deficit disorder with hyperactivity, most studies suffer from such methodological flaws as diagnostic and age heterogeneity of patients, small samples, lack of control, poor assessment procedures, lack of adequate description of subjects (regarding IQ, demographic data, diagnostic workup), inadequate monitoring (behavioral and laboratory), and inadequacy of study design, data analysis, and interpretation of results.

Second, our expectations of treatment in children differ from those in adults. In adult psychiatric patients, the goal of treatment is to diminish or abolish symptoms, or to normalize functions. In a developing organism such as the child, one also wishes to promote growth and development, which may be stunted or delayed by the psychiatric disorder. At our present state of knowledge, no treatment method can easily fulfill these expectations.

MAGDA CAMPBELL, IRA L. COHEN, AND RICHARD PERRY • Children's Psychopharmacology Unit, New York University Medical Center, New York, New York 10016. This work was supported in part by Public Health Service Grants MH-04665 and MH-32212 from the National Institute of Mental Health.

Keeping this in mind, we will present an overview of psychopharmacology in children, highlighting recent advances. For more exhaustive reviews, articles, chapters, or books will be suggested throughout the text.

Indications for Pharmacotherapy

Using the *Diagnostic and Statistical Manual,* (DSM-III, 1980)[1] of the American Psychiatric Association, the following are the diagnostic categories in which administration of psychoactive drugs has been found beneficial based on well documented research or on a clinical, empirical basis.

1. *Attention Deficit Disorder with Hyperactivity.* The superiority of psychomotor stimulants over placebo in children 6 to 12 years of age has been demonstrated in numerous well designed and controlled studies (for a review, see Conners & Werry, 1979). The behavioral response of younger children to the same drugs is not of the same magnitude and is more variable (Conners, 1975).

2. *Undersocialized Conduct Disorder, Aggressive Type.* This disorder frequently requires administration of a psychoactive agent, particularly when the child has failed to respond to psychosocial types of treatments and to environmental manipulations. Research is limited in this area of psychopharmacology; however, the few available studies and clinical experience indicate that stimulants are usually ineffective, and a neuroleptic may be indicated (for a review, see Campbell, Cohen, & Small, 1982).

3. *Schizophrenic and Schizophreniform Disorders.* These conditions are rare in prepubertal children; little research has been done in this area. It seems that neuroleptics, particularly the less sedative types, can be helpful as part of the total treatment.

4. *Pervasive Developmental Disorders: Infantile Autism, Childhood Onset Pervasive Developmental Disorder, and Atypical Pervasive Developmental Disorder.* The use of psychoactive drugs in autistic children is particularly controversial. There are those who state that these children fail to respond clinically to neuroleptics and that this is a feature that distinguishes autism from schizophrenia (Hanson & Gottesman, 1976; Ritvo, 1976). These statements are not based on systematic investigations, There is evidence based on well-controlled studies that a less sedative type of neuroleptic, such as haloperidol, is significantly superior to placebo in reducing the cardinal symptoms of infantile autism: withdrawal and stereotypies (Campbell, Anderson, Meier, Cohen, Small, Samit, & Sachar, 1978a; Campbell, Anderson, Cohen, Perry, Small, Green, Anderson, & McCandless, 1982: Cohen, Campbell, Posner, Small, Triebel, & Anderson, 1980). Some authors (Klein, Gittelman, Quitkin, & Rifkin, 1980a) state that the reduction of withdrawal and stereotypies has no clinical significance. This view reflects a failure to recognize the severity of infantile autism and its outcome.

5. *Affective Disorders.* Only recently has it been shown that prepubertal children can be reliably diagnosed as having major depressive disorder and fulfill the diagnostic criteria for depression seen in adults (Cytryn, McKnew, & Bunney, 1980; Puig-Antich, Blau, Marx, Greenhill, & Chambers, 1978). Such children have shown clinical improvement in response to imipramine or desipramine (Puig-Antich *et al.,* 1978; Puig-Antich, Perel,

[1]For a comprehensive comparison of DSM-III to the *International Classification of Diseases,* Ninth Revision (ICD-9, 1977), the reader is referred to a chapter by Gittelman-Klein, Spitzer, and Cantwell (1978).

Lupatkin, Chambers, Tabrizi, & Stiller, 1979; Weinberg, Rutman, Sullivan, Penick, & Dietz, 1973). Manic-depressive disorder is extremely rare in prepubertal children and no information is available.

6. *Stereotyped Movement Disorders.* Haloperidol has been found clinically helpful in chronic tic disorder in Tourette's disorder (Cohen, Shaywitz, Young, Carbonari, Nathanson, Lieberman, Bowers, & Maas, 1979a; Shapiro, Shapiro, & Wayne, 1973; Woodrow, 1974). More recently clonidine has been explored (Cohen, Young, Nathanson, & Shaywitz, 1979b).

7. *Other Disorders with Physical Manifestations.* The superiority of imipramine over placebo has been demonstrated in many double-blind trials conducted in children with the symptom of enuresis (Rapoport, Mikkelsen, Zavadil, Nee, Gruenau, Mendelson, & Gillin, 1980b; Shaffer, 1977); tolerance to this drug may develop (Rapoport *et al,* 1980b). However, because enuresis is frequently secondary and found in a variety of psychiatric disorders, it is desirable that the problem underlying this nonspecific symptom be investigated and treated accordingly (for a review, see Campbell, 1979; Mikkelsen, Rapoport, Nee, Gruenau, Mendelson, & Gillin, 1980; Rapoport *et al.,* 1980b). Conditioning procedures have been useful and have had longer lasting results than drugs (Dische, 1971; Forsythe & Redmond, 1970; Shaffer, 1977).

There is a paucity of literature on the use of drugs in sleep-walking disorder and sleep-terror disorder. It appears that the use of antianxiety drugs or imipramine may be helpful in some cases (Fisher, Kahn, Edwards, & Davis, 1973; Glick, Schulman, & Turecki, 1971; Pessikoff & Davis, 1971), though psychodynamically oriented treatments have also been explored in young children (Herzog, 1978).

Enuresis, somnambulism, nightmares, and *pavor nocturnus* were viewed as "disorders of arousal" in which the clinical phenomenon occurred during arousal from deep (slow-wave) sleep (Broughton, 1968). Mikkelson *et al.* (1980) did not confirm this in relation to enuresis.

8. *Mental Retardation Associated with Behavioral Disorders.* A trial of drug treatment may be indicated when behavior modification fails to result in decrease of symptoms of aggressiveness (directed against self or others), hyperactivity, impulsivity, or explosiveness. Learning itself may not be enhanced by drug treatment; actually, certain drugs or high doses may affect learning adversely (Lipman, DiMascio, Reatig, & Kirson, 1978; Sprague & Baxley, 1978). However, clinical experience indicates the retarded individual may become more amenable to special education or behavior modification, with the help of a stimulant, neuroleptic, or lithium carbonate (Campbell, Cohen, & Small, 1982; Campbell, Schulman, & Rapoport, 1978b; Ziring & Teitelbaum, 1980).

Classes of Drugs[2]

Neuroleptics

Neuroleptics or major tranquilizers are used less specifically in children than in adults, where they are prescribed almost exclusively for the treatment of schizophrenia and other psychoses; schizophrenia in prepubertal children is rare.

[2]The oral dosage range of some representative drugs is shown in Table 1.

There is a large literature on the use of the major tranquilizers in children. However, most of the reports are based on uncontrolled trials and often are contradictory. For extensive review, chapters by Winsberg and Yepes (1978), Campbell (1979), and Klein, Gittelman, Quitkin, and Rifkin (1980a,b) are suggested.

The following are conclusions from the literature and from clinical experience.

Neuroleptics reduce hyperactivity, stereotypies, tics, and, to some degree, aggressiveness in children of normal and subnormal intelligence. In hyperactive children with attention deficit disorder, the drugs of choice remain the stimulants. There is a moderate effect of these drugs in prepubertal children with schizophrenia (less than in adults), though systematic investigations are required.

There are five major classes of neuroleptic drugs or major tranquilizers: (1) phenothiazines; (2) thioxanthenes; (3) butyrophenones; (4) dihydroindolones; and (5) dibenzoxazepines.

1. *Phenothiazines.* This group consists of three subclasses: the aliphatics, the piperidines, and the piperazines. The aliphatics and piperidines have more marked sedative-hypnotic actions, while the piperazines have more activating and motor-stimulating properties. Other differences are in potency and untoward effects.

Of the phenothiazines, chlorpromazine and thioridazine are most frequently used for children.

Table 1. Representative Psychoactive Medications and Dosages in Children under 12 Years of Age[a]

Class	Oral dosage range (mg/day)
I. Neuroleptics (major tranquilizers)	
A. Phenothiazines	
1. Aliphatics	
chlorpromazine	10–200
2. Piperidines	
thioridazine	10–200
3. Piperazines	
fluphenazine	.25–16
trifluoperazine	1–20
B. Thioxanthenes	
thiothixene	1–40
C. Butyrophenones	
haloperidol	.5–16
D. Dihydroindolones	
molindone	1–150[b]
II. Antidepressants	
imipramine	25–225[c]
III. Stimulants	
dextroamphetamine	10–25
methylphenidate	30–60 (.3–.5 mg/kg)
magnesium pemoline	25–125 (1.9–2.7 mg/kg)
IV. Lithium Carbonate	450–1,500 and/or .6–1.2 mEq/1

[a]The latest issue of the PDR should be consulted, in general, for range of dosage. The dosage for adolescents is comparable to that in adults.
[b]Greenhill *et al.* (1980).
[c]In enuresis: for children under 12 years of age, 25–50 mg 1 hour before bedtime; for those over 12 years of age, 75 mg. For other indications (e.g., depression) daily dosage of imipramine should not exceed 5 mg/kg/day (Hayes *et al.*, 1975).

Chlorpromazine has been shown to reduce hyperactivity in school-age children of normal intellectual functioning in a placebo-controlled and double-blind study (Werry, Weiss, Douglas, & Martin, 1966). Aggressiveness, excitability, and distractibility were also reduced, but to a lesser degree. In a controlled crossover trial of 19 boys with hyperactivity and aggressiveness of long duration, dextroamphetamine (10 mg/day) was superior to chlorpromazine (75 mg/day), though both drugs yielded a significant decrease in severity of symptoms on parent and teacher ratings (Rapoport, Abramson, Alexander, & Lott, 1971). While dextroamphetamine produced changes in physical activity (grid crossings and combined pedometer measures), chlorpromazine failed to do so. As in the previous study, these children were out-patients and of normal intelligence; their ages ranged from 4.5 to 10.5 years (mean 8.2 years).

In a large sample of school-age hyperkinetic children ($N = 155$), thioridazine was found less effective than methylphenidate alone or in combination with it (Gittelman-Klein, Klein, Katz, Saraf, & Pollack, 1976b). However, all three drug treatments were significantly superior to placebo in controlling hyperactivity as rated by parents, teachers, and clinic staff. At the end of the 12-week treatment period, the mean daily dosage of thioridazine was 160 mg (4.54 mg/kg) and for methylphenidate 47 mg (1.66 mg/kg). In another well controlled study, thioridazine has been found to be superior to placebo and amphetamine in decreasing various symptoms, including aggressiveness in retarded children (Alexandris & Lundell, 1968).

In a small sample of aggressive and explosive school-age children, chlorpromazine was as effective as haloperidol or lithium in reducing symptoms of aggressiveness and explosiveness in doses of 100 to 200 mg/day, mean 150 mg/day (Campbell *et al.*, 1982).

Fish (1970) and others (Rapoport *et al.*, 1971) found that prepubertal psychotic and other severely disturbed children were often sedated by doses of chlorpromazine, which yielded decreases of target symptoms. Such sedation appeared to interfere, clincially, with the child's learning and functioning. Fish found this to be true particularly in the case of young, anergic, and retarded autistic children; it was for this reason that she began investigation of other types of neuroleptics. Administration of trifluoperazine, a less sedative type of phenothiazine, in a double-blind and controlled fashion, yielded increases in verbal production and alertness and decreases in withdrawal and anergy (Fish, Shapiro, & Campbell, 1966). However, therapeutic changes were seen only in those without speech. Interestingly, the more impaired children required higher doses of drug than the higher functioning children. This study involved a diagnostically homogenous sample of pre-school-age autistic children.

2. *Thioxanthenes.* Reports on chlorprothixene are anecdotal. Thiothixene was explored in both autistic and schizophrenic children. Because of the limitations of these studies (for a review, see Campbell, 1979), no definite conclusions can be made, though there is some evidence that thiothixene has a wide therapeutic margin. Also, it is a safe drug when administered on a short-term basis. It may be useful in children in that sedation does not occur at therapeutic doses.

3. *Butyrophenones.* Haloperidol was found to be effecitve in both high (0.05 mg/kg/day) and low (0.025 mg/kg/day) doses in reducing behavioral symptoms in hyperactive and aggressive outpatient boys of normal intelligence (Werry & Aman, 1975; Werry, Aman, & Lampen, 1976). In this double-blind crossover trial, both doses of haloperidol were as effecitve as methylphenidate (0.3 mg/kg/day); both drugs were superior to placebo. In a double-blind comparison with fluphenazine, haloperidol (mean dose 10.4 mg/day) was helpful in improving coordination, self-care, affect, and exploratory behavior in outpatient autistic children (Engelhardt, Polizos, Waizer, & Hoffman, 1973). There was no

placebo control. In a placebo-controlled, double-blind trial, haloperidol (in doses of 0.5 to 4.0 mg/day, mean 1.65 mg/day) was compared to behavior therapy and the combination of both treatments in 40 pre-school-age autistic children (Campbell, Anderson, Meier, Cohen, Small, Samit, & Sachar, 1978a). The drug alone was significantly superior to other treatments in reducing stereotypies and withdrawal, but only in those children who were 4.5 years of age and older. The combination of drug and behavior therapy (with emphasis on language acquisition) was superior to other treatments in facilitating imitative speech. These same effects of haloperidol on stereotypy and withdrawal were replicated by Cohen *et al.* (1980) using a within-subjects reversal design.

In low doses, haloperidol was helpful in reducing tics (Connell, Corbett, Horne, & Mathews, 1967) and the symptoms of Gilles de la Tourette's syndrome (Cohen, Shaywitz, Young, Carbonari, Nathanson, Lieberman, Bowers, & Maas, 1979a; Feinberg & Carroll, 1979; Shapiro *et al.,* 1973; Woodrow, 1974).

4. *Dihydroindolones.* A pilot study of molindone, involving 10 young retarded autistic children, indicates that this drug warrants further investigation in this population because of its low levels of sedation at therapeutic levels (Campbell, Fish, Shapiro, & Floyd, 1971). Currently, this drug is being explored in hospitalized aggressive children with conduct disorder (Greenhill, Hirsch, Halpern, & Spalten, 1980).

5. *Dibenzoxazepines.* Loxapine succinate was found to be as beneficial as haloperidol in reducing psychotic symptoms in adolescents with acute schizophrenia or chronic schizophrenia with exacerbation (Pool, Bloom, Mielke, Roniger, & Gallant, 1976). Both drugs were superior to placebo in this double-blind trial, where patients were randomly assigned to one of the three treatment conditions.

Untoward Effects of Neuroleptics. For a detailed review, a chapter by Klein *et al.* (1980b) is recommended. Of the immediate untoward effects of the neuroleptics, behavioral toxicity (particularly excessive sedation) is most commonly seen in children. Acute extrapyramidal symptoms (EPS) include: the parkinsonian complex (with tremor, cogwheel rigidity, excessive salivation, masklike face); acute dystonic reactions (involving the face, tongue, and jaw, oculogyric crises, torticollis, opisthotonos, difficulty in speech and swallowing); and akathisia. For the relief of parkinsonian symptoms, decrease of dosage is suggested rather than administration of antiparkinsonian drugs. Acute dystonic reactions are seen as frequently in pre-school-age as in school-age children, while other EPS are rarely seen in the younger age group.

It is common sense that if a child is clinically sedated by a neuroleptic his learning will suffer. However, the effects of this class of drugs on cognition, as measured in the laboratory, and their clinical relevance are still controversial (for a review, see Conners & Werry, 1979; Klein *et al.,* 1980a; Lipman, DiMascio, Reatig, & Kirson, 1978; Platt, Campbell, Green, Perry, & Cohen, 1981). While some studies clearly indicate that there are some deleterious side effects on performance (Werry *et al.,* 1966), others show that these effects are dose dependent (Campbell *et al.,* 1978a; Werry & Aman, 1975) and/or minimal (Platt *et al.,* 1981). At times, compromises have to be made. While higher doses of haloperidol controlled all or most of the symptoms in Tourette's disease, they also yielded clinical sedation and worsening of daily (including school) performance or functioning. Administration of lower doses resulted in small therapeutic effects without the excessive sedation (Shapiro, Shapiro, Brunn, & Sweet, 1978).

In a sample of 24 adults who were mentally retarded, IQ scores showed no differences whether obtained under standard or reinforcement conditions during chronic maintenance of neuroleptic drugs (Breuning & Davidson, 1981). However, after discontinuation of medication, significant increases were shown in IQ scores; this increment was greater under the reinforcement condition than under the standard condition.

Neuroleptic-induced abnormal movements (tardive dyskinesia, withdrawal emergent symptoms) represent the long-term, untoward effects of this class of drugs on the central nervous system (for a review, see Berger & Rexroth, 1980; Gualtieri, Barnhill, McGimsey, & Schell, 1980; "Tardive Dyskinesia: Summary of a Task Force Report of the American Psychiatric Association," 1980; studies in children include Engelhardt & Polizos, 1978; McAndrew, Case, & Treffert, 1972; Paulson, Rizvi, & Crane, 1975). Tardive dyskinesia is a neurological syndrome manifested in abnormal movements involving mainly the face (buccolingual masticatory syndrome), though other parts of the body can also be involved (choreoathetoid movements of the trunk and extremities). Movements of the face and tongue include facial grimacing, tremor of lips or tongue, puckering, licking, and the "bon-bon" sign. These movements are involuntary and rhythmic; their severity ranges from mild to incapacitating. At the present time, no satisfactory treatment is available (Berger & Rexroth, 1980). The "rabbit" syndrome (Villeneuve, 1972), an extremely rapid perioral tremor, may represent a late form of parkinsonian syndrome.

It is not clear whether neuroleptic-induced abnormal movements in children represent a variety of tardive dyskinesia, as seen in adults, or whether they occur only upon reduction or discontinuation of neuroleptic administration (withdrawal emergent symptoms, or WES; Polizos, Engelhardt, Hoffman, & Waizer, 1973).

All reports are based on retrospective findings and suffer from serious methodological problems. A review of the literature indicates that prevalence rates of tardive dyskinesia range from 5% to 56%. This enormous discrepancy can be due to a variety of factors, including demographic, diagnostic, ecological, and assessment techniques (Gardos, Cole, & LaBrie, 1977). The APA Task Force ("Tardive Dyskinesia," 1980) emphasized that

> Although it is essential that one be vigilant for early identification of tardive dyskinesia, it is important not to overlook other disorders in which psychiatric symptoms and involuntary movements may coexist and have no relationship to tardive dyskinesia. Once tardive dyskinesia is identified, efforts to rate its severity in a reliable manner are essential. (p. 1164)

In our experience with autistic children, stereotypies (including facial movements), reduced or suppressed by an effective neuroleptic such as haloperidol, will reemerge or worsen after drug discontinuation. In the absence of reliable and stable baseline (predrug) ratings, this can be mistaken for WES (Campbell, Anderson, Cohen, Perry, Small, Green, Anderson, & McCandless, 1982).

In a well designed study involving a small but intensively studied sample of patients, it was possible to distinguish tardive dyskinesia from neuroleptic-withdrawal dyskinesia (Breuning, Ferguson, & Cullari, 1981). In addition to dyskinesias, the following transient withdrawal emergent symptoms were observed: vomiting, anorexia, and weight loss.

Antidepressants

There are two major classes of antidepressants: the monoamine oxidase inhibitors (MAOI) and the tricyclics. Although the MAO inhibitors have been used in Europe in depressed children, there is no solid evidence of their therapeutic efficacy and, moreover, of their safety in children (for a review, see Annell, 1972). Systematic investigations of tricyclics, specifically of imipramine, have been done only in enuresis (Poussaint & Ditman,

1965). For reviews, see Shaffer (1977), Mikkelsen *et al.* (1980), and Rapoport, Mikkelsen, Zavadil, Nee, Gruenau, Mendelson, and Gillin, (1980b). Imipramine also has been evaluated with regard to attention deficit disorder in hyperactivity (Huessy & Wright, 1970; Rapoport, Quinn, Bradbard, Riddle, & Brooks, 1974; Waizer, Hoffman, Polizos, & Engelhardt, 1974; Werry, Aman, & Diamond. 1980; Winsberg, Bialer, Kupietz, & Tobias, 1972). There is only one well controlled study in school phobia of prepubertal nonpsychotic children, most of whom had associated depression (Gittelman-Klein & Klein, 1971). In these disorders, the superiority of imipramine over placebo has been well documented. However, for hyperactive children, the psychomotor stimulants remain the drugs of choice in view of the potential toxicity of imipramine (for a review, see Petti & Campbell, 1975; Winsberg, Goldstein, Yepes, & Perel, 1975). As for enuresis, underlying causes should be sought, wherever feasible, and conditioning treatments (buzzer system) explored because relapse after drug withdrawal is frequent. Use of antidepressants in prepubertal children has been critically reviewed by Rapoport and Mikkelsen (1978).

Since the late 1960s, numerous reports have appeared in the literature in regard to the efficacy of antidepressants in children with depression (for a review, see Conners, 1976; Klein *et al.,* 1980a; Schulterbrandt & Raskin, 1977). However, until recently, only a few attempts were made to validate the concept of depression in children and to diagnose this disorder by using criteria developed for adults (Puig-Antich *et al.,* 1978; Schulterbrandt & Raskin, 1977).

Weinberg *et al.* (1973) made the first attempt to specify and operationally define criteria of depression in children. This study was based on outpatients. The 19 depressed children who were treated with amitriptyline or imipramine in this open trial improved, while the remaining 15, whose parents refused treatment, failed to improve.

In an ongoing research project, Puig-Antich and associates found imipramine to be effective in reducing symptoms of depression in prepubertal children (Puig-Antich, Perel, Lupatkin, Chambers, Tabrizi, & King, 1979). As in adults, such clinical improvement in affective behavior is significantly related to imipramine and desmethylimipramine levels in plasma. Prior to this investigation, which was controlled and double blind, it was demonstrated that prepubertal children can be identified as having major depressive disorder using the unmodified Research Diagnostic Criteria of Spitzer, Endicott, and Robins (1975). In a pilot study, 6 of 8 such children responded to imipramine in doses of 2.0 to 4.5 mg/kg/day (Puig-Antich *et al.,* 1978).

Untoward Effects. Behavioral toxicity, anorexia, insomnia, dry mouth, and cardiovascular toxicity (Klein *et al.,* 1980a; Saraf, Klein, Gittelman-Klein, Gootman, & Greenhill, 1978; Winsberg, Goldstein, Yepes, & Perel, 1975) and possible epileptogenic properties (Petti & Campbell, 1975) were reported in children.

Psychomotor Stimulants

The amphetamines, methylphenidate, magnesium pemoline, deanol, and caffeine comprise this class of psychoactive drugs. Bradley's excellent open trials with amphetamine, reporting a "paradoxical" calming effect (Bradley, 1937; Bradley & Bowen, 1941), represent a wealth of information to this date (including the effect on affect). Since that time, efficacy of dextroamphetamine and methylphenidate over placebo in the treatment of hyperactive children has been documented in numerous well designed and well controlled studies, many using multiple assessment methods in the classroom, at home, in outpatient clinics, and in the laboratory situation (Conners & Taylor, 1980; Conners, Eisenberg, & Barcai, 1967; Conners, Rothschild, Eisenberg, Schwartz, & Robinson, 1969; Conners, Taylor, Meo, Kurtz, & Fournier, 1972; Gittelman-Klein & Klein, 1976; Rapoport, Quinn, Bradbard, Riddle, & Brooks, 1974; Satterfield, Cantwell, Lesser, & Podosin, 1972; Sprague, Barnes, & Werry, 1970). The decrease of behavioral target symptoms of hyperactivity and of distractibility, as rated by parents, teachers, and clinicians was usually accompanied by significant improvement in laboratory measures, which include performance change measures and motor activity (for a review, see Conners & Werry, 1979; Douglas, 1974; Klein *et al.,* 1980a). Although in most studies, behavioral and cognitive improvements are observed at the same dose, Sprague and Sleator (1975, 1977) found that optimal doses of methylphenidate for cognitive improvement (0.3 mg/kg/day) are lower than doses required to control maladaptive behaviors. It should also be noted that the positive effects of stimulants on laboratory tests measuring cognition and attention were not associated with improved academic achievement (Conners & Taylor, 1980; Conners & Werry, 1979; Gittelman-Klein & Klein, 1976).

More recently, magnesium pemoline was explored in hyperactive children. In a large, collaborative study (Page, Bernstein, Janicki, & Michelli, 1974a; Page, Janicki, Bernstein, Curran, & Michelli, 1974b) involving 413 hyperactive children, magnesium pemoline was found to be superior to placebo given in a single morning dose under double-blind conditions. Four individual studies confirmed these findings. However, significant differences from placebo were discernible only after 8–9 weeks of treatment and were noted only on some measures or were completely absent at 1 month (Conners & Taylor, 1980; Conners *et al.,* 1972; Dykman, McGrew, Harris, Peters, & Ackerman, 1976).

The most recent trial conducted with pemoline is an elegant study involving 60 hyperkinetic children of school age (Conners & Taylor, 1980). In this double-blind trial, the children were randomly assigned to pemoline, methylphenidate, or placebo over a period of 8 weeks. Methods of assessment included behavioral ratings, psychological tests, and achievement tests. Both pemoline (mean dose 60.4 mg/day, 2.25 mg/kg/day) and methylphenidate (22.0 mg/day, 0.82 mg/kg/day) were superior to placebo in all areas except in the achievement tests. Pemoline had a slower onset of clinical effect than methylphenidate, but its action seemed to be of longer duration; its clinical effect is perhaps slightly weaker than that of methylphenidate. The advantage of this drug is that it is given in a single morning dose. This study was able to replicate an earlier comparison of pemoline to dextroamphetamine (Conners *et al.,* 1972.) Only two open studies are available on the long-term (37–77 weeks) efficacy of this drug: Knights and Viets, 1975, and Page *et al.,* 1974a.

Use and efficacy of deanol in children was reviewed by Conners (1973) in a superb and most informative paper. A more recent study by Coleman, Dexheimer, DiMascio, Redman, and Finnerty (1976) reported modest overall results. On the basis of currently available reports, this drug has no place in the treatment of hyperactive children: the same is true for caffeine (for a review, see Klein *et al.,* 1980a).

There are some interesting theories about the mode of action of stimulants in hyperkinetic children. Gittelman-Klein and Klein (1973) suggest that these drugs enhance attentional processes; this helps the child to focus and to attend to his task. Satterfield, Cantwell, Saul, Lesser, and Podosin (1973) and Satterfield, Cantwell, and Satterfield (1974) present evidence that stimulants are therapeutically effective in a subgroup of hyperkinetic children with presenting evidence of underarousal of the central nervous system and low inhibitory control. It was thought by many, based on studies with adults, that hyperkinetic children have a "paradoxical" response to stimulants. This belief was recently disproved in a fine study by Rapoport. In an acute crossover design, under placebo-controlled, double-blind conditions, the effects of dextroamphetamine on cognition and behavior were compared in normal and hyperactive boys and normal college students (Rapoport *et al.,* 1980a). All groups showed a decrease of motor activity of various degrees, and, in general, the effects of dextroamphetamine were similar. However, while men reported euphoria, both groups of children experienced dysphoric effects.

In recent years several reports have emerged on the long-term efficacy of stimulants in children with attention deficit disorder associated with hyperactivity. All studies are retrospective (Weiss & Hechtman, 1979). Sleator *et al.* (1974) found that 26% of 42 children were able to function when switched to placebo after 2 years of treatment with methylphenidate. However, other follow-up studies (up to 5 years) indicate that hyperactive children receiving methylphenidate or chlorpromazine (and those who failed to respond and therefore received no medication) did not differ from each other on measures of antisocial behavior, academic performance, and emotional behavior (Weiss, Kruger, Danielson, & Elman, 1975). Hyperactivity decreased in all groups over the 5 years. Delinquent behavior was more frequent in these subjects than in controls. A 10-year follow-up indicates that although antisocial behavior decreased at this point in time, hyperactive children continue to have difficulties between 17 and 24 years of age when compared to controls (Weiss, Hechtman, Perlman, Hopkins, & Wener, 1979). A two-year assessment of hyperactive boys indicates that the combination of drug and psychological treatments resulted in behavioral and academic improvement (Satterfield, Satterfield, & Cantwell, 1980). It is difficult to evaluate the results of this study because the sample of 61 hyperactive boys represents those subjects who were available for follow-up; 31 patients dropped out in the first year of treatment, though they did not seem to differ on various measures from those who remained in the study.

Untoward Effects. Most common immediate untoward effects of the stimulants are insomnia, anorexia, weight loss, pallor, and behavioral toxicity, which includes dysphoria and drowsiness (Bradley, 1950; Winsberg *et al.,* 1972). Increases in heart rate and blood pressure were found in some children (Aman & Werry, 1975; Boileau, Ballard, Sprague, Sleator, & Massey, 1976); hallucinosis (Lucas & Weiss, 1971; Ney, 1967; Winsberg *et al.,* 1972), and tics (Golden, 1974) were also reported.

Inhibition of growth, a possible long-term untoward effect of chronic administration of stimulants, has been of concern since Safer and Allen's (1973) uncontrolled report. The findings are in discord, and what makes it difficult to evaluate the effects of stimulants on growth is that most patient samples are small. McNutt, Boileau, Cohen, and Sprague (1976) and von Neuman (1976) failed to observe growth suppression, while Weiss, Kruger, Danielson, and Elman (1975) did so. Satterfield, Cantwell, Schell, and Blaschke (1979) found a spurt of growth at year two, after an initial suppression of growth at year one. Roche, Lipman, Overall, and Hung (1979) gave an excellent critical review of this topic.

Anticonvulsants

At the present time, there is not sufficient evidence that antiepileptic drugs are effective in the treatment of behavioral disorders in children with abnormal EEG findings in the absence of a seizure disorder. For review, chapters by Conners and Werry (1979) and Stores (1978) are suggested.

Anxiolytics

The representatives of this class of drugs, meprobamate and the two benzodiazepines, chlordiazepoxide and diazepam, are most widely used in adults and in children. However, in children no systematic investigations were carried out to assess efficacy and safety of these drugs, including their usage in anxiety states (for review, see Gittelman-Klein, 1978; Klein *et al.,* 1980b).

Lithium

Although there is a modest amount of literature since the late 1950s on the use of lithium carbonate in children with a variety of behavioral disorders, there are only a few controlled studies available (for review, see Campbell *et al.,* 1978b; Lena, 1979; Youngerman & Canino, 1978). A pilot study (Campbell, Cohen, & Small, 1982) and preliminary results (of a well designed and placebo-controlled ongoing study) indicate that in hospitalized school-age children of normal intelligence diagnosed as conduct disorder, aggressive type, lithium has marked antiaggressive properties without significant untoward effect on cognition (Platt *et al.,* 1981). Data based on uncontrolled studies and clinical experience suggest that because of its possible antiaggressive property, lithium warrants further exploration in retarded children with severe symptoms of aggressiveness and/or self-mutilation, who have failed previously to respond to behavior modification and standard, psychoactive drugs (Campbell, Fish, Korein, Shapiro, Collins, & Koh, 1972; Dostal, 1972; Ziring & Teitelbaum, 1980).

Megavitamins

There is no evidence that high doses of vitamins yield significant improvement in infantile autism and other behavioral disorders of children (Arnold, Christopher, Huestis, & Smeltzer, 1978; Barnes, 1976). A recent study that claims therapeutic efficacy of megavitamins in autistic children has serious methodological flaws (Rimland, Callaway, & Dreyfus, 1978).

Dietary Treatment

Since Feingold's report in 1974, suggesting that food additives can cause behavioral symptoms, including hyperactivity and learning problems, there has been a tremendous, mainly emotional, storm of parents, their groups, and some professionals, concerning the behavioral toxicity of foods. Conners (1980), in a very thoughtful book, has analyzed and presented the available literature, including his own studies (Conners, 1980; Conners & Goyette, 1977; Conners, Goyette, Southwick, Lees, & Andrulonis, 1976; Goyette, Conners, Petti, & Curtis, 1978). At the present time, it appears that perhaps less than 5% of hyperactive children are sensitive behaviorally to artificial colors. In a small subgroup of such children, these food additives may also interfere with learning and cognition. Certainly, Feingold's dramatic findings were not confirmed by investigations of others, the results of which are quite inconsistent and more modest (Conners, 1980; Harley, Ray, Tomasi, Eichman, Matthews, Chun, Cleeland, & Traisman, 1978; Swanson & Kinsbourne, 1980;

Weiss, Williams, Margen, Abrams, Caan, Citron, Cox, McKibben, Ogar, & Schultz, 1980).

Behavioral Assessment, Treatment Monitoring, and Evaluation

Decisions on whether to use psychoactive agents in the treatment of behavioral disorders in children must be based on research that utilizes critical unbiased assessment procedures and appropriate experimental design. Sprague and Werry (1971) and Sprague and Baxley (1978) have enumerated the basic requirements of a clinical trial: (1) use of a placebo control; (2) random assignments of subjects to experimental conditions; (3) double-blind assessments; (4) standard dosage procedures; (5) standardized evaluation instruments with demonstrated reliability and validity; (6) appropriate statistical analysis of findings; and (7) the comparison of alternative treatments with the investigated drug. To this list may be added the attempt to precisely specify the sample in terms of basic demographic variables and diagnosis. With the exception of studies of children with attention-deficit disorder, most of the research in pediatric psychopharmacology has not met these basic requirements.

Presented below is an overview of assessment and design issues. For more comprehensive coverage, the interested reader is referred to Werry (1978), Conners and Werry (1979), Mann (1976), Doke (1976), Chassan (1979), and Klein *et al.* (1980a).

Delineation of the Characteristics of the Sample

Precise specification of the sample is required in order to identify subgroups of responders and nonresponders. In the case of behavioral disorders in childhood, this is made more difficult because of problems in diagnostic classification and developmental factors (Achenbach, 1978; Fish, 1968, 1969). The new *Diagnostic and Statistical Manual* (DSM-III, 1980) has not been validated. The classification system of the Group for Advancement of Psychiatry (GAP, 1966) has low interrater reliability (Beitchman, Dielman, Landis, Benson & Kemp, 1978). Investigators outside of the United States may use different criteria (Rutter, Lebovici, Eisenberg, Sneznevskij, Sadoun, Brooke, & Lin, 1969). Furthermore, multivariate techniques for identifying diagnostic groups must be more thoroughly researched (Achenbach, 1978). Diagnosis is essential because it statistically interacts with drug treatment. For example, stimulants have been shown to lead to improvements in 65–70% of children diagnosed by DSM-III (1980) as attention-deficit disorder with hyperactivity; yet a hyperactive psychotic child will show worsening of symptoms when placed on the same medication (Campbell, 1978; Fish, 1971). Similarly, developmental and intellectual factors may interact with diagnosis to determine the use of psychoactive drug treatment (Campbell & Cohen, 1981).

Historical Information

Decisions as to which medication is appropriate for a given child will depend, also, on the gathering of relevant historical information, as well as deciding on a diagnosis of the presenting problem. Previous reactions to the same or other medications in terms of behavioral and physiological changes, information on the child's medical status, and information as to the intactness of the child's family must all be considered and documented, where possible, by reports from private physicians or hospitals.

The ECDEU branch of the National Institue of Mental Health (Guy, 1976) has published a number of assessment instruments, some of which are designed to quantify the above relevant historical information. The Children's Personal Data Inventory (CPDI) consists of 55 items that yield demographic and social data concerning the child and his/her family. Campbell (1977) has developed an instrument to supplement the CPDI. This instrument includes information on the psychiatric status of the family as well as pre- and perinatal history for organicity. Such information may be useful for delineating subgroups of responders and nonresponders.

The Prior Medication Record (Guy, 1976) quantifies information about the psychotropic medication received by the child 1 month prior to entering the study, in addition to other drug and nondrug treatments.

Assessment of Behavior, Attention, and Learning

In order to evaluate the treatment efficacy of pharmacological agents, behavioral assessment instruments that are valid, reliable, and sensitive to drug effects must be used. Selection of such instruments must precede experimental design considerations. Further, such evaluations should be carried out in a double-blind fashion in order to eliminate systematic bias in reporting. In drug studies, maintaining the blind is enhanced by rating videotapes of patients with the sequence of assessment randomized for the raters. The instruments reported in the literature generally fall into two classes: "subjective" and "objective." In the former, the rater is required to provide an estimate of the severity of the child's global behavior or with respect to specific symptoms. Alternatively, an estimate of the change in the child's behavior as a result of treatment may be obtained. Use of such an instrument is predicated on the assumption that magnitude estimations of the observer are monotonically related to actual severity of the behavior of the child. Such a measure is similar to the method of "equal-appearing intervals" (Snodgrass, 1975) used in psychophysical studies. Such studies have shown that, at least with respect to sensory stimuli, the form of the relation between the behavior of the rater and the stimulus is monotonic. Whether one can make an inferential jump to the assessment of behavior from such psychophysical studies is not clear. None of the rating scales mentioned below has been "psychophysically" evaluated, that is, precisely which aspect (e.g., frequency, topography) of the child's behavior is measured by the rater has not been examined. Thus, the meaning of the severity estimates is unclear and not readily communicated to the scientific community. In addition, "halo effects" are a potential problem. Subjective rating scales are, however, convenient and have been shown to be sensitive to drug effects (Werry, 1978).

As noted earlier, the ECDEU branch of the National Institute of Mental Health has published a volume describing numerous rating instruments. Subjective rating scales for pediatric populations are among those described and include Conners' Teacher Questionnaire (CTQ) and Conners' Parent Questionnaire (CPQ), the Children's Psychiatric Rating Scale (CPRS), and the Clinical Global Impressions Scale (CGI). The Conners scales have been factor analyzed and norms are available for the CTQ (Werry, Sprague, & Cohen, 1975). The CPRS has not been factor analyzed and, therefore, the 63 items present problems in statistical analysis if all are analyzed for treatment effects (Campbell, Geller, & Cohen, 1977).

Objective assessment instruments utilize either human observers or mechanical devices to record behavior. In the former instance, then, subjectivity is reduced by requiring the rater to simply note presence or absence of a behavior. Even at this level, however, subjective factors such as observer drift and demand characteristics of the rating situation must be considered (Hersen & Barlow, 1976). Mechanical devices are not plagued by such problems, but their validity remains to be demonstrated. Typically, such devices (e.g., actometers) have been used to assess activity levels (Werry, 1978). Schulman, Stevens, and Kupst (1977), for example, have developed an actometer using microelectronic circuitry that can be freely worn by the child. A laboratory-based activity measure using pressure sensors has been investigated by Muller, Crow, and Cheney (1979). Davis, Sprague, and Werry (1969) assessed stereotyped head rocking with telemetry.

The Children's Behavioral Inventory (CBI) (Burdock & Hardesty, 1967) is an age-related checklist scale with developmental norms for children 1 to 15 years of age, which yields a behavioral profile of disturbance based on a 2-hour observation period. However, two studies (Campbell *et al.,* 1978a; Campbell, Small, Hollander, Korein, Cohen, Kalmijn, & Ferris, 1978c) have failed to show a sensitivity to drug effects. Cohen *et al.* (1980) developed an objective scale for assessment of autistic children utilizing interval recording techniques; this scale has normative values and has been shown to be sensitive to psychopharmacological intervention (Cohen, Campbell, McCandless, & Posner, 1980). Freeman, Ritvo, Guthrie, and Schroth (1978) have also developed an objective scale for autistic children based on interval recording techniques.

Ecological factors (i.e., the conditions under which ratings are performed) may significantly influence the results obtained. Variables such as time since ingestion of the medication, observation setting (e.g., ward, school, or home), and number of other individuals present may influence the result. Children diagnosed as Attention Deficit Disorder with hyperactivity may not exhibit hyperactive behavior in a one-to-one interview, while such behavior is very apparent in home or classroom situations. It has been noted by Christensen (1973), for example, that studies reporting minimal drug effects and excellent effects due to behavior modification were all performed in institutional settings with inpatients. On the other hand, studies noting significant drug effects were done with outpatients. Similarly, Campbell *et al.* (1978c) note significant effects of triiodothyronine on the behavior of autistic children as reported by parents, while the effect was much less when the same children were participating in an intensive therapeutic nursery program.

Learning measures may be influenced by psychoactive agents. This is of critical importance in children. Numerous studies have shown that for a large majority of children with attention-deficit disorder, stimulants improve cognitive performance (in terms of attention, learning, and memory), whereas neuroleptics tend to have the opposite effect (Aman, 1978). However, this result must be considered in light of the dosage administered. Werry and Aman (1975) note improvements in attention by haloperidol at low doses and deterioration at high doses. In autistic children, stimulants, as noted above, lead to deterioration in behavior. In one study (Campbell *et al.,* 1978a), haloperidol effected a significant increase in positive reinforced verbal imitation rates in young autistic children when compared with placebo. Other factors to be considered in interpreting the influence of drugs on learning are the simplicity of the tasks and the possible role of state-dependency (Overton, 1971). That is, what has been learned on drug may not be seen when the child is subsequently taken off medication. Tasks that are too simple may yield correct performance in a large majority of the children with no room for assessing improvement.

Tasks that have been shown to be sensitive to drug effects include reaction time, the Continuous Performance Task, Porteus Mazes, paired associate learning, Matching

Familiar Figures, and tests of short-term memory (Aman, 1978). We are currently examining the effects of haloperidol or placebo on free-operant, successive discrimination learning and stimulus overselectivity in pre-school-age autistic children using an automated operant control panel. Results to date indicate increased accuracy in children receiving haloperidol relative to placebo.

Assessment of Drug Side Effects

Clearly, determination of side effects to drug treatment is of extreme importance. Variables such as blood pressure, pulse rate, and body weight must be evaluated prior to and throughout treatment. Height should also be evaluated for possible long-term effects on physical growth. In this regard, normative values for height and weight are available from the National Center for Health Statistics (1976). Other side effects, including behavioral ones (e.g., sleepiness or changes in eating habits) may be assessed on the Dosage Record and Treatment Emergent Symptoms Scale and Treatment Emergent Symptoms Write-In Scale described by Guy (1976) at baseline and throughout treatment. Scales for measuring tardive dyskinesia have been developed for adults. For a review, Gardos, Cole, and La Brie (1977) is recommended. Whether such scales will be useful in children has yet to be determined.

Experimental Design and Data Analysis Considerations

Most research in psychopharmacology utilizes between groups designs in which two or more samples are compared on baseline and at the end of treatment, with results analyzed using conventional statistical tests of mean differences between groups. Such information is of value when the question is simply whether the average patient is likely to respond to a given treatment. However, problems exist with this approach. First, even patient groups that have the same diagnosis, agreed upon by two or more independent, experienced investigators, differ on a host of factors that may influence the results. Randomized assignment of subjects to conditions tends to reduce major group differences. However, this is typically the case only when sample sizes are large. For some rare diseases, such as infantile autism, finding large sample sizes presents difficulties. Prior stratification or, even, matching on hypothetically relevant variables, presents one solution to this problem. But the hypothetically relevant variables may turn out to be inappropriate. Second, this design does not permit the reliable identification of individual responders or nonresponders, because changes due to statistical fluctuation or treatment cannot be separated.

An alternative method of investigation is the systematic intensive study of a single subject or a group of subjects using a within-subjects design (e.g., ABAB) over time using repeated measures (Chassan, 1979; Hersen & Barlow, 1976). This is a technique popular among operant conditioners (Sidman, 1960). Such a strategy is extremely useful when the condition being treated is relatively chronic, rather than acute, when the drug has a relatively quick onset of action with little carry-over when withdrawn, and when the method of assessment is not readily influenced by practice effects. With this approach, individual responders are identified by the reversibility of their behaviors when the treatment is successively presented and withdrawn. Statistical procedures have been developed to analyze this type of data (Kazdin, 1976). Combining the intensive (within-subjects) and extensive (between-groups) designs may be most economical (Turner, Purchatzke, Gift, Farmer, &

Uhlenhuth, 1974). Just such a procedure was successfully utilized by Cohen *et al.* (1980) in an investigation of the effects of haloperidol on pre-school-age autistic children.

The importance of double-blind, placebo-controlled procedures has been emphasized throughout the literature. Two studies (Breuning, Ferguson, & Cullari, 1980; Campbell *et al.,* 1978c) demonstrate the significance of these variables.

Finally, more research is needed on assessing and, if possible, controlling the role of "idiosyncratic" variables on drug response. These factors include the sensitivity of each child to specific dosages, psychosocial and personality variables, and the inherent variability of the behavior of children (Conners, 1972).

Comparison of Drug Therapy with Other Treatments

We said at the outset that pharmacotherapy in children is an adjunct to other forms of treatment. A child will receive other treatments (environmental manipulation, parental counseling, remedial education, individual psychotherapy, etc.) depending on diagnosis, etiology, and associated handicaps. Drugs, for example, do not create intelligence or learning, but experience has shown that effective drug treatment can make a child more amenable to remedial work and special education. In several studies, however, academic performance did not improve with a drug. This applies to hyperactive as well as to overly anxious or aggressive children.

Unfortunately, efficacy of pharmacotherapy when used conjointly with other treatment modalities has not been well researched. The few reports that do exist involve the interaction of drug therapy with behavior therapy (which lends itself to this sort of research because it is relatively quantifiable and its conditions are reproducible).

Young and Turner (1965) treated a large sample of enuretic children with either the Eastleigh buzzer unit alone or in conjunction with dextroamphetamine or methamphetamine. Both drugs facilitated conditioning, with methamphetamine slightly superior to dextroamphetamine. Follow-up revealed that there was a greater rate of relapse in the combined-therapy groups—more so within the dextroamphetamine group—than in the conditioning-alone group. Kennedy and Sloop (1968) failed to replicate the finding that methamphetamine enhanced conditioning in normal or institutionzlized retarded children.

Christensen and Sprague (1973), in a placebo-controlled study, investigated the effects of methylphenidate and behavior therapy, administered alone and conjointly, in a group of twelve socially maladjusted children. Both therapies, used alone, significantly reduced the children's movements in their chairs. However, the combination of both therapies was superior in certain respects to behavior therapy alonne.

In two other studies (Conrad, Dworkin, Shai, & Tobiessen, 1971; Gittelman-Klein, Klein, Abikoff, Katz, Gloisten, & Kates, 1976a), the combination of stimulants and other therapies also proved superior to therapies administered alone. In the first study, which was placebo-controlled, combination of dextroamphetamine and tutoring was significantly superior for some variables to tutoring alone in a group of 68 school-age children with hyperkinesis and perceptual-cognitive impairment. The second paper involved a double-blind, placebo-controlled study of 34 hyperkinetic children of normal intelligence. The combination of methylphenidate and behavior therapy was superior, though not significantly to methylphenidate alone, which in turn was superior (significantly, on several measures of behavior) to behavior therapy with placebo.

Christensen (1973) also studied the effects of methylphenidate and behavior therapy in a group of 16 hyperkinetic, institutionalized retarded children, 9–15 years of age. A placebo-controlled, double-blind crossover design was used. Here too, therapies were administered alone and conjointly. The results demonstrated that behavior therapy was significantly superior to drug in reducing hyperactivity and other disruptive classroom behavior. Moreover, drug added little to the efficacy of conditioning when the two were administered conjointly.

Campbell *et al.* (1978a), in a double-blind, placebo-controlled study with pre-school-age autistic children, demonstrated the superiority of haloperidol in combination with conditioning over the therapies when administered individually. As noted above, those children in the combined-therapy group showed a significantly increased response in reinforced verbal imitative rates when compared to children who received the individual therapies.

It is clear from this survey that there is a paucity of research that explores the interaction of drug therapy with other modalities. This, as well as long-term follow-up, is needed in order to determine the most effective treatment regimen for a given patient.

Summary

An overview of psychopharmacological treatment in children with behavioral disorders was presented, and recent advances were highlighted. The role of psychoactive drugs in the treatment of children was viewed only as an adjunct to other treatment modalities

Careful clinical and laboratory monitoring is required in order to ensure that the drug does not interfere with the child's development and growth. Systematic and careful research is needed regarding the effects of drugs, particularly neuroleptics, on the child's cognition and academic work, and the possible long-term untoward effects on the central nervous system. Though neuroleptics and antianxiety drugs are widely used, there is a paucity of critical assessment of their therapeutic efficacy on behavioral symptoms in children.

With the exception of psychomotor stimulants, it is difficult to draw conclusions from the literature concerning the therapeutic efficacy of individual drugs. Reports suffer from such problems as lack of diagnostic criteria, diagnostically heterogeneous samples, lack of placebo control, and poor assessment procedures, to name a few.

We have reviewed drug treatment following two formats. First, a brief section on indications for pharmacotherapy was presented, organized following the DSM-III (APA, 1980) classification of psychiatric disorders in children. Cited were drugs that have been used in treatment of the various disorders. Secondly, the drugs, arranged by class, were more thoroughly discussed. Untoward effects were cited and a table was provided of representative drugs and their recommended dosage ranges.

The brevity of the last section, which dealt with efficacy of combining treatment modalities, results from the little attention that this area has attracted. The authors hope more work will be done in this promising direction.

References

Achenbach, T. M. Psychopathology of childhood: Research problems and issues. *Journal of Consulting and Clinical Psychology,* 1978, *46,* 759–776.

Alexandris, H., & Lundell, F. Effect of thioridazine, amphetamine and placebo on the hyperkinetic syndrome and cognitive area in mentally deficient children. *Canadian Medical Association Journal,* 1968, *98,* 92–96.

Aman, M. G. Drugs, learning and the psychotherapies. In J. S. Werry (Ed.), *Pediatric psychopharmacology: The use of behavior modifying drugs in children.* New York: Brunner/Mazel, 1978.

Aman, M. G., & Werry, J. S. The effects of methylphenidate and haloperidol on the heart rate and blood pressure of hyperactive children with special reference to time of action. *Psychopharmacologia (Berlin),* 1975, *43,* 163–168.

Annell, A. L. (Ed.). *Depressive states in childhood and adolescence.* Stockholm: Almquist & Wiksell, 1972.

Arnold, L. E., Christopher, J., Huestis, R. D., & Smeltzer, D. J. Megavitamins for minimal brain dysfunction: A placebo controlled study. *Journal of the American Medical Association,* 1978, *240,* 2642–2643.

Barness, L. A. Megavitamin therapy for childhood psychoses and learning disabilities. *Pediatrics,* 1976, *58,* 910–911.

Beitchman, J. H., Dielman, T. E., Landis, R., Benson, R. M., & Kemp, P. L. Reliability of the group for advancement of psychiatry diagnostic categories in child psychiatry. *Archives of General Psychiatry,* 1978, *35,* 1461–1466.

Berger, P. A., & Rexroth, K. Tardive Dyskinesia: Clinical, biological, and pharmacological perspectives. *Schizophrenia Bulletin,* 1980, *6,* 102–116.

Boileau, R. A., Ballard, J. E., Sprague, R. L., Sleator, E. K., & Massey, B. H. Effect of methylphenidate on cardiorespiratory responses in hyperactive children. *Research Quarterly,* 1976, *47,* 590–596.

Bradley, C. The behavior of children receiving benzedrine. *American Journal of Psychiatry,* 1937, *94,* 577–585.

Bradley, C. Benzedrine and dexedrine in the treatment of children's behavior disorders. *Pediatrics,* 1950, *5,* 24–37.

Bradley, C., & Bowen, M. Behavior characteristics of schizophrenic children. *Psychiatric Quarterly,* 1941, *15,* 298–315.

Breuning, S. E., & Davidson, N. A. Effects of psychotropic drugs on intelligence test performance of institutionalized mentally retarded adults. *American Journal of Mental Deficiency,* 1981, *85,* 575–579.

Breuning, S. E., Ferguson, D. G., & Cullari, S. Analysis of single-double blind procedures, maintenance of placebo effects, and drug-induced dyskinesia with mentally retarded persons. *Applied Research in Mental Retardation,* 1980 *1,* 175–192.

Broughton, R. J. Sleep disorders: Disorders of arousal? *Science,* 1968, *159,* 1070–1078.

Burdock, E. I., & Hardesty, A. S. Contrasting behavior patterns in mentally retarded and emotionally disturbed children. In J. Zubin & J. A. Jervis (Eds.), *Psychopathology of mental development.* New York: Grune & Stratton, 1967.

Campbell, M. Demographic parameters of disturbed children: A template to the CPDI and CSH—its rationale and significance. *Psychopharmacology Bulletin,* 1977, *13,* 30–33.

Campbell, M. The use of drug treatment in infantile autism and childhood schizophrenia: A review. In M. A. Lipton, A. DiMascio, & K. Killam (Eds.), *Psychopharmacology: A generation of progress.* New York: Raven Press, 1978.

Campbell, M. Psychopharmacology. In J. D. Noshpitz (Ed.), *Basic handbook of child psychiatry* (Vol. 3). New York: Basic Books, 1979.

Campbell, M., & Cohen, I. L. Psychotropic drugs in child psychiatry. In H. M. Van Praag (Ed.), *Handbook of biological psychiatry.* New York: Marcel Dekker, 1981.

Campbell, M., Fish, B., Shapiro, T., & Floyd, A. Study of molindone in disturbed preschool children. *Current Therapeutic Research,* 1971, *13,* 28–33.

Campbell, M., Fish, B., Korein, J., Shapiro, T., Collins, P., & Koh, C. Lithium and chlorpromazine: A controlled crossover study of hyperactive severely disturbed young children. *Journal of Autism and Childhood Schizophrenia,* 1972, *2,* 234–263.

Campbell, M., Geller, B., & Cohen, I. L. Current status of drug research and treatment with autistic children. *Journal of Pediatric Psychology,* 1977, *2,* 153–161.

Campbell, M., Anderson, L. T., Meier, M., Cohen, I. L., Small, A. M., Samit, C., & Sachar, E. J. A comparison of haloperidol and behavior therapy and their interaction in autistic children. *Journal of the American Academy of Child Psychiatry,* 1978, *17,* 640–655. (a)

Campbell, M., Schulman, D., & Rapoport, J. L. The current status of lithium therapy in child and adolescent psychiatry. *Journal of the American Academy of Child Psychiatry,* 1978, *17,* 717–720. (b)

Campbell, M., Small, A. M., Hollander, C. S., Korein, J., Cohen, I. L., Kalmijn, M., & Ferris, S. A. A controlled crossover study of triiodothyronine in young psychotic children. *Journal of Autism and Childhood Schizophrenia,* 1978, *8,* 371–381. (c)

Campbell, M., Anderson, L. T., Cohen, I. L., Perry, R., Small, A. M., Green, W. H., Anderson, L., & McCandless, W. H., Jr. Haloperidol in autistic children: Effects on learning, behavior, and abnormal involuntary movements. *Psychopharmacology Bulletin,* 1982, *18,* (1) 110–112.

Campbell, M., Cohen, I. L., & Small, A. M. Drugs in aggressive behavior. *Journal of the American Academy of Child Psychiatry,* 1982, *21,* 107–117.

Chassan, J. B. *Research design in clinical psychology and psychiatry* (2nd ed.). New York: Irvington Publishers, 1979.

Christensen, D. E. *Combined effects of methylphenidate (Ritalin) and a classroom behavior modification program in reducing the hyperkinetic behaviors of institutionalized mental retardates.* Doctoral dissertation, University of Illinois at Urbana-Champaign, 1973.

Christensen, D. E., & Sprague, R. L. Reduction of hyperactive behavior by conditioning procedures alone and combined with methylphenidate (Ritalin). *Behavior Research and Therapy,* 1973, *11,* 331–334.

Cohen, D. J., Shaywitz, B. A., Young, J. G., Carbonari, C. M., Nathanson, J. A., Lieberman, D., Bowers, M. B., & Maas, J. W. Central biogenic amine metabolism in children with the syndrome of chronic multiple tics of Gilles de la Tourette, *Journal of the American Academy of Child Psychiatry,* 1979, *18,* 320–341. (a)

Cohen, D. J., Young, J. G., Nathanson, J. A., & Shaywitz, B. A. Clonidine in Tourette's syndrome. *Lancet,* September 15, 1979, pp. 551–552. (b)

Cohen, I. L., Anderson, L. T., & Campbell, M. Measurement of drug effects in autistic children. *Psychopharmacology Bulletin,* 1978, *14,* 68.

Cohen, I. L, Campbell, M., McCandless, W., & Posner, D. *A timed objective rating scale for autistic children: Comparison of preschoolage patients and normal controls.* Paper presented at the annual meeting of the American Academy of Child Psychiatry, Chicago, Ill., October 1980.

Cohen, I. L, Campbell, M., Posner, D., Small, A. M., Triebel, D., & Anderson, L. T. Behavioral effects of haloperidol in young autistic children: An objective analysis using a within-subjects reversal design. *Journal of the American Academy of Child Psychiatry,* 1980, *19,* 665–677.

Coleman, N., Dexheimer, P., DiMascio, A., Redman, W., & Finnerty, R. Deanol in the treatment of hyperkinetic children. *Psychosomatics,* 1976, *17,* 68–72.

Connell, P. H., Corbett, J. A., Horne, D. J., & Mathews, A. M. Drug treatment of adolescent tiquers: A double-blind trial of diazepam and haloperidol. *British Journal of Psychiatry,* 1967, *113,* 375–381.

Conners, C. K. Pharmacotherapy of psychopathology in children. In H. C. Quay & J. S. Werry (Eds.). *Psychopathological disorders of childhood.* New York: Wiley, 1972.

Conners, C. K. Deanol and behavior disorders in children: A critical review of the literature and recommended future studies for determining efficacy. *Psychopharmacology Bulletin* (Special Issue: Pharmacotherapy of Children), 1973, 188–195.

Conners, C. K. Controlled trial of methylphenidate in preschool children with minimal brain dysfunction. In R. Gittelman-Klein (Ed.), Recent advances in child psychopharmacology. *International Journal of Mental Health,* 1975, *4* (No. 1–2), 61.

Conners, C. K. Classification and treatment of childhood depression and depressive equivalents. In D. M. Gallant & G. M. Simpson (Eds.), *Depression: Behavioral, biochemical, diagnostic and treatment concepts.* New York: Spectrum Publications, 1976.

Conners, C. K. *Food additives and hyperactive children.* New York: Plenum Press, 1980.

Conners, C. K. Artificial colors in the diet and disruptive behaviors. In R. N. Knights & D. Bakker (Eds.), *Treatment of hyperactive and learning disordered children.* Baltimore: University Park Press, 1980.

Conners, C. K., & Goyette, C. H. The effect of certified food dyes on behavior: A challenge test. *New Clinical Drug Evaluation Unit Intercom,* 1977, *7,* 18–19.

Conners, C. K. & Taylor, E. Pemoline, methylphenidate and placebo in children with minimal brain dysfunction. *Archives of General Psychiatry,* 1980, *37,* 922–930.

Conners, C. K., & Wells, K. C. Behavioral and physiological measurement of psychopharmacological effects in children. Read at the Annual Meeting of the American College of Neuropsychopharmacology, San Juan, Puerto Rico, 1977.

Conners, C. K., & Werry, J. S. Pharmacotherapy. In H. C. Quay & J. S. Werry (Eds.), *Psychopathological disorders of childhood* (2nd ed.). New York: Wiley, 1979.

Conners, C. K., Eisenberg, L., & Barcai, A. Effect of dextroamphetamine on children. *Archives of General Psychiatry,* 1967, *17,* 478–484.

Conners, C. K., Rothschild, G., Eisenberg, L., Schwartz, L. S., & Robinson, E. Dextroamphetamine sulfate in children with learning disorders. *Archives of General Psychiatry,* 1969, *21,* 182–190.

Conners, C. K., Taylor, E., Meo, G., Kurtz, M. A., & Fournier, M. Magnesium pemoline and dextroamphetamine: A controlled study in children with minimal brain dysfunction. *Psychopharmacologia,* 1972, *26,* 321–336.

Conners, C. K., Goyette, C. H., Southwick, D. A., Lees, J. H., & Andrulonis, P. A. Food additives and hyperkinesis: A controlled double-blind experiment. *Pediatrics,* 1976, *58,* 154–166.

Conrad, W. G., Dworkin, E. S., Shai, A., & Tobiessen, J. E. Effects of amphetamine therapy and prescriptive tutoring on the behavior and achievement of lower class hyperactive children. *Journal of Learning Disabilities,* 1971, *4,* 509–517.

Cytryn, L., McKnew, D., & Bunney, W. E. Diagnosis of depression in children: A Reassessment. *American Journal of Psychiatry,* 1980, *137,* 22–25.

Davis, K. V., Sprague, R. L., & Werry, J. S. Stereotyped behavior and activity level in severe retardates: The effect of drugs. *American Journal of Mental Deficiency,* 1969, *73,* 721–727.

Diagnostic and Statistical Manual of Mental Disorders (3rd ed.). Washington, D. C.: American Psychiatric Association, 1980.

Dische, S. Management of enuresis. *British Medical Journal,* 1971, *2,* 33.

Doke, L. A. Assessment of children's behavioral deficits. In M. Hersen & A. S. Bellack (Eds.), *Behavioral assessment: A practical handbook.* Oxford: Pergamon Press, 1976.

Dostal, T. Antiaggressive effects of lithium salts in mentally retarded adolescents. In A. L. Annell (Ed.), *Depressive states in childhood and adolescence.* Stockholm: Almquist & Wiksell, 1972.

Douglas, V. Differences between normal and hyperkinetic children. In C. K. Conners (Ed.), *Clinical use of stimulant drugs in children.* Amsterdam: Excerpta Medica, 1974.

Dykman, R. A., McGrew, J., Harris, T. S., Peters, J. E., & Ackerman, P. T. Two blinded studies of the effects of stimulant drug on children: Pemoline, methylphenidate, and placebo. In R. P. Anderson & C. G. Halcomb (Eds.), *Learning disability/Minimal brain dysfunction syndrome.* Springfield, Ill.: Charles C Thomas, 1976.

Engelhardt, D. M., & Polizos, P. Adverse effects of pharmacotherapy in childhood psychosis. In M. A. Lipton, A. DiMascio, & K. F. Killam (Eds.), *Psychopharmacology: A generation of progress.* New York: Raven Press, 1978.

Engelhardt, D. M., Polizos, P., Waizer, J., & Hoffman, S. P. A double-blind comparison of fluphenazine and haloperidol. *Journal of Autism and Childhood Schizophrenia,* 1973, *3,* 128–137.

Feinberg, M., & Carroll, B. J. Effects of dopamine agonists and antagonists in Tourette's disease. *Archives of General Psychiatry,* 1979, *36,* 979–985.

Feingold, B. F. *Hyperkinesis and learning difficulties (H-LD) linked to the ingestion of artificial colors and flavors.* Paper presented at the Annual Meeting of the American Medical Association, Section on Allergy, Chicago, June 24, 1974.

Fish, B. Methodology in child psychopharmacology. In D. H. Efron, J. O. Cole, J. Levine, & J. R. Wittenborn (Eds.), *Psychopharmacology, a review of progress, 1957–1967.* Washington, D.C.: Public Health Service Publication No. 1836, U.S. Government Printing Office, 1968.

Fish, B. Problems of diagnosis and the definition of comparable groups: A neglected issue in drug research with children. *American Journal of Psychiatry,* 1969, *125,* 900–908.

Fish, B. Psychopharmacologic response of chronic schizophrenic adults as predictors of responses in young schizophrenic children. *Psychopharmacology Bulletin,* 1970, *6,* 12–15.

Fish, B. The "one child, one drug" myth of stimulants in hyperkinesis: Importance of diagnostic categories in evaluating treatment. *Archives of General Psychiatry,* 1971, *25,* 193–203.

Fish, B., Shapiro, T., & Campbell, M. Long-term prognosis and the response of schizophrenic children to drug therapy: A controlled study of trifluoperazine. *American Journal of Psychiatry,* 1966, *123,* 32–39.

Fisher, C., Kahn, E., Edwards, A., & Davis, D. M. A psychophysiological study of nightmares and night terrors: The suppression of stage 4 night terrors with diazepam. *Archives of General Psychiatry,* 1973, *28,* 252–259.

Forsythe, W. I., & Redmond, A. Enuresis and the electric alarm: Study of 200 cases. *British Medical Journal,* 1970, *1,* 211–213.

Freeman, B. J., Ritvo, E. R., Guthrie, D., Schroth, P., & Ball, J. The behavior observation scale for autism. *Journal of the American Academy of Child Psychiatry,* 1978, *17,* 576–588.

Gardos, G., Cole, J. O., & La Brie, R. The assessment of tardive dyskinesia. *Archives of General Psychiatry,* 1977, *34,* 1206–1212.

Gittelman-Klein, R. Psychopharmacological treatment of anxiety disorders, mood disorders, and Tourette's disorder in children. In M. A. Lipton, A. DiMascio, & K. F. Killam (Eds.), *Psychopharmacology: A generation of progress.* New York: Raven Press, 1978.

Gittelman-Klein, R., & Klein, D. F. Controlled imipramine treatment of school phobia. *Archives of General Psychiatry,* 1971, *25,* 204–207.

Gittelman-Klein, R., & Klein, D. F. *The relationship between behavioral and psychological test changes in hyperkinetic children*. Presented at the 12th Annual Meeting of the American College of Neuropsychopharmacology, Palm Springs, California, December 1973.

Gittelman-Klein, R., & Klein, D. F. Methylphenidate effects in learning disabilities: I. *Archives of General Psychiatry,* 1976, *33,* 655–664.

Gittelman-Klein, R., Klein, D. F., Abikoff, H., Katz, S., Gloisten, A. C., & Kates, W. Relative efficacy of methylphenidate and behavior modification in hyperkinetic children: An interim report. *Journal of Abnormal Child Psychology,* 1976, *4,* 361–379. (a)

Gittelman-Klein, R., Klein, D. F., Katz, S., Saraf, K. R., & Pollack, E. Comparative effects of methylphenidate and thioridazine in hyperkinetic children: I. Clinical results. *Archives of General Psychiatry,* 1976, *33,* 1217–1231. (b)

Gittelman-Klein, R., Spitzer, R., & Cantwell, D. P. Diagnostic classifications and psychopharmacological indications. In J. S. Werry (Ed.), *Pediatric psychopharmacology. The use of behavior modifying drugs in children*. New York: Brunner/Mazel, 1978.

Glick, B. S., Schulman, D., & Turecki, S. Diazepam (Valium) treatment in childhood sleep disorders. *Disease of the Nervous System,* 1971, *32,* 565–566.

Golden, G. S. Case report—Gilles de la Tourette's syndrome following methylphenidate administration. *Developmental Medicine and Child Neurology,* 1974, *16,* 76.

Goyette, C. H., Conners, C. K., Petti, T. A., & Curtis, L. E. Effects of artifical colors in hyperkinetic children: A double-blind challenge study. *Psychopharmacology Bulletin,* 1978, *13,* 39–40.

Greenhill, L. L., Hirsch, M. L., Halpern, F., & Spalten, D. *Molindone hydrochloride in the treatment of aggressive, hospitalized children*. Paper presented at the Annual NCDEU-NIMH Meeting, Key Biscayne, Florida, May 27–29, 1980.

Gross, M. D., Growth of hyperkinetic children taking methylphenidate, dextroamphetamine or imipramine/desipramine. *Pediatrics,* 1976, *58,* 423–431.

Group for the Advancement of Psychiatry. *Psychopathological disorders in childhood: Theoretical considerations and a proposed classification.* Vol. 6, Report No. 62, June, 1966. New York: Mental Health Materials Center, Inc., 1966.

Gualtieri, C. T., Barnhill, J., McGimsey, J., & Schell, D. Tardive dyskinesia and other movement disorders in children treated with psychotropic drugs. *Journal of the American Academy of Child Psychiatry,* 1980, *19,* 491–510.

Guy, W. *ECDEU assessment manual for psychopharmacology,* revised, 1976. Rockville, Md.: DHEW Publication No. (ADM) 76-338, 1976.

Hanson, D. R., & Gottesman, I. I. The genetics, if any, of infantile autism and childhood schizophrenia. *Journal of Autism and Childhood Schizophrenia,* 1976, *6,* 209–234.

Harley, J. P., Ray, R. S., Tomasi, L., Eichman, P. L., Matthews, C. G., Chun, R., Cleeland, C. S., & Traisman, E. Hyperkinesis and food additives: Testing the Feingold hypothesis. *Pediatrics,* 1978, *61,* 818–828.

Hayes, T. A., Logan Panitch, M., & Barker, E. Imipramine dosage in children: A comment on "Imipramine and electrocardiographic abnormalities in hyperactive children." *American Journal of Psychiatry,* 1975, *132,* 546–547.

Hersen, M., & Barlow, D. H. *Single case experimental designs: Strategies for studying behavior change.* New York: Pergamon Press, 1976.

Herzog, J. M. *Sleep disturbance and father hunger in 18–28 month-old boys.* Paper presented at the 25th Annual Meeting of the American Academy of Child Psychiatry, San Diego, California, October 24–29, 1978.

Huessy, H. R., & Wright, A. L. The use of imipramine in children's behavior disorders. *Acta Paedopsychiatrica,* 1970, *37,* 194–199.

ICD-9, International Classification of Diseases. *Manual of the International Statistical Classification of diseases, injuries and causes of death* (Vol. 1). Geneva: World Health Organization, 1977.

Irwin, S. A rational framework for the development, evaluation, and use of psychoactive drugs. *American Journal of Psychiatry,* 1968, *124,* 1–19. (Supplement)

Kazdin, A. E. Statistical analyses for single-case experimental designs. In M. Hersen & D. H. Barlow, *Single-case experimental designs: Strategies for studying behavior change.* New York: Pergamon Press, 1976.

Kennedy, W. A. & Sloop, E. W. Methedrine as an adjunct to conditioning treatment of nocturnal enuresis in normal and institutionalized retarded subjects. *Psychological Reports,* 1968, *3,* 997.

Klein, D. F., Gittelman, R., Quitkin, F., & Rifkin, A. Diagnosis and drug treatment of childhood disorders. In D. F. Klein, R. Gittelman, F. Quitkin, & A. Rifkin (Eds.), *A diagnosis and drug treatment of psychiatric disorders: Adults and children* (2nd ed.). Baltimore: Williams & Wilkins, 1980. (a)

Klein, D. F., Gittelman, R., Quitkin, F., & Rifkin, A. Side effects of antipsychotic drugs and their treatment. In D. F. Klein, R. Gittelman, F. Quitkin, & A. Rifkin (Eds.), *A diagnosis and drug treatment of psychiatric disorders: Adults and children* (2nd ed.). Baltimore: Williams & Wilkins, 1980. (b)

Knights, R. M., & Viets, C. A. Effects of pemoline on hyperactive boys. *Pharmacology, Biochemistry and Behavior,* 1975, *3,* 1107–1114.

Lena, B. Lithium in child and adolescent psychiatry. *Archives of General Psychiatry,* 1979, *36,* 854–855.

Lipman, R. S., DiMascio, A., Reatig, N., Kirson, T. Psychotropic drugs and mentally retarded children. In M. A. Lipton, A. DiMascio, & K. Killam (Eds.), *Psychopharmacology: A generation of progress.* New York: Raven Press, 1978.

Lucas, A., & Weiss, M. Methylphenidate hallucinosis. *Journal of the American Medical Association,* 1971, *217,* 1079–1081.

Mann, R. A. Assessment of behavioral excesses in children. In M. Hersen & A. S. Bellack (Eds.), *Behavioral assessment: A practical handbook.* Oxford: Pergamon Press, 1976.

McAndrew, J. B., Case, Q., & Treffert, D. A. Effects of prolonged phenothiazine intake on psychotic and other hospitalized children. *Journal of Autism and Childhood Schizophrenia,* 1972, *2,* 75–91.

McNutt, B. A., Boileau, R. A., Cohen, M. N., Sprague, R. L., & von Neumann, A. *The effects of long-term stimulant medication on the growth and body composition of hyperactive children. II: Report on 2 years.* Paper presented at the Annual Early Clinical Drug Evaluation Unit Meeting, Psychopharmacology Research Branch, National Institute of Mental Health, Key Biscayne, Florida, May 20–22, 1976.

Mikkelsen, E. J., Rapoport, J. L., Nee, L., Gruenau, C., Mendelson, W., & Gillin, J. C. Childhood enuresis. I: Sleep patterns and psychopathology. *Archives of General Psychiatry,* 1980, *37,* 1139–1144.

Muller, P. G., Crow, R. E., & Cheney, C. D. Schedule-induced locomotor activity in humans. *Journal of the Experimental Analysis of Behavior,* 1979, *31,* 83–90.

National Center for Health Statistics (1976). *Monthly Vital Statistics Report,* Vol. 25, No. 3, supplement (HRA).

Ney, P. G., Psychosis in a child, associated with amphetamine administration. *Canadian Medical Association Journal,* 1967, *97,* 1026.

Overton, D. A. State-dependent or "dissociated" learning produced with pentobarbital. In J. A. Harvey (Ed.), *Behavioral analysis of drug action: Research and commentary.* Glenview, Ill.: Scott, Foresman, 1971.

Page, J. G., Bernstein, J. E., Janicki, R. S., & Michelli, F. A. A multi-clinic trial of pemoline in childhood hyperkinesis. In C. K. Conners (Ed.), *Clinical uses of stimulant drugs in children.* Amsterdam: Excerpta Medica, 1974. (a)

Page, J. G., Janicki, R. S., Bernstein, J. E., Curran, C. F., & Michelli, F. A. Pemoline (Cylert) in the treatment of childhood hyperkinesis. *Journal of Learning Disorders,* 1974, *7,* 498–503. (b)

Paulson, G. W., Rizvi, C. A., & Crane, G. E. Tardive dyskinesia as a possible sequel of long-term therapy with phenothiazines. *Clinical Pediatrics,* 1975, *14,* 953–955.

Pessikoff, R. B., & Davis, P. C. Treatment of *pavor nocturnus* and somnambulism in children. *American Journal of Psychiatry,* 1971, *128,* 778–781.

Petti, T. A., & Campbell, M. Imipramine and seizures. *American Journal of Psychiatry,* 1975, *132,* 538–540.

Platt, J. E., Campbell, M., Green, W. H., Perry, R., & Cohen, I. L. Effects of lithium carbonate and haloperidol on cognition in aggressive hospitalized school-age children. *Journal of Clinical Psychopharmacology,* 1981, *1,* 8–13.

Polizos, P., Engelhardt, D. M., Hoffman, S. P., & Waizer, J. Neurological consequences of psychotropic drug withdrawal in schizophrenic children. *Journal of Autism and Childhood Schizophrenia,* 1973, *3,* 247–253.

Pool, D., Bloom, W., Mielke, D. H., Roniger, J. J., & Gallant, D. M. A controlled evaluation of loxitane in seventy-five adolescent schizophrenic patients. *Current Therapeutic Research,* 1976, *19,* 99–104.

Poussaint, A. F., & Ditman, K. S. A controlled study of imipramine (tofranil) in the treatment of childhood enuresis. *Journal of Pediatrics,* 1965, *67,* 283–290.

Puig-Antich, J., Blau, S., Marx, N., Greenhill, L. L., & Chambers, W. Prepubertal major depressive disorder. A pilot study. *Journal of the American Academy of Child Psychiatry,* 1978, *17,* 695–707.

Puig-Antich, J., Lupatkin, W., Chambers, W., Perel, J., Tabrizi, M. A., & King, J. *Imipramine in prepubertal major depression.* Paper presented at the Annual NCDEU-NIMH Meeting, Key Biscayne, Florida, May 27–29, 1980.

Puig-Antich, J., Perel, J., Lupatkin, W., Chambers, W. J., Tabrizi, M. A., & Stiller, R. Plasma levels of imipramine (IMI) and desmethylimipramine (DMI) and clinical response in prepubertal major depressive disorder: A preliminary report. *Journal of the American Academy of Child Psychiatry,* 1979, *18,* 616–627.

Rapoport, J. L., & Mikkelsen, E. J. Antidepressants. In J. S. Werry (Ed.,), *Pediatric psychopharmacology: The use of behavior modifying drugs in children.* New York: Brunner/Mazel, 1978.

Rapoport, J., Abramson, A., Alexander, D., & Lott, I. Playroom observations of hyperactive children on medication. *Journal of the American Academy of Child Psychiatry,* 1971, *10,* 524–534.

Rapoport, J. L., Quinn, P., Bradbard, G., Riddle, D., & Brooks, E. Imipramine and methylphenidate treatments of hyperactive boys. *Archives of General Psychiatry,* 1974, *30,* 789–793.

Rapoport, J. L., Buchsbaum, M. S., Weingertner, H., Zahn, T. P., Ludlow, C., & Mikkelsen, E. J. Dextroamphetamine. Its cognitive and behavioral effects in normal and hyperactive boys and normal men. *Archives of General Psychiatry,* 1980, *37,* 933–943. (a)

Rapoport, J. L., Mikkelsen, E. J., Zavadil, A., Nee, L., Gruenau, C., Mendelson, W., & Gillin, J. C. Childhood enuresis, II. Psychopathology, tricyclic concentration in plasma and antienuretic effect. *Archives of General Psychiatry,* 1980, *37,* 1146–1152. (b)

Rimland, B., Callaway, E., & Dreyfus, P. The effect of high dose of vitamin B_6 on autistic children: A double-blind crossover study. *American Journal of Psychiatry,* 1978, *135,* 472–475.

Ritvo, E. R. Autism: From adjective to noun. In E. R. Ritvo (Ed.), *Autism: Diagnosis, current research and management.* New York: Spectrum Publications, 1976.

Roche, A. F., Lipman, R. S., Overall, J. E., & Hung, W. The effects of stimulant medication on the growth of hyperkinetic children. *Pediatrics,* 1979, *63,* 847–850.

Rutter, M., Lebovici, S., Eisenberg, L., Sneznevskij, A. V., Sadoun, R., Brooke, E., & Lin, T. Y. A triaxial classification of mental disorders in childhood. *Journal of Child Psychology and Psychiatry,* 1969, *10,* 41–61.

Safer, D. J., & Allen, R. P. Factors influencing the suppressant effects of two stimulant drugs on the growth of hyperactive children. *Pediatrics,* 1973, *51,* 660.

Saraf, K. R., Klein, D. F., Gittelman-Klein, R., Gootman, N., & Greenhill, P. EKG effects of imipramine treatment in children. *Journal of the American Academy of Child Psychiatry,* 1978, *17,* 60–69.

Satterfield, J. H., Cantwell, D. P., Lesser, L. I., & Podosin, R. L. Physiological studies of the hyperkinetic child. *American Journal of Psychiatry,* 1972, *128,* 1418–1424.

Satterfield, J. H., Cantwell, D., Saul, R. E., Lesser, L. I., & Podosin, R. L. Response to stimulant drug treatment in hyperactive children: Prediction from EEG and neurological findings. *Journal of Autism and Childhood Schizophrenia,* 1973, *3,* 36–48.

Satterfield, J. H., Cantwell, D., & Satterfield, B. T. Pathophysiology of the hyperactive child syndrome. *Archives of General Psychiatry,* 1974, *31,* 839–844.

Satterfield, J. H., Cantwell, D. P., Schell, A., & Blaschke, T. Growth of hyperactive children treated with methylphenidate. *Archives of General Psychiatry,* 1979, *36,* 212–217.

Satterfield, J. H., Satterfield, B. T., & Cantwell, D. P. Multimodality treatment. A two-year evaluation of 61 hyperactive boys. *Archives of General Psychiatry,* 1980, *37,* 915–918.

Schulman, J. L., Stevens, T. M., & Kupst, M. J. The biomotometer: A new device for the measurement and remediation of hyperactivity. *Child Development,* 1977, *48,* 1152–1154.

Schulterbrandt, J. G., & Raskin, A. (Eds.). *Depression in childhood: Diagnosis, treatment, and conceptual models.* New York: Raven Press, 1977.

Shaffer, D. Enuresis. In M. Rutter & L. Hersov (Eds.), *Child psychiatry, modern approaches.* London: Blackwell Scientific Publications, 1977.

Shapiro, A. K., Shapiro, E. S., Brunn, R. D., & Sweet, R. C. *Gilles de la Tourette Syndrome.* New York: Raven Press, 1978.

Shapiro, A. K., Shapiro, E., & Wayne, H. Treatment of Tourette's syndrome. *Archives of General Psychiatry,* 1973, *28,* 92.

Sidman, M. *Tactics of scientific research.* New York: Basic Books, 1960.

Sleator, E. K., von Neumann, A., & Sprague, R. L. Hyperactive children, a continuous long-term placebo-controlled follow-up. *Journal of the American Medical Association,* 1974, *229,* 316–317.

Snodgrass, J. G. Psychophysics. In B. Scharf & G. S. Reynolds (Eds.), *Experimental sensory psychology.* Glenview, Ill.: Scott, Foresman, 1975.

Spitzer, R. L., Endicott, J., & Robins, E. *Research Diagnostic criteria (RDC) for a selected group of functional disorders.* Unpublished manuscript, 1975.

Sprague, R. L., & Baxley, G. B. Drugs used for the management of behavior in mental retardation. In J. Wortis (Ed.), *Mental retardation* (Vol. 10). New York: Grune & Stratton, 1978.

Sprague, R. L., & Sleator, E. K. What is the proper dose of stimulant drugs in children? In R. Gittelman-Klein (Ed.), *Recent advances in child psychopharmacology, International Journal of Mental Health,* 1975, *4,* 75.

Sprague, R. L., & Sleator, E. K. Methylphenidate in hyperkinetic children: Differences in dose effects on learning and social behavior. *Science,* 1977, *198,* 1274–1276.

Sprague, R. L., & Werry, J. S. Methodology of psychopharmacological studies with the retarded. In N. R. Ellis (Ed.), *International review of research in mental retardation*. New York: Academic Press, 1971.

Sprague, R. L., Barnes, K. R., & Werry, J. S. Methylphenidate and thioridazine: Learning, reaction time, activity, and classroom behavior in disturbed children. *American Journal of Orthopsychiatry*, 1970, *40*, 615–628.

Stores, G. Antiepileptics (anticonvulsants). In J. S. Werry (Ed.), *Pediatric psychopharmacology. The use of behavior modifying drugs in children*. New York: Brunner/Mazel 1978.

Swanson, J. M., & Kinsbourne, M. Food dyes impair performance of hyperactive children on a laboratory learning test. *Science*, 1980, *207*, 1485–1487.

Tardive dyskinesia: Summary of a task force report of the American Psychiatric Association. *American Journal of Psychiatry*, 1980, *137*, 1163–1172.

Turner, D. A., Purchatzke, G., Gift, T., Farmer, C., & Uhlenhuth, E. H. Intensive design in evaluating anxiolytic agents. In J. Levine, B. C. Shiele, & W. J. R. Taylor (Eds.), *Principles and techniques of human research and therapeutics* (Vol. 8). Mt. Kisco, New York: Futura Publishing, 1974.

Villeneuve, A. The rabbit syndrome. A peculiar extrapyramidal reaction. *Canadian Psychiatric Association Journal*, 1972, *17*, 69–72.

Waizer, J., Hoffman, S. P., Polizos, P., & Engelhardt, D. M. Outpatient treatment of hyperactive school children with imipramine. *American Journal of Psychiatry*, 1974, *131*, 587–591.

Weinberg, W. A., Rutman, J., Sullivan, L., Penick, E. C., & Dietz, S. G. Depression in children referred to an educational diagnostic center: Diagnosis and treatment—preliminary report. *Journal of Pediatrics*, 1973, *83*, 1065–1072.

Weiss, B., Williams, J. H., Margen, S., Abrams, B., Caan, B., Citron, L. J., Cox, C., McKibben, J., Ogar, D., & Schultz, S. Behavioral responses to artifical food colors. *Science*, 1980, *207*, 1487–1489.

Weiss, G., & Hechtman, L. The hyperactive child syndrome. *Science*, 1979, *205*, 1348–1354.

Weiss, G., Kruger, E., Danielson, V., & Elman, M. Effect of long-term treatment of hyperactive children with methylphenidate. *Canadian Medical Association Journal*, 1975, *112*, 159–165.

Weiss, G., Hechtman, L., Perlman, T., Hopkins, J., & Wener, A. Hyperactives as young adults: A controlled prospective ten-year follow-up of 75 children. *Archives of General Psychiatry*, 1979, *36*, 675–681.

Werry, J. S. Measures in pediatric psychopharmacology. In J. S. Werry (Ed.), *Pediatric psychopharmacology. The use of behavior modifying drugs in children*. New York: Brunner/Mazel, 1978.

Werry, J. S., & Aman, M. G. Methylphenidate and haloperidol in children: Effects on attention, memory and activity. *Archives of General Psychiatry*, 1975, *32*, 790–795.

Werry, J. S., Weiss, G., Douglas, V., & Martin, J. Studies on the hyperactive child: III. The effect of chlorpromazine upon behavior and learning ability. *Journal of the American Academy of Child Psychiatry*, 1966, *5*, 292–312.

Werry, J. S., Sprague, R., & Cohen, M. Conners' Teacher Rating Scale for use in drug studies with children. *Journal of Abnormal Child Psychology*, 1975, *3*, 217–229.

Werry, J. S., Aman, M. G., & Lampen, E. Haloperidol and methylphenidate in hyperactive children. *Acta Paedopsychiatrica* (Basel), 1976, *42*, 26–40.

Werry, J. S., Aman, M. G., & Diamond, E. Imipramine and methylphenidate in hyperactive children. *Journal of Child Psychology and Psychiatry*, 1980, *21*, 27–35.

Winsberg, B. G., & Yepes, L. E. Antipsychotics. In J. S. Werry (Ed.), *Pediatric psychopharmacology. The use of behavior modifying drugs in children*. New York: Brunner/Mazel, 1978.

Winsberg, B. G., Bialer, I., Kupietz, S., & Tobias, J. Effects of imipramine and dextroamphetamine on behavior of neuropsychiatrically impaired children. *American Journal of Psychiatry*, 1972, *128*, 1425–1431.

Winsberg, B. G., Goldstein, S., Yepes, L. E., & Perel, J. M. Imipramine and electrocardiographic abnormalities in hyperactive children. *American Journal of Psychiatry*, 1975, *132*, 542–545.

Woodrow, K. M. Gilles de la Tourette's disease: A review. *American Journal of Psychiatry*, 1974, *131*, 1000.

Young, C. G., & Turner, R. K. CNS stimulant drugs and conditioning treatment of nocturnal enuresis. *Behaviour Research and Therapy*, 1965, *3*, 93–101.

Youngerman, J., & Canino, I. Lithium carbonate use in children and adolescents. *Archives of General Psychiatry*, 1978, *35*, 216–224.

Ziring, P. & Teitelbaum, L. *Affiliation with a university department of psychiatry: Impact on the use of psychoactive medication in a large public residential facility for mentally retarded persons*. Paper presented at the Conference on the Use of Medications in Controlling the Behavior of the Mentally Retarded. University of Minnesota, Minneapolis, Minn., September 22–24, 1980.

18

Preventive Strategies with Children and Families

Small Groups, Organizations, Communities

RICHARD A. WINETT, MICHAEL STEFANEK, AND ANNE W. RILEY

Introduction

Although the chapters in this volume attest to the rapid development of more effective assessment and treatment procedures for a wide range of childhood problems and disorders, these innovations continue to face the same problems of more traditional approaches. That is, it is very costly to treat any recalcitrant problem or disorder, and the "reach" of any psychotherapy intervention (either behavioral or more traditional therapy) is severely limited by the nature of that treatment modality (Rappaport & Chinsky, 1974). For at least two decades, mental health practitioners have been well aware of these limitations and have been urged to develop and implement preventive programs. In fact, prevention was supposed to be a key aspect of community mental health centers as they were implemented in 1963 (Kennedy, 1963).

Parts of the flexitime and family life work have been presented previously in the *Monthly Labor Review, Journal of Applied Behavior Analysis,* and the *American Journal of Community Psychology.*

RICHARD A. WINETT, MICHAEL STEFANEK, AND ANNE W. RILEY • Department of Psychology, Virginia Polytechnic Institute and State University, Blacksburg, Virginia 24061. Research reported on flexitime and family life was supported by Grant No. MH-30585 from the Center for Study of Metropolitan Problems of the National Institute of Mental Health.

A dramatic turn-around in the political climate since that time, the shortage of funds, and the difficulty of instituting new paradigms in a relatively entrenched mental health field (Rappaport, 1977) are all reasons why the move to prevention has been a slow one. Another reason has been that the concepts, strategies, and predicted outcomes in preventive mental health during the last two decades have often been unclear and have suffered from precipitously enacted programs (Heller, Price, & Sher, 1980).

One of the initial problems was the adoption without modification of the public health model that served so well in disease prevention. Readers are probably aware of the three levels of prevention in this model. Primary prevention involves reducing the incidence of new cases of the target disease in the population at large. Primary prevention often entails community-wide programs aimed at the entire, normal population. Secondary prevention involves reducing the duration and severity of a disorder by early treatment; such strategies most often focus on initial screening of high risk-populations, followed, where indicated, by early treatment. Tertiary prevention entails reducing the severity and disability of an established disorder. It is prevention in name only, and is best thought of as rehabilitation.

While these different approaches have been effective in disease prevention where certain factors can clearly be linked to specific diseases, the model is less workable in the mental health arena. It is simply not the case that we can frequently and reliably link specific, early social psychological variables with specific, later mental health problems. Limitations of applying the public health model to mental health concerns has become quite apparent, and has led to a paradigm shift in preventive mental health (Bloom, 1979).

Important new concepts include identification of stressful life situations or settings and programs to help individuals become more competent to deal with those situations or settings (a person-centered approach), or attempts to modify stressful settings and situations (a systems approach; Bloom, 1979). It is not necessary within this new conceptualization to have epidemiological data showing high correlations between specific stressors and (later) specific mental health problems (but, see the subsequent discussion). For example, dependent upon past history and current resources, loss of a spouse can have multiple outcomes: severe depression, drinking, death of the living spouse, or maybe only a short period of grief. Yet, it is clear that for most people, loss of a spouse will have some protracted mental health consequence, and providing ready access to mental health counseling before the surviving spouse's reaction becomes severe is one example of a preventive strategy.

The focus on building skills and competencies for stressful situations, or trying to modify stressful situations or settings themselves, can, however, be likened to effective public health measures. Skills and competency development for stress, in many ways, is analogous to inoculation procedures (see Meichenbaum, 1977). Modifying stress-producing settings or situations is similar to attempts to alleviate or eliminate environmental causes of disease. For example, it is generally agreed that modern sanitation practices have had more effect on disease prevention than any other public health measure (Dubos, 1974). If we agree that settings are the primary determinants of behavior, then the careful ecological assessment and modification of stress-producing settings should be a first priority in preventive mental health. In following this strategy, we will probably realize more widespread and beneficial outcomes (see discussion of this point in Wilson & O'Leary, 1980, pp. 37–40).

While the major interest now is in "health promotion" and "competency building," different approaches to achieve these global objectives have been identified. For example, Catalano and Dooley (1980) distinguished between "proactive primary prevention" and "reactive primary prevention." The goal of proactive approaches is to prevent occurrence of risk factors, and as we will indicate later, this is often a system-change approach. Reactive approaches primarily involve efforts to improve coping skills of people prior to or after exposure to stressors. The Presidential Task force (Task Panel on Prevention, 1978) and current federal funding (Plaut, 1980) have placed their priorities on more microlevel, reactive preventive approaches.

Obviously, reactive efforts are similar to traditional mental health practices. Even though this approach may have limitations in terms of scope and reach, in a period of political and fiscal conservatism, microlevel approaches probably have the best chance of implementation and public acceptance. An example of a microlevel effort, training normal children in problem-solving skills, will be detailed in the next section of this chapter. That set of interventions probably falls midway on a proactive-reactive continuum. Our commitment to broader setting and system-level proactive strategies is reflected in the last two sections of this chapter, which describe organizational and community change programs directed toward benefiting children and families.

However, movement away from a public health paradigm that called for a relatively strict one-to-one identification of early exposure to a contagion and later pathology (probably a caricature of that model) should not be construed as an endorsement of an amorphous, nonspecific approach to prevention. In terms of political feasibility, effectiveness, and the advancement of knowledge in the social sciences, what is needed are projects that identify the target problems, skills, or situations to be modified (Heller *et al.,* 1980). It may also be advisable at some levels to conduct and evaluate projects that focus on relatively specific risk factors. For example, a myriad of factors are making contemporary family life highly stressful. One of these factors is the possible mismatch between traditional structures of work, particularly its temporal aspects and changing family patterns. An assessment of problems encountered by single-parent and dual-earner families with young children suggests that more flexible work hours might alleviate some specific, predictable problems. Two field studies indicate that flexitime did, indeed, help with the specified problems, thus providing an example of more proactive, preventive intervention fulfilling at least proximal objectives. Note, however, that while this intervention was specific, it was not assumed that there was some one-to-one correspondence between work patterns and identifiable family pathology.

The objectives of this chapter are to present detailed examples of more proactive, preventive programs with children and families at the micro- and macrolevels. These are only examples of potential programs and are not presented as "the solutions" to a range of problems faced by children and families in contemporary society. Consistent with what we feel is a promotional approach, and not a precipitative campaign, is the commitment to careful program evaluation. Therefore, the next section will not only detail skills/problem-solving programs with children, but also review the methodological problems involved in evaluating these programs. The third section will explicate the methodology and outcomes of flexitime and family life studies. The final section will overview the structure and outcome measures involved in a potential multifaceted community program to help single parents. In that section, we first review political, social, and economic issues pertinent to efforts at the macrolevel, issues usually considered beyond the purview of mental health professionals. Within the present framework, however, these issues are seen as necessary variables to consider in assessing and intervening with family and childhood problems.

Background and Rationale

Despite the discussion above, couched in societal and community terms, it is important to maintain the idea that prevention is not necessarily equivalent to societal overhaul. As Bower (1963) noted, intervention not geared toward dissolution of prejudice, injustice, poverty, and economic discrimination can still be seen as consequential. Although community and organizational approaches to prevention hold great promise as viable primary prevention strategies, small group work has also been shown to be effective within a preventive framework (Shure & Spivack, 1979).

While it is obvious that the most effective approach will include families, schools, and recreational and organizational institutions, one setting in which much effort has already been fruitfully expended is the school system. There are a host of advantages in selecting this particular setting. In addition to the fact that it is the first social institution to service children in a given community, it necessarily influences development of a child in areas of interpersonal relationships with peers and adults, attitudes toward themselves and others, and self-perceived competence (Biber, 1961; Minuchin, Biber, Shapiro, & Zimiles, 1969). Finally, assuming implementation of a successful preventive strategy, the long-term impact implies beneficial effects for generations of children.

In contrast to other major social institutions to which the child is exposed, the family has distinct disadvantages in terms of primary prevention. Direct intervention in home settings is replete with logistical and technical problems. For example, access to the family poses problems because of the simple variable of geographic separation. These are obvious problems that are inherent in attempting intervention with hundreds of families in a small group format.

Granted that the school provides an overwhelmingly advantageous setting for primary prevention strategies, albeit not without a host of problems in its own right (Cowen, Trost, Lorian, Derr, Izzo, & Isaacson, 1975; Shure & Spivack, 1979), at least several questions present themselves as potential obstacles to implementation of effective primary prevention strategies: (1) What data exist linking poor adjustment early in life to later maladjustment? (2) What specific target areas (e.g., self-esteem, social skills) provide the most potential for fostering adjustment? (3) What type of intervention strategies are most effective? (4) Are there particular ages or grades to which these strategies should be addressed?

Certainly, the effort expended in developing and implementing primary prevention strategies would be futile if data relating problems in childhood to later adult dysfunction were nonexistent. A number of investigators have indicated that this relationship does, indeed, exist (Clarfield, 1974; Clarizio, 1969; Emmerich, 1966; Robbins, 1966). In addition, investigations undertaken within the confines of the school setting have shown the relationship of early maladjustment to academic and behavioral problems in later school years (Cowen, Pederson, Babigian, Izzo, & Trost, 1973; Spivack & Swift, 1977). Zax, Cowen, Rappaport, Beach, and Laird (1968) found that identification of potential for maladjustment can occur as early as the first grade, and that children so identified are performing less well than peer classmates as late as the seventh grade. Also, Chamberlin and Nader (1971) and Westman, Rice, and Bermann (1967), among others, found that nursery school behavior patterns were significantly related to later school functioning. In essence, then, data support the position that a relatonship exists between childhood maladjustment and later adjustment in life, in addition to the more circumscribed relationship between early and later school maladjustment. These data are extremely significant in terms of the rationale for implementation of preventive strategies. That is, it appears that children exhibiting poor adjustment are more likely to maintain such poor adjustment over time, but not to "outgrow" it. Hence, considerable effort needed for devising preventive strategies seems justified.

The question of what variables in the child's life predispose him/her to early school maladjustment and, consequently, what variables require most attention from primary prevention interventionists, is a crucial one. In selecting target areas, it is essential to delineate what Cowen (1977) has termed "pivotal competencies," or those competencies relating most directly to good adjustment. Several studies point directly to skills in peer relations as being a sensitive indicant of adequate adult adjustment (Kohlberg, Lacrosse, & Ricks, 1972; Roff, 1961; Spivack & Swift, 1977; Yule, 1977). For instance, Westman *et al.* (1967) found that observations based on the child's interpersonal relations bore more predictive significance than other indices in terms of future school adjustment. In addition, Cowen *et al.* (1973) found that children with poor social skills who were unpopular with peers were identified on a more frequent basis by mental health professionals and teachers as "high-risk." Finally, poor peer popularity has been related to increased rates of juvenile delinquency (Roff, Sells, & Golden, 1973) and early school dropout (Ullman, 1956).

In sum, peer relationships appear as a prominent variable (pivotal competency) when examining the longitudinal data for children's adjustment and later psychopathology. It seems warranted, then, to devise primary prevention strategies emphasizing development of those skills related to peer relationships and interpersonal functioning. Further, primary prevention programs devised for nursery, kindergarten, and early elementary school intervention seem reasonable, based on the ability to predict future maladjustment from data collected at these early age levels (Spivack & Swift, 1977; Stennett, 1965). However, the issue is not clear cut. It is essential, as Biber (1961) noted, that the intervention be calibrated to the developmental level of the target population. Hence, the question may not be what is the specific age from which predictions regarding adjustment or maladjustment can be made, rather, what are the primary prevention strategies available to use with various age populations?

Another question related to the issue of promoting primary prevention in the school setting deals with the type of intervention strategy chosen. Lemle (1976) describes three approaches to primary prevention in the schools: (1) specific curriculum additions; (2) modified environments; and (3) teacher training. The latter approach sorely lacks data, despite a certain intuitive appeal. Few examinations of the effects of teacher training on children have been reported. Studies in this area have emphasized training classroom teachers to increase self-rewarding behaviors of pupils (Felker, Stensyck, & Kay, 1973) or to teach children to take more responsibility for their behavior (DeCharms, 1972). The results have not been encouraging. In terms of the modified environment approach, research has focused principally on the open classroom environment. This has been and still is a hotly debated issue, but it suffices to say that no clear support exists for open environment classrooms (Lemle, 1976). However, it should be noted that there are promising developments with this approach. For example, Stallings (1975) found relationships between class atmosphere and children's persistence, cooperative behavior, and curiosity. In addition, Quilitch and Risley (1973) found that when social toys were present (toys designed for use by more than one youngster at a time), seven-year-olds engaged in social play 85% of the time, as opposed to 10% of the time when isolate toys (designed for use by one youngster at a time) were used. These examples certainly hold promise in light of their effect on peer relationships, but appear as relatively isolated examples of the effective use of modified environments in primary prevention research (see also, Winett, Battersby, & Edwards, 1975).

While teacher training and modified environment approaches may well prove beneficial with further investigation, the specific curriculum additions approach has been more frequently used and more stringently investigated in primary prevention efforts (Allen, Chinsky, Larcen, Lochman, & Selinger, 1976; Ojemann, 1960; Shure & Spivack, 1979; Stone, Hinds, & Schmidt, 1975). Table 1 briefly reviews the history of these programs described by Cowen (1977) as "competence building" (p. 6) strategies. Essentially, this process involves building resources and teaching specific skills needed to resolve personal problems. As Jason (1980) notes, the emphasis is on promoting adaptivity and strengthening competencies in affective (e.g., self-esteem), cognitive (e.g., problem-solving skills), and behavioral (e.g., social skills training) modalities.

Current Approaches

Based on data presently supporting the curriculum addition approach and the view of several investigators that it does, indeed, hold the most promise for primary prevention (Allen *et al.* 1976; Levine & Graziano, 1972), a closer examination of curriculum additions approaches seems warranted. The following questions may serve to add specificity to this examination: (1) What advances have occurred since inception of this approach into the school system, (2) What specific programs have been used, and what strategies have been most effective? (3) Do methodological weaknesses prevent an enthusiastic embrace of these approaches as clearly effective ones? (4) How have these approaches been evaluated, and do the evaluations denote changes significant enough to warrant continued use of such interventions? (5) What might the future hold with respect to implementation of these strategies in the school setting?

While results with this approach are not conclusive, the curriculum addition approach has progressed methodologically and increased in efficacy since Ojemann's initial efforts in the early 1960s (Ojemann, 1960; Ojemann & Snider, 1964). Ojemann's strategy entailed training in causal thinking (the ability to consider underlying motivations for behavior). The rationale for his strategy was that a causal understanding of human behavior (i.e., reactions that are sensitive to probable antecedent factors producing the behavior) enables one to cope more effectively with daily problems in living. Despite results purporting to show greater security, less anxiety, and greater acceptance of others as a result of training in causal thinking (Griggs & Bonney, 1970; Muus, 1960), methodological weaknesses in these studies limit their applicability.

In general, these studies suffered from suspect dependent measures. For example, Ojemann and Snider (1964) examined causal thinking with fourth- and fifth-grade children but included a poorly operationalized behavior checklist, which possessed low interobserver reliability (.69 and .67). Further, teachers implementing the program underwent 20 hours of group therapy during the summer preceding intervention. Hence, it is conceivable that group therapy experienced by the teachers made their interaction with students much more positive irrespective of the curriculum additions. In addition to the equivocal results obtained in this study (two of four fourth-grade experimental groups and three of four fifth-grade groups were significantly more causal posttreatment), the investigation failed to provide measures of maintenance.

Table 1. Summary Table of School Primary Prevention Approaches

Reference	Subjects $(n)_1$ and grade	Length and type of treatment	Dependent measures	Outcome	Follow-up
Ojemann (1960)	35, 4th grade 35, 5th grade 35, 6th grade	Training in causal thinking; one academic year	1. Problem situation test 2. Causal test (written measure)	Experimental group significantly more causal than control	None
Ojemann & Snider (1964)	206, 4th grade 212, 5th grade	Training in causal thinking; one academic year	1. Problem situation test 2. Observational report, items related to causal behavior	4th grade = 2 of 4 experimental classes significantly more causal than controls 5th grade = 3 of 4 experimental classes significantly more causal than controls	None
Stone, Hinds, & Schmidt (1965)	48, 3rd grade 48, 4th grade 48, 5th grade	Problem-solving skills (information seeking, generation of alternatives, setting goals); 1 week	1. Pre-post test measures of frequency of facts, choices, and solutions to problem situations (oral report)	3rd grade = Facts: significant difference in favor of experimental group; no difference on measures of choices and solutions between control and experimental groups 4th grade = Facts, choices, and solutions: significantly different in favor of experimental group	None
Allen, Chinsky, Larcen, Lochman, & Selinger (1976)	150, 3rd and 4th grades; 24 biweekly 30-minute lessons for 18 weeks	Social problem-solving training	1. Structured Real-life Problem situation 2. Problem Solving Measure (PSM) 3. In-class Assessment Measure (ICM), written quizzes testing learning of problem-solving components	1. Results inconclusive; favor experimental group 2. Significant difference favoring experimental group on PSM 3. No statistical interpretation provided for ICM	None
Shure & Spivack (1979)	131, nursery and kindergarten; daily 20-minute lessons for 3 months	Interpersonal cognitive problem-solving training (alternative solutions, consequential thinking)	1. Preschool Interpersonal Problem Solving Test (oral report measure of alternative solution thinking) 2. What Happens Next Game (oral report measure of consequential thinking) 3. Hahnemann Preschool Behavior Rating Scale	Significant difference favoring experimental groups on all measures	1 year
Shure & Spivack (1980)	219, nursery school	Interpersonal cognitive problem-solving training	Same as 1, 2, 3 above in addition to causal test	Significant difference favoring experimental groups on all measures	1 year

Stone, Hinds, and Schmidt (1975) also developed a prevention program that involved teaching problem-solving behavior using modeling and feedback through videotape procedures with third to fifth graders. Unfortunately, treatment effects were assessed using paper-and-pencil measures only, and the intervention itself was too short-lived to produce significant changes between control and experimental groups (total instructional and testing duration totalled 7 weeks), or at a minimum to adequately assess intervention. However, the study did attempt to operationalize a much discussed (problem-solving) intervention strategy by specifying both criterion variables and interventions used to effect change within a school setting.

Other programs designed to intervene in the areas of problem-solving thinking have been developed more recently (Allen *et al.,* 1976; Shure & Spivack, 1974; Shure & Spivack, 1980). Allen *et al.* (1976), working with third, fourth, and fifth graders, used classroom exercise, small group activities, and modeling videotapes. The intervention was carried out by teachers in a series of 24 biweekly, 30-minute lessons for 12 weeks. Six training units were incorporated into the program, including: (1) Problem Solving Orientation; (2) Problem Identification; (3) Generation of Alternatives; (4) Consideration of Consequences; (5) Elaboration of Solutions; and (6) Integration of Problem Solving Behavior. Results were disappointing in terms of overt behavioral adjustment, although trained children developed more positive expectancies regarding school experience and improved significantly in generating alternative solutions to problems in social situations. A positive addition to the evaluative measures involved a simulated behavior test. While the test was perhaps inappropriate (a child–adult problem was selected, as opposed to a child–child conflict), this type of test, properly designed and implemented, is certainly a more rigorous evaluation measure than those used in prior research (Ojemann, 1960; Roen, 1967).

Although programs such as the above and others (Gesten, Apadaca, Rains, Weissberg, & Cowen, 1979; McClure, Chinsky, & Larcen, 1978) show promise in developing skills tied intricately to later school and adult adjustment, the most rigorously evaluated program to date involves the interpersonal problem-solving skills approach of Shure and Spivack (1979), and Spivack, Platt, and Shure (1976). This approach has been implemented with latency-aged youngsters (Shure & Spivack, 1972), with adolescents (Platt, Spivack, Altmann, & Altmann, 1974) and with adults (Platt & Spivack, 1972). However, the research perhaps most relevant to the present discussion is the training of problem-solving skills with preschool and kindergarten children in a school setting (Shure & Spivack, 1979). The philosophy of this interpersonal cognitive problem-solving (ICPS) approach involves the belief that even very young children are able to think for themselves and solve everyday problems that arise, and that those children who can do this are more likely to be adjusted than those who cannot. In a series of seven studies (Spivack *et al.,* 1976), it was found that, independent of IQ or verbal skills, overly impatient children or children who displayed excessive control of behavior as measured by the Devereux Child Behavior Rating Scale (Spivack & Spotts, 1966) were particularly more deficient than their better adjusted peers in two skills: (1) ability to generate alternative solutions to an interpersonal problem; and (2) consequential thinking, or ability to see what might happen next in an interpersonal situation, as early as the age of 4.

Based on these findings, a logical next step involved formal training of these skills in a structured format with preschool children. As a general overview, the format of the program consists of daily 20-minute lessons in game form over a period of approximately 3 months. The early games involve simple word concepts designed for later association in problem-solving (e.g., meanings of words such as "not," "or," "different"). Following these initial training sessions, children are taught identification of, and sensitivity to, people's feelings, along with how their behavior affects others. After mastery of these skills, pictures and puppets depicting interpersonal situations are used as a means of helping children solve interpersonal problems. At this point, all solutions are accepted equally, while in later games the children decide for themselves whether an idea is a good one. Solutions are never reinforced for being good, rather for being different. In addition to the 20-minute formal sessions, the problem-solving approach is carried over during the day when real problems arise. That is, participants in the situation are stopped, questioned as to alternative solutions and possible consequences, and ultimately role-play the selected solution. In essence, then, children are taught *how,* not *what,* to think.

A particularly exciting investigation by these authors (Shure & Spivack, 1979) was implemented to answer several questions about the ICPS approach as a primary prevention strategy. This study was conducted over a two-year period and attempted to determine: (1) if ICPS training has holding power (i.e., do those trained in nursery school retain benefits without further intervention); (2) whether a program designed to teach ICPS skills affect these skills in the kindergarten years, as found to be the case in the nursery years (Spivack & Shure, 1974); and finally (3) if 2 years of training were better than 1 year, and, if so, which years were more potent. There were 134 children in the project, with 39 children (15 boys, 24 girls) trained in both nursery and kindergarten years. Thirty children (12 boys, 18 girls) were trained during the nursery school years, but in kindergarten, served as controls. Thirty other children (12 boys, 18 girls) were trained in kindergarten, but not in the nursery year. Finally, 35 children (15 boys, 20 girls) served as controls in both years. All children were black and attended inner-city day-care centers and kindergartens in Philadelphia. Pre–post measurement of skills included alternative solution thinking and consequential thinking, the first skills assessed by the *Preschool Interpersonal Problem Solving (PIPS) Test* (Spivack & Shure, 1974). This instrument involved eliciting from the child as many solutions as possible regarding two types of interpersonal problems; peer related and authority (mother) related. A child's score consisted of the total number of different relevant solutions given to both types of problems. Also, the *What Happens Next Game* (WHNG) was used to evaluate changes in consequential thinking. The format of this test also involved eliciting as many different consequences as possible to two types of interpersonal situations (grabbing toy from child, taking something from adult without asking). The score consisted of the total number of relevant consequences given to both types of interpersonal acts.

In addition, the *Hahnemann Preschool Behavior Rating Scale* was used by teachers to rate each child at the same times the testers administered the ICPS tests. This scale consisted of seven items, defining three behavioral factors (impatience, emotionality, dominance-aggression).

Results, based on all dependent measures (PIPS, WHNG, Hahnemann Rating Scale) indicated that a program to teach ICPS skills was as beneficial with 1 year of training as with two. In addition, nursery intervention was optimal since a greater total percentage of children trained at that point in time began kindergarten at a more positive behavioral level. However, if children were not trained in nursery school, results indicated behavioral adjustment could be affected via kindergarten training.

Despite these promising findings, several methodological difficulties were present. The chief weakness involved the lack of an adequate treatment control group. More specifically, could a less formal "group therapy" approach have resulted in the same changes? Perhaps merely talking about problem situations promoted behavioral adjustment, as opposed to the specificities involved in the alternative solutions and consequential thinking training. In addition, the students were tested on what was taught, conceivably an instance of "teaching the test." The "Structured Real Life Problem Situation" used by Allen *et al.* (1976) would have, in addition to the PIPS testing, been somewhat more convincing evidence of treatment efficacy. Finally, direct behavioral observations with regard to changes in overt social behavior of treated versus control children would have bolstered confidence in results of the study.

Despite the above weaknesses, methodological strengths in these studies exceed those of previous primary prevention attempts. For example, sex of the tester was controlled. That is, male and female testers, unaware of experimental group placement, administered the tests to equal numbers of boys and girls. Interrater reliability, ranging from .92 (irrelevancies in the WHNG) to .99 (repetitions and relevant solutions in the PIPS), was also high in their study. In addition, the authors report controlling for "halo effect" by instructing teachers to rate additional behaviors of the scale, unrelated to ICPS skills. If the "halo effect" were present, these nonrelated behavior categories would also change. Unfortunately, the authors did not report information on the results of this controlling factor. However, it should be noted that in a subsequent study (Shure & Spivack, 1980) these controls were established, and no "halo effect" was found. Thus, teachers apparently were not influenced by student participation in training sessions when making behavioral ratings.

Overall, the Shure and Spivack research indicates that training young children in problem-solving skills (more specifically, alternative solution and consequential thinking) can lead to increased ability to solve interpersonal problem situations as measured by the PIPS and WHNG tests. In addition, teachers see trained children as more adjusted on scales relating to emotionality, dominance-aggression, and impatience, as early as nursery school and kindergarten years. Granted that methodological shortcomings remain, and granted that no claim can be made that this approach is the *only* way to improve behavior, ICPS training is one means of primary prevention that has shown potential in improving and *maintaining* behavioral adjustment and problem-solving skills.

In summary, several key advances have been made since Ojemann's (1960) pioneering efforts. More precise specification of objectives and more direct measures of behavioral adjustment are evident in recent investigations (Allen *et al.,* 1976; Gesten *et al.,* 1979; Spivack & Shure, 1979). Of critical importance are the findings linking problem-solving skills as presented by the ICPS model (Spivack & Shure, 1974) with behavioral adjustment, a link necessary to provide a rationale for future primary prevention efforts. Even more exciting is the longitudinal evidence, indicating 2 year's holding power for the effects of problem-solving training (Shure & Spivack, 1979, 1980). This is especially encouraging, considering that new teachers were unaware of the children's prior training, and the generalization of effect from day-care nursery settings to kindergarten to first grade (i.e., three relatively dissimilar settings). Obviously, much longer term follow-ups on distal objectives are needed if such intervention is to be promoted as a truly preventive one.

Projects presented by Spivack and Shure over the past half dozen years represent one of the major school-based efforts in the primary prevention field. Other approaches (Allen *et al.,* 1976; Gesten *et al.,* 1979) also hold promise, but as yet lack sufficient data to match the ICPS approach as presented by Spivack and Shure. This is not meant to assert, however, that the potential of this approach has been exhausted. As noted above, methodological shortcomings exist, and evaluative measures can certainly be strengthened. In addition to comments made earlier regarding evaluation, use of such measures as the Health Resources Inventory (Gesten, 1976) could improve the quality of evaluation. This instrument represents a teacher measure of primary grade children's competency-related behavior. The HRI has not only discriminated between normal and disturbed children, but has sensitively differentiated competence levels within a normative sample. This instrument could prove extremely useful in future primary prevention interventions.

There is little doubt that these investigations have contributed to changing the nature of primary prevention programs from a nebulous, speculative area to a field well grounded in empirical data, with programs delineating the step-by-step processes needed to teach skills related to future adjustment. Finally, by increasing methodological rigor, implementing evaluative strategies beyond the precision afforded by behavioral checklists, and continuing to assess the extent to which changes in problem solving/social skills impact on future adjustment, primary prevention may well be evolving out of the infancy stage. At least with respect to primary prevention via small group strategies, the strides of investigators may already exceed the "baby steps" gait noted by Cowen (1977) when referring to progress in the field of primary prevention.

Alternative Work Patterns and Family Life—An Organizational Change Strategy

Overview of the Problem

The project described in this section was based, in part, on the ecological model delineated by Bronfenbrenner (1977, 1979), which called for investigations of the influence of more immediate settings (e.g., schools, child care, and work settings) and macrostructures on child development and family life. Of particular interest are studies that experimentally (or quasiexperimentally) alter settings or structures that are stress producing to assess the potential *benefits* and *costs* to children and families of such interventions. Certainly, one example of a pervasive and influential system is the structure of work in our society (Robinson, 1977). Analyses have indicated that the consistent temporal parameters (e.g., 8:30 A.M. to 4:30 P.M.) of work form rather reliable constraints and boundaries in our lives, so that the status of full-time working or nonworking outside of home is an excellent predictor of a person's everyday behavior and setting schedule (Robinson, 1977). For example, it is a relatively straightforward prediction that between 7:30–8:30 A.M. and 5–6 P.M. most working people are commuting. The schedule created by typical working hours, however, may be more or less functional for certain types of people. The dual-earner couple and/or the single-parent with young children may find that the typical work schedule is a poor match for their child care and home responsibilities (Hunt & Hunt, 1977). Thus, it may be stressful and possibly detrimental to family life and child development.

It has been proposed that flexible work hours ("flexitime"), a structure change in work organizations, may benefit families with young children. Under flexitime, people are given some degree of freedom regarding their arrival and departure time from work, although they generally have to be at work during some "core hours" during the day. In some flexitime systems, the hours of work can be varied each day as long as a designated amount is accrued during specified periods (Nollen, 1979).

Flexitime has been particularly proposed as a means to help the growing number of dual-earner and single-parent families with young children (Bronfenbrenner, 1979). The traditional male-breadwinner family is now a statistical minority (about 16% of married couples, 27% of all families). Of married women, 59% with school-aged children and 43% with preschoolers are employed (Johnson, 1980). These figures can be contrasted to only 13% of mothers with preschoolers working outside the home in 1948 (National Academy of Science, 1976), thus indicating a marked shift in work-family patterns (Keniston, 1977).

Despite these changes in work-family patterns, significant systems, such as schools and work settings, often have hours of operation that apparently assume that a caregiver is available (e.g., in the afternoon at specific times). More likely, many school and work settings simply do not consider child care responsibilities in formulating work schedules or policies (Bronfenbrenner, 1979).

Flexible work schedules may help working parents with young children by: (1) allowing for more child care coverage (less reliance on outside help) if parents work on somewhat overlapping schedules; (2) making it easier to arrange for a child to be picked up by a parent from a child care setting; (3) being able to arrive home about when the child returns from school; and (4) generally allowing working parents to more optimally schedule and coordinate their work and family life (see Holmstrom, 1972; Hunt & Hunt, 1977). Thus, the primary benefits for instituting flexitime for families have been articulated in terms of proximal objectives, while effects of long-term stress presumably caused by problems in coordinating work and home responsibiliies have been less clear.

Flexitime seems particularly promising as a family-oriented intervention for a number of other reasons. (1) If beneficial effects could be shown, then flexitime would be the type of structural change that could be instituted on a wide-scale with minimal costs in many work settings (Nollen, 1979). Thus, flexitime has many of the qualities of a proactive, preventive organizational change strategy (Catalano & Dooley, 1980). (2) Studies investigating the effects of flexitime on the work setting and other systems already suggest some positive outcomes. Indeed, the major rationale for flexitime is to provide workers with more control of their schedules in order to decrease tardiness, absences, and unnecessary leave. Hence, it should increase morale and productivity. (3) Flexitime (and staggered work hours) has been seen as an important adjunct to transportation management systems because if hours varied when people commuted to and from work, then transportation modalities may be less crowded and more efficient. Reduction of rush hour peaks may lead to energy savings and improved air quality.

Data from a number of case studies, in fact, indicate that such positive organizational and environmental outcomes generally do result from instituting flexitime (Nollen, 1979). These findings suggest that flexitime may be a relatively unique social innovation where benefits accrue *across* different systems.

However, as we have indicated in the introduction, it appears that various social innovations in the past deemed as preventive often suffered for a lack of specificity of objectives (either proximal or distal) and evaluation criteria. In addition, many programs were precipitously oversold regarding their capacity for prevention (Heller *et al.,* 1980). This has unfortunately been the case with flexitime, where insufficient assessments of benefits and costs have been coupled with extravagant claims, with little or no data to substantiate those claims (Winett & Neale, 1980a,b).

An assessment of family problems, in part attributable to the structure of work, indicates some areas where flexitime and other alternative work patterns (career-oriented, part-time work; flexiplace) could be beneficial. Of course, this does not imply that either the structure of work or alternative work patterns are the entire solution. Two major problems for working parents, as suggested above, are situational and time related (i.e., the ability to be with their children at certain places and the lack of time for particular activities). These

Table 2. Assessment of Antecedents and Consequences of Some Family Problems and Potential Policy Approaches

Antecedents (settings, systems, norms)	Problems (behavior, situations)	Consequences (outcomes)	Approaches (politics)
1. Inflation: High cost of housing; high expectations; move to sexual equality	1. Need for high income to live, and increase in dual-earner families as response to inflation and changing norms	1. Dual-earner families and problems to be noted	1. Curb inflation; revise mortgage policies, and alternative work patterns to be noted
2.	2. Family-related	2.	2.
A. Schedule of work; total hours	A. Getting child off to school/day-care[a]	A. Rushed and stressed; poor breakfast, etc.	A. Flexitime; part-time work; flexiplace
B. Schedule of work; total hours	B. Pick-up from school/day-care;[a] available after school	B. "Latch key syndrome"	B. Expand hours of school, day-care operation; flexitime; part-time work; flexiplace
C. Total hours, and to some extent schedule of work, lack of sharing of responsibilities between husband and wife	C. Chores,[a] child care responsibilities	C. Done at expense of other activities; done, perhaps inadequately	C. Reduced hours of work (part-time); flexitime, policies to emphasize parenting, not just women issues
	D. Family time;[a]dinner time;[a] evenings[a]	D. Stressful and limited lead to family problems?	D. Reduced hours of work (part-time); flexitime
E. Total hours, schedule of work	E. Personal time; exercise,[a] education[a] hobbies,[a] relaxation[a]	E. Stress, limited time; engaged in at expense of other activities; poorer health, particularly long-term; less advancement if no time for continuing education	E. More innovative flexitime; reduce number of hours (part-time); continuing education and exercise facilities at the worksite; flexiplace
3. Number of hours, labor market, values endorsing overwork	3. Stress on the job, high hours beyond full-time requirements	3. Less time for any of the above activities; stress; and family problems?	3. Career-oriented, part-time work with full benefits
4. Distance from work; commuting modality; number of days worked per week	4. Commuting[a]	4. From 2 to 3 hours per day involved and often wasted; major source of energy expenditure for the country	4. Flexitime to promote off-peak travel; part-time fewer days per week; work home (flexiplace); mix business and residential in suburbs and exurbs

[a] Possibly alleviated by flexitime.

include being with spouse and children, preparing dinner, doing other chores, engaging in recreation, and so on. As we will see later, the time dimension is of particular relevance.

Table 2 presents some of the possible antecedents of family problems as related to work, some of their consequences, and some possible policy approaches. Point one on the table, noting prevailing economic and consequent social conditions, is an important reminder that proposed changes in work or family problems have antecedents at the macrolevel. Interventions at that level may, in fact, be more appropriate (Catalono & Dooley, 1980). In addition, it is also clear from the assessment that problems noted are also linked to policies in other systems (e.g., hours of operation of schools or child care facilities, availability of education and recreational facilities, commuting patterns, and of course the continued inequities at home and work between men and women).

Nevertheless, it appears that certain family problems could be alleviated by flexitime. Note, however, that these problems are indicated in terms of parental behaviors and perceptions, and not in terms of the eventual target, aspects of child development. Thus, the project to be reported represents only a first phase in ascertaining benefits of flexitime on the most immediate proximal family indicators.

Flexitime Studies

In order to assess the effects of flexitime on families with young children, two longitudinal, quasiexperimental studies with about 100 volunteer workers from two large federal agencies in Washington, D.C., were conducted. Workers were either males from single-earner families, or males and females from dual-earner or single-parent families. Workers were primarily involved in administrative functions, represented a cross-section of job levels, had a mean age of 32 years, and were raising a mean of 1.7 children (whose mean age was 5.7 years).

In both studies, there were baseline periods (5–9 weeks) during which regular hours were in operation. Flexitime, then, was instituted across-the-board, or across departments within a short period of time. About half the workers opted to remain on their original hours of work, while the other half of the workers (with highly similar demographic characteristics) decided to adopt a minimal flexitime system that allowed them to alter their time of arrival and departure (earlier or later by an hour). During the flexitime period, workers were studied for periods of 14–28 weeks (see Winett & Neale, 1980b; Winett & Neale, 1981; and Winett, Neale, & Williams, 1982).

While a number of measures were used to assess impact of the flexitime system on family life, transportation, and the work setting, the two main measures were a time-activity log used before in cross-sectional research (Robinson, 1977) and a repeatedly administered 15-item survey. On this survey, participants rated the ease or difficulty on a seven-point scale in coordinating a number of aspects of work and family life (e.g., "The time I leave work makes it ____ to spend afternoon time with my child"—all closely tied to problems noted in Table 2).

The time-activity log completed twice during the work week involved an hour-by-hour delineation on a standard form of a participant's activities, settings, persons interacted with, secondary activities (eating dinner, but watching TV), and a rating of enjoyment on a five-point scale of each activity. Participants received training and feedback on form completion, and forms were hand delivered and hand retrieved. As described in detail elsewhere (Winett

& Neale, 1981; Winett, Neale, & Williams, 1979), these procedures resulted in about 93% of forms being completed and about 80% agreement between participant log entries and four *independent* corroboration sources. Log data were systematically reduced by coders, trained to 90% intercoder agreement criteria (see Winett & Neale, 1981), to nine main categories (A.M. and P.M.; time alone; with spouse; with children; with spouse and children; and at work) and 37 subcategories (e.g., time at dinner, exercise, TV). Thus, log data provided a mechanism to examine in detail how time was allocated to different activities, settings, and people, and how these time allocations were affected by flexitime. In addition, by performing two studies at different times with two agencies, we were able to assess the generality of our findings.

Results of Flexitime

The results were both positive and consistent at the two agencies, despite implementation of only a minimal flexitime system. Surprisingly, *all* workers who changed their schedule opted for an earlier schedule. These workers generally arose earlier in the morning (actually, some reduced their sleep time), minimally reduced family interaction time in the early morning, decreased commuting time, worked the same number of hours as before, but now arrived home earlier and spent about an hour more with their family in the late afternoon and evening.

Table 3 presents time outcomes for Agency Two for an early Spring baseline period and late Spring, Summer, and Fall flexitime periods for participants who changed their hours of work and participants who did not change their hours of work. Somewhat larger effects on overall or composite family time were recorded for Agency One, which had a flexitime program that permitted a larger change in work hours than at Agency Two.

Table 3. Mean Group Times for the Change and No-Change Groups during the Baseline and Flexitime Phases in Agency Two

	Change group (n = 24)				No-change group (n = 26)			
		Flexitime				Flexitime		
Variable	Baseline	Spring	Summer	Fall	Baseline	Spring	Summer	Fall
Time (hours) to:								
Arise	5.92	5.74[b]	5.74[b]	5.67[a]	6.09	6.08	6.18	6.16
Sleep	10.97	10.74	10.90	10.85	10.86	10.92	10.96	11.05
Start work	8.23	7.62[b]	7.63[b]	7.68[a]	8.13	8.01	8.05	8.09
End work	4.75	4.16[b]	4.16[b]	4.21[b]	4.85	4.84	4.81	4.84
Time (minutes) with:								
Children	76	89[a]	91[a]	90[a]	79	77	67[a]	90[a]
Spouse	72	64	58	62	66	71	81	75
Spouse and children	103	134[b]	147[b]	130[b]	96	90	110[a]	75[a]
Overall family	251	287[b]	296[b]	282[b]	241	238	259[a]	240
Commute home	63	60[a]	57[a]	55[a]	54	55	55	57

[a]Change in time by one-tailed t-test at $p < .05$.
[b]Change in time by one-tailed t-test at $p < .01$.

Figure 1 shows the relative consistency of the time change, by documenting time allocation data for the change and no-change groups for composite family time across 75 log recording days at Agency Two.

More importantly, rather than just a shift in schedule, flexitime apparently made some "quality of life" differences for participants in the studies. For example, throughout the baseline and flexitime phases of the studies, P.M. time was always rated as "more enjoyable" (on the logs) than A.M. time. Table 4 also shows results of ratings by the change and no-change groups at Agency Two for baseline and flexitime periods for items on the survey. Results at Agency One were virtually identical to those at Agency Two. Note that all changes were in the predicted direction and consistent with the assessment noted in Table 2. For example, flexitime was perceived as providing more time to spend with children in the afternoon, more time to spend with the spouse and children in the evening, and more time for friends, recreation, hobbies, chores, or educational pursuits. It was also perceived as resulting in more relaxed evenings and "easier" dinner time. Note also that items with activities (picking up a child from school or child care setting, commuting) beyond the purview of the limited flexitime program showed no change.

Constraints and Important Considerations in Planning Work and Family Programs

Despite positive findings, analyses of other data in the project and finer-grain analyses of log data indicated that more extensive changes in other policies and systems are needed if some of the problems of families are to be addressed. These latter findings are also congruent with the assessment in Table 2.

For example, even when women in the second study were working full-time outside

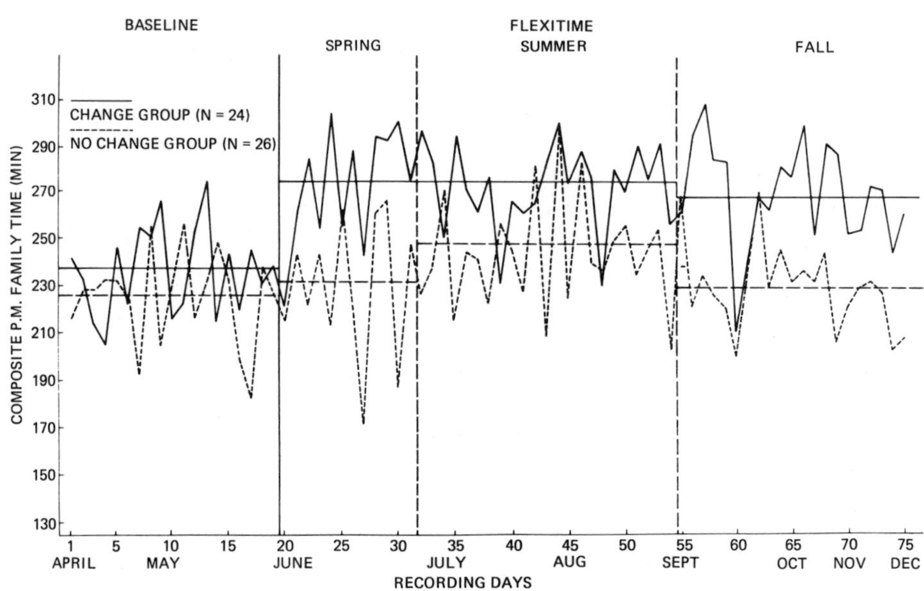

Figure 1. Composite family time for the change and no-change groups by recording day and phase of the study.

Table 4. Mean Group Score from the Work–Nonwork Survey across the Four Periods of Study Two

	Change group				No-change group			
	Pre	Spring	Summer	Fall	Pre	Spring	Summer	Fall
1. The time I start to work makes getting my child (children) to school or a child care setting ______.	4.1	4.0	4.0	4.0	4.0	3.9	3.9	4.0
2. If my child (children) should become ill during the day, my work situation makes it ______ to be sure the child is receiving care.	4.5	4.0	4.0	4.0	5.0	4.5	4.5	4.7
3. The time I *leave* work makes it ______ to spend afternoon time with my child.	5.8	3.4[b]	3.4[b]	4.2[a]	5.6	4.6	4.6	4.9
4. Because of my work hours, breakfast time with my child (children) is ______.	5.5	5.7	5.7	5.5	5.6	5.1	5.0	5.3
5. My work hours make picking up my child (children) after school or from a child care setting ______.	4.6	4.3	4.4	4.5	4.7	4.3	4.4	4.3
6. Because of my work hours, it is ______ to spend time with my spouse/partner during the work week.	4.7	3.2[b]	3.3[b]	3.5[a]	4.5	4.2	4.1	3.7
7. My work hours are such that it is ______ to see friends during the work week.	4.1	2.4[b]	2.9[a]	2.8[a]	3.9	3.3	3.2	3.3
8. My work hours are such that it is ______ to share lunchtime or a coffee break with friends at work.	3.9	3.8	3.7	3.5	4.2	3.6	3.9	4.0
9. Because of my work hours, commuting to and from work is ______.	4.5	3.6	3.5	3.5	4.1	3.7	3.6	3.5
10. The hours I work make having dinner with my spouse/partner and/or child (children) ______ during the work week.	3.6	2.6[a]	2.7[a]	2.7[a]	3.6	3.3	3.2	3.2
11. The hours I work make spending time in the evening with my child (children) ______.	4.1	2.4[b]	2.9[a]	2.8[a]	3.9	3.3	3.2	3.3

Continued

Table 4. (continued)

	Change group				No-change group			
	Pre	Spring	Summer	Fall	Pre	Spring	Summer	Fall
12. The hours I work make pursuing additional educational (formal and informal) opportunities ______.	5.1	3.6[b]	4.1[a]	4.0[a]	5.2	4.6	4.7	4.7
13. The hours I work make engaging in recreational pursuits and hobbies ______.	5.0	3.2[b]	3.7[b]	3.6[b]	4.8	4.4	4.4	4.4
14. The hours I work make completion of shopping and household chores ______.	5.0	3.1[b]	3.7[b]	3.6[b]	4.7	4.4	4.3	4.1
15. The hours I work make it ______ to have relaxed evenings during the work week.	4.5	3.0[b]	3.3[a]	3.2[a]	4.3	3.9	3.7	3.8

Note: 1 = very easy; 7 = very difficult
[a]Decrease in perceived difficulty by one-tailed t-test at $p < .05$.
[b]Decrease in perceived difficulty by one-tailed t-test at $p < .01$.

the home, two-thirds to three-quarters of child care and home chores, tapped by 29 separate items on a home interview (see Winett, Fuchs, Moffatt, & Nerviano, 1977), were still performed by them in these families. Some husbands of working wives limited themselves to three behaviors: taking out the garbage, locking the doors at night, and putting gas in the car! This situation led to much reported stress by working wives when husbands participated minimally in child care and home chores (see Berk & Berk, 1979). However, in families where men and women more equally shared child care and chores, stress was still reported as high, a result consistent with prior findings (Hunt & Hunt, 1977). The common denominator in explaining these results may simply be a lack of available time for both working and home and child care responsibilities.

Log data and a finer-grain analysis of subcategory data shed light on some temporal constraints and stresses of urban life for working parents with young children. Table 5 shows a composite workday schedule based on mean allocated time for participants from Agency Two. Note that only about 2 or, at most, 3 hours in the evening can be considered "free time." The rest of the time is almost all committed to daily maintenance activities. Thus, it is not surprising that participants frequently reported on the survey instrument that they felt constantly "rushed."

Analysis of subcategory data also showed some other more specific areas of concern. While participants reported relatively little television watching during the week ($\bar{x}$= 49 minutes: see Mankiewicz & Swerdlow, 1978), and apparently made efforts to spend dinner time with their family ($\bar{x}$ = 42 minutes), exercise and sports time (categorized broadly, with no emphasis on aerobic benefit) was limited to a mean of 17 minutes for men and only 4 minutes for women. Such limited engagement in exercise is now felt to be contributory to coronary heart disease (Cooper, 1977).

The study participants and their derived composite schedule are reasonably representative of the time and schedule constraints faced by parents who must commute to work in large urban areas (Robinson, 1977). Examination of the table illustrates the ecology of urban family life by showing how everyday behavior is largely a function of work schedule and commuting patterns. What is also striking, and noted above, is that there apparently is little "free time," suggesting that finding time for recreation and exercise, or taking more time for child care and home chores, has a high personal cost. Time each day is finite; more time for one activity means less time available for other activities.

Returning to Table 2 makes us keenly aware that other types of alternative work patterns may be more beneficial to families than flexitime (although evaluations of much more extensive flexitime systems are needed) because they do not just reproportion time, but actually *create* more time for the working parent. In particular, perhaps career-oriented, part-time work (with prorated benefits), not at half-time, but at 75% time, would be appealing to working parents because it would mean reasonable income and retention of career status but with fewer hours of work. Flexiplace can also be seriously considered in the future, particularly as more jobs revolve around computer-based information processing (Toffler, 1980).

These innovations should be implemented at first on a small scale, not only to assess their benefits and costs to families, but consistent with an ecological perspective to assess their effects across other systems (labor market, business, other organizations, transportation, energy) before widespread implementation. In addition, although it is difficult (Cowen, 1978), more distal objectives of work and family programs should be delineated and evaluated, perhaps with some long-term, follow-up methods. For example, if alternative work patterns reduce stress and provide more time for activities outside work, do families using alternative work patterns show a lower incidence of marital or health problems and a wider and more active span of interests? Also, are children from such families less likely to have academic or social problems or to manifest other kinds of behavior problems as children and later as adolescents? Such long-term, comprehensive studies are examples of the type of investigations that need to be done in the 1980s if alternative work patterns are to be legitimately promoted as preventive social innovations.

Finally, what is obviously needed from the perspective of prevention is more direct focus on macrolevel policies and structures that influence interplays between the world of work and family life.

Table 5. Composite Schedule of Participants Based on Log Data

Activity	Place	Time (hours)
Get up and breakfast	Home	.5
Commute to work and preparation	Car, bus, train, etc.	1.25
Work	Work	8.5
Commute home and preparation	Car, bus, train, etc.	1.25
Dinner, etc.	Home	1.0
T.V.	Home	1.0
Chores, kids, shopping, hobbies, classes, extra work, miscellaneous	Home and other	2.0
Get ready for bed	Home	.5
Sleep	Home	8.0
		24.0

Overview of Issues and Barriers

The preceding sections demonstrate viability of primary prevention programs at the small group and organization level. These levels of intervention, while clearly beyond the more typical one-to-one focus of therapists, are still within the purview of contemporary psychological conceptualization and intervention. But only rarely have mental health professionals expanded their values and perspectives and changed strategies to focus on community and institutional factors contributing to family and childhood problems (Rappaport, 1977). Macrolevel interventions are seen by the authors as potentially and necessarily within the domain of mental health professionals in collaboration with other professionals. Therefore, prior to describing an example of a macrolevel program, a discussion of the issues and forces influencing such primary prevention efforts seems important.

Ascertaining the future of prevention, particularly large-scale primary efforts, is difficult. In 1978 the President's Commission on Mental Health recommended that a center focused on primary prevention be established within the National Institute of Mental Health (Task Panel on Prevention, 1978). The Center on Prevention was subsequently established in 1979 and charged with coordinating and developing prevention efforts within the Institute. *Healthy People,* The Surgeon General's Report on Health Promotion and Disease Prevention (U.S. Department of HEW, 1979), is firmly based in an ecological approach to health that calls for adopting environments to fit the needs of people in addition to fostering the competency of individuals in dealing with life stressors. Despite these promising developments, however, current federal funding priorities for prevention are modest in scope, reflecting a practical commitment to research at the microsystem. There are conceptual, social, political, and economic reasons for this limited focus.

The paucity of hard scientific data on precursors to emotional problems is often cited as the major impediment to mental health prevention programs. While present knowledge of environmental influences on mental health is clearly substantial and does indicate areas for change (Zaw & Specter, 1974), research on the effects of life stress on development of disease and dysfunction is preliminary. The need for assessments of the impact of stressors, situations, and environments on individuals creates a demand for a relevant taxonomy to organize and communicate this information. The taxonomy can then be used as a basis for field experiments within the ecological framework described by Bronfenbrenner (1977, 1979).

Social, political, and economic impediments to prevention include: lack of a public mandate for prevention (Bloom, 1979); public reaction to programs designed to improve environments and situations not obviously relevant to the general public; reliance on the belief that there is a simple cause-and-effect relationship in the development of illness; belief that prevention is cost-prohibitive; and reaction of the public to "mental health" programs. By their nature, ecologically conceived primary prevention programs require substantial public involvement and, frequently, generous political and financial support (as assuredly do treatment programs). Meeting these requirements in a democracy mandates a sophisticated public understanding of health maintenance and the occurrence of ill-health. Presently, the short-run focus of the American political system and the substantial investment of the medical complex, governments, and corporations in treatment rather than prevention of illness are all factors limiting support for primary prevention. Large-scale preventive efforts entailing change in educational, occupational, and other settings, and in established institutional practices, will require political force to overcome these substantial barriers.

Raising the "public consciousness" so that a more ecological model of mental health is understood and accepted is one step toward removing obstacles to prevention efforts. The mass media communication process has the potential for meeting this goal and creating a demand for preventive services. The example of a macrosystem prevention program at the end of this section utilizes social marketing principles and mass media to reach such information dissemination goals.

Another impediment to primary prevention is seen in the lack of public sentiment for programs designed to remedy situations that do not directly affect the policy-determining middle class. An aspect of this egocentric attitude is more virulent as a middle-class view of the poor, which Ryan (1971) has characterized as "blaming the victim" (i.e., viewing the problems of poverty, health, social, and emotional adjustment among the poor or minority groups as of their own making). Rather than considering the environmental influences of poverty, such as crowding, alienation, lack of resources, and so forth, the belief is maintained that these problems are inherent in the deficient character of poor and minority groups, which character, in turn, is passed on to their children through poor parental practices. This strategy diverts attention from the institutional causes of the problems and absolves the rest of society of responsibility. An example of how "victim blaming" has influenced some of our most costly and positively conceived social programs will demonstrate its pernicious nature.

The Head Start program, which by 1970 was providing preschool experiences to over three million children of low socioeconomic status, is a prime example of a well meant but inadequately conceived program (Rappaport, 1977). It was intended to prepare poor children for greater success in school, and to provide medical, dental, and day-care services. The latter, secondary focus of the program was a success in that Head Start children have had a lower incidence of anemia, better nutritional practices, and more immunizations than comparable children who are not in Head Start (Department of HEW, 1979). However, the educational outcome seemed to be limited to an initial improvement among first graders that was not maintained in later school years (Rappaport, 1977).

These results pointed to deficiencies in the philosophy and structure of most schools, rather than to defects in children, because the data indicate that poor children can, indeed, profit as do other children from a well designed curriculum. Problems encountered upon entry to public school, including teacher expectancy and denial of the validity of minority cultures, are now understood to contribute to the school failure and alienation of minority and poor children (Baratz & Baratz, 1970). Possibly the most significant contribution of the Head Start programs is the awareness it has generated in some quarters, awareness that focusing solely on the victim and providing a one-dimensional approach to change (i.e., compensatory education) will not mitigate institutional forces responsible for poverty and family and childhood problems (Rappaport, 1977).

Issues in Cost-Accounting

Another impediment to prevention involves the limited training of mental health professionals in assessing the economic feasibility of their programs. However, in this era of health cost-containment, when the expense of prevention is frequently viewed as prohibitive, accurate assessment of costs and benefits is necessary. Such analysis is further mandated by the prevalent belief that in a competitive economy, investments in health should be reciprocated by increased productivity on the part of the treated individual. Adherence to this criterion indicates that an implicit or, occasionally, an explicit cost-accounting process is employed to determine "return on investment" (Newberger, Newberger, & Richmond, 1976). Two general forms of cost analysis can foster the aims of primary prevention. Behavioral cost-accounting of the mental health outcomes of various policy decisions can be utilized to determine how different policies contribute to the incidence of mental health consequences. An outline of such an analysis presented in Table 6 indicates the community consequences of alternative corporate decisions to reduce or stop production or sell a company.

Utilizing a behavioral cost-accounting procedure requires that: (1) the mental health outcomes of alternative policies be determined; (2) a point of reference be established by which to quantify value; and (3) the outcomes be weighed based on this valuing system. The preliminary work in predicting behavioral outcomes utilizes time series analysis to measure the correlation between longitudinal variance in societal changes and disorder (Catalano & Dooley, 1980). Particularly at the local level, inclusion of behavioral costs among accountable outcomes is a feasible procedure. The second and third steps require serious, public involvement to establish a reference point and weigh the outcomes. As this involves controversial social values, it will frequently be easier to obtain a consensus within a community than on a state or national level.

In addition to significant human costs, health outcomes have direct economic effects that must be considered as well. These include such measurable economic consequences as loss of productivity, cost of treatment or institutionalization, and increased public assistance costs. These measures are utilized in the second approach (cost benefit analysis) to determine whether the cost of intervention, the primary prevention effort, is less than the cost of nonintervention, or treatment.

Table 6. Evaluation of Policy Decisions Based on Behavioral Cost-Accounting

Policy alternative	Close local plant—all employees out of work	Reduce plant operations and work force by 40%	Sell plant but maintain work force
Outcomes	Community and job market unable to accommodate all workers	Relatively moderate impact on community and job market	Community and market stability maintained
	Increased stress on individuals and families	Most employees able to find work	No increase in unemployment or public assistance costs
	Increased pressure on spouses to provide income	Increased stress on families	Minimal stress effects on production employees
	Increased family disruption as parents seek jobs out of local area	Moderate or small increase in unemployment and public assistance costs	Various stress on managers of plant
	Increased demand for local support services: day care for children	Moderate or small increase in mental health problems	
	Increased unemployment and welfare costs		
	Increased depression, suicide, divorce, other mental health outcomes		
	Increased family abuse		

In analyzing the economic feasibility of a primary prevention program, the costs of producing it must be defined and the benefits (i.e., the costs averted or avoided) must be assessed. These can all be expressed in monetary terms. The costs and benefits must then be discounted to control for the fact that they do not accrue all at once and generally do not accrue uniformly over time. The basic tenet here is that, even ignoring inflation, a dollar today is valued more highly than a dollar tomorrow. An analyst must make current and future dollars commensurate to determine the present values of benefits and costs. This is achieved by discounting (diminishing) all benefits and costs that occur in the future. As preventive activities usually produce benefits well into the future, this is an important, and constraining concept. It also serves to explain how postponing costs can have the effect of containing them (Warner, 1979a). A final aspect of the cost-benefit methodology enables a valid assessment of the costs of the prevention program to be made despite the lack of precision inherent in determining the costs and benefits of illness or its absence. The procedure, a sensitivity analysis, involves repeating the cost and benefit calculations for the low, high, and best estimates of the costs and of the benefits. That is, if it is determined that there is a maximum error rate of 25% from the best estimate of the costs, the low and high estimates of this figure are computed to determine the economic feasibility of the program.

Economic evaluation of a preventive program will not always indicate that it is worth the expense, at least in monetary terms alone. Because costs are immediate and benefits are deferred, it appears on the surface that such analysis will rarely recommend a prevention proposal. However, several facts weigh in favor of prevention. First, the relative cost of prevention is much smaller than the cost of treatment in this era of escalating medical expenses. It is relevant to note that these costs are increasingly in the public domain. In 1979, 45% of medical expenditures were paid with public monies (Warner, 1979a). Second, the apparent treatment bias assumes an available, effective treatment without sustained costs. This is rarely true. Treatment of emotional problems, particularly in children, is an expensive, time-consuming endeavor. Developmental costs to a child may extend over a lifetime and possibly even result in later societal costs. Third, loss of productivity significantly increases the cost of illness. In 1980, expenditures on health care in this country will exceed $200 billion, and the productivity losses are valued at another $190 billion (Warner, 1979a)!

An example of the economics of the antismoking campaign on television from 1968–1970, prior to the ban on cigarette advertising, supports these notions. The impact of the antismoking messages apparently decreased cigarette consumption by 2–6%; they cost approximately $130 million in adjusted current dollars in donated air time. The annual economic health burden imposed by smoking is approximately $35 billion (Warner, 1976b). Employing a conservative 2% reduction in smoking to compute a comparable reduction in health consequences and costs, a savings of $700 million was realized. Even with the immense price-tag of $130 million, a net benefit of approximately $570 million was realized. Given the potential cost-savings of prevention programs with children and families, it behooves behavioral scientists to be thoroughly familiar with cost-accounting procedures for promotion and evaluation of their efforts.

Proposed Program: Rationale and Focus

The issues and concepts that have been discussed will be applied to the development of a macrosystems program directed toward the poor, particularly single-parent families.

A look at some recent statistics related to the single-parent population demonstrates the inadequacies of the current approach to poverty. Absolute poverty as measured by proportion of the population with annual incomes below "poverty level" has decreased from 20% in 1964 to 11.4% in 1978 (Lynn, 1978). Not surprisingly, however, only 8.7% of all white persons are living below this level, while 30.6% of all black persons are in this category (U.S. Bureau of the Census, 1980). If the uninterrupted growth in real income and real consumption are taken into account and poverty is defined as a relative state-deprivation of a standard of living enjoyed by others, then no progress has been made in alleviating poverty (Lynn, 1978). Further analysis of the antipoverty programs reveals an unequal distribution of benefits, with the households headed by a female of working age benefiting least (Lynn, 1978). Thus, potentially the most vulnerable segment of the poor (i.e., families of single-parent mothers) that currently comprises 50% of that population is most neglected by public assistance programs (U.S. Bureau of the Census, 1980).

What is needed if financial support equal to approximately 10% of the gross national product is not sufficient to reduce the extensive effects of poverty (Cook, 1978)? Analysis of the multifaceted nature of poverty must provide the basis for any intervention designed to reduce its debilitating consequences. This assessment indicates a need for changes at various levels of society, some of which are indicated in Table 7.

The discrepant income profiles for men and women and whites and minorities, shown in Table 8, suggest that possibly the best macrolevel strategy is the development of greater equity in education and the workplace. This approach to the problems of poverty requires a belief in the validity of cultural diversity and the right of individuals to equal access to the resources of society. Structuring the environment to facilitate the competent management of individual and societal resources is a primary objective of ecologically oriented, primary prevention efforts (Rappaport, 1977).

The national scope of these problems indicates that federal involvement is necessary for a viable primary prevention effort. However, the demand for cultural and community relevance and cost-effectiveness suggests that interventions developed within a local context will be the most successful (Catalano & Dooley, 1980).

Table 7. Ecological Evaluation of Poverty

Conditions of poverty	Possible approaches to reduce debilitating effects
Alienation	Societal acceptance of cultural validity; access by minorities to relevant training and education programs
Unskilled, low-pay jobs	Expansion of job market
Lack of adequate child care, mothers unable to work; inadequate supervision of children whose parents do work	Flexitime work schedules; after-school programs for children; expansion of day-care facilities in inner city and workplace; social support network that assumes child-care responsibilities
Working parents generally unavailable to children	Locate jobs near residential areas; provide incentives to keep businesses from "fleeing" cities; flexitime work schedules
Inadequate housing	Access to better paying jobs; improved apartment design
Welfare	Access for all citizens to resources of society; eliminate discrimination

Justification for focusing on single-parent families is also strong from a mental health perspective. Marital disruption has been closely identified with the distribution of psychopathology in the population. People undergoing marital disruption have been unequivocally identified as a high-risk group (Bloom, 1978). Some supportive evidence is found in studies of admissions to psychiatric facilities, which demonstrate rates consistently lower among married persons, intermediate among widowed and the never married, and highest among divorced and separated persons (Crago, 1971). Indications of the health-promoting environment of the marital state are found in reduced mortality rates from numerous, diverse physical diseases for all married persons (Syme, 1974). To date, little systematic evaluation of the variables mediating the health-protective nature of marriage has been done. One reasonable hypothesis proposes the particular supportive system of marriage as a facilitator both of coping with the environment (i.e., manipulating it to meet one's needs) and of adaptation (i.e., changing one's self in response to environmental demands). Viewed within this model, marriage facilitates and enhances "person–environment fit." An additional hypothesis is required to explain the high psychiatric admission rates of divorced and separated persons. The view of marital separation as an accidental life crisis constituting a significant stressor is consistent with Caplan's (1964) crisis theory. As discussion previously, severe stress may be a precipitant of illness. Further, it can be hypothesized that the effects of divorce are so deleterious because, unlike losing a spouse through death, there is no social norm for acknowledging the loss and supporting the individual.

These hypotheses are not mutually exclusive, and taken together they indicate a reasonable approach to primary and secondary prevention efforts. Should questions arise about their significance in a chapter on the prevention of psychopathology in children, one need only contemplate the potential effects of divorce on the remaining parent and the environment created for children. The child frequently experiences severe stress after these changes in the family support system. The actual losses are great and frequently multiple. In addition to loss of a parent, a child's friends, school, and neighborhood are often forfeited as well. Kelly and Wallerstein (1976) characterize divorce as a process of complexly related internal and external events that is frequently characterized by disequilibrium and that may approach disorganization in both the child and parent. The helplessness of the child, who has virtually no control in this situation, may be intensified by inconsistent parenting, especially during the first critical year. Wallerstein and Kelly (1976) and Kelly and Wallerstein (1976) relate the anger, confusion, and loneliness experienced by children they interviewed shortly after initial parental separation. These feelings, although universally experienced, were managed in various ways, depending on the age, behavioral style of the child, and family structure. In over half of the latency-aged children, there was a noticeable decline in school performance. Among these children, there was a concomitant decline in peer relationships of the late latency age group. At the follow-up of one year, the initial problem resolution of all the children was related to the age of the child at the time of divorce, with the late latency group fairing worst. Generally, 25–50% of children interviewed gave evidence of consolidation into troubled and conflicted behavior patterns. However, the remainder maintained their level of development or improved their psychological functioning. The various outcomes were related primarily to the postdivorce family strucure, the amount of support and gratification provided by the relationships, and the amount of sustained disequilibrium.

The impact of the quality of the family relationships is also demonstrated by Berg and Kelly (1979), who report that children in "accepting" single-parent families have comparable measured self-esteem to that of children in intact "accepting" families. Children in

Table 8. Selected Characteristics of Female-Headed Families

	All races	White	Black	Spanish origin[c]
Percentage of female heads of households, by race—1979[c]	14.0%	11.6%	40.5%	19.8%
Percentage total number of families below poverty level headed by female[a]	1959	1969	1977	
	14.5%	18.3%	24.8%	
Percentage female heads of households—1977	Work full-time		Worked all year	
	80.9%		54.9%	
Median income for families with children under 18—1978[b]	Intact husband—wife present		Female-headed	Male-headed
	$19,410		$7,035	$14,589

Sources:
[a]U.S. Bureau of the Census, 1979.
[b]U.S. Bureau of Labor Statistics, 1979.
[c]U.S. Bureau of the Census, 1980.

"rejecting" intact families have lower measured self-esteem. In a similar vein, the "emotional divorce" that precedes divorce, or sometimes exists within a prolonged marriage, has been posited to exact a greater toll on children than single-parent living.

While these findings indicate that divorce and single-parent living are clearly not pathological in and of themselves, the highly stressful nature of the divorce process may precipitate dysfunctional behavior, particularly in the absence of positive, interpersonal support.

Another frequent concomitant of divorce is an abrupt decline in economic resources. As can be seen in Table 8, this effect may be quite severe when children remain with the mother, which continues to be the case in the vast majority of dispositions. However, loss of status experienced by the female-headed, single-parent family has the potential for more than emotional consequences. The effects of poverty on physical and mental health are severe, diverse, and well documented (Department of HEW, 1979). The Joint Commission on the Mental Health of Children, Task Force VI (1973) addressed the environmental forces that impinge on children living in poverty, declaring that, particularly in the cities, these interact to promote a sense of defeatism, alienation, and hopelessness. Premature coping and defensive ability are required with the result that genuine mastery and flexible adaptability are forfeited.

While the actual number of persons in families living below "poverty level" has decreased since 1959, the number of female-headed families living in poverty has *increased.* This holds true for those living in near poverty as well (U.S. Bureau of the Census, 1979).

Clearly, the situation of female-headed families, especially those living near or below poverty, constitutes both a high-risk population and a high-risk situation. The interpersonal losses and the effects of financial instability may be ameliorated by the replacement of lost interpersonal attachments. This process of rebuilding the support network is integral for adaptation to divorce. Diverse social attachments facilitate social and recreational activities that rely on interpersonal contribution rather than monetary expense. Additionally, the formidable demands of dependent children can often be shared at mutual convenience, reducing both the financial burden and the time taken off from work. The mutuality of benefit within the support system appears to be a critical factor, one not attainable in traditional mental health support functions.

The lack of adequate social supports has been hypothesized as an explanation of Langer and Michael's (1962) findings that at every level of stress the low socioeconomic status group had an increased risk of psychiatric disorders. More recently, Berkman and Syme (1979), in a retrospective 9-year study of Alameda County adults, have demonstrated an inverse correlation between social and community ties and mortality rates. More precisely, the intimate ties of marriage and contact with friends and relatives were stronger predictors of health status than were ties of church and group membership. While clinical experiences with "enmeshed" family systems and the influence of psychoanalytic thought may have obscured the significance of family and kin social networks in the maintenance of creative adaptability and health, there is increasing evidence for the importance of social support. For example, recently, more focused studies of social support have found that this set of variables may be important in both alleviating stress in the work place and in maintaining appropriate child-rearing skills (LaRocco, House, & French, 1980; Wahler, 1980).

Cobb (1976) conceives of social support as information leading the subject to believe she or he is loved and cared for, she or he is esteemed and valued, and she or he belongs to a network of communication and mutual obligation. Fulfilling social support needs is usually a function of the primary group, traditionally exemplified by the family. The major axes of organization of this group are an instrumental system charged with the fulfillment of tasks and an expressive system geared to the satisfaction of individual needs and maintenance of solidarity. Dean and Lin (1977) hypothesize that to the extent an individual is able to maintain his expressive relations, she or he may be "protected" from illness-inducing stress. It is probably increasingly acceptable for some expressive support functions to be satisfied by contacts outside the immediate family system, providing an important source of support for single-parent families.

In considering the relevance of social support systems for primary prevention efforts, Bloom's (1978) comments deserve mention. He maintains that, in an ideal community, individuals are recognized as interdependent, each advantaged in some ways and disadvantaged in others. Further:

> The ideal community-wide prevention service is the deliberate development of comprehensive social support systems. [Such] a system is far more useful for creating a growth-inducing community than training and employing more caretakers. (Bloom, 1978, pp. 111–112)

The limited research evidence on the supportive functions of social networks indicates that it is not the mere quantity of social ties or frequency of interaction that determines their effectiveness (Berkman & Syme, 1979; Conners, Powers, & Bultena, 1979). Hirsch's (1980) study of 20 recently widowed women and 14 women who had recently returned to full-time university studies has relevance for the present proposal. He found that dense social networks, those characterized by a high degree of relatedness between the various members of a person's support network, provided relatively poor support on a number of measures. This structure of support may be represented by an extended family model, frequently considered ideal. Its association with less successful adaptation for individuals attempting to reintegrate themselves into society may be related to its homogeneity and curtailment of outside involvement. Alternatively, access to multidimensional relationships, those in which at least two kinds of activities or interests were shared, was related to higher self-esteem and greater tangible assistance and satisfaction from socializing. The social structure of individuals with a high number of multidimensional relationships was less dense. Hirsch assumes that, faced with the need to gain greater satisfaction outside their domestic lives (also the situation of recently divorced women), the women in his sample were best assisted by social networks that branched into the wider social environment.

Gottleib and Hall's (1980) suggestion that the social networks of low-income, sole-support mothers are frequently characterized by a small number of proximate and close-knit ties, is also relevant. Hirsch's (1980) data suggest that increasing the diversity of relationships and the dimensionality of existing relationships may enhance self-esteem and social satisfaction as well as providing necessary assistance (see also Wahler, 1980).

A comprehensive social network is fundamentally dependent on community acknowledgment of its desirability and a "vehicle" for its development. The mass media can be instrumental on both points. Its advantages in this context include the ability to reach even isolated single-parent families, to develop awareness of the impact of marital disruption, and to foster an understanding in the community of the effects of stress on health and the potential of social support systems in ameliorating this effect. The success of mass media in affecting such change in knowledge, attitude, and awareness is well documented (Rogers & Shoemaker, 1971). Meyer, Maccoby, and Farquhar (1980) maintain that, when appropriately used, mass media can successfully influence behavior as well. Certainly, its commercial effectiveness in shaping behavior is unmistakable, strongly recommending its use in prevention activities. The addition of a stepdown communication process involving face-to-face interactions is, however, frequently needed in persuading individuals to adopt new ideas or behaviors (Rogers & Shoemaker, 1971). In prevention programs, the active participation of community caregivers, social organizations, and key community members ensures that the message is passed on and discussed in familiar surroundings to increase its memorability, penetration, and action consequences.

The Stanford Three Community Study, designed as a multilevel mass communication effort to reduce the multiple risk factors associated with coronary disease, deserves mention as a model of this approach to prevention (Maccoby, Farquhar, Wood, & Alexander, 1977). Its success generated a second, larger intervention currently underway, the Five Community Study. Similar to the previous study, it is formulated within the framework of social learning (Bandura, 1977; Maccoby & Alexander, 1980), social marketing (Kotler & Zoltman, 1971; Solomon, 1979), and mass media communication (DeFleur & Ball-Rokeach, 1974; Maccoby & Alexander, 1980). A noteworthy addition to the second study is increased emphasis on community organizations and social networks in facilitating health behavior change.

A preventive intervention utilizing mass media will naturally constitute both primary and secondary prevention. While it is the secondary activities that best fit the current funding mold, contributions of a primary nature to the enhanced adaptability of the populace and community integration are possibly more significant. Perhaps the greatest current benefit of a preventive macrosystem intervention will result from program evaluation. Heller *et al.* (1980) suggest that the best way of overcoming social and political impediments to prevention programs is to collect evidence from demonstration projects that facilitate rational decision making. To ensure that evidence is as solid as field studies will permit, explicit specification of target groups, program elements, and expected outcomes is imperative. Lave and Lave (1977) evaluated the majority of preventive health care programs and noted that most analyses only attempted to ascertain whether the program changed the health status of the population at-risk. This, in itself, is a difficult task, involving two separate intervention programs. The second is to link proximal objectives such as behavior change with the ultimate reduction in incidence of the end-state goals (Heller *et al.,* 1980). However, evaluation must proceed beyond this assessment. As discussed previously, monetizing the effects and costs of the program is a necessary step in garnering public and political support for prevention programs.

Macrosystem Prevention Proposal

The proposed macrosystem program will be developed in light of the various social, political, and economic issues raised concerning prevention, and will be based on a non-victim-blaming, ecological model. The comprehensiveness of the program indicates that the mental health professional will be collaborating with other professionals and lay groups in its development and implementation. The proposed program most basically has two components (community organization and media) and has three major objectives: (1) to help, as noted in Table 9, the target single-parent population, and to prevent child behavior problems; (2) to organize the community around this objective; and (3) to increase awareness about the effects of stress in general and to develop a demand for more comprehensive social support systems.

Accepting the development of social support networks as a valid pursuit necessitates an appropriate method for development of social integration. Gottleib and Hall (1980) suggest that a set of key informants be identified in the community, people whom others nominate as knowledgeable about local social groupings. The information provided by this sample will allow investigators to characterize communication channels, density of the social networks, and so forth, and indicate feasibility of a full-scale social network study. This assessment clarifies needs and constraints of a community's social network, indicates interpersonal communication channels to be utilized, developed, and strengthened, and identifies key community members to involve in the development of social network. The assessment will be community-based; however, program development and community organization will focus on meeting single-parenting needs. It should be recognized that the problems of single parents are by no means limited to this group. For example, as more mothers enter the work force, increasing numbers of children return from school before a parent returns home. A community-supported cooperative program of after-school activities for children will meet needs of many families and facilitate social integration as well. The need for programs focused more exclusively on concerns of single parents may be identified. Issues such as child discipline, visiting the absent parent, financial management, and feelings of being overwhelmed by all the tasks and responsibilities are likely topics—ones that will best be dealt with in mutual help groups, some of which may appropriately include diverse members of the community.

The proposed setting for this subject is a moderate-sized urban area. For the sake of simplicity in this example, only one community within the setting would receive intensive interpersonal communication and social network development. However, providing different communities with alternative approaches to the development of social support systems appears to be an important research area. In either case, a control community within the targeted urban area that would not receive the step-down communication efforts and a no-treatment control outside the media range are necessary. In the interest of brevity, the intervention targets, program goals, and evaluation methods are outlined in Table 9.

The conceptual framework of the intervention maintains that there is a community need for an increased knowledge base regarding the concept and identification of stress, its maturational role in facilitating development of adaptation and coping strategies, as well as its inherent adaptation costs and its role in precipitating illness. Additionally, there is a need for knowledge and awareness of the dynamic interaction of individuals and environments and the environmental constraints on individuals and families. Further, the belief

Table 9. Outline of Comprehensive Social Network Development Program

	Secondary prevention focus	Primary prevention focus
Target	Single parents and their children within defined urban community	Urban population (all those receiving mass media input)
Intervention	Media	
	Increased knowledge of stress concepts	Media—same programs received
	Increased awareness of mediating role of support in facilitating coping and adaptation	
	Increased information on resources that provide support	
	Step-down communication-Increased impact of media messages feedback mechanism	Step-down communication-Informal; encourage greater acceptance and support of target group; encourage involvement in programs, personally satisfying support relationships
	Consolidate individual needs for program planning	
	Facilitate involvement in programs	
	Programs led or facilitated by community residents: mutual help groups, children's play groups, babysitting co-ops, teenage babysitting services, local child care for working mothers, support groups	
Goals	Proximal	Distal
	Reduce self-report of stress within target group	Decrease severity and no. of psychiatric treatment cases in the target area
	Increased knowledge, and awareness of stress, health and support concepts in general population	Decrease no. of child abuse and neglect cases in target area, reduce childhood problems
	Increased no. and utilization of formal and informal support activities	organizational and institutional change facilitating the person–environment fit
		Decrease Social integration and impact of community action.

that the acceptance of cultural diversity and equal access to resources facilitates individual, group, and community competence is an explicit foundation of this program. Finally, social support systems are viewed as a pivotal mechanism in allowing and encouraging individuals and families to initiate and persevere the positive coping and adaptation strategies.

An implicit assumption of social network development is that there is an awareness by community residents of the benefits to be derived from strengthening, increasing, or diversifying their social contacts. Fostering this awareness is a primary aim of the mass media communication effort. This objective can be accomplished using a sequential, multimedia approach. Initially, a few short television programs focusing on the single-parent family with the relevant stress, health, and social system concepts presented in vignettes would be broadcast. Additionally, short "commercials" relaying the same general message as well as specific information on support activities such as support groups, mutual-help groups, babysitting co-ops, after-school activity programs, parenting seminars, and so forth, would be broadcast. These would also be carried on radio and the information would be presented in newspapers as well. Consistent with the program's philosophy, as well as

Table 9. (continued)

	Single-parent target population	General population
Evaluation measures	1. Pre–post and follow-up; surveys of attitudes and information, re: stress, social relationships, parenting concerns, work patterns, media habits 2. Random sample interviews, to assess specific expectations and requirements of community 3. Pre–post and follow-up evaluation of stress, and coping, and adaptation strategies of random sample single-parent mothers and children 4. Social network analysis of a randomly selected sample of female single parents pre–post and at follow-up	1. Random samples, pre–post, and follow-up surveys of information, attitude and behaviors re: stress, social support, networks, situation of single-parent families as assessed by the community. 2. Pre–post and follow-up measures of: a. Rate, diagnosis and family structure and place of residence of individuals treated at local mental health clinics and psychiatric hospitals b. Child abuse and neglect cases, including relevant demographic information c. Incidence of juvenile delinquent behavior d. Assessment of no. and level of functioning of community organizations and mutual-help groups
Cost-benefit analysis	Production costs 1. Salaries of researchers, and paid community organizers, if appropriate 2. No. of hours volunteered 3. Clerical supplies 4. Postage costs 5. Media costs 6. Other overhead costs	Program benefits 1. Costs averted in health care expenses 2. Costs averted in child welfare expenses 3. Institutional and correctional agency costs averted 4. Contribution to community welfare provided by enhanced social integration (estimated)

Bandura's (1971) concepts of modeling, indigenous actors would be employed. Broadcast times would be determined by results of a viewing habits survey.

The interpersonal communication channels would be maintained by the key community resource people identified in the social network analysis, as well as by the caregivers in social and professional organizations. They would lead or facilitate the various support activities.

The impact of all these activities must be carefully assessed. The outcome criteria, as outlined in Table 9, are extensive, sampling pre–post changes on the individual, group, organizational, and community level. A follow-up evaluation is necessary as well. The substantive knowledge obtained could, in the future, outweigh the large investment required by such extensive evaluation. The final aspect of the program involves analyses of the costs and benefits, and is fundamental to the future of similar preventive interventions. Maintaining the ledger of production costs will be a demanding, and admittedly, time-consuming job. Clarity is imperative as attempts to replicate the program will benefit from an accurate accounting of all potential costs. Because this program is philosophically dependent on volunteer participation, many costs may be avoided. However, some record of the labor involved must be kept to reflect all potential costs. Assessing the benefits is a long-term endeavor, highly dependent on reliable evaluation measures. These are outlined in Table 9, but obviously would be developed to reflect the specific programs instituted.

Several comments are indicated in conclusion. The recommendation for a preventive program designed to develop comprehensive social support networks within a community does not presume that such a program is a panacea, but rather an active, multifaceted information and support system will permit and encourage individuals, especially those with a diminished social network, to initiate relationships that are mutually beneficial. Additionally, by increasing the competent interdependence of individuals, the strength of the community is enhanced. Further, the focus on single-parent families should not be misconstrued. The secondary program targets this known high-risk group. However, exclusive attention may implicate single-parent families as pathological, weak, or inadequate, thus possibly encouraging a victim-blaming phenomenon. Social network development is a comprehensive effort, and other focused support networks—of the elderly, for instance—may evolve as well. The concomitant goals of the primary intervention program attempts to ensure that social integration and enhanced community competence are the ultimate outcomes. At the same time, this type of macrolevel effort may be the most cost-effective way to help single-parent families and prevent relatively predictable family and childhood problems. Thus, as we noted at the beginning of this section, it is highly appropriate for mental health professionals to become involved in the development and implementation of complex, multilevel programs.

Summary

In this chapter, we have purposely presented a range of opinions, perspectives, and concrete approaches to the implementation and evaluation of primary prevention efforts. Quite obviously, professionals or lay persons interested in developing primary prevention programs must make a careful assessment and choice (based on their values, nature of the problems, resources available, and political constraints) on type of approach to be implemented, on proximal and distal objectives, on level of intervention and delivery system(s) that are necessary and practical, and on appropriate evaluation measures. These different possibilities are briefly summarized in Table 10.

We have also tried in this chapter to present the political, social, and fiscal realities of promoting primary prevention as we enter a period of marked conservatism. It is, however, our contention that all the factors shown in Table 10, plus the political, social, and economic context, are crucial variables in determining our conceptualizations of child and family problems and our attempts to alleviate such problems (Rappaport, 1977). While it is obviously difficult to assess the future of primary prevention and programs for families and children in a period of political transistion, several points in this chapter have been made that are probably more congruent with prevailing conservative attitudes:

1. Small group approaches as opposed to "Great Society" programs will probably be favored.
2. Local control and lack of federal mandates will probably also be favored, but such efforts *may* be multifaceted and multilevel.
3. Rigorous cost-accounting procedures will be needed to justify the development and existence of programs, most particularly, preventive programs, which seem to be "extras."
4. Programs delineated in this chapter or similar ones should be promoted as "pro-family" through competency building and/or stress reduction (as the authors, indeed, feel they are).

While these points suggest some optimism for prevention programs in the 1980s, we can only hope that a more ecological or systems-oriented approach (which in many ways is a more "liberal" perspective of human processes, and the basis for many of the ideas in this chapter) is not once again replaced by a more "conservative," victim-blaming stance (Ryan, 1971). An ecological position will continue the focus on strengths at multiple levels, the concern for person–environment fit, and analyses and modifications of stress producing settings and institutions. A return to a victim-blaming approach will unfortunately define the causes of family and childhood problems as deficits within the family and child, with major efforts directed toward very traditional modes of mental health conceptualization and treatment. The implicit and explicit philosophical foundations of a program obviously determine its objectives, implementation strategies, and ultimate worth to individuals and society.

Table 10. Summary of Considerations and Variables in Prevention Programs

Values/Perspective:	Source of problems seen within individuals, groups, organizations, communities, institutions
Approach:	Proactive, reactive
Proximal objectives:	Comptency building, stress reduction, modification of settings, social support, network building, community knowledge, awareness
Distal objectives:	Enhances child/family development, alternative settings, Community change, redistribution of resources
Level of approach:	Small Group, organizations, communities, regional, national, multilevel
Delivery system/channel:	Written media, face-to-face, multifaceted
Evaluation measures:	Tests, information and attitude surveys, ratings, behavioral observations, organizational agency, social indicators, indicators of networks and support, etc., maintenance of effects, cost-accounting (cost-effectiveness, cost-benefits)

Allen, G. J., Chinsky, J. M., Larcen, S. W., Lochman, J. E., & Selinger, H. V. *Community psychology in the schools: A behaviorally oriented multilevel preventive approach.* New York: Wiley, 1976.

Bandura, A. *Psychological modeling.* Chicago: Aldine-Atherton, 1971.

Bandura, A. *Social learning theory.* Englewood Cliffs, N.J.: Prentice-Hall, 1977.

Baratz, S., & Baratz, J. C. Early childhood intervention: The social science base of institutional racism. *Harvard Educational Review,* 1970, *40,* 29–50.

Berg, B., & Kelly, R. The measured self-esteem of children from broken, rejected, and accepted families. *Journal of Divorce,* 1979, *2,* 363–369.

Berk, R. A., & Berk, S. F. *Labor and leisure at home.* Beverley Hills, Calif.: Sage, 1979.

Berkman, L. F., & Syme, S. L. Social networks, host resistance and mortality. *American Journal of Epidemiology,* 1979, *109,* 186–204.

Biber, B. Integration of mental health principles in the school setting. In G. Caplan (Ed.), *Prevention of mental disorders in children.* New York: Basic Books, 1961.

Bloom, B. L. Marital disruption as a stressor. In D. G. Forgays (Ed.), *Primary prevention of psychopathology. Vol. II. Environmental influences.* Hanover, N.H.: University Press of New England, 1978.

Bloom, B. L. Prevention of mental disorders: Recent advances in theory and practice. *Community Mental Health Journal,* 1979, *15,* 179–191.

Bronfenbrenner, U. Toward an experimental ecology of human development. *American Psychologist,* 1977, *32,* 513–531.

Bronfenbrenner, U. *The ecology of human development: Experiments by nature and design.* Cambridge, Mass.: Harvard University Press, 1979.

Caplan, G. *Principles of preventive psychiatry.* New York: Basic Books, 1964.

Catalano, R., & Dooley, D. Economic change in primary prevention. In R. H. Price, R. F. Ketterer, B. C. Bader, & J. Monahan (Eds.), *Prevention in mental health: Research, policy, and practice.* Beverly Hills, Calif.: Sage, 1980.

Chamberlin, R. W., & Nader, P. R. Relationship between nursery school behavior patterns and later school functioning. *American Journal of Orthopsychiatry, 41,* 1971, 597–601.

Clarfield, S. P. The development of a teacher referral form for identifying early school maladaptation. *American Journal of Community Psychology,* 1974, *2,* 199–210.

Clarizio, H. F. (Ed.), *Mental health and the educative process.* Chicago: Rand McNally, 1969.

Cobb, S. Social support as a moderator of life stress. *Psychosomatic Medicine,* 1976, *38,* 300–314.

Conners, K. A., Powers, E. A., & Bultena, G. L. Social interaction and life satisfaction: An empirical assessment of late-life patterns. *Journal of Gerontology,* 1979, *34,* 116–121.

Cook, T. D. *Evaluation studies: Review annual. Vol. 3.* Beverly Hills, Calif.: Sage, 1978.

Cooper, K. H. *The aerobics way.* New York: Bantam Books, 1977.

Cowen, E. L. Baby steps toward primary prevention. *American Journal of Community Psychology,* 1977, *5,* 1–22.

Cowen, E. L. Some problems in community program evaluation research. *Journal of Consulting and Clinical Psychology,* 1978, *46,* 792–805.

Cowen, E. L., Pederson, A., Babigian, H., Izzo, L., & Trost, M. A. Long term follow-up of early detected vulnerable children. *Journal of Consulting and Clinical Psychology,* 1973, *41,* 438–446.

Cowen, E. L., Trost, M. A., Lorian, R. P., Derr, D., Izzo, L., & Issacson, R. *New ways in school mental health.* New York: Human Sciences Press, 1975.

Crago, M. A. Psychopathology in married couples. *Psychological Bulletin,* 1971, *77,* 114–128.

Dean, A., & Lin, N. The stress buffering role of social support. *Journal of Nervous and Mental Disease,* 1977, 165, 403–417.

DeCharms, R. Personal causation training in the schools. *Journal of Applied Social Psychology,* 1972, *2,* 95–113.

DeFleur, M. L., & Ball-Rokeach, S. Mass communication and persuasion. In M. L. DeFleur (Ed.), *Theories of mass communication* (3rd ed.). New York: Mackay, 1974.

Dubos, R. *Beast or angel?* New York: Charles Scribner's Sons, 1974.

Emmerich, W. Continuity and stability in early social development: Teacher ratings. *Child Development,* 1966, *37,* 17–27.

Felker, D. W., Stensyck, D., & Kay, R. A. The effects of a teacher program in self-concept enhancement on pupils' self concept, anxiety and intellectual achievement responsibility. *Journal of Educational Research,* 1973, *66,* 443–445.

Gesten, E. L. A health resources inventory: The development of a measure of primary grade children. *Journal of Consulting and Clinical Psychology,* 1976, *44,* 776–786.

Gesten, E. L., Apadaca, R., Rains, M., Weissberg, R., & Cowen, E. Promoting peer-related social competence in schools. In M. W. Kent & J. E. Rolf (Eds.), *Primary prevention of psychopathology, Volume III: Social competence in children.* Hanover, N.H.: University Press of New England, 1979.

Gottleib, B. H., & Hall, A. Social networks and utilization of preventive mental health services. In R. H. Price, R. F. Ketterer, B. C. Bader, & J. Monahan (Eds.), *Prevention in mental health: Research policy and practice.* Beverly Hills, Calif.: Sage, 1980.

Griggs, J. W., & Bonney, M. E. Relationship between "causal" orientation and acceptance of others, "self idea," "self congruency" and mental health changes for fourth and fifth grade children. *Journal of Educational Research,* 1970, *63,* 471–477.

Heller, K., Price, R. H., & Sher, K. J. Research and evaluation in primary prevention. In R. H. Price, R. F. Ketterer, B. C. Bader, & J. Monahan (Eds.), *Prevention in mental health: Research, policy and practice.* Beverly Hills, Calif.: Sage, 1980.

Hirsch, B. J. Natural support systems and coping with major life changes. *American Journal of Community Psychology,* 1980, *8,* 159–172.

Holmstrom, L. L. *Two two-career family.* Cambridge: Schenkman, 1972.

Hunt, J. C., & Hunt, L. L. Dilimmas and contradictions of studies: The case of the dual-career family. *Social Problems,* 1977, *24,* 407–416.

Jason, L. A. Prevention in the schools. In R. Price, R. Ketterer, B. Bader, & J. Monahan (Eds.), *Prevention in mental health: Research, policy, and practice.* Beverly Hills, Calif.: Sage, 1980.

The Joint Commission on the Mental Health of Children. *Social change and the mental health of children.* New York: Harper & Row, 1973.

Kelly, J. B., & Wallerstein, J. S. The effects of parental divorce: Experiences of the child in early latency. *American Journal of Orthopsychiatry,* 1976, *46,* 20–32.

Keniston, K. *All our children.* New York: Harcourt, Brace, Jovanovich, 1977.

Kennedy, J. F. *Message from the President of the United States relative to mental illness and mental retardation.* 88th Congress, First Session, U.S. House of Representatives Document No. 58. Washington, D.C.: U.S. Government Printing Office, 1963.

Kohlberg, L., LaCrosse, J., & Ricks, D. The predictability of adult mental health from childhood behavior. In B. B. Wolman (Ed.), *Manual of child psychopathology.* New York: McGraw Hill, 1972.

Kotler, P., & Zoltman, G. Social marketing: An approach to planned social change. *Journal of Marketing,* 1971, *35,* 3–12.

Langer, T. S., & Michael, S. T. *Life stress and mental health.* New York: Free Press of Glencol, 1962.

Lave, J. R., & Lave, L. B. Measuring the effectiveness of prevention. *Milbonk Memorial Fund Quarterly,* Spring 1977, *55,* 273–289.

LaRocco, J. M., House, J. F., & French, Jr., J. R. P. Social support: Occupational stress and health. *Journal of Health and Social Behavior.* 1980, *21,* 202–218.

Lemle, R. Primary prevention of psychological disorders in elementary and intermediate schools. *Journal of Clinical Child Psychology,* 1976, *5,* 26–32.

Levine, M., & Graziano, A. M. Intervention programs in elementary schools. In S. E. Golann & C. Eisdorfer (Eds.), *Handbook of community mental health.* New York: Appleton, 1972.

Lynn, L. A decade of policy development in the income maintenance system. In T. D. Cook (Ed.), *Evaluation studies review annual* (Vol. 3). Beverly Hills, Calif.: Sage, 1978.

Maccoby, N., & Alexander, J. Use of media in life-style programs. In P. Davidson (Ed.), *Behavioral medicine: Changing health life styles.* New York: Brunner/Mazzel, 1980.

Maccoby, N., Farquhar, J. W., Wood, P. D., & Alexander, J. Reducing the risk of cardiovascular disease: Effects of a community based campaign on knowledge and behavior. *Journal of Community Health,* 1977, *3,* 100–114.

Mankiewicz, F., & Swerdlow, J. *Remote control: Television and the manipulation of American life.* New York: Times Books, 1978.

McClure, L. F., Chinsky, J. M., & Larcen, S. W. Enhancing social problem solving performance in an elementary school setting. *Journal of Educational Psychology,* 1978, *70,* 504–513.

Meichenbaum, D. *Cognitive-behavior modification.* New York: Plenum Press, 1977.

Meyer, A. J., Maccoby, N., & Farquhar, J. S. Reply to Kosl and Leventhal *et al. Journal of Consulting and Clinical Psychology,* 1980, *48,* 159–163.

Minuchin, P., Biber, B., Shapiro, E., & Zimiles, H. *The psychological impact of school experience.* New York: Basic Books, 1969.

Muus, R. E. The effects of a one- and two-years causal learning program. *Journal of Personality,* 1960, *28,* 479–491.

National Academy of Sciences. *Toward a national policy for children and families. Report of the Advisory Committee on Child Development.* Washington, D.C.: Author, 1976.

Newberger, E. H., Newberger, D. M., & Richmond, J. B. Child health in America: Toward a rational public policy. *Milbonk Memorial Fund Quarterly,* 1976, *54,* 249–298.

Nollen, S. *New patterns of work.* Scarsdale, N.Y.: Work in America Institute, Inc., 1979.

Ojemann, R. H. Sources of infection revealed in preventive psychiatry research. *American Journal of Public Health,* 1960, *50,* 329–335.

Ojemann, R. H., & Snider, B. C. The effect of a teaching program in behavioral science on changes in causal behavior scores. *Journal of Educational Research,* 1964, *57,* 255–260.

Platt, J. J., & Spivack, G. Social competence and effective problem solving in psychiatric patients. *Journal of Clinical Psychology,* 1972, *28,* 3–5.

Platt, J. J., Spivack, G., Altmann, N., & Altmann, D. Adolescent problem solving thinking. *Journal of Consulting and Clinical Psychology,* 1974, *42,* 787–793.

Plaut, T. F. A. Prevention policy: The federal perspective. In R. H. Price, R. F. Ketterer, B. C. Bader, & J. Monahan (Eds.), *Prevention in mental health: Research, policy and practice.* Beverly Hills, Calif.: Sage, 1980.

Quilitch, H. R., & Risley, T. R. The effects of play materials on social play. *Journal of Applied Behavioral Analysis,* 1973, *6,* 573–578.

Rappaport, J. *Community psychology: Values, research, and action.* New York: Holt, Rinehart & Winston, 1977.

Rappaport, J., & Chinsky, J. M. Models for delivery of service from a historical and conceptual perspective. *Professional Psychology,* 1974, *5,* 42–50.

Robbins, L. M. *Deviant children grown up.* Baltimore, Md.: Williams & Wilkins, 1966.

Robinson, J. P. *How Americans use time: A social-psychological analysis of everyday behavior.* New York: Praeger, 1977.

Roen, S. R. Primary prevention in the classroom through a teaching program in the behavior sciences. In E. Cowen, E. Gardner, & M. Zax (Eds.), *Emergent approaches to mental health problems.* New York: Appleton-Century-Crofts, 1967.

Roff, M. Childhood social interactions and young adult bad conduct. *Journal of Abnormal and Social Psychology,* 1961, *63,* 333–337.

Roff, M., Sells, B., & Golden, M. M. *Social adjustment and personality development in children.* Minneapolis: University of Minnesota Press, 1972.

Rogers, E. M., & Shoemaker, F. F. *Communication of innovations* (2nd Ed.). New York: Free Press, 1971.

Ryan, W. *Blaming the victim.* New York: Random House, 1971.

Shure, M. B., & Spivack, G. Means-ends, thinking, adjustment, and social class among elementary school aged children. *Journal of Consulting and Clinical Psychology,* 1972, *38,* 348–353.

Shure, M. B., & Spivack, G. Interpersonal cognitive problem solving and primary prevention: Programming for preschool and kindergarten children. *Journal of Clinical Child Psychology,* 1979, *8,* 89–94.

Shure, M. B., & Spivack, G. Interpersonal problem solving as a mediator of behavioral adjustment in preschool and kindergarten children. *Journal of Applied Developmental Psychology,* 1980, *1,* 29–44.

Solomon, D. S. *Social marketing and health promotion: The Stanford heart disease prevention program community studies.* Paper presented to 31st Annual Convention of the Association for Advancement of Behavior Therapy, San Francisco, California, December, 14–16, 1979.

Spivack, G., Platt, J. J., & Shure, M. B. *The problem solving approach to adjustment.* San Francisco: Jossey-Bass, 1976.

Spivack, G., & Spotts, J. *Devereux child behavior rating scale manual.* Devereux, Penn.: Devereux Foundation, 1966.

Spivack, G., & Swift, M. "High risk" classroom behaviors in kindergarten and first grade. *American Journal of Community Psychology,* 1977, *5,* 206–221.

Spivack, G., & Shure, M. B. *Social adjustment of young children.* San Francisco: Jossey-Bass, 1974.

Stallings, J. Implementation and child effects of teaching practices on follow-through classrooms. *Monographs of the Society for Research on Child Development,* 1975, *40* (Serial No. 163).

Stennett, R. G. Emotional handicap in the elementary years: Phase or disease? *American Journal of Orthopsychiatry,* 1965, *35,* 444–449.

Stone, G., Hinds, W., & Schmidt, G. Teaching mental health to elementary school children. *Professional Psychology,* 1975, *6,* 34–40.

Syme, S. L. Behavioral factors associated with the etiology of physical disease: A social epidemiological approach. *American Journal of Public Health,* 1974, *64,* 1043–1045.

Task Panel on Prevention. *Task Panel Reports submitted to the President's Commission on Mental Health* (Vol. 4). Washington, D.C.: U.S. Government Printing Office, 1978.

Toffler, A. *Third wave.* New York: Morrow, 1980.

Ullman, C. A. Teachers, peers, and tests as predictors of adjustment, *Journal of Educational Psychology,* 1956, *48,* 257–267.

U.S. Bureau of the Census. *Current population reports,* Series P-60, No. 119. Washington, D.C.: U.S. Government Printing Office, 1979.

U.S. Bureau of the Census. *Current population reports,* Series P-20, No. 350, Population Profile of the United States. Washington, D.C.: U.S. Government Printing Office, 1980.

U.S. Bureau of Labor Statistics. *Monthly labor review,* 102 (3). Washington, D.C.: U.S. Government Printing Office, 1979.

U.S. Bureau of Labor Statistics. *Special labor force report: Marital and family characteristics of workers.* Washington, D.C.: U.S. Government Printing Office, 1979.

U.S. Department of Health, Education, and Welfare. *Healthy people: Surgeon general's report on health promotion and disease.* U.S. Public Health Service Publication No. 79-55071. Washington, D.C., 1979.

Wahler, R. G. The insular mother: Her problems in parent–child treatment. *Journal of Applied Behavior Analysis,* 1980, *13,* 207–220.

Wallerstein, J. S., & Kelly, J. B. The effects of parental divorce: Experiences of the child in later latency. *American Journal of Orthopsychiatry,* 1976, *46,* 256–269.

Warner, K. E. The economic implications of preventive health care. *Social Science and Medicine,* 1979, *13C,* 227–237. (a)

Warner, K. E. Clearing the airwaves: The cigarette ad ban revisited. *Policy Analysis,* 1979, *5,* 435–450. (b)

Westman, J. C., Rice, D. L., & Bermann, E. Nursery school behavior and later school adjustment. *American Journal of Orthopsychiatry,* 1967, *37,* 725–731.

Wilson, G. T., & O'Leary, K. D. *Principles of behavior therapy.* Englewood Cliffs, N.J.: Prentice-Hall, 1980.

Winett, R. A., & Neale, M. S. Modifying settings as a strategy for permanent, preventive behavior change: Flexible work schedules and family life as a case in point. In P. Karoly & J. J. Steffens (Eds.), *Improving the long-term effects of psychotherapy.* New York: Gardner Press, 1980. (a)

Winett, R. A., & Neale, M. S. Results of experiments on flexitime and family life. *Monthly Labor Review,* 1980, November, pp. 29–32. (b)

Winett, R. A., & Neale, M. S. Flexitime and family time-allocation: An analysis of a system change on individual data. *Journal of Applied Behavior Analysis,* 1981, *14,* 39–46.

Winett, R. A., Battersby, C. B., & Edwards, S. The effects of architectural change, individualized instruction, and group contingencies on the behavior and academic production of sixth graders. *Journal of School Psychology,* 1975, *13,* 28–40.

Winett, R. A., Fuchs, W. L., Moffatt, S. A., & Nerviano, V. J. A cross-sectional study of children and their families using different child care environments: Some data and conclusions. *Journal of Community Psychology,* 1977, *5,* 149–159.

Winett, R. A., Neale, M. S., & Williams, K. R. Effective field research procedures: Recruitment of participants and acquisition of reliable, useful data. *Behavioral Assessment,* 1979, *1,* 139–155.

Winett, R. A., Neale, M. S., & Williams, K. R. The effects of flexible work schedules on families with young children: Quasi-experimental, ecological studies. *American Journal of Community Psychology,* 1982, *10,* 49–64.

Yule, W. The potential of behavioral treatment in preventing later childhood difficulties. *Behavioural Analysis and Modification,* 1977, *2,* 19–32.

Zax, M., & Cowen, E. L. Abnormal psychology: Changing conceptions. New York: Holt, Rinehart, & Winston, 1976.

Zax, M., Cowen, E. L., Rappaport, J., Beach, D. R., & Laird, J. D. Follow-up study of children identified early as emotionally disturbed. *Journal of Consulting and Clinical Psychology,* 1968, *32,* 369–374.

Zax, M., & Spector, G. A. *An introduction to community psychology.* New York: Wiley, 1974.

Index